ST. MARY'S COLLEGE OF MARYLAND
ST. MARY'S CITY, MARYLAND 20686

ELITES IN AMERICAN HISTORY

VOLUME I: The Federalist Years to the Civil War

VOLUME II: The Civil War to the New Deal

VOLUME III: The New Deal to the Carter Administration

ELITES IN AMERICAN HISTORY

The New Deal to the Carter Administration

Philip H. Burch, Jr.

HOLMES & MEIER PUBLISHERS, INC.
New York ● London

First published in the United States of America 1980 by
Holmes & Meier Publishers, Inc.
30 Irving Place
New York, N.Y. 10003

Great Britain:
Holmes & Meier Publishers, Ltd.
131 Trafalgar Road
Greenwich, London SE10 9TX

Copyright © 1980 by Philip H. Burch, Jr.
All rights reserved

Library of Congress Cataloging in Publication Data

Burch, Philip H., Jr.
    The New Deal to the Carter administration.

    (*His* Elites in American history ; v. 3)
    Bibliography: p.
    Includes index.
    1. Business and politics—United States—History.
2. United States—Officials and employees—Appointment, qualifications, tenure, etc.—History.
3. United States—Politics and government—1933–1945.
4. United States—Politics and government—1945–
5. Elite (Social sciences)—United States—History.
I. Title. II. Series.
JK467.B87   vol. 3   322'.3'0973s [322'.3'0973]
ISBN 0-8419-0565-7   80-11528
ISBN 0-8419-0566-5 pbk.

Manufactured in the United States of America

To Dorothy S. Redden
with many thanks
for her aid and encouragement

Contents

	TABLES	ix
	PREFACE AND ACKNOWLEDGMENTS	xi
1	INTRODUCTION	1
2	THE NEW DEAL	13
	FDR's Socio-economic Status and Elite Support	20
	Major Administrative and Diplomatic Appointments	25
	Important Policy Actions	35
	Supreme Court Appointments and Actions	45
3	THE WORLD WAR II AND TRUMAN YEARS	69
	FDR's Major Administrative and Diplomatic Officials: 1940–1945	74
	Truman's Major Cabinet and Diplomatic Officials	80
	Important Policy Actions of the Truman Administration	91
	Supreme Court Appointments	106
4	THE EISENHOWER ADMINISTRATION	123
	Major Administrative and Diplomatic Appointments	127
	Important Policy Actions	146
	Supreme Court Appointments and Actions	152
5	THE KENNEDY-JOHNSON YEARS	169
	JFK's Major Administrative and Diplomatic Appointments	175
	Important Policy Actions of the Kennedy Administration	188
	Johnson and His Informal Inner Circle	192
	Top Officials of the Johnson Administration	197
	Important Policy Actions of the Johnson Administration	204
	Supreme Court Appointments and Actions	210
6	THE NIXON-FORD REGIME	231
	Nixon's Election and Informal Inner Circle	235
	Nixon's Major Administrative and Diplomatic Appointments	240
	Important Policy Actions of the Nixon Administration	258
	Top Officials of the Ford Administration	273
	Major Issues and Actions of the Ford Administration	278
	Supreme Court Appointments and Actions	280

7	**THE CARTER ADMINISTRATION**	307
	Carter's Political Rise and Major Ties	312
	Early Major Administrative and Diplomatic Appointments	316
	Major Issues and Actions	329
	Later Major Administrative and Diplomatic Appointments	338
8	**CONCLUSION**	359
	Geographic Background of Appointees	359
	Educational Background of Appointees	364
	Prior Governmental Experience of Appointees	369
	Economic and Occupational Backgrounds of Appointees	372
	Elite or Non-Elite Status of Appointees	378
	Circulation and Transformation of Elites	384
APPENDIX A	Primary Background Data of Major Cabinet and Diplomatic Officials: 1933–1980	399
APPENDIX B	Primary Background Data of Supreme Court Justices: 1933–1980	519
INDEX		535

TABLES

Table 1	America's Top 20 Manufacturing and Railroad Concerns in 1940	14
Table 2	America's Top 10 Banks and 5 Largest Life Insurance Companies in 1940	17
Table 3	America's Top 20 Industrial Concerns in 1952	71
Table 4	America's Top 10 Banks and 5 Largest Life Insurance Companies in 1952	72
Table 5	Early Allocation of World Bank Funds	96
Table 6	America's Top 10 Banks in 1960	124
Table 7	America's Top 30 Non-financial Firms in 1968	170
Table 8	America's Top 30 Financial Institutions in 1968	172
Table 9	America's Top 30 Non-financial Firms in 1976	232
Table 10	America's Top 30 Financial Institutions in 1976	233
Table 11	Percentage of High Federal Posts Held by People from Different States or Regions: 1789–1980	360
Table 12	Educational Background of High Federal Officials: 1789–1980	366
Table 13	Amount of Prior Governmental Experience of High Federal Officials: 1789–1980	370
Table 14	General Occupational Background and Elite (or Non-elite) Status of Major Cabinet and Diplomatic Officers: 1789–1980	374
Table 15	1789–1980 Summary Analysis of Elite Status of America's Major Cabinet, Diplomatic, and Supreme Court Officers	383

Preface and Acknowledgments

This work was begun in the early 1960s in an effort to explore some of the linkages between business and government as revealed by an examination of the makeup of the boards of directors of America's large corporations. This, I later discovered, was an approach which had not yet been employed in a thorough, systematic fashion, primarily because the requisite business directories were not available over a long period of time to be mined by various able historians and other social scientists. In part because of my orientation and training as a political scientist, my initial labors were confined to the post-1941 period, and focused largely on the federal recruitment process. However, as my work continued, the question naturally arose, what was the politico-economic linkage pattern in the preceding period? So I carried this general line of analysis back to the turn of the century, for most of which period a number of good business directories were available (along with a substantial set of secondary works); then to the late 1860s, for which years only *Poor's Railroad Manual* was available (to be supplemented by a wide variety of secondary sources); and finally, in one last major research effort, back through the pre-Civil War decades to 1789, for which years I had to rely largely on non-primary material, particularly biographical studies of high federal officials.

The initial aim of this study was to make a systematic analysis of the socio-economic background of the top appointive officials in the federal government over time in the hope that the data might be put to good use by other social scientists. Another equally important purpose was to employ these recruitment findings to make a rough general assessment of the distribution of power in the country and thereby shed some light on the "elitist" versus "pluralist" controversy which has been raging among political scientists and sociologists in recent decades. The analysis of major issues and events was undertaken somewhat later in an effort to show that there may be a significant relationship between the background of various high federal officials and their governmental actions, although it should be stressed that the latter acts do not constitute any kind of statistically sound sample, but are simply intended to demonstrate (rather than prove) that there is some connection between the two.

Because of the highly controversial nature of this work, I have deliberately eschewed much use of the voluminous archival material often mined by historians, preferring instead, aside from business directories, to rely almost exclusively on secondary sources, because, unlike the latter, the papers and correspondence of high federal officials cannot readily be checked.

The author of any such lengthy work owes a great deal to other people. I would like to express my special thanks to Tom Ferguson, now of M.I.T., for his highly supportive efforts during the critical late stages of this study. The author is also indebted to G. William Domhoff of the University of California (Santa Cruz); Michael Levy of Texas A. & M.; Ernie Reock, director of the Rutgers Bureau of Government Research and Services; Al Barnes, another stellar friend at the Bureau; and my two older children, Carol and David Burch, for their substantial aid and encouragement. Although I am not a member of this profession, I received considerable help from various members of Rutgers' fine history department, especially Sidney Ratner, Richard L. McCormick, Gerald Grob, Lloyd Gardner, Warren Susman, David Oshinsky, and Rudy Bell. Some of my political science colleagues were also supportive, notably Josef Silverstein, Steve Bronner, Anthony Champagne, Stanley Friedelbaum, Richard Mansbach, and Richard Wilson. None of these scholars is, of course, responsible for any errors contained in this study.

In addition, the author secured much sound counsel from two other people at Rutgers, Marlie Wasserman and J. Carl Cook. The staff at the Rutgers University Library was unfailingly helpful during the many years of research involved in this undertaking. The able and ever-cheerful Claire Luma did an extraordinary job of typing this manuscript, all on an overtime basis. I am also grateful to those sweet squash players at Rutgers for providing a welcome break in many a long workday.

CHAPTER 1

Introduction

The relationship between business and government is clearly an extremely important topic, particularly in highly industrialized countries. Yet, as indicated in the introduction to the first volume of this series, it is a subject which, for various reasons, has been badly neglected over the years by both serious researchers and more popular writers. While it is true that certain well-known historians, such as Charles A. Beard and more recently Gabriel Kolko, and some sociologists, notably C. Wright Mills and G. William Domhoff, have done considerable work in this area, they are the exceptions rather than the rule. And their research has been subjected to much criticism, rightly or wrongly, by other scholars in the social sciences, many of whom take strong issue with the elitist or "leftist" findings of such academic revisionists, but who generally do little in-depth analysis themselves, being content largely to accept the prevailing pluralist view of American government. Indeed, despite the impassioned pleas of such eminent scholars as Robert Dahl, most political scientists (who, in truth, know relatively little about the business world) and economists (who usually do not like to deal with the concept of power, particularly as it pertains to politics) have eschewed this important area as outside the scope of their respective disciplines.[1] In fact, as Dahl astutely observed in 1959, a virtual no-man's land has grown up between economics and political science, which, the work of certain conservative "public choice" theorists notwithstanding, has not been filled to this day.[2]

What can be done to improve this state of affairs? A look at the literature in the field reveals that a number of scholars in different disciplines have attempted to resolve this problem by dealing with such obviously important concepts as class, power, decision-making, and the distribution of governmental benefits (and burdens) over time.[3] But their efforts have not yet proved very fruitful, in considerable part because of the many knotty problems involved in trying to employ these often elusive terms. Hence the approach taken in this historical study of American politico-economic relations is one which focuses primarily on the role of various influential elites in American government. This is not to say that such crucial subjects as the distribution of power in a society, the allocation of economic benefits to different segments of the population, and the relation of elite groups to the class structure of a country should be slighted, but rather that a systematic analysis of the socio-economic background and affiliations of America's political elite may provide a more rewarding and reliable way of getting at such matters, particularly when it is combined, as it is here, with an examination of various major governmental actions.

Although remarkably few sound studies of elites have been published thus far, especially in economically advanced countries, this kind of research can do much to illuminate such key areas and issues as the number and relative power of different elite groups, their possible ties with one another, their socio-economic makeup and rates of change (or circulation, to use Pareto's term), the manner of their selection or recruitment, and their relations with other classes and less organized segments of the citizenry.[4] Such study can also shed considerable light on the extent to which there has been much equality of opportunity to hold high governmental office in the United States.[5]

Another reason for concentrating on the social and economic ties of a nation's political elite is to place governmental officials (and their chief advisors or confidants) in a more revealing setting than has been done to date. For, despite the emphasis placed on the economic basis of politics by Charles A. Beard in his early writings, the majority of American scholars have been content to refer to various governmental officers as "a former successful lawyer" or "an important businessman," without delving into their economic ties, or those of close kin or key business associates. And this is a grievous mistake. Where did such figures fit into the economic structure of the country at the time they were appointed or elected to high public office? Were they Establishment men, ardent reformers, or political "outsiders," as Jimmy Carter was widely touted to be during his 1976 presidential campaign? Without more pertinent data and discerning analysis, it is impossible to tell. Moreover, it is a basic premise of this study that a President may well be judged by the administrative, diplomatic, and judicial company he keeps— that is, by the type of people he picks to serve as his chief officers and advisors. In short, an in-depth analysis of a nation's top decision-makers should reveal much about the nature and locus of power in a society.

In this work, the term *governmental elite* has been defined primarily as the occupants of the nation's major Cabinet, diplomatic, and Supreme Court posts.[6] However, in dealing with the post-World War II years, the study has been expanded to include such increasingly important persons as the ambassadors to the Soviet Union and NATO and the directors of the CIA and the Bureau of the Budget (now the Office of Management and Budget).

The background data which have been collected for this largely positional analysis of high administrative, diplomatic, and judicial figures will emphasize the economic ties of an official (or of his close kin) at or near the time of his appointment to a federal post, particularly his primary business or occupational position, his major directorship ties, and, where relevant, certain key civic associations.[7] These links are probably more important than a person's distant social origins since they represent his (or her)[8] most recent, presumably predominant, economic allegiance.

These vital data, which have never been systematically mined over a long time, have been gathered for most officials from such generally reliable sources as *Who's Who in America*, the *Directory of Directors in the City of New York* (which contains data on a number of concerns located in other places), and the primary national business directories published during this period, mainly *Poor's* and *Moody's*.[9] Where appropriate, similar data have also been culled from such sources as the *Dictionary of American Biography*, the *National Cyclopaedia of American Biography*, and a substantial number of historical studies and political biographies. This information will be listed in systematic tabular form in two appendixes at the end of this volume, and even more importantly, will be analyzed in considerable depth and detail as an integral part of the text to see whether there are any key institutions, corporate clusters, or politico-economic alliances which have played a prominent role in the overall federal recruitment and decision-making process since the early 1930s.

A major distinction will also be made, to the extent possible, between what, for its time, would be described as big business on the one hand and small or medium-sized firms on the other. For despite the many problems involved, the reader is entitled to know whether the firms found to be closely linked to certain high federal officials are really large- or small-scale enterprises. And perhaps equally significant is a determination as to whether they are controlled by managerial or wealthy entrepreneurial interests, for which purposes the author will rely, where sound stockownership data does not exist, on an analysis of the makeup of the boards of directors of the companies in question. On the basis of such information, an assessment will be made, where data permit, of the economic elite or non-elite status of all high federal officials in the post-1933 period.[10]

Also, it should be noted that the author, unlike many social scientists, does not look upon the partners in America's major corporate law firms as merely able professionals. While this description may have fitted most attorneys up to the early post-Civil War years, this state of affairs was substantially altered, with the advent of the Industrial Revolution, by the growth of the big city law firms and their increasingly close links with major corporate and financial clients.[11] Thus while most lawyers practicing on their own, or with just a few associates, will be treated here as professional men, the top figures of the big firms must generally be regarded as either the allies or agents of important economic interests.

Another subject which will be emphasized in this work is that of elite family ties. This area has long been overlooked by American social scientists, perhaps because the very concept runs counter to the nation's democratic ethos. However, when one takes a close look at this topic, one cannot fail to be impressed by the frequency with which key family ties appear to play a vital role in a person's rise to high public office.

While the analysis of politico-economic relations will concentrate primarily on the corporate and kinship ties of high governmental officials, this does not mean that major long-recognized political considerations will be neglected. Other prior governmental service, various key party posts held, and pertinent geographic and ethnic factors will be noted both in the text and in the biographical tables found at the end of this volume. In other words, it is readily conceded that many appointments to high governmental office are made wholly or largely for political reasons. Yet a substantial number also appear to have been the result primarily of economic influence.[12]

Since the socio-economic background of people usually has a marked effect on their actions, it is imperative to look at the role of high federal officials from yet another standpoint—namely, that posed by the problem of possible "conflict of interest." As the generally conservative Bar Association of the City of New York rightly pointed out in its report on *Congress and the Public Trust*, the term *conflict of interest* should be defined broadly to include more than the assumption of an obligation on the part of a public official to merely abstain from lining his pockets (or those of family or friends); even more important, he should try to avoid being placed in any position which would result in the impairment of his independent judgment, so that governmental decisions could be made in what is generally termed the "public interest."[13] With this in mind, the New York bar association concluded that members of Congress should not serve as officers, directors, trustees, or partners in any commercial enterprise—a recommendation which could be extended, for the same reasons, to all high administrative, diplomatic, and judicial officials.[14] Indeed, some feel that the real problem with the appointment of businessmen (or other wealthy or "friendly" figures) to high posts in government is not so much overt corruption (which, as a rule, occurs only sporadically), but the intrusion of improper (pro-business) bias into the formulation and implementation of governmental policy.[15]

Because of the strong possibility that the appointment of pro-corporate federal officials may have a profound effect on the governmental decision-making process, this volume contains an analysis of a selected set of major events in the post-1933 period to see what, if any, relationship exists between the socio-economic background of high governmental authorities and their actions in office.[16] In short, this study will provide a rough test of the relative impact of the federal recruitment pattern on the government's policy-making process and, to a considerable extent, on the general distribution of benefits in the nation.

For example, as the first volume of this work shows, up to the Civil War the top posts in the federal government were controlled by various wealthy elite figures. This was true even during the hallowed age of Jacksonian democracy, which, according to many historians, represented an era of equalitarianism in which the western frontiersmen and urban working classes, led by Old Hickory and his followers, wrested political control from long-privileged property interests. In fact, at only one point during these early years did elite forces claim under 80 percent of the major Cabinet and diplomatic offices of the nation, and that was not until the late 1850s, in the administration of Pennsylvania's James Buchanan. And although the total number of people appointed was much smaller, almost the same percentage of positions on the United States Supreme Court was held by upper-class leaders during the pre-Civil War period.

Moreover, the governmental actions of these early leaders would frequently appear to have been dictated by a desire to protect or promote their economic holdings or those of other wealthy people. For instance, one of the most hotly contested acts of the entrepreneurially oriented Washington administration was its decision to fully fund the public debt of both the federal and state governments, most of whose securities were, because of many uncertainties, selling at only a fraction of their original face value. After much heated debate involving charges of widespread speculation on the part of certain wealthy, probably well-informed figures, this plan was finally passed, much to the benefit of various large securities holders, a number of whom were close friends or associates of the influential Secretary of the Treasury, Alexander Hamilton, or other members of the administration. It was roughly this same set of forces which had much to do with the creation of the First Bank of the United States, a quasi-public institution, formed, at the urging of Hamilton, to help stabilize the country's monetary system, and also to serve the needs of the young Republic's major businessmen, the merchants of the nation's larger cities.

Similarly, several decades later, after the relatively quiescent "era of good feelings," another epic battle occurred when Andrew Jackson became President of the United States, for this fiery Tennessee leader decided to destroy the Second Bank of the United States, which had been chartered shortly after the War of 1812 to provide the country with some kind of central bank (albeit one which was dominated primarily by private interests). This bitter controversy has generally been portrayed in one of three ways. Some historians claim that it was basically a struggle which pitted the debt-ridden farmers and urban working classes against the alleged "monied aristocracy"; other scholars have depicted it as essentially a clash between two strong-willed men, the impetuous Jackson and the haughty, patrician president of the Bank of the United States, Nicholas Biddle; and still other writers maintain that it represented primarily a conflict between rising entrepreneurial interests, especially the newer state banks, and a long-entrenched economic elite centered heavily in Philadelphia, which was then the nation's financial capital. As is often the case, there is some truth to each of these contentions. But judging from the highly elitist background of most of Jackson's major Cabinet officers and the pioneering work of such researchers as Bray Hammond, it would appear that it was rival elite forces, particularly those located in New York City, which were mainly responsible for Jackson's unrelenting and ultimately successful campaign to destroy the Second Bank of the United States.[17]

A number of major actions taken later in the pre-Civil War period either revolved around, or directly impinged upon, the issue of slavery, which most Northerners viewed mostly in moral terms. Yet as Volume I shows, important economic forces were also at work. For instance, the primary reason Illinois's ambitious Senator Stephen A. Douglas introduced his controversial Kansas-Nebraska Act of 1854, which reopened the long-suppressed slavery question, was that he was allied with certain influential railroad leaders who were extremely eager to build one or more routes to the Pacific Coast; Douglas agreed, so long as at least one line would have Chicago as its eastern terminus, for it was here that he had amassed some of his largest landholdings, which were sure to increase tremendously in value if Chicago became a great railroad nexus.[18]

Two other key governmental acts taken during the critical pre-Civil War decade revealed economic interests working in the very opposite direction—that is, to help "keep the lid on" the slavery issue. This clearly was the primary consideration behind the adoption of the famous Compromise of 1850, in which various concessions were made to both the pro-slavery and the abolitionist forces when Congress was compelled to decide on the status of the Western territory acquired in the recent Mexican War. In the great debate over this issue, such important leaders as Daniel Webster were probably not acting as idealistic or farsighted statesmen defending the cause of national unity, but rather as the spokesmen of Northeastern business interests, or "Cotton Whigs," who placed the preservation of normal intersectional trade relations above the plight of an enslaved people. The same interpretation could be placed on the actions of the defendant in the famous Dred Scott decision, for this individual, John F. A. Sanford, was a prominent New York City (and former St. Louis) businessman who may have been pressured by other economic interests in the North to strongly contest this case in yet another attempt to keep the long-simmering division over slavery from erupting into a bloody internecine conflict.

The second volume of this study begins with Lincoln's election, an event which signified a major, albeit rarely stressed, shift in American politico-economic relations. For the President not only picked almost all of his Cabinet, diplomatic, and judicial officials from the North, but he recruited more overtly pro-business (mainly railroad) figures into his administration than had been the practice in most pre-Civil War regimes. Lincoln himself was an attorney who had derived a good deal of his income during the previous decade from recently established railroad concerns, particularly the big Illinois Central line. Thus it is not surprising that most of his top officials were drawn from these and other emerging economic interests.

This recruitment pattern was followed, with certain minor variations, by all of America's presidents (aside from New Jersey Democrat Woodrow

Wilson, who had to contend with the influence of the strong agrarian-based Bryan wing of the party) from the Civil War to the New Deal. In all, about 84 percent of the major Cabinet and diplomatic officials appointed between 1861 and 1933 and around 87 percent of the Supreme Court Justices selected during this 72-year period were either representatives of or closely allied with upper-class interests.

The marked pro-business (and especially pro-railroad) orientation of the federal government during this economically pivotal period can be seen in many of the actions taken by different presidential regimes, usually regardless of which party was in power. For instance, it was probably no accident that by far the greatest acreage in railroad land grants in American history were given out while Lincoln was in office. That railroad forces, which represented the nation's first "big business" (but were no monolithic body), wielded considerable influence in the Democratic party was also vividly revealed some 30 years later by the way in which the second Cleveland administration handled the famous Pullman strike of 1894. In this bitter dispute President Cleveland was persuaded by his conservative Attorney General (and Boston corporate lawyer), Richard Olney, to send in federal troops to break the strike, though such action had not been requested by Illinois governor John Peter Altgeld. From a politico-economic standpoint, the most disturbing aspect of this unfortunate affair was the fact that although he was an influential Cabinet official, Olney had continued to serve as a director and general counsel of two major railroads, one of which was based in Chicago. Hence he was hardly a neutral party in the proceeding.

The era spanned by the years between the mid-1890s and 1933 was marked by even greater change, both economically and politically. Indeed, this period has been described by most historians as one which saw the sudden spawning, frequently through giant mergers, of the first great industrial "trusts" and also, many have claimed, the rise of "finance capitalism" in the country. It was during this period that the nation's first billion-dollar company, the United States Steel Corp., was created, mainly through the efforts of J. P. Morgan & Co., and that the Rockefeller-dominated Standard Oil Co. grew to huge, quasi-monopolistic proportions. Even more significant, the House of Morgan emerged during these critical years as a potent politico-economic force in American life, for under the direction of its legendary leader this influential complex came to control a number of large financial and industrial enterprises, although it often had to contend with the power of rival business interests such as the Rockefellers and railroad magnate E. H. Harriman.

When Theodore Roosevelt became President in 1903, following the assassination of his Republican predecessor Wiliam McKinley, this ambitious New York patrician seized upon much of the populist and progressive discontent then at work in the country. He lashed out against the "malefactors of great wealth," to use his phrase, and backed a number of major reform measures. Because of his much-publicized steps against certain vast business combines, he was extolled, by both the contemporary press and many later historians, as a great "trustbuster."

More recent researchers, however, have severely questioned Roosevelt's reputation as an economic reformer. And on the basis of his overall record as President, they would appear to be correct, particularly with regard to his actions against large corporate interests. For Roosevelt actually initiated a much smaller number of antitrust suits, especially against big companies, than his conservative successor, William Howard Taft, who held office for a considerably shorter period. In addition, Roosevelt made a curious distinction between what he described as "good trusts" and "bad trusts." Upon close inspection, the good trusts usually turned out to be Morgan-dominated concerns, while the bad ones were what might be referred to as non-Morgan trusts, such as the Rockefeller-controlled Standard Oil Co. and E. H. Harriman's Union Pacific Railroad.

William Howard Taft's administration refused to make any such distinctions, and in 1911 went so far as to file antitrust charges against two Morgan-controlled (or affiliated) firms, the United States Steel Corp. and the International Harvester Co., against which Roosevelt had refused to act. This bold move so enraged Roosevelt that he decided to reenter national politics and directly challenge Taft for the Republican presidential nomination in 1912. When Roosevelt failed in this dramatic bid, he quit the party, thereby creating a split in the GOP ranks that resulted in the election of the Democratic nominee, Woodrow Wilson.

Wilson was a man of considerably different mold from most earlier occupants of the White House, for he had been a scholar and university president who, following a breach with his school's board of trustees, had turned his hand to politics and been elected governor of New Jersey. Although Wilson is often depicted as a reformer, he actually had a good deal of support from various conservative quarters, first particularly from New York publisher George Harvey (who looked on Wilson as someone to repel the progressive William Jennings Bryan) and later from such men as Texas political leader (and former businessman) Edward M. House. The Wilson administration was a rather unusual one, in part because it contained a substantial number of non-elite figures holding major Cabinet and diplomatic posts. In fact, this marked the first time in American history that the representation of elite interests in high federal office fell as low as 57 percent. But this more pluralistic recruitment policy was not entirely Wilson's doing, for some of the officials included in his regime had been virtually forced upon the administration by the Bryan-led agrarian wing of the Democratic party.

The complex nature of the influences at work on Wilson can be seen in two of the major reform measures which were adopted during the early years of his administration: the creation of the Federal Reserve System (a kind of quasi-public central bank) and of the Federal Trade Commission (an independent regulatory agency designed to police business practices), both of which were the end product of considerable compromise hammered out between liberal and conservative interests. However, America's entry into the First World War during Wilson's second term of office so channeled the nation's energies in other more pressing directions that little thought was, or could be, given to unresolved domestic issues.

With the end of the somewhat atypical Wilson administration, which suffered heavily from its attempts to convince the country that it should join the newly formed League of Nations after World War I, the United States returned to what has generally been described as a period of "normalcy," that is, an era marked by the rule of three Republican presidents—Harding, Coolidge, and Hoover—each of whom was either favorably disposed toward or closely allied with influential economic forces.[19] Indeed, such was the weight of business interests in these regimes that one man, Pittsburgh banker and industrialist Andrew W. Mellon, served as Secretary of the Treasury for 11 of these 12 years, a span of high Cabinet office almost unmatched in American history.

In the 1920s the most important actions taken by the federal government lay in the realm of domestic finance. To the surprise of some, the Harding administration was initially thwarted by liberal forces in Congress in its attempts to reduce the fairly sizable tax burden which had been imposed for the first time on both rich people and major corporate interests by the Wilson regime to help finance the nation's recent war effort. But in the mid-1920s, President Coolidge and his Secretary of the Treasury Andrew Mellon were able to overcome this resistance and secure the passage of a key fiscal measure which drastically reduced the rates of both the federal estate (i.e., inheritance) tax and the progressively conceived income surtax, and completely abolished the recently enacted federal gift tax.

In addition, and perhaps even more important in the long run, the Coolidge-Mellon administration (as some have described it) managed, with the help of certain key figures in Congress, particularly Pennsylvania's Senator David A. Reed (who was closely allied with the Mellon interests), to obtain a tremendous boost in the depletion allowance granted to extractive industries, mostly oil and mining firms, since 1913. In 1926 this subsidy was raised from an average of about 5 percent of these corporations' gross income to a lucrative, arbitrarily arrived-at 27.5 percent, a standard which remained in effect for over 40 years. Scant wonder, then, that many rich and powerful interests in America viewed Andrew Mellon as the greatest Secretary of the Treasury since Alexander Hamilton.

When Herbert Hoover became President in 1929, he followed the same general pro-corporate recruitment pattern, appointing to high office such elite figures as Wall Street lawyer Henry L. Stimson and Boston Brahmin attorney Charles Francis Adams, whose daughter had married J. P. Morgan, Jr. Presented with two openings on the Supreme Court a little later, Hoover made appointments of a similar sort. As Chief Justice he picked the able Charles Evans Hughes, who had held a number of important governmental positions over the years (the most prominent of which was as Secretary of

State in the early 1920s), but who had also served recently as a major counselor for the Rockefeller interests. And, after one rebuff, Hoover filled the other 1930 Court opening with Philadelphia lawyer and former Teapot Dome special investigator Owen J. Roberts, who in the past few years had sat on the board of such giant concerns as A.T.&T. and the Equitable Life Assurance Society (America's third largest life insurance company).[20]

When the Great Depression struck, President Hoover's reaction to this debacle was of a distinctly limited nature, for he was badly hampered by the conservative counsel he constantly received from his chief advisors and his own firm belief, wealthy businessman that he had been, in "rugged individualism" and the importance of voluntary rather than governmental action. For example, the Hoover regime was strongly opposed to granting direct relief to America's many needy citizens because it clung to the archaic view that this financial burden was the sole responsibility of private charity and the state and local units of government. In short, because of the conservative, pro-corporate orientation of Hoover and his key advisors, the President acted on much too small a scale and was too inflexible to deal effectively with the Depression, thereby losing the political support of the vast majority of the American people and paving the way for the emergence of a leader who was more willing to undertake drastic remedial measures.

Notes

1. Aside from Marxist scholars, whose work is often marred by their analytical slant, the only group of economists who in recent years seem willing to recognize the existence of power relationships in the worlds of business and politics are the so-called institutional economists who, under a now broadened organizational aegis, publish the *Journal of Economic Issues*.

2. See Robert A. Dahl, "Business and Politics: A Critical Appraisal of Political Science," *American Political Science Review* (March 1959), p. 9. Dahl went on to say that "one can debate whether this no-man's land should be occupied by the discipline now called economics or the discipline now called political science; but it is difficult to argue persuasively that it should not be occupied at all by the social sciences."

3. For a survey of the work of historians, political scientists, sociologists, and economists in this general area, see the Introduction to Volume I of this study.

4. For an incisive discussion of these questions, see T. B. Bottomore, *Elites and Society* (Middlesex, Eng.: Penguin Books, 1964), passim.

5. Because of the immense difficulties involved in trying to ascertain in any precise manner the relative ability or expertise of those people chosen to hold high office over the years, the author has decided to eschew this obviously important matter. Another reason for skirting this subject is that skill or developed intelligence is often closely related to a person's socio-economic background. Similarly, the author does not intend to deal with the perplexing questions of

ambition and personality, given the present inchoate state of research in these areas, and the fact that there is no way to apply these terms to officials in times past.

6. With a few exceptions, this study will not deal with members of Congress, partly because of the problem posed by the sheer weight of numbers, and also because they are elected on a state or district basis and not from any national pool of political aspirants. Nor will much attention be given to the nation's top military leaders, for aside from the early post-World War II years, they have been of only moderate importance. Another set of officials who will receive scant treatment in this work are the top figures of the independent regulatory agencies, most of whom have very different backgrounds than the major Cabinet, diplomatic, and Supreme Court officers; also they have exerted less influence in national affairs. Finally, the Post Office Department is not included, both because of its essentially second-tier status and because it was transformed in the early 1970s into a very different type of governmental unit.

7. Because of the light it may shed on the distribution of politico-economic power at the time, due note will be made of any figure who is known through published sources to have been formally offered, but chose not to accept, appointment to an important Cabinet, diplomatic, or judicial post, for in certain cases the actual occupant of this office was a second or third choice of the President and his chief advisors. The role of major party fundraisers and presidential campaign managers will also be discussed at various points, to the extent that the data, often spotty, permit.

8. The masculine form of pronouns will generally be used in this work because up to the mid-1970s only two women were appointed to high federal office. This represents less recognition than that accorded to blacks and most other ethnic groups in America.

9. Although theoretically a person is elected to a board of directors (or trustees), the term *appointed* has generally been employed in this study because it more accurately describes this process.

10. Since there is no widely accepted definition of the term *economic elite*, the author had to rely largely on his knowledge and experience in this area, and the rough scale he has employed is, of necessity, a relative one, pitched to fit the level of economic development in the country. A person associated with a sizable financial institution or industrial firm in a major metropolitan center, such as Minneapolis, would, for example, be classified as a national economically elite figure. A man such as FDR's first Attorney General, Homer Cummings, who served on the board of the First Stamford National Bank & Trust Co., would not be so viewed. The determination of an official's personal or family wealth is, of course, a much more difficult matter, and one is compelled here to rely on relevant statements found in various published sources—hardly an ideal approach, but the best possible one under the circumstances. A breakdown of the general occupational and elite (or non-elite) status of every major Cabinet and diplomatic official of each administration in the post-1933 years and every Supreme Court justice who held office during this period is given in the appendices.

11. See Beryl H. Levy, *Corporation Lawyer: Saint or Sinner?* (Philadelphia: Chilton, 1961), p. 43.

12. In those cases where both political and economic considerations may have been involved, some understandable differences of opinion may arise as to their relative weighting, although these hopefully will be resolved by further study.

13. See the Association of the Bar of the City of New York, *Congress and the Public Trust* (New York: Atheneum, 1970), pp. 39–40.

14. That such ties are of considerable importance even with regard to the appointment of ex-governmental officials as corporate directors may be seen from the fact that when former Secretary of the Treasury John B. Connally was elected to the board of Pan-American World Airways in March 1973, it was reportedly with the view that he would serve as "Pan-Am's ambassador to Washington." See the *New York Times* (March 11, 1973), Sect. 3, p. 1.

15. See Edwin M. Epstein, *The Corporation in American Politics* (Englewood Cliffs, N.J.: Prentice-Hall, 1969), p. 35. In fact, as one scholar has recently observed, "it is much easier for

businessmen, where required, to divest themselves of stocks and shares as a kind of *rite de passage* into government service than to divest themselves of a particular view of the world and the place of business in it." See Ralph Miliband, *The State in Capitalist Society* (New York: Basic Books, 1969), p. 59.

16. The major issues and events examined in the course of this work do not, of course, constitute a representative sample of all important political actions (how could this be determined?), but have been selected simply to show through many illustrations that there may indeed be a connection between the socio-economic background of governmental leaders and their decisions made in office. Nor is it claimed that the treatment of issues and events represents an in-depth analysis of these topics. Space did not permit more than brief summaries, although most of the case studies are based on the work of a number of scholars. But, hopefully, enough evidence has been presented to make a persuasive case regarding these relationships, or at least spark other researchers to pursue these matters further.

17. See Bray Hammond, *Banks and Politics in America* (Princeton, N.J.: Princeton University Press, 1957).

18. See David M. Potter, *The Impending Crisis, 1848–1861* (New York: Harper & Row, 1976), pp. 145–76, especially 168–70.

19. The Democratic party meanwhile had fallen back into conservative hands. In 1924, after an unprecedented stalemate between two prime contenders, the Democrats selected as their presidential candidate Wilson's former Ambassador to Great Britain, John W. Davis, who since returning to private life in 1921 had been a senior partner in the "Morgan" law firm of Davis, Polk, Wardwell, Gardiner & Reed. And in 1928 the party nominated New York governor Alfred E. Smith to serve as its standard bearer, but by this time he had lost most of his liberalism and had become closely associated with such conservative figures as John J. Raskob, who was a vice-president of both E. I. du Pont de Nemours & Co. and the du Pont-controlled General Motors Corp.

20. Shortly before he stepped down from the Presidency, Hoover also appointed an able non-elite figure, New York's Benjamin Cardozo, to the Supreme Court, but this was a rather unusual move on his part. For a revealing analysis of the influential economic forces which, perhaps typically, worked quietly earlier in the 1920s to secure the selection of a wealthy corporate lawyer (Pierce Butler) to the High Court, see David J. Danelski, *A Supreme Court Justice Is Appointed* (New York: Random House, 1964), passim.

CHAPTER 2

The New Deal

When Franklin Delano Roosevelt took office in 1933, America was in the throes of the greatest depression in the nation's history. More than 15 million workers had lost their jobs, and in some cities in the Northeast well over half the labor force was unemployed. The national income had fallen by at least 40 percent, and the purchasing power of farmers had been reduced by fully 50 percent. Thousands of farmers lost their land for want of sufficient funds to pay their taxes or mortgage bills. In the cities many people were forced to live in shantytowns (or "Hoovervilles") and wait in long breadlines for a meager handout from hard-pressed private charities and local governmental units. Indeed, a majority of those in need received no assistance at all.[1] In addition, 5,000 banks had collapsed, wiping out the savings of nearly 9 million persons. As one commentator put it, "never in modern times...had there been so widespread unemployment and such moving distress from sheer hunger and cold."[2]

The Depression also did much to undermine America's weak labor movement, which was represented primarily by the highly conservative, craft-dominated American Federation of Labor (AFL). Thanks in no small part to an aggressive anti-union drive led mainly by the National Association of Manufacturers (NAM) in the postwar years, organized labor had suffered a severe drop in membership, from roughly 5 million workers in 1920 to about 3.6 million members by the end of the decade. As Irving Bernstein has observed, these were lean years for the labor movement.[3] With the advent of the Depression this downward trend worsened, so that by 1933 there were well under 3 million union members in the entire country. And the rolls of the AFL had plummeted to only a little over 2.1 million members, in contrast to its early postwar total of more than 4 million. Thus by the time Roosevelt took office, the labor movement was in a sorely troubled state.

The Depression also had a marked impact on most of the nation's leading industrial concerns, though not nearly to the same extent as it had on middle- and low-income groups. Some of America's largest manufacturing firms suffered a significant reduction in their overall assets, while many others barely held their own economically during these trying times. In like manner, the Depression had a clearly retarding effect on most of the nation's larger railroads (see Table 1). Despite adverse economic conditions, however, there emerged during these years a number of sizable firms in such relatively new fields as aviation, radio, and motion pictures, and these enterprises spawned other important entrepreneurial interests.

There was, not surprisingly, comparatively little growth in the public utility sector during the Depression. The most noteworthy development here was

TABLE 1

America's Top 20 Manufacturing and Railroad Concerns in 1940 (and their assets in certain preceding years)

1940 Rank	Manufacturing Firm	1929 Assets ($ millions)	1933 Assets ($ millions)	1940 Assets ($ millions)
1.	Standard Oil Co. of N.J.	1,767	1,912	2,072
2.	U.S. Steel Corp.	2,286	2,103	1,855
3.	General Motors Corp.	1,184	1,316	1,536
4.	Socony Vacuum Oil Co. (formerly Standard Oil of N.Y.)	708	990	940
5.	E. I. du Pont de Nemours & Co.	542	606	801
6.	Bethlehem Steel Corp.	802	649	764
7.	Standard Oil Co. of Ind.	697	677	757
8.	Ford Motor Co.	761	639	713
9.	Texas Corp.	610	497	675
10.	Standard Oil Co. of Calif.	605	568	623
11.	Anaconda Copper Mining Co.	764	692	607
12.	Gulf Oil Corp.	431	428	523
13.	General Electric Co.	429	375	491
14.	International Harvester Co.	384	349	444
15.	Republic Steel Corp.	162	268	405
16.	Kennecott Copper Corp.	338	319	395
17.	Shell Union Oil Co. (subsidiary of Royal Dutch Co.)	662	658	384
18.	Union Carbide & Carbon Corp.	354	306	365
19.	Consolidated Oil Corp. (the former Sinclair Consolidated Oil Corp.)	401	361	344
20.	American Tobacco Co.	265	289	298

	Railroad			
1.	Pennsylvania Railroad	2,078	2,182	2,396
2.	Southern Pacific Co.	2,278	2,381	1,867
3.	New York Central Railroad	1,722	1,826	1,844
4.	Atchison, Topeka, & Sante Fe Railway	1,263	1,271	1,318
5.	Baltimore & Ohio Railroad	1,111	1,212	1,222
6.	Union Pacific Railroad	1,196	1,176	1,214
7.	Northern Pacific Railway	866	842	843
8.	Great Northern Railway	852	851	837
9.	Chicago, Milwaukee, St. Paul & Pacific Railway	787	783	779
10.	Chesapeake & Ohio Railway	550	696	764
11.	Illinois Central Railroad	761	776	746
12.	Missouri Pacific Railroad	631	665	697
13.	Chicago & Northwestern Railway	690	673	693
14.	Chicago, Burlington, & Quincy Railroad	712	681	687
15.	Southern Railway	692	641	632
16.	Norfolk & Western Railway	542	553	578
17.	Erie Railroad	601	626	565
18.	Louisville & Nashville Railroad	545	532	537
19.	New York, New Haven & Hartford Railroad	601	592	531
20.	Chicago, Rock Island & Pacific Railway	512	549	527

NOTE: The data in this table, which provides a list of the top concerns in these two areas, have been drawn from the various appropriate *Moody's* manuals. The second part of the above list is somewhat misleading in that several of these railroads were subsidiaries or affiliates of other large lines. For instance, a substantial block of stock in the Illinois Central Railroad was owned by the Union Pacific system, and the Louisville and Nashville Railroad was even more closely linked with the Atlantic Coast Line. With regard to the industrials, it should be noted that General Motors was controlled by the du Pont interests, and a number of other manufacturing firms were dominated by various wealthy families, such as the Guggenheims. The ranking in this table was made on the basis of 1940 assets. To have chosen a year in the early 1930s would have given a rather distorted picture of most companies' financial affairs.

the creation by the early 1930s of a number of huge public utility holding companies, some of which spanned vast areas, especially in the eastern and central sections of the country. One of the largest such complexes operated under the guidance of the Morgan-dominated United Corp., which, although it had assets of less than $600 million, controlled five of the top twelve public utilities in the nation in 1933.[4]

> Commonwealth & Southern Corp., which, as the 5th-ranked firm in this field, had assets of roughly $1.13 billion and covered much of Michigan, most of Alabama and Georgia, a sizable part of Mississippi and Tennessee, and a portion of Ohio and western Pennsylvania.
>
> United Gas Improvement Co., which, as the 8th-ranked public utility, had assets of $815 million and controlled various large concerns, especially in the northeastern section of the country, such as the Philadelphia Electric Co.
>
> Columbia Gas & Electric Corp., which, as the 9th-ranked public utility, had assets of about $730 million and covered much of Ohio and West Virginia, plus a part of western Pennsylvania.
>
> Public Service Corp. of N.J., which, as the nation's 11th-ranked public utility, had assets of a little over $700 million and covered most of the densely populated sections of New Jersey.
>
> Niagara Hudson Power Corp., which, as the 12th-ranked public utility, had assets of about $660 million and covered a sizable portion of upper New York state.

Given the wretched plight of many people during this period, it is not surprising that such giant networks soon became a conspicuous target for political attack and reformist measures.

In one area—finance—there was substantial growth on the part of big concerns. This was particularly true of the major banks and insurance companies, which, in some cases because of mergers, grew at a rather startling rate after the first part of the Depression (see Table 2).[5] Moreover, within this important sector various potent economic forces emerged or gained vastly expanded influence, while certain others, such as the House of Morgan, clearly lost ground.[6] For example, the two biggest banks in the country—Chase and the National City Bank of New York—were controlled by the two major branches of the Rockefeller family and their chief allies (in the case of the National City Bank, the Stillman-Rockefeller and Taylor-Pyne families). And the nation's largest life insurance company, Metropolitan, was closely aligned through long-standing reciprocal directorship ties with the Chase National Bank, which was headed by an influential Rockefeller in-law, Winthrop W. Aldrich, son of onetime Senate leader Nelson W. Aldrich.

Perhaps even more important from a politico-economic standpoint was the recognition and influence achieved by a number of fairly close-knit New York Jewish investment banks, only one of which, Kuhn, Loeb & Co., had represented a real force in the pre-World War I period (primarily in the

TABLE 2

America's Top 10 Banks and 5 Largest Life Insurance Companies in 1940
(and their assets in certain preceding years)

1940 Rank	Commercial Bank	1929 Assets ($ millions)	1933 Assets ($ millions)	1940 Assets ($ millions)
1.	Chase National Bank, N.Y.C.	1,715	1,715	3,824
2.	National City Bank, N.Y.C.	2,206	1,387	3,095
3.	Guaranty Trust Co., N.Y.C.	2,017	1,420	2,719
4.	Bank of America, Calif.	1,055	941	1,818
5.	Continental Illinois Bank & Trust Co., Chicago	1,177	747	1,620
6.	Bankers Trust Co., N.Y.C.	818	737	1,579
7.	Central Hanover Bank & Trust Co., N.Y.C.	769	697	1,398
8.	First National Bank, Chicago	459	643	1,238
9.	Manufacturers Trust Co., N.Y.C.	508	507	1,050
10.	Chemical Bank & Trust Co., N.Y.C.	423	449	958
	Insurance Company			
1.	Metropolitan Life Insurance Co., N.Y.C.	3,011	3,861	5,358
2.	Prudential Insurance Co. of America, Newark	2,267	2,835	4,264
3.	New York Insurance Co., N.Y.C.	1,666	2,011	2,870
4.	Equitable Life Assurance Society, N.Y.C.	1,179	1,521	2,564
5.	Mutual life Insurance Co., N.Y.C.	991	1,120	1,485

NOTE: These figures were taken from *Moody's Bank & Finance Manual* for the appropriate years and represent the best data available in the area. However, they are probably on the low side since the large trust funds controlled primarily by the big commercial banks were not included in the totals reported in various major financial directories. The cutoff point of five was established for the top life insurance companies because there was only one other concern, the Northwestern Mutual Life Insurance Co., that came close in size to the above five.

railroad field in alliance with E. H. Harriman). The two most prominent banks to rise to power in the late 1920s and early 1930s were Lehman Brothers and Goldman, Sachs & Co.[7] These concerns were heavily involved in financing the growth of many of the nation's larger retail trade companies and various other relatively new enterprises, which most long-established, predominantly WASP firms shied away from as unduly risky or non-prestigious ventures. For instance, in the 1930s Robert Lehman (of Lehman Brothers) served on the board of the Associated Dry Goods Corp., Gimbel Brothers, Inc., and the May Department Stores Co., while John M. Hancock (one of the few non-Jewish partners in Lehman Brothers at this time) was a director of the American Stores Co., W. T. Grant Co., and Sears, Roebuck & Co. Similarly, Sidney Weinberg (of Goldman, Sachs) was an influential director of the General Foods Corp., National Dairy Products Corp., and Sears, Roebuck & Co.

The critical links that held this group together were provided mainly by a set of interlocking family ties forged over the years. For example, one son of Mayer Lehman, the "founding father" of this economically elite family, married a daughter of mining magnate Adolph Lewisohn, one of whose children married into the Kuhn-Loeb family; another of Lehman's sons wed a daughter of Nathan Straus, a longtime high official in R. H. Macy & Co., whose son had married a member of the Goldman-Sachs family; and still another Lehman son wed a daughter of Charles Altschul, a partner in Lazard Frères (a then less important, but closely linked firm).[8] Moreover, one of Mayer Lehman's grandchildren married a partner in Kuhn, Loeb, Benjamin Buttenweiser, while another, Harold M. Lehman, married a member of the well-established Seligman family, one of whose members had also married into the Kuhn-Loeb family.[9] Indeed, so complex were these relations that Stephen Birmingham devoted an entire book to the subject, "*Our Crowd.*" Given the strong anti-Semitic feeling that had long pervaded the upper echelons of the American business community—and, one suspects, the WASP-dominated Republican party—it is not surprising that these and other newly emergent economic forces, such as the Giannini banking interests, should have allied themselves with the Democratic party, which provided them with greater access to high government officials.

Another major development during the Depression years was the creation of a new economic organization, the Business Advisory and Planning Council (or as it was named in early 1935, the Business Advisory Council [BAC]).[10] This little-known body, which was theoretically part of the Department of Commerce, was established in June 1933 in an apparent effort to forge favorable relations between the nation's corporate interests and the newly installed Democratic administration of Franklin D. Roosevelt. Initially, this roughly 40-to-50-man body was composed of an interesting mixture of big business executives, such as Walter Gifford of AT&T and

Alfred P. Sloan, Jr., of General Motors, and an almost equal number of small businessmen, such as T. Austin Finch, president of the Thomasville Chair Co. of North Carolina, and A. P. Greensfelder, head of the Fruin-Colnon Construction Co. of St. Louis. A number of the early members of the Business Advisory Council were associated as directors with the U.S. Chamber of Commerce, and a few, such as California's John B. Elliott and Michigan's Henry Heimann, appear to have been picked because of their close ties to the Democratic party. Although little research has been done on the BAC, one study indicates that the three most important men in its early operation were Gerard Swope, its first chairman, who was president of the General Electric Co. (and a director of the National City Bank of New York); Walter C. Teagle, president of the Standard Oil Co. of New Jersey (in which the Rockefeller family and allied forces still owned almost 18 percent of the stock); and Henry I. Harriman, who was president of the U.S. Chamber of Commerce and a high official of the New England Power Association (in which the Chase National Bank and New York-based Phipps interests indirectly held a substantial interest).[11] Thus the BAC's initial core of leaders was drawn primarily from the nation's top economic interests.

There was, however, considerable turmoil and dissension within the ranks of the BAC in its early years. To some extent this was due to a feeling on the part of various small business figures on the Council that their interests were not well represented or effectively served by the BAC in its dealings with the federal government. But there was also a tremendous amount of opposition in certain major business circles to many of Roosevelt's economic policies, especially after the early halcyon days of the National Recovery Administration (NRA) and the end of the so-called first, fairly conservative New Deal. This turmoil led to the resignation from the BAC of such notable figures as Pierre S. du Pont, the board chairman of E. I. du Pont de Nemours & Co. (and a director of the indirectly family-dominated General Motors Corp.); St. Louis businessman Robert L. Lund (who was a member of the executive committee of the NAM); John J. Raskob, a du Pont vice-president (and director of both General Motors and the Morgan-allied Bankers Trust Co.); Alfred P. Sloan, Jr., the president of General Motors (and a director of the du Pont Co., Johns-Manville, and Pullman, Inc.); and Francis B. Davis, Jr., the head of the du Pont-controlled U.S. Rubber Co. (and, not surprisingly, a director of the du Pont company). Moreover, judging from the course of events, it also led to the creation of the vehemently anti-Roosevelt American Liberty League, a group apparently organized by the du Pont family, many high figures in the House of Morgan, and a substantial number of people associated with the NAM.[12]

Thus by the latter part of the 1930s much had changed within the Business Advisory Council. Most of its reactionary members had left the organization, and after some major policy clashes with FDR's more liberally oriented "second New Deal" administration, the BAC came to be increasingly dominated by big business interests, whose politico-economic influence extended far beyond the confines of the Department of Commerce.

FDR'S SOCIO-ECONOMIC STATUS AND ELITE SUPPORT

The man who took over the reins of the presidency in 1933 was an unusual political figure in that he was a wealthy patrician who never had been extensively involved in the world of big business or high finance. In no small part because of his prestigious family background, Roosevelt had been able to secure an appointment, at the age of 31, as Assistant Secretary of the Navy in the Wilson administration after only two years of public office as a New York state legislator. Having served fairly well in this capacity for almost eight years, Roosevelt was chosen, largely because he came from a critical state, as the Democratic vice-presidential nominee in 1920. Although this campaign resulted in a resounding defeat for his party, it helped to spread Roosevelt's name and image around the country. Shortly after, he was stricken with polio, which left him partially paralyzed, his legs almost useless. Yet even this crippling handicap could not long suppress Roosevelt's long-simmering political ambition. In 1928 he ran for governor of New York and won by a narrow margin. Two years later he was reelected by the largest majority in the state's history, a victory that provided him with a promising springboard to higher national office.

But what sort of man was Franklin Delano Roosevelt? Was he simply the Democratic counterpart of his distant Oyster Bay cousin, Theodore Roosevelt, or did he represent a different set of socio-economic forces? Judging from the available data, the answer would seem to be the latter. While the Hyde Park Roosevelts had accumulated a considerable amount of money over the years (primarily through various railroad, coal, and real estate ventures in the post-Civil War period), unlike the Oyster Bay Roosevelts, not a single member of FDR's family (except the Delanos) had been an important figure in the business world in recent decades.[13] Instead, most of the Hyde Park Roosevelts had been content to live largely on their inheritance, investments, and minor directorships, as country gentlemen on their estates along the Hudson River. In fact, their overall fortune, by the time of FDR's death, reportedly amounted to no more than a relatively modest $1 million.[14]

Moreover, during his eight years of private life in the 1920s, Roosevelt had formed few noteworthy business links for a man with his elitist background. He was first affiliated, on a part-time basis, with the fairly small but well-connected New York law firm of Emmet, Marvin & Roosevelt, but this association was terminated on mutually friendly terms in 1924, at which point Roosevelt entered into a partnership with Basil O'Connor, a man with no major corporate links.[15] Neither connection played a very important part in Roosevelt's life during this period.[16] Instead, he devoted a substantial amount of his time to serving as the New York vice-president of the medium-sized Fidelity and Deposit Co. of Maryland. This association is quite revealing, for if Roosevelt had been closely linked with any major segment of the New York business community prior to his election to high public office, he would hardly have taken a post with this little-known Baltimore-based concern.[17] Hence it seems fair to describe Roosevelt as a politically ambitious patrician who had no key corporate ties or rigidly fixed economic views, although he was apparently a fiscal conservative at heart.[18] Perhaps for those reasons he had to overcome considerable opposition in certain influential business circles to win his party's presidential nomination in 1932.[19]

While Roosevelt himself had no important corporate ties, the same cannot be said of some of his lesser-known relatives, such as his uncle, Frederic A. Delano, who had played a very supportive role when FDR was recovering from his attack of polio. After spending many years in business (primarily railroading), Delano had turned largely to civic activity and in the early 1930s served as deputy chairman of the Federal Reserve Bank of Richmond, treasurer of the Carnegie Endowment for International Peace, and a trustee and officer of the Brookings Institution, an increasingly influential research body which was then funded partly by the Rockefeller Foundation. Even more important, FDR's first cousin, Lyman Delano, was the board chairman of the big Louisville and Nashville Railroad and its parent company, the Atlantic Coast Line Railroad, which apparently had long been controlled by New York and Baltimore interests linked in part through the marriage of Delano's father to a member of the latter city's wealthy Walters family.[20]

The Hyde Park Roosevelts also had very close ties to the enormously wealthy Astor family, whose fortune derived largely from New York City real estate. FDR's half-brother, James R. Roosevelt, had married a daughter of *the* Mrs. William Astor, a dominant figure in New York's high society. Although he died in the late 1920s, this link reinforced the common economic interests of the two families, especially in the Delaware and Hudson (Railroad) Co. Furthermore, following the death of his first wife, FDR's father married the dughter of the influential Warren Delano, whose brother Franklin (for whom FDR was named), had married William Astor's sister. Laura, thereby providing a double link between these elite forces. Thus the Delanos and Astors had long been considered part of the same family circle.[21] To show that the Astors now had diverse interests, one need only point out that in the early 1930s FDR's good friend Vincent Astor served on the board of such big firms as the Chase National Bank, Illinois Central Railroad, International Mercantile Marine Co., Western Union Telegraph Co., and the considerably smaller County Trust Co. of New York (a board that included a number of wealthy Democratic party figures such as John J. Raskob and, up to this election as New York's lieutenant-governor in 1928, Herbert Lehman).[22]

It would also appear that several powerful economic forces were closely allied with the Roosevelt administration. The most important of these was the aforementioned socio-economic complex of Jewish investment bankers and associated interests now known as "our crowd."[23] But the Rockefeller interests also became quietly allied with the Roosevelt regime.[24] Moreover, these two key business complexes did not operate in isolation, but were linked to some extent through an influential economic intermediary, W. Averell Harriman, the transportation-banking magnate whose role in the Roosevelt administration has been much underrated.[25]

Harriman was by now closely affiliated with Lehman Brothers through his involvement with the Aviation Corp., which was created in an ill-fated effort to assemble a major network of airlines across the country. In 1932, its last year of operation under these auspices, its two top officers were W. Averell Harriman, a senior partner in Brown Brothers Harriman & Co. and a high executive of both the Union Pacific Railroad and the Illinois Central Railroad, and Robert Lehman, a top figure in Lehman Brothers.[26] The big board of directors of the Aviation Corp. also included such "friendly" figures as David K. E. Bruce, a Mellon in-law and Harriman ally, Matthew C. Brush, president of the American International Corp. (and a director of the Lazard-Lehman-controlled General American Investors Co.), Paul Mazur of Lehman Brothers, Samuel F. Pryor, and R. H. M. Robinson, the last two of whom served on the board of the Harriman-dominated American Ship & Commerce Corp. The able Harriman was probably well aware of the importance of political connections and Democratic presidential prospects, for the only non-New York figure to serve as an outside director of his American Ship & Commerce Corp. in 1930 was Van Lear Black, the Baltimore businessman who was a close friend and (up to 1928) chief employer of Franklin D. Roosevelt.

Harriman's other major tie to "our crowd" was through Kuhn, Loeb & Co., which firm had served as his father's chief financial advisor, particularly with regard to the Union Pacific Railroad.[27] In 1932 Harriman sat on the board of the Manhattan Co., which controlled both the large Bank of Manhattan and the somewhat smaller International Acceptance Bank, enterprises in which Kuhn Loeb clearly had a substantial interest (James P. Warburg served as the vice-chairman of the first company and as president of the second, while his uncle, Felix M. Warburg, graced the boards of both enterprises).[28] The close-knit nature of these relations can also be demonstrated through an examination of the makeup of the 1932 board of the Union Pacific Railroad:[29]

	Name (and primary affiliation)	Secondary Ties
Board Chairman	W. Averell Harriman	
Chairman, Executive Committee	Fannin W. Charske	Director of the Bank of Manhattan

The New Deal 23

President	C. R. Gray	
Outside Directors	Charles B. Seger (a recent high official of the Union Pacific)	Director of the International Acceptance Bank, Western Union Telegraph Co., and the Harriman-dominated Merchant-Sterling Corp.
	E. Roland Harriman (Averell's younger brother who was also a partner in Brown Brothers Harriman)	
	Robert A. Lovett (a partner in Brown Brothers Harriman, who married a member of the Brown family)	
	Robert W. Goelet (a wealthy New York real estate figure who was related to the Harrimans)	Director of the Illinois Central Railroad and the Guaranty Trust Co.
	David K. E. Bruce (a wealthy Baltimore–New York figure who married a member of the Mellon family)	Director of the W.A. Harriman Securities Corp.
	James P. Warburg (vice-chairman of the Manhattan Co. and president of the International Acceptance Bank)	Director of the Harriman-controlled American Ship & Commerce Corp.
	Newcomb Carlton (president of the Western Union Telegraph Co.)	Director of the International Acceptance Bank, Chase National Bank, and Metropolitan Life Insurance Co.
	Charles A. Stone (board chairman of Stone & Webster, Inc.)	Director of the International Acceptance Bank and the International Mercantile Marine Co.
	Henry Bruere (president of the Bowery Savings Bank of N.Y.)	
	James H. Perkins (president of the City Bank Farmers Trust Co., affiliate of the National City Bank of N.Y.)	
	Heber J. Grant (a high official in the Mormon Church and its various economic enterprises)	

There is little doubt, then, that Harriman was closely linked to Kuhn, Loeb and its economic allies.[30]

Moreover, Harriman was, although rarely noted, on intimate terms with some important leaders of the Rockefeller forces.[31] For instance, in a much-ignored article, *Fortune* magazine reported in the early 1930s that the wealthy Percy Rockefeller (a son of John D.'s less famous brother, William) served on a number of major boards, such as the Anaconda Copper Mining Co., Western Union Telegraph Co., and the National City Bank of New York, and that his close friends included Charles E. Adams, who was board chairman of the U.S. Industrial Alcohol Co. and president of the Air Reduction Co.; Frederick B. Adams, who was a high official of the Air Reduction Co., Cuban Dominican Sugar Corp., and the Atlantic Fruit and Sugar Co. (and had married a member of the Delano family); Frederic W. Allen, a partner in Lee, Higginson & Co. (and a director of the Chase National Bank and the Harriman-dominated Merchant-Sterling Corp.); Samuel F. Pryor, a high official of the Remington Arms Co. (and a director of the Chase National Bank and the Merchant-Sterling Corp.); and W. Averell Harriman.[32]

The general nature of the Rockefeller- "our crowd" coalition can be seen by the following analysis of the 1932 board of the American International Corp., a medium-sized financial holding company:[33]

American International Corp.

	Corporate Directors (and major affiliation)	Important Secondary Ties
President	Matthew C. Brush	Director of the Aviation Corp., General American Investors Co., and Manhattan Co.
Outside Directors	Percy A. Rockefeller	Director of the National City Bank of New York
	Albert H. Wiggin (high official of the Chase National Bank)	
	H. G. Freeman (up to 1931, president of the Chase Securities Corp., subsidiary of the Chase National Bank)	1932 director of the Chase Securities Corp.
	Beekman Winthrop (partner, Robert Winthrop & Co., N.Y.C.)	Director of the National City Bank of New York
	Gordon Auchincloss (New York lawyer who was Winthrop W. Aldrich's best friend)	Director of the Chase National Bank
	Frank Altschul (partner, I Lazard Frères)	President of the General American Investors Co. and a director of the Chase National Bank

Arthur Lehman (partner, Lehman Brothers)	Vice-president of the General American Investors Co.
Frederic W. Scott (partner, Richmond banking firm of Scott & Stringfellow)	Director of the General American Investors Co. and the Louisville & Nashville Railroad
Buford Scott (partner in Scott & Stringfellow and son of F. W. Scott)	
George H. Walker (up to recently, president of W. A. Harriman & Co.; now a partner in G. H. Walker & Co.)	Director of the Atlantic Fruit & Sugar Co.
Robert K. Cassatt (Philadelphia businessman)	Director of the Cuban Dominican Sugar Corp.
Pierre S. du Pont (board chairman, E. I. du Pont de Nemours & Co.)	
John J. Raskob (vice-president of the du Pont Co.)	

It is this constellation of forces which quietly emerged as a major influence in the New Deal administration of Franklin Delano Roosevelt.

MAJOR ADMINISTRATIVE AND DIPLOMATIC APPOINTMENTS

In selecting his Cabinet, Roosevelt made a number of decisions which clearly indicated that his administration was going to be considerably different from that of most of his predecessors. After some calculation, he chose as Secretary of State a longtime leader of the anti-tariff forces in the South, Tennessee's courtly and highly conservative Cordell Hull.[34] Unlike many other men who had held this position, Hull was, thanks mainly to his father's substantial funds, primarily a political figure. He had served for over 20 years in the House of Representatives and then briefly (in the early 1930s) in the United States Senate. His law practice was rather limited, being confined essentially to several small towns in Tennessee. In short, Hull had no major formal business ties, in contrast to most preceding Secretaries of State who since 1900 had included such prominent pro-corporate statesmen as John Hay, Elihu Root, Philander Knox, Robert Lansing, Charles Evans Hughes, Frank Kellogg, and Henry L. Stimson.[35] However, it should be noted that Hull, who was picked largely for geo-political reasons, was not a man on whom Roosevelt relied heavily. FDR frequently chose to work more closely with some of Hull's more seasoned, patrician top aides, such as

Under Secretary of State William Phillips and his (1936) successor, Sumner Welles, both of whom were related to the Astor family.[36]

After suffering at least one rebuff, Roosevelt chose New York industrialist William H. Woodin to serve as his first Secretary of the Treasury.[37] Woodin had comparatively little experience in government (two briefly-held state posts). Instead, he had spent the bulk of his career as a high official of the big American Car and Foundry Co., and also more recently as board chairman of the almost equally large American Locomotive Co. In addition, he was up to the early 1930s a director of a number of major economic enterprises, such as the du Pont-controlled General Motors Corp., the Harriman-dominated American Ship and Commerce Corp., the Cuba Co. (a big Caribbean holding company that was controlled by largely New York forces), the Rockefeller-dominated Remington Arms Co., and the influential Federal Reserve Bank of New York. Furthermore, Woodin had served as a key party fundraiser in 1932, and had been a trustee of the Warm Springs Foundation (a charitable body created to run the health spa later made famous by FDR), along with such political or economic notables as Louis McHenry Howe, Basil O'Connor, Henry Morgenthau, Jr., Russell Leffingwell of J. P. Morgan & Co., Herbert Straus of R. H. Macy & Co., and Harvey Gibson, a non-Morgan New York banker who served up to the early 1930s on the board of the American Smelting and Refining Co. and the Wright Aeronautical Corp.[38] Thus Woodin was a very well-connected figure whose chief ties would appear to have been with the Rockefeller-Harriman (and "our crowd") complex, rather than with the House of Morgan.[39]

Woodin, however, held office only until December of 1933 when he resigned largely because of age and ill health. As his successor, the President chose a longtime friend and Dutchess County neighbor, Henry Morgenthau, Jr., who had served in various special (non-economic) capacities under Roosevelt when he was governor of New York. Since the start of the New Deal Morgenthau had acted first as head of the newly formed U.S. Farm Credit Administration, a second-tier post he had been awarded after he had failed, because he was a New Yorker, in his efforts to become Secretary of Agriculture, and then briefly, when Woodin became increasingly ill, as Under Secretary of the Treasury. But most of Morgenthau's experience, both in public and private life, had been in the realm of farming. In fact, he had devoted most of his time in the preceding 12-year period to publishing a New York-based journal known as the *American Agriculturalist*. Apparently Morgenthau owed his appointment as Secretary of the Treasury largely to his friendship with Roosevelt and to his wealthy father's influence and support, for the latter had long been a substantial fundraiser for the Democratic party. Moreover, unknown to many, Morgenthau had two major family links to a crucial source of money for the Democrats, New York's close-knit set of Jewish investment bankers. The younger Henry Morgenthau's wife was a member of the Lehman family (her mother was a sister of Arthur and Herbert Lehman), and Henry's nephew, Jules Ehrich, had married one of Philip

Lehman's sisters. In addition, Morgenthau's father had long been a major stockholder and director of the Underwood Typewriter Co. (or, as it was known after 1928, the Underwood Elliott Fisher Co.), which board included, up to 1928, such figures as Philip Lehman, a brother-in-law of Jules Ehrich; Maurice Wertheim, who had married the younger Henry Morgenthau's sister, Alma; and Waddill Catchings, a top official in Goldman, Sachs.[40] Thus, if one can consider the 1906 appointment of Oscar Straus as Secretary of Commerce and Labor a politico-economic aberration, it can be said that Henry Morgenthau, Jr., was the first representative of this important ethnic group to attain high Cabinet office.[41]

Roosevelt's original choice for Attorney General was Montana's progressive Senator Thomas J. Walsh, a longtime Helena lawyer with no known corporate ties—if anything, he had an anti-business bias. But the intrepid Walsh, who had played a vital role in exposing the Teapot Dome scandal, died a few days before he was to assume office. Roosevelt then appointed Connecticut lawyer Homer Cummings, who had never held a major state or federal post, but was a longtime state Democratic leader and onetime national party chairman. He had been slated to be governor-general of the Philippine Islands, a relatively obscure position. As a private attorney, Cummings had built up a substantial practice in one of Connecticut's smaller cities, Stamford, where he had been associated with a number of mostly local business enterprises. As such, he was a less progressive figure than Roosevelt's first choice for the position, and he may have been on close terms with at least one prominent business leader.[42] Although a last-minute selection, Cummings held office for almost six years, until early 1939, when he resigned to return to private practice.

Cummings was replaced as Attorney General by another primarily political figure, Frank Murphy, who had held a series of governmental posts over the years, the most recent of which were as governor-general of the Philippines (from 1933 to 1936) and as governor of Michigan (from 1936 to 1938). In fact, Murphy had spent a total of 15 years in public office, and had practiced law in Detroit for only comparatively short periods of time, before and after the First World War. Although he was a close personal friend of the Chrysler family (which had economic links to pro-New Deal forces), Murphy had no formal corporate ties and, perhaps because of his Irish (nonelite) background and many years of public service, recognized the gross economic grievances of organized labor in these troubled times.[43]

For Secretary of War (which, because of the nation's pressing domestic problems, was not viewed as a very important post), Roosevelt chose one of his earliest and most steadfast supporters, Utah's George Dern, who had served as governor of his state for the preceding nine years. Though picked primarily for political reasons, Dern was also a well-established local business figure (as was his father before him), having served at various times as a high official of at least one mining concern, a small public utility, and a minor manufacturing firm, the Consolidated Wagon and Machine Co.[44]

Moreover, although he severed most of his economic ties by 1933, Dern continued to sit on the board of the First Security Trust Co. of Salt Lake City (which was controlled by a much larger company long dominated by Marriner S. Eccles, who had recently been appointed head of the Federal Reserve Board) throughout his years in Cabinet office. Yet, in retrospect, the most interesting aspect of his appointment was the fact that he was the first representative of the Far West to hold this position in the post-Civil War era.

When Dern died suddenly in 1936 in the midst of the presidential election campaign, Roosevelt promoted the Secretary's chief aide, Harry Woodring, another Westerner, to the top post. Before becoming Assistant Secretary of War in 1933, Woodring, thanks to much American Legion support, had served briefly as governor of Kansas and, like Dern, had been an ardent early backer of Roosevelt in his rise to national power. But unlike Dern (and many other Cabinet members over the years), Woodring was essentially a small town figure, for he had spent much of his adult life as an executive of the First National Bank of Neodesha, Kansas (which had a population of about 3,000 in the mid-1930s).[45] In short, neither Dern nor Woodring had the same sort of background as their mostly Eastern, big-city-based predecessors.

The position of Secretary of the Navy was also filled in a manner that did not fit the usual pattern. In considerable part because Virginia's conservative Senator Carter Glass chose not to accept the post of Secretary of the Treasury, Roosevelt decided, in an apparent effort to placate this influential leader, to appoint his Democratic colleague in the Upper House, Claude Swanson, to this prestigious Cabinet post.[46] Like Cordell Hull, Swanson was known mainly for his political activities, for he had served as a United States Senator since 1910, and before that as governor of his state and as a Virginia Congressman. Swanson was in private life what might best be described as a country lawyer, having practiced for many years in his hometown of Chatham (which in the early 1930s had only a few thousand people). This, again, was in marked contrast to the background of most of the post-Civil War occupants of this office, who generally were Northern business-oriented figures, such as Swanson's immediate predecessor, Charles F. Adams, a Boston Brahmin who had served on the board of the American Sugar Refining Co., AT&T, and the John Hancock Mutual Life Insurance Co., and whose daughter had married the son of the great J. P. Morgan.

After holding this post for a little over six years, the aged Swanson died in 1939. He was replaced by his top aide, Charles Edison, who prior to his appointment as Assistant Secretary of the Navy in 1936 had been president of Thomas A. Edison, Inc., a medium-sized New Jersey-based concern founded by his famous father, Thomas Alva Edison, some years after he had lost control of his original enterprise, the Edison Electric Light Co., to powerful New York and Boston interests led by J. P. Morgan & Co. (which then formed, by merger, the giant General Electric Co.). But this selection was not one of great economic note, for Edison, though fairly wealthy, had no other major business connections, and because of his father's loss of his electric company many years earlier, he probably had little use for such financial forces as the House of Morgan.

In an obvious effort to defer to Western interests and provide another sign of political assurance for his liberal supporters, President Roosevelt first offered the position of Secretary of the Interior to New Mexico's pro-New Deal Senator, Bronson Cutting (who had been born into a wealthy New York family), and then to California's progressive Republican Senator, Hiram Johnson. When both refused the post, it was awarded to a politically active and independent Chicago lawyer, Harold Ickes, who had long been identified with the Progressive party movement in Illinois, and who in recent years had been much involved in the civic battle waged against the reportedly piratical utility magnate, Samuel Insull. Since Ickes had led Illinois's Progressive forces into Roosevelt's camp in the 1932 election, he had a strong claim to a high office in the new administration. Equally important, given the temper of the times, Ickes belonged to a law firm (Ickes, Lord, Wise & Cobb) that had no significant ties to big business. From all accounts, Ickes more than justified Roosevelt's faith in him, for throughout his many years in office he ran the Department of the Interior in a sound and scrupulous fashion, favoring no special group or major economic interest.

When it came time to select a Secretary of Agriculture, Roosevelt was seriously torn between his close friend Henry Morgenthau, Jr., who coveted a Cabinet post, and the more politically acceptable sectional choice, Iowa's Henry A. Wallace, whose deceased, firmly Republican father had served in this capacity in the early 1920s. In the end the President bowed to the pressure generated by the nation's larger farmers, especially that exerted by the powerful American Farm Bureau Federation, and picked Wallace because he was believed to be in closer touch with the economic needs of America's agricultural interests.[48] One reason farm leaders supported Wallace was that he had spent over 20 years dealing with many of their problems as a high-level executive of the widely read Midwestern farm journal long published by the Wallace family.[49] In this sense, Wallace's selection was a rather traditional appointment. But he was apparently a less conservative figure than his father and most other members of his family, and in the late 1930s made a major break with the commercially dominated Farm Bureau.[50]

For Secretary of Commerce, an office generally awarded to an acknowledged spokesman of the business community, President Roosevelt chose, reportedly at the urging of some Southern leaders and William G. McAdoo, a Washington, D.C., lawyer, Daniel Roper, who had long been active in Democratic party affairs and had held a number of second- and third-tier posts in the Wilson administration. Since the early 1920s he had spent the bulk of his time working as a partner in the Washington law firm of Roper, Hagerman, Hurrey & Dudley, a now-defunct concern which, judging from existing published sources, had no ties to major corporate interests.⁵¹ Hence it is widely believed that Roper, unlike many of his Republican predecessors, was not closely associated with the business community.

But a more careful look at Roper's party record reveals that he had long been allied with some very important political and financial figures in the Democratic camp. For instance, in 1924 he was an integral part of a potent group led by Bernard Baruch and New York lawyer Thomas L. Chadbourne, which worked extremely hard that year to win the presidential nomination for Wilson's former Secretary of the Treasury (recently turned California attorney) William G. McAdoo.⁵² Roper remained a close friend of both Baruch and Chadbourne, particularly the latter, throughout the post-World War I period and frequently received the benefit of their sound "insider" financial counsel.⁵³ Although Chadbourne was not a well-known figure (certainly not compared to Baruch), he was the senior partner in a New York law firm (Chadbourne, Staunchfield & Levy) that often represented the Guggenheim interests, and he was closely linked with Baruch's friend Herbert Bayard Swope and other important businessmen in various stock market ventures.⁵⁴ To illustrate, in 1933 Chadbourne served on the board of such major concerns as the Adams Express Co., Manufacturers Trust Co., Mack Trucks, and Otis Elevator Co., all of which were linked with pro-New Deal forces.⁵⁵ In addition, Roper's son-in-law, South Carolina businessman David Coker, was a longtime director of the Federal Reserve Bank of Richmond, the deputy chairman of which was FDR's uncle, Frederic A. Delano.⁵⁶ Thus Roper was on closer terms with important figures in the business community than has been generally assumed.⁵⁷

When, because of his advancing years, Roper stepped down from office in late 1938, he was replaced by another apparently odd choice for the Commerce post. This appointee, Harry Hopkins, had no formal corporate ties or business experience. Instead he had held two important welfare posts under Roosevelt's New Deal government—as head of the Works Progress Administration (WPA), and director of the Federal Emergency Relief Administration—and before that he had served briefly as a high official of New York state's Temporary Emergency Relief Administration. Prior to the early 1930s Hopkins had been in charge of such civic enterprises as the New York Tuberculosis Association and the Association for Improving the Condition of the Poor in New York City. In fact, Hopkins was the only Secretary of Commerce in the nation's history who could be classified as a social worker.

But despite this unusual background, Hopkins had recently developed some powerful friends in the business community, men such as W. Averell Harriman, John D. Hertz (a partner in Lehman Brothers, board chairman of the Omnibus Corp., and a director of the Consolidated Aircraft Corp., Madison Square Garden Corp., Paramount Pictures, Inc., Studebaker Corp., and Tide Water Associated Oil Co.), Bernard Baruch, and Herbert Bayard Swope (a Baruch associate who was a director of the Brooklyn Manhattan

Transit Corp. and Columbia Broadcasting System).[58] Of these ties, the most important was with W. Averell Harriman who, realizing that Roosevelt had come to rely heavily on Hopkins' advice in many areas, felt that as Secretary of Commerce Hopkins could provide business leaders with effective access to the President. Indeed, in what may have been a pivotal effort to attain this objective, Harriman, as head of the Business Advisory Council, managed to secure the unanimous support of this influential body for Hopkins' appointment.[59] Further evidence of Harriman's role in this affair may be found in the fact that the man Hopkins soon chose to serve as his top aide, Edward J. Noble, was the head of the comparatively small Life Savers Corp., but had, more importantly, been a director of the medium-sized (pro-New Deal) Commercial National Bank and Trust Co. of New York and, back in the early 1930s, a board member of the Harriman-Lehman-dominated Aviation Corp.[60]

President Roosevelt took an unprecedented step and appointed a woman, Frances Perkins, to the now critical post of Secretary of Labor. This choice was made over the opposition of organized labor, which did not view her as a bona fide representative of its interests.[61] Rather she was a social worker who, like Hopkins, had turned governmental administrator. She had served as either a member or the head of the New York State Industrial Board from 1923 to 1929, and since then in the more influential capacity of State Industrial Commissioner, which experience undoubtedly gave her much insight into labor relations. Yet although Miss Perkins' sympathies lay more with labor than with management, it is interesting to note that she was on intimate terms with some prominent people in the New York business and social world. For instance, she was a longtime friend of W. Averell Harriman's sister, Mary H. Rumsey, who had become much involved in civic and political affairs since her husband's death in 1922. In fact, they shared a house in Washington up to the latter's accidental death in December 1934.[62] Miss Perkins was also on close terms with New York businessman (and onetime civic and city official) Henry Bruere, who was the president of the big Bowery Savings Bank, treasurer of the moderate reform group known as the Twentieth Century Fund, and a recently appointed director of the Harriman-dominated Union Pacific Railroad.[63] Thus there could be some question about the strength of Miss Perkins' commitment to the cause of America's long-depressed working classes.

In the realm of foreign affairs the recruitment pattern was of a rather mixed nature too. As his first Ambassador to Great Britain, FDR chose a wealthy Kentucky figure, Robert W. Bingham, who had no significant governmental experience, but who had contributed a substantial amount of money to Roosevelt's 1932 election campaign. Bingham had come into most of his wealth some years earlier when he married the widow of Henry M. Flagler, a onetime Standard Oil magnate and later major Florida developer. She died shortly after their marriage, leaving Bingham with a very sizable fortune, part of which he used to buy one of Louisville's best-known newspapers, the

Courier-Journal. This organ had been one of FDR's strongest supporters in the South in 1932. Bingham also served up to 1933 as a director of several Kentucky-based concerns, the most important of which was the Louisville and Nashville Railroad; this enterprise and its parent company, the Atlantic Coast Line Railroad, were controlled by a close-knit set of Baltimore and New York interests led by the interrelated Walters and Delano families. In fact, the Louisville and Nashville's board chairman was FDR's first cousin. Thus while Bingham did not have as many major business ties as most of his diplomatic predecessors at the Court of St. James, he had at least one key corporate link.

Bingham held office for over four years, after which his health deteriorated rapidly and he was forced to return to the United States. President Roosevelt chose as his replacement another wealthy, ambitious figure, Irish-American entrepreneur Joseph P. Kennedy. Partly because of his recent handsome financial support of the Democratic party, Kennedy had been appointed the first chairman of the Securities and Exchange Commission (SEC), a New Deal agency created to oversee the operations of the stock market, and later head of the U.S. Maritime Commission, another newly established body. However, Kennedy was mainly a self-made businessman who had gotten his start in Brahmin-dominated Boston, but who later moved his base of operations to New York and Hollywood, where he had a greater chance to achieve fame and fortune. When he first became prominent in the late 1920s, Kennedy was associated, either alone or with other groups (such as Lehman Brothers), with several sizable concerns in the nascent motion picture industry—namely, the Film Booking Offices of America, Keith-Albee-Orpheum Corp., and Pathé Exchange, Inc.[64] In the early 1930s, after severing his Hollywood ties (with a profit of at least $5 million), Kennedy returned to New York City to resume his stock market activities. In one such venture he worked closely with Bernard Baruch and Herbert Bayard Swope.[65] Later, between his two governmental stints in Washington, Kennedy served as a consultant to two major corporations, RCA and Paramount Pictures, the latter of which was closely linked with New York's Lehman Brothers.[66] Hence it seems fair to describe Kennedy as a wealthy entrepreneurial "out-group" figure, who secured his appointment as Ambassador to Great Britain primarily because of his financial links and resources.[67]

President Roosevelt chose another wealthy non-WASP figure and major Democratic party fundraiser, New York's Jesse Straus, as his first Ambassador to France.[68] Unlike many New Deal leaders, Straus had no governmental experience. He had been the longtime head of R. H. Macy & Co., a big family-dominated retail trade concern, and more recently had served as a director (or trustee) of the New York Life Insurance Co. and Bowery Savings Bank. But an even more important factor in Straus's appointment was that he had many key family ties in the elite Jewish circle now known as "our crowd." His brother Percy was related through the

Abraham family to the Schiffs and Warburgs of Kuhn, Loeb & Co., and Percy apparently took Jesse's seat on the board of the New York Life Insurance Co. when the latter was appointed Ambassador to France. One of Straus's cousins, Sissie Straus, had married into the Lehman family, and her brother, Nathan, had wed a member of the wealthy Sachs family (of Goldman, Sachs). Still another cousin, Roger Straus, had married a daughter of Daniel Guggenheim and was a high official of the American Smelting and Refining Co. Indeed, President Roosevelt would have been hard pressed to find anyone who had more socio-economic links to one major sector of the New York business community than Jesse Straus.[69]

Straus served as Ambassador to France for a little over three years before he became ill and was compelled to return home. As his successor Roosevelt chose another man of substantial means, Philadelphia's William C. Bullitt, who, unlike Straus, had considerable experience in foreign affairs and had been acting, since recognition was granted in 1933, as our representative to the Soviet Union. Bullitt had inherited a large amount of money from his family, whose fortune had been amassed through the efforts of his long-deceased grandfather, John C. Bullitt, who had been connected with a number of important enterprises such as the Northern Pacific Railroad. But because of a controversial diplomatic episode during the latter part of the Wilson regime and his marriage to the widow of Soviet sympathizer John Reed, William Bullitt had been virtually ostracized by Philadelphia's conservative economic establishment and had, as a consequence, spent most of the post-World War I years living abroad as an affluent man of leisure.[70] Thus, though very wealthy, he was considered something of an outsider, like many other New Dealers.[71]

Roosevelt also had a set of informal advisors unlike any which had previously aided a chief executive, the famous "brains trust." Although none of these people held a top-tier formal post in the administration (the White House then had only a meager staff), some exerted a great deal of influence in various high-level proceedings, especially during the critical early part of Roosevelt's first term in office. The "brains trust" was a mixed group with no hard-and-fast membership. It got its name from the fact that for the first time in history a president had recruited a significant number of academic figures to aid in his administration.

Initially, the most important person in this informal advisory body was Raymond Moley, a professor of public law at Columbia University who, because of the personal jealousy of Roosevelt's longtime private secretary, Louis McHenry Howe, was not awarded a White House post, but was instead appointed (at least for the record) an Assistant Secretary of State.[72] Yet such was Moley's influence at the outset that he was entrusted with the recruitment of several other members of the original "brains trust." Moley, however, did not long remain an official member of the administration, largely because, although he had a liberal image, he soon proved to be essentially a conservative, particularly in fiscal matters. One reason for

Moley's financial orthodoxy may be that, although he was primarily an academician, he had nonetheless become friendly with such elitist figures as F. Trubee Davison (whose family had long been associated with the House of Morgan), W. Averell Harriman, and apparently Vincent Astor.[73] Hence it is not surprising that after Roosevelt abandoned the gold standard and, in effect, subverted the London Economic Conference (for which many financial leaders had held high hopes), Moley resigned from office in late August 1933 to take an editorial post with a new national magazine owned by the Harriman and Astor interests.[74]

Two other early prime movers in the "brains trust" were Rexford G. Tugwell and Adolf A. Berle, Jr., both of whom were recruited by Moley and were, like him, members of the Columbia University faculty.[75] Tugwell, who was placed in the Department of Agriculture because of his long-term interest in this area, was a professor of economics who was widely regarded as a liberal thinker, in part because of the many articles he had written for *The New Republic*. Berle, a New York attorney and well-known professor of corporate law, was an able and ambitious man who, though he had married well, had never become a partner in a well-established corporate law firm and apparently harbored some ill feeling toward such concerns and their big business clients.[76] Perhaps because he was a director of the Taussig family-dominated American Molasses Co.,[77] Berle was, in the eyes of most corporate executives, a less "radical" official than Tugwell (who was a staunch advocate of economic planning).

Another early influential advisor, closely linked with the "brains trust" (though not considered one of its integral figures), was New York banker James P. Warburg, who had turned down a bid to become Under Secretary of the Treasury, but nonetheless rendered much valuable assistance, particularly on industrial and financial matters, during the first part of the New Deal administration.[78] Warburg was a member of a rich and well-connected family. His father (Paul) was a longtime partner in the famous banking house of Kuhn, Loeb, his mother was a Loeb, and his uncle was Jacob Schiff, the man mainly responsible for Kuhn, Loeb's rise to power. With the support of his family, James P. Warburg had become involved with commercial banking after World War I and had for some time been president of the International Acceptance Bank of New York (which had recently become a subsidiary of the Manhattan Co.). He also served in the early 1930s as a director of the Union Pacific Railroad and (along with William H. Woodin, the newly appointed Secretary of the Treasury) the American Ship and Commerce Corp., both of which were controlled by the Harriman interests.[79] Hence, although initially friendly to the New Deal, Warburg clearly fell into the conservative camp.[80] And as the Roosevelt administration engaged increasingly in numerous economic experiments and innovative programs to try to lift the nation out of the Depression, Warburg gradually lost favor with the President, who came to rely more and more on the advice of men such as

Harvard law professor Felix Frankfurter and two of his youthful protégés, Benjamin Cohen and Thomas Corcoran.[81]

IMPORTANT POLICY ACTIONS

Because of the unusual, mixed background of the people appointed to serve as either high federal officials or informal advisors in the Roosevelt administration, it is essential to analyze their influence on the more important actions taken by this regime, confronted as it was by the greatest economic crisis in the nation's history. Initially, as various historians have pointed out, many of the major acts of the New Deal were of a distinctly conservative nature, both because of Roosevelt's own aristocratic (and to some extent, pro-business) background and because of the even more orthodox economic thinking of most of his key early advisors, who carried more weight than the various liberal members of his administration. This was clearly demonstrated in the first part of 1933 when, at the urging of such conservatives as financial director Lewis Douglas, Roosevelt made severe cuts in the proposed budgets of almost every department and submitted a sharply pruned appropriations bill to Congress.

But the most far-reaching action undertaken by Roosevelt in 1933 was the establishment of the National Recovery Administration (NRA). This agency was designed, through the formulation and implementation of industrial and production codes, to help stimulate business, increase purchasing power (in part by a provision granting labor the right to organize and bargain collectively), and thus pull the nation out of the Depression.[82] The program was based on the concept of a cartelized economy (an idea ardently espoused by both Bernard Baruch and GE president Gerard Swope), and was dominated by influential corporate interests almost from its inception.[83] Indeed, according to one authority, businessmen such as utility executive Henry I. Harriman, who was president of the U.S. Chamber of Commerce and a member of the Business Advisory Council, and former New York banker Fred Kent, who was treasurer of the research-oriented National Industrial Conference Board and also a member of the BAC, had a major hand, along with Roosevelt advisor Raymond Moley, in the original drafting of the National Industrial Recovery Act. Then men such as budget director Lewis Douglas, Hugh Johnson, a close friend and business associate of financier Bernard Baruch, and Donald Richberg, a former Chicago labor lawyer, whipped the bill into its final form.[84]

Of even greater note was the fact that the operation of the NRA was dominated by big business or pro-business figures. For example, as the chief administrator of the new agency, President Roosevelt chose Hugh Johnson, who, while he had been associated with small business up to the late 1920s, was most likely appointed to this important post because he was one of Bernard Baruch's chief economic and political aides.[85] Since 1929, when he lost his position with the Moline Implement Co. because of a merger, Johnson was little more than a well-paid employee of Baruch ($25,000 a year was a handsome salary during the Depression), and, in fact, remained on Baruch's payroll two months after he became head of the NRA.[86] Other early high officials of the NRA included Arthur D. Whiteside, who was president of the newly formed Dun and Bradstreet, Inc., and W. Averell Harriman, who, as noted earlier, was one of the original prime movers in the BAC and a key figure in the economic coalition closely allied with the New Deal (in fact, Harriman so overshadowed NRA boss Hugh Johnson as a businessman that it raises a serious question about the nature of their relationship).[87] Furthermore, according to Bernard Bellush, no well-qualified labor and consumer representatives were appointed to any vital post in the NRA during its brief existence.[88]

Another insight into the politico-economic nature of the NRA can be gained from the fact that the first head of its rather ineffective Consumers' Advisory Board was the wealthy, civic-minded Mary H. Rumsey, who was W. Averell Harriman's sister and a close friend of Secretary of Labor Frances Perkins.[89]

The NRA's Industrial Advisory Board, on the other hand, was dominated by the BAC. Indeed, to quote Kim McQuaid, the conservative Hugh Johnson "... proposed that the BAC provide all of the personnel of the IAB from among its own membership on a rotating basis. BAC members enthusiastically accepted the invitation, and Walter Teagle was selected as the first chairman of the new NRA advisory agency."[90] As a result, during the crucial summer months of 1933 BAC members Teagle, Swope, Kirstein, and H. I. Harriman (who was also president of the U.S. Chamber of Commerce) spent almost all of their time in Washington in a concerted effort to give form and substance to the NRA. That their labors were largely successful may be seen from the following analysis of the make-up of the NRA's Industrial Advisory Board in early 1935:[91]

	Name (and primary business affiliation)	Major Organizational Links (as directors or their equivalents)
Chairman	George H. Mead (president, Mead Corp., Ohio)	BAC
Other Members	Henry S. Dennison (president, Dennison Mfg. Co., Mass.)	BAC and 20th Century Fund
	Lew Hahn (former head, Hahn Department Stores, Inc., N.Y.)	BAC
	Henry I. Harriman (board chairman, New England Power Assn., Boston)	BAC and U.S. Chamber of Commerce (USCC)

George H. Houston (president, Baldwin Locomotive Works, Phila.)	NAM and National Industrial Conference Board
Henry P. Kendall (president, Kendall Co., Boston)	BAC
deLauncey Kountze (board chairman, Devoe & Raynolds Co., N.Y.)	BAC
Morris E. Leeds (president, Leeds & Northrup Co., Phila.)	BAC and American Association for Labor Legislation
Rivers Peterson (editor, *Hardware Retailer*, Ind., a spokesman apparently for the National Retailers Council)	
Rudolph Rauch (unidentified member)	
Roger B. Shepard (president, Finch, Van Slyck & McConville, an apparently small St. Paul business concern)	
George A. Sloan (president, Cotton Textile Institute)	(Sloan became a member of the BAC in 1936)
Harold C. Smith (president, Illinois Tool Works, Chicago)	BAC and NAM
R. Douglas Stuart (vice-president, Quaker Oats Co., Chicago)	BAC
Gerard Swope (president, General Electric Co., N.Y.)	BAC
Myron C. Taylor (board chairman, U.S. Steel Corp., N.Y.)	BAC
Walter C. Teagle (president, Standard Oil Co. of N.J., N.Y.)	BAC and USCC
Sidney J. Weinberg (partner, Goldman, Sachs & Co., N.Y.)	BAC
William P. Witherow (president, Witherow Steel Co., Pa.)	BAC and USCC

McQuaid's analysis of the IAB's minutes reveals that "...the Industrial Advisory Board exercised a powerful, often a determining, influence over the fundamentals of NRA industrial and labor policy."[92] Thus, contrary to what some scholars have claimed, the NRA was not dominated by such groups as the U.S. Chamber of Commerce and other lesser economic forces, but by the BAC and major corporate interests.

Still further evidence of the disproportionate power exerted by big business in this area may be seen in the make-up of the NRA's seven-man National Labor Board (NLB), which was created to preside over disputes arising out of all (now legally sanctioned) labor organization and collective bargaining activities. At the outset it consisted of its chairman, New York's progressive Senator Robert F. Wagner, three labor representatives—the AFL's William Green, the United Mine Workers' John L. Lewis, and Columbia University professor Leo Wolman—and three important corporate executives—GE president Gerard Swope (who was the first chairman of the BAC), Walter C. Teagle, the president of Standard Oil of New Jersey (and a major figure in both the BAC and U.S. Chamber of Commerce), and a lesser known official, Louis E. Kirstein, who was a vice-president and general manager of Filene's department store in Boston.[93] Filene's was actually a subsidiary of the much larger Federated Department Stores, Inc., which was probably dominated by Cincinnati's Lazarus family and New York's "our crowd." Moreover, although only a second-tier official, Kirstein served on the board of the RKO subsidiary of RCA, along with Monroe Gutman, Arthur Lehman, and Paul Mazur (all of Lehman Brothers), Elisha Walker of Kuhn, Loeb, Frederick Strauss of J. & W. Seligman & Co., GE board chairman Owen D. Young, and Herbert Bayard Swope. Hence it is clear that small business was poorly represented on this labor-management body. However, as it turned out, the NLB was soon reduced to impotence for want of effective authority and the bitter resistance of certain key corporate interests, apparently spearheaded by influential members of the NAM.[94]

Big business's domination of the NRA also extended to the various industry boards created by this agency, for Hugh Johnson turned over much of the responsibility for formulating and implementing the NRA's economic codes to business leaders or other friendly forces.[95] For example, the Cotton Textile National Industrial Relations Board was headed by a New York writer and researcher named Robert Bruere, whom one scholar has described as too weak to cope with the widespread problems of this strongly anti-union industry.[96] Though it is not mentioned in most accounts, one reason for Bruere's ineffective performance may have been that his brother, Henry, was president of the big Bowery Savings Bank and a director of the New York Life Insurance Co. and of the Harriman-dominated Union Pacific Railroad. Henry Bruere was also apparently a close friend of Secretary of Labor Frances Perkins, who was on intimate terms with Harriman's sister. Thus when NRA official Robert Bruere received complaints about the textile industry's failure to live up to the labor provisions of his board's code, he merely forwarded them to George A. Sloan, the president of the Cotton Textile Institute (and a recently elected director of the Southern Railway), who usually concluded that there was nothing amiss.[97] Scant wonder, then, that organized labor viewed the NRA as an instrument created largely for the benefit of big business.[98] Fortunately for labor and the general public, this agency was declared unconstitutional by the Supreme Court in 1935, mainly because of certain flaws in its enabling legislation.

Other important measures dealing with financial reform were adopted in the first few years of Roosevelt's administration. The first of these had to do with the operation of the nation's banks, many of which were in desperate straits as a result of the Depression and, in certain cases, shady management practices. In fact, a large number of banks had collapsed, creating a massive run on these institutions and wiping out the savings of thousands of middle- and low-income families. To bring a temporary halt to this disastrous downward spiral, President Roosevelt declared a brief bank holiday shortly after he assumed office.

Moreover, Congress, under the prodding of certain leaders who had long been dissatisfied with federal oversight of the nation's banks, had begun through a subcommittee a major probe into this area during the last year of the Hoover regime. The Congressional investigation received a substantial boost in early 1933 when former New York assistant district attorney Ferdinand Pecora, a dedicated progressive with no noteworthy economic ties, was hired as chief counsel of the subcommittee.[99] Among its first targets were the heads of two big commercial banks which in the postwar years had engaged in a considerable amount of dubious speculative activity—Charles E. Mitchell, board chairman of the National City Bank of New York, and Albert H. Wiggin, a longtime high official of the Chase National Bank (a Morgan-oriented concern up to 1930). To give further impetus to this inquiry, Wiggins was, because of his former ties, reportedly "thrown to the wolves" by Chase's recently emerged top interests, the John D. Rockefeller family.[100] These influential forces were, in fact, the first to break the ranks of Wall Street's bitter opposition to a bill introduced earlier by Virginia's Senator Carter Glass providing for the separation of commercial and investment banking. They apparently decided to support the measure for two reasons: to restore the prestige of the nation's much criticized big banks, and, though it was never publicly acknowledged, to undercut the enormous power power of the House of Morgan, a complex that had been built in part around the integration of commercial and investment banking.[101] Indeed, it was Rockefeller in-law Winthrop W. Aldrich, the recently appointed head of the Chase National Bank, who was credited in many circles with the astute maneuvering which brought the giant firm of J. P. Morgan & Co. within the range of questioning of the Pecora subcommittee, thereby generating further pressure for the passage of this measure.[102] Thus Congress was persuaded to adopt the Glass-Steagell Act of 1933, which provided not only for the separation of commercial and investment banking, but also, at the urging of Vice President John Nance Garner and various Congressional leaders, for the creation of the Federal Deposit Insurance Corp. to safeguard the savings of America's badly buffeted middle- and low-income families.

Another area into which the Roosevelt administration moved soon after it assumed office was that of securities regulation. In the boom fever of the roaring 1920s, many Americans had invested considerable money in wildly touted corporate stocks. But, unlike certain "insiders," their financial hopes were often badly dashed, particularly after the great crash of October 1929. In an effort to protect the investing public, FDR created several task forces to come up with remedial measures. The upshot was the passage in early 1933 of what might be called a "truth in securities" law designed to eliminate many of the dubious, if not fraudulent, tactics involved in the sale of corporate stock. However, many felt that this legislation fell far short of what was required, since it did not cover the operation of the nation's stock market, which had long been marked by questionable practices. As a result, further study was undertaken by Congressional investigators, in the course of which Richard Whitney, the president of the New York Stock Exchange, was called to testify about this body's general mode of operation.[103] Many found his statements unconvincing. Spurred on by the growing drive for reform, President Roosevelt drew upon a variety of advisors to aid in drafting a law that would provide for effective federal oversight of the nation's stock markets. These men included several members of the "brains trust," such as Adolf Berle, Benjamin Cohen, Thomas Corcoran, and Felix Frankfurter, Secretary of Commerce Daniel Roper and his top aide, John Dickinson, as well as Yale University professor William O. Douglas and former Federal Trade Commissioner Huston Thompson. Among the "outside" advisors brought in to help whip the bill into final shape were such influential figures as W. Averell Harriman, Paul Mazur of Lehman Brothers, and three members of major New York law firms—Arthur H. Dean of Sullivan & Cromwell, Alexander I. Henderson of Cravath, deGersdorff, Swaine & Wood, and Roland L. Redmond of Carter, Ledyard & Milburn, who had married into the Delano family and was a director of the Louisville and Nashville Railroad.[104] Eventually, a bill emerged with sufficient backing to secure its passage. This provided for the creation of an independent regulatory body known as the Securities and Exchange Commission (SEC). As a result of its initial staffing and support, this agency soon managed to eliminate many of the unsavory trading practices which had previously existed in the often "insider"-dominated financial world.[105]

Still another important measure, adopted shortly after the establishment of the SEC, was the Banking Act of 1935, which dealt largely with the reorganization of the Federal Reserve System (a matter initially skirted by the Roosevelt administration). According to all accounts, the principal author of this bill was FDR's newly appointed governor of the Federal Reserve Board, Marriner S. Eccles, who, unlike his predecessors, represented rising banking and entrepreneurial interests in the West.[106] As Arthur Schlesinger has observed, Eccles was a provincial tycoon by the age of 40, "...the head of a holding company controlling 26 banks in the Rocky Mountain area [the First Security Corp.], the president of milk, sugar, lumber, and construction companies, and the director of hotels, railroads, and insurance companies."[107] Eccles and other "outsiders" had long felt that, all legal provisions notwithstanding, the Federal Reserve Board in Washington had been dominated by the various regional Reserve banks, particularly the influential New York Federal Reserve Bank, which was reportedly closely linked with the House of Morgan.[108] Hence, he drafted legislation which clearly bolstered the authority of both the President of the United States and the Federal Reserve System's national board of governors, and in the process removed its two ex officio members, the Secretary of the Treasury and the Comptroller of the Currency. With the support of some powerful dissident figures in the financial community such as California's A.P. Giannini, the head of the Bank of America, he managed to secure sufficient votes to attain the passage of this controversial measure, much to the dismay of major banking forces in the East.[109]

Economic interests probably also played an important part in a number of the actions taken by the New Deal in the foreign policy area, as for example in the formulation of the reciprocal trade program that was adopted as part of Roosevelt's "good neighbor" policy in the early 1930s. One reason this measure was strongly advocated by many economic and political leaders was that the Central American-United States sugar trade had fallen off drastically after the onslaught of the Depression and the passage of the Smoot-Hawley Tariff Act of 1930 which, thanks to the efforts of the beet sugar bloc in Congress, had raised the duty on imported cane sugar to its highest point since the turn of the century.[110] However, various American businessmen had large holdings in Cuban-based sugar operations (over $600 million, all told), and they were understandably eager to protect their investments and increase the shipment of sugar into the United States.[111] In fact, many of these people were closely allied with the economic coalition that was backing FDR. In 1933, for example, the big Atlantic Fruit and Sugar Co. was headed by Frederick B. Adams, who was also the president of the West Indies Sugar Corp. (the recently reconstituted Cuban-Dominican Sugar Corp.), a director of the Louisville and Nashville Railroad, and whose wife was a member of the Delano family. The "outside" members of the Atlantic Fruit and Sugar Company's board included Roosevelt kinsman Vincent Astor, Percy A. Rockefeller, Samuel F. Pryor, a high official of the probably Rockefeller-dominated Remington Arms Co. (and a director of Chase National Bank and Harriman-controlled Merchant-Sterling Corp.), and Robert W. Goelet, a wealthy Harriman kinsman who was a director of the Illinois Central and Union Pacific railroads. Furthermore, both Under Secretary of State William Phillips and Assistant Secretary of State (and 1933 Ambassador to Cuba) Sumner Welles were related to the Astor family; Secretary of State Cordell Hull and Secretary of Commerce Daniel Roper were friendly to sugar interests; New Deal (and Cuba) advisor Adolf Berle was a director of the American Molasses Co., which used Cuban sugar; and FDR's first Secretary of the Treasury, William Woodin, had been a board member of the Cuba Co., which controlled many enterprises in that country.[112] Thus, although it is difficult to show exactly how influence is exercised, one cannot help but feel, given these politico-economic links, that these officials had much to do with the success of the Roosevelt administration in securing a reduction in the tariff and an expansion of trade with Cuba and other Latin American states. Both objectives were achieved through the adoption of the new reciprocal trade program.

Toward the end of the "first" New Deal (roughly the first two, fairly conservative years of the Roosevelt regime), another very different kind of measure was adopted in the form of the Social Security Act of 1935. Most accounts of the events leading up to the enactment of this epic statute have placed great emphasis on the amount of business opposition it encountered. For instance, Arthur Schlesinger has made much of the fact that the NAM, National Industrial Conference Board, and General Motors president (and du Pont ally) Alfred P. Sloan, Jr., all strove vigorously to defeat this plan.[113] However, more recent research, particularly that conducted by G. William Domhoff, has shown that there was also considerable support for the proposal in other influential quarters, especially in the BAC and the American Association for Labor Legislation (an older, much less elitist group that had long urged the adoption of such a measure), and that the NAM's opposition reflected the narrow and shortsighted position of various small- and medium-sized concerns and certain arch-conservative big business interests which had recently taken over the NAM.[114]

There would appear to be a great deal of truth to Domhoff's claim. For instance, when the Social Security proposal was coming under heavy attack in the spring of 1935, a sizable delegation of key corporate leaders, all of whom were members of the BAC, made a special visit to the White House to reemphasize their support of the measure to a favorably disposed Roosevelt, perhaps partly because they feared that some form of the more radical Townsend plan might otherwise be adopted.[115] The Social Security program had also been given a critical boost at an earlier juncture, in late 1934 when, in the face of presidential caution or indifference, Standard Oil's Walter Teagle, GE's Gerard Swope, Eastman Kodak's Marion Folsom, and certain other executives serving on the advisory council of Roosevelt's Committee on Economic Security (most of whom were members of the BAC) came out strongly for its adoption.[116] In fact, according to one recently published study, the BAC "...was the staunchest advocate within the business community of a social security system."[117] When the Social Security system was finally enacted by Congress (albeit with a regressive mode of financing), President Roosevelt chose as its first head a former New Hampshire governor, John G. Winant, who was a vice-president of the American Association for Labor Legislation, a member of the elitist-dominated board of the Brookings Institution, and a man with some influential New York family ties in his own right.[118]

Another major piece of legislation adopted, after much travail, in 1935 was the famous Wagner Act, which for the first time in American history provided effective guarantees of the right of workers to organize and bargain collectively with their employers. Actually, this right had, by law, been granted to labor under Section 7(a) of the National Industrial Recovery Act, which such important groups as the Business Advisory Council and Chamber of Commerce agreed to support in return for the AFL's acceptance of the NRA's economic cartelization program. In an effort to resolve the many disputes that soon arose as a result of this clause, President Roosevelt had created a seven-man National Labor Board. However, this part-time body never had any control over the enforcement of its decisions, for this power lay with the top officials of the business-dominated NRA and the Department of Justice. As a result, by early 1934 the National Labor Board had arrived at a serious impasse because of the refusal of various big companies, especially some associated with the NAM, to comply with its rulings.[119]

At this juncture the still cautious Roosevelt decided to abolish the badly harried NLB and, with the support of Congress, established a three-man National Labor Relations Board, which was to be made up of more objective, fulltime officials. But this body was given no more power than its predecessor; it could do little other than investigate. Nonetheless, under the direction of its two patrician chairmen—Wisconsin Law School dean Lloyd K. Garrison, a former New Yorker with family ties to the influential Jays and the Villards (who had long owned the liberal journal *The Nation*), and his successor, Philadelphia attorney Francis Biddle, who was a member of one of that city's "first families"—this sparsely endowed agency struggled to forge some sort of effective national labor policy.[120] Yet it too had only limited success, especially against the more influential larger companies.[121]

The Board's rulings, nevertheless, proved to be of considerable value, for they were the source of many substantive and procedural provisions that were incorporated into a much stronger measure, the Wagner Act. This legislation had been introduced in 1934 against the will of a still fairly conservative FDR, but by the spring of 1935 it had gathered increasing support in Congress. Then, President Roosevelt, sensing the political trend, finally abandoned his cautious position and, with the backing of men like Biddle, threw his weight behind the bill, which was strongly pushed by New York's progressive Senator Robert F. Wagner and such groups as the American Association for Labor Legislation.[122] And it is well that Roosevelt did, because it was only after a vigorous legislative struggle, in which most major business spokesmen (including many BAC leaders) were arrayed in bitter opposition, that this controversial measure was passed.

The Wagner Act ushered in a new era in American politico-economic relations. For not only did this law encourage labor organization, it made collective bargaining compulsory on the part of the employer and, by its wording, did much to weaken, if not destroy, the quasi-captive company union.[123] As a result of this legislation, labor union membership grew from a rather modest total of 3,728,000 in 1935 to nearly 9,000,000 by 1940. Equally important, the new law marked a turning point in labor's involvement in political affairs. In the 1936 election the major unions contributed substantial funds to the campaign of Franklin Delano Roosevelt and other friendly Democrats, thus forging a link that has not been severed to this day.[124]

Other noteworthy changes were made about this time in the realm of taxation. President Roosevelt, reacting largely to growing radical pressures generated by such forces as Huey Long's "share-the-wealth" movement, did much to secure the enactment of a bill that boosted the income tax on individuals to an all-time high of 75 percent on incomes of over $5 million.[125] In addition, following a 1934 increase, Congress, at the President's request, raised the federal estate (i.e., inheritance) tax to an unprecedented 70 percent and, to help curb gross evasion, reimposed a federal gift tax, which was pegged at a level of 52.5 percent.[126] As one might expect, these progressive measures exacerbated the conflict between the now leftward-leaning Roosevelt administration and wealthy business interests in America.

A last major law adopted during this period was the Public Utility Holding Company Act of 1935. As pointed out earlier, a number of huge utility holding companies had been created before the Depression by influential financial and entrepreneurial interests. Indeed, government officials found that by the early 1930s economic concentration in this area had reached the point where a mere thirteen holding companies controlled, directly or indirectly, about 75 percent of the privately-owned electric power in the country, and that the three largest combines—the United Corp., Electric Bond and Share Co., and Midwestern-based Insull group (the first two of which were closely linked with the House of Morgan)—had 40 percent of the total.[127] By 1935 Roosevelt, who had clashed with utility interests while he was governor of New York, had begun to turn away from his general pro-business orientation and had decided that the time was ripe to break up these vast, often highly complex enterprises, and thereby undermine the strength of the economic forces associated with them.[128] However, the measure designed to achieve this goal ran into a great deal of opposition in Congress, largely because of intense lobbying efforts by a number of major utility executives, the most prominent of whom were Wendell Willkie of the Commonwealth and Southern Corp. and Philip H. Gadsden of the United Gas Improvement Co., both of which were controlled by the Morgan-dominated United Corp.[129] As a result, the bill's original mandatory "death sentence" clause was significantly softened, and it was instead specified that all holding companies more than twice removed from their operating companies were to be dissolved. In addition, the Securities and Exchange Commission was given the discretionary authority to eliminate all interlocking enterprises that were not deemed to be in the public interest. Though the implementation of this act took some time to work out, it ultimately had considerable effect. And like some other New Deal measures, it would seem to have been most vigorously applied initially against certain big Morgan-dominated concerns, particularly the United Corp., which by 1940 had been drastically reduced in size and was in the process of divesting itself by governmental edict of its subordinate operational units.

Thus it is not altogether surprising that the bitter resentment generated in various business circles by the passage of this and other major reform measures in the mid-1930s led to the creation of a politically extreme group known as the American Liberty League, which, by all accounts, was dedicated primarily to defeating Roosevelt in his upcoming bid for reelection in 1936.[130] This organization was dominated by a very small but influential segment of the business community, for much of its money and most of its leadership came from a coalition of the du Pont interests, the still powerful House of Morgan, and certain arch-conservative forces in the NAM.[131] Yet despite its vast financial support, this reactionary effort was a dismal failure because Roosevelt had now established himself as an extremely popular figure in American politics, and he crushed his Republican opponent, former Kansas governor Alf Landon, in the 1936 presidential election.

Badly strained as politico-economic relations were by this time, the gap between major business interests and the Roosevelt regime grew even worse in the late 1930s, partly because of the administration's much-expanded antitrust activity and its overt support of the famous TNEC investigation into the concentration of corporate wealth and power in the United States. It was because of this general trend, plus the Roosevelt administration's drastic move against the private power industry and its increasing ties with organized labor, that the Republican party turned, thanks to a well-financed "dark horse" drive, to big business executive (and political neophyte) Wendell Willkie as its presidential candidate in 1940. Willkie had led the much publicized fights against the Public Utility Holding Company Act of 1935 and the TVA, and had thus acquired a great deal of public recognition. Not surprisingly, his bid failed. But in failing it was still important, not from the standpoint of Willkie's widely praised effort to deprive Roosevelt of an unprecedented third term, but because Willkie was closely associated with the House of Morgan (although rarely noted, he even graced one of its major bank boards).[132] In retrospect, his defeat marked the end of an era, extending back to Grover Cleveland's second term, in which this financial complex had wielded great power. Willkie, in fact, was the last presidential candidate to be strongly linked with the House of Morgan, which, having lost much support and prestige during the hectic New Deal years, entered into a period of sharp decline, and never again exerted great influence in American politico-economic affairs.

SUPREME COURT APPOINTMENTS AND ACTIONS

Not only did the Roosevelt regime bring about many changes in high-level federal recruitment and governmental policy, it also produced a major realignment in the socio-economic makeup of the U.S. Supreme Court.

Because of the long-term nature of these appointments, this shift did not take place until over four years after Roosevelt assumed office in 1933.

At the outset of the New Deal the Supreme Court was clearly dominated by conservative, pro-business figures. At the top this dominance was manifested in the person of Chief Justice Charles Evans Hughes, who, though he had held many prominent governmental posts over the years (ranging from governor of New York to Secretary of State), had since 1916 become increasingly associated with corporate interests. Indeed in the late 1920s, prior to his appointment as a judge of the Permanent Court of International Justice, he had served as an attorney for the American Petroleum Institute and the Standard Oil Company of New Jersey, as a trustee of the Rockefeller Foundation (which had substantial holdings in Standard Oil), and as a councillor (i.e., official advisor) of the National Industrial Conference Board.[133] His son, Charles Evans Hughes, Jr., who was a member of his father's former law firm, was a director of the New York Life Insurance Co. up to 1934, and another of his partners, Richard E. Dwight, served on the board of Merck and Co. up to 1937. Hence until jarred by certain events into taking a more positive attitude toward various public policy questions in the late 1930s, Hughes frequently adopted a fairly conservative stance on important politico-economic issues brought before this high tribunal.

Also on the Court were four arch-conservative jurists, frequently referred to as the "Four Horsemen," who had been appointed long before Hughes and represented a powerful pro-business bloc. One of these men was Wyoming's Willis Van Devanter, who had served for six years as an Assistant Attorney General and seven years as a federal judge before the First World War. He also had been associated, before the turn of the century, with a Cheyenne law firm which regularly handled the state affairs of the influential Union Pacific Railroad, and this experience apparently had considerable effect on his economic outlook.[134]

Another closely allied justice was James C. McReynolds, who had been President Wilson's first Attorney General, but soon proved to be a very abrasive force within the Cabinet and, in an ill-advised move, had been "kicked upstairs" to a seat on the United States Supreme Court. McReynolds was a former Nashville (and later, briefly, New York City) lawyer, in which pre-1903 capacity he had served as a legal advisor to the Illinois Central Railroad.[135]

The other two highly conservative jurists, George Sutherland and Pierce Butler, were appointed in the early 1920s when the business-dominated Harding administration was in power. Both had been closely linked with banking and other business interests in their home states. For example, although a Washington, D.C., attorney from 1917 to 1922, former Utah Senator George Sutherland was a board member of the Mormon-controlled Deseret Savings Bank of Salt Lake City up to his appointment to the Supreme Court. He also served as a vice-president of the fairly small Home

Trust and Savings Co. of that city from about 1910 to 1926.[136] And St. Paul attorney Pierce Butler, whose selection was strongly urged by various important business and legal figures, was a millionaire as a result of his corporate law practice and family business.[137] In fact, he had long been regarded as one of the best railroad lawyers in the Northwest, and had served on the board of a major bank and a utility company in St. Paul prior to his appointment to the High Court.

These four arch-conservative justices were usually joined in their rulings by another longtime corporate lawyer, Owen J. Roberts, who had received considerable acclaim as the chief investigating and prosecuting official in the famous Teapot Dome scandal in the 1920s (which was a major reason why he was appointed to the Court). But Roberts was primarily a Philadelphia attorney who had devoted most of his efforts over the years to representing various business interests. As a matter of fact, he had served since the mid-1920s as a board member of the Franklin Fire Insurance Company (which was an affiliate of a larger New York-based company), the Equitable Life Assurance Society (of New York), the Bell Telephone Co. of Pennsylvania, and, shortly before his appointment to the High Court, as a director of Pennsylvania Bell's huge parent company, AT&T.[138] Given these associations, one could have predicted that Roberts would generally align himself with the conservatives on the Court, thereby providing this group with a majority during the first part of the Roosevelt regime.

The three liberal or moderate justices on the Supreme Court in the early New Deal years were Louis D. Brandeis, Benjamin Cardozo, and Harlan Fiske Stone. Brandeis was a former Boston attorney who had once represented some big business enterprises, but who by 1910 had become a dedicated advocate of the progressive cause.[139] It was largely for this reason that, despite the bitter opposition of the American Bar Association and various powerful corporate interests, he was appointed by President Wilson to the nation's highest court. Another liberal figure who had only recently been elevated to this tribunal was New York's Benjamin Cardozo, who, unlike Brandeis, had never been an influential corporate lawyer, but had served for 18 years (from 1914 to 1932) in a major state judicial capacity. The third member of this group, Harlan Fiske Stone, had a very mixed background, having been both a Wall Street lawyer (though only briefly with a top-tier firm) and a dean of the Columbia University law school. The latter experience apparently did much to mitigate the marked pro-business bias found in so many corporate attorneys appointed to high judicial posts.[140] Thus, from a socio-economic standpoint, this trio was quite different from the majority faction on the Supreme Court.

Because none of the nine justices died or resigned during the first four years of the New Deal, the Court remained dominated by its strong conservative majority up to the late 1930s. And this conservative coalition wreaked havoc in the mid-1930s on many of the emergency measures that were adopted as economic reform or recovery devices by the pragmatic Roosevelt regime. For instance, in the famous *Schechter Poultry Corp.* v. *United States* case the Court did away with the NRA by taking an extremely narrow view of the interstate commerce clause and also ruling (perhaps rightly in this regard) that this act represented an improper delegation of legislative power. In another important case it, in effect, abolished the Agricultural Adjustment Administration, which had been established in an effort to alleviate the economic plight of many American farmers, through what one learned dissenting judge described as a "tortured construction of the Constitution." In addition, to quote a set of highly respected historians, the Court "... rejected the railroad retirement plan on the curious theory that there was no legitimate connection between interstate commerce and the welfare of those who conducted it, while the Bituminous Coal Act went into the judicial wastebasket because the Court, in the Carter case, insisted that coal mining was a purely local business. It invalidated congressional legislation to protect farm mortgages on the ground of conflict with the esoteric 'due process' clause of the Fifth Amendment and nullified the Municipal Bankruptcy Act on the assumption that such legislation invaded the domain of the states—even though the Act required state consent, which many states had already given."[141] Indeed, at no time in the past had the Supreme Court overruled so many acts of Congress in such a short period.

Faced with these and other judicial verdicts that threatened to scuttle a large part of the New Deal program, President Roosevelt took a drastic step in early 1937. He submitted to Congress a reform plan which would give him the power to enlarge the Supreme Court to a maximum membership of fifteen by appointing one new judge for each justice who, having passed the age of seventy (and having served for at least ten years), failed to retire. This extraordinary measure created a storm of controversy, for it was a transparent attempt to alter the politico-economic makeup of this august body and seemed to interject much ideology and partisanship into its proceedings. Such was the opposition to this measure that it was defeated without ever getting out of committee. But in the end it accomplished its political purpose. Sensing now that the Court's excessive negativism would lead only to disaster, Chief Justice Hughes shifted noticeably in his rather conservative line of thinking, and Philadelphia's Owen J. Roberts made an abrupt about-face and began to approve measures he had formerly adjudged to be unconstitutional. For instance, nine months after the Court had struck down a New York minimum wage law (in *Morehead* v. *New York*), it sustained a similar act of the state of Washington (in the *West Coast Hotel Co.* v. *Parrish*). The Court went on to uphold the National Labor Relations Act of 1935 and the recently established Social Security program. In short, the Court was thereafter very careful about declaring acts of Congress unconstitutional and rarely imposed its economic judgment over that of the nation's duly elected representatives.

About this time a significant change took place in the overall makeup of the Supreme Court. In mid-1937 Wyoming's conservative justice Van Devanter, reacting apparently to the pressures generated by the President's "court-packing" plan, decided to step down from office, thereby providing FDR with his first opportunity to fill an opening on this body. Roosevelt chose Alabama's Hugo Black, who was a very different kind of figure from his predecessor. Black had served for over a decade in the United States Senate, where he had compiled an extremely liberal, pro-New Deal voting record. Perhaps even more important, in his twenty years (1907–1927) as a Birmingham lawyer, Black had never been connected with any large corporate or wealthy interests; indeed, he had been retained at times to represent various labor groups in his home city and state.[142] As many New Deal leaders hoped, Black went on to become one of the most progressive spokesmen in the history of the Supreme Court.

Not long after, another opening occurred on the High Court when the reactionary George Sutherland finally bowed to the changing temper of the times and submitted his resignation. As his successor, the President selected Kentucky's Stanley F. Reed, who had held a series of governmental posts in the course of the previous decade, ranging from counsel to Herbert Hoover's Federal Farm Board to U.S. Solicitor General in 1935. Prior to 1929 Reed had been a private attorney, which experience provided him with a rather mixed background. He had, for instance, represented numerous agricultural co-ops and certain small hometown enterprises, such as the Bank of Maysville. But he had also served as local counsel for the big Chesapeake and Ohio Railway.[143] Hence Reed turned out to be something of a centrist figure on the Court. Yet even this was a marked improvement over the strongly negative position generally taken by his Republican predecessor.

Within a matter of months two other vacancies occurred on the Supreme Court. The first was created by the untimely death of New York's liberal justice, Benjamin Cardozo, who had served on this tribunal for only six years. After some deliberation President Roosevelt chose the highly regarded Felix Frankfurter as his successor. Unlike most other Supreme Court justices, this man had spent comparatively little time in private legal practice or even, after 1913, in any noteworthy formal government capacity. Instead, the able Frankfurter had served since 1914 as a Harvard University law professor, in which role he had established a reputation as a fairly liberal thinker. His teaching career had also been interspersed with an unusual amount of civic activity. Frankfurter was one of the founders of the American Civil Liberties Union, a legal advisor of the NAACP (National Association for the Advancement of Colored People), and an attorney for the National Consumers' League.[144] In addition, during the preceding New Deal years he had acted informally as one of Roosevelt's chief "brain trusters," advising the President on executive appointments, various speeches, and the formulation of legislative policy, particularly on securities regulation and the Public Utility Holding Company Act. Yet, ironically, Frankfurter turned out, through his adherence to a strict interpretation of the Constitution and perhaps because of certain social or civic links, to be a more conservative jurist than Roosevelt and many others had expected.[145]

The other opening on the Court occurred about six months later when the liberal Louis D. Brandeis felt compelled to resign because of his advanced age (he was 82). To succeed him, Roosevelt picked another man who had relatively little contact with the business world, William O. Douglas, a Westerner who had spent much of his time since graduating from law school in 1925 in academic institutions—Columbia and Yale—rather than in corporate law firms.[146] Unlike Frankfurter, he had chosen early in his career to accept a full-time position in the federal government—first as a staff aide and then as an official member of the Securities and Exchange Commission, an agency he headed from 1937 to 1939. Thus Douglas was another New Deal appointee to the Supreme Court who brought a very different set of values to this long elitist-dominated body.

The last opening on the Court during Roosevelt's second term occurred at the very end of 1939 when Minnesota's rock-ribbed conservative, Pierce Butler, died after seventeen years of what might be described as pro-business service. Roosevelt lost no time in appointing his progressive Attorney General, Frank Murphy, to take Butler's place. As indicated earlier, Murphy had no major formal business ties (although he was a close friend of the Chrysler family). Instead, he had devoted the bulk of his professional life to public affairs, having most recently held such posts as governor-general of the Philippines (1933–1936), governor of Michigan (1936–1938), and then finally as a Cabinet member. Over the years Murphy had demonstrated that he was a compassionate man with a real concern for the needs of working people. With this appointment Roosevelt finally managed to secure a Supreme Court in which liberal forces prevailed for the first time in the nation's history. Indeed, as John Schmidhauser has pointed out, this represented the beginning of a new era in Supreme Court affairs, one which could almost be described as a revolution in both the judicial appointment process and the types of decisions rendered by this important body.[147]

In recent decades there has been a good deal of debate as to whether or not the New Deal represented a revolution in American politico-economic affairs. In the eyes of a number of scholars, the many changes brought about by the Roosevelt regime were of such a profound and enduring nature as to warrant being called a "revolution."[148] Other more critical or radical figures, however, have charged that the New Deal was an essentially conservative regime which was forced by the pressure of the Depression to adopt some long-overdue political and economic policies primarily to bolster a shaky social order.[149] In fact, one writer has gone so far as to claim that "the liberal reforms of the New Deal did not transform the American system; they conserved and protected American corporate capitalism, occasionally by absorbing parts of threatening programs. There was no significant redistribution of power in American society...."[150] Given these widely disparate assessments, what can be said about the New Deal? Was it a much misunderstood campaign directed by the wily Roosevelt to save the nation's capitalist system? Or did it really make a number of major changes in the politico-economic order of the country?

One way of getting at this matter is to examine the background and socio-economic links of the people appointed to high office during the New Deal and compare these findings with those of previous regimes. Such an analysis reveals, for example, that there was only a moderate difference in the percentage of college-educated persons appointed to key administrative and diplomatic posts by President Roosevelt and his three conservative Republican predecessors (Harding, Coolidge, and Hoover)—85 percent, as contrasted with 70 percent. Similarly, if one ignores the Coolidge "carryovers" from the Harding administration, there was but a slight difference in the proportion of administrative and diplomatic officials with significant prior governmental experience; 50 percent of Roosevelt's appointees had such a background, as compared to 55 percent of those selected by his three presidential predecessors. The really important difference in the recruitment pattern of these regimes lay in the corporate and family connections of their officials. About 80 percent of the major Cabinet and diplomatic officers of the Harding, Coolidge, and Hoover administrations had key socio-economic ties, whereas no more than 47 percent of the New Deal appointees had such elitist links.[151] Even more revealing, no elite figures were appointed to the Supreme Court during this period.

To take a much longer perspective, it is manifest that the New Deal represented a marked shift in the federal recruitment process from that which existed (with certain variations) throughout the post-Civil War period. Indeed, although the New Deal had a significant number of elite leaders, it was the most pluralistic administration in American history. Never before was such a variety of persons brought into high posts in the federal government—people such as social workers Frances Perkins and Harry Hopkins, political reformer Harold Ickes, and college professors Felix Frankfurter and William O. Douglas.

In addition, a number of new economic interests rose to the fore during the New Deal years, a major development which has long been overlooked by American scholars. The New Deal was a period in which the House of Morgan received several telling blows that triggered its decline, and such other elite forces as the Rockefeller interests and the financial complex now known as "our crowd" emerged as powerful politico-economic factions. Democratic officials with such out-group links included Henry Morgenthau, Jr. (a man with close family ties to New York's major Jewish investment bankers), Jesse Straus (a high executive in the big retail trade concern of R. H. Macy), and Joseph P. Kennedy (an ambitious Irish-American entrepreneur). Furthermore, by 1935 there was a noticeable split in the business community between various arch-conservative leaders (many of whom were part of the NAM), who bitterly opposed most New Deal proposals, and more moderate executives (frequently affiliated with the BAC), who were generally willing to work with the Roosevelt administration. In short, the New Deal era witnessed a major realignment of the nation's top economic interests—or to put it in Pareto's terms, a circulation of elites.

With regard to policy matters, it is also clear that after a rather cautious start the New Deal, upon coming under attack from certain pro-corporate quarters such as the American Liberty League, veered sharply to the left and enacted a number of measures which brought about many critical changes in American society—a shift generally described as the rise of the welfare state, with its concomitant growth of government as a major force in economic affairs. These acts included the establishment of the Social Security program, the Securities and Exchange Commission, the Rural Electrification Administration (a large-scale agricultural aid program), and the adoption of a law that led ultimately to the dissolution of most of the big public utility holding companies. Perhaps even more important was the passage of the Wagner Act, which guaranteed the right of the nation's workers to organize and bargain collectively with their employers, a provision that did much to stimulate the growth of organized labor and thereby create a partial counterbalance to the power long held by business interests in America.[152]

Thus although the New Deal got off to a slow start and lasted, as a major reform movement, for only a comparatively short period (from 1935 to 1940), it nonetheless wrought many significant changes in the economic and political life of the nation. And while numerous authorities have undoubtedly overemphasized the magnitude and character of this transformation, it was obviously a watershed period.[153] Millions of Americans transferred their allegiance to the Roosevelt regime and its post-NRA reformist policies. Organized labor became both a major electoral and financial force in national politics and a strong ally of the Democratic party. Furthermore, while the New Deal certainly did not destroy or severely impair the power of big business, it did lock horns with some potent interests on various crucial issues such as the Public Utility Holding Company Act. Even if the initial primary objective of the Roosevelt administration was to preserve and protect "corporate capitalism," as some critics have claimed, the New Deal was nevertheless responsible, in its more "leftist" second stage, for the introduction of a number of noteworthy reforms which helped create a more equitable and viable society. Hence the best judgment one might make of this period is probably that of William Leuchtenburg, who has described the New Deal as "a halfway revolution."[154]

Notes

1. See Frank Freidel, "The New Deal in Historical Perspective," in Abraham S. Eisenstadt, *American History: Recent Interpretations*, 2nd ed. (New York: Crowell, 1969), Book II, p. 377. In 1929, about 71 percent of the American people had incomes of less than $2,500, the sum then considered necessary for a decent standard of living. As to income distributions, the

24,000 families that made over $100,000 a year in 1929 had a total income over three times as great as the 5.8 million poorest families in the United States.

2. See William E. Leuchtenberg, *Franklin D. Roosevelt and the New Deal, 1932–1940* (New York: Harper & Row, 1963), pp. 19–33.

3. For more on the economic lot of the working man during this period, see Irving Bernstein, *The Lean Years: A History of the American Worker, 1920–1933* (Boston: Houghton Mifflin, 1950).

4. The author has not presented a list of the top public utilities in the country because such a ranking would not be very meaningful in light of the operation of such giant holding companies as the United Corp.

5. Mutual funds and pension funds were at this time still in their infancy. In late 1929, for instance, the largest mutual fund in the country had assets of only $41 million, and the industry as a whole had an aggregate of only $140 million. Although certain savings banks were considerably larger, not even the two biggest—New York City's Bowery Savings Bank and Emigrant Industrial Savings Bank—ranked among the top ten banks by the late 1930s. It is difficult to assess the overall size and importance of the nation's major investment banks and brokerage houses, partly because of their special economic role and partly because the first-named line of activity had just been established as a separate financial field, thanks to the passage of some early New Deal legislation.

6. However, the Morgan interests had certainly not been reduced to a weak or minor state by the late 1930s, for two top ten concerns, the Bankers Trust Co. and Guaranty Trust Co., were still closely linked with this financial complex, as were both the First National Bank of New York (the 12th-ranked commercial bank in the country) and the Mutual Life Insurance Co. (and to a lesser extent, through directorship ties, the Prudential Insurance Co. of America). The three banks and J.P. Morgan & Co. had total assets of a little over $6 billion in 1940.

7. For more on these two investment banks, which have usually had fairly close working relations, see Arthur H. D. Smith, *Men Who Run America* (Indianapolis: Bobbs-Merrill, 1935), pp. 111–118, Barry Supple, "A Business Elite: German-Jewish Financiers in Nineteenth Century New York," *Business History Review* (Summer 1957), pp. 143–178, and Stephen Birmingham, *"Our Crowd": The Great Jewish Families of New York* (New York: Harper & Row, 1967), pp. 389–408.

8. Another well-known Jewish family, the Guggenheims, also had fairly close ties with a number of these families, but was never really an integral part of "our crowd," perhaps in part because its primary interest was in mining rather than investment banking. For a chart that depicts many of these links, see Barry Supple, *op cit.*, p. 165.

9. Though these elite families were primarily involved with investment banking over the years, some had expanded the scope of their operations in the pre-New Deal period into other key financial areas. For example, by the early 1930s the Lehman and Goldman-Sachs interests had forged important links with New York's big Manufacturers Trust Co., and the Warburgs (of Kuhn, Loeb & Co.) had secured a major stake in the big Bank of Manhattan.

10. Another business organization, the NAM, underwent a marked shift during this period. This rightist and staunchly anti-labor body had been dominated up to the early 1930s by small and medium-sized business enterprises. However, between 1933 and 1935 the NAM was, in effect, taken over by large arch-conservative corporate interests, vehemently opposed to a number of the early economic measures of the New Deal. The more moderate (though still basically conservative) U.S. Chamber of Commerce, on the other hand, did not change appreciably during the 1930s; its board of directors continued to be made up of roughly an equal mix of big, medium, and small business interests. For more on the NAM and its striking politico-economic shift during the early New Deal, see the author's "The NAM as an Interest Group," *Politics and Society* (Fall 1973), pp. 97–102.

11. See Kim McQuaid, "The Business Advisory Council of the Department of Commerce, 1933–1961: A Study of Corporate/Government Relations," in Paul Uselding (ed.) *Research in*

Economic History (Greenwich, Conn.: JAI Press, 1976), Vol. 1, p. 173, and for the above stockownership data, see the U.S. Temporary National Economic Committee, Monograph No. 29, *The Distribution of Ownership in the 200 Largest Nonfinancial Corporations* (Washington, D.C.: U.S. Government Printing Office, 1940), pp. 1114–21 and 1328–29. Judging from other evidence, New York banker-businessman W. Averell Harriman and Wall Street financier Sidney Weinberg played even more important roles in the organization and early operation of the Business Advisory Council. Harriman was the only person to serve on the executive committee of the BAC from 1933 through 1940, three years as a vice-chairman and three as chairman. The man who served for the next longest period (six years) on the BAC's executive committee was Sidney Weinberg, a partner in Goldman, Sachs & Co. and a major party fundraiser for FDR in both 1932 and 1936. According to two fairly recent sources, the BAC was the organizational brainchild of the influential Sidney Weinberg. See *Dun's Review* (December 1976), p. 71, and the *New York Times*, July 24, 1969, p. 34.

12. See the author's article on the NAM, *op. cit.* Strong evidence of this linkage may be found in the fact that a majority of the members of the Liberty League's executive committee in the mid-1930s were associated, in one way or another, with one of these three economic interests, and also that the only female member who did not come from a major northeastern city, Mrs. James Ross Todd of Louisville, was the mother-in-law of Morgan partner S. Parker Gilbert.

13. In contrast to the Hyde Park Roosevelts, none of whom sat on a major board of directors in the post-World War I period, George Emlen Roosevelt, one of the leading members of the Oyster Bay clan, served in the mid-1930s as a vice-president of the Bank for Savings in the City of New York and as a director of the Chemical Bank & Trust Co., Guaranty Trust Co., and Southern Pacific (Railroad) Co.; and his recently deceased father, William Emlen Roosevelt, was a former director of the Bank of New York, Central Union Trust Co., Chemical National Bank, and the International Telephone & Telegraph Corp. Franklin Roosevelt's marriage to a member of the more business-oriented Oyster Bay branch of the family does not really weaken this distinction because Eleanor Roosevelt did not especially identify with her "root" family.

14. See Stephen Hess, *American Political Dynasties* (Garden City, N.Y.: Doubleday, 1966), p. 171.

15. Although the author is not sure what significance should be attached to this tie, one of Roosevelt's initial (post-World War I) law partners, Langdon P. Marvin, was a longtime director of the Metropolitan Life Insurance Co., which linkage would presumably place Marvin in an economic faction, after 1930, friendly to the Rockefeller interests. Significantly, most of the clients of Roosevelt's second law firm seem to have been relatively small retail trade companies, which must have suffered badly as a result of the Depression.

16. See Frank Freidel, *Franklin D. Roosevelt: The Ordeal* (Boston: Little, Brown, 1954), pp. 141–51.

17. In fact, according to one source, the Fidelity and Deposit Co. hired Roosevelt largely for his name, in an effort to build up its bond business in the New York area. Roosevelt was also later appointed president of a newly created organization called the American Construction Council, but this was a nonsalaried, primarily public relations post. See Kenneth S. Davis, *FDR: The Beckoning of Destiny, 1882–1928* (New York: Putnam's, 1971), pp. 627–29 and 700–02.

18. Like many others, Roosevelt had engaged in various speculative ventures during this period, and in the late 1920s had served on the board of a number of small business concerns such as the Sanitary Postal Service Co. and Photomaton, Inc. The second company was headed by New York financier and realtor Henry Morgenthau, Sr., and included the latter's son among its directors. Roosevelt's most important links in the 1920s were as a member of the National Civic Federation and the board of overseers of Harvard University. However, because of his attack of polio he did not serve very long in either capacity.

19. The conservative "stop Roosevelt" coalition rallied behind the candidacy of Wilson's former Secretary of War and Cleveland attorney Newton D. Baker, who was, by 1932, a

director of the Baltimore & Ohio Railroad, Cleveland Trust Co., and Mutual Life Insurance Co. According to one recent study, this drive was firmly supported by such business leaders and corporate lawyers as A. Lincoln Filene (a Boston merchant), Owen D. Young (the board chairman of GE and a high official of RCA), Melvin Traylor (the president of the First National Bank of Chicago and a director of GE), Robert Woodruff (the president of the Georgia-based Coca-Cola Co.), Thomas W. Lamont (a senior partner in J. P. Morgan & Co.), John W. Davis and Frank L. Polk (two partners in the "Morgan" law firm of Davis, Polk, Wardwell, Gardiner & Reed), Norman H. Davis (an important figure in the Council on Foreign Relations and a director of the Bank of New York & Trust Co.), and Wall Street financier Bernard M. Baruch (a board member of the Baltimore & Ohio RR and the Guggenheim-controlled American Smelting & Refining Co.). Davis, Polk, and Young were also directors of the Council on Foreign Relations, which would indicate that Morgan interests had a good deal of influence on this body. In addition, Filene was the president of the Twentieth Century Fund, a moderate reform group, and both Newton D. Baker and Owen D. Young were members of its board of trustees. For a brief analysis of this abortive coalition, see Elliot A. Rosen, *Hoover, Roosevelt, and the Brains Trust* (New York: Columbia University Press, 1977), pp. 36–37 and 235–45.

20. In 1932 two of the seven outside directors of this line, New York lawyer Roland L. Redmond and Rockefeller ally Frederick B. Adams, had also married into the Delano family. That Lyman Delano was closely associated with Baltimore financial forces is also evident from the fact that he served on the board of this city's big Safe Deposit & Trust Co. from 1933 through 1940.

21. See Kenneth S. Davis, *op. cit.*, pp. 28–29, and also Harvey O'Connor, *The Astors* (New York: Knopf, 1941), p. 211.

22. Vincent Astor was also a member of the Democratic National Finance Committee in 1932. Up to the late 1920s Herbert Lehman was a partner in his family's investment banking firm and a director of such fairly sizable concerns as Abraham & Straus, Inc., Franklin Simon & Co., Jewel Tea Co., Pierce Petroleum Corp., and the Studebaker Corp.

23. For example, although Sidney Weinberg of Goldman, Sachs never held an official position in the New Deal (he declined one major ambassadorial post), he played an important role behind the scenes and served as assistant treasurer of the Democratic National Committee in both 1932 and 1936.

24. For a recent extended treatment of this hitherto neglected subject, see Thomas Ferguson, *Critical Realignment: The Fall of the House of Morgan and the Origins of the New Deal* (New York: Oxford University Press, forthcoming).

25. Harriman and FDR had been friends for a long time, and Eleanor Roosevelt had known Harriman and his sister, Mary, for three decades. The two Harrimans were strong early supporters of FDR's presidential drive. (See Larry I. Bland, "W. Averell Harriman: Businessman and Diplomat, 1891–1945," unpublished University of Wisconsin dissertation, 1972, pp. 80–82 and passim.) Harriman was also probably on very close economic terms with the Astor family, for the Harriman interests had secured a major stake in the Delaware and Hudson Co. about 15 years earlier, thereby associating themselves with an enterprise long identified with the Astor and Roosevelt clans.

26. In 1933 the financially troubled Aviation Corp. underwent a major reorganization and a considerable part of its assets were sold to the newly formed Pan-American Airways Corp., the top official of which was John Hay Whitney's lesser known brother, C. V. Whitney, and whose board of directors included Robert Lehman and FDR's cousin Lyman Delano.

27. In part because of his bitter feud with the House of Morgan, E. H. Harriman had also allied himself, in the years just before his death in 1909, with the Rockefeller forces, as can be seen from the fact that he served on the board of the Colorado Fuel & Iron Corp. and the National City Bank of New York.

28. That Roosevelt had been strongly backed in recent years by "our crowd" and other "out-group" forces may be seen from the fact that the Democratic finance committee for his 1930 gubernatorial reelection campaign was jointly managed by Henry Morgenthau, Sr. (about

whom more will be said shortly), and Howard S. Cullman, a then relatively minor figure (whose only important corporate tie was as a director of the probably Warburg-controlled International Acceptance Bank, and whose brother, Joseph, had marriage ties to "our crowd"). Actually, Cullman did most of the party fundraising in this campaign. See Bernard Bellush, *Franklin D. Roosevelt as Governor of New York* (New York: Columbia University Press, 1955), p. 157, and *Forbes* (August 15, 1965), p. 30.

29. The Harriman interests and other friendly forces apparently also had a substantial stake in the Western Union Telegraph Co. at this time, for its board of directors included W. Averell Harriman, Charles B. Seger, Henry W. DeForest (an old friend of E. H. Harriman), Robert S. Lovett (the former longtime head of the Union Pacific Railroad), John M. Schiff (of Kuhn, Loeb & Co.), Vincent Astor, and several Rockefeller representatives.

30. Judging from one recent book, Harriman was also apparently on fairly close terms with Bernard Baruch's longtime friend and associate, former New York publisher Herbert Bayard Swope. See Alfred A. Lewis, *Man of the World: Herbert Bayard Swope* (Indianapolis: Bobbs-Merrill, 1978), pp. 180–193.

31. Harriman also served on the board of the Morgan-dominated Guaranty Trust Co. up to 1940. But this link, in the author's opinion, does not necessarily mean that Harriman was on good terms with the Morgan interests. He may simply have bought enough shares to procure a seat on this board to provide himself with a kind of strategic observation post.

32. See *Fortune* (December, 1931), pp. 58–59. For further evidence of these ties, one need only look at the makeup of the boards of the above-named industrial enterprises. For example, Rockefeller, Allen, Pryor, Harriman kinsman R. W. Goelet, John McHugh (a high official of the Chase National Bank), and Matthew C. Brush (head of the closely allied American International Corp.) represented a majority of the "outside" directors of the Air Reduction Co.

33. The author is inclined to view the two du Pont representatives on this board as anomalous figures by 1933 because of their lukewarm, if not hostile, feelings toward FDR.

34. Only a few other persons were seriously considered for this position, the most prominent of whom was Owen D. Young, who was board chairman of the General Electric Co. (a concern dominated by Boston interests and the House of Morgan), deputy chairman of the Federal Reserve Bank of New York, a director of General Motors, a trustee of the Rockefeller Foundation, and a director of the Council on Foreign Relations. However, because of Young's big business background, he was ruled out by the President, who feared that his selection would generate a storm of protest by liberal and progressive forces. See Arthur M. Schlesinger, Jr., *The Crisis of the Old Order, 1919–1933* (Boston: Houghton Mifflin, 1957), p. 467, and Frank Freidel, *Franklin D. Roosevelt: Launching the New Deal* (Boston: Little, Brown, 1973), p. 145.

35. Apparently because of his marked conservatism, Hull's appointment as Secretary of State was, according to his biographer, warmly praised by such "middle-of-the-road" Democrats (and CFR leaders) as Norman H. Davis, John W. Davis, and Frank L. Polk (the last two of whom were influential Morgan law partners). The first-named Davis was a director of the Bank of New York, Seaboard Air Line Railway, and the much smaller Tennessee Central Railway, and was, according to Frank Freidel, such a close friend of Hull's that he could walk into the latter's office almost unannounced. See Harold B. Hinton, *Cordell Hull* (Garden City, N.Y.: Doubleday, 1942), p. 211, and Frank Freidel, *Franklin D. Roosevelt: Launching the New Deal*, p. 145.

36. At the urging of FDR, Hull picked as his second-ranking official a longtime career diplomat, William Phillips, who had served as Assistant Secretary of State (1917–1920), as Under Secretary of State (1922–1924), and then (until 1929) as Ambassador to Belgium and Canada. Phillips did not hold any federal office between 1929 and 1933, but was called back from private life to work under Hull. When Phillips relinquished this post in 1936 to become Ambassador to Italy, he was replaced by Sumner Welles, another New York patrician who had been an American diplomat up to 1925, when he resigned from the foreign service to devote himself primarily to writing. Eight years later Welles was appointed Assistant Secretary of State

by his close friend Franklin Delano Roosevelt, at whose 1905 wedding he had served as a page. Phillips had married into New York's wealthy Astor family, and Welles's grandmother was a sister of *the* Mrs. William Astor. See Annette Townsend, *The Auchmuty Family of Scotland and America* (New York: Grafton Press, 1932), p. 41, and Jules R. Benjamin, *The United States and Cuba: Hegemony and Dependent Development, 1880–1934* (Pittsburgh: University of Pittsburgh Press, 1974), p. 73.

37. Roosevelt first offered this post to Virginia's longtime Democratic leader Carter Glass, a conservative (Lynchburg) newspaper publisher who had held this position during the last years of the Wilson regime. But because of his status as one of the founders of the Federal Reserve System, Glass decided not to join the administration so as to preserve his right to act as a government critic if he chose. During the heat of the 1932 Democratic nominating convention this key Cabinet post was also offered, perhaps as a matter of political strategy, to an influential member of the "stop Roosevelt" coalition, Melvin Traylor, who was president of the First National Bank of Chicago (and a director of GE and two big Midwestern companies, the U.S. Gypsum Co. and the Standard Oil Co. of Indiana). Traylor declined, partly because he felt that he could not afford the financial sacrifice involved. See Elliot A. Rosen, *op. cit.*, pp. 255 and 257.

38. Up to 1930 Gibson was president of the New York Trust Co., and thereafter served as head of the Manufacturers Trust Co. For more on the make-up of the Warm Springs Foundation in the late 1920s, see Kenneth S. Davis, *op. cit.*, p. 808, and Antony C. Sutton, *Wall Street and FDR* (New Rochelle, N.Y.: Arlington House, 1975), p. 66.

39. Further evidence of this orientation may be seen in the fact that when the strongly pro-Democratic County Trust Co. of New York was established in 1926, Woodin was a member of its original board of directors (albeit only briefly), along with such influential businessmen as Vincent Astor and Herbert Lehman. See Harvey O'Connor, *The Astors*, pp. 341–42.

40. Arthur Lehman apparently replaced his cousin Philip on the Underwood board in 1929, by which time the Schley family (which was associated with the Chase National Bank) had acquired a substantial interest in this renamed firm. That Roosevelt himself was on close terms with both of the Morgenthaus can be inferred from the fact that he and Henry Morgenthau, Jr., served in the late 1920s on the board of Photomaton, Inc., a small concern headed (and presumably dominated) by Henry Morgenthau, Sr. The elder Morgenthau also served as a trustee of the Equitable Life Assurance Society from 1915 to 1921, but this link was of a much shorter and more distant nature and of considerably less significance.

41. A more diverse set of interests was represented in the second-ranking post in the Treasury Department during the New Deal years. The first man to serve as Under Secretary of the Treasury during this period was a conservative Washington lawyer, Dean Acheson, one of whose senior partners, J. Harry Covington, was a director of the Guggenheim-controlled Kennecott Copper Corp. However, Acheson only held office for about six months because of a major policy dispute with the President. Following a brief stint by Henry Morgenthau, Jr., this position was filled by Brahmin leader T. Jefferson Coolidge, a former vice-president of the First National Bank of Boston (and a director of the United Fruit Co., Boston & Maine Railroad, and Suffolk Savings Bank). And in the latter part of the 1930s this post was held by John W. Hanes, a scion of a North Carolina textile family, who prior to his federal appointment had been a partner in the New York banking house of Charles D. Barney & Co., a high official of the (Seligman-controlled) Selected Industries, Inc., and up to 1937 a director of the International Mercantile Marine Co., Glenn L. Martin Co. (New York-dominated), Missouri-Kansas-Texas Railroad, Pan-American Airways, and Tri-Continental Corp. (the Seligman-run parent company of Selected Industries, Inc.). Moreover, in the early 1930s Hanes had served as a director of the Aviation Corp., which was then dominated by the Harriman and Lehman interests. Thus Hanes apparently had close ties to "our crowd" and other allied forces. In fact, the only non-economic figure to hold this second-tier post during the New Deal period was Columbia law school professor Roswell Magill, who served in this capacity for about 20 months in 1937–1938.

42. Cummings' most notable business connection was his directorship link with the First Stamford National Bank & Trust Co., a concern headed by Schuyler Merritt, the longtime chief executive officer of the fairly large, locally based Yale & Towne Mfg. Co.

43. Although Murphy has always been viewed as a liberal leader, he had long been on intimate terms with the Chrysler family (he had been the best man at the wedding of Walter Chrysler's daughter in 1924, and was later godfather of her first child). Indeed, while Murphy was a municipal official in Detroit in the mid and late 1920s, he was the recipient of substantial funds from the Chrysler Corp. (through a legal retainer) or various members of the Chrysler family. Chrysler was, as already indicated, closely allied with certain influential forces friendly to the New Deal, as may be seen by the make-up of its board and Walter Chrysler's directorship ties. For more on Murphy's relations with the Chrysler family, see Sidney Fine, *Frank Murphy: The Detroit Years* (Ann Arbor: University of Michigan Press, 1975), pp. 84 and 193-94, and J. Woodford Howard, Jr., *Mr. Justice Murphy* (Princeton, N.J.: Princeton University Press, 1968), p. 22.

44. Dern was reportedly appointed to this office rather than the one for which he was originally considered, that of Secretary of the Interior, because it was felt that his previous mining and utility ties might create a conflict of interest and political problem for the Roosevelt administration.

45. Woodring was reportedly brought into this bank by its president, J. C. McDonald, who was also head of the Standard Oil Co. of Kansas, a fairly small concern not affiliated with any of the giants of the industry. Because of a clash over utility rates while he was governor, Woodring was, moreover, an acknowledged foe of the big Cities Service Co. See Keith D. McFarland, *Harry H. Woodring* (Lawrence: University Press of Kansas, 1975), pp. 13 and 73.

46. For a study which describes the conservative Swanson's close alignment with the long-established Democratic oligarchy in Virginia, see Allen W. Moger, *Virginia: Bourbonism to Byrd, 1870-1925* (Charlottesville: University Press of Virginia, 1968), passim.

47. Neither of Ickes' two top aides during this period, Oscar Chapman (a relatively unknown Denver lawyer) and Charles West (a former Ohio Congressman and Denison University professor), had any significant corporate ties.

48. See Frank Freidel, *Franklin D. Roosevelt: Launching the New Deal*, pp. 151-52, and Christiana M. Campbell, *The Farm Bureau and the New Deal* (Urbana: University of Illinois Press, 1962), pp. 61-62.

49. In the 1930s Wallace's two top aides were men who were not directly involved in agriculture, but were knowledgeable authorities in this area, former Columbia University professor Rexford Tugwell (about whom more will be said later) and Montana State College economist M. L. Wilson.

50. For instance, unlike his father and uncle (John), the younger Henry Wallace never served on a local bank board, much less any other more important enterprise. For more on Wallace's later badly strained relations with the Farm Bureau, see Christiana M. Campbell, *op. cit.*, pp. 84 and 185.

51. Very little has been written about Daniel Roper, so this inference may simply reflect the paucity of pertinent material. However, one rarely noted study did find that Roper had represented several Cuban sugar companies at a U.S. Tariff Commission hearing just a few weeks before his appointment to Cabinet office. See Robert F. Smith, *The United States and Cuba* (New York: Bookman, 1960), p. 143.

52. See Robert K. Murray, *The 103rd Ballot* (New York: Harper & Row, 1976), pp. 42-43 and David Burner, *The Politics of Provincialism: The Democratic Party in Transition, 1918-1932* (New York: Knopf, 1968), p. 119.

53. Although Roper was a Southerner, he served on the board of the relatively small, New York-based Marlin-Rockwell Corp. from 1919 to 1923, actually as president of the concern for a year, apparently because of the influence of Thomas L. Chadbourne. In 1928 Roper still

referred to Chadbourne as his most intimate friend. See Daniel C. Roper, *Fifty Years of Public Life* (Durham, N.C.: Duke University Press, 1941), pp. 208 and 223.

54. See Harvey O'Connor, *The Guggenheims*, p. 443, and E. J. Kahn, Jr., *The World of Swope* (New York: Simon & Schuster, 1965), pp. 321 and 334.

55. Chadbourne was also board chairman of the International Mining Corp. and a director of the Marlin-Rockwell Corp. and the Zonite Products Corp., but these were comparatively small concerns. By 1933 Baruch's relations with Roper had reportedly cooled, most likely because the latter, unlike Baruch, had supported FDR.

56. Coker, who was also a director of one of the smaller subsidiaries of the Seaboard Air Line Railway, was chosen to be a member of the influential Business Advisory Council shortly after its creation in 1933, which link was probably also of prime importance.

57. Roper was given a second Assistant Secretary of Commerce. Neither of the first two men to hold this dual set of offices, former University of Pennsylvania law professor (and onetime William G. McAdoo law partner) John Dickinson, and Springfield, Mo., attorney Ewing Mitchell, had any significant business connections or experience. When these officials resigned in 1935, another non-economic figure, South Carolina engineer John M. Johnson, was chosen to fill one of the posts. The other, New York executive Ernest Draper, did not appear to be closely linked with major corporate interests either, for he was just a vice-president of the Hills Bros. Co., a small (probably privately owned) food company. But he had also been a member of the BAC, and in the early 1920s he had been president of the reformist-oriented American Association for Labor Legislation. In 1938, Draper was replaced by another New York business (and civic) figure, Richard C. Patterson, Jr., who had been an executive vice-president of NBC in recent years, the 1937 president of the elite-dominated Citizens Budget Commission, and a director of the fairly large Central Savings Bank.

58. Swope, who was the brother of the president of GE, was also head of a small enterprise called Polo Magazine, Inc., of which John Hertz served as a director. For more on these relations, see Henry H. Adams, *Harry Hopkins* (New York: Putnam, 1977), pp. 119, 124, 149, 154, and 156, Larry I. Bland, "W. Averell Harriman," p. 104, and Richard Oulahan, *The Man Who... The Story of the 1932 Democratic Convention* (New York: Dial Press, 1971), p. 77.

59. See Henry H. Adams, *op. cit.*, p. 149. From the above it is clear that the author does not subscribe to Kim McQuaid's view that the BAC was a relatively weak and ineffective body during most of the New Deal years. See Kim McQuaid, *op. cit.*, pp. 178–81.

60. Because of Hopkins's wide-ranging informal governmental responsibilities, both foreign and domestic, Noble virtually ran the Department of Commerce from mid-1939 to mid-1940; Hopkins himself spent very little time on the job—less than 30 days during this period. See Kim McQuaid, *op. cit.*, p. 182, and Henry H. Adams, *op. cit.*, p. 153.

61. Organized labor's representation came primarily through Miss Perkins's two top aides, Edward F. McGrady and Charles V. McLaughlin, both of whom were longtime union leaders.

62. See George Martin, *Madam Secretary: Frances Perkins* (Boston: Houghton Mifflin, 1976), pp. 269 and 278–79, and Larry I. Bland, *op. cit.*, pp. 77 and 82.

63. Bruere served briefly in late 1933 as FDR's credit coordinator and apparently as an executive assistant to Secretary of the Treasury William H. Woodin. For more on the relations between the Brueres and Frances Perkins (and her husband, Paul Wilson), see George Martin, *op. cit.*, pp. 123, 130, 170, and 326.

64. See David E. Koskoff, *Joseph P. Kennedy: A Life and Times* (Englewood Cliffs, N.J.: Prentice-Hall, 1974), p. 31.

65. See Richard J. Whalen, *The Founding Father: The Story of Joseph P. Kennedy* (New York: New American Library, 1964), pp. 132–33, and Alfred A. Lewis, *Man of the World*, p. 194.

66. See David E. Koskoff, *op. cit.*, p. 79.

67. Unlike President Roosevelt, Kennedy subscribed to the appeasement policy espoused

by British Prime Minister Neville Chamberlain, in large measure out of a fear that a major conflict among the Western European powers would deal a serious, if not fatal, blow to the existing capitalist system. See David E. Koskoff, *op. cit.*, pp. 281–83, and Richard J. Whalen, *op. cit.*, p. 234.

68. For more on the financial contributions of the Straus family, see Ferdinand Lundberg, *America's Sixty Families* (New York: Vanguard Press, 1937), p. 455.

69. See Stephen Birmingham, *op. cit.*, pp. 7–12 and 332.

70. See Beatrice Farnsworth, *William C. Bullitt and the Soviet Union* (Bloomington: Indiana University Press, 1967), pp. 72–73. Bullitt's brother, Orville, had served for some time on the board of the (medium-sized) Muskogee Co., a Midwestern railroad holding company. This concern was controlled by the wealthy Ingersoll family, which had long been linked with the Democratic party.

71. The appointment pattern with regard to America's other major ambassadorial post, Germany, was quite different from that of Britain and France. After first offering the Berlin post to former Democratic presidential candidate James M. Cox (who graciously refused), Roosevelt appointed University of Chicago historian William E. Dodd. After holding this important post for over four years Dodd was recalled in the late 1930s, largely because of his strong anti-Nazi views. He was replaced by a more neutral career diplomat, Hugh Wilson, who served until the latter part of 1938, when, because of increasing hostility, America's ties with Germany were formally severed.

72. Another of Roosevelt's original political advisors, Samuel Rosenman, has not been included in this influential group because he was appointed to a major New York state judicial post in the first part of 1932, which prevented him from playing an important role in New Deal affairs (at least up to 1936, when he was asked to provide more counsel).

73. See, for instance, Raymond Moley, *The First New Deal* (New York: Harcourt, Brace & World, 1966), pp. 65 and 312.

74. The origins of this move go back to the first part of 1933 when the wealthy Mary H. Rumsey decided, because the press was generally hostile to Roosevelt, to establish a major pro-New Deal newspaper. In this endeavor she was joined by her brother, W. Averell Harriman, and his friend (and sometimes business associate) Vincent Astor. In fact, they tried to buy the *Washington Post* early in the year, but lost out in the bidding to former financier Eugene Meyer, who had a sizable stake in the Allied Chemical (& Dye) Corp. In May 1933 the trio made plans with Moley to produce their own national weekly magazine, which was to be called *Today* and be devoted largely to public affairs. Two years after Mary Rumsey's accidental death, Harriman and Astor merged this organ into *Newsweek* and thereby gained control of the latter enterprise. See Larry I. Bland, "W. Averell Harriman," pp. 82 and 84.

75. According to Moley, the inner core of the "brains trust" also included Hugh S. Johnson, James F. Byrnes, and Key Pittman. The first of these figures (who was a close friend and employee of New York financier Bernard Baruch) will be discussed in more detail at a later point in conjunction with his work as head of the National Recovery Administration. The latter two were United States Senators (from South Carolina and Nevada respectively), and as such they played somewhat different roles from the other members of this informal advisory body. Yet it is interesting to note that both Byrnes and Pittman were also part of a coterie of Congressional leaders intimately associated with the influential Baruch. See Raymond Moley, *The First New Deal*, p. 18, Margaret Coit, *Mr. Baruch* (Boston: Houghton Mifflin, 1957), p. 331, and Carter Field, *Bernard Baruch: Park Bench Statesman* (New York: McGraw-Hill, 1944), p. 268.

76. See, for instance, Berle's biting comments about the legal profession in the first (1933) *Encyclopedia of the Social Sciences* (New York: Macmillan, 1933), Vol. 9, pp. 340–45. These views contrast sharply with those espoused by a more prosperous Berle in the post-World War II period.

77. See the *Directory of Directors in the City of New York: 1933* (New York: Directory of Directors Co., 1933), pp. 65 and 1070. Since this company was privately owned, it was not

listed in any of the major business manuals, but it was apparently a medium-sized enterprise. In the latter part of 1933 Berle was also appointed to the board of two other small concerns, the Savings Bank Trust Co. of New York and the closely linked Institutional Securities Corp.— financial ties that probably reinforced his increasing conservatism. In addition, Berle had married the daughter of wealthy New York businessman Cortlandt Bishop, but the latter's economic interests were not of a major scope. See Richard S. Kirkendall, "A. A. Berle, Jr.: Student of the Corporation, 1917-1932," *Business History Review* (Spring, 1961), p. 47.

78. See William E. Leuchtenburg, *op. cit.*, p. 38, and Frank Freidel, *Franklin D. Roosevelt: Launching the New Deal*, passim.

79. Up to the early 1930s this financier's father, Paul M. Warburg, and another kinsman, Mortimer L. Schiff, also served on the board of the Western Union Telegraph Co., in which the Harriman forces had long held a major stake.

80. Another important pro-business figure in the critical early months of the administration was Lewis W. Douglas, a former Arizona Congressman who served as Roosevelt's first director of the Bureau of the Budget. A good deal of Douglas's conservatism undoubtedly stemmed from the fact that he came from a wealthy family that had substantial mining interests in the West, the most prominent of which was the Phelps Dodge Corp. Deeply disturbed by Roosevelt's pragmatic fiscal policy, Douglas soon followed Raymond Moley's lead and resigned from office in August 1934. (It was Douglas who exclaimed, after Roosevelt abandoned the gold standard, "Well, this is the end of Western civilization.")

81. Both Cohen and Corcoran were former New York lawyers. The first had his own private practice, while the latter had been associated, from 1927 to 1932, with an apparently second-tier law firm known as Cotton & Franklin. They were generally considered to be fairly liberal Frankfurter protégés.

82. For two major studies of this agency, see Ellis W. Hawley, *The New Deal and the Monopoly Problem* (Princeton, N.J.: Princeton University Press, 1966), pp. 19-146, and Bernard Bellush, *The Failure of NRA* (New York: Norton, 1975), passim. Bellush claims (see pp. 6-17) that the program was devised in part to counteract Alabama Senator Hugo Black's more radical industrial recovery act, which was built around the concept of a 30-hour work week and had the strong support of the still fairly conservative leadership of the AFL. The latter body apparently agreed to accept the trade association (or cartelization) feature of this legislation in exchange for industry's acquiescence to labor organization and collective bargaining, although business often later reneged on this matter. For more on the first point, see Kim McQuaid, "Corporate Liberalism in the American Business Community, 1920-1940," *Business History Review* (Autumn 1978), p. 355.

83. See Robert F. Himmelberg, *The Origins of the National Recovery Administration* (New York: Fordham University Press, 1976), pp. 190-208.

84. See Ellis W. Hawley, *op. cit.*, p. 42. Hawley has also pointed out (p. 23) that Moley consulted extensively with Bernard Baruch and Alexander Sachs (an executive of a financial concern controlled by Lehman Brothers) before he attempted to prepare a first draft of this controversial legislation. Furthermore, by NRA head Hugh Johnson's own admission, he had a number of discussions with Alexander Sachs about various possible recovery measures for nearly a year prior to the adoption of this extraordinary economic rehabilitation program, and Sachs served briefly as the first head of the NRA's research and planning division. As it turned out, the ambitious Richberg, after being appointed as the second-ranking official of the NRA, soon turned his back on the labor movement and sided largely with business interests in agency proceedings. See Hugh S. Johnson, *The Blue Eagle from Egg to Earth* (Garden City, N.Y.: Doubleday, Doran, 1935), p. 196, and Thomas E. Vadney, *The Wayward Liberal: A Political Biography of Donald Richberg* (Lexington: University Press of Kentucky, 1970), pp. 107-128 and 153.

85. Johnson had been a high official of the Moline Plow (or Implement) Co. up to 1929 when it was merged into the larger Minneapolis Steel & Machinery Co., which was then

renamed the Minneapolis-Moline Power Implement Co. At the time of his appointment as head of the NRA Johnson was a director of an even smaller New York-based company known as Durium Products, Inc. But these were comparatively minor links.

86. See Carter Field, *Bernard Baruch: Park Bench Statesman* (New York: McGraw-Hill, 1944), p. 85, and Elliot Rosen, *op. cit.*, pp. 311–12. Although often portrayed as an influential presidential advisor, Baruch may have functioned primarily in the capacity of politico-economic intermediary for certain groups in the business community, especially "our crowd" and allied interests. For example, one of Baruch's most trusted associates was former newspaperman Herbert Bayard Swope, who was a close friend of W. Averell Harriman and a brother of GE's president, Gerard Swope. Another person long linked with Baruch was his former World War I aide, John M. Hancock, who was now a senior partner in Lehman Brothers, board chairman of the Jewel Tea Co., a director of a number of other major business enterprises, and apparently a more important figure than Baruch himself. For similar comments regarding Baruch's World War I role as the government's chief economic coordinator, see Robert D. Cuff, "Bernard Baruch: Symbol and Myth in Industrial Mobilization." *Business History Review* (Summer 1969), pp. 115–33.

87. After his appointment as (chief?) administrative officer of the NRA in late 1933, Harriman was given particular responsibility for recruiting industrial personnel for the agency, which may help to account for the marked corporate domination of this important body. See Kim McQuaid, "The Frustration of Corporate Revival during the Early New Deal," *The Historian* (August 1979), p. 694.

88. See Bernard Bellush, *op. cit.*, p. 45.

89. The NRA also had a Labor Advisory Board, but it apparently was not much more effective than that established for consumers.

90. See Kim McQuaid, "Corporate Liberalism in the American Business Community, 1920–1940," *Business History Review* (Autumn 1978), p. 358.

91. See Bernard Bellush, *op. cit.*, pp. 33, 46, and 69.

92. See Kim McQuaid, "Corporate Liberalism," p. 358.

93. At Wagner's request, in October 1933 President Roosevelt expanded this seven-man body by adding two more labor men and two other business leaders. One of the latter was T. Austin Finch, president of North Carolina's Thomasville Chair Co. and a member of the BAC. The other was Illinois' Edward Hurley, head of the Hurley Machine Co., a director of the U.S. Chamber of Commerce, and a member of the BAC. Hurley, however, died about a month later, and his place was quickly taken by Delaware industrialist Pierre S. du Pont, who, not surprisingly, was also a member of the BAC.

94. See Bernard Bellush, *The Failure of NRA*, pp. 100–03, and Thomas E. Vadney, *The Wayward Liberal*, p. 132.

95. According to McQuaid, in the fall of 1933 Hugh Johnson told Walter Teagle, the head of the NRA's Industrial Advisory Board, that putting the administration of national industrial codes in the hands of public officials would create "too bureaucratic" a setup. Rather, the regulation of industry would best be achieved through the use of rotating panels of outstanding businessmen who would oversee the operation of the codes. See Kim McQuaid, "The Frustration of Corporate Revival during the Early New Deal," *The Historian* (August 1979), p. 694.

96. See Bernard Bellush, *op. cit.*, pp. 44 and 127.

97. See Bernard Bellush, *op. cit.*, pp. 44, 55, and 127.

98. Ellis Hawley has arrived at a similar verdict (*op. cit.*, pp. 53–71 in particular), although, in the author's judgment, he does not sufficiently stress the role played by the BAC. For instance, when Roosevelt finally felt compelled in late 1934 to remove the often impetuous and biased Johnson from his high post and created instead a five-man control board, the President chose a prominent member of the BAC, S. Clay Williams, the former chief executive

of the R.J. Reynolds Tobacco Co., as his replacement. And, according to Hawley (see p. 108), this new NRA board acted against business wishes only twice during the first six months of its existence.

99. While serving as assistant district attorney, Pecora had rejected a number of offers from Wall Street law firms and resisted opportunities to supplement his modest salary by outside practice. For more on Pecora, and the origin and general conduct of this investigation, see William H. Harbaugh, *Lawyer's Lawyer: The Life of John W. Davis* (New York: Oxford University Press, 1973), pp. 319–35.

100. See Peter Collier and David Horowitz, *The Rockefellers: An American Dynasty* (New York: Holt, Rinehart & Winston, 1976), p. 161.

101. *Ibid.*, and also Ferdinand Lundberg's *America's Sixty Families*, p. 461.

102. See Ralph F. DeBedts, *The New Deal's SEC: The Formative Years* (New York: Columbia University Press, 1964), p. 44. Some observers also felt that in his position as chief counsel, Pecora was highly selective, if not clearly partisan, in his choice of firms to probe, focusing heavily on certain large pro-Republican houses, while carefully avoiding such New Dealish enterprises as Lehman Brothers and Brown Brothers Harriman. See, for example, Susan E. Kennedy, *The Banking Crisis of 1933* (Lexington: University Press of Kentucky, 1973), p. 109. For a more detailed analysis of the interplay of economic forces behind this financial measure, see Thomas Ferguson, *Critical Realignment*, passim.

103. The New York Stock Exchange was probably closely aligned with certain key financial forces, as may be seen from the fact that its (post-1930) president, Richard Whitney, was the head of a small brokerage firm which often acted as the agent for other larger houses, a director of the Corn Exchange Trust Co. of New York, and, perhaps most important of all, a brother of George Whitney, who was a senior partner in J. P. Morgan & Co. and a director of such key companies as General Motors and the United Corp. (the Morgan-dominated public utility holding company). For more on this point, see Ralph F. DeBedts, *op. cit.*, p. 146, and Matthew Josephson, *The Money Lords: The Great Finance Capitalists, 1925–1950* (New York: Weybright & Talley, 1972), pp. 92–94.

104. See *Fortune* (June 1940), pp. 91 and 120, Ralph F. DeBedts, *op. cit.*, pp. 56–82 and 144–50, and Michael E. Parrish, *Securities Regulation and the New Deal* (New Haven, Conn.: Yale University Press, 1970), pp. 108–44 and 187–94. Other leaders who backed this drive against the NYSE's "old guard" were Chase National Bank head Winthrop W. Aldrich, Paul V. Shields, E. A. Pierce (two lesser-known figures), and John W. Hanes, who was later appointed to the SEC and then to the second-ranking post in the Treasury Department.

105. According to Ralph DeBedts (*op. cit.*, p. 78), the Roosevelt government originally wanted to have the Federal Trade Commission act as the administrative agency overseeing securities regulation. But this idea was strongly opposed by Wall Street interests, who favored a newly created special body. In the end their views apparently prevailed. However, aside from the appointment of Joseph P. Kennedy as the Commission's first (15-month) chairman and John W. Hanes, none of the people placed on the SEC in the 1930s had any significant economic ties. For more on Kennedy's appointment to the SEC, see Alfred A. Lewis, *Man of the World*, p. 219.

106. Eccles's immediate (1933–1934) predecessor was a Roosevelt appointee, Eugene R. Black, a Georgian who had most recently served as head of the Federal Reserve Bank of Atlanta. From 1929 to 1933 this Washington post had been filled by former New York financier (and later high federal official) Eugene Meyer, whose major economic interest was then centered in the big Allied Chemical & Dye Corp., and whose brothers-in-law, George W. Blumenthal and Alfred A. Cook, served on the board of such large concerns as the Continental Insurance Co., New York Trust Co., and Chicago, Rock Island & Pacific Railway.

107. See Arthur M. Schlesinger, Jr., *The Politics of Upheaval* (Boston: Houghton Mifflin, 1960), p. 238, and also Sidney Hyman, *Marriner S. Eccles* (Stanford, Calif.: Stanford University Graduate School of Business, 1976), passim.

108. See, for instance, Arthur M. Schlesinger, Jr., *The Politics of Upheaval*, pp. 292–93.

109. See Sidney Hyman, *op. cit.*, pp. 174 and 323. Eccles also had a firm ally in the administration in the person of Secretary of War George Dern, who had long graced the board of one of the banks in Eccles's big Utah-based financial chain.

110. The acknowledged spokesman for the American beet sugar bloc was Utah's able and aggressive Senator Reed Smoot, who was indirectly allied with such interests in his home state. For example, Smoot served on the board of two Mormon-controlled banks in Salt Lake City and the Zion's Cooperative Mercantile Institution, whose head also served as president of the Utah-Idaho Sugar Co. Smoot became a director of this big sugar company shortly after he left the Senate in 1933. For a much acclaimed account of this 1930 legislative struggle, see E. E. Schattschneider, *Politics, Pressures and the Tariff* (New York: Prentice-Hall, 1935); for a more recent analysis of the close-knit economic operations of the Mormon Church, see *Fortune* (April 1964), pp. 136–39 and 166–72.

111. Indeed, a sugar cartelization plan was promoted in 1930–1931 by New York lawyer Thomas Chadbourne, who was a longtime friend of Bernard Baruch and FDR's first Secretary of Commerce, Daniel Roper. The plan failed for want of sufficient cooperation by certain nations.

112. For more on all of the above officials except Phillips, see Jules R. Bernstein, *The United States and Cuba: Hegemony and Dependent Development, 1880–1934* (Pittsburgh: University of Pittsburgh Press, 1974), p. 89, and Robert F. Smith, *The United States and Cuba: Business and Diplomacy, 1917–1960* (New York: Bookman, 1960), pp. 142–143.

113. See Arthur M. Schlesinger, Jr., *The Coming of the New Deal*, p. 311.

114. See G. William Domhoff, *The Higher Circles: The Governing Class in America* (New York: Random House, 1970), pp. 212–16, and Philip H. Burch, Jr., "The NAM as an Interest Group," *Politics and Society* (Fall 1973), pp. 101–03. One sign that the AALL was far from a radical body may be seen in the fact that New York corporate lawyer Thomas Chadbourne served as president of this organization for six years during the 1920s. A number of other figures associated with this body also had important economic links.

115. See G. William Domhoff, *op. cit.*, pp. 214–15, and the *New York Times* (May 3, 1935), p. 1. The U.S. Chamber of Commerce and the National Retail Dry Goods Association also supported the Social Security program, although their backing was probably not as important as that of the BAC. Curiously, organized labor initially took little interest in this measure and jumped on the legislative bandwagon at a rather late date. See Arthur J. Altmeyer, *The Formative Years of Social Security* (Madison: University of Wisconsin Press,1966), pp. 32–33.

116. See J. Douglas Brown, *An American Philosophy of Social Security* (Princeton, N.J.: Princeton University Press, 1972), pp. 21–22.

117. See Robert M. Collins, "Positive Business Responses to the New Deal: The Roots of the Committee for Economic Development, 1933–1942," *Business History Review* (Autumn 1978), p. 374.

118. Of the other nine "outside" trustees of the Brookings Institution in 1935, only two (Morton D. Hull and John C. Merriam) had no important socio-economic ties, and four (Jerome D. Greene, Vernon Kellogg, Alanson B. Houghton, and Clarence P. Dodge) were apparently on friendly terms with the Rockefeller family (the first two being linked through the Rockefeller Foundation and the last through the Phelps Dodge interests). Winant was also related, through his wife, to the rich Taylor-Pyne family, which still had significant stockownership in the National City Bank of New York.

119. The arch-conservative NAM never relented in its opposition to this agreement, thereby signaling an early split in the ranks of the business community. See Irving Bernstein, *The New Deal Collective Bargaining Policy* (Berkeley: University of California Press, 1950), p. 34.

120. Garrison, whose liberalism was apparently derived from his idealistic family line and the Villards, had married the daughter of Pierre Jay, who had served as chairman of the Federal

Reserve Bank of New York from 1914 to 1926, and since 1930 had been head of the recently established Fiduciary Trust Co. and a trustee of the Bank for Savings in New York City. The second-ranking official of the Fiduciary Trust Co., John R. Simpson, was closely associated with a number of figures in "our crowd," primarily through his involvement in the Van Raalte Co. Biddle was related to most of Philadelphia's top-tier families, including the Dukes and the Drexels; his law firm had frequently been retained by the Pennsylvania Railroad and the Berwind-White Coal Mining Co.

121. As one authority has pointed out, under the NRA employer-sponsored company unions grew at a much faster rate than independent collective bargaining units. See Milton Derber, "The New Deal and Labor," in John Braeman, Robert H. Bremmer, and David Brody (eds.), *The New Deal* (Columbus: Ohio State University Press, 1975), p. 133, and also James A. Gross, *The Making of the National Labor Relations Board* (Albany: State University of New York Press, 1974), pp. 93–94.

122. It was in part because of the views and persuasiveness of the NLB's recent chairmen, Biddle and Garrison, that Senator Wagner was induced to include a section in the bill requiring companies to bargain collectively with their employees. However, the act was largely the product of the dedicated efforts of Senator Wagner, who, after his disappointing experience with FDR a year earlier, did not bother to consult the White House about this pro-union measure. Nor did he, interestingly, receive much support from Secretary of Labor Frances Perkins. See James A. Gross, *op. cit.*, pp. 91 and 139, J. Joseph Huthmacher, *Senator Robert F. Wagner and the Rise of Urban Liberalism* (New York: Atheneum, 1968), pp. 166–91, Irving Bernstein, *Turbulent Years: A History of the American Worker, 1933-1941* (Boston: Houghton Mifflin, 1970), pp. 323–42, G. William Domhoff, *op. cit.*, pp. 234–44, Bernard Bellush, *op. cit.*, p. 170, and Thomas E. Vadney, *op. cit.*, pp. 151–52.

123. The act also transformed the NLRB into a permanent agency, and to emphasize the impartiality of this reconstituted body, President Roosevelt chose as its first chairman a former University of Pittsburgh law professor, J. Warren Madden, who had no noteworthy socioeconomic ties.

124. In 1936 the newly formed CIO (Congress of Industrial Organizations) contributed the then enormous sum of $770,000 to Roosevelt's campaign, which made it, by far, the party's biggest single financial backer. Business, on the other hand, turned sharply away from the Democrats. See William E. Leuchtenburg, *op. cit.,* p. 188.

125. Near the end of the Hoover administration this tax had been pushed up to 55 percent on incomes in excess of $1 million in a belated effort to help finance some much needed anti-Depression measures.

126. There were also some significant upward revisions in the corporate tax during the New Deal years, but these were of less importance than those described above.

127. See Arthur M. Schlesinger, Jr., *The Politics of Upheaval*, pp. 303–04.

128. On the first point, see Bernard Bellush, *Franklin D. Roosevelt as Governor of New York* (New York: Columbia University Press, 1955), pp. 212–240. Roosevelt had long had a strong interest in providing electric power at reasonable rates to various segments of the population, particularly those who lived in non-urban or economically depressed areas, as already evinced by his earlier creation of the TVA and the Rural Electric Administration. For more on the development of the former program, see Thomas K. McCraw, *TVA and the Power Fight, 1933-1939* (Philadelphia: Lippincott, 1971).

129. This struggle is described in considerable detail in Philip Funigiello's book, *Toward a National Power Policy: The New Deal and the Electric Utility Industry, 1933-1941* (Pittsburgh: University of Pittsburgh Press, 1973), pp. 32–121. However, Funigiello makes no mention of the fact that these two companies were, in effect, subsidiaries of the United Corp., the financial linchpin of the Morgan utility empire, which relationship was of tremendous import in explaining the role of the opposition leaders in this bitter battle.

130. For the only lengthy study of this body, which expired soon after the 1936 election, see

George Wolfskill, *The Revolt of the Conservatives: A History of the American Liberty League, 1934-1940* (Boston: Houghton Mifflin, 1962), passim. This analysis, while it does indicate that the du Pont forces were behind the Liberty League, does not probe deeply into the other linkages which formed the financial nexus of this organization. There is no evidence that the 1936 Republican presidential candidate, Kansas Governor Alf Landon (who was merely a small oil operator), was connected with this reactionary body. Nevertheless, a substantial amount of the money that was raised for Landon's campaign apparently came from such rightist sources, for, as Wolfskill has pointed out (see p. 206), one-third of the 21-man Republican National Finance Committee in 1936 was closely associated with the Liberty League. It should also be noted that the top aide of Landon's campaign manager, Topeka lawyer John D. M. Hamilton, was former J. P. Morgan official Charlton MacVeagh, whose father had up to recently been a longtime partner in the "Morgan" law firm of Davis, Polk, Wardwell, Gardiner & Reed, and whose brother was still a member of this concern.

131. See Philip H. Burch, Jr., "The NAM as an Interest Group," *Politics and Society* (Fall, 1973), pp. 101-03.

132. Willkie sat on the board of the Morgan-dominated First National Bank of New York both before and after his presidential nomination (to be precise, in 1940 and 1943-1944). Moreover, his close friends included Perry Hall (a vice-president of Morgan, Stanley & Co.), Thomas W. Lamont (vice-chairman of J. P. Morgan & Co.), S. Sloan Colt (president of the Bankers Trust Co.), George Howard (president of the United Corp.), Henry Luce and Russell Davenport (the head and a high official of Time, Inc.), Roy Howard (a co-owner of the Scripps-Howard newspapers), Gardner and John Cowles (the Midwestern-based publishers of *Look* magazine and two widely read newspapers), Sinclair Weeks (a New England industrialist), and Samuel F. Pryor, Jr. (a Connecticut Republican party chieftain with various major corporate ties). It should also be noted that the two youthful GOP leaders who did much to promote Willkie's candidacy, Oren Root, Jr., and Charlton MacVeagh, were both previously associated with Morgan concerns (the former with the New York law firm of Davis, Polk, Wardwell, Gardiner & Reed, and the latter, up to 1934, with J. P. Morgan & Co.). See Donald B. Johnson *The Republican Party and Wendell Willkie* (Urbana: University of Illinois Press, 1960), pp. 47-49, Oren Root, *Persons and Persuasions* (New York: Norton, 1974), pp. 18-29, Warren Moscow, *Roosevelt and Willkie* (Englewood Cliffs, N.J.: Prentice-Hall, 1968), pp. 53-68, and Matthew Josephson, *The Money Lords*, pp. 271-73.

133. See Peter Collier and David Horowitz, *op. cit.*, pp. 165-69, John Hoff Wilson, *American Business and Foreign Policy: 1920-1933* (Lexington: University Press of Kentucky, 1971), p. 298, and Henry J. Abraham, *Justices and Presidents* (New York: Oxford University Press, 1974), p. 188.

134. See Lewis L. Gould, *Wyoming: A Political History, 1868-1896* (New Haven, Conn.: Yale University Press, 1968), p. 213.

135. See Leon Friedman and Fred L. Israel (eds.), *The Justices of the United States Supreme Court, 1789-1969* (New York: Chelsea House, 1969), Vol. III, p. 2025.

136. The able Sutherland might also be viewed as a pro-Establishment figure, for he had been president of the American Bar Association in 1917 and had served on the board of the elitist-dominated Carnegie Endowment for International Peace up to 1925.

137. For much insight into Butler's background and his many influential political and economic supporters for this high office, see David J. Danelski, *A Supreme Court Justice is Appointed*, passim. Also, in the 1930s, Butler's son, Francis, served on the board of the First Trust Co. of St. Paul, which was an affiliate (i.e., subsidiary) of the big First National Bank of that city.

138. Roberts was also reported to be on very close terms with the Pennsylvania Railroad and the Philadelphia banking house of Drexel & Co., a Morgan-affiliated firm that counted Roberts' former brother-in-law, Thomas S. Gates, among its senior partners. Gates was a director of the Pennsylvania Railroad, Penn Mutual Life Insurance Co., and the United Gas Improvement Co., one of the big operational subsidiaries of the Morgan-dominated United

Corp. In fact, according to a recent source, Roberts once served as legal counsel to the Pennsylvania Railroad. See Henry J. Abraham, *op. cit.*, p. 189, Drew Pearson and Robert S. Allen, *The Nine Old Men* (New York: Doubleday, Doran, 1936), pp. 147–48, and G. Edward White, *The American Judicial Tradition* (New York: Oxford University Press, 1976), p. 211.

139. For more on this able and unusual figure, see Alpheus T. Mason, *Brandeis: A Free Man's Life* (New York: Viking Press, 1946).

140. The bulk of the time that Stone spent in private practice was with Satterlee, Canfield & Stone, which firm, although it counted J. P. Morgan's son-in-law as one of its senior partners, apparently never handled a large volume of work for big business interests. Stone's only corporate link over the years was with the small Atlanta & Charlotte Air Line Railway.

141. See Samuel Eliot Morison, Henry Steele Commager, and William E. Leuchtenberg, *The Growth of the American Republic* (New York: Oxford University Press, 1950), Vol. 2, p. 512.

142. Black came from a relatively modest, if not humble, background; as one author has observed, "Black did not get accustomed to inside plumbing until he was twenty years old." See Leon Friedman and Fred L. Israel, *op. cit.*, Vol. III, p. 2322, John P. Frank, *Mr. Justice Black* (New York: Knopf, 1949), pp. 21–22, Virginia V. Hamilton, *Hugo Black: The Alabama Years* (Baton Rouge: Louisiana State University Press, 1972), p. 83, and Gerald T. Dunne, *Hugo Black and the Judicial Revolution* (New York: Simon & Schuster, 1977), pp. 94–102, in particular.

143. See Leon Friedman and Fred L. Israel, *op. cit.*, Vol. III, p. 2374, and the *National Cyclopaedia of American Biography*, Vol. E, p. 61.

144. See Leon Friedman and Fred L. Israel, *op. cit.*, Vol. III, p. 2404.

145. One possible reason for Frankfurter's fairly conservative stance on the Supreme Court may have been that he was also a longtime close friend of former (1929–1933) Secretary of State and wealthy New York attorney Henry L. Stimson, and of another Wall Street lawyer, Grenville Clark, who was a senior partner in the top-tier firm of Root, Clark, Buckner & Ballantine (and a member of a family associated with Clark, Dodge & Co.). Furthermore, up to the mid-1920s Frankfurter had served as a trustee of the Institute for Government Research, a Washington-based organization which, after a set of mergers in 1927, became known as the Brookings Institution. For more on Frankfurter's friends, see Liva Baker, *Felix Frankfurter* (New York: Coward-McCann, 1969), pp. 24–28 and 239.

146. Douglas was associated briefly (in 1925–1926) with the Wall Street law firm of Cravath, Henderson & deGersdorff. But this was a comparatively short stint; he left in the latter part of 1926 to take up law practice in his hometown of Yakima, Washington. After a few months there he accepted a teaching post at Columbia University.

147. See John R. Schmidhauser, *The Supreme Court: Its Politics, Personalities, and Procedures* (New York: Holt, Rinehart & Winston, 1960), p. 31.

148. See, for instance, Carl N. Degler, *Out of Our Past* (New York: Harper & Row, 1959), pp. 379–416, and Mario Einaudi, *The Roosevelt Revolution* (New York: Harcourt, Brace & Co., 1959), passim.

149. See "The Myth of the New Deal" in Ronald Radosh and Murray N. Rothbard (eds.), *A New History of Leviathan* (New York: Dutton, 1972), pp. 146–87.

150. See "The New Deal: The Conservative Achievements of Liberal Reform," in Barton J. Bernstein (ed.), *Toward a New Past* (New York: Random House, 1968), p. 264, and for a similar view, see William Appleton Williams, *The Contours of American History* (Cleveland: World Publishing 1961), p. 439.

151. The latter percentage would be even lower if such officials as Henry Wallace, tentatively classified as an elite leader, were found on further study to be non-elite figures.

152. From a long-range standpoint, the author would challenge Barton Bernstein's claim (see p. 264 of *Toward a New Past*) that the benefits of the New Deal did not extend significantly beyond the middle classes, for, in truth, the increased economic leverage provided by the

government's protection and promotion of organized labor, buoyed by the post-1941 growth in prosperity, eventually lifted many families out of the lower-income brackets and made them part of a much enlarged middle class. At the same time, however, the author agrees with Bernstein's assertion that there was no noteworthy shift in the distribution of wealth during this period (or even later years), largely because of various major loopholes in the country's income, gift, and estate tax systems.

153. To argue, as some scholars have, that the New Deal should have accomplished much more—wiping out poverty, eliminating unemployment, nationalizing the banks, etc.—is to engage in a good deal of retrospective speculation. There were limits to what the New Deal could achieve during this brief period (although they clearly were not reached), and on many issues the Roosevelt regime ran into stiff opposition, which forced it to retreat or compromise. For a telling critique of some revisionist writings, see Jerold S. Auerbach, "New Deal, Old Deal, or Raw Deal: Some Thoughts on New Left Historiography," *Journal of Southern History* (February 1969), pp. 18–30, and also for a less hostile survey, Richard S. Kirkendall, "The New Deal as Watershed: The Recent Literature," *Journal of American History* (March 1968), pp. 839–52.

154. See William E. Leuchtenburg, *Franklin D. Roosevelt and the New Deal*, p. 347.

CHAPTER 3

The World War II and Truman Years

As the politically stormy, Depression-ridden 1930s drew to a close, the attention of the Roosevelt administration was increasingly directed to the threat posed to America's national security by the aggressive Axis powers. In the early 1940s the stunning military successes of Germany and Japan were so sweeping that it appeared they might ultimately conquer the entire world. Though severely hampered by a strong isolationist sentiment in the United States, the Roosevelt regime firmly supported the hard-pressed Allied forces, led by Great Britain, China, and the Soviet Union.

America's abrupt entry into the war in late 1941 quickly united the country and permitted the government to take a series of unprecedented steps to effectively coordinate the nation's military and industrial defense effort. Because of a shortage of essential raw materials such as rubber, gas rationing was imposed for the first time in American history. An Office of Price Administration was established by federal edict to restrain inflationary pressures created by the diversion of a tremendous amount of material into the production of vital military goods. Another important agency was created in the form of the War Production Board, which was given extraordinary powers to oversee and direct the nation's massive economic mobilization. At the same time the War and Navy departments underwent a vast expansion in their size and range of responsibility. To direct these now critical agencies, a sizable number of able executives were recruited on short notice from various sectors of the economy, especially from the business and legal communities. Through such efforts the country built up a huge military machine (capped by the development of the atomic bomb) that played a decisive role in defeating the Axis powers in 1945.

But even with the return of peace and the accession of a new President, Missouri's Harry S. Truman, America was unable to return to its less hectic prewar conditions, particularly in the realm of foreign relations. Soon after the cessation of hostilities it became clear that the United States and the Soviet Union had emerged from this momentous conflict as the two strongest

69

nations in the world and that they held bitterly opposed views on most international economic and political issues. As a result, the murderous "hot war" of Axis versus Allied powers was succeeded by an extremely tense "cold war" in which the capitalist-dominated democracies, led by the United States, were arrayed against the Soviet Union and its Communist-controlled satellite countries. In the late 1940s, Russia was joined in this struggle by Red China, following a bitter civil war which resulted in a rout of the Nationalist forces of Chiang Kai-shek. The antipathy between the Communist and free worlds erupted into open warfare during the closing years of the Truman administration when the Republic of South Korea was invaded by the North Korean army, an act that led first to the dispatch of a substantial number of American troops and shortly thereafter to the unexpected intervention of Red China. Eventually, the conflict ended in a military stalemate. Thus the Korean war represented a peak in the long-simmering hostility which existed between the capitalist and Communist bloc countries in the postwar period.

The international situation also led the United States to revamp its defense establishment and to create a number of government agencies designed to cope with postwar problems. One of the most important acts merged the War and Navy departments in the late 1940s into a much larger Cabinet-level agency, the Department of Defense, which body now had its own air arm. At about the same time the government also established a top-secret unit known as the Central Intelligence Agency (CIA), which was directed to delve into any matters that might pose a threat to America's national security and, presumably, take whatever countermeasures were necessary. Another very different kind of agency was created with the support of friendly nations, and that was the World Bank (officially known as the International Bank for Reconstruction and Development). It was authorized to extend loans to various needy or worthy countries to promote their overall economic development. In 1948, following the Communist takeover of Czechoslovakia, yet another important agency, the Economic Cooperation Administration, was established by federal authorities to conduct a massive aid and relief program, called the Marshall Plan, to shore up the war-ravaged and faltering Western European democracies. And in 1950 the American government set up the Office of Defense Mobilization to deal with the Korean War. Thus, under the press of changing, often hostile world conditions, the United States was required in the postwar period to create a number of new or substantially revised government agencies, most of which were concerned with defense and national security.

The extraordinary climate of conflict and international tension did much, not surprisingly, to spur the growth of many industries in the United States, particularly those that produced planes, guns, tanks, petroleum, and other essential material for the nation's now highly mechanized military establishment. Table 3 shows the growth of the country's top twenty manufacturing and merchandising concerns between 1940 and 1952, all but two of

TABLE 3
America's Top 20 Industrial Concerns in 1952

1952 Rank	Corporation	1940 Assets ($ millions)	1952 Assets ($ millions)
1.	Standard Oil Co. of N.J.	2,072	5,049
2.	General Motors Corp.	1,536	4,001
3.	U.S. Steel Corp.	1,855	2,988
4.	Socony Vacuum Oil Co.	940	2,011
5.	Standard Oil Co. of Ind.	757	1,964
6.	Ford Motor Co.	713	1,758
7.	Texas Co.	675	1,736
8.	E. I. du Pont de Nemours & Co.	801	1,731
9.	Gulf Oil Corp.	523	1,627
10.	Bethlehem Steel Corp.	764	1,610
11.	General Electric Co.	491	1,580
12.	Standard Oil Co. of Calif.	623	1,407
13.	Sears, Roebuck & Co.	nearly 350	1,362
14.	Westinghouse Electric Corp.	241	1,195
15.	International Harvester Co.	444	1,091
16.	Union Carbide & Carbon Corp.	365	1,072
17.	Cities Service Co.	338*	1,047
18.	Sinclair Oil Corp. (formerly Consolidated Oil Corp.)	344	1,035
19.	Phillips Petroleum Co.	227	923
20.	Chrysler Corp.	268	914

*Excluding its public utility subsidiaries.

which benefited from vastly expanded sales to America's armed forces. With the possible exception of U.S. Steel, the economic development of these companies, and of many other large manufacturing firms, was striking (even when allowance is made for the effect of inflation).[1] Their growth far exceeded that of the utility industry.[2] And it was also in sharp contrast to that of the railroad industry, which in real dollar terms did not grow at all during this time.[3] (As a matter of fact, four lines that had been in the 1940 "top 20" ranking—the Illinois Central, Chicago and Northwestern, Erie, and Chicago, Rock Island and Pacific—actually declined in assets.) Clearly, it was during this period that big manufacturing came of age in America.

Another area of activity which witnessed considerable growth between 1940 and 1952 was finance. Many large commercial banks and insurance companies more than doubled in size during these years. Buoyed by California's postwar population explosion, the Giannini-dominated Bank of America grew at an even faster rate, so that by 1952 it ranked, according to official figures, as the largest commercial bank in the country (see Table 4).[4]

TABLE 4
America's Top 10 Banks and 5 Largest Life Insurance Companies in 1952

1952 Rank	Bank	1940 Assets ($ millions)	1952 Assets ($ millions)
1.	Bank of America, Calif.	1,818	8,202
2.	National City Bank, N.Y.C.	3,095	6,117
3.	Chase National Bank, N.Y.C.	3,824	5,743
4.	Guaranty Trust Co., N.Y.C.	2,719	3,149
5.	Manufacturers Trust Co., N.Y.C.	1,050	2,949
6.	First National Bank, Chicago	1,238	2,829
7.	Continental Illinois Bank & Trust Co., Chicago	1,177	2,801
8.	Bankers Trust Co., N.Y.C.	818	2,137
9.	Security-First National Bank, Los Angeles	687	2,017
10.	Chemical Bank & Trust Co., N.Y.C.	958	2,048
	Insurance Company		
1.	Metropolitan Life Insurance Co., N.Y.C.	5,358	11,593
2.	Prudential Insurance Co. of America, Newark, N.J.	4,264	10,219
3.	Equitable Life Assurance Society, N.Y.C.	2,564	6,572
4.	New York Life Insurance Co., N.Y.C.	2,870	5,326
5.	John Hancock Mutual Life Insurance Co., Boston	1,054	3,541

Spurred on by an economy fueled first by a major war and then by feverish international tension, the nation's top financial institutions grew at an accelerated pace during this critical twelve-year period. Despite some regional shifts, most of the huge concerns—six of the "top 10" banks and four out of five biggest insurance companies—retained their headquarters in the New York metropolitan area, the country's longtime financial capital.

Another notable development during this period was the increasing institutionalization of the nation's top business leadership. Until the early 1930s, America's primarily Eastern-dominated economic structure had been characterized by a number of important, often rival, groups, the most potent of which were the House of Morgan and two less influential formal organizations, the NAM, which had been controlled up to the mid-1930s by small and medium-sized concerns, and the U.S. Chamber of Commerce, a body with very mixed representation.[5] However, as pointed out in the preceding chapter, in 1933 a new organization, the Business Advisory Council (BAC), was created to improve communications between the New Deal administration and various segments of the corporate community. After a brief early period of intimacy, especially during the NRA days, its relations with the later "leftish" Roosevelt regime cooled perceptibly, and it exerted less influence on the federal government during the latter part of the 1930s. However, as America was drawn into the rapidly expanding Second World War, the BAC emerged as an enormously important politico-economic group, thrashing out top policy, advising major governmental agencies (particularly those concerned with the management of the nation's war effort), and serving, without public notice, as a key federal recruitment channel.[6] By this time the BAC had clearly evolved into an organization that was thoroughly dominated by large corporate interests, so it was viewed in some economic circles with grave suspicion.[7]

It was perhaps for this reason that when a number of prominent figures in the big business community decided to take some early steps to cope with the various probable postwar problems, such as widespread unemployment and the specter of another major depression, they chose in 1942 to create another organization, which has since been known as the Committee for Economic Development (CED). This initially small body, which was made up of men who, unlike the NAM's leaders, had come to accept most of the reforms adopted by the New Deal and the need for a certain amount of governmental intervention in the operation of the economy, grew largely out of the BAC.[8] Of the first eighteen trustees of the CED, nine were members of the BAC, including the former group's first chairman, Paul Hoffman, who was president of the Studebaker Corp.[9] Another trustee, Quaker Oats Co. president John Stuart, had a brother and fellow company officer, R. Douglas Stuart, who also belonged to the BAC. Moreover, at least 80 percent of the corporate representatives on the board of the CED, which had expanded to well over 100 members by the early 1950s, were drawn from the ranks of big business. Equally important, the close links between the CED and the BAC were maintained in the ensuing years, through both direct and indirect ties. Thus it can be said that the BAC-CED axis, as one business journal has described this interlocked complex, has represented America's true economic establishment since the early 1940s.[10]

Another organization which became increasingly prominent about this time was the prestigious Council on Foreign Relations (CFR). Although accounts differ, this group would appear to have played a relatively minor role in the formulation of American foreign policy up to the late 1930s. But as the war clouds gathered over Europe and Asia, the Council became directly enmeshed in the diplomatic and war preparation efforts of the Roosevelt administration, both formally, through such mechanisms as the CFR's officially funded War and Peace Studies Project, and informally, through the so-called Century group.[11] The latter body reportedly did much to bring about the controversial destroyer deal, whereby the United States gave beleaguered Britain fifty badly needed ships in exchange for permission to build a number of military bases on its possessions in the Western hemisphere. The Council created five special study groups to deal with various major phases of America's war mobilization and diplomatic strategy.

Overall, these groups attended 362 meetings with high federal officials in the course of the conflict and prepared a total of 682 separate documents for the State Department and the President.[12] Indeed, so close were the relations between the Council and the administration that these groups were, in effect, absorbed into the State Department by 1942.[13]

FDR'S MAJOR ADMINISTRATIVE AND DIPLOMATIC OFFICIALS: 1940–1945

In the first part of this critical five-year period, the Roosevelt Cabinet was made up of a number of holdovers from the preceding, domestically oriented phase of his administration—officials such as Secretary of State Cordell Hull, Secretary of the Treasury Henry Morgenthau, Secretary of the Interior Harold Ickes, and Secretary of Labor Frances Perkins (only one of whom, Morgenthau, could be described as an elitist figure)—plus a larger set of new appointees. Perhaps the most important of these was the able, albeit elderly, Henry L. Stimson, who, though a Republican, was persuaded by the President to become Secretary of War in mid-1940. Thus this now critical department was placed in the hands of a man who, unlike isolationist Harry Woodring, was fully aware of the need for greater military preparedness.[14] Stimson was a highly respected, time-tested official, having served as a Cabinet member in two earlier administrations—as Secretary of War in the last half of the Taft regime, and as Secretary of State under Herbert Hoover. However, over the years he had worked primarily as a Wall Street lawyer, although by the 1930s his relationship with his longtime firm of Winthrop, Stimson, Putnam & Roberts had been reduced to merely that of "counsel." He also had various wealthy, influential kinsmen in the New York area, the most prominent of whom was his cousin, Landon K. Thorne, who served on the board of the Morgan-dominated First National Bank, the considerably smaller Federal Insurance Co., and, from 1943 on, the Southern Pacific Railroad.[15] In short, the able and experienced Stimson was clearly an Establishment figure.[16]

At about the same time the President appointed a new Secretary of the Navy to replace New Jersey industrialist Charles Edison, who held office for less than a year before resigning to run for governor of his home state. As his successor, Roosevelt picked another business-oriented official, former Illinois publisher Frank Knox, who, like Stimson, was conscripted from the ranks of the Republican party in an effort to secure bipartisan support for the nation's rapidly expanding war mobilization program. As publisher of the *Chicago Daily News*, Knox had fairly close ties to major business interests. For example, three of the eight outside members of the *Daily News* board were either officers or directors of the big Pure Oil Co., a firm apparently dominated by the wealthy Dawes family, and a fourth, John Stuart, president of the Quaker Oats Co., was linked through his brother with the BAC.[17] Knox himself served up to 1940 as a director of Chicago's City National

The World War II and Truman Years 75

Bank and Trust Co., a $185-million concern, also probably controlled by the Dawes family. Thus, although regarded by some as a progressive figure, Knox was, in fact, a pro-corporate official.

Because of the crisis conditions that prevailed, a number of other able men with pro-business views were brought into these two key departments during the war. They were as follows:

Under Secretary of War	Robert P. Patterson, N.Y. (1940–1945)	Federal judge (1930–1940); partner, N.Y.C. law firm of Webb, Patterson & Hadley (1922–1929) and Murray, Aldrich & Webb (1929–1930), to which practice he returned in the late 1940's; Webb was a longtime director of the New York Trust Co.
Asst. Secretary of War	John J. McCloy, N.Y. (1941–1945)	Federal defense post (1940–1941); partner, N.Y.C. law firm of Cravath, deGersdorff, Swaine & Wood (1929–1940); brother-in-law of Lewis W. Douglas, president of the Mutual Life Insurance Co. and a trustee of the Rockefeller Foundation; another brother-in-law, John S. Zinsser, on board of J.P. Morgan & Co. (1943 on)
Asst. Secretary of War for Air	Robert A. Lovett, N.Y. (1940–1945)	Federal defense post (1940–1941); partner, N.Y.C. banking house of Brown Brothers Harriman & Co. (1926–1940); director of the Union Pacific Railroad (1926–1940) and the New York Trust Co. (1926–1940)
Under Secretary of Navy	James V. Forrestal, N.Y. (1940–1944)	Federal defense post (1940); high official, N.Y.C. investment banking firm of Dillon, Read & Co. (1916–1940, president 1938–1940); director of the Chase Securities Corp., an affiliate of the Chase National Bank (1930–1931)

Under Secretary of Navy	Ralph A. Bard, Ill. (1944–1945)	Assistant Secretary of the Navy (1941–1944); board chairman, Eversharp, Inc., Chicago (1940–1942); president, Ralph A. Bard & Co., Chicago (1934–1941); director of the Mead Corp., Ohio (1933–1935), the head of which company was an influential charter member of the BAC
Asst. Secretary of Navy	Ralph A. Bard, Ill. (1941–1944)	See above entry
	H. Struve Hensel, N.Y. (January 1945 on)	Federal defense posts (1941–1945); member, N.Y.C. law firm of Milbank, Tweed & Hope (1933–1941), the last-named partner of which was a trustee of the Metropolitan Life Insurance Co.
Asst. Secretary of Navy for Air	Artemus L. Gates, N.Y. (1941–1945)	No prior governmental experience; president, New York Trust Co. (1931–1941); director of American Smelting & Refining Co. (1932–1942), Time, Inc. (1932–1941), and Pan-American Airways Corp. (1940–1941); brother-in-law of Harry P. Davison, VP of J.P. Morgan & Co. and a director of the American Brake Shoe & Foundry Co., Standard Brands, Inc., and Montgomery, Ward & Co.; another brother-in-law F. Trubee Davison, served on the board of the Mutual Life Insurance Co.

The above data show that most of the second-tier posts in the nation's defense establishment during the Second World War were occupied by men who were either Wall Street lawyers or bankers, a recruitment pattern that would seem to indicate that this financial hub was the locus of much talent and economic influence in American society.[18]

A somewhat less important post which had to be filled on two occasions during this critical five-year period was that of Attorney General. This position became vacant in 1940 when Michigan's Frank Murphy was appointed to the Supreme Court. As his successor, Roosevelt selected another staunch New Dealer, Robert H. Jackson, who had served in several prominent legal capacities in the administration, most recently as U.S. Solicitor General (1938–1940). Unlike most high-level appointees to America's wartime defense establishment, Jackson was not an elitist figure. Quite the contrary. He was essentially a small town (Jamestown, New York) lawyer who, while he had certain economic ties, had been aligned with small business interests in his home town, some of which had fought zealously against various large corporations that posed a threat to their operations or existence.[19] Jackson, however, held office only briefly; in July 1941 he too was appointed to the U.S. Supreme Court. For his replacement Roosevelt turned logically to the second-ranking official in the Justice Department, Solicitor General Francis Biddle, who had served recently as a federal judge (1939–1940) and earlier as chairman of the National Labor Relations Board (1934–1935). But Biddle had spent most of his working life with a well-established Philadelphia law firm, which counted among its most important clients the Pennsylvania Railroad and the Berwind-White Coal Mining Co.[20] In addition, he was a wealthy patrician who had many elite family ties in the Philadelphia area.[21] However, like his predecessor Robert Jackson, Biddle served as a trustee of the fairly liberal (non-elite dominated) Twentieth Century Fund during all of his years as a high official in the Justice Department.

Another Cabinet post which had to be filled in 1940 was that of Secretary of Commerce. The incumbent, Roosevelt's confidant, Harry Hopkins, had become increasingly involved in his informal role as chief aide and advisor to the President, particularly in the realm of foreign policy. FDR selected Texas executive Jesse Jones, who was a very different sort of person from Hopkins, the social worker turned dedicated New Dealer. Jones was clearly a more conventional choice in that he was a wealthy entrepreneur who had served during most of the financially-troubled mid and late 1930s as chairman of the Reconstruction Finance Corp., an agency created by the Hoover administration to help shore up badly sagging enterprises.[22] He had a variety of major business interests—he was the longtime head of Houston's big National Bank of Commerce (a position he held through his Cabinet years), the president of an influential local newspaper, the *Houston Chronicle*, and the owner of a large number of commercial buildings in several Texas cities, as well as some in New York City.[23] Hence this Cabinet post was obviously in "safe" economic hands during most of the World War II years.[24]

The same, however, cannot be said of the, to some, less prestigious post of Secretary of Agriculture. After Henry Wallace's election as Vice President in 1940, this position was offered to Claude Wickard, an Indiana farmer of relatively modest means. Although Wickard had served in the department for the preceding seven years, he was not, interestingly, on good terms with the influential, big-farmer-dominated American Farm Bureau Federation (AFBF). In fact, Wickard soon became anathema to the AFBF, and as a penalty for his independence, he ultimately "...paid the price by becoming a nearly impotent bystander in his own department when the main functions of the department were later placed under the War Food Administration headed [initially] by Chester C. Davis,"[25] an official who was one of the original trustees of the CED.

One last major Cabinet appointment made toward the end of World War II was that of Secretary of State, a post long held by Tennessee political leader Cordell Hull. After many years of service in this capacity (during the last part of which Roosevelt had relied increasingly on such influential aides as Harry Hopkins),[26] Hull resigned from office. He was replaced by a former corporate executive, Edward R. Stettinius, who since the start of the war had held various key posts in the federal government, most notably that of Under Secretary of State. But Stettinius was essentially a big businessman, for he had been a high official of the General Motors Corp. from 1926 to 1934 and then, for the next six years, of the U.S. Steel Corp. He also had served in recent years as a director of the Metropolitan Life Insurance Co., as a member of the Business Advisory Council, and as a trustee of the Brookings Institution.[27] Although some scholars have described Stettinius as little more than a figurehead, it would nevertheless appear that the State Department was directed by a pro-business leader during the closing stages of World War II.[28]

America's major wartime ambassadors were, on the other hand, a rather mixed lot.[29] For example, in the first part of 1941, following the welcomed resignation of our pro-appeasement Ambassador to Great Britain, Joseph P. Kennedy, President Roosevelt chose a very different type of figure, John G. Winant, an enlightened Republican, to serve as his successor. Originally from New York, Winant had the good fortune to marry into the Russell and Pyne families ("old money"),[30] and fairly early in life decided to embark on an unusual career for a man of his background. He moved to New Hampshire where, in addition to acquiring two Concord newspapers and a local oil company, he became active in state politics. In fact, he was thrice elected governor of New Hampshire, in which role he compiled a fairly liberal record. Upon the completion of his last term in office, Winant was appointed by President Roosevelt as the first chairman of the Social Security Board, after which he went to work for the International Labor Organization (another indication that he was of a liberal persuasion). Since the mid-1930s Winant had also served on the board of the elitist-dominated but politically moderate Brookings Institution, along with such prominent leaders as former Secretary of War Dwight F. Davis (whose son-in-law, William McChesney Martin, Jr., was the new head of the New York Stock Exchange), Marshall Field, Corning glass manufacturer Alanson B. Houghton (who sat on the board of the Metropolitan Life Insurance Co.), Princeton University president Harold W. Dodds (who sat on the board of the Prudential Insurance Co.

of America), and Washington attorney Dean Acheson.[31] So, although Winant was a liberal, he had close ties with various members of America's emerging politico-economic establishment.

Out of necessity, the United States established closer relations with the Soviet Union during the crucial World War II years. The first Ambassador to Russia in the early 1940s was Lawrence A. Steinhardt, a well-connected New York corporate lawyer who had recently acted as our emissary to Sweden and Peru.[32] Steinhardt held this post up to November 1941, when he was replaced by retired Admiral William H. Standley. Though a longtime military man, Standley had recently forged other important ties, for he had served on the board of the Pan American Airways Corp. in the early 1940s and was a member of the Century group, which was closely linked with the Council on Foreign Relations.[33] Then in the fall of 1943, Roosevelt appointed a big business executive, W. Averell Harriman, to act as our Ambassador to the Soviet regime. Like Edward R. Stettinius, Harriman had held various defense and foreign policy posts in the wartorn early 1940s. But Harriman also had many key economic ties. He had served as a high official in the New York banking house of Brown Brothers Harriman & Co. (and its predecessor concern) since 1920, as board chairman of the Harriman family-controlled Union Pacific Railroad from 1932 through 1945, as chairman of the executive committee of the probably family-dominated Illinois Central Railroad up to 1942, as a member of the potent Business Advisory Council from 1933 through 1945 (he was its chairman in the late 1930s), and as a director of the American Ship and Commerce Corp., Guaranty Trust Co. of New York, and Western Union Telegraph Co. up to 1940. Hence he was clearly a spokesman for many of America's top corporate interests.

As one might expect, America's economic mobilization program after Pearl Harbor was dominated by big business forces. Look, for example, at the men chosen to run the War Production Board (WPB), a special ad hoc agency created in January 1942 after our abrupt entry into the world conflict and the realization that our divided industrial efforts were generating considerable waste and confusion. The man who directed the highly complex WPB operation during most of the war was Donald M. Nelson, the executive vice-president of Sears, Roebuck & Co. Probably even more important, Nelson was a member of the influential Business Advisory Council and a director of the Harriman-controlled Union Pacific Railroad.[34] In 1943, at the height of the war effort, the other officials of the WPB were:

Assistant to the Chairman	Sidney J. Weinberg (partner, Goldman, Sachs & Co., N.Y.C.)	Member of the executive committee of the BAC and a director of Sears, Roebuck & Co. and many other companies
Executive Vice-Chairman	Charles E. Wilson (president, General Electric Co., whose boss, Philip D. Reed, was a member of the BAC)	Director of the Guaranty Trust Co., N.Y.C. (up to 1942)

Vice-Chairman	Ralph J. Cordiner (1939–1942 president, Shick, Inc.; also a former high official of GE)	
Operations Vice-Chairman	Donald D. Davis (president, General Mills)	Boss, James F. Bell, on board of AT & T and an original (1942) trustee of the CED
Programs Vice-Chairman	Julius A. Krug (longtime federal and state government official)	
Vice-Chairman, International Supply	William L. Batt (president, S.K.F. Industries, Phila.)	Member of the executive committee of the BAC
Vice-Chairman, Civilian Requirements	Arthur D. Whiteside (president, Dun & Bradstreet, Inc., N.Y.C.)	Up to 1940, member of the BAC
Rubber Director	William M. Jeffers (president, Union Pacific Railroad)	
Director, Bureau of Planning and Statistics	Stacy May (official, Rockefeller Foundation)	Member of the BAC; also married a member of the Harkness family (of the Standard Oil Co.)
General Counsel	John Lord O'Brian (partner, Buffalo Law firm of O'Brian, Hellings, Ulsh & Morey)	Director of the Equitable Life Assurance Society (of N.Y.C.)

Thus there is little doubt that the management of the nation's war production effort was firmly in the hands of major corporate interests, whose special resources and abilities probably contributed a good deal to making America an "arsenal of democracy."[35]

TRUMAN'S MAJOR CABINET AND DIPLOMATIC OFFICIALS

Franklin Roosevelt died shortly after the start of his fourth term in office, just a few months before the Allies achieved total victory over the Axis powers. Because the maneuvers of certain influential conservatives in the Democratic party had managed to force the liberal Henry Wallace off the 1944 ticket, FDR's death brought to power Harry S. Truman, who reportedly represented a compromise selection at the 1944 national convention.[36] But Truman was quite unprepared for the massive leadership burden abruptly thrust upon him. He had held office as Vice President for only a brief period, less than three months. In addition, although he had previously served as a United States Senator from Missouri for about ten years (during which time he had compiled a fairly liberal voting record), he had not been prominently involved in many major legislative matters. Indeed, his most conspicuous activity had been as chairman of a special committee created to investigate the operation of the nation's war mobilization program, in the course of which he earned a reputation for unusual perseverance and integrity. To some, even this was surprising, for Truman had long been regarded as a product of the malodorous Missouri Democratic machine which had been headed, up to recently, by Thomas J. Pendergast. Actually, Truman was a rather plebeian figure who had never gone to college. Instead, he had been involved in his early years in various minor, mostly ill-fated, commercial ventures in the Kansas City and Independence areas. The most notable of these was a small haberdashery business, which failed after a few years, leaving him with a substantial debt. Although Truman was never a staunch liberal, he grew in stature and confidence as the years progressed.[37] Moreover, to the dismay of his many critics, Truman proved to be a forceful President, although he was frequently thwarted on domestic issues by a conservative Congress. Though he was given virtually no chance to retain his high office in 1948, Truman waged an extremely vigorous campaign against the able but overconfident Eastern Republican Establishment candidate, Thomas E. Dewey, and stunned most pundits by scoring a decisive victory.

When Truman assumed the Presidency in April 1945, he had relatively little experience in foreign affairs and thus had to rely heavily on the advice of men in high posts in the State Department. Some of these were career officials; others were individuals whom Truman appointed from outside the diplomatic ranks. The political and occupational backgrounds of the three men chosen to serve as Secretary of State during the Truman years were as follows:

James F. Byrnes (1945–1947)	Director, Office of War Mobilization (1943–1945); Associate Justice, U.S. Supreme Court (1941–1942); U.S. Senator, S.C. (1931–1941)
George C. Marshall (1947–1949)	Longtime (1901–1945) high-ranking U.S. Army officer; special representative of the President in China (1945–1946)
Dean G. Acheson (1949–1953)	Under Secretary of State (1945–1947); Assistant Secretary of State (1941–1945); Under Secretary of the Treasury (May–November 1933); partner, Washington law firm of Covington, Burling, Rublee, Acheson & Shorb (1926–1941 and 1947–1949)

This summary account is somewhat misleading, for two of these figures, Byrnes and Acheson, were on friendly terms with certain important economic interests. James F. Byrnes was a good friend of New York financier Bernard Baruch and a charter member of the exclusive Jefferson Island Club, an informal conservative clique which included such influential political figures as Virginia's Harry Byrd, Mississippi's Pat Harrison, and Arkansas' Joseph Robinson.[38] And while Dean Acheson had been praised for his knowledge and expertise in foreign affairs (gained mainly through his six years of service in two high State Department posts), it should be pointed out that this patrician figure had spent a much longer period working for a well-established Washington, D.C., corporate law firm, known by the late 1940s as Covington, Burling, Rublee, Acheson and Shorb.[39] Although the growing politico-economic role played by Washington lawyers was little noted at the time, some of Acheson's partners had close ties with major business enterprises. For instance, John G. Laylin had served since 1947 as a director of the J. Henry Schroder Banking Corp. of New York, which had long been linked with one branch of the Rockefeller family through the investment banking house of Schroder, Rockefeller & Co. In addition, Acheson's law firm had added a new partner to its ranks in 1945 in the person of John Lord O'Brian, who had long served on the board of the Equitable Life Assurance Society of New York, a big mutual concern that had what might be called a Rockefeller orientation. In 1949 another partner, Gerhard A. Gesell, was elected to the board of W. R. Grace & Co., a large New York company whose head had served since 1907 as a director of the Stillman-Rockefeller-dominated National City Bank. Also, Acheson himself had served since 1940 as vice-chairman of the Washington-based, pro-Establishment Brookings Institution and had been a prominent member, up to 1941, of the "Century group," an informal body closely linked with the Council on Foreign Relations.[40]

However, there is much more to this recruitment pattern than can be found by a look at the backgrounds and associations of the Secretaries of State themselves. Byrnes's top aide, for example, was Dean Acheson, who reportedly wielded considerable power in Washington when Byrnes was out of the country attending numerous diplomatic conferences.[41] Similarly, during much of the time that former Army General George C. Marshall was Secretary of State, his principal advisor was New York financier Robert A. Lovett, who had held a major defense post during World War II, but who had, probably more importantly, been a longtime partner in the influential banking house of Brown Brothers Harriman & Co. and a director of the Harriman-controlled Union Pacific Railroad.[42] When Acheson was in charge of America's foreign relations, the two persons who served as Under Secretaries of State were James E. Webb and David K. E. Bruce, both of whom has some experience in governmental affairs. Webb was a protégé of former North Carolina governor and Washington lawyer O. Max Gardner, who, until his death in 1946, had many important links, particularly with textile and transportation interests.[43] Bruce came from a wealthy Maryland family and had a brother, James, who served on the board of such major concerns as the Avco Manufacturing Corp., American Airlines, Chemical Bank and Trust Co. of New York, Commerical Credit Co. of Baltimore, General American Investors Co. (which was controlled by New York's top Jewish investment banking interests), National Dairy Products Corp., and the Republic Steel Corp.[44]

A number of new posts were also created in the State Department during

Acheson's four-year term in office, the most important of which were various Assistant Secretaries of State. There was one for United Nations affairs (a post filled by John D. Hickerson, a career diplomat), one for Inter-American affairs (filled by Edward G. Miller, Jr., a partner in the Wall Street law firm of Sullivan & Cromwell), one for European affairs (filled by George W. Perkins, a former Marshall Plan official, who served up to the late 1940s as treasurer of Merck & Co. and as a director of the trust affiliate of the National City Bank of New York), one for Far Eastern affairs (filled successively by three State Department officials, William W. Butterworth, Dean Rusk, and John M. Allison), and one for Near Eastern, South Asian, and African affairs (filled through most of this period by George C. McGhee, who had held various governmental posts since 1941, but whose father-in-law, E. L. DeGolyer, was a well-known Texas oilman and entrepreneur).[45] Hence it would appear that the State Department was very much in pro-business hands, particularly during the latter part of the Truman administration.

The pattern of appointment in the Treasury Department in the postwar period was somewhat different in that there were not as many elite figures recruited for its high posts. Shortly after he took office, President Truman selected as his new Secretary of the Treasury former Kentucky Democratic leader Fred M. Vinson, who, unlike his predecessor, had no noteworthy socio-economic ties and was generally viewed as a political moderate. Vinson was originally a small town (Ashland) lawyer, who had served since the early 1930s as a Kentucky Congressman, a federal judge, and most recently as a high defense official. In the course of these years he had become quite friendly with Senator Truman (they were both inveterate poker players). Vinson, however, held this office for only about a year. When Chief Justice Harlan Fiske Stone died, the President decided to elevate the affable Vinson to this key post in an effort to restore harmony to the strife-ridden Supreme Court. As Vinson's successor at the Treasury, Truman chose another friend, Missouri banker and governmental official John W. Snyder. Indeed, Truman and Snyder had been on intimate terms since they had been in the army together in World War I.[46] Up to the early 1940s Snyder had worked for a number of small banks in Missouri and had also held a series of relatively minor federal posts. From 1943 to 1945, however, he had served as a vice-president of the fairly large First National Bank of St. Louis, and then in April 1945, just before Truman became President, he was appointed director of the Office of War Mobilization and Reconstruction, an agency now concerned primarily with the nation's conversion to a peacetime economy. Perhaps even more important, from 1945 through 1953 (that is, during his entire term as Secretary of the Treasury), Snyder was an active member of the Business Advisory Council, an unusual linkage which was probably established to provide better communications between this elitist-dominated body and America's top financial official.[47]

With the escalation of the cold war in the postwar period, no arm of

American government was considered more essential than the nation's defense establishment. Nevertheless, in the two years following the defeat of the Axis powers, no major changes were made in its organizational structure, although there were certain shifts in high-level personnel. For example, when the venerable Henry L. Stimson stepped down as Secretary of War in September 1945, he was suceeded by his top aide, Robert P. Patterson, who had been a Wall Street lawyer before he became a federal judge in 1930.[48] In the mid-1940s the post of Secretary of the Navy was filled by an even more overtly pro-business official, James V. Forrestal. Prior to lending his talents to the nation's war effort, Forrestal had been associated with the New York investment banking firm of Dillon, Read & Co. for many years, ultimately becoming president of this concern. Although an influential financier, Forrestal did not serve, curiously, on any key boards of directors in the mid or late 1930s. But he was prominently involved in certain big business ventures, such as the 1928 merger of the Dodge auto empire into the Chrysler Corp., and, like various other non-Morgan figures, he had strongly supported the securities legislation adopted after the so-called Pecora investigation. Furthermore, it would appear that Forrestal was recruited largely through the efforts of New Deal "brain truster" Thomas Corcoran, who before joining the Roosevelt administration had been a member of the law firm which served as general counsel to Dillon, Read & Co.[49] Thus during the early Truman years these two important defense departments, War and Navy, were run by men who clearly had elitist links.

Because of international and domestic pressures, there was in 1947 a massive reorganization in this area which resulted in the creation of a new superordinate Department of Defense and the abolition, in name at any rate, of the old War Department. The new agency was given considerable power to coordinate the policies of the three principal (still civilian-led) branches of the armed forces—Army, Navy, and Air Force. Although it initially met with much internal opposition, the Department of Defense quickly became a crucial part of the federal government. An analysis of the people appointed to its top post is quite revealing, for this Cabinet position was generally filled by officials with close ties to the business community. They were as follows:

James V. Forrestal (1947–1949)
Secretary of the Navy (1944–1947); Under Secretary of the Navy (1940–1944);
longtime high official of Dillon, Read & Co.;
no major directorship ties since the early 1930s

Louis A. Johnson (1949–1950)
Assistant Secretary of War (1937–1940);
longtime partner in Clarksburg (W.V.) law firm of Steptoe and Johnson (which also had offices in Charleston and Washington, D.C.);
director of the Consolidated Vultee Aircraft Corp., Calif. (1942–1949) and the General Aniline & Film Corp. (1944–1949)

George C. Marshall (1950–1951)	Secretary of State (1947–1949); longtime high-ranking Army officer; director of Pan-American World Airways, Inc. (1949–1950) and member of the BAC (1949–1951)
Robert A. Lovett (1951–1953)	Deputy Secretary of Defense (1950–1951); Under Secretary of State (1947–1949); Assistant Secretary of War for Air (1941–1945); partner, New York investment banking firm of Brown Brothers Harriman & Co. (1926–1941, 1946–1947, 1949–50); director of Union Pacific Railroad (1926–1940, 1946–1947, 1949–1950), New York Trust Co. (1924–1940), and New York Life Insurance Co. (1949–1953); also a trustee of the CED (1949–1950) and the Rockefeller Foundation (1949–1953)

Three of these men had longstanding links with various large economic enterprises, and the one official who had a non-business background, former Army General George C. Marshall, had by the late 1940s become a member of the Business Advisory Council and a director of Pan-American World Airways.

In addition, a number of the other high officials in the revamped defense establishment had important corporate connections. For instance, the three Deputy Secretaries of Defense during the latter part of the Truman administration were Robert Lovett; Stephen Early, FDR's former press secretary who had taken a position with the Morgan-Mellon-dominated Pullman, Inc. in the postwar period; and William C. Foster, a former Commerce Department and Marshall Plan official. At first glance, Foster would appear to have been recruited from the ranks of small business, the Pressed and Welded Steel Products Co. of New York. However, since he had also served as a trustee of the CED from about the time of his appointment to federal office through 1953, he was obviously on good terms with many of America's major corporate executives.

This pattern also prevailed, though to a lesser extent, in the selection of the three military service secretaries.[50] For example, one of the three persons to act as Secretary of the Army during this period was Gordon Gray, who, up to 1947, was president of the small Piedmont Publishing Co. of Winston-Salem, North Carolina. But Gray had elite family links, for both his brother and uncle, Bowman and James A. Gray, were high officials of the R. J. Reynolds Tobacco Co. Similarly, of the three people to hold the post of Secretary of the Navy in the late 1940s and early 1950s, two were clearly corporate figures—Franklin P. Matthews (an Omaha lawyer and businessman who had long sat on the board of the Northwestern Bell Telephone Co., a subsidiary of AT&T) and Dan Kimball (a California-based officer of the Aerojet General subsidiary of Ohio's General Tire and Rubber Co.).[51] Even more striking were the backgrounds and affiliations of the men who served as Secretary and Under Secretary of the Air Force:

Secretary of the Air Force		Under Secretary of the Air Force	
W. Stuart Symington (1947–1950)	Assistant Secretary of War (1946–1947); P or BC, Emerson Electric Mfg. Co., St. Louis (1938–1945); director of the Mississippi Valley Trust Co., St. Louis (1943–1950); son-in-law of wealthy James W. Wadsworth (who married a daughter of former Secretary of State John Hay)	Arthur S. Barrows (1947–1950)	P or VC, Sears, Roebuck & Co. (1942–1947), lesser company official before that
Thomas K. Finletter (1950–1953)	former foreign economic aid official (1943–1944 and 1948–1949); also special assistant to Secretary of State (1941–1943); partner, N.Y.C. law firm of Coudert Brothers (1926–1950, except for WWII years and 1948–1949); director of the fairly small American Machine and Metals, Inc. (1932–1948), N.Y.C. publishing house of Reynal & Hitchcock, Inc. (1947), and Coty, Inc. (1949–1950); also a director of the Council on Foreign Relations (1944–1953)	John A. McCone (1950–1951)	P of Joshua Hendy Corp., Calif. (1949–1950); BC of Pacific Far East Line (1950–1951); P of California Shipbuilding Corp. (1941–1948); P of Bechtel-McCone Corp. (1937–1945); director of Curtiss-Wright Corp. (1949–1950), W. A. Bechtel Co. (up to the late 1940s), and the Bechtel-controlled Industrial Indemnity Co. (1945–1952)
		Roswell L. Gilpatric (1952–1953)	Partner, N.Y.C. law firm of Cravath, Swaine & Moore and predecessor concerns (1931–1951)

Thus there was, overall, a substantial amount of business representation and influence in the nation's vastly expanded defense establishment in the postwar years. In fact, one could say that America's "military-industrial complex" emerged during this critical period.[52]

Given this pattern of appointments, one might expect that there would be a good deal of business support for the Defense Department, both as a way of maintaining the security of the United States and as a means of indirectly aiding the nation's industrial growth. And such indeed was the case. But there were also some charges of favoritism and possible corruption in the operation of this agency, particularly with regard to the award of military contracts. The most important instance occurred in 1949 when America's second Secretary of Defense, Louis A. Johnson, a former West Virginia (and Washington, D.C.) lawyer, chose to bring a halt to the Navy's supercarrier construction program and instead decided to approve the Air Force's request for more B-36 long-range bombers; this $183 million contract was awarded to the financially distressed Consolidated Vultee Aircraft Corp. This decision initially created a furor, in large measure because it was soon discovered that Johnson had served, up to the late 1940s, as a director of this California-based company (he had also been the principal Democratic party fundraiser for the Truman-Barkley ticket in 1948).[53]

Although a formal Congressional investigation was made of the matter, little came of it. Yet certain disturbing questions can still be raised about Louis Johnson's seven-year tie with Consolidated Vultee.[54] Mr. Johnson claimed, for example, that he became a member of the board in 1942 at the personal request of the President—to act, in effect, as Roosevelt's "eyes and ears" with regard to this company's overall defense production.[55] But if Johnson had acted merely as the President's informal supervisory agent, why did his law firm receive more than $90,000 in legal fees from Consolidated Vultee over this seven-year period?[56] And, as one astute Republican asked, why would a California-headquartered and New York-controlled company employ a law firm whose main office was in West Virginia, of all places?[57] Were there no other able lawyers close at hand? Hardly. Hence one cannot help but think that Johnson served on Consolidated Vultee's board primarily for politico-economic reasons. In any case, this episode points up the conflict-of-interest dangers inherent in a recruitment process which relies so heavily on people with close ties to powerful corporate interests, especially when such officials are involved in military procurement.

Most of Truman's other Cabinet positions were filled by men who did not have such potentially troublesome ties. Two of the three persons to serve as Attorney General were clearly non-elite figures, former Dallas lawyer Thomas Clark, who had served for the preceding eight years in various Justice Department posts and apparently had no major economic connections, and James P. McGranery, a former federal judge, government official, and Philadelphia attorney, who before the early 1940s had represented a number of the city's police and firemen unions. In fact, the only occupant of this Cabinet office who might be viewed as having attained elite status was Rhode Island's J. Howard McGrath, a wealthy Providence lawyer with substantial local business interests.[58]

The men who served as Secretary of the Interior under Truman were also a mixed lot. Initially this post was held by New Deal appointee Harold Ickes, an outspoken progressive. When he resigned in 1946, following a sharp split with the President over the proposed Navy Department appointment of

California oilman Edwin Pauley, Truman passed over Ickes' longtime liberal top aide, Oscar Chapman, and picked another former government official with a more conservative bent, Julius Krug. Although he had no noteworthy socio-economic ties, Krug was by now considered a protégé of New York financier Bernard Baruch.[59] However, in 1949 Krug felt compelled to resign as Secretary of the Interior, largely because he had lent only token support to Truman's reelection campaign, which many had written off as a lost cause. As his successor, the President turned to the previously ignored Oscar Chapman, who had spent over sixteen years as a high official of this agency.

A rather similar pattern prevailed in the Department of Agriculture. Two people held this top post under the Truman administration, and both had rather modest backgrounds. The first was Clinton P. Anderson, a former New Mexico Congressman and head of an Albuquerque insurance agency. Once in office, however, the politically ambitious Anderson chose to ally himself with the big farmer-dominated American Farm Bureau Federation.[60] Apparently for political reasons, he was replaced shortly after Truman's 1948 reelection campaign by Colorado rancher Charles F. Brannan, who for the previous eight years had held two high posts in the Department of Agriculture where he had demonstrated that his sympathies lay with the less affluent smaller agrarian interests, especially those represented by the National Farmers Union.

Although Truman's relations with organized labor were at times badly strained, in part because of the rash of strikes which took place in the early postwar period, the two men he chose to serve as Secretary of Labor were well-known liberals, although neither was a union official. The first man to hold this position was Truman's close friend Lewis Schwellenbach, a former federal judge, United States Senator, and Seattle lawyer, whose pre-1940 clientele had included interests closely associated with the Brotherhood of Locomotive Engineers.[61] When Schwellenbach died in 1948, he was replaced by Maurice J. Tobin, who had served up to 1937 as a relatively minor official of the New England Telephone and Telegraph Co. (an AT&T subsidiary), but had then been elected mayor of Boston and later governor of Massachusetts. In public office he showed that he was a firm advocate of labor and social welfare legislation. Thus during the Truman years the Department of Labor was directed by men who strongly supported the union cause.

Indeed, aside from the "great triumvirate" of State, Treasury, and Defense, the only department which had a significant amount of business representation during the Truman administration was that of Commerce, as one might expect given its orientation. Initially, this Cabinet post was held by New Deal carryover Henry A. Wallace, a former Iowa agriculturist turned dedicated political progressive, who had been awarded the office more or less as a consolation prize after he had been forced off the Democratic national ticket in 1944 by conservative pressures. But because of his radical views and budding presidential ambitions, Wallace soon became embroiled in a number of bitter controversies with influential officials in both business and government circles. After publicly criticizing Truman's "hardline" anti-Soviet policy, he was fired by the President in late 1946. As his replacement, Truman chose W. Averell Harriman, who had held various high federal posts in the preceding years, particularly during World War II. He was also a major financier and railroad executive. For instance, he had served as a top official in the New York banking house of Brown Brothers Harriman & Co. up to 1946 (and thereafter as a limited partner), as board chairman of the Union Pacific Railroad (1932–1946), as chairman of the executive committee of the Illinois Central Railroad (1931–1942), as a director of the Merchant-Sterling Corp., a family-controlled investment company (up through his Cabinet years in the late 1940s), and as a member of the elitist Business Advisory Council (1933–1945).[62] When Harriman stepped down from the Commerce post in May 1948, he was succeeded by Ohio lawyer-businessman Charles Sawyer, a well-known state Democratic leader and recent Ambassador to Belgium. Sawyer's economic ties were much less important than Harriman's. He served from the late 1920s through 1953 (that is, including his term in office) as a director of the American Thermos Bottle Co. and Kemper-Thomas Co., two fairly small Ohio concerns.[63] However, he also had long-term legal and entrepreneurial links with major Cincinnati businessmen, William Procter (of the Procter & Gamble interests) and Powel Crosley, Jr., a wealthy radio and baseball figure.[64]

In summary, during the Truman years the State, Defense, Treasury, and Commerce departments were dominated by big business forces, whereas other less vital departments such as Justice, Labor, Interior, and Agriculture were directed by men drawn from a variety of sources, many of whom were still firmly committed to the domestic goals of the New Deal.

In the realm of diplomatic affairs, the appointments, though somewhat mixed, were primarily elitist. For example, as America's Ambassador to Great Britain, President Truman chose to rely for about a year on the liberal patrician incumbent John G. Winant, who had devoted considerable time to public service over the years, but who also sat, through the mid-1940s, on the board of the prestigious Brookings Institution. When he stepped down from office in early 1946, he was replaced for a brief period (approximately six months) by W. Averell Harriman. In the fall of 1946, following Harriman's selection as Secretary of Commerce, this key diplomatic post was given to another elitist figure, Lewis W. Douglas, a onetime Arizona Congressman and early New Deal director of the Bureau of the Budget, who in more recent years had been head of the Mutual Life Insurance Co. of New York (one of the few such executives ever to hold such a high federal post).[65] Douglas had many other important ties, for he was a Phelps Dodge heir, a director of General Motors, and a trustee of both the Rockefeller Foundation and Council on Foreign Relations, and one of his brothers-in-law, John S. Zinsser, sat on the board of J. P. Morgan & Co., while another, John J. McCloy, served in a similar capacity with the Union Pacific Railroad. When

Douglas resigned in 1950, he was succeeded by another major executive, Walter S. Gifford, the recently retired head of AT&T, who had served for many years as a director of the Morgan-dominated U.S. Steel Corp. and the similarly controlled First National Bank of New York. Like Douglas, Gifford was a trustee of the Rockefeller Foundation. This diplomatic post was thus very much in the hands of Establishment interests during the Truman years.[66]

America's Ambassadors to France, on the other hand, were drawn more from the career ranks. President Truman was content to rely on longtime foreign service officer Jefferson Caffrey up to 1949. At this point Caffrey was replaced by a clearly elite figure, David K. E. Bruce, who had been born into a well-connected Maryland family, had married initially into great wealth, and established various influential business ties, the most important of which were with W. Averell Harriman.[67] In the postwar period, however, Bruce had devoted most of his time and talents to the federal government. Yet it should be noted that although he had severed all his economic links, Bruce continued to serve as a trustee of the Brookings Institution. Moreover, his brother, James, who was the Ambassador to Argentina, sat on the board of a number of large business enterprises such as the Avco Manufacturing Corp., American Airlines, Chemical Bank and Trust Co. of New York, General American Investors Co., National Dairy Products Corp., and Republic Steel Corp.[68] When Bruce stepped down as Ambassador to France in March 1952, he was succeeded by a career diplomat, James C. Dunn, who had married into the wealthy Armour (meat-packing) family of Chicago, and thus may have shared their upper-class views.

This appointment pattern was in marked contrast to that which prevailed with regard to the Soviet Union during these troubled years. Aside from one early emissary, W. Averell Harriman (who left Russia in January 1946), this key diplomatic post was held by two former high-ranking military men—Army General Walter Bedell Smith and Admiral Alan Kirk—and one able foreign service officer, George F. Kennan, who served for only a short period before he was declared *persona non grata* by Communist authorities.

In the immediate postwar period the United States did not, of course, maintain normal diplomatic relations with its vanquished adversaries, Germany and Japan. Instead, it designated special officials to preside over these countries until their national sovereignty was restored. One such emissary, after 1949, was the U.S. High Commissioner to West Germany, John J. McCloy, a Wall Street lawyer who had served in the early 1940s as Assistant Secretary of War and later as president of the World Bank.[69] McCloy was a rising and well-connected figure in the business world. He had served in the mid-1940s as a director of the Union Pacific Railroad and as a trustee of the Rockefeller Foundation, as had one of his brothers-in-law, Lewis Douglas, the Ambassador to Great Britain. A second brother-in-law, John S. Zinsser, was board chairman of Sharp and Dohme, Inc., a Philadelphia pharmaceutical concern, and sat on the board of J. P. Morgan & Co.

Another major diplomatic post created about this time was that of

Ambassador to NATO, the North Atlantic Treaty Organization, which was established in the latter part of 1949 to shore up Western Europe's armed forces against a possible Soviet attack. Both men who held this position during the Truman years had long been associated with the New York business community—Charles M. Spofford, a longtime partner in the "Morgan" law firm of Davis, Polk, Wardwell, Sunderland & Kiendl, and William H. Draper, Jr., who had been a high-ranking official in James Forrestal's old firm of Dillon, Read & Co. (except for his nine years of service in the federal government in the 1940s). Hence, even in this special post America's top economic interests were strongly represented.[70]

IMPORTANT POLICY ACTIONS OF THE TRUMAN ADMINISTRATION

Probably the most important act of the early Truman administration was the decision to drop the newly developed atomic bomb on two Japanese cities in August 1945. Until recently, it had been widely believed that this action was necessary to induce the Japanese government, which was still dominated by tenacious militaristic interests, to surrender as quickly as possible, thereby obviating the need for a bloody American invasion. Thus it was generally argued that Truman's seemingly callous decision, which was strongly urged upon him by most of his more experienced military and political advisors, actually saved many lives in the long run, especially those of American troops.

However, this judgment has recently become subject to considerable criticism. In 1965, for example, political economist Gar Alperovitz published a provocative, carefully researched study which clearly indicated that by 1945, a badly beaten Japan would have soon surrendered without resort to a massive and costly invasion, and that in the final stages of the war, as American policymakers came increasingly to view the Soviet Union as an extremely hostile, expansionist threat to other nations, the primary objective of this bombing was no longer military but political.[71] In other words, the atomic bombs were dropped, without warning or less devastating demonstration, on two densely populated centers to accomplish two objectives. The first was an (as it turned out, futile) effort to bring the war to a quick close before the Russian army, recently freed from the German front, could invade Manchuria; the second objective was to convince the Soviet Union that in the postwar world of international politics the United States held the upper hand, since it had the "ultimate" weapon.[72]

One key question that ought to be raised in this regard is whether the decision to drop the atomic bombs was arrived at objectively, or whether it was unduly influenced by politico-economic considerations. It is generally agreed that the newly installed Harry S. Truman had little knowledge of or experience in foreign affairs and was forced to rely heavily on the views and judgment of his top military and political advisors.[73] This group, because of its largely pro-business background, felt strongly that the Soviet Union represented a serious threat to the capitalist Western states. One of Truman's most vigorous anti-Communist advisors was W. Averell Harriman, our Ambassador to the Soviet Union, who believed that the United States was faced with "a barbarian [i.e., Russian] invasion of Europe," a view undoubtedly reinforced by Harriman's longstanding business ties.[74] Another influential "hard-liner" was Under Secretary of State Joseph C. Grew, an elite-linked career diplomat then in charge (in the temporary absence of Edward R. Stettinius) of the State Department. Grew was already convinced that a future war with the Soviet Union was almost certain.[75] Other key figures in this critical policymaking process were Secretary of War Henry L. Stimson, Secretary of the Navy James Forrestal, Assistant Secretary of War John J. McCloy, Assistant Secretary of the Navy Ralph Bard, Stimson aide Harvey H. Bundy (a former Boston lawyer), the newly appointed Secretary of State James F. Byrnes, several high-ranking military men such as George C. Marshall, Admiral William D. Leahy, and General Leslie Groves, and some distinguished American scientists who had been involved in the development of the bomb, chief of whom were Vannevar Bush, Karl T. Compton, and James B. Conant.[76] Of the above-named civilian officials, all but one, James F. Byrnes,[77] had been intimately associated with the world of business, usually big business. Most, in fact, were former New York City figures. In contrast to certain prominent scientists who had serious reservations about the use of the bomb, especially on large population centers, these pro-business leaders were almost unanimous in recommending that the bomb be dropped on Japan.[78]

By far the most important official in this group was Secretary of War Henry L. Stimson, a onetime Wall Street lawyer, for it was he who prepared or approved many of the policy statements on the atomic bomb. He also had a great deal to do with the creation and staffing of the so-called Interim Committee, a little-known ad hoc body established in the spring of 1945 to consider all aspects of the proposed use of this awesome weapon.[79] A look at the background of some members of this group may tell much about its overall politico-economic orientation. One of its most influential participants was a man named George L. Harrison, who for some reason has not been adequately identified in any of the books written on this subject, and was not even listed as a federal official in either the *U.S. Government Manual* or *Congressional Directory* during this period (although he has described himself in *Who's Who in America* as a special assistant and civilian consultant to the Secretary of War).[80] Further investigation reveals that Harrison was an extremely potent figure in financial circles, much more so than Forrestal or Stimson had ever been. Indeed, he was the recently appointed president of the New York Life Insurance Co., the nation's fourth largest insurance company, and a presumably still active director of the First National Bank of New York (along with Stimson's cousin, Landon K. Thorne).[81] Another person who frequently sat in, at Stimson's request, on the meetings of the Interim Committee was the Secretary's longtime friend, Arthur W. Page, who, like Harrison, was a neophyte in government.[82] But Page was no insignificant figure either. Rather, he was a vice-president of AT&T; in fact, he was an unusually important official, for no other executive of this giant company, not even its president, served on more major corporate boards—namely, the Chase National Bank, Continental Oil Co., Kennecott Copper Corp., Prudential Insurance Co., and Westinghouse Electric & Manufacturing Co. Thus, while we do not know precisely what impact each of these individuals had on the Committee's proceedings, one cannot help but think that their marked pro-business background and affiliations must have had considerable effect on their thinking regarding the use of the atomic bomb as an, in part, anti-Soviet measure in the closing stages of the war.[83] Perhaps equally disturbing, no other segment of American society had this kind of opportunity to influence the government's deliberations on this critical matter.

Another major development in the early postwar years was the creation, through American-led negotiations, of the International Bank for Reconstruction and Development (the World Bank), an agency sorely needed. As its formal title indicates, this institution had a dual purpose. The participants at the Bretton Woods conference recognized that "... at the conclusion of hostilities, there would be a pressing need for international capital to finance both the reconstruction of productive facilities destroyed by the war and an increase in productivity and living standards in the underdeveloped areas of the world."[84] Its charter thus expressly stated that "the resources and facilities of the Bank shall be used exclusively for the benefit of members with equitable consideration to projects for development and projects for reconstruction alike." According to various sources, however, it was understood that the World Bank's initial emphasis would be on the urgent problems of reconstruction.[85]

Initially, the Bank was authorized to raise up to $10 billion, a then huge sum, close to 90 percent of which was subscribed by the early 1950s. A substantial part of this money was obtained from American sources, mainly through the sale of long-term securities. This financial procedure almost automatically imposed certain severe constraints on the Bank's general mode of operation, for from the outset considerable emphasis was placed on an applicant's ability to repay, much to the detriment of many poorer countries.[86] In the late 1940s United States shareholders owned nearly 40 percent of the stock in the Bank and British interests had over 15 percent, which combined total gave these two countries great power in this important enterprise.[87]

The Bank's bylaws granted substantial authority to its board of governors, which consisted of one representative from each member country. However, as Mason and Asher have pointed out, the board, because of its unwieldy size, has never been an effective policymaking body. As they put it, the board was "... too large a body to do more than ratify proposals put to it and serve as a general indicator of trends of thought. It meets only once a year, and the annual Bank-Fund gathering serves chiefly as a fraternal get-together for the international financial community."[88] In their view, the real "board" of the World Bank consisted of its executive directors, of whom there were initially twelve, five who were appointed (one by each of the five members who had the largest number of voting shares) and seven who were elected (by the other less influential governors). Since the executive directors met more often than the board, they came to play a more significant role in the affairs of the Bank. But, according to Mason and Asher, since the departure of the Bank's first president (who held office for only six months), this body, too, "... has concerned itself primarily with the problems that the president chooses to put before it." During its early decades, the World Bank's agenda consisted mostly of projects "... on which the staff work had already been done, and the board could only say 'yes' or 'no' to the recommendations made by the president."[89] In short, the president was clearly the central figure in the Bank's proceedings, so an analysis of the backgrounds of the men holding this post should reveal much about the operation and locus of control of the institution.[90]

After at least one abortive recruitment effort, the World Bank chose as its first president onetime Wall Street financier Eugene Meyer, who had apparently severed almost all his earlier major corporate ties and by the late 1920s had become chairman of the board of governors of the Federal Reserve System.[91] He later bought a controlling interest in the *Washington Post*.[92] As a former businessman turned government official, Meyer would seem to have been an ideal choice for this important position. However, because of personal and policy clashes (particularly with the Bank's American executive director, Emilio Collado), he did not last long as president. Upset by these disputes, he resigned in December 1946, before any loan applications could even be acted on. His replacement was former New York lawyer and Assistant Secretary of War, John J. McCloy, who, upon stepping down from his defense post in 1945, had become a partner in the Wall Street law firm of Milbank, Tweed, Hope, Hadley & McCloy.[93] He had also recently become a member of the board of the Union Pacific Railroad, the Empire Trust Co. of New York, and the Rockefeller Foundation (the last affiliation he maintained throughout his years with the World Bank). Of these ties, the last was probably the most important, for McCloy's new law firm was the longtime legal arm of the John D. Rockefeller family and its primary financial enterprise, the Chase National Bank (or as it is now known, Chase Manhattan Bank).[94] When McCloy stepped down from the World Bank post in 1949 to become U.S. High Commissioner to Germany, he was succeeded by someone drawn from the same economic quarter, Georgia-born Eugene Black, who had recently acted as the American executive director of the World Bank (replacing the controversial Collado), but had served for a much longer period (14 years) as a vice-president of the Chase National Bank.[95]

Judging by these and later appointments, it thus seems fair to conclude that the World Bank was strongly influenced, if not dominated, by American financial interests, particularly those associated with the Rockefeller family.[96]

Given this highly skewed pattern of appointments, it is not surprising that a disproportionate amount of the money loaned by the World Bank during the Truman years went to certain Western European nations (and their politico-economic allies or colonies) rather than to the underdeveloped countries (see Table 5).

In these early years, substantial amounts of the World Bank's funds were channeled into the reconstruction of the war-ravaged economies of Western Europe rather than into a comparable effort to build up the industrial structure or improve the standard of living of the so-called backward countries—a debatable, but partially defensible policy. However, it is hard to explain why a country such as Australia, which was not impoverished and had been virtually untouched by the war, got more money than India and Pakistan combined. Or why such repressive regimes as the Belgian Congo, Southern Rhodesia, and the Union of South Africa should have been awarded such large sums, in contrast to what was given to Ethiopia and Iran.[97] One likely explanation may be that of Mason and Asher, who said "... there can be little doubt that the countries that were to hold a majority of the stock were concerned primarily with the reconstruction objective."[98] To this one could add another possibly equally important factor—namely, the economic orientation of the men chosen to run this financial enterprise. They were quite favorably disposed toward the highly industrialized or pro-American countries and were much less receptive to the needs of "unfriendly" or politically unstable areas.

Another noteworthy development of the early postwar years was the creation and high-level staffing of a very different type of federal governmental unit, the Central Intelligence Agency. The CIA was clearly a product of the Cold War, for it was organized in 1947 to protect and improve America's national security through the conduct of various foreign political and military detection and espionage activities.

Because of the extremely critical and largely clandestine nature of its activities, the CIA has always operated under a veil of secrecy. Very little is known about either its work or its key personnel; in fact, until recently the only government data given out about this agency were the names of its top two officials. Judging from this information, the management of the agency was originally placed in the hands of former high-ranking Army and Navy officers, perhaps because it was felt that they were most qualified to evaluate the military data collected by CIA sources. For example, the first director was Rear Admiral Roscoe Hillenkoetter, a longtime naval intelligence officer, and his top aide was General Edwin K. Wright.[99] When Hillenkoetter stepped down in 1950, he was succeeded by retired General Walter

TABLE 5
Early Allocation of World Bank Funds

	World Bank Loans, up to early 1953 ($ millions)	Estimated Population (millions)		World Bank Loans, up to early 1953 ($ millions)	Estimated Population (millions)
Belgium	16	9	Brazil	130	49
Denmark	40	4	Chile	17	6
France	250	41	Colombia	55	11
Italy	10	46	El Salvador	13	2
Luxembourg	12	0.3	Mexico	100	24
Netherlands	229	10	Nicaragua	5	1
Subtotal	557	110	Paraguay	5	1
Australia	150	8	Peru	4	8
Belgian Congo	70	11	Uruguay	33	2
Southern Rhodesia	28	2	Subtotal	361	104
Union of South Africa	80	11	India	114	342
Subtotal	885	142	Pakistan	31	80
Iceland	4	0.1	Thailand	25	18
Iraq	13	5	Subtotal	530	544
Turkey	51	20	Ethiopia	9	15
Total	953	167	Total	539	559

NOTE: These data were taken from the appendix found on pp. 216–222 of *The International Bank for Reconstruction and Development: 1946–1953*. Certain adjustments have been made to delete loans that were apparently processed after the Truman years. The above totals are somewhat misleading, in that certain countries received little or no funds because they were unwilling or unable to join the World Bank immediately. Pakistan, for instance, did not join the Bank till 1950, and Germany and Japan did not until 1952. Great Britain apparently made special arrangements for the provision of substantial capital prior to signing the Bank's articles of agreement. Brazil's total may be especially misleading, for almost 70 percent of this money was granted for one particular purpose, to expand the facilities and services provided by the Brazilian Traction, Light & Power Co., Ltd., a major concern controlled by Canadian interests.

Bedell Smith, who had recently served as the American Ambassador to Russia, where he presumably had gained considerable insight into Soviet affairs.

At this juncture a significant shift began to take place in the recruitment practices of the CIA. Certain prominent civilian figures were now brought into its upper echelons. For instance, in 1950 General Wright was replaced as deputy director by New York businessman and former attorney William H. Jackson, who had served in recent years as a partner in the privately-owned investment concern of J. H. Whitney & Co. (the top official of which was the wealthy grandson of former Cabinet members John Hay and William C. Whitney) and as a director of the Bankers Trust Co. of New York, the Great Northern Paper Co. (probably Whitney-controlled), and the Spencer Chemical Co. of Kansas City.[100] When Jackson decided to return to the financial world in 1951, his place was taken by Allen W. Dulles, who had been a longtime partner in the top-tier New York law firm of Sullivan & Cromwell, which included among its clients the huge Standard Oil Co. of New Jersey.[101] Dulles had also served as a director of the J. Henry Schroder Banking Corp. in the late 1930s and early 1940s, and of the American Bank Note Co. in 1950–1951. Furthermore, he had long been intimately associated with the elite-dominated Council on Foreign Relations, most recently as its president.[102] Thus it would appear that during the latter part of the Truman years business interests had begun to establish significant ties with the CIA.

Another act taken under the Truman administration was the adoption of the massive American-financed Marshall Plan. This program was conceived and implemented because Western Europe was on the brink of economic collapse in 1947 and appeared to be threatened by Communist pressures from within and without. A number of countries had not recovered from the devastation wrought by World War II, despite substantial aid provided by the United Nations Relief and Rehabilitation Administration. As a consequence, there was much discontent and political unrest, particularly in France and Italy, where the Communist party had a large following and considerable appeal.

To counteract these conditions, the Truman administration formulated, upon the advice of a special committee, a gigantic recovery program and submitted it to Congress in December 1947 with an urgent recommendation that it appropriate some $17 billion in economic aid over a four-year period. The legislators at first rebelled against this staggering request. But after the dramatic Communist takeover of Czechoslovakia in early 1948, Congress quickly passed a set of financial measures, which ultimately totaled $12 billion. To distribute these funds, Congress chose not to rely on the State Department (which was viewed as too slow moving by various prominent political and economic figures), but to create an independent body called the Economic Cooperation Administration. In retrospect, this program must be judged a success, for within a few years there was an aggregate increase of 37 percent in the industrial output of the Marshall Plan countries and a 25 percent boost in their agricultural production, which growth obviously did much to bolster democracy in Western Europe.

According to one political scientist, the Economic Cooperation Administration was a striking example of pluralism at work in American government and foreign relations, with much effective participation on the part of business, labor, and agriculture, the nation's three most important politico-economic interests.[103] As to that claim, however, it should be pointed out that much of the early work on this proposal was done, at the direction of Under Secretary of State Robert Lovett, by such officials as William Clayton, Lewis Douglas, Paul Nitze, and Willard Thorp, all of whom had close ties to the business community.[104] The Marshall Plan was later put into more concrete form and given an important boost by the President's specially appointed Committee on Foreign Aid, which was headed by Secretary of Commerce W. Averell Harriman. The makeup of this body reveals a great deal about the major forces behind the Marshall Plan; its members, grouped by general occupational category, were as follows:

Chairman	W. Averell Harriman (a longtime partner in Brown Brothers Harriman & Co.; also recent Ambassador to Russia and Great Britain)	Active member of BAC (1933–1945); graduate member thereafter
Other Members	Hiland Batcheller (president, Alleghany Ludlum Steel Corp., Pa.)	Member of BAC (up to 1945); made a trustee of the CED later in 1947
	W. Randolph Burgess (vice-chairman, National City Bank of N.Y.)	Director of the Mutual Life Insurance Co.
	John L. Collyer (president, B. F. Goodrich Co., Ohio)	Chairman of the BAC; trustee of CED; director of J. P. Morgan & Co.
	Granville Conway (president, Cosmopolitan Shipping Co., an apparently small New York concern; also a former longtime federal maritime official)	
	Chester C. Davis (president, Federal Reserve Bank of St. Louis; also a former high official of the Department of Agriculture)	Vice-chairman of the CED; active member of the BAC (up to 1946), graduate member thereafter

Richard R. Deupree (president, Procter & Gamble Co., Ohio)	Member of the BAC; trustee of the CED; also director of the Baltimore & Ohio Railroad and the Coca-Cola Co.
Paul G. Hoffman (president, Studebaker Corp., Ind.)	Chairman of the CED; member of the executive committee of the BAC; director of the New York Life Insurance Co.
Robert Koenig (president, Ayrshire Collieries Corp., a medium-sized Indiana company)	
Owen D. Young (former longtime head of GE)	Onetime trustee of the Rockefeller Foundation and director of GM; two top officials of GE also served as trustees of the CED in 1947, and one of these was a member of the BAC
Robert E. Buchanan (dean, Iowa State College)	
Melville F. Coolbaugh (president, Colorado School of Mines)	
Calvin B. Hoover (dean, Duke University)	Member of CED's research advisory board
Edward S. Mason (dean, graduate school of public administration, Harvard University)	Member of CED's research advisory board
Harold G. Moulton (president, Brookings Institution)	Son had married a daughter of the head of the Harris Trust & Savings Bank of Chicago
William I. Myers (dean, agricultural school, Cornell University)	Trustee of the Rockefeller Foundation and Mutual Life Insurance Co.
Robert G. Sproul (president, University of California, Berkeley)	Trustee of the CED and the Rockefeller Foundation
George Meany (secretary-treasurer, AFL)	
James B. Carey (secretary-treasurer, CIO)	
Robert M. LaFollette, Jr. (former U.S. Senator, Wisc.)	

In sum, of the ten business members of this committee, all but two—Conway and Koenig—were linked with one or both arms of America's economic establishment (the BAC and CED) or one of the major financial institutions in New York City. More surprising is the fact that at least four of the seven academic members of this body were associated with the CED or the Rockefeller Foundation. And Harold Moulton's ties bring this total even higher. In short, no fewer than thirteen of the twenty members of the so-called Harriman Committee were drawn from one influential segment of society.[105] Furthermore, as one researcher has noted, even this body's executive secretary, Richard M. Bissell, Jr., "...had been close to the CED ever since he had helped to draw up the original plans for it," while serving as an aide to the Secretary of Commerce.[106]

Certain members of Congress also gave special attention to the passage of this epic plan. In the Upper House the matter was handled largely by Michigan's Senator Arthur H. Vandenberg, a former Grand Rapids newspaperman who had no major corporate ties, but was on very friendly terms with CED chairman Paul Hoffman.[107] In the House of Representatives the proposal was studied, and ultimately strongly supported, by a select committee headed, to all intents and purposes, by Massachusetts Congressman Christian A. Herter, another seemingly non-elite figure. Yet such was not really the case, for Herter had, like Paul Nitze, married a member of New York's famous Pratt family, whose fortune had been built largely around the Standard Oil Co. And perhaps not coincidentally, the House select committee's top staff aide was Harvard professor William Yandell Elliott, who had been an active member of the BAC up to the mid-1940s and was still accorded "graduate" status in that body in 1947.[108] With this kind of support, plus a widely shared concern over Europe's precarious condition, it is not surprising that the Marshall Plan was approved by a conservative-dominated Congress.

The Marshall Plan was not only formulated largely by big business or pro-business figures, it was also run primarily by them.[109] The three men who served as the top officials of the Economic Cooperation Administration (or as it was later known, the Mutual Security Agency) during the Truman years were closely linked with America's economic establishment.[110]

ECA Administrator	Paul G. Hoffman (1948–1950)	President of Studebaker Corp. (1935–1948); also chairman of the CED (1942–1948)	Trustee of the CED (1948–50); member of the BAC (1941–1946 and 1947–1950); director of the New York Life Insurance Co. (1945–1950)
	William C. Foster (1950–1951)	Former Under Secretary of Commerce; president, small Pressed & Welded Steel Products Co., N.Y.	Trustee of the CED (1947–1951)

Director, Mutual Security Agency	W. Averell Harriman (1951–1953)	Former Secretary of Commerce and special representative of ECA, Europe; longtime partner, Brown Brothers Harriman & Co.	Director of the Council on Foreign Relations (1950–1953); active member of the BAC (1933–1945), graduate member thereafter; director of the Merchant-Sterling Corp., New York (1945–1953)

The ECA's first mission chiefs to the four most important European countries were also drawn from the ranks of big business:

ECA Mission Country	ECA Chiefs		
United Kingdom	Thomas K. Finletter (longtime partner in New York law firm of Coudert Bros.)		Director of the Council on Foreign Relations (1944–1950)
France	David K. E. Bruce (pre-WWII Baltimore and Pittsburgh business figure; later federal official)		Brother (James Bruce) director of American Airlines, Chemical Bank & Trust Co. of New York, National Dairy Products Corp., and Republic Steel Corp.
West Germany	Robert M. Hanes (wealthy North Carolinian, family fortune from hosiery business)		Director of the Southern Railway; brother (John W. Hanes) a director of Bankers Trust Co. of New York, Johns-Manville Corp., and the United States Lines
Italy	James D. Zellerbach (president, Crown Zellerbach Corp., Cal.)		Trustee of the CED (1947–1950); director of Rayonier, Inc. and Wells Fargo Bank

In light of this obviously elite recruitment pattern, it would seem almost absurd to refer, as Hadley Arkes does, to the Marshall Plan as a "pluralistic" operation.[111] Theodore Lowi would also seem to have been wide of the mark when he subtitled his section of *The End of Liberalism* dealing with the Marshall Plan, "How to Avoid an Establishment in Foreign Economic Policy."[112]

Not long after the development of the Marshall Plan there was a major shift in American foreign policy, to one which placed much greater emphasis on "containing" whatever expansionist thrusts were made by the Soviet Union and/or its Communist allies by, if necessary, strong military force. The origins of this policy have generally been attributed to the famous anonymous (Mr. X) article, "The Sources of Soviet Conduct," which appeared in the July 1947 issue of *Foreign Affairs*, the influential organ of the Council on Foreign Relations. In this article, reportedly written by longtime career diplomat George F. Kennan (who had just been appointed to the newly created post of chief of the State Department's policy planning staff), it was argued that Soviet pressure against non-Communist countries must be contained by appropriate countermeasures, an idea which was soon enthusiastically adopted by the nation's key government and economic leaders. Kennan's primary line of argument was that Soviet power posed mainly a *political* threat to Western nations and must therefore be contained largely by political rather than by military means. However, because of certain ambiguities in the article, his argument was twisted by various officials to emphasize the need for an enormous rearmament drive. Yet there was at the same time much pressure, emanating especially from a cost-conscious Congress, to hold defense spending down to a relatively moderate level.

So this matter stood until the latter part of 1949 when American leaders were severely stunned by two momentous events: the successful detonation of the Soviet Union's first atomic bomb and the sudden defeat of Chiang Kai-shek's forces in China by the Communist armies of Mao Tse-tung. As a result of these disturbing developments, President Truman issued a special directive calling for a thorough review of America's international objectives and military capabilities through the collaborative efforts of the Departments of State and Defense. Secretary of State Dean Acheson, who believed that Russia posed a grave military threat to American interests around the world, took this opportunity to replace the less hawkish George F. Kennan as chief of the department's policy planning staff with the more military-minded Paul Nitze, a former New York investment banker turned high federal official. And it was primarily through the efforts of such figures as Nitze and Acheson that, after a six-weeks study, a crucial report was made, over the objection of the more economy-minded Defense Secretary, Louis Johnson, to President Truman, calling for vastly increased military outlays of at least $35, if not $50, billion a year.[113] Though National Security Council Document 68 was not immediately formally endorsed by the President, primarily because of the nation's antipathy to high taxes, it did much to set the stage for the truly vast escalation in defense spending which took place later in the 1950s.

According to Paul Hammond, much of the difference between the policy advocated by Kennan and Charles Bohlen and that advanced by Paul Nitze (and, one might add, Dean Acheson), can be explained by their backgrounds, by the fact that "...Kennan and Bohlen, unlike Nitze [and Acheson], were foreign service officers and Soviet experts."[114] Unfortunately, Hammond does not pursue this matter any further, leaving his readers with the impression that the key to this dichotomy lay in a particular kind of training and experience. But this line of analysis neglects other, perhaps more important factors. For instance, Acheson was a wealthy patrician who had spent the bulk of his adult life with Washington's leading corporate law firm, Covington, Burling, Rublee, Acheson & Shorb, several partners of which were closely associated with various New York-based business enterprises.[115] Perhaps equally significant, before the war Paul Nitze had been an executive in the investment banking firm of Dillon, Read & Co., and had married into New York's wealthy Pratt family, whose fortune had long been linked with the Standard Oil interests. Although a federal official since the early 1940s, Nitze had continued to serve on the boards of the St. Louis–San Francisco Railway and the Chicago, Rock Island & Pacific Railroad up to 1946, a sign that he was reluctant to sever some of his major economic ties. His brother-in-law, Walter Paepcke, was head of the Container Corp. of America (which had 1950 assets of about $75 million) and a director of the United States Gypsum Co. Hence one might argue that it was in part because of their pro-business background that Nitze and Acheson took such a strong anti-Communist stand.

In any event, America was shortly thereafter suddenly drawn into a bloody war in the Far East when, without much provocation, Communist forces launched a massive invasion of the Western-supported Republic of South Korea. Though not initially prepared to counter such an assault, the United States (with UN backing) was able to beat back the Red armies after much hard fighting. Once again, a number of emergency ad hoc agencies were created to deal with the crisis, the most important of which was the Office of War Mobilization.[116] And much as in World War II, this agency was run largely by men who were recruited from big business circles. The first (1950–1952) director of the Office of Defense Mobilization was Charles E. Wilson, president of the General Electric Co., who also served as a trustee of the CED, a director of the Guaranty Trust Co. of New York, and was a former (1943–1947) active member of the BAC. His two most influential aides were men of almost equal rank—Sidney J. Weinberg, the well-known senior partner in Goldman, Sachs & Co., who was a longtime member of the BAC and a director of such large corporations as the Continental Can Co., GE, and Sears, Roebuck, and former Army General Lucius D. Clay, who was board chairman of the Continental Can Co., a member of the BAC, and a director of the Lehman Corp., the Newmount Mining Corp., and the Marine Midland Trust Co. of New York. Thus once again, in time of national emergency the federal government turned to big business circles, one of the primary sources of talent in the country.

In domestic affairs, other more diverse economic interests exercised a good deal of influence. For example, there was a protracted struggle before Congress could be persuaded to pass the Employment Act of 1946. While not officially committing the government to the goal of full employment for all able-bodied citizens (as was proposed in the controversial first draft of the bill), this law clearly indicated that federal officials were now much concerned about the overall economic health of the nation, especially the supply of jobs, and it created a special three-man council to provide the President with sound counsel on this subject. According to one much-cited study, numerous groups were involved in this bitter legislative battle, the most important of which were the NAM, U.S. Chamber of Commerce, National Farmers Union, National Planning Association (a moderate civic body made up of people drawn from various quarters), and a coalition of certain prominent liberal and labor forces that Stephen Bailey has aptly described as the "lib-lab" lobby.[117]

The end result of this extended debate and pressure group activity was the adoption of a compromise measure which satisfied none of the contending parties. The NAM and Chamber of Commerce remained opposed to any such legislation, whereas liberal interests felt that the original, fairly strong bill had been badly diluted to get sufficient support to secure its passage. Although it may be true, as Stephen Bailey contends, that the NAM and the "lib-lab" lobby were the two primary contending forces, it would also appear that certain other potent interests, particularly the CED, quietly played a crucial role in the latter stages of these proceedings and may well have tipped the scale in favor of the passage of a significantly softened bill.[118] Indeed, as one authority put it, while the CED spoke softly, "...it carried *the* big stick" (italics added).[119]

President Truman's appointments to the Council of Economic Advisers (CEA), the agency established to carry out the provisions of the Employment Act of 1946, were of a markedly different nature from those made to various high defense and foreign policy posts during this period.[120] The first chairman of the CEA was a well-known, moderately conservative economist named Edwin G. Nourse, who had long been associated with the Brookings Institution.[121] The other two original members were Leon Keyserling, an acknowledged New Dealer, who had served both as a federal housing official and as a legislative aide (in the mid-1930s) to New York's liberal Senator Robert Wagner, and John D. Clark, who had given up a successful business career in mid-life to join the academic profession and eventually became dean of the University of Nebraska's school of business administration.[122] The latter men held office throughout the Truman years. However, Nourse, who did not share the President's economically moderate views, resigned in 1950, at which point the ambitious, activist-oriented Keyserling assumed the chairmanship of the Council. Keyserling's place was taken first by a University of Chicago professor and onetime Treasury Department official, Roy Blough, and then in the last year of the Truman regime by Robert C. Turner, another Midwestern economics professor, who had formerly worked for the federal government. Yet, although this was a different recruitment pattern from that which prevailed in many other agencies, it should be recognized that, in part because of the President's limited knowledge of such matters and his preoccupation with foreign policy issues, this body did not carry much weight during the Truman administration.[123]

Another important, primarily domestic agency which was created during this period was the Atomic Energy Commission (AEC). This five-man body was established in 1946, shortly after the first atom bombs were dropped, to assume control, under the President, of all development and future use of this new, potentially dangerous form of energy. Because of the critical nature of its administrative and scientific responsibility, it was expressly provided that the AEC would be wholly civilian-controlled. As its initial chairman, President Truman picked a governmental official long used to dealing with engineering and scientific matters, David E. Lilienthal. This able executive had worked for the previous fifteen years with the Tennessee Valley Authority, the last five as chairman of this federally-backed regional development agency. The other four original members of the Atomic Energy Commission were as follows:

Robert F. Bacher	Former Cornell and MIT physics professor, who during the war had helped to develop the first atomic bomb
William W. Waymack	Longtime (1918–1946) high official of the Des Moines *Register & Tribune* (a Cowles-controlled newpaper); deputy chairman of the Federal Reserve Bank of Chicago (1942–1946); trustee of the Carnegie Endowment for International Peace (1941–1948)
Sumner T. Pike	Commissioner of the U.S. Securities & Exchange Commission (1941–1946); VP of the NYC financial firm of Case, Pomeroy & Co. (1928–1939); director (up to 1940) of Selected Industries, Inc. (an investment concern closely affiliated with the Tri-Continental Corp. and J. & W. Seligman & Co.)
Lewis L. Strauss	Partner in the New York investment banking firm of Kuhn, Loeb & Co. (1929–1946); director of the C.I.T. Financial Corp. (1937–1946), General American Transportation Corp. (1932–1946), Hudson-Manhattan Railroad Co. (1939–1945), U. S. Leather Co. (1926–1947), and the U.S. Rubber Co. (1929–1946)

The first two commissioners, Bacher and Waymack, served only until the late 1940s, when they were replaced by Henry D. Smyth, an Internationally known Princeton University physics professor, and Gordon Dean, a University of Southern California law professor, who earlier in the decade had been a law partner of Connecticut Senator Brien McMahon, one of the Congressional "fathers" of the Atomic Energy Commission.[124]

As it turned out, no especially important decisions were made by the AEC in the first years of its existence. However, in the latter part of 1949, upon learning that the Russians had successfully tested their first atomic bomb, various high federal officials, such as Dean Acheson and most top military men, became much concerned about America's need to develop an even more formidable weapon, the hydrogen bomb. There was, nevertheless, considerable opposition to such a drastic (and, some thought, perilous) move, both in the nation's scientific community and in the AEC itself, particularly on the part of Henry Smyth and the agency's liberal chairman, David Lilienthal. But thanks to the energetic efforts of certain figures, this opposition was overcome, for President Truman soon became convinced of the need for such action. And it is interesting to note that the person who labored most vigorously, within both the AEC and the administration generally, to secure support for the building of the H-bomb was Lewis Strauss, the commissioner with the closest links to big business.[125]

SUPREME COURT APPOINTMENTS

During the 1940–1952 period, the recruitment pattern for the Supreme Court was quite different from that which prevailed with regard to many of the nation's top defense and foreign policy posts, and was actually more akin to that found in various domestic agencies. In fact, it would be fair to say that the appointments made to the High Court represented a continuation of the pluralistic policy initiated by FDR of selecting men who, in contrast to the practice of preceding presidents, had no noteworthy socio-economic ties.

This trend can be seen in the types of persons chosen to serve as Chief Justice. This position was held at the outset of the era by the able, though hardly progressive, Republican, Charles Evans Hughes, who had held many high governmental posts over the years, including that of Secretary of State in the early 1920s. He had also spent a considerable amount of time after 1916 working as a Wall Street lawyer, particularly for the Rockefeller interests. Hughes stepped down from office in 1941, primarily because of age and ill health, and was replaced by one of the Court's most distinguished sitting judges, Harlan Fiske Stone. Stone had served on the Supreme Court since 1925, following a brief stint as U.S. Attorney General. Prior to his entry into the federal government, he worked in an unusual dual capacity, as dean of the Columbia law school (from 1910 to 1923) and as a Wall Street lawyer, mostly with a second- or third-tier firm known as Satterlee, Canfield & Stone. Judging from all accounts, it was the Columbia affiliation which provided the intellectual basis for his development into one of the Court's first modern liberal spokesmen. Stone, however, died in April 1946, after serving less than five years. At this juncture President Truman, in an effort to restore harmony to a tribunal badly divided by personal animosities, chose one of his close political associates, the amiable Frederick M. Vinson, to take over as the Court's chief magistrate. Unlike many of his predecessors, Vinson had no notable socio-economic links, in private life having been a small-town (Ashland, Kentucky) lawyer. Since 1924 he had held an almost uninterrupted string of government posts of a widely varied sort, the most critical of which was that of Secretary of the Treasury (in 1945–1946). While not an avowed liberal, Vinson generally took a moderate position on the role of government in American society and did not attempt to repeal the New Deal.

A majority of the other justices who were serving on the Supreme Court at the start of this period were men with remarkably few pro-business ties. Of the old-timers, only a couple had had significant economic links prior to their elevation to the bench. The most conspicuous of these was Philadelphia's Owen J. Roberts, who had been both a corporate attorney (whose clients once included the Pennsylvania Railroad and the big banking house of Drexel & Co.) and, up to 1918, a University of Pennsylvania law professor. He had also been closely affiliated with certain major business enterprises, having served as a director (or trustee) of the Equitable Life Assurance Society and AT&T. However, the five New Deal appointees—Hugo Black, Stanley Reed, Felix Frankfurter, Frank Murphy, and William O. Douglas— were all well-known governmental or academic figures with no important socio-economic connections.[126] With the exception of Frank Murphy (who died in 1949), all these more liberal jurists served on the Supreme Court throughout the World War II and Truman years.

Much to the satisfaction of liberal forces, the first justice to step down from the Court in the early 1940s was the aged former Tennessee lawyer, James C. McReynolds, the last of the so-called four horsemen who had done so much to block progressive legislation over the years. As his replacement, President Roosevelt selected longtime South Carolina lawyer and political leader James F. Byrnes, who had served his state both in the House of Representatives (in 1911–1925) and the United States Senate (in 1931–1941). Byrnes was a fairly conservative figure, as one might expect of a close friend of Bernard Baruch. But he served for only a little over a year when the President, who was greatly in need of additional help during the hectic wartime years, asked him to join his administration as, in effect, an "Assistant President" responsible for resolving various major mobilization problems.

As Byrnes's successor, Roosevelt picked a man of a very different mold, Wiley B. Rutledge, who had no connections with either the political or business world. He had spent most of his adult years a a law school professor or dean at several Midwestern universities before he was appointed to the U.S. Court of Appeals in 1939. Throughout his career Rutledge had been a firm New Deal supporter, which was probably one of the primary reasons for his selection.[127]

When Rutledge died prematurely in 1949, President Truman turned to another well-known Midwesterner, Sherman Minton, who, like Rutledge, had served as a federal judge during most of the 1940s and before that as a United States Senator from Indiana. He was also a close friend of Truman from their years together in the Senate. Though originally a small-town (New Albany, Indiana) lawyer, Minton had established a reputation during his political career as a staunch New Dealer. Ironically, he turned out to be one of the Court's more conservative members.[128]

Another opening on the Supreme Court occurred in 1941 as a result of Roosevelt's elevation of the distinguished Harlan Fiske Stone to serve as Chief Justice. To fill the vacancy this created, FDR picked his able Attorney General, Robert H. Jackson, a man who had held several high governmental posts since the early days of the New Deal. Up to the mid-

1930s, Jackson had been a small-town lawyer in Jamestown, New York, where he had been closely associated with a number of small business enterprises, some of which he had represented in legal battles against such corporate giants as AT&T. This experience did much to shape his early views about the power of big business in American life.[129] In the previous three years, while he was holding the two top posts in the Justice Department, Jackson had served as a trustee of the Twentieth Century Fund, a group with a moderate, if not liberal, orientation. However, like Frankfurter and Minton, Jackson shifted to the right once he was on the Court. He also later became engaged in a bitter personal and political feud with progressive Justice Hugo Black, thereby exacerbating relations within this body.

In 1945 the last of the Court's pre-New Deal justices, Owen J. Roberts, stepped down from the bench because of his advanced age. After one rare retracted offer, President Truman decided to fill this vacancy with a Republican, former Ohio lawyer and political leader Harold Burton, who had served for the previous four years as a United States Senator (in which role he had worked closely with Truman), and for five years before that as mayor of Cleveland.[130] Unlike many of his Republican predecessors on the High Court, Burton was not a dedicated conservative. Nor could he be considered an elite figure, for his legal connections had not been with top-tier firms and he had never served on the board of a major corporation. Instead, he was what might best be described as a middle-of-the-roader, probably because of his trying experiences in dealing, as mayor, with the grievous welfare and unemployment problems of Cleveland during the latter stages of the Depression.[131]

The last opening on the Supreme Court during the Truman administration occurred in 1949 when Michigan Justice Frank Murphy died after nine years on this tribunal. To replace him, President Truman chose his Attorney General, Tom Clark, who, in the eight years prior to his appointment to Cabinet office, had held a variety of posts in the Justice Department. Before that he had been a Dallas attorney. However, his practice had apparently never included any of the big oil or other large business enterprises that were emerging in Texas. Although not an elite figure, Clark turned out to be more conservative than most of the other men appointed to the Court since the mid-1930s, particularly on national security matters. Perhaps this can be traced to the rightist ideological climate of his home state and the fact that he was a former protégé of Texas Senator Tom Connally.[132]

In retrospect, it is clear that almost all the men appointed to the Supreme Court in the 1940s were persons who, while not as liberal as most of those chosen by Roosevelt in the late 1930s, still stood in marked contrast to those selected by Republican presidents in previous years. In appointments to major Cabinet and diplomatic office, however, the Truman administration represented a significant shift from Roosevelt's New Deal government.[133]

Although about 80 percent of these officials in both administrations had college degrees, there were some noteworthy differences in the proportions of those who had considerable government experience and key socio-economic ties. For example, almost 85 percent of Truman's top appointees had a significant amount of political or administrative experience, in comparison to roughly 50 percent of high officeholders during the New Deal era—a shift which may be explained by the fact that a number of Truman's chief aides and advisors were men brought into the government by Roosevelt.[134] Moreover, about 55 percent of Truman's key officials had influential corporate or family connections, whereas no more than 47 percent of the high-ranking New Deal figures had such ties.

A closer look at the defense and foreign policy areas of the Truman administration reveals even greater contrasts with FDR's pre-1940 regime. In these sectors many more business-oriented elite figures were recruited, not only during the crisis-ridden war years, but also in the postwar period. Over 70 percent (22 out of 31) of Truman's chief defense and foreign policy officials had elitist links, the bulk of them with America's rapidly evolving business establishment.[135] Thus, while New Deal forces continued to exercise considerable influence in the domestic area (although they were often thwarted by the conservative coalition in Congress), the nation's major corporate interests, having reestablished good working relations with the federal government during the war years, remained very much in control of the key defense and foreign policy posts during the Truman administration.

Further, judging from an analysis of the special agencies created and vital decisions made during these trying years, it would certainly appear that the elite backgrounds and affiliations of many of the chief Cabinet and diplomatic officials had a great deal to do with the actions taken by the federal government during the closing stages of World War II and in the early postwar years. The conservative, pro-corporate ties of a large number of these leaders may have had a marked effect on their decision to drop, without warning, two atom bombs on Japan in the very last months of the war in the Pacific, a decision that may have been taken at least partly because of an exaggerated fear of the political threat posed by the Soviet Union rather than for strictly military reasons. The next few years witnessed the adoption of a number of other important measures which revealed that corporate interests had much influence in American government. For example, the World Bank, which was created to provide aid to both the war-ravaged and underdeveloped areas of the world, was, with one brief exception, directed by a set of men who were closely allied with the Rockefeller forces. And the Marshall Plan, which was established to shore up a badly sagging Western Europe, was virtually run by major business and legal figures who were an integral part of America's BAC-CED-dominated economic establishment. In short, in both foreign policy and national security matters, it was elite leaders who played the key roles in the Truman administration.

Notes

1. Because corporate assets were used as the fiscal standard in Table 3, no aircraft companies made the "top 20" list in 1952, although one such firm (the Boeing Airplane Co.) actually had a larger volume of sales than the 19th-ranked Phillips Petroleum Co.

2. In point of fact, only five public utilities in the country had assets of over $1 billion—namely, AT&T (an over $10 billion giant), the Pacific Gas & Electric Co., the Consolidated Edison Co. of New York, the Commonwealth Edison Co. of Illinois, and the American Gas & Electric Co. The last four concerns had assets of between $1 and $2 billion.

3. The only transportation concerns to grow significantly during this period were the airlines, which had emerged from their prewar "infant industry" stage, but were still considerably smaller than the major railroads.

4. These figures are somewhat misleading in that they do not include the often substantial assets managed by the trust departments of these big commercial banks. Although no pertinent data were reported on this subject until the 1960s, the author suspects that the Bank of America (which has never had huge trust funds) was probably not the largest commercial bank in the country. This honor undoubtedly rested with one of the major New York City concerns.

5. The National Civic Federation did represent an earlier type of business, labor, and civic leadership structure, but its effectiveness was of relatively brief duration (from roughly 1900 to 1912). The later-established National Industrial Conference Board was primarily a research-oriented agency, although it did have some significant ties to the BAC.

6. Very little was written about this organization up to 1960, an extraordinary gap in journalistic and academic coverage considering the power wielded by this body. For a brief, at times misleading, analysis of this group's activity from the Roosevelt through the Eisenhower administrations, see Hobart Rowen, "America's Most Powerful Private Club," *Harper's* (September 1960), pp. 79–84.

7. In 1940 and 1945, for example, over 80 percent of this body's active (nonacademic) membership was made up of the top officials of various big business enterprises such as Eastman Kodak, Anaconda Copper, Procter & Gamble, Quaker Oats, and R. J. Reynolds Tobacco. By the early 1950s, this figure had risen to more than 85 percent. Similarly, all but a few of the members of the BAC's key 15-man executive committee represented big business interests during this period. A complete list of the names (but not the corporate affiliations) of the, at most 60, active members of the BAC may be found in the annual reports of the Department of Commerce, except for the World War II years.

8. For an incisive account of the origins of the CED, see Robert M. Collins, "Positive Business Responses to the New Deal: The Roots of the Committee for Economic Development, 1933–1942," *Business History Review* (Autumn 1978), pp. 369–91. While Collins places great weight on the role of the BAC in this organizational development, he also emphasizes the intellectual contribution made by a set of liberal officials at the University of Chicago, and another less well defined group of businessmen led by Beardsley Ruml, a former academic who was now the treasurer of R. H. Macy & Co. and chairman of the Federal Reserve Bank of New York. There was considerable input from various figures at the University of Chicago, the most important of whom was William Benton, who served as the first vice-chairman of the CED. Benton, a onetime advertising executive, was reportedly appointed to this post because the organization wanted someone who did not have a Wall Street or "big business" label. See Sidney Hyman, *The Lives of William Benton* (Chicago: University of Chicago Press, 1969), especially pp. 266 and 316, and for a brief general description of the origins of the CED, Karl Schriftgiesser, *Business and Public Policy: The Role of the Committee for Economic Development, 1942–1967* (Englewood Cliffs, N.J.: Prentice-Hall, 1967), pp. 1–4, and also his *Business Comes of Age* (New York: Harper & Bros., 1960), pp. 1–29.

9. The other eight joint BAC-CED members were William L. Clayton (a former Texas cotton magnate who was presently serving as a high federal official), Ralph E. Flanders (president of the relatively small Jones & Lamson Machine Co. of Vermont), Marion B. Folsom (treasurer of the Eastman Kodak Co.), Clarence Francis (president of the General Foods Corp.), Charles R. Hook (president of the American Rolling Mill Co.), Harrison Jones (vice-president of the Coca-Cola Co.), Thomas B. McCabe (president of the Scott Paper Co.), and Reuben R. Robertson (executive vice-president of the Champion Paper & Fibre Co.). In contrast, only one representative of the U.S. Chamber of Commerce, Seattle's Eric A. Johnston, was on the original CED board, and only one man, Armco's Charles R. Hook, might be viewed as an emissary of the NAM (and even that is debatable).

The NAM probably represented the center of "rightist" thinking in the business community since the late 1930s, even though its make-up changed noticeably, from the standpoint of size, as the years progressed. In the post-World War II period it was dominated by a coalition of small and medium-sized concerns and various large family-controlled corporations, which interests were highly conservative and never became reconciled to the reformist measures adopted by the New Deal. For more on this latter point, see Philip H. Burch, Jr., "The NAM as an Interest Group," *Politics and Society* (Fall 1973), pp. 97–130.

10. See "Who Speaks for Business?" *Dun's Review* (November 1969), pp. 46–47 and 121. As this article points out, the executive branch of the federal government has not been very responsive over the years to the views of the NAM and Chamber of Commerce, in contrast to its receptivity to the ideas and influence of the BAC and CED.

11. The primary leaders of the Century group, which was apparently created to help counter the country's deep-rooted isolationist sentiment and the activities of the America First Committee, were Francis P. Miller (the organization director of the New York-based Council on Foreign Relations), Lewis W. Douglas (the president of the Mutual Life Insurance Co. and a trustee of the Rockefeller Foundation and the CFR), Whitney Shepardson (a vice-president of the International Railways of Central America and the treasurer of the CFR), Will Clayton (a Texas cotton magnate who had served since 1938 as head of the Houston regional study committee of the CFR and was a prominent member of the BAC), Allen W. Dulles (a partner in the Wall Street law firm of Sullivan & Cromwell, secretary of the CFR, and a director of the J. Henry Schroder Banking Corp.), Dean G. Acheson (a partner in the Washington law firm of Covington & Burling who was soon appointed Assistant Secretary of State), and Henry P. Van Dusen (a New York theologian who was a close friend of Francis Miller). See Mark L. Chadwin, *The Hawks of World War II* (Chapel Hill: University of North Carolina Press, 1968), pp. 32–73.

12. For a detailed analysis of these and other related activities of the CFR, see Laurence H. Shoup and William Minter, *Imperial Brain Trust: The Council on Foreign Relations and United States Foreign Policy* (New York: Monthly Review Press, 1977), pp. 118–25 in particular. However, the book probably presents an exaggerated or erroneous picture of the Council's early expansionist (i.e., imperialistic) plans.

13. See the *New York Times* (November 21, 1971), Section VI, p. 124; for more on the CFR's place in America's postwar politico-economic establishment, see Douglas Cater, *Power in Washington* (New York: Random House, 1964), p. 247.

14. This appointment was reportedly engineered largely by FDR's recently selected Supreme Court Justice (and longtime informal governmental advisor) Felix Frankfurter and their mutual friend, Grenville Clark, who was a senior partner in the New York law firm of Root, Clark, Buckner & Ballantine, a director of the fairly small Fiduciary Trust Co. of New York City, and in the early 1930s a board member of the probably Harriman-dominated American-Hawaiian Steamship Co. See Liva Baker, *Felix Frankfurter*, pp. 239–40, and Norman Cousins and J. Garry Clifford (eds.), *Memoirs of a Man: Grenville Clark* (New York: Norton, 1975), pp. 15–17.

15. The 73-year-old Stimson had not served on any major corporate board since he stepped down from that of the (probably Morgan-dominated) American Superpower Corp. in 1927 to

become governor-general of the Philippines. Since 1933 his close friend and law partner Bronson Winthrop had served as a director of the big Bank of Manhattan, in which the Warburg family of Kuhn, Loeb & Co. had until recently held a major stake.

16. With regard to civic ties, while Stimson never served as a key officer or director of the Council on Foreign Relations, he did act as chairman of one of its special study committees in the mid-1930s.

17. The most prominent member of the family, Charles G. Dawes, had served as Vice President of the United States under Calvin Coolidge, and then for the first three years of Hoover's term as Ambassador to Great Britain.

18. Although these officials were undoubtedly very able, there were surely many other equally capable people who might have been recruited from other cities or economic backgrounds.

19. The most noteworthy of these was the Jamestown Telephone Corporation, which had once been engaged in an extended battle with an arm of AT&T's Bell Telephone system, a struggle that may have done much to color Jackson's way of thinking about corporate giants. At times Jackson had also reportedly acted as an attorney for the Central Labor Council in his home town, another possible countervailing influence. Further evidence of Jackson's generally liberal outlook may be found in the fact that he served on the board of the Twentieth Century Fund during the years he held high administrative office. See Eugene C. Gerhart, *America's Advocate: Robert H. Jackson* (Indianapolis: Bobbs-Merrill, 1958), pp. 38–41.

20. See Francis Biddle, *A Casual Past* (Garden City, N.Y.: Doubleday, 1961), pp. 330 and 353.

21. Biddle had also served for many years on the board of the Philadelphia Contributionship for the Insurance of Houses from Loss by Fire. This quaintly titled company was a small concern but had tremendous social status. Biddle was a member of the same family that had produced the famous financier Nicholas Biddle back in Andrew Jackson's time. For more on the Biddles, see Nathaniel Burt, *First Families* (Boston: Little, Brown, 1970), pp. 93–112 and 383–85.

22. Jones also served in two less conspicuous capacities in the Roosevelt regime, as Federal Loan Administrator (in 1939–40), and since 1936 as a high official of the Export-Import Bank, an agency designed to stimulate foreign trade.

23. See Bascom N. Timmons, *Jesse H. Jones* (New York: Henry Holt, 1954), pp. 83 and 115–19.

24. In the first part of 1945 Jones, whose relations with Roosevelt had become strained over the years, was forced to resign from office in order to make a suitable place for former Vice President Henry A. Wallace, who, because of considerable pressure from conservative quarters, had been pushed off the Democratic ticket in 1944.

25. Grant McConnell, *The Decline of Agrarian Democracy* (Berkeley: University of California Press, 1953), p. 122; see also Dean Albertson, *Roosevelt's Farmer, Claude R. Wickard in the New Deal* (New York: Columbia University Press, 1961), passim. Davis was also president of the Federal Reserve Bank of St. Louis and a former high official of the Agricultural Adjustment Administration.

26. One noted historian claims that "during the last five years of Roosevelt's life, Hopkins was usually his most influential advisor in foreign affairs; he was called 'Roosevelt's own personal Foreign Office.'" See Alexander De Conde, *The American Secretary of State: An Interpretation* (New York: Praeger, 1962), p. 29.

27. In addition, Stettinius's brother-in-law, Juan Trippe, was president of the Pan American Airways Corp. and sat on the board of the Metropolitan Life Insurance Co. and the Chrysler Corp. And perhaps equally revealing, Stettinius's brother, William, served up to his death in the late 1930s as a director of the Worthington Pump & Machinery Corp., whose board included during all or part of this decade such key pro-New Deal figures as W. Averell Harriman, David

K. E. Bruce, and New York financier Louis F. Rothschild, who had married a member of the Guggenheim family.

28. Alexander De Conde has placed Stettinius in this unflattering category (see his *The American Secretary of State*, p. 110). Even if this assessment is correct, it ignores the connections of other high-level officials such as Under Secretary of State (and career diplomat) Joseph C. Grew. For example, his brother Henry served on the board of the State Street Trust Co., and his cousin married the son of the great J. P. Morgan. Stettinius's three most important Assistant Secretaries of State, James C. Dunn, William L. Clayton, and Nelson A. Rockefeller, were also elite figures (Dunn through his marriage into the wealthy Armour family and Clayton through his linkage with the BAC and CED).

29. Our wartime ambassadors to Vichy France were two rather typical emissaries, William D. Leahy, a former high-ranking naval officer (who served in this capacity in the early 1940s), and toward the end of the war, career diplomat Jefferson Caffrey. America had severed relations with Nazi Germany in the late 1930s and thus had no representatives in Berlin during the first half of the 1940s.

30. See, for example, Bernard Bellush, *He Walked Alone: A Biography of John Gilbert Winant* (The Hague: Mouton, 1968), p. 53.

31. In addition, according to a recent source, Winant was a member of one of the numerous study groups which were created by the Council on Foreign Relations in 1940 to help deal with the growing threat posed to the nation's security by Axis aggression. See Laurence H. Shoup and William Minter, *Imperial Brain Trust*, p. 121.

32. Up to 1933 Steinhardt had been a member of the New York law firm of Guggenheimer & Untermyer, which had long been headed by his uncle, Samuel Untermyer, a noted attorney who had served for many years as counsel to the Guggenheim interests. Steinhardt's cousin and former law partner, Alvin Untermyer, was a director of the big Consolidated Oil Corp.

33. For more on the CFR-Century group association, see Francis Pickens Miller, *Man from the Valley* (Chapel Hill: University of North Carolina Press, 1972), p. 94.

34. Nelson was one of the few retail trade executives appointed to serve as a high federal official in the entire post-New Deal period, and the author suspects that the primary reason for his selection was that he was one of the few merchants in the country who was a member of the BAC.

35. One should not infer from the appointment pattern that there was any conspiracy or impropriety involved in the operation of the WPB. However, the government's recruitment efforts did not extend very far, certainly not to various small- or medium-sized businesses, which probably could have supplied more talent than was secured from these sources.

36. According to most accounts, the "dump Wallace" movement was initiated largely by independent California oilman (and Democratic party treasurer) Edwin Pauley and several other conservative leaders. These men were primarily concerned with eliminating any chance that Wallace might become President of the United States rather than with naming a particular successor, so long as the latter was a "safe and sound" figure. Originally, various conservative spokesmen wanted South Carolina's James F. Byrnes as Roosevelt's running mate in 1944, but he lost out because of sectional considerations and strong labor opposition. Truman was then accepted as a compromise candidate. See, for instance, Bert Cochran, *Harry Truman and the Crisis Presidency* (New York: Funk & Wagnalls, 1973), pp. 3–8, and Jonathan Daniels, *The Man of Independence* (Philadelphia: Lippincott, 1950), pp. 232–54.

37. See Alonzo Hamby, *Beyond the New Deal: Harry S Truman and American Liberalism* (New York: Columbia University Press, 1973), pp. 41–44.

38. See Margaret Coit, *Mr. Baruch*, pp. 321–35 and 530, and James F. Byrnes, *All in One Lifetime* (New York: Harper & Brothers, 1958), pp. 204–07. As evidence of this link, when Byrnes was asked to establish the Office of War Mobilization in 1943, he immediately turned for aid and advice to two Northern businessmen, John M. Hancock of Lehman Brothers, who

was a director of 19 corporations, and Fred Searls, a vice-president of the Newmount Mining Corp. Both men were close associates of Bernard Baruch.

39. Acheson's mother was a member of the wealthy Gooderham family, which had long held a significant interest in the Canadian whiskey company of Hiram Walker-Gooderham & Worts, Ltd., and various other enterprises in that country.

40. See Mark L. Chadwin, *op. cit.*, pp. 32–113, especially 58–59.

41. See Gaddis Smith, *Dean Acheson* (New York: Cooper Square Publishers, 1972), pp. 25–26. Three other prominent officials in the State Department in the immediate (1945–1947) postwar period were Spruille Braden (who served up to 1936 on the board of the Harriman-dominated American Ship & Commerce Corp.), William Benton (who was one of the original trustees of the CED), and William L. Clayton (a former Texas cotton merchant, who was also a trustee of the CED and, up to 1945, a member of the BAC). But none of these individuals was as important as Acheson.

42. Another top aide of Marshall, and later of Dean Acheson, was Assistant Secretary of State for Economic Affairs Willard L. Thorp, a former Dun & Bradstreet figure and later chairman of the big General Public Utilities Corp. Judging by the public record, he continued to serve on the latter board throughout his years as a State Department official.

43. See Joseph L. Morison, *Governor O. Max Gardner* (Chapel Hill: University of North Carolina Press, 1971), pp. 139–48, 246, and 256.

44. David K. E. Bruce had originally married into the Mellon family and had served on the board of various Mellon-controlled corporations in the 1930s. But this relationship ended when Bruce and his wife were divorced in 1945.

45. In the late 1940s and/or early 1950s De Golyer, who was the head of the most renowned oil consultation service in the world, served on the board of the (Dillon-controlled) U.S. and Foreign Securities Corp., Empire Trust Co. of New York, Louisiana Land and Exploration Co., Republic Natural Gas Co., Texas Eastern Transmission Corp., and Southern Pacific Railroad. It was during this period that a major governmental policy was adopted, with McGhee as an important participant, granting oil companies operating abroad a big reduction in their domestic tax burden. See the *New York Times*, January 31, 1974, pp. 1 and 18, and John M. Blair, *The Control of Oil* (New York: Random House, 1976), pp. 196–203.

46. For more on this relationship, see Bert Cochran, *Harry Truman and the Crisis Presidency*, p. 122, and Robert J. Donovan, *Conflict and Crisis: The Presidency of Harry S. Truman, 1945–1948* (New York: Norton, 1977), p. 23.

47. As already indicated, the vast majority of the members of the BAC were the chief executives of big business concerns, whereas Snyder was merely one of his bank's 24 vice-presidents. Thus one assumes he was awarded BAC status to secure more business influence in the Truman administration. Most of the second-tier figures in the Treasury Department were longtime career officials. The two exceptions were A. L. M. Wiggins, a former South Carolina businessman (and director of the big Atlantic Coast Line Railway), who served as Under Secretary of the Treasury in 1947–1948, and William McChesney Martin, Jr., who acted as Assistant Secretary of the Treasury from 1949 to 1951. Martin was a St. Louis broker who became president of the New York Stock Exchange before entering the federal government in 1945. He had married the daughter of the recently deceased Dwight F. Davis, a former Secretary of War and Brookings Institution board chairman.

48. Patterson was originally tapped for his high wartime defense post by the same men who promoted Stimson's candidacy for Secretary of War in 1940, Supreme Court Justice Felix Frankfurter and Wall Street lawyer Grenville Clark. Up to 1930 Patterson had been a partner in the firm of Webb, Patterson & Hadley and its later successor, Murray, Aldrich & Webb. Following a Rockefeller-inspired merger in the early 1930s, this concern was known as Milbank, Tweed, Hope & Webb. After he stepped down from the War Department in 1947, Patterson formed a new law firm with one of his former partners, Vanderbilt Webb, who was a longtime director of the New York Trust Co. and a postwar vice-president of Rockefeller Center, Inc. For

more on Patterson's early law firms and later selection as a federal official, see Paul Hoffman, *Lions in the Street* (New York: Dutton, 1973), pp. 77–80, Liva Baker, *op. cit.*, p. 240, and Norman Cousins and J. Garry Clifford, *op. cit.*, p. 17.

49. For more on Forrestal's New Deal ties, see Robert G. Albion and Robert H. Connery, *Forrestal and the Navy* (New York: Columbia University Press, 1962), pp. 2–7. Forrestal's top aide in the early postwar years was a non-elitist figure named John L. Sullivan, who had been a Manchester (New Hampshire) lawyer before joining the federal government in 1939. Sullivan was also a longtime friend of Secretary of the Navy Frank Knox, who had once run a newspaper in Manchester.

50. Although these now second-tier defense posts were no longer accorded Cabinet status, they were still important positions, deserving of special attention.

51. Matthews had also served for about a decade as a director of the U.S. Chamber of Commerce. In fact, he was one of the few high Defense Department officials to be associated with this organization in the postwar period.

52. The author does not subscribe to the thesis advanced by Paul Koistinen that the military-industrial complex had its roots in an earlier era. For more on this line of argument, see Paul A. C. Koistinen, "The 'Industrial-Military' Complex in Historical Perspective: World War I," *Business History Review* (Winter 1967), pp. 378–403, and also his later article, "The 'Industrial-Military' Complex in Historical Perspective: The Inter War Years," *Journal of American History* (March 1970), pp. 819–39.

53. According to one source, the "miracle" for Floyd Odlum, Consolidated Vultee's new controlling stockholder, "... was what happened to his B-36 bomber. Overnight it emerged from comparative obscurity to become the Air Force's favorite child." Large orders for military aircraft (which totaled more than $300 million) were, as *Fortune* put it, "rudely snatched away" from other prime contractors, such as Boeing, Northrup, and North American. See "Mr. Odlum Gets the Business," *Fortune* (September 1949), pp. 90 and 138, and Carl W. Borklund, *Men of the Pentagon: From Forrestal to McNamara* (New York: Praeger, 1966), pp. 71–79.

54. Johnson's directorship link with the General Aniline & Film Corp. was of a much less significant nature, for this concern was not heavily involved in military procurement.

55. See U.S. Congress, House of Representatives, Armed Services Committee, *Investigation of the B-36 Bomber Program* (Washington, D.C.: U.S. Government Printing Office, 1949), pp. 476–77. When Johnson was first appointed to this board in August 1942, he was acting as Roosevelt's special representative to India, a position he held until December of that year. It would thus seem difficult for him to have served initially as the President's informal corporate overseer under these conditions.

56. See House Armed Services Committee, *op. cit.*, p. 489. Johnson was also paid $23,000 for his seven years' service as a director.

57. See House Armed Services Committee, *op. cit.*, p. 494. Johnson was the only person on the board who did not come from either California or New York. Consolidated Vultee had been controlled since October 1947 by the New York-based Atlas Corp., which was headed by financier Floyd Odlum, a longtime big contributor to the Democratic party. Prior to that time this concern had been dominated by a syndicate led by entrepreneur Victor Emanuel, another influential Democrat. It is interesting to note that up to 1947 Consolidated Vultee's board also included another well-known figure, George E. Allen, who has usually been depicted as a kind of Democratic "court jester," but, according to Arnold Rogow, actually served as a major party fundraiser. See Arnold Rogow, *James Forrestal* (New York: Macmillan, 1963), p. 279.

58. For more on McGrath, see Robert S. Allen and William V. Shannon, *The Truman Merry-Go-Round* (New York: Vanguard Press, 1950), pp. 108–110.

59. See Robert J. Donovan, *Conflict and Crisis* (New York: Norton, 1977), pp. 183–84, and Alonzo L. Hamby, *op. cit.*, p. 73. Truman originally tried to allay liberal anger over Ickes' resignation by first offering this post to Supreme Court Justice William O. Douglas, who was a

116 Elites in American History

native of the Far West and had a longstanding interest in conservation matters, but Douglas could not be induced to step down from the High Court.

60. See Allan J. Matusow, *Farm Policies and Politics in the Truman Years* (Cambridge, Mass.: Harvard University Press, 1967), pp. 68–70 and 169, and Alonzo L. Hamby, *op. cit.*, pp. 75, 223, and 303–06.

61. See Arthur F. McClure, *The Truman Administration and the Problems of Postwar Labor, 1945-1948* (Rutherford, N.J.: Fairleigh Dickinson University Press, 1969), p. 51, and Alonzo L. Hamby, *op. cit.*, p. 56. However, some of the people chosen to act as Under Secretary of Labor during the Truman years were men who appeared to have had pro-corporate ties, such as Keen Johnson (a former governor of Kentucky, who served in the mid-1940s as an officer of the Reynolds Metals Co.) and Michael J. Galvin (a longtime partner in the Boston law firm of Herrick, Smith, Donald, Farley & Ketchum).

62. Harriman continued to serve on the board of the Illinois Central Railroad until he was appointed to Cabinet office. His brother Roland was also a longtime close business associate and a director of both the Anaconda Copper Mining Co. and the Mutual Life Insurance Co.

63. Additional evidence that the Department of Commerce was controlled by pro-corporate interests may be found in the fact that the three persons to hold the post of Under Secretary during the Truman administration were Alfred Schindler, the executive director of the CED's St. Louis office in 1943–1944; William C. Foster, who was a trustee of the CED throughout this period; and Cornelius Vanderbilt Whitney (a brother of financier John Hay Whitney), who served as board chairman of the Hudson Bay Mining & Smelting Co., Ltd., from 1931 through 1950 and was the former head of Pan American Airways.

64. See Charles Sawyer, *Concerns of a Conservative Democrat* (Carbondale: Southern Illinois University Press, 1968), pp. 39–77. Sawyer's law firm of Dinsmore, Shohl, Sawyer & Dinsmore still served apparently as general counsel to the Procter & Gamble Co. In addition, Sawyer owned a number of radio stations in the eastern part of the country, and for a brief time had controlling interest in the Ansonia Brass and Copper Co.

65. Douglas was not Truman's first choice for this position. He initially appointed onetime (1928–1933) North Carolina Governor O. Max Gardner, who in early 1946 had been appointed Under Secretary of the Treasury. During the intervening period Gardner had been a Washington (D.C.) attorney who had acted as general counsel to the Cotton Textile Institute, as president of the fairly small Cleveland Cloth Mills of North Carolina, as a lawyer-lobbyist for a number of large business concerns, and, in the mid-1940s, as a director of the big Sperry (Gyroscope) Corp., whose head, Thomas A. Morgan, was a board member of the Lehman Corp. and Pan-American Airways. Gardner was also a longtime close friend of John W. Hanes, a North Carolina textile heir turned New York financier, who had served as Under Secretary of the Treasury in the late 1930s. However, Gardner died suddenly, just before his departure for Great Britain. See Joseph L. Morrison, *Governor O. Max Gardner, pp. 131–203.*

66. It is interesting that these two ambassadors had ties to both the Morgan and Rockefeller forces, the two economic camps with the greatest stake in American foreign relations.

67. Bruce had married (and later divorced) the daughter of the rich former Secretary of the Treasury Andrew W. Mellon, and served, up to the late 1930s or early 1940s, on the board of the Mellon-controlled Aluminum Co. of America and Westinghouse Electric & Mfg. Co.

68. In addition, both David and James Bruce were substantial contributors to Truman's poorly funded presidential campaign in 1948. See Robert J. Donovan, *op. cit.*, p. 419.

69. McCloy was the first civilian to exercise direct governmental authority over West Germany. His counterpart in Japan was the victorious Pacific war General Douglas MacArthur.

70. Two other important posts were also created in the late 1940s, those of Ambassador to the United Nations and Ambassador to the Organization of American States. The first position

was filled until 1952 by Vermont's former conservative Senator, Warren Austin, while the latter office was held by State Department careerists.

71. Alperovitz agrees with the later finding of the U.S. Strategic Bombing Survey that "Japan would have surrendered even if the atomic bombs had not been dropped, even if Russia had not entered the war, and even if no invasion had been planned or contemplated." According to Walter Schoenberger, Air Force General "Hap" Arnold had recommended that the bomb be dropped first, not on a major urban center, but in some large harbor around Japan, so as to demonstrate its frightening effects without taking such a terrible toll in lives and later human suffering. See Gar Alperovitz, *Atomic Diplomacy: Hiroshima and Potsdam* (New York: Simon & Schuster, 1965), pp. 237–38, and Walter S. Schoenberger, *Decision of Destiny* (Athens: Ohio University Press, 1969), p. 261.

72. The super-secret atomic bomb was originally developed strictly as a fearsome military weapon, and it was not until the last few months of the war that high government officials began to think in terms of its political potential. Up to the time of the Potsdam Conference and the first successful test of the atomic bomb, most of Truman's military and political advisors were strongly in favor of Russian involvement in the war against Japan. But when the first atomic bomb was successfully detonated, all this changed, particularly since it was clear that Japan was now close to defeat.

73. For another study which reinforces Alperovitz's general line of analysis and places particular stress on Truman's inexperience and uncertainty in the foreign policy area, see Martin J. Sherwin, *A World Destroyed: The Atomic Bomb and the Grand Alliance* (New York: Knopf, 1973), especially pp. 146–64.

74. See Alperovitz, *op. cit.*, pp. 22–30, and Sherwin, *op. cit.*, p. 155.

75. See Alperovitz, *op. cit.*, p. 27. Grew had numerous important socio-economic ties. For instance, his first cousin, Jane Norton Grew, had married the son of the great J. P. Morgan.

76. For a study which stresses some of these politico-economic connections, see John C. Donovan, *The Cold Warriors: A Policy-Making Elite* (Lexington, Mass.: Heath, 1974), pp. 32–57.

77. Even this well-known South Carolina leader was a close friend of New York financier Bernard Baruch, who was a native of Byrnes's home state, where he still maintained a huge estate and often entertained prominent political and economic figures.

78. Interestingly, the one former businessman in this group who reversed his position and took issue with the decision to drop the atomic bomb, without advance warning, on Japan was Chicago executive Ralph Bard, the man with the least salient corporate connections. But his plea, like that of various concerned scientists, was largely ignored. (See Alperovitz, *op. cit.*, pp. 149–50.) It should also be noted that a number of scientists, particularly those who served on the Interim Committee's official technical advisory panel, were strongly disposed toward the use of the bomb. Some of these, perhaps not coincidentally, had close links with the nation's top economic leaders over the years; for example, former MIT dean Vannevar Bush had been a trustee of the Brookings Institution and a graduate member of the BAC, and MIT president (and physicist) Karl T. Compton was a trustee of both the Brookings Institution and the Rockefeller Foundation, and had also been an active member of the BAC during the early New Deal years.

79. Stimson was somewhat less "hawkish" than most of Truman's other advisors in this area, perhaps because he had not been actively associated with the business world for some time.

80. According to one study, Harrison served as deputy chairman of the Interim Committee and, in the absence of Stimson, actually conducted at least one of its meetings in the spring of 1945. He apparently played a critical role throughout its proceedings. For instance, it was he who made the judgment that the Franck report of the concerned scientists who objected to the proposed use of atomic bombs on Japanese cities was not important enough to warrant consideration by the Interim Committee. See Walter S. Schoenberger, *Decision of Destiny*, pp. 117–50, and Elting E. Morison, *Turmoil and Tradition: A Study of the Life and Times of Henry L. Stimson* (Boston: Houghton Mifflin, 1960), p. 624.

81. Harrison was still listed in 1945 in *Moody's* and various other business manuals as holding these two economic posts, although one cannot tell from existing sources what proportion of his time was devoted to these activities while he was acting as one of Stimson's top aides. It should also be noted that another of Stimson's special assistants in the War Department (and a key Interim Committee figure), former Brahmin lawyer Harvey H. Bundy, apparently continued to serve as a director of the Boston-controlled Tampa Electric Co., although he did resign from the board of the State Street Trust Co. when he entered the federal government in 1941. Joseph C. Grew's brother Henry was also a member of the latter board.

82. See Schoenberger, *op. cit.*, pp. 125, 128, 136, 147, and 266.

83. The author does not find Herbert Feis's defense of our decision to drop a second atomic bomb on Nagasaki very convincing, certainly not in terms of the number of lives lost and his own admission that this action merely brought the war to a close a few weeks earlier. As Martin Sherwin has emphasized, the second bomb was surely not necessary. See Herbert Feis, *The Atomic Bomb and the End of World War II* (Princeton, N.J.: Princeton University Press, 1966), pp. 199–200, and Sherwin, *op. cit.*, pp. 235–37.

84. See *The International Bank for Reconstruction and Development: 1946–1953* (Baltimore: Johns Hopkins University Press, 1964), p. 4.

85. See Edward S. Mason and Robert S. Asher, *The World Bank Since Bretton Woods* (Washington, D.C.: Brookings Institution, 1973), pp. 22–23, and *The International Bank for Reconstruction and Development: 1946–1953*, p. 8. Judging from the former study, there would not appear to have been a firm consensus about this matter. The less developed nations feared that if too much stress were placed on reconstruction, "the Bank would never get around to development."

86. Two authorities have recently observed that the World Bank was "...at least in its initial stages, far from being a bona fide international institution, since the United States supplied most of its loanable funds and was by far the predominant market for Bank securities." See Mason and Asher, *op. cit.*, p. 28.

87. See *The International Bank for Reconstruction and Development: 1946–1953*, pp. 229–30, and Mason and Asher, *op. cit.*, pp. 800–02. When the financial influence of France was added to that of the United States and Britain, it pushed this voting power to considerably more than 50 percent.

88. See Mason and Asher, *op. cit.*, p. 63.

89. See Mason and Asher, *op. cit.*, p. 63.

90. *Ibid.*

91. According to a Brookings study, the first choice for this position was Lewis Douglas, the president of New York's big Mutual Life Insurance Co. However, because certain objections were raised—mainly about his association with what was frequently referred to as "big business," "Wall Street," and "international financiers"—Douglas decided to withdraw his name from consideration. Steve Weissman claims that the post was offered even earlier to Assistant Secretary of State William Clayton (who was an active member of the Business Advisory Council and a trustee of the CED), and Edward E. Brown, the board chairman of the First National Bank of Chicago (and an active member of the BAC). See Mason and Asher, *op. cit.*, pp. 40–41, and Steve Weissman and members of the Pacific Studies Center and the North American Congress on Latin America, *The Trojan Horse: A Radical Look at Foreign Aid* (Palo Alto, Cal.: Ramparts Press, 1975), pp. 47–48.

92. Meyer had also been the largest stockholder and, indirectly, a dominant force in the Allied Chemical & Dye Corp., and in 1945 he was made a trustee of the CED. In addition, his brother-in-law, Wall Street lawyer Alfred A. Cook, sat on the board of the New York Trust Co. and Allied Chemical & Dye Corp. (in the latter case, probably as Meyer's representative). For more on Meyer's role in this big industrial enterprise, see Edmund L. Van Deusen, "You'd Hardly Know Allied Chemical," *Fortune* (October 1954), pp. 119–23 and 161–71.

93. According to Weissman, several other men—namely, William Clayton, W. Averell Harriman, and New York Federal Reserve Bank president Allan Sproul—were asked to take this job before McCloy could finally be persuaded to accept. See Weissman et al., *op. cit.*, pp. 48–49.

94. As is the practice with most large law firms, this tie is not listed in the *Martindale-Hubbell Law Directory*. For a recent treatment of the relationship, see Paul Hoffman, *Lions in the Street*, pp. 18 and 83.

95. Lest one think this selection was largely accidental, it should be noted that Black, who had spent 16 years climbing up the managerial ladder at Chase, was reluctant to take this prestigious, but more tenuous, position with the World Bank until he was persuaded to do so by the former's board chairman, Winthrop W. Aldrich, who was a Rockefeller kinsman (and a trustee of both the Rockefeller Foundation and the Metropolitan Life Insurance Company). See *Fortune* (August 1954), pp. 114 and 168.

96. Black served as president of the World Bank for 12½ years, until the end of 1962, when he was replaced by New York financier George D. Woods, who was the head of a major investment banking concern known as the First Boston Corp. He was also a director or trustee of the Rockefeller Foundation, the Chase International Investment Corp. (an affiliate of the Chase Manhattan Bank), and various other lesser business enterprises. Woods held this post until 1968 when he was succeeded by the recently resigned Secretary of Defense, Robert McNamara, whose only significant tie at the time was as a newly elected trustee of the Ford Foundation. This skewed recruitment pattern clearly runs counter to the claim found in Mason and Asher, *op. cit.*, p. 95.

97. These differences may stem, in part, from uneven request rates or other such factors. But much cannot be so explained. For instance, Iran asked for a loan of $250 million in 1946, but despite much extended negotiation did not receive any funds until 1957, by which time a pro-American regime was firmly entrenched.

98. See Mason and Asher, *op. cit.*, p. 23.

99. Newspaper columnist Stewart Alsop has claimed that these military men served essentially as the titular heads of the CIA and that it was actually a civilian figure, Frank Wisner, a former partner in the well-known Wall Street law firm of Carter, Ledyard & Milburn, who really ran the agency—an intriguing assertion which requires further study. See Stewart Alsop, *The Center* (New York: Harper & Row), p. 193.

100. Judging from business sources, Jackson continued to serve on the last board while acting as deputy director of the CIA. Although no federal directory so indicates, another prominent official in the early 1950s was New York executive Kingman Douglass, who also apparently maintained his affiliation with Dun & Bradstreet throughout his years as an assistant director of the CIA. (See the *New York Times*, October 10, 1971, p. 85.) In addition, there were two other persons who served as deputy director of the CIA under Allen Dulles. They were Loftus Becker, a partner in the New York law firm of Cahill, Gordon, Zachry & Reindel, and Walter R. Wolf, a former senior vice-president of the City Bank Farmers Trust Co. (a subsidiary of the National City Bank of New York). Wolf continued to grace the board of this big trust company while he held his CIA post, although this hardly seemed necessary to maintain suitable "cover." See the *New York Times* (May 19, 1963), p. 86, and various (post-1953) issues of *Who's Who in America*.

101. See Paul Hoffman, *op. cit.*, p. 80. Allen Dulles's older brother, John Foster Dulles, was the senior partner of this concern, and also served as board chairman of the Rockefeller Foundation and (up to 1949 or 1950) as a director of the American Agricultural Chemical Co., Babcock & Wilcox Co., Bank of New York, and the International Nickel Co. of Canada, Ltd. The Dulles brothers were nephews of Wilson's second Secretary of State, Robert Lansing.

102. Popular impressions to the contrary, the Council on Foreign Relations was not dominated, up to the early 1950s, by the still-rising Rockefeller forces, but included a number of people closely associated with the House of Morgan.

103. See Hadley Arkes, *Bureaucracy, the Marshall Plan and the National Interest* (Princeton, N.J.: Princeton University Press, 1972), especially pp. 103, 213, 222, and 326.

104. See Harry B. Price, *The Marshall Plan and Its Meaning* (Ithaca, N.Y.: Cornell University Press, 1955), p. 46. The backgrounds of Ambassador Douglas and Robert Lovett have already been described. Clayton was a trustee of the CED and had, up to recently, been an active member of the BAC. Assistant Secretary of State Willard Thorp still sat on the board of the General Public Utilities Corp. Paul Nitze had married a member of the wealthy Pratt family (which had been associated for many years with the Standard Oil interests), and had, up to World War II, been a vice-president of Dillon, Read & Co. In addition, although a federal official since the early 1940s, he had served as a director of the St. Louis–San Francisco Railway and Chicago, Rock Island & Pacific Railroad up to 1946.

105. For another study which has emphasized these links, see David W. Eakins, "Business Planners and America's Postwar Expansion," in David Horowitz (ed.), *Corporations and the Cold War* (New York: Monthly Review Press, 1969), pp. 164–66.

106. See Karl Schriftgiesser, *Business Comes of Age* (New York: Harper & Brothers, 1960), p. 128.

107. *Ibid.*, p. 132.

108. See Harry B. Price, *op. cit.*, pp. 51–54.

109. This is not to say that various corporate executives became involved in the Marshall Plan primarily to promote the sales of their particular companies or even those of American business generally. They were probably much more concerned about stemming the Communist tide in Western Europe. But for a contrary line of analysis, see Joyce and Gabriel Kolko, *The Limits of Power* (New York: Harper & Row, 1972), particularly pp. 359–83.

110. The three men who held the second-ranking post in this agency were William C. Foster, Richard M. Bissell, Jr. (a well-known CED aide), and Howard Bruce, who was the longtime head of the Baltimore National Bank, board chairman of both the Maryland Drydock Co. and Worthington Pump & Machinery Corp., a member of the BAC (from 1948 through 1950), and a director of the Baltimore & Ohio Railroad, Glenn L. Martin Co., and United States Lines.

111. See Hadley Arkes, *Bureaucracy, the Marshall Plan and the National Interest*, passim. However, Arkes did note (see pp. 270–71) that small business interests received short shrift in this operation.

112. See Theodore J. Lowi, *The End of Liberalism* (New York: Norton, 1969), p. 161.

113. It is ironic that on this occasion various high authorities in the State Department were actually advocating much higher military expenditures than were the nation's top defense officials—a case of certain civilian figures being more hawkish than the hawks.

114. See Warner R. Schilling, Paul Y. Hammond, and Glenn H. Snyder, *Strategy, Politics, and Defense Budgets* (New York: Columbia University Press, 1962), p. 308. John C. Donovan has another explanation of Acheson's hard-line foreign policy views—namely, that he had succumbed to the "Munich syndrome." There is undoubtedly a certain amount of truth to this. But, as indicated above, there were probably other forces at work too. See John C. Donovan, *The Cold Warriors*, p. 103.

115. The original senior partner in the firm, J. Harry Covington, had also served as a director of the Kennecott Copper Corp. up to his death in the early 1940s. Furthermore, one of Acheson's daughters had married a son of Boston lawyer (and World War II Stimson aide) Harvey H. Bundy, who in 1949–1950 sat on the board of the Boston Five Cents Savings Bank (which had assets of about $230 million), the Merchants National Bank of Boston (which had assets of almost $150 million), and the medium-sized Tampa Electric Co.

116. Another influential agency during the Korean War was the Defense Production Administration, which was headed by Buffalo lawyer Manly Fleischmann, a director of the big Equitable Life Assurance Society.

117. See Stephen K. Bailey, *Congress Makes a Law: The Story Behind the Employment Act of 1946* (New York: Columbia University Press, 1950), passim.

118. Another major measure adopted shortly thereafter was the Taft-Hartley Act of 1947, which was passed over President Truman's veto by a strong anti-labor bloc in Congress. This hotly disputed bill was sponsored largely by arch-conservative interests such as the NAM (which actually drafted certain key sections of it) and Ohio's Senator Robert A. Taft, who represented the "old guard" in American business and politics. The more moderate CED, on the other hand, favored a distinctly milder measure, but in this instance its efforts proved unavailing. While Taft had no formal ties to the NAM, he had served briefly as a board member of the Baltimore & Ohio Railroad prior to being elected to the United States Senate in the late 1930s, and as a director of such Cincinnati concerns as the Gruen Watch Co., Central Trust Co., and Covington and Cincinnati Bridge Co. for an even longer period (in the case of the last two companies, up through 1947). Furthermore, although it is rarely noted, a strong anti-labor feeling may have permeated the wealthy Taft family. For instance, it was the Senator's father-in-law, railroad lawyer Lloyd Bowers, who instituted the injunction proceedings which ultimately led to the trial and imprisonment of Eugene V. Debs for his role in the Pullman strike of 1894. For more on the Taft-Hartley Act and the economic links and views of Robert A. Taft and other members of his family, see Karl Schriftgiesser's *Business and Public Policy*, pp. 161–62, and his *Business Comes of Age*, p. 141, R. Alton Lee, *Truman and Taft-Hartley* (Lexington: University of Kentucky Press, 1970), pp. 63–66, James T. Patterson, *Mr. Republican: A Biography of Robert A. Taft* (Boston: Houghton Mifflin, 1972), pp. 61 and 503–09, and Irving Bernstein, *The Lean Years*, p. 190.

119. See Karl Schriftgiesser, *Business and Public Policy*, p. 20, also his *Business Comes of Age*, pp. vii and 99, and Sidney Hyman, *The Lives of William Benton*, pp. 300–01. Bailey made few references to the CED in his study, in large part because it operated very quietly and not as an ordinary pressure group. Yet in his concluding remarks, Bailey noted (see p. 238) that the CED, U.S. Chamber of Commerce, and the relatively unknown Machinery and Allied Products Institute "...were of great importance in shaping the substance of the final bill." Bailey, unfortunately, did not delve into the politico-economic nature of the CED, which even then was a key component of America's emerging economic establishment. He seems to have labored under the erroneous impression that the NAM reflected the thinking of most major corporate leaders.

120. During the postwar years the Bureau of the Budget was also directed largely by men who had no noteworthy socio-economic ties. And the President's own administrative staff, which was still relatively small, was made up primarily of personal friends and political figures. Even former St. Louis attorney Clark Clifford, one of Truman's ablest advisors, had no important corporate connections.

121. See Edward S. Flash, Jr., *Economic Advice and Presidential Leadership: The Council of Economic Advisers* (New York: Columbia University Press, 1965), p. 21, and Hugh S. Norton, *The Employment Act and the Council of Economic Advisers, 1946–1976* (Columbia: University of South Carolina Press, 1977), pp. 107–112.

122. Since the early 1940s Clark had also served on the board of the American National Bank of Cheyenne (a medium-sized concern) and as a director of the Omaha branch of the Federal Reserve Bank of Kansas City, links that might indicate a pro-business leaning. However, he had also been associated politically with Wyoming's liberal Senator Joseph O'Mahoney, and perhaps partly for this reason, did not generally take a conservative line.

123. One reason the liberally oriented Council of Economic Advisers did not have more influence in administration affairs was because of the effective counterforce posed by the recently appointed head of the Federal Reserve System, Scott Paper Co. president Thomas B. McCabe, who was a member of the BAC and a trustee of the CED.

124. Dean became chairman of the AEC when Lilienthal relinquished this post in 1950. Dean's place was, in turn, taken by T. Keith Glennan, who since 1947 had been head of the

Case Institute of Technology. Lewis Strauss also resigned in 1950, and was replaced by another New York businessman, Thomas E. Murray, the longtime president of the Metropolitan Engineering Co. (and a former director of the Chrysler Corp. and the Bank of New York). Sumner Pike was succeeded in 1952 by Eugene Zuckert, a onetime Harvard Business School professor, who had held various posts in the federal government since 1945.

125. See Richard G. Hewlett and Francis Duncan, *A History of the United States Atomic Energy Commission* (University Park: Pennsylvania State University Press, 1969), Vol. II, pp. 362–409. The assets of the four companies with which Strauss was connected in 1946 totaled over $850 million. Strauss's place on the board of the United States Leather Co. was taken almost immediately by his brother, L. Z. Morris Strauss, who was also a director of the (then small) Polaroid Corp. and the much larger Studebaker Corp.

126. The only one of these New Deal appointees to serve on a corporate board preceding his appointment to the High Court was Kentucky's Stanley Reed, and his affiliation was with the Bank of Maysville, a small hometown institution.

127. See Leon Friedman and Fred L. Israel (eds.), *The Justices of the United States Supreme Court, 1789–1969*, Vol. IV, pp. 2595–97.

128. See Friedman and Israel, *op. cit.*, Vol. IV, p. 2699, and Henry J. Abraham, *Justices and Presidents*, pp. 224 and 231.

129. See Eugene C. Gerhart, *America's Advocate: Robert H. Jackson*, p. 38, and Friedman and Israel, *op. cit.*, Vol. IV, pp. 2543–62.

130. Initially, this post was offered to former federal judge and high-ranking defense official Robert Patterson, but Truman quickly realized that he sorely needed Patterson to replace Henry Stimson as Secretary of War, and persuaded Patterson to accept this important Cabinet office instead.

131. See Friedman and Israel, *op. cit.*, Vol. IV, pp. 2617–18.

132. According to various reports, Clark grew considerably in stature in his later years on the Court. See Henry J. Abraham, *op. cit.*, pp. 229–30.

133. The first half of the 1940s is not treated here because World War II created many atypical conditions in governmental recruitment and operation.

134. In the computation of these figures, George C. Marshall has been counted twice, as Secretary of State and as Secretary of Defense. W. Averell Harriman has also been treated as a multiple officeholder, as Ambassador to Great Britain and to the Soviet Union, and as Secretary of Commerce.

135. This is a higher percentage than that arrived at by Gabriel Kolko in *The Roots of American Foreign Policy*. He found that over a longer span (1944–1960), approximately 60 percent of the key positions in the State and Defense (or War) Departments were occupied by men associated with corporate law firms, big banks, and other business enterprises (see pp. 18–21).

CHAPTER 4

The Eisenhower Administration

In 1952 the American people turned away from the Democratic party and elected an idolized World War II general, Dwight D. Eisenhower, as President of the United States. Indeed, such was Eisenhower's popularity that he was reelected by an even greater margin (almost 10 million votes) in 1956, thereby giving the Republican party eight years of uninterrupted rule.

Aside from the areas of civil rights and the cold war, the Eisenhower administration has generally been characterized as a period of relative tranquility in which the nation attempted to return to a course of moderation after two decades of rather turbulent Democratic control. The amiable Eisenhower was widely proclaimed to be a middle-of-the-roader, or to use another politically appealing phrase, as a man who believed in "dynamic conservatism." Few new domestic programs were initiated under Eisenhower, and his foreign policy was designed primarily to contain the real or imagined threats posed by various Communist forces in the world.

There was also relatively little change in the economic structure of the country during this period. Outside of a marked increase in relative size, there was only one noteworthy alteration in the makeup of the nation's "top 20" industrial firms (half of which were still oil companies), and that was the emergence of IBM, which by 1960 had assets of over $1.5 billion, as a new member of this elite group.[1] There was, likewise, little shift in the overall ranking of America's major public utilities, for AT&T remained in a class by itself in this area. Perhaps the most noteworthy development here was the rapid growth of a number of big natural gas companies in the southwestern section of the country. In the realm of transportation, the railroads, following a long-term trend, continued to lag.[2] But the nation's larger airlines had grown in assets to the point where three of these comparatively new concerns—American Airlines, Pan-American World Airways, and United Air Lines—had climbed into the "top 20" category.

The world of finance, however, deserves special attention because of certain mergers which took place during this period and because of the unusual, partially concealed power exercised by some of these institutions.

123

For example, in 1955 the Bank of Manhattan was merged into the Rockefeller-controlled Chase National Bank, which thereby moved up one notch in the national rankings. At the same time, the Stillman-Rockefeller-dominated National City Bank took over the long Morgan-linked First National Bank of New York, which transaction marked a further decline in the steadily eroding influence of the House of Morgan. Four years later, two friendly firms, the Guaranty Trust Co. and J.P. Morgan & Co., joined forces to form the Morgan Guaranty Trust Co., while the Chemical Bank & Trust Co. bought out the (probably Harkness-dominated) New York Trust Co. Hence in 1960 the nation's "top 10" banks were as shown in Table 6.

Also by 1960 three giant life insurance companies—Metropolitan, Prudential, and Equitable—had each amassed more than $10 billion in assets, and would thus appear to have overshadowed almost all of the nation's large commercial banks.[3] Yet this was not really the case, for, unknown to most people outside the financial community, many of these big banks had huge unreported trust funds that often dwarfed their officially stated assets. For instance, in 1961 it was reliably estimated that the Morgan Guaranty Trust Co. had about $8.5 billion in its trust department, in addition to its reported total assets of $4.4 billion.[4] Even some of the seemingly smaller Wall Street concerns, such as the Bank of New York and the United States Trust Co., both of which had formally declared assets of well under $1 billion, had trust

TABLE 6

America's Top 10 Banks in 1960

	1952 Assets ($ millions)	1960 Assets ($ millions)
1. Bank of America, Cal.	8,202	11,942
2. Chase Manhattan Bank, N.Y.C.	5,743*	9,260
3. First National City Bank, N.Y.C.	6,117*	8,668
4. Chemical Bank New York Trust Co.	2,048*	4,540
5. Morgan Guaranty Trust Co., N.Y.C.	3,149*	4,424
6. Manufacturers Trust Co., N.Y.C.	2,949	3,974
7. Security First National Bank, Los Angeles	2,017	3,594
8. Bankers Trust Co., N.Y.C.	2,137	3,430
9. First National Bank, Chicago	2,829	3,136
10. Continental Illinois National Bank & Trust Co., Chicago	2,801	2,886

*These represent, in the above order, the 1952 pre-merger totals of the Chase National Bank, National City Bank, Chemical Bank & Trust Co., and the Guaranty Trust Co.

NOTE: This list may be misleading in one respect, for it does not include any bank holding companies, one of which, the California-based Western Bancorporation, had assets of over $5 billion.

department funds of $5 billion or more, and hence deserved to be ranked in or near the nation's "top 10."[5] Indeed, such were the financial resources of these firms that by 1960 institutional investors, led mainly by the commercial banks, held almost 25 percent of the shares listed on the New York Stock Exchange, and this trend was accelerating at a sharp rate.[6]

Another noteworthy development during the Eisenhower years was the changing nature of the leadership of one of the nation's most important civic groups, the New York-based Council on Foreign Relations.[7] Up to the early 1950s the CFR had been dominated by a number of influential economic forces, one of which was the House of Morgan. By 1953, however, the key positions in the CFR had been taken over by men who were either a part of or closely aligned with the rising Rockefeller interests, as may be seen in the following summary description of its top officials:[8]

Board Chairman	John J. McCloy (board chairman, Chase Manhattan Bank)	Trustee of the Rockefeller Foundation (up to 1959); director of various major corporations
President	Henry M. Wriston (former president, Brown University; post-1955 president of the CFR-backed American Assembly)	Trustee of the Northwestern Mutual Life Insurance Co.; son, Walter B. Wriston, a high official of the Stillman-Rockefeller-dominated (First) National City Bank of New York
Vice-President	David Rockefeller (high executive, Chase Manhattan Bank)	
Treasurer	Elliott V. Bell (chairman of the executive committee, McGraw-Hill Publishing Co.)	Trustee of the New York Life Insurance Co. and the CED; post-1955 director of the Chase Manhattan Bank
Secretary	Frank Altschul (board chairman, General American Investors Co., a concern controlled largely by Lehman Bros.)	Trustee of the CED

The executive director of the CFR was a much lesser-known figure, George S. Franklin, Jr., who at first glance would appear to have had no such elitist links. However, Franklin had been David Rockefeller's roommate in college and had married one of his cousins, the former Helena Edgell—still another sign that the CFR was firmly allied with the Rockefeller interests.[9]

The man who led the country during this eight-year period was not the usual type of person to be elected President, but rather was someone who, for the first time since the early post-Civil War years, was elevated to this position primarily because of the fame he had achieved as a military leader in a major war. General Eisenhower, a West Point graduate, had spent almost all his adult life as an Army officer in a career that was capped first by his successful command of the Allied forces in Europe during World War II, and then, for the next three years, as George C. Marshall's replacement as Army Chief of Staff.

In 1948 Eisenhower resigned from the Army to become president of Columbia University, a post offered to him largely at the instigation of IBM head Thomas J. Watson (who was a trustee of the CED and a director of the Guaranty Trust Co.), either in an effort to improve the school's financial status through Ike-inspired fundraising activities or as part of an attempt to groom Eisenhower for a presidential nomination.[10] Whatever the original intent, while Eisenhower was president of Columbia, a drive was quietly organized in various major business circles to build up substantial support for the General as the Republican party's 1952 candidate. Much of this effort was reportedly carried out by such relatively minor figures as William H. Burnham, a partner in F.S. Smithers & Co. (a small brokerage house) and Clifford Roberts, a partner in Reynolds & Co. (a second-tier securities firm probably controlled by the wealthy Reynolds tobacco family). However, judging from much other evidence, it would appear that the most influential forces behind this promotional campaign were those of big business. For instance, in December 1949 Burnham arranged for a special dinner at which Eisenhower was to meet, as Peter Lyon has put it, such important men "... as the chairman of Standard Oil of New Jersey, the president of six other big oil corporations (Standard of California, Texaco, Socony-Vacuum, and the like), the executive vice-president of J.P. Morgan & Co., the presidents of another ten assorted corporations, and a stray Vanderbilt."[11] Moreover, Eisenhower had been introduced even earlier, through a special study group, to various key figures in the Council on Foreign Relations, and a plan was devised in the fall of 1949 to create a new organization known as the American Assembly (in essence, the CFR study group expanded through the addition of other leaders), whose primary purpose was reputedly to build up the presidential prospects of Dwight D. Eisenhower.[12] In short, even at this early stage Ike had tremendous support in the business community.

In December 1950 Eisenhower stepped down as president of Columbia in order to assume the role of supreme commander of the newly authorized NATO forces in Europe. This, of course, removed him from the domestic political scene. Nevertheless, strenuous efforts continued to be made to boost his stock as the party's best "centrist" choice for the Republican presidential nomination in 1952. For example, in the summer of 1951 a group known as "Citizens for Eisenhower" was formed to generate grass-roots support for the General. This organization was directed by such prominent businessmen as Wall Street financier John Hay Whitney (one of whose partners, James F. Brownlee, was vice-chairman of the CED), New York investment banker

Sidney J. Weinberg (a longtime member of the BAC), former Studebaker executive Paul Hoffman (who was both a member of the BAC and a trustee of the CED), and W. Alton Jones, the president of the Cities Service Co., who was one of Ike's close friends and regular golfing companions.[13]

With this kind of influential backing, the Eisenhower forces were able to repel the challenge of the party's right wing, which ardently supported Ohio's Senator Robert A. Taft, and to secure the presidential nomination for the extraordinarily popular general, who then went on to score a smashing victory over his more liberal and intellectually inclined Democratic opponent, former Illinois Governor Adlai Stevenson.[14] Hence although the American people elected Eisenhower President primarily because of his rol as a military leader, it was the nation's business establishment which had been mainly responsible for initiating and promoting his candidacy. Furthermore, Eisenhower was himself formally linked with the country's major economic interests, for he had served as a trustee of the CED from 1950 to 1952, and his brother, Milton, an academic figure, had been associated with this group in the late 1940s.[15] Thus Eisenhower was probably as much at home among corporate executives as he was with high-ranking military men.

MAJOR ADMINISTRATIVE AND DIPLOMATIC APPOINTMENTS

When the Republicans took over the federal government, there was an almost complete restaffing of the top administrative positions, as one might expect after two decades of Democratic rule. For the premier post of Secretary of State Eisenhower chose, curiously, a man he hardly knew, former Wall Street lawyer (and postwar diplomatic troubleshooter) John Foster Dulles.[16] Much has been written about this controversial figure, most of which has dealt with his diplomatic background and accomplishments and his strong moralistic bent. Dulles's father had been a minister, and his son was, as a result, much inclined throughout his life to take an almost Calvinistic view of the world, and of America's enemies in particular. Dulles's family was also steeped in diplomatic affairs. His uncle, Robert Lansing, had been Woodrow Wilson's second Secretary of State, and his maternal grandfather, John W. Foster, had served briefly in a similar capacity under Benjamin Harrison (in addition to holding a number of other prominent diplomatic posts). These men provided the young Dulles with easy entree to many important Washington circles during the Wilsonian years and gave him the opportunity to participate in some of the high-level negotiations that were conducted at the end of the war in Europe. In the post-World War II period, following more than twenty years of successful legal practice, Dulles, though not a Democrat, was asked by President Truman to handle a series of major diplomatic assignments, the most important of which was the conclusion of a peace treaty with our recent military foe, Japan.

However, these sides of Dulles's life have probably been overemphasized, and while some studies mention the fact that he was a former highly paid partner in the New York law firm of Sullivan & Cromwell, they do not give proper stress to this concern's place in the business and legal world. Dulles was actually the senior partner in one of the world's largest corporate law firms, one which was closely linked to various key segments of the business community. Its most important client was probably the Standard Oil Co. of New Jersey.[17] And Dulles himself served until about 1950 as a director of the American Agricultural Chemical Co., American Bank Note Co. (two medium-sized concerns), the big Babcock & Wilcox Co., and the International Nickel Co. of Canada, Ltd., in which various American interests had large holdings. Moreover, Dulles sat up to 1953 on the board of the Bank of New York, which had, by conservative estimate, several billion dollars in trust funds in addition to its formally disclosed assets of $464 million. After many years as a trustee, Dulles also served in the early 1950s as board chairman of both the Carnegie Endowment for International Peace and the Rockefeller Foundation, which was the biggest single stockholder (roughly 3.5 percent) in the Standard Oil Co. of New Jersey. Clearly, Dulles was an integral part of America's big business establishment.[18]

Dulles presided over the State Department longer than any man before him in the twentieth century, except for Cordell Hull, who never exercised much influence on foreign policy. But in the spring of 1959 he was stricken with cancer and forced to step down. As his successor, President Eisenhower selected a longtime Massachusetts political leader and onetime Boston newspaper editor, Christian A. Herter, who had served for a decade (1943–53) as a member of Congress, then for four years as governor of Massachusetts. In 1957 he had been tapped to become Dulles's chief aide, a position that made his later elevation to Secretary of State an apparently logical move.[19]

Herter did not have a great deal of experience in diplomatic affairs, merely that of an intelligent and concerned Congressman who had served briefly (for two years) on the House Foreign Affairs Committee. Why then, one might ask, was he chosen for these two high State Department posts? One reason may have been his elite family links. Herter had, like Paul Nitze, married into the wealthy Pratt family of New York City, which clan had once been heavily involved in both the ownership and operation of the early Standard Oil companies (one of Mrs. Herter's uncles, Herbert L. Pratt, had been president or board chairman of the Standard Oil Co. of New York up to 1934).[20] Furthermore, one of Herter's sons, Christian, Jr., who was a Boston lawyer, served on the board of the New York-based Foreign Policy Association, the two top officials of which were Eustace Seligman, a senior partner in Sullivan & Cromwell, and Emile Soubry, an executive vice-president of the Standard Oil Co. of New Jersey.[21] Thus, though not as overtly pro-business as John Foster Dulles, Christian Herter was no less an elitist.[22]

In the Treasury Department major corporate interests took over the reins of control in most emphatic fashion, as may readily be seen by a glance at the following summary portraits (which are more complete than those found in most official sources):

Secretary of the Treasury

George M. Humphrey (1953–1957) — No prior governmental experience; president, M. A. Hanna Co., Cleveland (1929–1952); board chairman, Pittsburgh Consolidation Coal Co. (1947–1952); executive committee chairman of the National Steel Corp. (1930–1952); exec. comm. chairman of Industrial Rayon Corp. (1942–1952); member of the BAC (1942–1952, all but the first year of which as a member of its executive committee); trustee of the CED (1950–1952); director of the Phelps Dodge Corp. (1938–1952) and National City Bank of Cleveland (1934–52)

Robert B. Anderson (1957–1961) — Deputy Secretary of Defense (1954–55); Secretary of the Navy (1953–54); president of Ventures, Ltd. (1956–1957); official or director, Dresser Industries, Inc. (1956–1957); general counsel or general manager, W. T. Waggoner estate, Texas (1937–1953);

Under Secretary of the Treasury

Marion B. Folsom (1953–1955) — No prior governmental experience; treasurer, Eastman Kodak Co. (1935–53); president, Eastman Savings & Loan Assn. of Rochester (1947–1952); member of the BAC (1936–1949 and 1951–1955, vice-chairman 1945–1949); trustee of the CED (1943–1952, chairman or vice chairman 1945–1952); director of Rochester Savings Bank (1931–1949) and Lincoln Rochester Trust Co. (1946–1949)

H. Chapman Rose (1955–56) — Assistant Secretary of Commerce (1953–55); partner, Cleveland law firm of Jones, Day, Cockley & Reavis (1939–52, except during World War II); director of Brush Beryllium Co. (at least 1948–52) and two other lesser concerns (at least 5 years)

Fred C. Scribner, Jr. (1957–1961) — General counsel, Treasury Department (1955–1957); general counsel, Republican

Anderson (cont.)	president, Mid-Continent Oil & Gas Association (1947–1951); deputy chairman, Federal Reserve Bank of Dallas (1946–1952); member of BAC (1956–1960); trustee, CED (1956–1957); director of the Hanover Bank, N.Y. (1957), American Overseas Investing Co. (1957), Missouri-Pacific Railroad (1956–1957), and two Canadian banks (1957)	Scribner (cont.)	National Committee (1952–1955); partner, Hutchinson, Pierce, Atwood & Scribner, Portland, Me., law firm (1935–55);-president vice-president and treasurer, Bates Manufacturing Co., Me. (1946–55); secretary and director, Rockland-Rockport Lime Co. (1935–55)

The first two top-tier officials to be appointed to the Treasury Department in 1953 were men who were intimately associated with the nation's business establishment. George M. Humphrey, who was a BAC-CED figure, had been strongly recommended to Eisenhower (who had never previously met him) by Ike's friend, former Army General Lucius Clay, and financier Sidney Weinberg, both of whom were BAC leaders.[23] Unlike Marion Folsom, who did not hold a top-tier high corporate post,[24] Humphrey was an extremely important business leader. In fact, he was the most influential figure to serve as Secretary of the Treasury since the days of Andrew Mellon, for Humphrey headed a huge economic complex controlled by the M. A. Hanna Co. (the company founded by McKinley's major backer, Mark Hanna). It included such giant concerns as the National Steel Corp. (one of the nation's five biggest steel companies), the Pittsburgh Consolidation Coal Co. (the nation's largest coal company), the Hanna Mining Co., and probably the National City Bank of Cleveland.[25] Not surprisingly, Humphrey soon emerged as one of the dominant figures in Eisenhower's Cabinet, especially in financial matters.[26] When Folsom stepped down as Under Secretary of the Treasury in 1955 to become head of the Department of Health, Education and Welfare, he was replaced by Ohio attorney H. Chapman Rose, who, prior to his appointment as Assistant Secretary of the Treasury in 1953, had been a partner in the Cleveland law firm of Jones, Day, Cockley & Reavis, which concern had long served as general counsel to the M. A. Hanna Co. and various other enterprises in the area.[27] In short, Rose was one of Humphrey's lawyers.

When Humphrey resigned his Cabinet post shortly after the start of Eisenhower's second term of office, he was succeeded by another elite figure,

Robert B. Anderson, who had been a longtime Texas businessman (primarily oil and finance) before his entry into the Defense Department in 1953.[28] The ambitious Anderson apparently did not find this agency much to his liking, for he served in it for only about 2½ years. At this juncture Anderson chose to sever a number of his Texas ties and become much more of a New York Establishment figure. Although he was appointed head of a comparatively small Canadian holding company, Ventures, Ltd., and a high executive of a Texas-based company, Dresser Industries, he also became a member of the board of the Rockefeller-dominated American Overseas Investing Co., the big Hanover Bank of New York, and the Missouri-Pacific Railroad.[29] Even more revealing was the fact that Anderson served as a trustee of the CED in 1956–1957 and as a member of the BAC from 1956 through 1960 (his years of Cabinet office). Thus Anderson was as closely linked to America's business establishment as his more famous predecessor.[30]

In like manner, the Defense Department was virtually taken over by major corporate interests during the Eisenhower years. Look, for example, at the following politico-economic analysis of the occupants of the top two positions in the Pentagon during this eight-year period of Republican rule:

Secretary of Defense		Deputy Secretary of Defense	
Charles E. Wilson (1953–1957)	No prior governmental experience; president, General Motors (1941–1953, vice-president 1929–1940); member of the BAC (1947–1951; member of executive committee 1950–1951); director of the National Bank of Detroit (1942–53)	Roger M. Kyes (1953–1954)	No prior governmental experience; high-ranking executive, General Motors (1948–53); apparently no other major corporate links
		Robert B. Anderson (1954–1955)	Secretary of the Navy (1953–1954); various Texas business connections
		Reuben R. Robertson, Jr. (1955–1957)	No prior governmental experience; high-ranking official, Champion Paper & Fibre Co., Ohio (1946–1957, vice-chairman 1956 on); member of the BAC (1951–1955, one of its 4 vice-chairmen, 1953–1955); director of the Procter & Gamble Co. (1949–55), B. F. Goodrich Co. (1953–55), and Cincinnati &

		Robertson (*cont.*)	Suburban Bell Telephone Co., subsidiary of AT&T (1952–55)
Neil H. McElroy (1957–1959)	No prior governmental experience; president, Procter & Gamble Co., Ohio (1948–1957, lesser official, 1929–1947); member of the BAC (1957–59); director of the General Electric Co. (1950–57) and Chrysler Corp. (1953–57)	Donald A. Quarles (1957–1959)	Secretary of the Air Force (1955–1957); Assistant Secretary of Defense for Research and Development (1953–1955); executive, Western Electric Co., subsidiary of AT&T (1919–1953)
Thomas S. Gates, Jr. (1959–1961)	Secretary of the Navy (1957–1959); Under Secretary of the Navy (1953–1957); longtime official of Philadelphia investment banking firm of Drexel & Co. (partner 1940–1953, limited partner 1953–1961); director of the Scott Paper Co., Pa. (1937–1959) and International Basic Economy Corp. (1947–1954)	James H. Douglas, Jr. (1959–1961)	Secretary of the Air Force (1957–1959); Under Secretary of the Air Force (1953–1957); partner, Chicago law firm of Gardner, Carton & Douglas (1934–1953); director of the Metropolitan Life Insurance Co. (1942–1953), American Airlines (1951–1952), and Chicago Title & Trust Co. (1939–1953)

As already noted, two of Eisenhower's three Secretaries of Defense were, or had been, formally affiliated with the Establishment-dominated Business Advisory Council. And the third, Thomas S. Gates, Jr., was a member of a Philadelphia banking firm which prior to World War II had long been linked with New York's House of Morgan. In addition, Gates had served up to 1954 as a director of the Rockefeller-controlled International Basic Economy Corporation.[31]

The same kinds of links characterized most of the figures who served as Deputy Secretary of Defense during this period. Robert B. Anderson had been Deputy Chairman of the Federal Reserve Bank of Dallas and, for a much shorter period of time, a director of the Southwestern Bell Telephone Co., an AT&T subsidiary.[32] His successor, Reuben Robertson, was not only a major executive, but a prominent member of the BAC and a director of B. F. Goodrich, Procter & Gamble, two Canadian banks, and a southern Ohio subsidiary of AT&T.³³ While Eisenhower's last Deputy Secretary of Defense, James H. Douglas, Jr., was not connected with the BAC or CED, he was the only Chicago lawyer (out of over ten thousand) to serve on the board of a major New York City financial institution, Metropolitan Life, in the postwar period, a probably important factor in his recruitment and rise as a federal official.

The same appointment pattern also prevailed to a considerable extent in the selection of the three civilian armed service secretaries during the Eisenhower administration, as may be seen by the following brief biographical sketches:

Secretary of the Army		*Secretary of the Navy*	
Robert T. Stevens (1953–1955)	No prior governmental experience; president or board chairman, J. P. Stevens & Co. (1929–1953); chairman, Federal Reserve Bank of New York (1949–1952); member of the BAC (1941–1955, chairman, 1951–1952); director of the Mutual Life Insurance Co. (1938–52), General Foods Corp. (1946–52), General Electric Co. (1947–52), and New York Telephone Co., an AT&T subsidiary (1946–52)	Robert B. Anderson (1953–1954)	See text
		Charles S. Thomas (1954–1957)	Under Secretary of the Navy (January–August 1953); Assistant Secretary of Defense for Supply and Logistics (1953–1954); high official, Foreman & Clark, Inc., Los Angeles (1932–1953); director of Broadway-Hale Stores, Inc., Los Angeles (1947–52), Lockheed Aircraft Corp. (1946–52), and the Pacific Finance Corp. (1948–52); former member of the Republican National Finance Committee
Wilbur M. Brucker (1955–1961)	General counsel, Defense Department (1953–1954); partner, Detroit law firm of Clark, Klein, Brucker & Waples (1937–1954); director of First Federal Savings & Loan Association, Detroit (1938–1954)	Thomas S. Gates, Jr. (1957–1959)	See text
		William B. Franke (1959–1961)	Under Secretary of the Navy (1957–59); Assistant

134 Elites in American History

Franke (*cont.*)	Secretary of the Navy (1954–1957); special assistant to Secretary of Defense (1951–52); partner, New York accounting firm of Franke, North, Hannon & Withey, (1928–54); head, John Simmons Co., Newark (1938–54) and General Shale Products Corp., N.Y. (early 1950s); director of Julius Kayser & Co., N.Y.C. (1945–53) and Carolina, Clinchfield & Ohio Railway (1946–52)

Secretary of Air Force

Harold E. Talbott (1953–1955)	No prior governmental experience; member of the Republican National Finance Committee; board chairman, Standard Cap & Seal Corp., N.Y.C. (1934–52); vice-president Talbott Co., N.Y.C. realty firm (1942–52); director of the Chrysler Corp. (1928–52), Mead Corp. (least 1921–52), Electric Autolite Co. (1935–52), Madison Square Garden Corp. (1936–52), and Baldwin-Lima-Hamilton Corp. (1951–52)
Donald A. Quarles (1955–1957)	See text
James H. Douglas, Jr. (1957–1959)	See text
Dudley C. Sharp (1959–1961)	Under Secretary of the Air Force (1959); other Defense Department posts (1955–59); high official, Mission Manufacturing Co., Houston (1927–55); president, Texas Fund, Inc. (1950–55)

These data plainly show that many of the officials chosen to serve as Secretary of the Army, Navy, or Air Force were elite figures, with ties to major business groups or large corporations. Even such a comparatively minor executive as Charles S. Thomas, who was merely head of a small Los Angeles department store, had more than one key link to influential economic interests, for he had served on the board of both the Lockheed Aircraft Corp., one of the Navy's biggest contractors, and the Pacific Finance Corp., a concern apparently dominated by Lockheed interests.[34]

Hence the nation's business establishment had a great deal to do with the top-tier staffing of the three most important departments in the Eisenhower administration. Much of the recruitment for high federal office was obviously channeled through such influential organizations as the BAC and CED, with an assist in the foreign policy area from such institutions as the Council on Foreign Relations and the Rockefeller Foundation. In fact, as one financial journal later pointed out, the Business Advisory Council "... really came into its own when BC member (he joined as president of Columbia University) Dwight Eisenhower entered the White House."[35] According to this source, "the actual selection of the Cabinet was done when the Council held its fall meeting at the posh Cloister at Sea Island, Georgia, just after the election. As Eisenhower pondered the possible choices, Sidney Weinberg and General Lucius Clay, then chairman of the Continental Can Co., shuttled back and forth between Sea Island and the new President's vacation retreat at the nearby Augusta National Golf Club."[36]

This account, while accurate as far as it goes, tells only part of the story. It fails to mention the other half of the core of America's powerful business establishment, the closely allied CED, which probably played an equally important role in this recruitment process.[37] It was no accident that the two men who served as Secretary of the Treasury during the Eisenhower administration had been associated with both the BAC and CED, or that the first two Secretaries of Defense were, or had been, members of the BAC. Nor was it a matter of chance that Eisenhower's first Secretary of State, John Foster Dulles, was a well-connected Wall Street lawyer (and former board chairman of the Rockefeller Foundation), and his successor, Christian Herter, was a socio-economic elite figure. These three departments were, in short, very much under the influence of America's major corporate interests.[38]

A number of the other Cabinet posts in the Eisenhower administration were, however, not filled by such elite figures. Ike's first Attorney General, Herbert Brownell, Jr., was a New York lawyer who, while he had some corporate ties, was known primarily for his work as a national political strategist. Although Brownell was a partner in a Wall Street law firm known as Lord, Day & Lord, this was, at best, a second-tier concern, and none of Brownell's directorships were of a particularly significant nature.[39] The canny Brownell had, more importantly, served as manager of Thomas E. Dewey's two presidential campaigns in 1944 and 1948. In this connection he had been chairman of the Republican National Committee in the mid-1940s, although he reportedly had been forced to maintain a low profile in 1952 for fear of arousing the wrath of many of Taft's anti-Establishment Midwestern supporters.[40] When Brownell decided to step down as Attorney General in 1958, he was replaced by another primarily political figure, William P. Rogers, who had held a number of governmental posts over the years, the most prominent of which was as Brownell's top aide in the Justice Department. For a brief period in the early 1950s Rogers had also been a partner in the New York law firm of Dwight, Royall, Harris, Koegel & Caskey.

However, this concern did not rank among the giants in the field, as shown by the fact that none of its senior partners served on the board of a major corporation during this period.

The position of Secretary of the Interior was also filled during the Eisenhower administration by men whose business connections were of comparatively little significance, as seen by the following summary analysis of the two occupants of this office:

Secretary of the Interior	Political and Social Background
Douglas J. McKay (1953–1956)	Governor of Oregon (1949–1953); state legislator (1934–1949, except during World War II); owner, Douglas McKay Chevrolet auto agency, Salem (1927–1955); apparently no major directorship ties
Fred Seaton (1956–1961)	Assistant Secretary of Defense for Legislative Affairs (1953–1955); U.S. Senator, Nebraska (1951–1953); state legislator (1945–1949); president, Seaton Publishing Co. and other newspaper and broadcasting companies, Hastings, Nebraska (since 1937); apparently no "outside" directorship ties

In short, it seems fair to say that these two leaders were appointed largely for geo-political reasons, as representatives of the Western section of the country, which had come to look upon the Interior Department as its special preserve.

As one might expect, the position of Secretary of Agriculture was occupied throughout the Eisenhower administration by another Westerner, Utah's Ezra Taft Benson. This highly conservative executive had no prior government experience.[41] He had instead worked for almost twenty years as a high official of various farm cooperative organizations, many of which were even then very sizable economic enterprises.[42] Benson was also a rather prominent figure in the Mormon Church, a close-knit body which had long controlled numerous business concerns in Utah and has been described as a "theocratic corporation."[43] Perhaps of even greater importance in explaining Benson's marked pro-business and "big farmer" thinking was the fact that he had served from 1946 to 1950 as a trustee of the Farm Foundation, a Chicago-based organization which was apparently dominated by a number of big food processing and farm supply companies favorably disposed toward large-scale, heavily mechanized agriculture. For instance, in the early 1950s the foundation's board was made up of such big businessmen as Ralph Budd, the longtime former head of the Chicago, Burlington and Quincy Railroad; John Stuart, the board chairman of the Quaker Oats Co.; and Chris L. Christensen, a high executive of the Chicago-based Celotex Corp. (all three of whom were directors of the International Harvester Co.); and such farm spokesmen as Oscar Johnston, who was president of the Delta Pine and Land

Co., the largest plantation in the entire South (he was also a director of the Illinois Central Railroad); and Allan B. Kline, the president of the influential American Farm Bureau Federation. In fact, the strong support of Kline and the AFBF was reportedly a crucial factor in Benson's selection as Secretary of Agriculture.[44] It is not surprising then that Benson advocated policies which generally favored the large farmers and the big food processing and farm supply interests.[45]

The Departments of Commerce and Labor were manned at the top by people who were believed to be responsive to the particular needs and desires of their organizational constituencies.[46] This is readily demonstrated by the following comparative analysis of the types of persons appointed to these key posts during the Eisenhower years:

Secretary of Commerce		*Secretary of Labor*	
Sinclair Weeks (1953–1958)	Little governmental experience (although a prominent Republican party official); president or board chairman, United-Carr Fastener Corp., Boston (1930–1952); also high official, Reed & Barton Corp. (1923–1953); director of the First National Bank of Boston (1927–1952), Gillette Co. (1941–1952), West Point Manufacturing Co. (1938–1950), Atlas Plywood Corp. (1939–1953), Pacific Mills (1940–1952), and the Pullman Co. of Chicago (1948–52)	Martin P. Durkin (January–October 1953)	No prior governmental experience; president, United Association of Journeymen Plumbers and Steamfitters of U.S. and Canada (1943–1953); state director for labor, Illinois (1933–early 1940s); director of Labor Union Life Insurance Co. (1944–1953)
		John P. Mitchell (1954–1961)	Assistant Secretary of the Army (1953); various federal welfare and personnel posts (1936–1945); vice-president, Bloomingdale's department store, subsidiary of Federated Department Stores, Inc. (1947–1953); director of personnel and industrial relations, R. H. Macy & Co., N.Y.C. (1945–1947); no outside corporate directorship links

Secretary of Commerce

Lewis L. Strauss (1958–1959)	Chairman, Atomic Energy Commission (1953–1958); member of AEC (1946–1950); consultant and financial advisor to Rockefellers (1950–1953); partner, Kuhn, Loeb & Co., N.Y.C. (1929–1947); director of the Industrial Rayon Corp. (1951–1953), General Tire & Rubber Co. (1951–1952), General American Transportation Corp. (1932–1946 and 1951–1952), Rockefeller Center, Inc., (1951–1953), and RCA (first part of 1953)
Frederick H. Mueller (1959–1961)	Under Secretary of Commerce (1958–1959); Assistant Secretary of Commerce (1955–1958); longtime partner, Mueller Furniture Co., Grand Rapids, Mich. (1914–1955); president, Furniture Mutual Insurance Co. (1941–1955); director of Peoples National Bank, Grand Rapids (1949–1958)

Organized labor was initially represented in Eisenhower's Cabinet by Martin P. Durkin, the former president of an AFL union of plumbers and steamfitters (and a longtime Democrat).[47] When he resigned ten months later in protest against the conservative orientation of the administration, he was replaced by a postwar industrial and labor relations executive of two big New York City department stores, John P. Mitchell, a man who had considerable governmental experience, primarily in the New Deal and World War II years. Though perhaps not a totally objective figure, Mitchell nonetheless held office until the end of this Republican regime.[48]

Up to the latter stages of the Eisenhower administration, the Department of Commerce was controlled by big business interests. Although neither of the concerns with which the first Secretary of Commerce, Sinclair Weeks, had held office were really large firms, he had a number of significant ties with major industrial and financial enterprises such as the Gillette (Safety Razor) Co. and the First National Bank of Boston.[49] Furthermore, as a well-connected businessman, he had served as chairman of the Republican National Finance Committee from 1947 to 1952, which undoubtedly did much to enhance his prospects for a Cabinet post. After holding office for over five years, Weeks decided to step aside in the fall of 1958. As his replacement, Eisenhower picked former New York financier Lewis Strauss, who, after having served as one of the original members of the Atomic Energy Commission in the Truman administration, had returned to the federal government a few years later when Eisenhower appointed him chairman of this important body. Strauss's ability to secure high federal office under both Democratic and Republican regimes is somewhat unusual, but may well have stemmed from the fact that he had shifted his economic allegiance during the intervening years. Before his initial appointment to the AEC, Strauss had been a partner in one of New York's major Jewish investment banking houses, Kuhn, Loeb & Co., and a director of the "our-crowd"-dominated C. I. T. Financial Corp., both of which concerns carried great weight in Democratic circles. But by the early 1950s Strauss had severed these ties and become a financial advisor to the Rockefeller brothers, who were influential supporters of the Republican party. Despite their backing, the able but often abrasive Strauss was unable to obtain Cabinet approval from a Democratically controlled Senate, in part because of the vigorous opposition of Oklahoma's powerful Robert Kerr (whose own uranium interests, which were a growing part of the Kerr-McGee Oil Industries, may not have been aided by the policies espoused by Strauss when he was AEC chairman). Stunned by this setback, Strauss had no alternative but to resign from office, which he did in mid-1959. He was succeeded by his chief aide, Frederick H. Mueller, a retired businessman who had served as a high departmental official since 1955. Before his entry into the federal government, Mueller had been a partner in the Mueller Furniture Co., president of the Furniture Mutual Insurance Co., and a director of the Peoples National Bank of Grand Rapids—all minor enterprises. Thus it was only toward the latter part of the Eisenhower administration that the top leadership of the Department of Commerce passed into the hands of someone who could be said to represent the interests of America's small businessmen.

A new Cabinet-level agency was also created at the outset of the Eisenhower administration—the Department of Health, Education and Welfare (HEW). Though established to provide aid and advice in three key social service areas, this agency was initially staffed at its highest levels by people who had a pro-business orientation.[50] The first Secretary of HEW was Mrs. Oveta Culp Hobby, who may have been chosen in part because it was felt that a woman was especially suited for the essentially "domestic" concerns of the new department. However, Mrs. Hobby was a wealthy Texas business executive (and former Southern Democrat) who had served for over fifteen years as a high official of the conservative *Houston Post*. And the first Under Secretary of HEW was Nelson A. Rockefeller, who had held various State Department posts during the Second World War, but had devoted most of his time over the years to acting as head of Rockefeller Center, Inc. (which had assets in the mid-1950s of about $150 million) and, since 1947, as president of the family-dominated International Basic Economy Corp.[51] He had also been a trustee of the CED. When Mrs. Hobby stepped down from office in 1955, she was succeeded by Establishment leader Marion Folsom, a former Eastman Kodak executive who had recently served as Under Secretary of the Treasury, but was, more importantly, a longtime key figure in both the BAC and CED.[52] Hence, up to the mid-1950s, when the appointment pattern began to change in favor of professional interests, the Department of Health, Education and Welfare was directed primarily by people whose sympathy and support for progessive measures had discernible limits.[53]

In summary, while a number of the more domestically oriented departments were headed by people drawn from various clientele groups, the influence of the nation's business leadership clearly extended in the first part of the Eisenhower administration to the newly created Department of Health, Education and Welfare, as well as to the Department of Commerce. When this fact is coupled with the heavily business-oriented recruitment pattern found in the Departments of State, Treasury, and Defense—the "big three" of the federal government—it is misleading, if not erroneous, to make light, as some studies have done, of the appointment power exerted by major corporate interests in the post-New Deal period.[54]

The influence of big business can also be seen in the pattern of appointments to the nation's two most important ambassadorial posts during the Eisenhower administration:

Ambassador to Great Britain		*Ambassador to France*	
Winthrop W. Aldrich (1953–1956)	No prior governmental or diplomatic experience; president or board chairman, Chase National Bank, N.Y.C. (1932–1953); director of the Metropolitan Life Insurance Co. (1938–52), Westinghouse Electric Corp. (1934–52), International Paper Co. (1944–52), New York	C. Douglas Dillon (1953–1957)	No prior governmental or diplomatic experience; high official, Dillon, Read & Co. (1938–1953); president, United States & Foreign Securities Corp., N.Y.C. (1947–1953); director of the Amerada Petroleum Corp. (1947–1953)

Ambassador to Great Britain		*Ambassador to France*	
	Central Railroad (1948–52), and AT&T (1931–52); trustee of the Rockefeller Foundation (1936–51); married daughter of former New York lawyer Charles B. Alexander (a longtime director of the Equitable Life Assurance Society and the Equitable Trust Co.); sister married John D. Rockefeller, Jr.		
John Hay Whitney (1956–1961)	No prior governmental or diplomatic experience; partner, J.H. Whitney & Co., N.Y.C. investment concern (1947–61); board chairman, Freeport Sulphur Co. (1949–1956); publisher, *New York Herald Tribune* (1958–1961); member of the BAC (1953–1961); director of the Great Northern Paper Co. (1951–1957)	Amory Houghton (1957–1961)	No prior governmental or diplomatic experience (father had been Ambassador to both Great Britain and Germany in the 1920s); president or board chairman, Corning Glass Works, N.Y. (1930–56); trustee of the CED (1949–1956); director of the Metropolitan Life Insurance Co. (1940–1961), National (or First National) City Bank of New York (1933–1957), Erie Railroad (1942–1956), and Investors Management Co. (1946–53)

It would have been hard to find four more elitist figures than these officials, none of whom had any governmental or diplomatic experience. Three of the four were from New York City, and the other, Amory Houghton, was an executive from an upstate family which had long maintained close ties with certain major New York City financial institutions, particularly the Metropolitan Life Insurance Co. and the National (or First National) City Bank.[55] All were extremely wealthy. Aldrich was the son of former Rhode Island Senator Nelson W. Aldrich; his sister married John D. Rockefeller's only son (hence Aldrich's affiliation with the Chase National Bank); and he himself had married the daughter of a well-connected New York City lawyer, Charles B. Alexander, who had served up to his death in 1927 on the board of the Rockefeller-controlled Equitable Trust Co. and the Equitable Life Assurance Society. John Hay Whitney was a scion of a number of rich, interrelated families. His paternal grandfather, William C. Whitney, had been a major Wall Street figure and first-term Cleveland Cabinet member; his maternal grandfather was former Secretary of State John Hay; and his granduncle, Oliver H. Payne, was one of the founders of the Standard Oil Co. Given this lineage, it is not surprising that John Hay Whitney's fortune was estimated, shortly after he stepped down from office, to have been about $250 million.[56] C. Douglas Dillon represented newer wealth, most of which had been amassed by his father, Clarence Dillon, who was primarily responsible for the early growth and development of the investment banking house of Dillon, Read & Co. Much of his money had been channeled into the family-dominated United States and Foreign Securities Corp., a firm which, with its international subsidiary, had assets of almost $100 million, and was very closely linked with a number of the above interests.[57] Amory Houghton was a member of a wealthy upstate family which owned over 50 percent of the stock of the Corning Glass Works, which had assets of almost $140 million.[58] Most of these diplomatic figures also had direct or close indirect ties with the BAC or CED.[59]

Ike's appointments as Ambassador to Russia, however, were of a very different nature. His first emissary was a longtime career diplomat, Charles E. Bohlen, who, though he had married into one of Philadelphia's established families, was chosen largely because of his experience and widely recognized ability.[60] He was succeeded in 1957 by another highly regarded foreign service officer, Llewellyn Thompson. The selection of such professionals to serve in Moscow was probably dictated by the fact that the administration felt it could not afford to have ill-informed amateurs in this critical post.

In the 1950s normal diplomatic relations were reestablished with Germany (West Germany) after a war-imposed breach of many years. Again, our initial representatives appear to have been chosen mainly because of their knowledge and ability. For instance, our first emissary to Germany was longtime (1933–1953) Harvard University president James B. Conant, an academic of international repute.[61] Yet it should also be noted that Conant was on friendly terms with many of America's top economic leaders, for in September 1952 he had been elected a trustee of the CED, a position he held throughout his years of diplomatic service. In 1957 Conant was succeeded by another man of marked ability, David K. E. Bruce, a wealthy Maryland figure who had given up a business career in the early 1940s and had devoted much of his time in the postwar years to the federal government (although, as indicated in Appendix A, his brother had many key corporate ties). Toward the end of the Eisenhower administration, Bruce was replaced by career diplomat Walter Dowling, a man with no major socioeconomic links.

The position of Ambassador to NATO was, in contrast, held largely by men who had strong business backgrounds. Only the first of Eisenhower's three emissaries, former New York executive John C. Hughes, was not clearly linked with important economic interests. Hughes had merely been head of a fairly small textile concern known as McCampbell and Co. and a director of the considerably larger, closely affiliated Graniteville Co. of South Carolina. The other two Ambassadors to NATO were essentially Wall Street figures:

George W. Perkins (1955–1957)	Assistant Secretary of State (1949–1953); E.C.A. official (1948–1949); treasurer, Merck & Co., N.J. (1929–1947); married a member of the Merck family; trustee of the Foreign Policy Association (mid-1950s); director of the City Bank Farmers Trust Co., subsidiary of the National City Bank of New York (1935–1949)
W. Randolph Burgess (1957–1961)	Under Secretary of the Treasury (1953–1957); high official, National City Bank of New York (1938–1952); director of IT&T (1948–1953), Mutual Life Insurance Co. (1941–1952), and Union Pacific Railroad (1948–1952)

As under Truman, most of our Ambassadors to NATO, in short, were elite figures with close ties to New York-based business.[62]

During this period a number of new key posts were also created in the federal government. For instance, a marked increase was made in the administrative staff of the White House during the Eisenhower years, thanks largely to the creation of a sizable set of special aides and advisors to the President in both the domestic and foreign policy areas.[63] No position was more important than that of Special Assistant to the President for National Security Affairs, for this official had unusual access to the Oval Office and also acted as secretary to the National Security Council, a key policymaking body. Almost all of the people who held this post during the Eisenhower years were influential business (or pro-business) figures, as may be seen by a look at the following biographical summaries:

Robert Cutler (1953–1955)	No prior governmental experience; president, Old Colony Trust Co., an affiliate of the First National Bank of Boston (1946–1953); partner, Boston law firm of Herrick, Smith, Donald & Farley (1928–1940); director of the Boston Five Cents Savings Bank (1949–1953)

144   Elites in American History

Dillon Anderson
(1955–1956)
No previous governmental experience;
partner, Houston law firm of Baker, Botts, Andrews & Shepard (1940–1955, member of firm 1929–1940);
also board chairman, Electro-Mechanical Research, Inc., of Conn. (at time of appointment to this federal post);
trustee of the Carnegie Endowment for International Peace (1953–1956);
director of the Westinghouse Electric Corp. (1954–1955) and Texas National Bank of Houston (1954–1955)

William H. Jackson
(August–November 1956)
Deputy director, CIA (1950–1951);
partner, J.H. Whitney & Co., N.Y.C. (since 1947);
partner, New York law firm of Carter, Ledyard & Milburn (1934–1947);
director of the Spencer Chemical Co., Kansas City (1948–1956) and Thomas Industries, Inc., Kentucky (1954–1955)

Robert Cutler
(1956–1958)
Special Assistant to the President for National Security Affairs (1953–1955);
president or board chairman, Old Colony Trust Co., an affiliate of the First National Bank of Boston (1946–1953, 1955–1956);
director of the Boston Five Cents Savings Bank (1949–1953, 1956–1957) and the Raytheon Manufacturing Co. (1955–1956)

Gordon Gray
(1958–1961)
Director, Office of Defense Mobilization (1957–1958);
Assistant Secretary of Defense for International Security Affairs (1955–1957); Assistant Secretary and then Secretary of the Army (1947–1950);
president, University of North Carolina (1950–1955);
head of the Piedmont Publishing Co., North Carolina (since 1935);
trustee of the CED (1952–1957);
Gray family long associated with the R. J. Reynolds Tobacco Co.

The first man to assume this important position, Robert Cutler, had served as one of Eisenhower's 1952 political campaign strategists. Judging from official sources, Cutler's primary economic tie was of only moderate, if not minor, significance, for the Old Colony Trust Co., a managerial affiliate of the First National Bank of Boston, had stated assets of less than $11 million. However, Old Colony actually had a vast amount of (unreported) trust funds, much of which were invested in major business enterprises. Indeed, according to Cutler's own testimony, Old Colony was, around the time of his appointment to high federal office, the largest trust operation in the United States outside of New York City.[64] Clearly, then, Cutler was a prominent business figure.

In 1955, after serving for two crisis-packed years, Cutler decided to return to business life. He was replaced by another relatively inexperienced person,

Dillon Anderson, a longtime Houston corporate attorney, whose only prior governmental service was as a special advisor to the National Security Council for the previous two years.[65'] Anderson, whose law firm did much work for oil companies, was a member of the board of the Texas National Bank of Houston, Westinghouse Electric Corp., and the Carnegie Endowment for International Peace (a less important and prestigious body than the Council on Foreign Relations) when he was appointed as Special Assistant to the President for National Security Affairs. Yet there was another economic link which may have been of even more significance in Anderson's elevation to this key post, for, although a Texas lawyer, he served as board chairman of a comparatively small (120 employees) Connecticut concern known as Electro-Mechanical Research, Inc., an enterprise closely associated with certain wealthy Rockefeller interests.[66]

After a little more than a year, Anderson stepped down from his federal post, which was then taken by a New Yorker, William H. Jackson, a partner in J. H. Whitney & Co. (a family investment firm) and recent (1950-1951) deputy director of the CIA. Jackson did not hold office very long. He was succeeded in November 1956 by Robert Cutler, who was called back from his post as board chairman of the Brahmin-dominated Old Colony Trust Co. In mid-1958, Cutler was replaced by yet another well-connected, though more experienced, official, Gordon Gray, who had held a number of high positions in the federal government in the postwar period, and had served in the early 1950s as president of the University of North Carolina. But probably of greater weight in his selection were the facts that Gray was a member of a wealthy Southern family which had a major stake in the R. J. Reynolds Tobacco Co. and had served, from 1952 to 1957, as a trustee of the CED.[67]

In like manner, the Bureau of the Budget was taken over to a considerable extent by business interests during the Eisenhower years, although most of these officials were not drawn from the nation's top economic ranks.[68] This set of appointments, in fact, marked a significant shift from that of Harry Truman, who had generally selected men with a good deal of governmental experience and almost no noteworthy socio-economic ties. Eisenhower's four directors of the Bureau of the Budget were: Joseph M. Dodge, the longtime president of the Detroit Bank (one of the top 25 banks in the country); Rowland R. Hughes, a former comptroller and vice-president of the National City Bank of New York; Percival F. Brundage, a high-ranking official in the big accounting firm of Price, Waterhouse & Co. (and recent president of the prestigious National Bureau of Economic Research); and Maurice H. Stans, a onetime partner in the much smaller Chicago accounting house of Alexander Grant & Co.[69] Thus one would expect that little but conservative counsel came from this quarter during the Eisenhower years.[70]

Moreover, in 1953 the top post in the CIA was given for the first time to an overtly pro-business figure, former Wall Street attorney Allen Dulles, who was the younger brother of the newly appointed Secretary of State, John

Foster Dulles, and a member of the same New York law firm, Sullivan & Cromwell.[71] Dulles had served for the two preceding years as a deputy director of the CIA. However, he was clearly a pro-business figure, for he had served from 1937 to 1943 as a director of the J. Henry Schroder Banking Corp. (a concern with close ties to the Rockefeller interests) and in 1950-1951 as a board member (replacing his brother) of the American Bank Note Co. In addition, Dulles had long been a trustee of the Establishment-dominated Council on Foreign Relations and, in fact, served as its president from 1947 to 1951. Although Dulles did relinquish this last post when he assumed high federal office, he continued to act as a trustee of this influential body throughout his (over 8-year) tenure as head of the CIA.

According to government sources, Dulles's top aide in the agency was General Charles P. Cabell, a longtime career Air Force (or Air Corps) officer. But there were many more high-level officials in the CIA than the published records reveal, and most of them were apparently wealthy, pro-business figures. For instance, one of the deputy directors during this period was Robert Amory, Jr., whose Brahmin father was a vice-president of a large textile concern, Springs Mills, and a director of the American Mutual Liability Insurance Co. and various lesser firms. Other important figures in the Dulles-led CIA included William P. Bundy, who had married a daughter of Dean Acheson, and whose father, Harvey H. Bundy, was a Boston corporate lawyer; Richard M. Bissell, Jr., a former ECA official who had elite family links and served as a member of the CED's research advisory board throughout the 1950s; and John A. Bross, who had married the daughter of a former New Hampshire governor and Brookings Institution board chairman, New England businessman Robert Bass.[72] Thus during the Eisenhower years the CIA would seem to have been dominated by upper-class figures, most of whom had gone to prestigious Eastern prep schools and had various ties, frequently through close kin, to a number of America's major corporate interests.[73]

IMPORTANT POLICY ACTIONS

A number of major actions taken by the Eisenhower administration, both in the foreign and domestic areas, reflect its strong support for pro-business forces. One such act was the CIA's clandestine intervention in Iran in the early 1950s. This controversial event had its origins in 1951 when the government of this then-impoverished country decided to nationalize the extensive holdings of the big British-owned, Anglo-Iranian Oil Co., which, it was widely felt, had long pursued a highly exploitative policy, paying a relatively light tax to the Iranian government, while charging more for oil there than in Britain itself. As a result, the democratically elected regime of liberal-leftist leader Mohammed Mossadegh took over the domestic operation of Anglo-Iranian Oil. This action stunned the major Western powers, many of which had huge holdings in this region, and soon led to the imposition of a boycott of Iranian oil by the big European and American companies, which latter interests were not averse to gaining a piece of Britain's lucrative operation in Iran.

So matters stood till the spring of 1953 when the Eisenhower administration apparently decided that the Mossadegh regime, which was now alleged to be currying Communist support, should be replaced, by force if necessary, by a government more amenable to Western enterprise. To attain this objective, the CIA dispatched one of its top undercover agents, Kermit Roosevelt (a scion of the wealthy Oyster Bay Roosevelts), to direct its anti-Mossadegh maneuvers in Iran.[74] CIA director Allen Dulles flew to Switzerland to be in a better position to oversee this operation. It was highly successful. Mossadegh was ousted and put into prison, and various anti-Western dissident groups were effectively stilled through repressive police tactics. Even more important from an international standpoint, a new consortium of major oil companies was organized to take over Iran's denationalized oil industry as, in effect, an economic partner of the country's newly installed, more authoritarian government. By negotiation, five American oil companies—Jersey Standard, Gulf, Socony-Vacuum (now Mobil), Texaco, and Standard Oil of California—secured a substantial 40 percent stake in this new enterprise, all this largely as a result of the political coup engineered by the CIA, whose director had been recruited from a law firm which represented Standard Oil of New Jersey.[75]

Another glaring example of United States intervention in the politico-economic affairs of an underdeveloped nation occurred less than a year later in the tiny Central American state of Guatemala. This country had been run in the postwar period by a democratically elected, reform-oriented government headed since 1951 by former Army officer Jacobo Arbenz Guzman. His administration was dedicated to breaking up the large, often unused, landholdings of wealthy citizens and foreign economic interests, and redistributing the land among the peasants. However, it was initially hampered in this endeavor by a series of frustrating delays.

But in the early 1950s the Arbenz government took decisive action against the nation's largest landholder, the American-controlled United Fruit Co. It expropriated 234,000 acres of the company's uncultivated land on the country's west slope, and shortly thereafter announced its intention to seize an additional 173,000 acres of idle land owned by this quasi-monopolistic concern along the Caribbean coast.[76] Arbenz had also proved to be receptive to the influence of some Communist leaders in his domestic reform program, mainly in the areas of education, agriculture, and social security. This set of events was so disturbing to powerful politico-economic forces in the United States that in the latter part of 1953 the Eisenhower administration decided to organize a counterrevolution in Guatemala. This task was assigned by the President and his chief advisors to the CIA. After considerable planning and preparation, which included the provision of arms and aircraft, the agency managed to launch a successful assault, led by exiled Army Colonel Castillo

Armas, which soon brought about the ouster of the Arbenz regime and its replacement by a right-wing military junta.[77] And to no one's surprise, this body promptly abolished Guatemala's Congress, abrogated the voting rights of the great mass of poorly educated people, did away entirely with the agrarian reform program, and, to the satisfaction of the junta's primary political and financial backers, returned most of the expropriated property to its former owners, the United Fruit Co. and the country's wealthy major landholders.

Although all this is now a matter of history, there are some disturbing aspects about the Eisenhower administration's involvement in this furtive affair.[78] For example, as pointed out earlier, Allen Dulles had served as a director of the J. Henry Schroder Banking Corp. from 1937 to 1943 (at which point he was replaced by another Sullivan & Cromwell partner, Delano Andrews), and as a longtime trustee and high official of the influential Council on Foreign Relations.[79] One of Dulles's close associates in the CFR, Whitney H. Shepardson, had also served up to the early 1940's as a vice-president of the International Railways of Central America, an enterprise in which United Fruit had a very substantial interest.[80] Furthermore, the position of board chairman of the International Railways of Central America had long been held by a high official of the J. Henry Schroder Banking Corp., a concern apparently aligned with United Fruit.[81] In short, it seems clear that CIA director Allen Dulles was on good terms with the major American economic interests involved in this Guatemalan dispute.

In addition, the man who served as Special Assistant to the President for National Security Affairs, former Boston banker Robert Cutler, had very close ties to United Fruit. As already noted, he had been president of the Old Colony Trust Co., a major arm or affiliate of the big First National Bank of Boston. In fact, his boss, Old Colony Trust's chairman T. Jefferson Coolidge, also served as board chairman of United Fruit, most likely because this financial institution had large stockholdings in the Boston-controlled banana company.[82] Moreover, a sizable number of the "outside" directors of United Fruit sat on the board of either Old Colony Trust or the First National Bank of Boston.[83] Hence Robert Cutler could hardly have been a neutral party in the high-level proceedings which led to the decision to organize a counterrevolution in Guatemala, whose leftist-leaning government had been so rash as to expropriate a substantial amount of land belonging to the United Fruit Co.

Business interests also played an influential role in the domestic affairs of the Eisenhower administration, sometimes in ways surprising to anticorporate critics. For instance, a number of business leaders were much involved in helping to bring about the fall of Wisconsin's demagogic Senator Joseph R. McCarthy in 1954. In the late 1940s and early 1950s this ambitious and unscrupulous figure took full advantage of the cold war hysteria and proceeded to terrorize a number of key government agencies, especially the State Department, by making a series of wild charges about Communist infiltration and influence. In the process, McCarthy built up a large following among the general public and the mass media, particularly the rightist Hearst and McCormick newspaper chains. Although his sensational allegations were clearly damaging to the government and the nation's public image, most political leaders, Democrats and Republicans alike, were afraid or reluctant to challenge the tyrannical Wisconsin Senator.[84]

In addition, McCarthy had the backing of some big businessmen, such as the reactionary Texas oil millionaire H. L. Hunt and Sears Roebuck executive Robert E. Wood, who had been a prime mover in the prewar isolationist America First Committee.[85] But most major corporate executives apparently viewed him with disdain, or at least with mixed feelings, favoring his anti-Red line while deploring his extremist tactics. However, when McCarthy made a brutal public assault in 1954 on Secretary of the Army Robert T. Stevens, a former textile magnate who had been a longtime member of the BAC (and whose brother was a trustee of the CED), America's top economic leaders closed ranks and turned sharply against the Wisconsin Senator, exerting considerable influence on leaders in both parties to take action against him.[86] It was probably no accident that the man who formally introduced the censure motion against McCarthy in the Senate was closely allied with important economic interests, Vermont Senator Ralph Flanders, a longtime (1942–1954) trustee of the CED and a former vice-chairman of the BAC.[87] And substantial business pressure was brought to bear on many other members of the Senate during the censure proceedings.[88] Thus, as one conservative source later noted, the nation's powerful business establishment "...played a significant behind-the-scenes role in ending the career of Senator Joseph McCarthy."[89]

In another major step in mid-1954, President Eisenhower appointed a special committee to study the highway needs of the nation because these facilities had become badly strained as a result of the postwar surge in automobile usage. In a remarkably short time, just four months later, this group reported to the President that the country required a massive new interstate highway program. This extraordinary plan was quickly adopted by Congress, in part because of the great wave of favorable publicity generated for it, with the encouragement of the oil and auto industries, in the nation's major news media.

Yet, in retrospect, there would seem to be considerable doubt as to whether this huge project—the largest public works program in American history (it was originally estimated to cost $27 billion, but turned out to be much more)—was designed solely or even primarily to promote the public interest. Consider, for example, the economic makeup of the five-man body that conceived the plan:

President's Advisory Committee on a National Highway Program

Lucius D. Clay (chairman)	Former high-ranking Army officer and close friend of President Eisenhower; now board chairman of the big Continental Can Co.; member of the executive committee of the BAC

150 *Elites in American History*

S. Sloan Colt	President of the Bankers Trust Co. of New York; trustee of the CED (1948–1954)
William A. Roberts	President of the Allis-Chalmers Manufacturing Co. (which made construction equipment as well as farm machinery)
Stephen D. Bechtel	President of the Bechtel Corp., a California-based construction company; vice-chairman of the BAC (1954)
David Beck	President of the International Brotherhood of Teamsters

Although presidential advisory bodies have often been extolled for their reported representation of diverse interests, this group was obviously not so structured.[90] Indeed, a close look at the above committee reveals an intriguing pattern. Its chairman, Lucius Clay, was a director of General Motors, which (then) du Pont-controlled concern had a significant stake in these proceedings. S. Sloan Colt was the president of a financial enterprise which had long been linked with the House of Morgan, GM's major bankers.[91] Stephen D. Bechtel was a director of the Continental Can Co., and just a few months before his appointment to this presidential committee, he had been elected to the board of J. P. Morgan & Co., the first Westerner to be so honored. Thus it seems clear that the so-called Clay committee was dominated by forces which were closely allied with or friendly toward the auto industry and highway construction interests.

A few years later, after Russia had stunned the world with its successful launching of a space satellite, another important advisory commission was created to deal with the question of America's overall level of defense spending, which a number of leaders now felt was too low to keep pace with the growing military strength of the Soviet Union. This special body, generally referred to as the Gaither Committee, was composed of an interesting mixture of people: several business executives, a few men selected because of their special expertise (such as Robert Prim of Bell Telephone Labs), and four persons who were essentially academic figures—James P. Baxter, president of Williams College; Robert D. Calkins, head of the Brookings Institution; James A. Perkins, a vice-president of the Carnegie Corp.; and Jerome Weisner of MIT.

The group was originally headed by H. Rowan Gaither, a San Francisco lawyer who was presently serving as chairman of both the Ford Foundation and the Rand Corporation.[92] However, Gaither became ill shortly after assuming his post, so the direction of this study fell largely to the committee's co-chairmen, both of whom were elite figures. One of these officials was New England industrialist Robert C. Sprague, who was head of the medium-sized Sprague Electric Co. of Massachusetts, chairman of the Federal Reserve Bank of Boston, and a director of the United Carr Fastener Corp. (a concern headed up to 1953 by Secretary of Commerce Sinclair Weeks). The other de facto director was William C. Foster, a former (1951–1953) Deputy Secretary of Defense, who now served as a high official of the Olin

Mathieson Chemical Corp. (and as a board member of the BAC, CED, Detroit Edison Co., and Marquardt Aircraft Co.). A special eleven-man advisory panel was also created to assist the committee in its deliberations. This body included a number of well-known figures and former governmental officials such as Robert Lovett, John J. McCloy, and MIT president James R. Killian, Jr., as well as the president of CBS, Frank Stanton, who was affiliated with both the BAC and CED. In short, the committee probably had a marked orientation toward increased spending from the outset of its proceedings.

This group came up with an important (but still unpublished) report which strongly urged a drastic increase in defense spending, particularly for air defense. However, its recommendations met with considerable opposition in certain influential quarters of the Eisenhower administration and in some powerful segments of the business community, which forces either wanted to hold down federal expenditures or advocated other options. For example, Treasury Department authorities were engrossed with balancing the budget, while Secretary of State John Foster Dulles placed great weight on less expensive strategic weapons. Because of this split in high-level government (and business) ranks, no agreement was reached on this controversial topic during the latter part of the Eisenhower regime, although the report probably did help to set the stage for massive boosts in defense spending in the years ahead.[93]

Although defense pressures made it impossible for the Eisenhower administration to achieve any noteworthy reductions in the overall federal tax burden, there was one very important financial act taken in the late 1950s, and that was the adoption of the oil import quota system.[94] Actually, various attempts had been made some years earlier to stem the flow of less costly crude oil brought in from abroad by big American concerns, imports which had been vastly increased in recent years by such relative "newcomer" or "maverick" firms as Sinclair, Phillips, Signal, Tidewater, and the Sun Oil Co. But these initial efforts produced rather meager results. Despite the protests of domestic oil producers, the Eisenhower administration chose to rely primarily on a voluntary restriction program, which, as one might predict, was not very effective.[95]

However, by 1959 the long-established international companies had lost considerable ground, particularly in relative terms, to the aggressive "newcomers" (or "intruders," as Anthony Sampson has described them). In fact, the latter's share of the nation's crude oil imports had jumped from 32 percent in 1954 to about 55 percent in 1958.[96] The President was then persuaded, under legislative authority adopted during this period, to impose a mandatory oil import quota system. This was of substantial help to both independent domestic producers, the most obvious beneficiaries, and the influential international giants, for the latter concerns apparently fared quite well in the government's subsequent issuance of valuable oil "import tickets." The primary losers were, of course, the "newcomers" and the

American consumer. The program has since been estimated to have cost the public about $4 billion a year up to 1973, when the scheme was finally scrapped because of a sharply escalating oil crisis and much Congressional and public pressure.[97]

A closer look at the adoption of this program, however, raises certain questions about the impartiality of at least one of Eisenhower's key advisors. This was Secretary of the Treasury Robert B. Anderson, who was a Texas oilman turned, in part, Northeastern (and Canadian) financier.[98] As pointed out earlier, prior to his first appointment to high federal office in 1953, Anderson had been employed for 16 years as either attorney or general manager for the W. T. Waggoner estate, a major ranching enterprise which encompassed more than half a million acres in north Texas and was found to be the source of tremendous oil reserves.[99] He had also served in the late 1940s and early 1950s as the president of the Mid-Continent Oil and Gas Association (which reportedly had been the original source of the drive for a vastly expanded oil depletion allowance in 1926) and as a director of the American Petroleum Institute. When Anderson stepped down from the Defense Department in the mid-1950s, he assumed a number of other important business posts, becoming a major officer of Dresser Industries, Inc. (a big oil industry supplier), and a director of the American Overseas Investing Co. (a Rockefeller-dominated firm), the Hanover Bank of New York, and a member (or trustee) of the BAC and CED.[100] Thus Anderson had close ties to both of the major economic interests which benefited greatly from Eisenhower's decision to impose a mandatory oil import quota system in the late 1950s.[101]

SUPREME COURT APPOINTMENTS AND ACTIONS

The Supreme Court during the Eisenhower years presented an interesting contrast to the administration itself, in considerable part because two of the President's appointees turned out to be more progressive figures than he had anticipated. At the outset of this period the Chief Justice was Fred M. Vinson, a pleasant, mildly conservative former Kentucky lawyer and political leader who had been appointed by Truman, as had Justices Burton, Clark, and Minton. The remaining Justices (Black, Douglas, Frankfurter, Jackson, and Reed) had been picked in the late 1930s or early 1940s by Franklin Roosevelt. As previously noted, none of these officials had ever been associated with major corporate interests, and only a few had been linked with even small economic enterprises. In short, thanks largely to the New Deal, the Supreme Court now had a very different composition from that which existed in earlier times, when business influence was dominant.

Shortly after assuming office, Eisenhower was presented with a golden opportunity to alter the new ideological orientation of the Court when Chief Justice Vinson died of a heart attack in the fall of 1953. As his successor, the President chose, on the advice of key party counselors, a highly popular Californian (and one of his recent political backers), Earl Warren, who had spent most of his adult years in public office. Warren had served for fourteen years as Alameda County district attorney, then briefly (from 1939 to 1943) as state attorney general, and finally for an unprecedented three terms (1943–1953) as governor of California, in which role he had emerged, much to the consternation of onetime conservative supporters, as an increasingly liberal leader.[102] In addition, Warren, who came from a lower-middle-class family, never had any noteworthy socio-economic ties. Probably for these reasons, he turned out, to the dismay of the President and many of his chief advisors, to be a thoroughly progressive figure on the High Court, and did much to make this body into an even more liberal force in governmental affairs, particularly in the realm of civil rights. Indeed, it was shortly after Warren took office that the Supreme Court handed down its most important decision of the Eisenhower era when it ruled unanimously in the now classic case of *Brown* v. *Board of Education of Topeka* that racial segregation in the nation's public schools represented a violation of the equal protection of the laws clause of the 14th Amendment of the Constitution. In retrospect, it was clearly this ruling which ignited the civil rights movement and led ultimately to a marked improvement in social and educational equality in the United States.

Soon after this case was decided, Eisenhower got another chance, as a result of the sudden demise of Justice Jackson, to put someone of a more conservative mold on the High Court. Again acting largely on the advice of his chief political and legal counselors, particularly Attorney General Herbert Brownell and retiring New York Governor Thomas E. Dewey, the President decided to appoint a highly regarded New York lawyer, John Marshall Harlan. Harlan had only limited governmental and judicial experience (six months as a U.S. Circuit Court judge),[103] but was recognized as a man of marked ability. In addition, by way of historical advantage, his grandfather had been one of the Court's most distinguished jurists in the late 19th and early 20th centuries. However, unlike his grandfather, who was a former Louisville, Kentucky, lawyer with no major socio-economic ties, John Marshall Harlan was not simply an able big city attorney, but a longtime partner in one of New York City's most important corporate law firms— Root, Ballantine, Harlan, Bushby & Palmer. He also served (1947–1954) as a board member of the United States Trust Co. of New York, which had substantial stockholdings in various large corporations.[104] Given this background, it is not surprising that Harlan generally allied himself with the conservative forces on the Supreme Court.[105]

In 1956 another opening occurred on the Supreme Court when Indiana's Sherman Minton decided to resign after serving without distinction for seven years on this prestigious body. At the urging of various Eastern leaders and the American Bar Association, President Eisenhower chose as his replacement a well-regarded New Jersey lawyer and jurist, William J. Brennan. Like Earl Warren, Brennan may have been picked partly for political reasons: he was a Democrat and a Roman Catholic, two facts which no doubt loomed large in a presidential election year. However, unlike Harlan, Brennan had served for a significant period of time (seven years) in two prominent judicial posts, as a judge of the New Jersey Superior Court and Supreme Court. Up to 1949 he had also been a partner in one of Newark's major corporate law firms, Pitney, Hardin, Ward & Brennan, as it was then known.[106] Yet, despite this concern's business ties, Brennan turned out, to Ike's surprise, to be a very liberal judge, perhaps because he had been born into a lower-income family, and his father had been one of Newark's more important labor leaders, an uncommon background for a Supreme Court justice.[107]

Shortly thereafter, Eisenhower received yet another opportunity to redress the ideological balance of the Supreme Court when Kentucky's aged Associate Justice Stanley Reed felt compelled to step down from the bench. To replace him, the President decided to select someone who would, in his view, represent "middle America." After a vigorous promotional campaign had been waged by such Missouri leaders as newspaper publisher Roy Roberts, Eisenhower picked one of Kansas City's more conservative corporate attorneys, Charles Whittaker, who also happened to be a close friend of the President's brother, Kansas City banker Arthur Eisenhower. Though a self-made man (he got his law degree at night school), Whittaker had risen to the top of one of Kansas City's leading law firms, which served as counsel for a number of major business enterprises such as the Union Pacific Railroad, Montgomery Ward, and the City National Bank and Trust Co. of Kansas City (a concern dominated by the same interests, the Kemper family, that controlled Arthur Eisenhower's bank).[108] Whittaker, however, had rather limited judicial experience, having served for only a few years (in the mid-1950s) as a federal judge. He proved to be a distinct disappointment on the High Court—he wrote about one opinion a year—and stepped down from the bench in the early 1960s.

Eisenhower's last Supreme Court selection was made in the late 1950s, following the resignation of Ohio's Harold Burton, a somewhat conservative Truman appointee. To succeed him, the President picked a man, Potter Stewart, who had served for the last five years as a U.S. Circuit Court judge, and perhaps more important, came from a family which had been very active in public affairs (his father had been mayor of Cincinnati and later Chief Justice of the Ohio Supreme Court).[109] Stewart had also been a partner (1947–1954) in one of Cincinnati's most prominent law firms, Dinsmore, Shohl, Dinsmore & Todd which had long acted as general counsel for the big locally based Procter and Gamble Co.[110] Perhaps as a result of this mixed background, Stewart emerged as a kind of conservative "swing" man on the Court, a role which presumably brought some satisfaction to the President.

Eisenhower's appointees, however, did not bring about a major change in the general outlook of the Supreme Court. In part because of a few New Deal carryovers, the High Court continued to have a fairly liberal orientation throughout the 1950s.

In summary, while the Supreme Court was made up of lawyers drawn from various, mostly non-elite, walks of life, the upper ranks of the executive branch of government during the Eisenhower years were filled largely by men who had major socio-economic links. Of Eisenhower's top executive and diplomatic officials, over 80 percent had key economic or family ties, the highest proportion of such officials to be so recruited since the business-dominated Harding, Coolidge, and Hoover regimes.[111] Nearly 40 percent of these elitist figures were closely associated with the BAC, CED, or CFR (as contrasted with only about 28 percent in the Truman administration), and many of the remainder had other Establishment ties.[112] As was the case with the Truman administration, the bulk of these officials were concentrated in the most important departments in the federal government—State, Treasury, and Defense. Furthermore, a number of new posts were created under Eisenhower, such as Special Assistant to the President for National Security Affairs, and many of these were filled by prominent business (or pro-business) figures.

A substantial number of Eisenhower's major officials also had relatively little or no governmental experience prior to their appointment to high federal office. Indeed, a majority of them were, in effect, drawn directly from large economic enterprises and corporate law firms, in contrast to the 15 percent so recruited in the Truman administration. In fact, only two members of Eisenhower's original Cabinet—Secretary of State John Foster Dulles and Secretary of the Interior Douglas McKay—had a significant amount of experience in government up to 1953 (and some might argue that Dulles's previous diplomatic record was overrated). This recruitment pattern clearly represented a marked shift from the two preceding Democratic regimes.

It should also be pointed out that although there was little difference between the Eisenhower and Truman administrations in the proportion of high-level appointees who had attended college, there was a profound difference in the types of schools they had attended. Little more than 25 percent of Truman's top executive and diplomatic officials had gone to a prestigious Ivy League (or "little Ivy League") school. On the other hand, over 50 percent of the major Cabinet members and diplomatic emissaries picked by Eisenhower had graduated from such elite institutions. Hence while some writers have described President Eisenhower as "the centrist from mid-America," he would instead appear to have been a firm ally of America's powerful economic establishment.

The highly elitist background of many of the top officials of the Eisenhower administration probably had much to do with certain major actions taken while Ike held office. For instance, it seems clear that the decisions made to have the CIA help plan and support the overthrow of democratically-elected leftist regimes in Iran and Guatemala were strongly influenced by the fact that three of Eisenhower's chief advisors—Secretary of State John Foster Dulles, CIA director Allen Dulles, and Special Assistant to the President for National Security Affairs Robert Cutler—were closely allied with firms which had a significant economic stake in these proceedings.

Similarly, on the domestic scene, one might well raise a question as to whether the massive interstate highway program adopted in the mid-1950s was solely in the public interest when the chairman of the special five-man commission that conceived the plan was Lucius Clay, a director of General Motors, and two other members of this ad hoc group were closely associated with a big New York-based banking complex which acted as financial advisor to GM.

However, not all of the economic pressure exerted on the Eisenhower administration was for such questionable purposes. After Wisconsin Senator Joseph R. McCarthy made a scurrilous attack on certain high officials in the Defense Department, the nation's business leadership worked assiduously behind the scenes to help bring about his downfall. But, as a rule, the politico-economic influence applied during this period was not of this nature; it was intended to provide substantial benefits to major segments of the business community. This was again demonstrated toward the end of the 1950s when, at the urging of such officials as Secretary of the Treasury Robert B. Anderson (who was closely linked with both Texas oil interests and the Rockefeller forces), the Eisenhower administration imposed a mandatory oil import quota system. This program was designed to protect both the independent Texas oil producers and the big international oil companies (which were being challenged abroad by various second-tier concerns), and cost the American consumers billions of dollars before it was terminated in 1973. In short, despite some contrary claims, the Eisenhower administration was clearly a business-dominated regime.

Notes

1. *Fortune* magazine has published its famous "top 500" ranking since 1955, although this tabulation, unlike the author's, is based on volume of sales rather than assets.

2. By 1960 the nation's largest railroad, the Pennsylvania, had been eclipsed by almost all the "top 10" industrial concerns. Moreover, the New York Central Railroad, which had long been dominated by the Vanderbilt-Morgan interests, was taken over in 1954, after a bitter proxy battle, by a coalition of new economic forces, led by Texas oilmen Clint Murchison and Sid Richardson.

3. One other financial enterprise, a mutual fund known as Investors Diversified Services, Inc., had sufficient assets (around $3 billion) to rank with some of the "top 10" banks. Yet this complex, which was controlled by the Kirby family, did not play a very significant role in the nation's economic affairs, perhaps because it was not closely associated with Establishment interests. As a matter of fact, America's second largest mutual fund, the Massachusetts Investors Trust, wielded more power in the business world, probably because it was dominated

The Eisenhower Administration   157

by Boston Brahmins. Still, most mutual funds did not carry much weight in important economic circles.

4. The Chase Manhattan Bank is reported to have handled almost 10 percent of all corporate and union pension funds in the country. And the Bankers Trust Company had over $3 billion in its biggest (AT&T) pension fund account alone. The banks outside of the Northeast did not have such mammoth trust funds. For example, in 1961 it was estimated that the Bank of America had only about $2.5 billion to $3 billion in such accounts. See *Fortune* (November 1961), p. 135, and *Forbes* (October 1, 1961), p. 22.

5. See *Fortune* (November 1961), p. 135, and *Trusts and Estates* (February 1964), p. 174. It was not until the late 1960s, following a Congressional investigation led by Texas populist Wright Patman, that accurate, systematic information was compiled as to the magnitude of these holdings.

6. See *Business Week* (December 6, 1969), p. 184, and for a more general treatment of the subject, Daniel J. Baum and Ned B. Stiles, *The Silent Partners: Institutional Investors and Corporate Control* (Syracuse, N.Y.: Syracuse University Press, 1965), passim. These concerns, however, do not usually have the amount of voting power indicated by their shareholdings, although it is still substantial. The large investment banks and brokerage houses such as Lehman Brothers and Merrill Lynch also handle billions of dollars worth of securities each year, but only on a short-term basis.

7. There was relatively little change in either of the two closely linked groups, which represented the heart of America's big business "establishment," the BAC and CED, except that the latter body increased somewhat in size during the Eisenhower years.

8. The influence of the Rockefeller family also extended beyond such formal bodies as the CFR and sometimes worked in more indirect or subtle fashion. For instance, by 1960 the Rockefeller brothers owned 40 percent of a 1,000,000-acre cattle ranch in the rich Mato Grosso region of Brazil, which they operated jointly with that country's ambassador to the United States, former banker Walther Moreira Salles. See *Time* (June 20, 1960), p. 76, and Peter Collier and David Horowitz, *The Rockefellers*, p. 706.

9. See *The New Yorker* (January 9, 1965), p. 64, and the *New York Times* (June 15, 1950), p. 66 and November 21, 1971, Sect. VI, pp. 130–31. The less important Foreign Policy Association, on the other hand, was oriented more toward the National (or First National) City Bank in the postwar period.

10. See Herbert S. Parmet, *Eisenhower and the American Crusade* (New York: Macmillan, 1972), pp. 13–14, Peter Lyon, *Eisenhower: Portrait of the Hero* (Boston: Little, Brown, 1974), pp. 373–74, and for the latter point of view, Marquis Childs, *Eisenhower: Captive Hero* (New York: Harcourt, Brace, 1958), p. 107.

11. A year later Eisenhower was invited to dinner by Clarence Dillon, the retired founder of Dillon, Read & Co. At this affair the guests included Russell C. Leffingwell, the board chairman of both the CFR and J. P. Morgan & Co.; John M. Schiff, a senior partner in Kuhn, Loeb & Co.; John D. Rockefeller, Jr.; Ohio industrialist Harvey Firestone; and financier Jeremiah Milbank, who was a director of the Chase Manhattan Bank, Metropolitan Life Insurance Co., and Southern Railway. Similar meetings were also arranged in such other large cities as Boston and Minneapolis. See Peter Lyon, *op. cit.*, pp. 380–414, especially 408.

12. See Peter Lyon, *op. cit.*, p. 407.

13. As yet another example of the extraordinary efforts made to promote Ike's presidential stock around the country, the board chairman of the Standard Oil Co. of California resigned all posts (save one directorship) in January 1952 to work almost full time on Eisenhower's candidacy. See Peter Lyon, *op. cit.*, p. 433.

14. It was to placate the dissident Taft supporters that Eisenhower, at the urging of his Eastern advisors, picked California Senator Richard M. Nixon, a rabid anti-Communist, to serve as his running mate.

15. As Columbia University president, Ike had also sat on the board of the (roughly $350 million) Central Savings Bank of New York in 1950–1951, and one of his more conservative brothers, Edgar, served as a director of the big St. Regis Paper Co. from 1954 through 1961. For more on Ike's key sources of support, see Herbert S. Parmet, *op. cit.,* p. 33.

16. According to one recent source, Eisenhower's first choice for this position was former Wall Street lawyer and World Bank head John J. McCloy, who was about to step down as U.S. High Commissioner to West Germany, but Senator Taft vetoed him as being too close to the "international bankers" and "Roosevelt New Dealers." See Peter Collier and David Horowitz, *op. cit.*, p. 271.

17. See Paul Hoffman, *Lions in the Street,* p. 80.

18. In addition, Dulles's brother (and law partner), Allen, was president of the Council on Foreign Relations up to 1951, when he became deputy director of the Central Intelligence Agency.

19. Herter's two immediate predecessors as Under Secretary of State were former Army General (and recent high federal official) Walter Bedell Smith and Western oilman Herbert Hoover, Jr., who in the early 1950s had been head of a subsidiary of the Union Oil Co. of California and a director of the latter company and the Southern California Edison Co. Hoover's brother, Allan, was also president of a (probably American-controlled) foreign concern known as Compania Minera de Guatemala, S.A., and a director of the Connecticut-based Pitney-Bowes, Inc. Herter's successor in this important post was former New York financier and recent (1953–57) Ambassador to France C. Douglas Dillon, who, prior to his entry into the federal government, had been a high official of Dillon, Read & Co., president of the family-controlled United States & Foreign Securities Corp., and a director of the Amerada Petroleum Corp.

20. Also interestingly, Herter's uncle, a physician, had been treasurer of the Rockefeller Institute for Medical Research up to his death in 1910. And one of Mrs. Herter's cousins, Richardson Pratt, who had served as assistant treasurer of the Standard Oil Co. of New Jersey up to 1945, still sat on the board of the big United States Trust Co., along with many other elite figures.

21. Herter himself served as a trustee of the Boston-based World Peace Foundation throughout his years in office. However, this organization had comparatively few major businessmen on its board, and was more of a true civic group than the Council on Foreign Relations.

22. Most of the other high officials in the State Department during the Eisenhower years were career diplomats, except for the following: San Francisco lawyer Herman Phleger, who was the department's 1953–1957 legal advisor (and a director of the Union Oil Co. of California, American Trust Co. of San Francisco, Fibreboard Products, Inc., and Matson Navigation Co., which last three links he maintained up through 1957); Phleger's successor, Loftus Becker, who was a partner in the New York law firm of Cahill, Gordon, Reindel & Ohl; Becker's successor, Eric Hager, who was a partner in the Wall Street law firm of Shearman & Sterling & Wright; Gerald C. Smith, the 1957–1961 Secretary of State for Policy Planning, whose father-in-law, William G. Maguire, was head of the big Panhandle Eastern Pipe Line Co. (and a director of the National Distillers and Chemicals Corp.); and Walter S. Robertson, the 1953–1959 Assistant Secretary of State for Far Eastern Affairs, who was a longtime partner in the Richmond investment banking firm of Scott & Stringfellow (and a director, throughout the 1950s, of the Robertson Chemical Co. and, up to 1955, of the Camp Manufacturing Co.). Robertson's business partner, Buford Scott, was a director of the Continental Insurance Co. of New York.

23. See Peter Lyon, *op. cit.*, p. 466, and Herbert S. Parmet, *op. cit.*, p. 171. Humphrey had actually been a longtime Taft supporter.

24. Indeed, if one were to ignore Folsom's BAC and CED ties, W. Randolph Burgess, the newly appointed Under Secretary of the Treasury for Monetary Affairs, would appear to be a

more influential figure, for Burgess was a longtime high official of the National City Bank of New York and a director of IT&T, the Union Pacific Railroad, and Mutual Life Insurance Co.

25. The Hanna interests were also on friendly terms with the Mellon forces, which had a substantial stake in the Pittsburgh Consolidation Coal Co. One of Humphrey's close business associates, Hanna executive George H. Love, was a director of the Mellon National Bank & Trust Co.

26. Humphrey's overall influence was undoubtedly aided by the fact that one of the Hanna-dominated companies, the Industrial Rayon Corp., counted among its directors Harry F. Byrd, Jr., a Winchester, Virginia, newspaper publisher who was the son of the conservative Southern Democrat Harry F. Byrd, a key member of the Senate Finance Committee.

27. See Dean E. Mann and Jameson W. Doig, *The Assistant Secretaries* (Washington, D.C.: Brookings Institution, 1965), p. 39.

28. Before joining the Defense Department, Anderson had worked for sixteen years as a general manager or attorney for the relatively unknown, but extremely rich, Waggoner estate, which apparently had assets of about $300 million in 1953. See *Fortune* (November 1955), p. 47.

29. Anderson's links with the Rockefeller interests were also later shown by the fact that in 1957 he borrowed $84,000 from Nelson Rockefeller to buy stock in the latter's International Basic Economy Corp. The loan was repaid at 3 percent interest just before Anderson was appointed Secretary of the Treasury. See the *New York Times* (October 29, 1974), p. 1.

30. Anderson's Under Secretary of the Treasury, Fred Scribner, was much more of a political figure. He was essentially a Portland, Maine, lawyer and local businessman, who had served as his state's Republican National Committeeman from 1948 to 1956 and as general counsel to the Republican National Committee from 1952 to 1955.

31. It is interesting to note that Wilson's immediate superior, Alfred P. Sloan, Jr., served on the board of J. P. Morgan & Co. from 1943 through 1957, and that McElroy's boss, R. R. Deupree, was also a director of J. P. Morgan & Co. Moreover, Gates became president of the recently formed Morgan Guaranty Trust Co. when he stepped down as Secretary of Defense in 1961.

32. Roger Kyes and Donald Quarles had no such important outside ties, but were basically management men. Kyes was obviously brought in by his boss, Charles Wilson. Donald Quarles apparently had no such overt sponsorship. Yet it should be noted that his firm, the Western Electric Co., ranked as one of the country's major defense contractors.

33. Robertson served as president of the Champion Paper & Fibre Co. up to 1955 when he assumed his high Defense Department post, at which point he became vice-chairman of this big concern, a presumably less demanding position, though one still posing a possible conflict of interest.

34. Thomas returned to the board of the Lockheed Aircraft Corp. shortly after his resignation as Secretary of the Navy, which pattern of affiliation would certainly seem to raise a question about his role as a high federal official.

35. See "The Blue Ribbon Business Council," *Dun's Review* (January 1970), p. 39. This article is mistaken in describing Eisenhower as a formal member of the BAC at this time (he was awarded honorary status in 1962). However, on the basis of the evidence, one might argue that he was a de facto member of this elite body (which was simply known as the Business Council after 1961).

36. *Ibid.* Also see Hobart Rowen, *The Free Enterprisers: Kennedy, Johnson and the Business Establishment* (New York: Putnam, 1964), p. 62.

37. In all, the CED had, by 1957, placed a total of 38 figures in the federal government, and it reportedly played a critical role in shaping the economic policies of the Eisenhower administration. For instance, as Karl Schriftgiesser has observed, "six days before the President-elect moved his command post from his New York hotel to the White House, a small

group of CED colleagues brought him a carefully prepared nine-page statement of 'views on the areas of economic policy most in need of attention.' " See Karl Schriftgiesser, *Business Comes of Age*, p. 162.

38. In sharp contrast to this appointment pattern, Ike's defeated Republican opponent, Senator Robert Taft, reportedly urged that the position of Secretary of Defense be given to an arch-conservative Chrysler Corp. executive, B. Edwin Hutchinson, who was a trustee of two right-wing civic groups, the American Enterprise Association and the Foundation for Economic Education (and who later became a member of the editorial advisory committee of the John Birch Society's magazine, *American Opinion*). Similarly, one of the people Taft recommended for Secretary of Labor was, almost incredibly, Clarence Manion, the reactionary dean of the Notre Dame Law School (he also later became a member of the editorial advisory committee of *American Opinion*). Taft's other unheeded Cabinet suggestions were Virginia's Senator Harry Byrd for Secretary of the Treasury and Mormon business and religious leader Vernon Romney for Secretary of the Interior. See James T. Patterson, *Mr. Republican*, p. 583.

39. It is true that one of Brownell's partners, George deF. Lord, did serve, up to his death in 1950, on the board of the United States Trust Co. of New York, a company with a large amount of undisclosed trust funds. But this was the only important affiliation of any member of this firm. Brownell himself served in the late 1940s or early 1950s as a director of the National Retailers Mutual Insurance Co., which was a New York subsidiary of the Kemper-controlled Lumbermens Mutual Casualty Co. of Chicago, and the World Trade Corp., a firm created in the late 1940s by the New York legislature in an early abortive effort to promote the development of a mammoth World Trade Center. The latter company was headed by New York banker Winthrop W. Aldrich up to its demise in 1949.

40. See Peter Lyon, *op. cit.*, p. 431.

41. Benson was the only Eisenhower Cabinet member who was generally acknowledged to be a Taft man; like some other supporters of this Ohio leader, he later joined the John Birch Society.

42. For an analysis of the "agribusiness" group with which Benson was last affiliated, see Wesley McCune, *"Who's Behind Our Farm Policy?* (New York: Praeger, 1956), pp. 60–65.

43. See *Business Week* (November 23, 1957), pp. 108–116, and for a more detailed analysis, *Fortune* (April 1964), pp. 136–39 and 166–72.

44. See Edward L. Schapsmeier and Frederick H. Schapsmeier, *Ezra Taft Benson and the Politics of Agriculture, 1953–1961* (Danville, Ill.: Interstate Printers & Publishers, 1975), p. 14. For more on Benson's inner circle of informal advisors, the most important of whom was apparently William I. Myers, the dean of the college of agriculture at Cornell University (and a director of several large corporations), see *ibid.*, pp. 47–48, and Wesley McCune, *op. cit.*, pp. 290–95.

45. For instance, a later study found that Benson, unlike his predecessor, Charles Brannan, was closely allied with the big farmer-dominated AFBF and three of his major department appointees were representatives of this potent group. See Dean E. Mann and Jameson W. Doig, *op. cit.*, p. 49.

46. Two Brookings researchers have described Labor and Commerce as "clientele" agencies, and, without overtly applying this term, arrived at a similar judgment with regard to Agriculture and Interior. Yet they were, curiously, content to refer to the Treasury Department as an agency dominated by "specialists" or "technicians," although the data presented earlier in this chapter would indicate that this body was just as much a "clientele" agency as either Commerce or Labor, if not more so. See Mann and Doig, *op. cit.*, pp. 37–56, and Dean E. Mann, "The Selection of Federal Political Executives," *American Political Science Review* (March 1964), p. 90.

47. It was Durkin's appointment which led to the quip that Ike's Cabinet was initially composed of eight millionaires and a plumber, a charge that was not quite accurate, for Ezra Taft Benson did not have that kind of money.

48. Mitchell's two Assistant Secretaries of Labor were Arthur Larson, a former Cornell and University of Pittsburgh law professor (a presumably neutral official), and James T. O'Connell, a vice-president of the fairly large Publix Shirt Corp. of New York.

49. Weeks had also been associated with the arch-conservative NAM and American Enterprise Association, but apparently underwent a conversion during his years in federal office, for shortly after he resigned from the Cabinet, he became a member of the more moderate Establishment-oriented BAC. Weeks's top aide in the department was another prominent Eisenhower backer, Western businessman Walter Williams, who had been president of a small Seattle banking concern known as Continental, Inc. However, the primary reason Williams was appointed Under Secretary of Commerce was most likely that he had been an important figure in the CED.

50. This skewed pattern even manifested itself in the selection of Ike's Postmaster-General, Arthur E. Summerfield, who was a prominent Michigan party official and the recent chairman of the Republican National Committee. Summerfield was the longtime owner of a Flint Chevrolet agency, and his son served, from 1955 through 1961, on the board of the Genesee Merchants Bank & Trust Co. (and its predecessor concern), which was headed throughout this period by GM executive Harlow H. Curtice. The elder Summerfield was, moreover, a close friend and neighbor of Curtice, who was a member or trustee of both the BAC and CED. See *Fortune* (December 1955), p. 144.

51. See *Fortune* (February 1955), p. 140. Although no longer an active corporate executive, Rockefeller continued to serve on the board of Rockefeller Center during his two years with HEW.

52. Folsom had also been a director of the Federal Reserve Bank of New York (1949–1953) and the U.S. Chamber of Commerce (1941–1948). However, the latter affiliation was apparently of little significance. In fact, the Chamber of Commerce had almost no representation in the upper echelons of the Eisenhower administration, and the NAM did not fare much better.

53. In 1955 the position of Under Secretary of HEW was assumed by a professional educator, Herold C. Hunt. He was followed by a trio of non-economic figures—University of Delaware president John A. Perkins, former Ohio Wesleyan University president (and recent federal official) Arthur S. Flemming, and Bertha Adkins, a well-known Maryland Republican leader. Flemming, in fact, took over as head of the department in the latter part of 1958, when Folsom chose to step aside.

54. For instance, in a study which focused on sub-Cabinet recruitment, Dean Mann and Jameson Doig maintained that personal relationships rather than institutional affiliations played the primary role in appointments to high federal office in the 1945–1961 period. But the evidence presented in this and the preceding chapters clearly runs counter to this claim. See Dean E. Mann with Jameson W. Doig, *The Assistant Secretaries*, p. 83.

55. About a year after Houghton had been appointed Ambassador to France, his cousin, Arthur A. Houghton, Jr., was elected to the board of the Rockefeller Foundation. Perhaps not coincidentally, Aldrich's two predecessors as Ambassador to Great Britain, Lewis Douglas and Walter Gifford, also served as trustees of the Rockefeller Foundation.

56. See *Fortune* (October 1964), p. 115. One cannot explain this highly skewed appointment pattern by arguing that it takes a great deal of money, over and above one's governmental salary, to serve in either of these diplomatic posts, for there were a rather surprising number of wealthy men in the country, no less than 27,000 millionaires, many of whom would probably have been willing to accept such a prestigious appointment.

57. Its outside directors included Frederick H. Ecker, the former head of Metropolitan Life; financier Robert Winthrop, who was a director of the National City Bank of New York; and Curtis E. Calder, a public utility executive who also sat on the board of this big bank. The United States and Foreign Securities Corp. owned about 5 percent of the stock of the Amerada Petroleum Corp., a large concern of which Dillon had been a director. Dillon was also a close friend and business associate of Laurence Rockefeller. On this last point, see Peter Collier and David Horowitz, *The Rockefellers*, pp. 295–98.

58. See the 1958 *Moody's Industrial Manual*, p. 669.

59. Although the well-connected Winthrop Aldrich did not really need such links, his nephew and bank associate, David Rockefeller, was a vice-president of the Council on Foreign Relations, and the latter's brother, Nelson Rockefeller, served as a trustee of the CED from 1947 to 1953, when he was appointed Under Secretary of HEW. Dillon was the only one of the four ambassadors who was not affiliated in some way with one of the nation's top economic or civic organizations.

60. For more on Bohlen's marriage ties, see E. Digby Baltzell, *Philadelphia Gentlemen* (New York: Free Press, 1958), pp. 95, 125–26, and 440.

61. Conant actually served as John J. McCloy's successor as U.S. High Commissioner for West Germany up to 1955, when upon normalization of diplomatic relations, he was formally designated as our ambassador to this nation.

62. Perkins' business links were further strengthened by the fact that the vice-chairman of Merck & Co. was John S. Zinsser, who was a brother-in-law of two important business (and former diplomatic) officials: John J. McCloy, who was now board chairman of the Chase Manhattan Bank, and Lewis W. Douglas, who was board chairman of the Mutual Life Insurance Co. The last two men were also longtime trustees of the Rockefeller Foundation. And the president of the (First) National City Bank was James Stillman Rockefeller. For more on the Rockefeller interests in the latter bank, see *Fortune* (September 1965), p. 138, Martin Meyer, *The Bankers* (New York: Weybright & Talley, 1974), p. 436, and the *New York Times* (November 7, 1973), p. 93.

63. Many of these men were able, experienced governmental officials, such as former New Hampshire Governor Sherman Adams, who, up to his scandal-induced resignation in 1958, acted as Eisenhower's chief administrator or general manager. Some other White House aides or advisors had important economic ties, such as Meyer Kestnbaum, the head of Chicago's big retail trade concern of Hart, Schaffner & Marx (who served as a director of the Chicago and Northwestern Railway from 1944 through 1961, and as a trustee of the CED from 1948 through 1961); Clarence Randall, a longtime high executive of the Inland Steel Co. (who served as a director of the Bell & Howell Co. from 1957 through 1961, the Chicago, Burlington & Quincy Railroad from 1956 through 1961, the First National Bank of Chicago from 1953 to 1956, and as a member of the BAC from 1952 to 1956); and President Eisenhower's first general counsel, former New Jersey lawyer Bernard Shanley (whose most important directorship tie was with the Public Service Electric & Gas Co.).

64. See Robert Cutler, *No Time for Rest* (Boston: Little, Brown, 1966), p. 73.

65. Though never so listed in any government directories, Anderson was one of the seven members of a special set of consultants to the National Security Council appointed in early 1953 to help improve its operations. The other initial six advisors were James B. Black, president of the Pacific Gas & Electric Co. (and a director of the Chemical Bank & Trust Co. of New York. Equitable Life Assurance Society, Shell Oil Co., Southern Pacific Railroad, U.S. Steel Corp., and a number of San Francisco concerns); John Cowles, president of the *Minneapolis Star & Tribune* (who had formal ties with the BAC. Ford Foundation, General Mills, and various other Midwestern concerns); Eugene Holman, president of the Standard Oil Co. of New Jersey (and a vice-chairman of the BAC); Charles A. Thomas, president of the Monsanto Chemical Co. (who was a director of two St. Louis banks and the Southwestern Bell Telephone Co., a subsidiary of AT&T); Deane Malott, president of Cornell University (who had formal ties with the BAC, General Mills, B. F. Goodrich Co., and Owens-Corning Fiberglas Corp.); and David B. Robertson, president of the Brotherhood of Locomotive Firemen and Engineers (the token labor representative?). Black had long been involved with the BAC, and Thomas became a member of this body in 1955. The National Security Council's advisory committee has been described by knowledgeable insiders as "the seven wise men." See the *New York Times* (March 12, 1953), p. 22 and (March 21, 1965), p. 86.

66. In 1955 the three "outside" directors of Electro-Mechanical Research were Ernest M. Brannon, a Washington, D.C., attorney, Godfrey Rockefeller, a limited partner in the

investment banking concern of Clark, Dodge & Co. (and a director of the probably Whitney-dominated Freeport Sulphur Co.), and George A. Percy, another partner in Clark, Dodge (and a director of the Pallas Corp., a small Rockefeller-backed company).

67. For more on the role of the Gray family in the R. J. Reynolds Tobacco Co., see *Fortune* (December 1957), p. 242, and *Forbes* (December 1, 1971), p. 36.

68. Though dominated by academic economists, Eisenhower's Council of Economic Advisers (CEA) also took a decided turn to the right during these years. Its first chairman was Arthur F. Burns, a Columbia University professor and a research director of the National Bureau of Economic Research, who was an avowed anti-Keynesian. His two fellow members were Neil H. Jacoby, dean of the Graduate School of Business Administration at UCLA (and a member of the research advisory board of the CED), and Walter W. Stewart, a former New York businessman who had served as head of the Rockefeller Foundation from 1941 to 1950. In the mid-1950s Burns's place as chairman was taken by his Columbia colleague, Raymond Saulnier, who, like his predecessor, had been associated with the National Bureau of Economic Research. The four persons to serve, largely or wholly under Saulnier, as members of the CEA were: Joseph S. Davis, a Stanford University economist; Paul McCracken, a University of Michigan professor (and a director of a sizable investment company known as Group Securities, Inc., in the mid-1950s); Henry C. Wallich, a Yale University economist (who was a member of the CED's research advisory board in the late 1950's); and Karl Brandt, another Stanford University economist (who, after stepping down from this post in the early 1960s, joined the board of the arch-conservative Foundation for Economic Education).

69. Dodge, who had served briefly as a director of the Detroit branch of the Federal Reserve Bank of Chicago, had been strongly recommended for this White House post by Continental Can Co. head (and BAC member) Lucius Clay, who, as a military commander, had worked closely with Dodge in U.S.-occupied West Germany in the early postwar period.

70. A number of other special agencies also operated in much the same manner. The Atomic Energy Commission was, for example, directed by a combination of businessmen and scientists. As for corporate interests, the AEC's chairman for the first five years of the Eisenhower administration was Lewis Strauss, a recent financial advisor to the Rockefeller family. His successor was West Coast shipbuilder John A. McCone, head of the medium-sized Joshua Hendy Corp. (and a recent director of the Bechtel-controlled Industrial Indemnity Co., the California Bank, and the Pacific Mutual Life Insurance Co.). As a result of Russia's successful launching of a space satellite, the United States created in 1958 the National Aeronautics and Space Administration in an effort to catch up in this area. Most of the top officials of this agency were drawn initially from the scientific ranks, as seen by the appointment of its first head, Dr. T. Keith Glennan, the former president of the Case Institute of Technology.

71. Several other special defense and foreign policy agencies continued to operate during the Eisenhower years. These included the Office of Defense Mobilization (ODM) and the Mutual Security Agency (a body known after 1955 as the International Cooperation Administration). However, most of these were run by men who were primarily political or governmental figures rather than economic notables. Yet there were some exceptions to this appointment pattern, such as Victor Cooley, the former head of the Southwestern Bell Telephone Co. (a subsidiary of AT&T), who served as deputy director of the ODM from 1953 to 1957; William M. Rand, a high-ranking executive of the Monsanto Chemical Co. (and a director of various major Boston concerns), who served in 1953–1954 as a deputy director of the Mutual Security Agency; and John B. Hollister, the late Senator Taft's longtime law partner, who was the first head of the International Cooperation Administration. Hollister sat on the board of a number of large corporations, the most important of which was the New York Life Insurance Co. He was also a trustee of the arch-conservative American Enterprise Association.

72. See various post-1960 issues of *Who's Who in America* and, with regard to Bissell, Peter Wyden, *Bay of Pigs: The Untold Story* (New York: Simon & Schuster, 1979), p. 14, and any of the many reports of the CED during this period.

73. See, for example, Stewart Alsop, *The Center* (New York: Harper & Row, 1968), pp.

204–205, and the *New York Times* (July 1, 1973), Sect. VI, p. 35. Indeed, according to the first source, "there was a time [primarily in the 1950s and early 1960s] when the CIA was positively riddled with old Grotonians...".

74. See, for instance, David Wise and Thomas B. Ross, *The Invisible Government* (New York: Random House, 1964), pp. 110–114. These writers maintain "there is no doubt at all that the CIA organized and directed the 1953 coup that overthrew Premier Mohammed Mossadegh and kept Shah Mohammad Reza Pahlavi on his throne." They claim that Kermit Roosevelt "is still known as 'Mr. Iran' around the CIA...."

75. See Paul Hoffman, *Lions in the Street*, p. 80. The British Petroleum Co. (the corporate successor of the Anglo-Iranian Oil Co.) was allotted a much reduced 40 percent share in this enterprise, the Royal Dutch Shell Co. was granted a 14 percent stake, and another smaller concern, the Compagnie Française des Pétroles, got a rather scanty 6 percent. Unfortunately, very little has been revealed about the extended proceedings which led to the establishment of this consortium, although later testimony has shown that Secretary of State Dulles placed a sharp limit on participation by America's smaller independent oil companies. See the *New York Times* (March 29, 1974), p. 47.

76. The United Fruit Co. had nearly 100,000 employees, more than 90 percent of whom were Latin Americans. According to one reliable source, the company imported about 57 percent of all bananas sold in North America in the late 1950s, and had once handled 75 percent of the total. See *Fortune* (March 1959), p. 99.

77. The coup was reportedly directed by CIA operative Frank Wisner, who, up to 1947, had been a member of the Wall Street law firm of Carter, Ledyard & Milburn, a once top-tier concern which had declined considerably in the postwar period. See the *New York Times* (July 1, 1973), Sect. VI, p. 35.

78. The CIA also backed an abortive effort in the late 1950s to overthrow President Sukarno of Indonesia because he had taken an increasingly strong stance against various foreign-owned businesses in his country. Among the CIA's less nefarious activities in the 1950s was the payment of large sums of money to support friendly political parties in other countries, such as in Italy where an average of $3 million a year was covertly channeled into the coffers of the ruling Christian Democratic party. For more on the latter, see the *New York Times* (May 13, 1973), p. 3.

79. In 1953 the board of the J. Henry Schroder Banking Corp. included Delano Andrews; George A. Braga, who was president of the Manati Sugar Co. and two other interrelated concerns; Charles W. Gibson, a vice-president of the Rockefeller-oriented Air Reduction Co.; John G. Laylin, a partner in the Washington law firm of Covington & Burling (with which former Secretary of State Dean Acheson was long associated); Avery Rockefeller, president of a closely affiliated banking firm known as Schroder, Rockefeller & Co.; and Albert L. Williams, a high IBM official. The board of the Manati Sugar Co. included Gerald F. Beal, the president of the J. Henry Schroder Banking Corp. and board chairman of the International Railways of Central America; Alfred Jaretski, Jr., another partner in Sullivan & Cromwell; and Henry E. Worcester, a recently retired executive of United Fruit.

80. In the early 1940s Shepardson served as treasurer of the CFR, while Dulles was its secretary. Both men were affiliated, as trustees, with the CFR when the Guatemalan coup was carried out.

81. In 1959 this post was taken over by James McGovern, the general attorney for the United Fruit Co., which still held 48 percent of the stock in this rail line, which carried most of United Fruit's products from interior to port in Guatemala.

82. Coolidge's father was actually one of the organizers of the United Fruit Co. For more on a number of the figures involved in this affair, see Laurence H. Shoup and William Minter, *Imperial Brain Trust*, pp. 195–99.

83. Up to 1950 one of the United Fruit Company's directors was business executive Thomas D. Cabot, whose brother, career diplomat John M. Cabot, held the post of Assistant

Secretary of State for Inter-American Affairs from March 1953 to March 1954, a few months before the Guatemalan coup. Thomas Cabot also served on the board of the First National Bank of Boston throughout this period. For more on John M. Cabot's hostility toward the Arbenz regime, see Cole Blasier, *The Hovering Giant: U.S. Responses to Revolutionary Change in Latin America* (Pittsburgh: University of Pittsburgh Press, 1976), pp. 160–64.

84. For a good overall treatment of this subject, see Robert Griffith, *The Politics of Fear: Joseph R. McCarthy and the Senate* (Rochelle Park, N.J.: Hayden, 1970), p. 197–238.

85. McCarthy had a number of backers in the business world, but most were maverick figures or strong supporters of right-wing groups. For a survey of corporate views on this controversial figure, see *Fortune* (April 1954), pp. 156–58 and 180–94.

86. See *Dun's Review* (January 1970), p. 40, and Hobart Rowen, "America's Most Powerful Private Club," *Harpers* (September 1960), p. 84. The article in *Dun's Review* claims that the BAC exerted much pressure on Eisenhower to take a strong stand against McCarthy, something he had been unwilling to do. But since the President chose to work largely behind the scenes in this affair, it is difficult to gauge the effect of this influence. Big business's other efforts against McCarthy probably had greater impact, particularly in the Senate.

87. For an assessment of the importance of Flanders' censure motion and a description of the financial and operational support given to the anti-McCarthy drive by such business leaders as Paul Hoffman (who was a trustee of the CED and a former member of the BAC), see Robert Griffith, *op. cit.*, pp. 270–79.

88. For instance, there was a 23-man citizens group formed under the leadership of Studebaker head Paul Hoffman and Philadelphia banker Howard Petersen, which, among other things, sent a telegram to every United States Senator to urge strong support of the McCarthy censure motion. Of the 14 business members of this committee, six were trustees of the CED, two others were affiliated with one of the regional federal reserve banks, and another was New York insurance company executive Lewis Douglas. Some of the non-corporate members of this group were also associated with such elitist interests. Moreover, in their special efforts to reach Arkansas's conservative Senator John McClellan, who represented a pivotal figure among the uncommitted Democrats in the Upper House, the McCarthy censure backers turned to Philadelphia businessman C. Jared Ingersoll, who controlled a railroad company located in Arkansas and adjoining states. See Robert Griffith, *op. cit.*, pp. 272 and 281, and the *New York Times* (July 23, 1954), p. 24.

89. See *Dun's Review* (January 1970), p. 40, and also Richard M. Fried, *Men Against McCarthy* (New York: Columbia University Press, 1976), p. 291.

90. See, for instance, Thomas E. Cronin and Sanford D. Greenberg (eds.), *The Presidential Advisory System* (New York: Harper & Row, 1969), p. 105. However, for a more incisive contrary analysis, see Frank Popper, *The President's Commissions* (New York: Twentieth Century Fund, 1970), pp. 15–19.

91. In 1954, the outside directors of General Motors included five representatives of the du Pont interests, two high officials of J. P. Morgan & Co., Lewis W. Douglas (the president of the "Morgan-oriented" Mutual Life Insurance Co.), and Pittsburgh banker Richard K. Mellon (who had married a daughter of Seward Prosser, a former head of Bankers Trust and a onetime director of General Motors). Furthermore, GM executive Alfred P. Sloan, Jr., sat on the board of J. P. Morgan & Co.

92. Although Gaither had married a member of the wealthy Castle family of Hawaii and sat on the board of the Pacific National Bank of San Francisco, he was probably asked to serve as the initial chairman of this committee because of his Ford Foundation and Rand Corp. ties.

93. See John C. Donovan, *op. cit.*, pp. 144–47.

94. In 1953 the Eisenhower administration also moved to resolve the tidelands oil controversy by passing legislation which, except for previous treaty obligations, gave the states control over the first three miles of the Continental Shelf, with the federal government granted jurisdiction over all resources beyond that point. According to one source, the man responsible

for the development of this legislative package was Houston attorney Dillon Anderson, who was a partner in Texas's largest corporate law firm of Baker, Botts, Andrews & Shephard, which had many ties to Southwestern oil interests. See *Newsweek* (February 13, 1956), p. 30.

95. The long-established 27½ percent oil depletion allowance remained intact throughout this period, in part because of the strong support it continued to receive in the Senate Finance Committee, which included among its key members Oklahoma's influential Robert Kerr (the board chairman of Kerr-McGee Oil Industries), Louisiana's Russell Long (whose family had major petroleum holdings), and Florida's George Smathers (whose law firm counted among its clients the Gulf Oil Corp.). In 1957 another "Southern Rim" Senator was added to this committee, New Mexico's Clinton P. Anderson, who about this time was appointed to the board of directors of the New York publishing firm of Henry Holt & Co., which was controlled by the Murchison oil interests of Texas. On this latter point, see *Fortune* (December 1959), pp. 104–105.

96. Conversely, the import share of the big international oil companies dropped from about 68 percent in 1954 to a little over 45 percent four years later. See Edward H. Shaffer, *The Oil Import Program of the United States: An Evaluation* (New York: Praeger, 1968), pp. 15–23, Douglas R. Bohi and Milton Russell, *Limiting Oil Imports* (Baltimore: Johns Hopkins University Press, 1978), pp. 10–62, and Anthony Sampson, *The Seven Sisters* (New York: Viking, 1975), pp. 146–47.

97. To get some idea of the magnitude of this subsidy, one need only note that the federally protected domestic oil cost almost twice as much as that imported from the (pre-OPEC) Middle East. See *Fortune* (June 1969), p. 106. For other accounts of this matter, see Ronnie Dugger, "Oil and Politics," *Atlantic Monthly* (September 1969), p. 77, and Gerald D. Nash, *United States Oil Policy, 1890–1964*, pp. 202–206.

98. The State Department was, of course, also involved in these proceedings. Up to early 1959 it was headed by John Foster Dulles, whose former New York law firm had long represented the Standard Oil Co. of New Jersey and Under Secretary of State Christian Herter, who had married into a family which had been closely associated with the development of this giant concern. However, because of Dulles's illness he may not have played a very important role in this affair.

99. See John Bainbridge, *The Super-Americans* (Garden City, N.Y.: Doubleday, 1971), p. 366, and *Fortune* (November 1955), p. 47. Anderson was also apparently a much-favored protégé of Texas oil magnate Sid Richardson, who reportedly persuaded Eisenhower to appoint him to his first high federal post (Secretary of the Navy) in 1953. See Alfred Steinberg, *Sam Johnson's Boy: A Close-up of the President from Texas* (New York: MacMillan, 1968), p. 620; Ann Fears Crawford and Jack Keever, *John B. Connally: Portrait in Power* (Austin, Texas: Jenkins, 1973), p. 81, and John M. Blair, *The Control of Oil* (New York: Random House, 1976), pp. 173–75.

100. For more on Anderson's later financial ties to the Rockefeller interests, see the *New York Times* (October 29, 1974), p. 1.

101. Another issue which was fiercely debated during the Eisenhower years concerned the proposed liberalization of America's foreign trade. This extended dispute has been described by Bauer, Pool and Dexter as essentially a legislative deadlock, created by deep-seated divisions in the business community. However, judging from the available evidence, these scholars did not pay proper heed to the important role probably played, albeit quietly, by the nation's two most influential economic groups, the BAC and CED (the latter is mentioned only four times in their analysis, the former not at all). In fact, almost all of the non-governmental figures frequently referred to in their study were affiliated with one or another of these elite groups. This issue was ultimately resolved in favor of the nation's major corporate interests in the early 1960s. See Raymond A. Bauer, Ithiel de Sola Pool, and Lewis A. Dexter, *American Business and Public Policy: The Politics of Foreign Trade* (New York: Atherton Press, 1963), passim.

102. For instance, in 1945, long before it was popular, Warren publicly advocated a system of prepaid state health insurance. Hence his appointment to the Supreme Court actually pleased

some conservative California Republicans, such as Vice President Richard Nixon and Senate majority leader William F. Knowland, for it effectively removed Warren from the state political scene. See Henry J. Abraham, *Justices and Presidents*, p. 237.

103. Harlan had also served briefly in the early 1950s as the chief counsel of the New York State Crime Commission, but this was his only other significant governmental experience.

104. By the mid-1960s the United States Trust Co. had total assets of about $6 billion (see *Trusts and Estates*, (February 1965, p. 160). Some indication of the overall influence of Harlan's law firm may be found in the fact that one of its senior partners, Arthur A. Ballantine, sat on the board of the New York Life Insurance Co. and the New York Trust Co., and that Elihu Root, Jr., had long served as a director of AT&T and the Mutual Life Insurance Co. Just before his appointment to the U.S. Circuit Court, Harlan had represented the du Pont family in the first round of its antitrust fight with the federal government to retain its indirect control of General Motors. See John P. Frank, *The Warren Court* (New York: Macmillan, 1964), p. 102, and Paul Hoffman, *Lions in the Street*, p. 65.

105. See Henry J. Abraham, *Justices and Presidents*, p. 243.

106. One senior partner, Waldron M. Ward, had served for many years as board chairman of the big Howard Savings Institution and as a director of the National Newark & Essex Banking Co. and the New Jersey Bell Telephone Co. Brennan is also reported to have represented a number of major concerns in the New York metropolitan area, particularly with regard to labor matters. See John P. Frank, *The Warren Court*, p. 117.

107. See Leon Friedman and Fred L. Israel (eds.), *The Justices of the United States Supreme Court, 1789–1969*, Vol. IV, p. 2851. When Eisenhower was later asked if he had made any mistakes while he had been President, he replied, "Yes, two, and they are both sitting on the Supreme Court." See Henry J. Abraham, *Justices and Presidents*, p. 246.

108. See Friedman and Israel, *op. cit.*, Vol. IV, p. 2894. One of Whittaker's law partners, Henry N. Ess, had served for many years as a director of the City National Bank & Trust Co.

109. Stewart also apparently married into considerable money, and was reported to be the wealthiest member of the Court in the late 1970s. See *Time* (May 28, 1979), p. 16.

110. Its senior partner, Frank Dinsmore, was a director of Procter & Gamble up to 1956 when he resigned because of his advancing age.

111. Although a substantial number of such people were appointed to important posts under Truman, the proportion was not as high as it was under Eisenhower. For example, only one of the three persons who served as Secretary of State under Truman and only one of his two Secretaries of the Treasury could be classified as elite figures, whereas all of these officials in the Eisenhower administration were drawn from the upper ranks of American business and society. (These percentages exclude five persons whose elite or non-elite status cannot be readily determined.)

112. Aside from the so-called clientele Departments of Labor, Commerce, Interior, Agriculture, Justice, and (now) HEW, there were only six people appointed to high posts in the Eisenhower administration who did not fall into one or another of the above categories. These were Detroit lawyer Wilbur Brucker, New York accountant William Franke (who was appointed Secretary of the Navy near the end of the administration), Texas businessman Dudley Sharp (who was made Secretary of the Air Force at an almost equally late date), and three career diplomats—Charles E. Bohlen, Llewellyn Thompson, and Walter Dowling. Also note that the socio-economic status of four of these six figures could not be determined.

CHAPTER 5

The Kennedy-Johnson Years

The eight-year period following the Eisenhower administration was marked by a number of important economic and political developments. Nowhere was there more striking change than in the industrial sphere. Indeed, primarily because of the war in Vietnam, manufacturing firms grew at a truly remarkable rate during this period, some mainly through expanded production and sales, others mostly through the absorption of various, usually lesser, concerns. IBM was a prime example of the first kind of corporation. It grew from about $1.5 billion in assets in 1960 to more than $6.7 billion by 1968, a spectacular rise that made it America's seventh largest manufacturing firm (sixth, if volume of sales is used as a standard). But there were many other companies which chose to expand through mergers, some to such an extent that they came to stand as symbols of a new form of economic enterprise, the giant conglomerate. One of the best known of these was the International Telephone & Telegraph Corp., which, under the aggressive leadership of its president, Harold Geneen, took over a host of other companies and in the process transformed itself into more of a manufacturing firm than a public utility. Similarly, in the 1960s several railroads broadened the scope of their operations to counteract their declining passenger business, altering their names to reflect this fact; the Chicago and Northwestern Railway, for example, became Northwest Industries, Inc., and the Atchison, Topeka & Santa Fe Railway was transformed into Santa Fe Industries, Inc.

As a matter of fact, the mid and late 1960s witnessed the greatest wave of corporate mergers in the nation's history. Not all represented the absorption of small or medium-sized concerns by larger units. A number of these transactions involved one big company buying out another. For instance, the Union Oil Co. of California took over the Pure Oil Co. (which had assets of $766 million), the Atlantic Refining Corp. acquired the Richfield Oil Corp. (which had assets of $450 million), the McDonnell Aircraft Corp. bought out the Douglas Aircraft Co. (which had assets of $565 million), Montgomery Ward and Co. merged with the Container Corp. of America (which had assets of nearly $400 million), and the Texas-based conglomerate, Ling-

Temco-Vought, Inc., acquired a controlling interest in the Jones and Laughlin Steel Corp. (which had assets of almost $1.1 billion).[1] The greatest merger of this period was undoubtedly that effected, after much negotiation with high federal officials, between two of the giants of the transportation industry, the Pennsylvania Railroad and the New York Central Railroad, to form the mammoth Penn Central Co.[2]

As a result of these developments, the 1968 makeup of America's thirty largest non-financial concerns represented a truly staggering array of corporate wealth (see Table 7).

TABLE 7
America's Top 30 Non-financial Firms in 1968

1968 Rank	Company	1960 Assets ($ millions)	1968 Assets ($ millions)
1.	AT&T	22,558	40,151
2.	Standard Oil Co. of N.J.	10,090	16,786
3.	General Motors Corp.	7,838	14,010
4.	Ford Motor Co.	3,757	8,953
5.	Texaco Inc.	3,647	8,687
6.	Gulf Oil Corp.	3,843	7,498
7.	Mobil Oil Corp.	3,455	6,871
8.	IBM	1,535	6,743
9.	Penn Central (RR) Co.	4,856	6,524
10.	Sears, Roebuck & Co.	2,149	6,508
11.	United States Steel Corp.	4,627	6,391
12.	General Telephone & Electronics Corp.	2,205	6,157
13.	Standard Oil Co. of Cal.	2,782	5,770
14.	General Electric Co.	2,522	5,744
15.	Standard Oil Co. of Ind.	2,926	4,737
16.	Chrysler Corp.	1,369	4,398
17.	Shell Oil Co. (a foreign-controlled firm)	1,885	4,230
18.	ITT	924	4,022
19.	Tenneco Inc. (the former Tennessee Gas Transmission Co.)	1,734	3,888
20.	Consolidated Edison Co. of N.Y.	2,963	3,845
21.	Pacific Gas & Electric Co.	2,501	3,815
22.	E. I. du Pont de Nemours & Co.	2,949	3,289
23.	Union Carbide Corp.	1,713	3,209
24.	Southern Pacific (RR) Co.	2,017	2,923
25.	Phillips Petroleum Co.	1,647	2,889
26.	Southern California Edison Co.	1,343	2,755
27.	Ling-Temco-Vought, Inc.	93	2,648
28.	Commonwealth Edison Co., Ill.	1,737	2,624
29.	Marcor, Inc. (the merger successor of the Container Corp. of America and Montgomery Ward & Co.)	740	2,618
30.	Eastman Kodak Co.	899	2,565

Thus by the late 1960s only two railroads ranked among the "top thirty" non-financial firms in the country, and only one company engaged entirely in retail trade (Sears, Roebuck) fell into this select category.[3] Furthermore, no more than six "top 30" concerns could be classified as public utilities, and two of these—the General Telephone and Electronics Corp. and Tenneco— were considered by *Fortune* to be industrial enterprises because more than 50 percent of their revenue was derived from manufacturing or mining.[4] Only one public utility, AT&T, stood out as an economic giant of enormous importance from a national rather than regional standpoint. In short, the majority of America's biggest non-financial enterprises in the 1960s were manufacturing firms, and by far the largest proportion of these were major oil companies.

Although none of the companies which are generally thought of as heavy defense contractors (Boeing, Lockheed, etc.) made the "top 30" ranking, a significant number of the concerns listed in Table 7 were among the nation's chief suppliers of military hardware (although such sales made up only a small percentage of their overall volume of business).[5] For example, GE, AT&T, General Motors, and Ling-Temco-Vought constituted four of the top ten Defense Department contractors in 1968, and GE, IBM, and Chrysler were three of the ten largest contractors with the National Aeronautics and Space Administration.[6] In addition, GE, AT&T, Union Carbide, and E. I. du Pont de Nemours and Co. were four of the top five contractors with the Atomic Energy Commission in 1968. Thus it is clear that a number of the nation's biggest industrial firms did a substantial volume of business with the government's major defense (and defense-oriented) agencies in the 1960s.

During the latter part of this period systematic data were compiled and published for the first time, thanks primarily to the efforts of Texas Congressman Wright Patman, on the amount of trust funds held by America's large commercial banks; these figures, when combined with the assets long reported in the major directories, gave a more accurate picture of the true size of the nation's "top 30" financial institutions (see Table 8).

Despite what many writers have claimed about the alleged demise of "finance capitalism," the major banks and insurance companies still occupied a crucial place in American business life. Indeed, a number of the trust departments of the banks listed in Table 8 were larger than many of the nation's top industrial concerns.[7] And while it is true that a sizable amount of this (trust) money was invested in non-voting stock, these big institutions have apparently wielded considerable influence in corporate affairs, as may be inferred from the fact that many of their high-ranking officials (or their legal representatives) have served on the boards of various large industrial companies over the years.[8] These institutions have far eclipsed the much-publicized mutual funds, whose power has been vastly overrated. In fact, the only other set of financial firms of much importance in America were certain influential (mainly New York) investment banks, such as the First Boston Corp., Lehman Brothers, Lazard Frères, Morgan, Stanley & Co., and Carl

TABLE 8
America's Top 30 Financial Institutions in 1968

		Overall Assets ($ millions, including trust funds)	Trust Fund Component of Overall Assets ($ millions, as of late 1967)
1.	Chase Manhattan Bank, N.Y.C.	31,657	13,644
2.	First National City Bank of N.Y.C.	28,379	10,872
3.	Morgan Guaranty Trust Co., N.Y.C.	25,993	16,825
4.	Bank of America (National Trust & Savings Association), Cal.	25,151	3,696
5.	Prudential Insurance Co. of America	25,111	—
6.	Metropolitan Life Insurance Co.	24,601	—
7.	Bankers Trust Co., N.Y.C.	17,942	11,091
8.	Manufacturers Hanover Trust Co., N.Y.C.	16,510	7,338
9.	Equitable Life Assurance Society, N.Y.C.	13,093	—
10.	Chemical Bank New York Trust Co.	12,959	4,593
11.	Mellon National Bank & Trust Co., Pittsburgh	11,520	7,630
12.	First National Bank, Chicago	11,387	5,430
13.	Continental Illinois National Bank & Trust Co.	11,310	5,137
14.	New York Life Insurance Co.	9,579	—
15.	First National Bank of Boston (and its Old Colony Trust Co. affiliate)	8,964	5,561
16.	John Hancock Mutual Insurance Co., Boston	8,865	—
17.	United States Trust Co., N.Y.C.	8,762	8,399
18.	Western Bancorporation (a California bank holding company)	8,496	2,137
19.	Aetna Life & Casualty Co., Conn.	7,985	—
20.	Security First National Bank, Los Angeles	7,831	2,213
21.	National Bank of Detroit	6,930	3,427
22.	Wells Fargo Bank, San Francisco	6,590	1,897
23.	Crocker-Citizens National Bank, San Francisco	6,386	2,081
24.	Wilmington Trust Co., Del.	6,066	5,625
25.	Cleveland Trust Co.	5,891	3,605
26.	Northern Trust Co., Chicago	5,842	4,542
27.	Irving Trust Co., N.Y.C.	5,732	1,656
28.	Harris Trust & Savings Bank, Chicago	5,636	3,869
29.	Northwestern Mutual Life Insurance Co., Wisc.	5,476	—
30.	Marine Midland Banks, Inc. (a New York bank holding company)	4,943	2,472

M. Loeb, Rhoades & Co.[9] These concerns, along with the big banks and insurance companies, have been the dominant forces in American finance in the postwar period.

Several other post-1960 developments of an economic (or politico-economic) nature deserve special comment. One of these had to do with a politically induced change in the Business Advisory Council and its formal relationship with the federal government (in theory, the BAC was a central advisory committee for the Department of Commerce). From the late 1930s to the early 1960s, the BAC was almost entirely dominated by major corporate interests. For instance, out of the 59 active members of this elite body in 1960, all but three were high-ranking executives of big companies. And two of these three men, who were officials of small or medium-sized concerns, had directorship ties with large corporations.

However, when a more liberal Democratic regime headed by John F. Kennedy came into power in 1960, a difference of opinion soon emerged as to the proper role and makeup of the BAC. The new administration's Secretary of Commerce, Luther Hodges (a former North Carolina governor and business executive who was not closely linked with the BAC), took the position, initially with the President's blessing, that the BAC should include more small businessmen and that its meetings should be open to the press when governmental officials were participating in its proceedings. This proposal met with bitter opposition. Rather than accede to the request, the BAC chose to sever its formal tie with the Department of Commerce and to reconstitute itself as a completely independent body, henceforth simply to be known as the Business Council.[10] But for various reasons (such as the President's apparent need for substantial business support), these strained relations did not last long and the White House soon extended the olive branch to these corporate leaders.[11] In fact, the Business Council emerged from this affair in a better position in some respects than it had formerly enjoyed under the Eisenhower regime, for it was now permitted, if not encouraged, to set up liaison committees with most of the major departments of the federal government, as well as with the Council of Economic Advisers and the White House itself.[12] In short, the BAC had regained its highly privileged status. As one member put it, "only the name has been changed."[13]

One noteworthy development which took place somewhat earlier was the merger in 1955 of the nation's two largest labor unions, the American Federation of Labor and the Congress of Industrial Organizations, to form the giant AFL-CIO. Although this huge body did not carry much weight in the fairly conservative Eisenhower administration, by 1960 it claimed a total of 15 million members, roughly one-fifth of the American labor force. Hence one might expect that with the election of a strongly labor-backed Democratic regime in 1960, this massive union would exert considerable influence in the appointment practices and general policymaking of the new administration.

The 1960 presidential election pitted two very different kinds of men against each other. The Democratic candidate, John F. Kennedy, was a comparatively youthful and appealing figure who was the product of a family of great wealth and political ambition. The patriarch of this clan was FDR's controversial pre-World War II Ambassador to Great Britain, Joseph P. Kennedy, an Irish-American who had been brought up in Boston, but had been badly slighted by that city's highly inbred Brahmin establishment and thus sought his fortune elsewhere.[14] In the course of his career Joseph P. Kennedy amassed a great deal of money, first through various (at times, questionable) stock market ventures and the production of a number of second-rate movies, later in the 1930s, after Prohibition was repealed, as a whiskey importing agent, and finally in the postwar period as a major real estate operator whose holdings were concentrated primarily in Chicago and New York City.[15] Indeed, by about 1960 the elder Kennedy had compiled a huge fortune, estimated to be close to $300 million (although some informed observers put it considerably higher).[16]

In large part because of his great desire to achieve public recognition (perhaps to compensate for slights received earlier in the business and social worlds), Joseph Kennedy strongly encouraged his sons to enter politics. Thus shortly after John F. Kennedy finished his World War II tour of military duty, he ran for a seat in the House of Representatives and won handily, thanks partly to his father's money and political connections with various Irish leaders in the Boston area. Then in 1952 John F. Kennedy was elected to the United States Senate after a hard-fought race in which he bested Brahmin incumbent Henry Cabot Lodge, once again with the help of his father's fortune and many important politico-economic ties. Four years later, in an effort to gain greater national recognition, Kennedy made a strong but futile bid to become his party's vice-presidential candidate. Very much encouraged by this showing, he embarked, with the support of various close friends and family members, on a four-year quest to capture the Democratic presidential nomination in 1960 through a carefully planned campaign which featured many public appearances and various promotional devices.[17] With this backing, Kennedy was able to score several key primary victories over his financially beleaguered liberal opponent, Hubert Humphrey, and to win the nomination, despite the belated efforts of two other formidable adversaries, Senate majority leader Lyndon Johnson, and the more intellectual Adlai Stevenson, who could not overcome the handicap of being a two-time presidential loser.[18]

Kennedy's Republican opponent in the 1960 election was former Vice President and onetime California Congressman Richard Nixon, who had shrewdly exploited his position as the nominally second-ranking figure in the Eisenhower administration to build up support among the party regulars and in various influential segments of the business community. Such was Nixon's strength in major economic circles that he was able to beat back the challenge of New York's fairly liberal Governor, Nelson A. Rockefeller, who, despite his great wealth, failed to secure the support of many important corporate officials, apparently because they felt he was too liberal or independent.[19] Nixon, who came from a family of modest means, not only had the support, as a zealous anti-Communist, of the conservative wing of the Republican party, he also had the strong endorsement of most of America's top economic leaders. These included Horace Flanigan, board chairman of the Manufacturers Trust Co. of New York; Walter Thayer, president of the recently created Whitney Communications Corp. and a partner in the New York investment firm of J. H. Whitney & Co. (one member of which was associated with the BAC, and another with both the CED and, interestingly, the Chase Manhattan Bank); and New York financier Sidney J. Weinberg, who until the early 1950s had been a major fundraiser and high-level corporate recruiter for the Democratic party.[20] To gain electoral appeal in the Northeast, Nixon selected as his running mate former Massachusetts Senator Henry Cabot Lodge, who, since his defeat by Kennedy in 1952, had gained much acclaim and publicity by serving as America's Ambassador to the United Nations during the Eisenhower administration. Yet it was the Democratic ticket of John F. Kennedy and Lyndon B. Johnson (who, despite his identification with Texas oil interests, had been picked in a shrewd effort to carry the South)[21] which emerged victorious in an extremely close election.

JFK'S MAJOR ADMINISTRATIVE AND DIPLOMATIC APPOINTMENTS

When Kennedy took office in January 1961, the liberal forces in the country, having suffered through eight lean years under Eisenhower, were hopeful that they would be well represented in the new Democratic regime, in part because Kennedy's campaign oratory had created the expectation that he would forge some kind of New Deal, one which, to use his words, would constitute a New Frontier in American politics. However, in many respects the nation's progressive forces were to be disappointed.

At the outset of his administration Kennedy turned heavily for advice to Robert A. Lovett, a New York investment banker whom he barely knew and who had not even voted for him.[22] Lovett was undoubtedly a very able and knowledgeable man, having served as Under Secretary of State under George C. Marshall and as Secretary of Defense in the closing years of the Truman administration. But as David Halberstam has pointed out, Lovett was also "...the very embodiment of the Establishment," a man who had spent most of his life as a partner in the major Wall Street banking house of Brown Brothers Harriman & Co., and had acted as chairman of the executive committee of the Harriman-controlled Union Pacific Railroad since 1953.[23] In addition, Lovett had served in recent years as a board member of the Columbia Broadcasting System, Freeport Sulphur Co., New York Life Insurance Co., North American Aviation, Inc., and Rockefeller Foundation, and, up to 1957, as a trustee of the CED.

There were a number of avowed aspirants for the key post of Secretary of State, chief of whom were former presidential candidate Adlai Stevenson, Connecticut's liberal onetime Ambassador to India Chester Bowles, postwar diplomat David K. E. Bruce, and Arkansas Senator J. William Fulbright. But ultimately the choice boiled down to David Bruce, a Maryland patrician whose brother had many important corporate ties, and Lovett's warmly supported candidate, Dean Rusk, a mild-mannered Georgia-born figure who had held two academic posts in the prewar period and had been a second-echelon official in the State Department during the Truman administration.[24] This had led to his appointment as president of the Rockefeller Foundation in 1952, a position he attained largely at the urging of John Foster Dulles, with whom he had worked in the negotiation of the Japanese peace treaty. In this capacity Rusk came to know a number of prominent people in both the civic and business worlds, such as Foundation chairman John D. Rockefeller III, Lewis W. Douglas (the recently retired head of the Mutual Life Insurance Co. and a brother-in-law of Chase executive John J. McCloy), and President-elect Kennedy's influential advisor Robert Lovett.[25] Apparently the support of these and other similar figures did much to secure Rusk's appointment as Secretary of State.

As one might expect with a change in parties, a number of new people were appointed to high posts in the State Department in the early 1960s, some of them selected by Kennedy himself rather than by Dean Rusk. One of these was Connecticut's progressive leader Chester Bowles, who had strongly backed Kennedy in the 1960 campaign and had gained some diplomatic experience by serving as Ambassador to India in the early 1950s. He was awarded the post of Under Secretary of State. Bowles was also, interestingly, a trustee of the Rockefeller Foundation; indeed, he was probably its most liberal member. However, Bowles did not last long as Rusk's top aide. By December 1961 he had been eased out of this office and appointed Ambassador-at-large, a seemingly impressive, but not really vital post. He was replaced at State by a rather unusual figure, George W. Ball, who, prior to his appointment as Under Secretary of State for Economic Affairs earlier in the year, had been a member of a Washington law firm which had its main office in New York, where it was known as Cleary, Gottlieb, Steen & Hamilton. This was what might be called a second-tier firm which represented a number of fairly large American concerns such as Royal McBee (a typewriter and office supply company) and, up to at least 1959, Pan-American World Airways. The firm also counted among its clients a variety of foreign business enterprises such as the Venezuelan Chamber of Commerce and the European Coal and Steel Community, which gave it a distinctly international flavor.[26]

Most of the other major posts in the State Department were filled during the Kennedy years by longtime career officials, the bulk of whom had held fairly prominent positions in the preceding administration. One exception was George C. McGhee, a Texas oilman and diplomatic official under

Truman, who was appointed to the comparatively new post of Under Secretary of State for Political Affairs. From the mid-1950s to the early 1960s McGhee had a number of noteworthy economic links, for he was apparently the sole owner of the McGhee Production Co. (a Texas oil company of undetermined size), a director of Petroleum Reserves, Inc. (a small concern probably dominated by the New York-based investment firm of William A. M. Burden & Co., the senior partner of which was a director of the Council on Foreign Relations), and a trustee of the CED and the Brookings Institution.[27] Thus McGhee, who held this high-level post till May of 1963 (when he assumed other diplomatic duties), was obviously an elite figure.[28]

As his Secretary of the Treasury, Kennedy chose (after an abortive effort to recruit Robert Lovett) another wealthy New York figure whom he hardly knew, C. Douglas Dillon.[29] This was a curious appointment, for Dillon had served for eight years in the Eisenhower regime, first as Ambassador to France and later as a high State Department official, and was thus one of the few people in American history to hold posts in successive administrations controlled by two different parties. (Indeed, he had even been a big contributor to Nixon's presidential campaign.) Dillon was on intimate terms with many of the nation's major business leaders, especially the Rockefeller interests.[30] Prior to his appointment as our chief emissary to Paris, he had been president of Dillon, Read & Co. (a New York investment banking firm founded by his father) and the family-dominated U.S. and Foreign Securities Corp. (in which the Dillon interests probably had a significant stake). More recently (in 1960–1961), Dillon served as a trustee of the Rockefeller Foundation, which body would appear to have played an important part in the high-level federal recruitment process in the postwar period.[31]

For the very demanding post of Secretary of Defense, Kennedy picked, on the advice of various prominent business figures, Ford Motor Co. executive Robert S. McNamara. This man had built a record in economic circles as an extraordinarily able administrator, as almost a "human computer." He had entered the employ of Ford in 1946 as one of a group of highly touted Harvard Business School "whiz kids" and had proceeded to climb rapidly up the corporate ladder. In late 1960 (just five weeks before his appointment as Secretary of Defense), McNamara had been elected president of the Ford Motor Co., the first president to come from outside the Ford family. McNamara was therefore somewhat reluctant to accept this key federal post, but after consulting with a number of important people such as investment banker (and Ford Motor Co. director) Sidney Weinberg, and, of course, Henry Ford himself, he agreed to take over the management of the nation's huge Defense Department.[32]

Most of the other top posts in the Defense Department were also filled by influential figures drawn from the ranks of business or business-oriented law firms. McNamara's Deputy Secretary of Defense was New York attorney Roswell Gilpatric, who, although he had served a brief stint as Under

Secretary of the Air Force in the early 1950s, was essentially a Wall Street lawyer. Indeed, his firm (Cravath, Swaine & Moore) served as general counsel for such large concerns as the Bethlehem Steel Corp., Chemical Bank New York Trust Co., Minneapolis-Honeywell Regulator Co., IBM, National Sugar Refining Co., and Time, Inc. (a partner, Maurice T. Moore, was a brother-in-law of magazine publisher Henry Luce).[33]

The first Secretary of the Navy was a man of a different stripe, Texas lawyer John B. Connally, who was best known as a close friend and political ally of Vice President Lyndon B. Johnson. But Connally had also branched out in the 1950s to become a powerful politico-economic figure in his own right. More to the point, he had become closely linked with certain major oil interests in Texas, most notably as attorney for the big independent oil operator Sid Richardson, who, up to his death in 1959, was a close friend of an even richer figure, Clint Murchison.[34] Strong evidence of this association may be found in the fact that Connally sat on the board of the now largely Texas-controlled New York Central Railroad from 1959 to 1961, most likely as a replacement for Richardson. Connally, however, resigned as Secretary of the Navy in late 1961 in order to run for governor of Texas. He was replaced by another representative of that state, Fred Korth, a high-ranking official of the (medium-sized) Continental National Bank of Fort Worth, who had served briefly as Assistant Secretary of the Army at the end of the Truman administration. Korth was not without his "outside" ties either. He served in the early 1960s as a director of the Bell Aerospace Corp., a major defense-oriented arm of Textron, Inc., and of the Texas and Pacific Railway, a subsidiary of the Missouri-Pacific Railroad. In the latter connection, Korth may have acted as an agent of the above Texas oil interests, for when he stepped down from this board to enter the Defense Department, his place was apparently taken by Perry R. Bass, a nephew and former business partner of Sid Richardson. Thus during most of the Kennedy administration the Navy Department would appear to have been run by men closely aligned with important politico-economic interests in Texas.

The position of Secretary of the Air Force was held by a person who had considerably more experience in governmental affairs, Eugene Zuckert. He had served as Assistant Secretary of the Air Force from 1947 to 1952, and then for two years as a member of the Atomic Energy Commission. Upon leaving the federal government in 1954, Zuckert had established a law practice and a management consulting service in Washington, both of which he ran until the end of the decade. At this point he became board chairman of the Nuclear Science and Engineering Corp., a relatively small Pittsburgh-based concern which was backed by various major financial interests, chief of which was probably New York's Lehman Brothers, a concern with great politico-economic influence.[35]

The first Secretary of the Army was Elvis J. Stahr, Jr., an academic with no elite ties. He had most recently served as president of West Virginia

University. But Stahr, it should be noted, was not Kennedy's first choice for this post (that was IBM president Thomas J. Watson, Jr.).[36] Moreover, he served only until July 1962, when he was induced to leave the government by the lure of another prestigious academic post. Stahr was succeeded by Cyrus Vance, a former New York attorney who had, since the outset of the administration, been acting as general counsel of the Defense Department. He had also been employed in the late 1950s as a part-time counsel for a major subcommittee of the Senate Armed Services Committee (largely because he and his more influential senior law partner, Edwin L. Weisl, were close associates of Senate majority leader Lyndon B. Johnson). Like Roswell Gilpatric, Vance was basically a Wall Street lawyer, though his firm—Simpson, Thacher and Bartlett—represented a different set of interests. Its clients included two of New York's most important financial institutions, Lehman Brothers and the Manufacturers Hanover Trust Co. (the product of the 1961 merger of the Hanover Bank and the Manufacturers Trust Co.).[37] In addition, the West Virginia-born Vance had attended the "right" schools and had married into New York's wealthy (W. & J.) Sloane family. In fact, although Vance's father-in-law, John Sloane, had retired as a corporate executive in 1955, he served up to 1961 as a director of the big United States Trust Co. and was a still active board member of the much smaller, but also elitist-dominated, Atlantic Mutual Insurance Co.

Most of the other members of Kennedy's Cabinet were very different types from those appointed to the Departments of State, Treasury, and Defense, as the following summary analysis makes clear:

Attorney General

Robert F. Kennedy, Mass. (1961 through 1963)	Chief counsel, Senate Committee to Investigate Improper Activities in Labor-Management Relations (1957–1959); other lesser federal posts (1951–1956); no experience in private law practice; no formal corporate ties; younger brother of the President and his 1960 campaign manager; married into Chicago's wealthy Skakel family, which controlled the big privately owned Great Lakes Carbon Corp.

Secretary of the Interior

Stewart L. Udall, Ariz. (1961 through 1963)	U.S. Congressman, Arizona (1955–61); partner, Tucson law firm of Udall & Udall (1948–1954); no major socio-economic ties; father was a longtime justice of the Arizona Supreme Court

180   Elites in American History

Secretary of Agriculture

Orville S. Freeman, Minn. (1961 through 1963)	Governor of Minnesota (1955–1961); partner, Minneapolis law firm of Larson, Lindquist, Freeman & Fraser (1947–1955); no major socio-economic ties

Secretary of Labor

Arthur J. Goldberg, Ill. (1961–1962)	No prior governmental experience; partner, Chicago law firm of Goldberg, Devoe, Shadur & Mikva (1947–1961); general counsel of the CIO (1948–1961); director of the Amalgamated Trust & Savings Bank of Chicago, a union-controlled concern (1948–1961)
W. Willard Wirtz, Ill. (September 1962 through 1963)	Under Secretary of Labor (1961–1962); partner, Stevenson, Rifkind & Wirtz, Chicago law firm (1955–1961); also partner, New York law firm of Paul, Weiss, Rifkind, Wharton & Garrison (1958–1961); professor of law, Northwestern University (1946–1954 and 1939–1942); no major socio-economic ties

Secretary of Commerce

Luther H. Hodges, N.C. (1961 through 1963)	Governor of North Carolina (1954–1960); Lieutenant-Governor of North Carolina (1952–1954); gen. manager or vice-president (North Carolina area), Marshall Field & Co. (1938–1950, lesser official before that); director of the American Thread Co. (1952–1955)

Secretary of Health, Education and Welfare

Abraham Ribicoff, Conn. (1961–July 1962)	Governor of Connecticut (1955–1961); Connecticut Congressman (1949–1953); partner, Ribicoff, Ribicoff & Kotkin, Hartford law firm (1941–1954); no major socio-economic ties
Anthony J. Celebrezze, Ohio (July 1962 through 1963)	Mayor of Cleveland (1953–1962); Cleveland lawyer, individual practice (1939–1952); no major socio-economic ties

Of these eight Cabinet officials, only one could be described as an elite figure, and that was the President's brother, Robert F. Kennedy, who, although he had never applied his legal training outside of government, was appointed Attorney General, primarily because of his close political and personal relationship with the nation's newly elected chief executive.[38] Like his brother, Robert Kennedy was heir to one of America's great, albeit recently acquired fortunes. Furthermore, he had married into another wealthy family, the Skakels, who controlled the Great Lakes Carbon Corp., a company which probably had a gross income of over $100 million a year.[39] Yet neither of these two rich families had any noteworthy formal links with the country's leading business institutions and executives; in a sense, they were "outsiders." Hence, it seems fair to say that while their vast family resources were of enormous value in promoting the political rise of the Kennedy clan, Robert Kennedy's appointment to Cabinet office was made purely for personal and political reasons and not because he had the backing of America's economic establishment.[40]

Similarly, the selection of Orville Freeman and Stewart Udall to serve as heads of the Departments of Agriculture and Interior did not stem from any pressure exerted by major corporate interests. Both men were chosen because of long-established geo-political considerations, and neither had any significant socio-economic ties. Similarly, the two men who held office as Secretary of Health, Education and Welfare, Abraham Ribicoff and (after July 1962) Anthony Celebrezze, were clearly political choices, probably made in part for ethnic reasons.[41] In fact, Celebrezze was America's first Italian-born Cabinet official. Neither man had graduated from college (though both later obtained law degrees), nor had either established any marked economic links.

In his initial appointment as Secretary of Labor, President Kennedy obviously strove to satisfy key union leaders by selecting a lawyer who had long been identified with the labor movement, Arthur Goldberg. The economic allegiance of this man was readily revealed by the fact that he had served as general counsel for the CIO (and its post-1955 component of the AFL-CIO) from 1948 to 1961, and for a like period as a director of the Amalgamated Trust and Savings Bank of Chicago, a comparatively small concern controlled by the Amalgamated Clothing Workers of America and run for the benefit of its union members. When the able and ambitious Goldberg was appointed to the Supreme Court in the latter part of 1962, he was replaced by his top aide in the department, W. Willard Wirtz, a man without any ties to the labor movement. Since 1955 Wirtz had been a partner in a Chicago law firm with former Illinois Governor Adlai Stevenson. This was a rather unusual concern, for it was linked with the much bigger and better known New York firm of Paul, Weiss, Rifkind, Wharton & Garrison, which had long had strong Democratic ties and, unlike most prominent firms, many Jewish partners.[42] Neither of these concerns was closely associated with America's top corporations; rather, they derived the bulk of their support from various lesser enterprises.⁴³ Wirtz had also spent a number of years up to the mid-1950s as a law professor at Northwestern University, which experience probably gave him a fairly objective view of labor-management relations, in contrast to that of people generally picked by Republican regimes.

Even the traditionally pro-business post of Secretary of Commerce was filled during the Kennedy administration by a man who was not intimately associated with the top ranks of big business. This official, former North Carolina governor Luther Hodges, was picked for two reasons: to give the South some representation in the Cabinet, and to satisfy the "politico-economic" requirements of this office by selecting someone who was a part of the business world. Hodges had been an essentially second-tier national official of the Chicago-based retail trade concern of Marshall Field and Co. However, he retired from this firm in 1950 and a few years later decided to run for high executive office in his home state, in which effort he was eminently successful. At no time in his career was Hodges affiliated with a concern that was linked with the organizational heart of America's economic establishment, the BAC and CED.⁴⁴

In sum, most of the domestically oriented Cabinet posts in the Kennedy administration were filled, as they were in the Truman regime, by people without close ties to major corporate interests. Yet big business continued to hold sway over State, Treasury, and Defense, all lofty words about the democratic vistas of the New Frontier notwithstanding.

In the realm of foreign affairs, the appointment policy of the Kennedy administration clearly placed considerable weight on ability and experience, although some of the emissaries chosen also had noteworthy socio-economic ties. For example, as Ambassador to Great Britain, President Kennedy picked the seasoned diplomat David K. E. Bruce, who had held a number of important federal posts in the postwar period such as Ambassador to France (1949–1952), Under Secretary of State (1952–1953), and Ambassador to West Germany (1957–1959). However, Bruce was also a wealthy patrician who, although he had given up a business career in the early 1940s, had a brother (James) who maintained an impressive array of corporate connections and had apparently long acted as a major Democratic party fundraiser.⁴⁵ At the time of his brother's appointment to the Court of St. James, James Bruce served on the board of the Avco Manufacturing Co., American Airlines, Continental Insurance Co., the Lehman-Lazard Frères-dominated General American Investors Co., Republic Steel Corp., Revlon, and U.S. Industries. In short, David Bruce had both strong professional and politico-economic support for his appointment to this premier diplomatic post.

As his initial Ambassador to France, President Kennedy made a rather unusual choice, for in a sharp break with tradition he selected a former high-ranking military man, General James M. Gavin. A West Point product, Gavin had spent almost his entire career in the United States Army, rising ultimately to the rank of Lieutenant-General. Upon his retirement in 1958, Gavin, like a number of other ex-officers, took a position in the business community, becoming a high executive of Boston's fairly large management consulting firm of Arthur D. Little, Inc. In addition, he served as a director of the medium-sized Merchants National Bank of Boston (known after 1960 as the New England National Bank) and the big New York-based American Electric Power Co. Thus this former Army officer had forged some ties with important economic interests. However, Gavin held diplomatic office for only about a year and a half before he decided to return to private life. His replacement was a man with much more experience in this area, Charles E. Bohlen, a moderately wealthy, highly respected career diplomat who had served as Ambassador to the Soviet Union in the mid-1950s and then, toward the later part of the Eisenhower administration, as a special assistant to the Secretary of State for Soviet Affairs.

President Kennedy also chose to rely heavily on professional personnel for the nation's emissaries to West Germany and the Soviet Union. Although appointed by the preceding Republican regime, America's Ambassador to West Germany, Walter Dowling, was retained in office until April 1963. He was then succeeded by George C. McGhee, a man who had both a significant amount of diplomatic experience, most recently as Under Secretary of State for Political Affairs, and a number of noteworthy economic ties (as a trustee of the CED up to 1961, and as a director of a fairly small concern known as Petroleum Reserves, Inc., which was probably dominated by New York's influential William A. M. Burden interests). In like manner, Kennedy retained career diplomat Llewellyn Thompson as Ambassador to the Soviet Union. When Thompson stepped down from this post in mid-1962, he was replaced by another high State Department official, Foy Kohler, who had been acting for the previous three years as Assistant Secretary of State for European Affairs.

As American Ambassador to NATO, President Kennedy chose a person with limited experience, Thomas K. Finletter, who had served briefly as a Marshall Plan official and a Defense Department executive during the Truman administration. Through most of the postwar period, Finletter had been a member of a New York law firm, Coudert Brothers, which could, at best, be ranked in the second tier of Wall Street's legal community and was hardly of sufficient importance to warrant Finletter's selection as NATO emissary. Finletter was more likely picked because he was a longtime director of the influential Council on Foreign Relations.

Because of the United States' increasing involvement in the political and military affairs of South Vietnam, a special look should be taken at the types of people chosen to serve as Washington's representatives to this embattled country. In the early 1960s the American Ambassador was longtime career diplomat Frank E. Nolting, Jr. But when conditions worsened in Vietnam in the summer of 1963, the President felt compelled to make a change. Apparently in an effort to gain bipartisan support for his foreign policy,

Kennedy appointed former UN Ambassador Henry Cabot Lodge to replace Nolting. Like many men drawn from outside the departmental ranks, Lodge was an elitist figure, as could be inferred from his name. He had also served since 1961 as a director of the Foreign Policy Association (a New York-based civic group) and the big John Hancock Mutual Insurance Co., along with such other influential Brahmins as Lloyd D. Brace (board chairman of the First National Bank of Boston), corporate executive Thomas Cabot, and financier Ralph Lowell.

For his White House staff, President Kennedy picked a number of men who had previously worked for him, either as legislative assistants or as high-level campaign officials—men such as Theodore Sorensen, his longtime Senate aide and advisor, Arthur Schlesinger, Jr., a well-known Harvard historian, and Lawrence O'Brien, another staunch Kennedy backer who was placed in charge of patronage matters and Congressional relations. However, the most important member of his staff turned out to be a person who had almost no contact with Kennedy before his election, former Harvard dean McGeorge Bundy. Bundy had not even been a part of the so-called Cambridge group of some twenty-five intellectuals who fed ideas to Kennedy during his campaign.[46] Although he had written almost no serious scholarly works during his academic career, Bundy was, judging from all accounts, an extremely able man, with a strong strain of intellectual arrogance. As David Halberstam has put it, Bundy "...had been a legend in his time at Groton [one of the nation's most exclusive prep schools], the brightest boy at Yale, [and] dean of Harvard College at a precocious age...."[47] Indeed, at Harvard he rose from lecturer to the prestigious post of dean of the faculty in just four years.

Able though he was, Bundy was undoubtedly helped enormously by the fact that he had been born into a wealthy Boston Brahmin family, which on his mother's side was a part of that city's fabled Lowell clan.[48] In addition, his father, Harvey H. Bundy, was a longtime partner in Boston's top-tier law firm of Choate, Hall & Stewart, and served as a high official of the (New York-based) Foreign Bondholders Protective Council from 1953 to 1962, board chairman of the Carnegie Endowment for International Peace from 1952 to 1958 (he succeeded John Foster Dulles), president of the Boston-based World Peace Foundation from 1946 to 1954, and as a director of the big Boston Five Cents Savings Bank and the Merchants (or New England Merchants) National Bank of Boston.[49] Also, McGeorge Bundy's older brother, William, a high State Department official, had married Dean Acheson's daughter, and his younger sister, Katherine, had married into the socially prominent Auchincloss family of New York, thereby establishing a link with the President's wife.[50] Furthermore, Bundy's father had served as a top aide to Henry L. Stimson when this Establishment leader was Secretary of War in the early 1940s and during the last half of his term of office as Secretary of State under Herbert Hoover, an experience that brought the elder Bundy in contact with many important business and government officials.⁵¹ Bundy thus brought to the position of Special Assistant to the President for National Security Affairs both a highly elitist background and an unusually strong, self-confident character. As a result, he soon emerged as a more decisive and powerful figure in the administration than the mild-mannered Secretary of State, Dean Rusk.

As head of the CIA, President Kennedy initially retained the Republican director, Allen Dulles, a former Wall Street lawyer who still served as a director of the Council on Foreign Relations. Although the early planning was undertaken during the last year of the Eisenhower regime, it was in considerable part at the urging of the pro-business Allen Dulles and one of his elitist top aides, Richard M. Bissell, Jr. (a recent CED advisor), that the newly installed Kennedy administration was persuaded to support a CIA-backed invasion of Cuba, which under the leftist leadership of Fidel Castro had recently seized a number of large American-owned properties there.⁵² The Bay of Pigs invasion was a dismal failure. But it had far-reaching effects within the Kennedy administration, and soon led to the removal of Dulles as head of the CIA.⁵³

As his replacement, President Kennedy chose another distinctly pro-business figure, former West Coast industrialist John A. McCone. Although he had previously served as Under Secretary of the Air Force (in 1950–1951) and as Chairman of the Atomic Energy Commission (from mid-1958 to late 1960), McCone had spent most of his life in an executive or entrepreneurial capacity. He had been a high official of the Bechtel-McCone Corp. from 1937 to 1945 and a medium-sized California steamship company, the Joshua Hendy Corp., from 1945 to 1958. In addition, McCone had served during much of the postwar period as a director of such California-based concerns as the Bechtel-controlled Industrial Indemnity Co., the (United) California Bank of Los Angeles, and the Pacific Mutual Life Insurance Co. Upon stepping down from his AEC post, McCone had been appointed to the board of Trans World Airlines (apparently as part of a New York-backed financial takeover of this big enterprise) and, perhaps even more importantly, to the board of the Standard Oil Co. of California. Thus it would appear that, after the embarrassing Bay of Pigs debacle, President Kennedy, although obviously upset with the CIA for its bungling, merely replaced one pro-business official with another.⁵⁴

President Kennedy also made several important appointments dealing with the critical issue of arms control during the first part of his administration. These selections revealed much about his overall orientation in diplomatic and defense affairs. For example, as his special advisor on disarmament (a newly created post) he picked a man who epitomized the American Establishment, New York banker John J. McCloy.⁵⁵ As already noted, this able individual had served in three noteworthy governmental positions in years past: as a top aide to Secretary of War Henry L. Stimson during World War II, as president of the World Bank in the late 1940s, and as U.S. High Commissioner to West Germany from 1949 to 1952. However, McCloy was now primarily a major financial figure. He served as board chairman of the Rockefeller-dominated Chase Manhattan Bank from 1953 to 1960, when he became head of its overseas affiliate, the Chase International Investment Corp. He was also a director of Metropolitan Life, Allied Chemical, AT&T, and Westinghouse Electric. In addition, McCloy was board chairman of the Ford Foundation and a trustee of the Rockefeller Foundation. McCloy served as special advisor on disarmament only until the fall of 1961, when a more formal governmental mechanism was created to deal with this knotty diplomatic problem—namely, the U.S. Arms Control and Disarmament Agency. To head this agency, President Kennedy chose a onetime government official, William C. Foster, who had served as Under Secretary of both Commerce and Defense in the Truman administration and had been a key Marshall Plan administrator. Upon leaving the federal government, Foster had become a major business executive. He had, for example, acted as a second-tier official of the big Olin Mathieson Chemical Corp. from 1955 to early 1961, at which point he was appointed board chairman of the (medium-sized) United Nuclear Corp., a concern probably dominated by the Rockefeller interests.[56] Foster had forged an impressive array of politico-economic links in recent years. He had served as a trustee of the CED from 1946 to 1961, as an active member of the BAC from 1953 to 1957 (after which he assumed "graduate" status), and since 1959 as a director of the Council on Foreign Relations. Obviously, Foster was on very close terms with America's economic establishment.

President Kennedy was compelled to pick a new head of the World Bank when its longtime president, former Chase National Bank official Eugene Black, reached retirement age in 1962. Kennedy's selection was an even more prominent New York financial figure, George D. Woods, board chairman of the First Boston Corp., a big investment bank. Woods had many key corporate ties. He served as a director (or trustee) of the Rockefeller-dominated Chase International Investment Corp. from 1959 to early 1963, the Rockefeller Foundation from 1960 up to almost the end of his term of office as president of the World Bank, the Rockefeller-oriented Transoceanic-AOFC, Ltd. (and its predecessor concern) from 1958 to 1961, the Rockefeller-controlled International Basic Economy Corp. in the latter part of 1962, the Kaiser Steel Corp. from 1951 to 1962, the Commonwealth Oil Refining Co. from 1957 to 1962, the Campbell Soup Co. from 1958 to 1963, the New York Times Co. from 1960 to 1962, and the (Pitcairn-controlled) Pittsburgh Plate Glass Co. in the early 1960s. Thus, in view of the first set of ties, it seems fair to say that during the New Frontier years the presidency of the World Bank was merely shifted from one Rockefeller representative to another.[57]

The influence of corporate interests was much less marked in the operation and top-tier staffing of various special domestic agencies. Only the recently formed (post-Sputnik) National Aeronautics and Space Administration showed any significant sign of such economic forces at work, and this was manifested primarily in the appointment of James E. Webb as its head. Webb had gained considerable experience in the federal government under the Truman administration, for he had served as director of the Bureau of the Budget in the late 1940s and as Under Secretary of State from 1949 to 1952. Since that time Webb had been associated primarily with the business world; from 1952 to 1961 he had been an assistant to the president of the Kerr-McGee Oil Industries, a large firm controlled primarily by Oklahoma's influential Senator Robert Kerr.[58] In addition, although he was never a major corporate executive, Webb served as a trustee of the CED from 1956 to 1961 and for an even longer period as a director of the big McDonnell Aircraft Corp., a concern that relied largely on defense business. Hence, although NASA had many able engineers and scientists on its staff, the top office in the agency, which by now was an integral part of the military-industrial complex, was held by a man with key economic and political ties.[59]

In line with the domestic appointment pattern of most postwar Democratic regimes, the Bureau of the Budget was run under Kennedy by men whose backgrounds were primarily governmental or academic. The first director of this agency was David Bell, who had secured much valuable experience in this area through his work as a major White House aide in the Truman administration. Since the early 1950s Bell had been a professor of economics at Harvard University, and apparently had little contact with the business community prior to his elevation to this high federal post in 1961. Later in the following year, Bell was asked to take over the management of the recently revamped Agency for International Development. His place as head of the Bureau of the Budget was assumed by another non-elite figure, Kermit Gordon, who had been a professor of economics at Williams College prior to his appointment to the President's Council of Economic Advisers in 1961.

The CEA was also dominated during the Kennedy years by a group of fairly liberal, professionally trained economists, foremost of whom was Walter W. Heller, a professor of economics at the University of Minnesota who had served as a fiscal advisor to Orville Freeman when he was governor of that state. The other two newly appointed members of the CEA were the aforementioned Kermit Gordon and Yale University professor James Tobin, both of whom were more liberal than their Republican predecessors (one of these. Karl Brandt, soon became a major economic advisor to Barry Goldwater). For various political and professional reasons, Gordon and Tobin served only briefly. Their replacements—Gardner Ackley, a University of Michigan economist, and John P. Lewis, an Indiana University professor- were men of the same mold. The Council of Economic Advisers, however, was a relatively new agency staffed largely by academics, so it never had the power or prestige of the Treasury Department and was not able to exert as much influence in financial affairs as Cabinet spokesman C. Douglas Dillon, a former Wall Street banker.[60]

Thus, judging by its major administrative and diplomatic appointments, the overall orientation of the Kennedy administration was not one of flaming liberalism, but one of fiscal restraint and caution, with numerous concessions made to important corporate interests.[61]

IMPORTANT POLICY ACTIONS OF THE KENNEDY ADMINISTRATION

While President Kennedy did have a brief, much-publicized confrontation with one of the nation's largest concerns, United States Steel, over a proposed price hike, in the end big steel quietly got its way.[62] The record of the Kennedy administration must be judged by more lasting measures. For instance, although the President talked much about the need for tax reform during his first two years in office, he did not push particularly hard for it, both because of his conservative instincts and his precarious political position stemming from the extraordinarily close 1960 election. However, in 1963 Kennedy did make a major attempt to provide tax relief to both private citizens and corporate interests through a substantial, though pro-upper class, personal income tax cut for the former and massive investment credit program for the latter.[63] To help generate economic and political support for this measure, the President created a special Businessmen's Committee for Tax Reform, the initial composition of which was quite revealing, for it again showed that certain interests wield great influence in American life:[64]

Co-chairmen	Henry Ford, II, board chairman, Ford Motor Co.	Active member of the Business Council; director of GE and the General Foods Corp.
	Stuart T. Saunders, president, Norfolk & Western Railway, a subsidiary of the Pennsylvania Railroad (of which appointed head one month later)	Active member of the Business Council and a trustee of the CED
Vice-chairmen	M. W. Cresap, Jr., president, Westinghouse Electric Corp.	Trustee of the CED; director of the Mellon National Bank & Trust Co.
	Sam Fleming, president, Third National Bank of Nashville	Director of the Louisville & Nashville Railroad
	Frazar B. Wilde, board chairman, Connecticut General Life Insurance Co.	Vice-chairman of the CED: director of the Bankers Trust Co. of New York
Other executive committee members	Frederick R. Kappel, board chairman, AT&T	Chairman of the Business Council; vice-chairman of the CED; director of the Chase Manhattan Bank, the Metropolitan Life Insurance Co., and the General Foods Corp.

David Rockefeller, president, Chase Manhattan Bank	Trustee of the Equitable Life Assurance Society
Gardiner Symonds, board chairman, Tennessee Gas Transmission Co.	Vice-chairman of the National Industrial Conference Board; active member of the Business Council; trustee of the CED; director of several large companies
J. Harris Ward, board chairman, Commonwealth Edison Co., Ill.	Director of the New York Life Insurance Co. and several other large companies

As one might infer from this kind of support, President Kennedy's tax reform bill was not a very progressive measure.[65]

Another major, very different kind of decision during the Kennedy years was the award, by administrative act, of a hotly contested multi-billion dollar defense contract for the construction of a revolutionary (movable wing) fighter plane for the Navy and the Air Force known as the TFX. The two main contenders for this enormous contract were the big Boeing Airplane Co. of Seattle and an ad hoc team composed of the General Dynamics Corp., a New York-based concern with large plants in Texas and Southern California, and the considerably smaller Grumman Aircraft Engineering Corp. Both bidders went through a series of grueling tests. Although the competition was fairly close, the Air Force Council and System Source Selection Board, two long-established evaluation panels made up of high-ranking military and professional men, voted to award the coveted contract to Boeing on the grounds of better design and lower cost. Indeed, in the fourth and final evaluation, "there was," to quote one authority, "...unanimity—absolutely no dissent—up through the entire military chain of command, in recommending the Boeing Company."[66] Yet, for the first time in Pentagon history, the top civilian officials in the Defense Department expressly rejected the counsel of their chief military advisors and, after a series of hurried meetings, decided, largely on the basis of their "rough" judgment and McNamara's special emphasis on the "commonalty" factor (i.e., like parts and plane for both the Navy and Air Force), to award the contract to the financially troubled General Dynamics Corp.[67]

This turned out to be a disastrous decision. Partly because of the radical nature of the proposed craft, many technical problems arose in the course of its construction, problems which high Pentagon officials did much to screen from public and Congressional view. Moreover, despite the best efforts of Secretary McNamara and other important Defense Department figures, the plane failed to meet numerous key design and operational standards and was given extremely poor ratings by test pilots in its early trial runs. As a result, after billions of dollars had been expended on this dubious project, the program was terminated in the late 1960s when Congress refused to authorize any additional funds for the craft. Thus, instead of getting the originally planned 1,700 "path-breaking" planes (officially known as F-111s) at a cost of approximately $6 billion, the Pentagon obtained about 500 fighters for a total outlay of almost $7.9 billion. Many of these aircraft were plagued with operational problems.[68]

But even more disturbingly, there would seem to have been a gross conflict of interest involved in the award of this contract, the full extent of which was not revealed until a Senate study was released (after considerable delay) to the general public in early 1970. According to all accounts, four high-ranking civilian officials—Secretary of Defense Robert McNamara; Deputy Secretary of Defense Roswell Gilpatric, a former partner in the Wall Street law firm of Cravath, Swaine & Moore; Secretary of the Navy Fred Korth, a longtime major executive of the Continental National Bank of Fort Worth; and Eugene Zuckert, a Washington lawyer and management consultant who had recently served as board chairman of the Nuclear Science and Engineering Corp.—were, in different degrees, responsible for the reversal of the recommendation of the Source Selection Board and Air Force Council that this job be given to Boeing.

Of these four, one man in particular, Roswell Gilpatric, has been singled out for his highly questionable role in the award of this lucrative contract to General Dynamics, a concern apparently not averse to using political influence to achieve its objectives.[69] Contrary to the impression he initially gave Senate probers of having previously done only a limited amount of work for both competing firms, Gilpatric had actually served for over two years, immediately prior to his appointment as Deputy Secretary of Defense, as a major legal (and policy?) advisor to General Dynamics in a number of important matters, even though his law firm did not then act as general counsel to this corporation.[70] In all, he devoted roughly one-quarter of his time from the latter part of 1958 through 1960 to the affairs of General Dynamics, for which service his law firm received a total of $111,000.[71] Furthermore, Gilpatric attended 18 of the 31 regular and special meetings held by the board of directors of General Dynamics between 1958 and December of 1960, so that, although never so listed, he was, as the Senate subcommittee concluded, "...a de factor member of the board of directors" during this period.[72] Moreover, Gilpatric did not cease (non-social) contact with his law firm when he entered the Pentagon. By his own admission, he made 17 phone calls to one of his former partners, Maurice T. Moore, between January 24, 1961, and March 19, 1963, a number of which concerned General Dynamics.[73] Also, interestingly, Maurice T. Moore was elected to the board of directors of General Dynamics just four weeks after the big TFX contract was awarded to this company, at which time Cravath, Swaine & Moore became the general counsel to this corporation.[74] Thus, without even considering the role played by the other three high-ranking officials in this affair, it seems fair to conclude that economic influence was a major factor in the decision to award the TFX contract to General Dynamics and that Roswell Gilpatric was clearly enmeshed in a gross conflict of interest.[75]

Another issue in which the Kennedy administration was involved was the communications satellite controversy. Most knowledgeable authorities strongly favored the creation of some form of communications satellite system, partly to secure the benefits of such advanced technology, and partly to keep ahead of the Russians in this critical area. The basic question was, how should such a system be organized? Many liberals in Congress argued that this vital program should be run by a government agency under the control of democratically elected officials. Various other people, fearing governmental waste or inefficiency, wanted the system placed in private hands. The Kennedy administration sided with the latter, much larger, group, although it initially opposed the efforts of the big communications carriers to have a substantial voice in the management of this enterprise. Indeed, to prevent the carriers from exercising a baneful influence on the company organized to operate the system, the President originally proposed that their stock would carry no voting rights. However, after much fierce debate and political infighting, the common carriers, led by AT&T, managed, with the help of Oklahoma Senator and oilman Robert Kerr, to kill this idea. Full voting rights were granted to all shareownership interests. In the end, Congress passed a law that provided for the creation of an essentially privately-owned Communications Satellite Corp., to be governed by a fifteen-man board of directors. Six of these officials were to be elected by the common carriers, six by the other stockholders in the corporation, and because of a late amendment (allegedly inserted to allay liberal critics), three "public" directors were to be chosen by the President with the advice and consent of the Senate.[76]

At the outset, it was difficult to know where control resided in this important enterprise, in part because a number of the men picked by the President to serve as the first directors and formal incorporators of this federally chartered concern were relatively insignificant figures, chosen perhaps to create a favorable public image.[77] Most of them served for only about a year, in what was apparently little more than a brief shakedown period. However, some indication of where power lay in this corporation in its critical early years may be found in the fact that its first board chairman was Leo D. Welch, who had just retired as head of the Standard Oil Co. of New Jersey, and was a former high official and still active director of the (First) National City Bank of New York.[78] In addition, he had recently served as a trustee of the CED. Thus Welch was clearly on good terms with the leaders of America's economic establishment, of which AT&T was an integral part.

The Kennedy administration was, of course, involved in the war in Vietnam.[79] When Kennedy assumed office, the American government had, under former President Eisenhower's "limited risk" policy, fewer than a thousand men stationed in this beleaguered nation, almost all of whom served as military advisors to various units of the South Vietnamese armed forces. By the latter part of 1963 the Kennedy administration, despite gnawing doubts about the viability of the Diem regime, had sharply increased the number of army personnel (who now were permitted to engage in combat activities), to well over 16,000. These steps were reportedly taken because the President and many of his military and diplomatic advisors strongly subscribed to an exaggerated containment policy (later described as the "domino" theory) which placed great weight on a military solution to this internecine conflict and tended to overlook the serious weaknesses of the unpopular and often repressive South Vietnamese government.[80]

By the summer of 1962, conditions had deteriorated to the point where President Kennedy felt compelled to make a change in our diplomatic representation to this country. He replaced incumbent emissary Frederick Nolting, a postwar career official who had become closely identified with the authoritarian regime of Ngo Dinh Diem and his family, with a patrician Republican, Henry Cabot Lodge, who had served as American Ambassador to the United Nations under Eisenhower and had recently been elected to the board of the John Hancock Mutual Life Insurance Co. of Boston.[81] But the situation in South Vietnam only continued to worsen, and it soon became evident that a change in the national leadership of the South Vietnamese government was imperative. The Diem regime, however, stubbornly refused to step aside, much to the annoyance of American officials. Hence the Kennedy administration gave its approval to Ambassador Lodge and the CIA to encourage a military coup to oust these obstinate rulers. This action, to the surprise of the President, led to the murder of Premier Ngo Dinh Diem and his brother. As it turned out, this was the last major act of the Kennedy administration, for within a month, President Kennedy was assassinated.

JOHNSON AND HIS INFORMAL INNER CIRCLE

The death of John F. Kennedy brought to power a very different type of person from those men who had served as chief executive in the post-Civil War period. Lyndon Baines Johnson, who had been added to the 1960 Democratic ticket strictly for geopolitical reasons, was the first man from the South to hold this high office in almost a hundred years. Johnson came from a relatively poor family. He did not attend a prestigious Ivy League college, or even the less expensive University of Texas, but instead went to the Southwest Texas State Teachers College. After teaching school for a number of years, Johnson was fortunate enough in the early 1930s to obtain a position as secretary to a newly elected Texas Congressman, Richard Kleberg, the wealthy son of the owner of the fabled King Ranch. This experience gave him his first taste of national politics and implanted in the ambitious Johnson a strong desire to run for high office himself. In 1937, with the sudden demise of the Congressman in his district, he received his chance to achieve his objective, and was elected to the House of Representatives. Because of his background and the temper of the times, Johnson was in these early years an avowed New Dealer, faithfully supporting most of the measures advocated by America's highly popular President, Franklin D. Roosevelt, who took a strong interest in Johnson's career and reportedly had a marked influence on his thinking on various major governmental issues.

Johnson served in the House of Representatives until 1948 when, seizing on a good opportunity, he won an extremely close election to replace the politically fading "Pappy" O'Daniel as a United States Senator from Texas. Johnson soon emerged as a masterful legislative strategist, and by the mid-1950s was the acknowledged leader of the Democratic party in the Senate. Indeed, he was the most influential figure in this body during the latter part of the decade, thanks in part to his alliance with such potent forces as Oklahoma's Senator Robert Kerr.

However, it should be emphasized that during this period Johnson was no longer the New Deal liberal of his early political years.[82] According to Evans and Novak, the basic reason for this shift was that with the end of the war Texas was overwhelmed by a great oil and gas boom which quickly pushed cotton and cattle, the traditional mainstays of the economy, into a subordinate status. Unlike some political leaders, such as Texas Senator Tom Connally,[83] Lyndon Johnson soon managed to forge a number of crucial links with influential figures in the oil and gas industry, the first and foremost of which was his intimate tie with the famous Brown brothers (George and Herman) of Houston. These two men had not only built up a huge contracting firm known as Brown and Root, Inc., in the postwar period, but had also expanded their activities into the natural gas field by buying one of the "'Big Inch'' lines in the late 1940s (previously a government-owned facility built during World War II to transport natural gas to the Northeast) and transforming it into the big Texas Eastern Transmission Corp.[84]

Johnson's other major link with such interests was established a few years later when his longtime close friend and political aide John B. Connally became the general attorney for Texas oil magnate Sid Richardson. Connally retained this position up to Richardson's death in 1959, at which time he became the executor for the latter's multimillion-dollar estate. Connally remained loyal to both Richardson and Johnson. From 1959 to 1961 he served as the former's replacement as a director of the New York Central Railroad. He also acted as one of Johnson's key campaign managers during his abortive 1960 presidential drive. For this effort he was subsequently rewarded with the post of Secretary of the Navy. Thus when Johnson was suddenly forced to assume the reins of presidential leadership in November 1963, he had already demonstrated that he was an extremely able and ambitious politician with more conservative than liberal leanings.

Yet as President of the United States Johnson appeared, to many, to be a distinctly progressive figure, at least with regard to domestic issues. In his first year or two in office he managed to secure the passage of a number of important (though probably long overdue) measures, such as the much acclaimed "war on poverty," more effective civil rights legislation, substantially increased aid for education, and Medicare and Medicaid. On the basis of this record, some scholars have even gone so far as to compare Lyndon Johnson with Huey Long as a vigorous economic dissenter, if not a Southern radical.[85] However, in the latter part of 1964 *Fortune*, a thoroughly conservative source, came to quite the opposite conclusion. It claimed that within a year of the time he had assumed the Presidency, Lyndon Johnson had built up a bridge of confidence "...between the White House and the upper echelons of industry that had not been equaled by any Democratic President since Grover Cleveland."[86]

Given such a marked difference of opinion, how does one make a valid judgment about this complex public official? One way is to take a close look at the various men who served as his key informal advisors, especially during his early years in executive office.[87] One such man was New York lawyer Edwin L. Weisl, who had served, along with John Connally, as manager of Johnson's unsuccessful 1960 presidential drive.[88] Weisl had met Johnson back in the late New Deal days and had acted for a considerable period as his principal legal and business advisor. Not surprisingly, in late 1963 he was appointed as the President's chief Democratic agent in New York state.[89] Indeed, such was their relationship that Weisl looked upon Lyndon Johnson as virtually a member of his own family. Weisl, moreover, was no ordinary New York City lawyer, but was one of the senior partners in the top-tier firm of Simpson, Thacher & Bartlett, which had long served as general counsel for Manufacturers Hanover Trust Co. (or as it was known up to 1961, the Manufacturers Trust Co.) and the investment banking house of Lehman Brothers, to name just two of its most important clients.[90] In fact, Weisl was so closely linked to the latter concern that, according to *Fortune*, he was sometimes referred to as "Lehman's eighteenth partner."[91] Weisl had also served up to 1961 as a director, and then for five years as chairman of the executive committee of the Paramount Pictures Corp. (a concern which was merged into the giant conglomerate, Gulf and Western Industries, in 1966). In short, Weisl was a strongly pro-business figure.

Another probably even more important advisor to Johnson was Washington lawyer Abe Fortas, who was a senior partner in the influential firm of Arnold, Fortas and Porter, a concern founded by two former New Deal officials in the mid-1940s. Although this firm had a well-merited reputation for taking up many liberal causes, especially in the civil rights area, it also did a good deal of work for various major business enterprises. For instance, Fortas served from 1962 to 1966 as a vice-president, director, and general counsel of the Texas-based Greatamerica Corp., a newly formed holding company which controlled a number of insurance companies, two banks (one being the big First Western Bank and Trust Co. of California), and after 1964 Braniff Airways. He was also a director of the large Federated Department Stores for roughly the same period.[92] Both of these concerns, it should be observed, had ties to Lehman Brothers.[93] Hence Fortas, too, had important economic links, although they were primarily with non-Establishment firms.

Most of Johnson's other major informal advisors were, like Abe Fortas, Washington lawyers. Two of them belonged to the same firm, Corcoran, Foley, Youngman & Rowe. Thomas G. Corcoran was a member of FDR's circle of key aides and advisors in the mid and late 1930s, in which role he gained much valuable experience about the intricate operations of the federal government. However, after the war he turned his hand to a different line of activity and soon emerged as one of Washington's leading counselors to corporate interests. His most important client was the big Tennessee Gas Transmission Co. (now known as Tenneco), and he reportedly did considerable work for such major concerns as the United Fruit Co. and Pan-American World Airways.[94] His partner, James H. Rowe, Jr., was also retained for many years by Burlington Industries, one of the nation's largest textile concerns.[95]

Another key Johnson advisor was Washington attorney Clark Clifford, a self-made man who had earned his political spurs by serving as special counsel to President Truman from 1946 to 1950. The astute Clifford later followed the lead of a number of other former high federal officials and set up his own legal practice. Indeed, he was perhaps the most successful of these influential figures, for he represented at various times such wealthy interests as the du Pont family (in its efforts to ease the fiscal impact of the Supreme Court's ruling that it must relinquish its huge holdings in General Motors), the General Electric Co. (in its attempts to counter the federal government's charge of illicit corporate price-fixing), and the El Paso Natural Gas Co. (in an antitrust dispute).[96]

Johnson's relationship with the business community may also be assessed by looking at the support he received from various quarters when he ran for reelection in 1964, as contrasted to that given to his Republican challenger, Barry Goldwater. However, it should be stressed that Goldwater was not the usual type of moderate (or moderately conservative) candidate put forward by the Establishment-dominated Eastern wing of the Republican party. Instead, after a series of bitter battles in which Goldwater was first challenged by New York's rich governor, Nelson Rockefeller, and then, shortly before the convention, by Pennsylvania's wealthy governor, William Scranton,[97] the Republican party yielded to its more extreme elements and nominated Arizona's arch-conservative Senator, whom most Americans viewed as a politically reckless and antediluvian figure. Confronted with this choice, the vast majority of the nation's major business executives threw their support wholeheartedly behind Democratic incumbent Lyndon Johnson, who they felt sure (particularly on the basis of his record in the Senate) was a more responsible and moderate leader.[98] Note, for example, the top leadership of the ad hoc group known as the National Independent Committee for President Johnson and Senator Humphrey (Johnson's vice-presidential running mate), created in the fall of 1964 to help generate support for the Democratic slate among the country's most influential businessmen:[99]

Robert B. Anderson	Former (1957–1961) Secretary of the Treasury; limited partner, New York investment banking house of Carl M. Loeb, Rhoades & Co.; director of Dresser Industries and Goodyear Tire & Rubber Co.; trustee of the CED
Carter L. Burgess	Board chairman, American Machine & Foundry Co.; director of American Airlines, Ford Motor Co., and the Morgan Guaranty Trust Co.; vice-chairman of the Business Council
John T. Connor	President, Merck & Co.; director of the Communications Satellite Corp. and General Foods Corp.; vice-chairman of the Business Council; trustee of the CED
Henry Ford II	Board chairman, Ford Motor Co.; director of the General Foods Corp.; active member of the Business Council
Henry H. Fowler	Former (1961–1964) Under Secretary of the Treasury; Washington lawyer
Edgar F. Kaiser	President, Kaiser Industries Corp.; director of the Bank of America; active member of the Business Council
Thomas S. Lamont	Vice-chairman, Morgan Guaranty Trust Co.; director of the Phelps Dodge Corp. and Texas Gulf Sulphur Co.
Ralph Lazarus	President, Federated Department Stores, Inc.; director of the General Electric Co. and the Gillette Co.; active member of the Business Council; trustee of the CED
Robert Lehman	Senior partner, Lehman Brothers; director of the Associated Dry Goods Corp., Gimbel Bros., Pan-American World Airways, Twentieth Century-Fox Film Corp. and United Fruit Co.
John. L. Loeb	Senior partner, Carl M. Loeb, Rhoades & Co.; director of the Allied Chemical Corp. and Distillers Corp.–Seagrams, Ltd.; married a member of the Lehman family
Sidney J. Weinberg	Senior partner, Goldman, Sachs & Co.; director of the Continental Can Co., Champion Papers, Inc., Ford Motor Co., and McKesson & Robbins, Inc.; trustee of the CED; up to 1961 a vice-chairman of the Business Council

With this array of financial support, the Democratic party in 1964 became for the first time in recent history the overwhelming favorite of the corporate "fat cats," while the Goldwater-led Republican party was, in a striking shift, forced to depend primarily on small contributors for its financial support.[100] Although this major politico-economic realignment was created in part by big business's fear of the extremist Goldwater, it nonetheless shows that Lyndon Johnson was on very good terms with the nation's top business leaders, for they could easily have sat on their hands during this election.

TOP OFFICIALS OF THE JOHNSON ADMINISTRATION

Upon assuming office after Kennedy's assassination, President Johnson understandably made a special effort to keep most high federal officials in their posts, at least until after the 1964 election, in order to give the country confidence in his political leadership. He retained Secretary of State Dean Rusk in his important Cabinet position throughout this administration, in large measure because Rusk shared his hawkish views on foreign policy. However, there were now some major differences within the State Department as to the wisdom of providing more military support to the shaky pro-Western regime in South Vietnam. One group of officials, led by Assistant Secretary of State for Far Eastern Affairs Roger Hilsman, argued that the basic weakness of this Asian government was political (its repressive and generally corrupt nature) rather than military, and that vastly increased aid would in the end prove unavailing. But President Johnson would have none of this talk, for he and many of his advisors were convinced that America's national image would be gravely damaged if South Vietnam fell. He also believed that our enormous military power would soon crush the insurgent guerrilla forces. Hence Hilsman, who was a former academic and governmental figure, was, as David Halberstam has put it, "a marked man" from the very outset of the Johnson administration and was pressured into resigning even before the 1964 presidential campaign got under way. His replacement, William P. Bundy, the older brother of the President's Special Assistant for National Security Affairs, was a man more to Johnson's liking. Unlike his sometimes abrasive brother, William Bundy had spent the bulk of his adult life in the federal government, first (from 1951 to 1961) as a second-echelon official of the CIA, and then (in the early 1960s) as a high-level Defense Department executive dealing with international security matters. A patrician by birth (his recently deceased father had been a Boston corporate lawyer), Bundy had cemented his Establishment ties through his marriage in the early 1940s to Dean Acheson's daughter. He was also apparently viewed favorably by many top business and civic leaders in the country, for about the time of his appointment to this key State Department post he was made a director of the elitist-dominated Council on Foreign Relations.[101]

Another important change in the upper echelons of the State Department was made a few years later when Under Secretary of State George Ball resigned, in large measure because of his growing disillusionment with the war in Vietnam. Ball, a former partner in a second-tier New York and Washington law firm, was not closely tied to what might be called America's foreign policy establishment, and as the war in Southeast Asia degenerated into a costly stalemate, he soon became known as the sharpest "inside" critic of Johnson's militaristic policy. He apparently hoped that his resignation in a Congressional election year would be taken as a sign of serious dissent in this critical area. But his essentially symbolic act had little effect on the administration's approach to the Vietnamese conflict. Ball was quickly replaced by the recently appointed Attorney General Nicholas

Katzenbach, who was a very different sort of figure. Before joining the Justice Department in 1961, Katzenbach had been a law professor, first at Yale (1952 to 1956) and then at the University of Chicago (1956 to 1961). While Katzenbach may have had some doubts about the wisdom of our Southeast Asia policy, unlike Ball he never chose to rock the boat and at times took a strongly hawkish line. Though rarely noted, Katzenbach had, through his wife, the former Lydia Stokes (whose family had been involved in the founding of the Phelps Dodge Corp.), a number of noteworthy links with various elite figures, the most prominent of which was his wife's cousin, Isaac N. P. Stokes, a partner in the Wall Street law firm of Webster, Sheffield, Fleischmann, Hitchcock & Chrystie.[102] Thus Katzenbach may have been less inclined than his predecessor to challenge the thinking of Establishment-oriented leaders.[103]

The last major shift in the State Department was made in the mid-1960s when W. Averell Harriman was eased out of his post as Under Secretary of State for Political Affairs and given the prestigious, but much less important, position of Ambassador-at-large. The basic reason for this move was that, unlike many other elite figures, Harriman had become a severe internal critic of the administration's Southeast Asia policy.[104] He was replaced by Eugene V. Rostow, who had served as a Yale University law professor for over twenty years, during the last ten of which he had acted as dean of its law school. Rostow was the brother of former MIT economist Walt W. Rostow, the recently appointed extremely hawkish Special Assistant to the President for National Security Affairs (he had taken over this post from the haughty Brahmin McGeorge Bundy, whose relations with Lyndon Johnson had become somewhat strained). Eugene Rostow had also found time during his later years (1962–1966) as Yale law school dean to serve on the board of a fairly small Texas oil company known as the Texstar Corp., which might indicate that he too was of the "right" politico-economic mold.[105]

The Treasury Department was another agency in which a number of major personnel changes were made during the early Johnson years. The incumbent Secretary, C. Douglas Dillon, had stayed on after Kennedy's assassination at Johnson's request to provide continuity in this position. But in the spring of 1965, following Johnson's landslide victory over Barry Goldwater, the wealthy Dillon felt compelled, because of personal (rather than ideological) differences with the President, to resign.[106] After making two abortive, but revealing, efforts to find a suitable successor, Johnson finally settled on a relatively obscure Washington attorney named Henry H. Fowler, who had served for three years as Under Secretary of the Treasury before he returned in the first part of 1964 to his old law firm of Fowler, Leva, Hawes & Symington.[107] However, as indicated earlier, Fowler had been associated, for over two years prior to his entry into the Kennedy government, with the big business–dominated CED through his participaton on its specially constituted National Commission on Money and Credit.[108] In addition, he was reportedly in almost daily contact with various Wall Street bankers during the first part (if not the entire span) of his term of office as Secretary of the Treasury.[109] Thus, although Fowler did not seem to be closely linked with America's major business and financial forces, he was obviously their staunch ally.[110]

Only one change was made in the top post at the Pentagon during the Johnson years, and that took place in March 1968 when the highly efficient Robert McNamara was, in effect, forced out of office by the President, largely because he had recently turned dovish on the war in Vietnam.[111] He was replaced by one of Johnson's longtime close informal advisors, Washington lawyer-lobbyist Clark M. Clifford, who, in addition to being a well-paid consultant to various key corporate interests (such as the General Electric Company and the du Pont family), had the reputation of being a strong "hardliner" in international affairs. Clifford accepted the domino theory and had opposed earlier bombing pauses in the bitter Vietnamese war, which struggle, he believed, was essential to contain the expansionist forces of Communist China.[112] In short, Clifford was just as strongly committed to the pursuit of the war in Vietnam as McNamara had been during the early years of the Johnson administration.[113]

There was, however, a considerable turnover in the second-tier positions in the Defense Department during these deeply troubled years. The scandal-tainted Deputy Secretary of Defense, Roswell Gilpatric, stepped down from office in the first part of 1964, to be replaced by Cyrus Vance, a former New York lawyer who had been acting as Secretary of the Army since 1962. As pointed out earlier, Vance was an extremely well-connected attorney, having been a partner in the Wall Street firm of Simpson, Thacher & Bartlett, which had served as general counsel to Manufacturers Hanover Trust, Lehman Brothers, and many other large enterprises (one of its senior partners, Edwin L. Weisl, was a longtime advisor to the President).[114] A loyal Johnson supporter, Vance served as Deputy Defense Secretary until mid-1967, when he resumed his New York law practice. He was replaced by a firm hard-liner, Secretary of the Navy Paul Nitze, a onetime New York investment banker (Dillon, Read & Co.), who had devoted much of his time in the postwar period to serving in various high defense and foreign policy posts.[115] Nitze was in some ways even more closely linked to the business community than Vance. He served until shortly after his entry into the federal government on the board of two major railroads; his (now deceased) brother-in-law, Walter Paepcke, had built up one of the nation's largest corporations, the Container Corp. of America;[116] and Nitze himself had married into the wealthy Pratt family, which had been associated with the Standard Oil interests for many years and one of whose members still served on the board of the big United States Trust Co. of New York.

Much the same sort of men were in control of the Department of the Army during much of the Johnson administration. When Cyrus Vance was elevated to the key post of Deputy Secretary of Defense in the first part of 1964, his place was taken by his top aide, Stephen Ailes, who, prior to his assumption of federal office in 1961, had been a partner in one of Washington's second-tier law firms, Steptoe and Johnson.[117] Hence Ailes would appear to have been a largely non-economic selection. However, he served in this capacity for only about a year and a half, when he was replaced by a more elitist figure, Stanley R. Resor, a former New York lawyer with very little experience in governmental affairs. Resor had been a partner in a fairly prominent Wall Street law firm known (since 1962) as Debevoise, Plimpton, Lyons & Gates.[118] But perhaps even more important, he had many influential family connections. His brother-in-law, Gabriel Hauge, was the president of Manufacturers Hanover Trust, a high official of the Council on Foreign Relations, a trustee of the CED, and a director of American Metal Climax. Resor himself had married into the wealthy Pillsbury (flour) family of Minneapolis, one member of which had long served as a director of the Northwest Bancorporation, a big bank holding company in the Midwest.[119]

The position of Secretary of the Air Force was held by a different type. The man who occupied this post at the time of Kennedy's assassination, former Washington lawyer and management consultant Eugene Zuckert, continued to serve until the latter part of 1965 when, probably because he had already been in office for almost five years, he chose to resign and reenter the business world. He was replaced by a former academic, University of California physicist Harold Brown, who had been acting for the previous four years as the Defense Department's director of engineering and research. Although he had no business (or pro-business) background, the able Brown clearly shared the hawkish views of most high Pentagon officials. As late as March 1968, Brown still sided with the Joint Chiefs of Staff, Johnson's personal military advisor General Maxwell D. Taylor, presidential aide Walt W. Rostow, and Under Secretary of State Nicholas Katzenbach in strongly opposing any cutback in America's massive bombing raids in Vietnam.[120]

Most of the other key (non-diplomatic) posts in Johnson's administration were filled by non-elite figures. The heads of three major "clientele" agencies—Secretary of Agriculture Orville Freeman, Secretary of Interior Stewart Udall, and Secretary of Labor W. Willard Wirtz—were Kennedy carryovers who were retained during Johnson's five-plus years as President. Some of the other departments, however, had a greater turnover. Robert Kennedy stayed on as Attorney General only until the fall of 1964 when, having had his Vice Presidential hopes dashed by Johnson's refusal to consider any of his Cabinet members as a possible running mate, he rather bitterly resigned from the government.[121] After a brief delay he was replaced by his top aide, Nicholas Katzenbach, who was a former Chicago and Yale University law professor, with at least one noteworthy socio-economic tie (the Stokes family). However, Katzenbach served in this capacity for just a little over a year and a half. He was then induced by President Johnson to assume the second-ranking post in the State Department. Katzenbach was succeeded, in turn, by his Deputy Attorney General, Ramsey Clark, who, prior to his entry into the Justice Department (in 1961), had been a Dallas lawyer and whose father was a member of the United States Supreme Court. Although from a fairly conservative state, Clark was not a pro-business figure; in fact, he proved to be a progressive official.

Another agency marked by considerable turnover was the Department of Health, Education and Welfare. When Johnson took over the reins of executive leadership, this major administrative unit was headed by former Cleveland mayor Anthony J. Celebrezze, who had reportedly been picked by President Kennedy largely for ethnic reasons. Though Celebrezze had not demonstrated much managerial ability, Johnson was apparently reluctant to make a change initially for fear of alienating a significant segment of the electorate in the urban Northeast. But with the passage of new legislation providing more financial support for both health and education, Johnson felt compelled in the summer of 1965 to find a more capable person for this key post.[122] He picked New York's John W. Gardner, the head of one of America's largest foundations, the Carnegie Corp., who, although he had no prior governmental experience, had done much to focus attention on the nation's educational needs.[123]

The Department of Commerce was yet another agency marked by frequent change in its upper echelons during the Johnson years. Aside from Kennedy incumbent and former North Carolina businessman Luther Hodges (who served only until two months after the 1964 presidential election), all of its top officials were drawn from the ranks of big business:

John T. Connor (1965–1967)	No prior governmental experience; president, Merck & Co., N.J. (1955–1965, lesser company official before that); director of General Foods Corp. (1962–1965), General Motors Corp. (1964–1965), and Communications Satellite Corp. (1963–1964); trustee of the CED (1956–1965); an active member of the Business Council (1962–1967); a prime mover in the (big business–dominated) National Independent Committee for President Johnson and Senator Humphrey in 1964
Alexander B. Trowbridge (1967–1968)	Assistant Secretary of Commerce (1965–1967); high official, South American subsidiaries of the Standard Oil Co. of N.J. (1959–1965); official, Cal-Tex Oil Co., joint subsidiary of Texaco and the Standard Oil Co. of Cal. (1954–1958); no major (outside) directorships
Cyrus R. Smith (1968–1969)	No prior governmental experience; board chairman, American Airlines (1946–1968); director of the Chase Manhattan Bank (1954–1966); graduate member of the Business Council

Thus Johnson's three appointees as Secretary of Commerce were not only recruited from large corporations, but had been connected with New York-based concerns.[124] This was in marked contrast to the pattern which had prevailed in Democratic administrations since the late 1940s, for neither Truman's last Secretary of Commerce, Charles Sawyer, nor Kennedy incumbent Luther Hodges, had such important ties.[125] This would certainly seem to indicate that Johnson, despite his promotion of a liberal domestic program, had forged close links with the nation's top economic interests, and that the politico-economic breach which had developed between corporate leaders and the Kennedy administration in the early 1960s over the role and make-up of the Business Advisory Council and the steel price hike controversy had been effectively healed.

In the realm of foreign affairs, Johnson adhered to a very different appointment policy. Eschewing a massive shakeup in our representation abroad, he chose to retain all the American emissaries to the major European powers. Two of these officials were longtime career diplomats, Charles E. Bohlen, Ambassador to France, and Foy D. Kohler, Ambassador to Russia.[126] Some of the others had both a considerable amount of diplomatic experience and key socio-economic ties. America's Ambassador to Great Britain, David K. E. Bruce, for example, had already been U.S. emissary to France (1949–1952) and West Germany (1957–1959). His brother James had long served on the board of a number of large corporations, such as Avco, American Airlines, General American Investors, Republic Steel, and U.S. Industries, the majority of which concerns had strong Democratic ties. Our Ambassador to West Germany, George C. McGhee, was a man of similar mold. Although he had less diplomatic experience than Bruce, McGhee probably had better economic links, for he had not only served as a director of a relatively small (New York-based) oil company known as Petroleum Reserves, but he had also been a trustee, up to the early 1960s, of the CED and Brookings Institution.[127] In short, both Bruce and McGhee had close ties to influential economic interests.[128]

Perhaps the most important diplomatic position during this trying period was that of Ambassador to South Vietnam. At the outset of the Johnson administration this post was held by the Boston Brahmin and Republican party leader Henry Cabot Lodge, who in 1961 had been appointed to the board of John Hancock Mutual Life. However, Lodge asked to be relieved of these duties in the summer of 1964 in order to make a (futile) bid for the Republican presidential nomination. He was thereupon replaced by a highly respected figure, General Maxwell D. Taylor, who had been called out of a brief retirement in the early 1960s to serve, first as a White House military advisor, and then as Chairman of the Joint Chiefs of Staff. Though primarily a military man, Taylor had also served briefly as board chairman of the Mexican Light and Power Co., Ltd. (in 1959–1960, before it was taken over by the Mexican government), and as a director of a set of financial concerns controlled by Calvin Bullock, Ltd. Hence he was not just a retired Army general. But despite his background, Taylor soon became disenchanted with the increasing use of American ground forces in the war (he strongly favored stepped-up air assaults), and resigned his post in mid-1965. At this juncture

President Johnson reappointed the still hawkish Henry Cabot Lodge, who served as America's emissary to Saigon until the first part of 1967, during which period the war in Vietnam was sharply escalated. By this time, however, Lodge was beginning to feel the effects of the arduous demands of this job, and he decided to return for a while to private life.

As his replacement, President Johnson chose a onetime major business executive, Ellsworth Bunker, who, since his retirement in 1951 as president of the fairly large National Sugar Refining Co., had served in several prominent diplomatic capacities: Ambassador to Italy (in 1952–1953), Ambassador to India (from 1956 to 1961), Ambassador to the Organization of American States (in the mid-1960s), and most recently Ambassador-at-large.[129] However, Bunker also maintained a number of noteworthy business ties over the years, the most conspicuous of which was with the elitist-dominated Atlantic Mutual Insurance Co. of New York, and as time went on. he even added a few corporate links to his collection.[130] In the early 1960s, for example, he was elected to the board of the Lambert International Corp. (an investment company controlled by Belgian magnate Jean Lambert), and perhaps more revealingly, to the board of the financially troubled Curtis Publishing Co., most likely as part of a group headed by the investment banking firm of Carl M. Loeb, Rhoades & Co.[131] Thus some influential figures outside the federal government were probably kept well informed about both military and politico-economic developments in Vietnam during these critical years.[132]

As for other posts, President Johnson chose, upon assuming office, to retain John A. McCone as director of the CIA. This former West Coast shipbuilder had, as pointed out earlier, a number of noteworthy economic ties, the most significant of which were as a director, up to the late 1950s or early 1960s, of the Bechtel-controlled Industrial Indemnity Co., the California Bank of Los Angeles, and the Pacific Mutual Life Insurance Co. Moreover, in 1960 McCone had been elected to the board of TWA (apparently as part of a New York-based takeover of this airline from the eccentric magnate, Howard Hughes), and, perhaps even more important in light of later events in Indonesia, the Standard Oil Co. of California.[133] McCone, however, resigned in early 1965, most likely because of his age. He was replaced by a recently retired former naval officer, Admiral William F. Raborn, Jr., who had served for the last year and a half as a vice-president of the Aerojet-General Corp., a California-based subsidiary of the big General Tire and Rubber Co. of Ohio. But Raborn, who had no experience in intelligence matters, reportedly did not turn out to be an effective director of the CIA and was persuaded to step aside after little more than a year in office. He was succeeded by his deputy director, Richard Helms, who was acclaimed as the first real professional ever to head the agency. But although Helms had worked his way up through the agency, he also had an elite background. His maternal grandfather, Gates W. McGarrah, had been the head of New York's Mechanics and Metals National Bank until its merger into the (then Morgan-dominated) Chase National Bank in 1926, about which time he was elected board chairman of the powerful Federal Reserve Bank of New York. Moreover, after holding another financial post in the early 1930s, he served as a director of such large enterprises as the Bankers Trust Co. up to his death in 1940. In short, Helms was a part of what has been referred to as the wealthy "St. Grottlesex" (elite Eastern prep school) network that had dominated the upper echelons of the CIA for many years.[134]

Most of the other more domestically oriented special agencies of the federal government were manned primarily by non-elite figures during the Johnson years. The Bureau of the Budget was, for example, headed during most of this period by former academicians Kermit Gordon and Charles Schultze.[135] Yet there was one nationally chartered body which moved increasingly under the control of certain influential private interests, and that was the recently created Communications Satellite Corp.[136] This shift was discernible not only in the election to its board of a sizable number of representatives of the nation's common carriers (especially AT&T), as prescribed by federal law, but also in the selection of a new board chairman. When former Jersey Standard executive Leo D. Welch relinquished this post in 1965, he was replaced by retired General James McCormack, who since entering civilian life in 1955 had served as a high-ranking official of MIT. However, McCormack had also sat up to the mid-1960s on the board of a number of sizable concerns, such as the United Nuclear Corp. and Geophysics Corp. of America (both of which were probably dominated by the Rockefeller forces), the State Street Bank & Trust Co., Federal Reserve Bank of Boston, and the New England Telephone and Telegraph Co., a subsidiary of AT&T.[37] Thus the board chairman of this key enterprise had some revealing economic links.

IMPORTANT POLICY ACTIONS OF THE JOHNSON ADMINISTRATION

President Johnson has generally been described as a dedicated liberal, particularly on domestic matters, who came a cropper because of his disastrous expansion of the war in Vietnam. It is certainly true that Johnson, especially during his early years in office, was able to secure the enactment of a number of progressive measures, most notably in the areas of health, education, welfare, and civil rights, the likes of which had not been seen since the famous first "one hundred days" of the New Deal. But this does not mean that Johnson was a dedicated liberal in the mold of Estes Kefauver or the pre-1964 Hubert Humphrey. Rather, Johnson was one of the most astute politicians ever to occupy the White House and knew full well that, as a Southerner with an extremely mixed record, he needed a legislative program that would build support in the more liberal industrial Northeast. Moreover, the ambitious Johnson, who, partly because of his family background, clearly had empathy for the underprivileged, also strongly desired to be adjudged a great leader, like his early political idol Franklin D. Roosevelt. So it is not surprising that he vigorously backed such innovative measures as Medicare and Medicaid and launched his much-heralded "war on poverty." Still, there is reason to suspect that the anti-poverty program was conceived more for political than humanitarian reasons, that is to boost Johnson's stock in a presidential election year. As Evans and Novak have pointed out, "Johnson's War on Poverty was more a slogan, a concept, a laudable desire than a carefully structured plan of action," and "the excruciating problems of how the poor could best and most systematically be lifted from the rut of poverty were glossed over in the mad rush to put a program on paper and hurry it through Congress."[138] In light of this analysis, it seems fair to characterize Johnson as essentially a conservative figure who nevertheless, for personal and political reasons, strongly supported a number of progressive programs during his early years as President of the United States.

Another revealing, and often overlooked, indicator of the politico-economic orientation of the Johnson regime may be found in the realm of antitrust activity. During LBJ's administration the nation witnessed a great wave of corporate mergers, particularly in the industrial area, as may be seen by the following figures:[139]

	Total Number of Manufacturing and Mining Mergers	Number of Large (over $10 million) Companies Acquired	Assets Involved in Large Mergers ($ millions)
1960	844	51	1,535
1961	954	46	2,003
1962	853	65	2,251
1963	861	54	2,536
1964	854	73	2,303
1965	1,008	64	3,254
1966	995	76	3,329
1967	1,496	138	8,259
1968	2,407	174	12,580
1969	2,307	138	11,043
1970	1,351	91	5,904
1971	1,001	59	2,460
1972	911	60	1,886

Though many of the more important large mergers were of a conglomerate nature, a significant number involved firms in closely related or identical fields, and were, therefore, subject to federal sanction. Yet comparatively little action was taken against such mergers by the Antitrust Division of the Justice Department under the Johnson administration (although, curiously, the more independent Federal Trade Commission began about this time to adopt a firmer stance against this marked trend toward increasing economic concentration).[140] As one business magazine pointed out in 1966, the

Antitrust Division seemed to ignore mergers that in years past might have raised serious hackles.[141] Note, for example, the following selective list of large (over $250 million) industrial mergers consummated during the 1960s:[142]

Year of Merger	Acquiring Company	Acquired Company	Assets of Latter Concern ($ millions)
1963	FMC (Food Machinery & Chemical) Corp.	American Viscose	335
1965	Union Oil Co. of Cal.	Pure Oil	766
1966	Continental Oil	Consolidation Coal	446
1966	Atlantic Refining	Richfield Oil	450
1966	Phillips Petroleum	Tidewater Oil (western manufacturing and marketing properties)	305
1967	McDonnell Aircraft	Douglas Aircraft	565
1967	Tenneco	Kern County Land Co.	254
1967	North American Aviation	Rockwell Standard	391
1968	Montgomery Ward	Container Corp. of America	397
1968	Ling-Temco-Vought	Jones & Laughlin Steel	1,093
1968	Loew's Theatres	P. Lorillard Co.	375
1968	ITT	Rayonier	296
1968	Sun Oil	Sunray DX Oil Co.	749
1968	American Standard	Westinghouse Air Brake	303
1969	General Host	Armour	561
1969	Amerada Petroleum	Hess Oil & Chemical	492
1969	Atlantic Richfield	Sinclair Oil	1,851
1969	Lykes Bros. Steamship Co.	Youngstown Sheet & Tube	1,027

Of these eighteen giant mergers, thirteen were approved during the Johnson administration. Four of them involved the amalgamation of big oil companies, while another resulted in the union of two large aircraft companies.[143] Yet only one of these transactions—Phillips Petroleum's purchase of Tidewater Oil's western refining and distribution facilities—received even a halfhearted challenge from the Justice Department.[144]

It was also during these years that the largest merger in American history took place. After much high-level negotiation and maneuver, the giant Pennsylvania and New York Central railroad systems (and certain other financially troubled Northeastern lines) were joined to form, with President Johnson's blessing, the gigantic Penn-Central Co.[145] Thus, although Johnson clearly worked hard to secure the passage of a number of worthy measures for many underprivileged segments of American society, his administration failed to effectively enforce the nation's antitrust laws, which policy was of substantial benefit to certain major business interests.

Further evidence of Johnson's pro-corporate leanings can be found in the fact that when in the late 1960s he created a special commission to study the organization and operation of the deficit-ridden Post Office Department, he appointed mostly big business leaders to serve on this body:[146]

	Commission Members (and their primary occupational affiliations)	Major Organizational and Directorship Ties
Chairman	Frederick R. Kappel (recently retired board chairman, AT&T)	Member of executive committee of the Business Council; trustee of the CED; director of the Chase Manhattan Bank and Metropolitan Life Insurance Co.
Other Members	George P. Baker (dean, Harvard Graduate School of Business Administration)	Director of the Lockheed Aircraft Corp., Mobil Oil Corp., and First National Bank of Boston
	David E. Bell (vice-president, Ford Foundation; former director of the Bureau of the Budget)	
	Fred J. Borch (president, GE)	Vice-chairman of the Business Council and the CED
	David Ginsburg (partner, Ginsburg & Feldman, a small Washington law firm, of which the other partner was a former aide to President Johnson)	
	Ralph Lazarus (board chairman, Federated Department Stores, Ohio)	Vice-chairman of the Business Council; trustee of the CED; director of the Chase Manhattan Bank and GE
	George Meany (president, AFL-CIO)	
	J. Irwin Miller (board chairman, Cummins Engine Co., Ind.)	Member of executive committee of Business Council; trustee of the CED (up to 1966); director of AT&T, Chemical Bank New York Trust Co., and Equitable Life Assurance Society
	W. Beverly Murphy (president, Campbell Soup Co., N.J.)	Member of executive committee of the Business Council; director of AT&T
	Rudolph A. Peterson (president, Bank of America, Cal.)	Trustee of the CED and the National Industrial Conference Board

Of the ten members of this ad hoc body, six were prominently associated with one or both of America's two most influential economic groups, the Business Council and the CED, and another member, Harvard business school dean George P. Baker, served on the board of three large companies. Although it was not until 1971 that a law was passed implementing the recommendations of this commission, it was apparently largely as a result of the original work and later legislative support of this special task force that a public corporation was created to take over the operation of the much-troubled postal department.

In sharp contrast to his domestic victories, LBJ's decision to sharply expand the war in Vietnam led to tremendous internal dissension and ultimately his political downfall. In the spring and summer of 1965, however, things looked quite different. Johnson and his chief advisors were, with few exceptions, supremely confident that the United States could readily defeat the Communist-led Vietcong forces, which were threatening to overwhelm the ineffective South Vietnamese armies, by a commitment of about 100,000 additional men to our existing military component of 73,000 soldiers. Domino theorists believed that this massive boost would stem the Communist tide in all of Southeast Asia. Judging from all accounts, the primary reasons for Johnson's fateful decision to drastically upgrade the war effort was his widely shared assumption that, through vastly superior firepower, the United States would quickly crush the Communist-backed guerrilla movement. Furthermore, many leaders believed that a failure to do so would seriously damage America's "image" around the world and possibly open up the rest of this valuable (or potentially valuable) region to Red domination.[147]

Most of Johnson's early hawkish advisors were former or still active pro-business figures. For instance, the primary participants at one important meeting in July 1965 (at which it was decided to increase America's military commitment to South Vietnam to close to 200,000 men) included, in addition to the President and Joint Chiefs of Staff, Dean Rusk, George Ball, Robert McNamara, Secretary of the Army Stanley Resor (a recent Wall Street lawyer with many prominent socio-economic ties), Secretary of the Navy Paul Nitze (who had various key family links), Secretary of the Air Force Eugene Zuckert (a man with lesser connections), and his heir-apparent, Harold Brown (a hawkish technocrat), plus three essentially civilian figures—Clark Clifford, the chairman of the President's Foreign Intelligence Advisory Board (who counted many potent corporate interests among his clients) and two members of the President's panel of consultants on foreign affairs: Arthur H. Dean, a partner in Sullivan & Cromwell (and a director of the CFR and several large corporations) and former Chase Manhattan Bank head John J. McCloy (board chairman of the CFR).[148] Shortly after, a prestigious national committee was created to back the President's aggressive military policy in Vietnam. Its ranks were studded with influential Establishment figures: the chairman was Arthur Dean, and its members included such well-known leaders as Dean Acheson, Eugene

Black (the former head of the World Bank, now a director of the Chase Manhattan Bank and various other large corporations), Gabriel Hauge (president of Manufacturers Hanover Trust, treasurer of the CFR, a trustee of the CED, and a brother-in-law of Secretary of the Army Stanley Resor), William B. Murphy (president of Campbell Soup, chairman of the Business Council, and a director of AT&T), David Rockefeller (president of the Chase Manhattan Bank and a vice-president of the CFR), and James R. Killian, Jr. (the longtime head of MIT and a director of AT&T and General Motors).[149] When federal taxes had later to be raised to sustain the vastly expanded conflict, it was again to Establishment leaders that Johnson turned for aid in his efforts to get Congress to provide the requisite funds. Of the thirteen businessmen Johnson persuaded to head this lobbying drive, eleven were members of the Business Council.[150] In short, President Johnson clearly had the strong support of the nation's top business leaders for his policy of escalating the war in Vietnam.

With the firm backing of America's military and economic establishment, the war continued to grow in scope and intensity, despite increasing public protests. By the first part of 1968 the United States had nearly 500,000 men in Vietnam. And yet, though both high Pentagon officials and military commanders frequently assured the nation that the war was being won, the enemy's strength and will to resist had not really been weakened. This was demonstrated most emphatically at the end of January 1968 when the Communist-led forces launched the so-called Tet offensive, temporarily seizing many urban centers and catching the American and South Vietnamese armies completely off guard.

Taken aback by this startling development, President Johnson decided to replace his able, though increasingly dovish, Secretary of Defense, Robert McNamara, with one of his longtime close friends and political advisors, Clark Clifford, an astute Washington lawyer with numerous wealthy corporate clients, who was generally regarded as an ardent supporter of the war.[151] But much to Johnson's surprise, once Clifford took over the Defense Department and began to investigate the conflict more carefully, his hard-line views started to wane. At the President's behest, Clifford agreed to head a special study group created to evaluate General Westmoreland's most recent request for even greater military funds and personnel. This critical probe raised many doubts in Clifford's mind as to the wisdom and feasibility of our Southeast Asian policy. Indeed, he became convinced that our role in Vietnam should be substantially reduced, and in the ensuing weeks he labored strenuously, both inside and outside the administration, to generate support for his new position.

Thus when on March 22, 1968, President Johnson convened a two-day meeting of his little-known but highly influential Senior Informal Advisory Group on Vietnam (made up of such former key officials and elite figures as Dean Acheson, George Ball, McGeorge Bundy, C. Douglas Dillon, Arthur Dean, Abe Fortas, Arthur Goldberg, Henry Cabot Lodge, John J. McCloy,

Maxwell Taylor, and Cyrus Vance) to assess the military situation, he received a rude shock. Instead of warmly supporting the war, as most of these men had up to the Tet offensive, the majority now expressed firm opposition. Only a few members of the group (mainly Abe Fortas and Maxwell Taylor) still adhered to a hard-line strategy.[152] The still hawkish President Johnson was stunned by this advice, but, perhaps because of its source, he apparently accepted it.[153] He had also been stung by the recent announcement of New York Senator Robert Kennedy, whom Johnson had long viewed as a bitter rival, that he planned to enter the race for the Democratic presidential nomination on an antiwar platform.[154] Less than a week after he had met with his elite advisory group, Johnson announced to the nation that he would not seek reelection and was ordering a sharp reduction in America's military commitment to Vietnam, thereby setting the government on a course of action which would lead ultimately to the United States' disengagement from this disastrous conflict.[155]

SUPREME COURT APPOINTMENTS AND ACTIONS

In contrast to the high turnover that characterized the executive branch of government during the Kennedy and Johnson years, there was relatively little change in the make-up of the Supreme Court. California's liberal Republican Earl Warren was still Chief Justice. Five other Associate Justices remained in office throughout this period. Two of these were fairly conservative jurists—John Marshall Harlan, a former Wall Street lawyer, and Potter Stewart, who up to 1954 had been a partner in one of Cincinnati's more important corporate law firms. But the other three Associate Justices who served throughout the 1960s were confirmed liberals—William Brennan, who was one of Eisenhower's alleged judicial errors, and Hugo Black and William O. Douglas, two avowed New Dealers who had no important socioeconomic links. Thus there was a strong liberal nucleus on the High Court during the Kennedy and Johnson years.

The first opening on the Supreme Court during this period occurred in April 1962 when Charles Whittaker, a former Kansas City corporate lawyer (and 1954–1957 federal judge), decided to retire after holding office for only five years, during which brief span he displayed little initiative. He was replaced by a former Denver attorney, Byron R. White, who had been active in Kennedy's 1960 presidential campaign and after the election had been appointed Deputy Attorney General under Robert Kennedy. Unlike Whittaker's, White's law firm of Lewis, Grant & Davis apparently had no major economic ties. Hence, although White did not turn out to be as liberal a jurist as many had expected, he was, nonetheless, a distinct improvement over his rather modestly endowed, pro-business predecessor.

The next opening on the Court occurred shortly thereafter when the distinguished Justice Felix Frankfurter was compelled to step down because of his advanced age. He was succeeded by Arthur Goldberg, who had served as Secretary of Labor for the past twenty months. Before his appointment to Cabinet office, Goldberg had acted as general counsel for the CIO (1948–1955), and then as the chief legal advisor of the industrial union department of the AFL-CIO. His selection was especially significant from an economic standpoint, for although there had been since the 1930s some persons appointed to the High Court who had marked sympathies for the working man, Goldberg was the first official formally affiliated with the labor movement to be so chosen.

Goldberg, however, served on the Court for only a short time. In July 1965 President Johnson, who was desirous of creating a new opening, persuaded him to become American Ambassador to the United Nations, a position enticingly portrayed as of great importance to the nation in trying times. The President then appointed his longtime friend and political advisor, Abe Fortas, to this key post.[156] Like Johnson, Fortas had been introduced to national politics during the New Deal and had climbed up the governmental ladder very quickly. At the remarkably early age of 32, he was named Under Secretary of the Interior, which high office he held until 1946. But at this juncture Fortas decided to leave the federal government and set up a Washington law practice with two other well-known ex-New Dealers, Thurman Arnold and Paul Porter. Over the years this firm had prospered, both professionally and financially. It established, for example, a national reputation through its *pro bono* work, handling many civil rights cases. Yet despite this liberal image, the Fortas law firm also developed close ties to certain influential business interests in the postwar period, particularly in the 1960s when the Democratic party was in power. For instance, in addition to his law firm's representation of such major corporate clients as the Coca-Cola Co., Fortas himself served from 1961 to 1965 as a director of the large ($636 million) Federated Department Stores and, for roughly the same period, as a vice-president and board member of a Texas-based holding company known as the Greatamerica Corp., which by the mid-1960s controlled several insurance companies, a big West Coast bank, and Braniff Airways.[157] As a result, in his years on the High Court Fortas often broke sharply with the liberals in many cases which pitted business against the federal government.[158]

The last opening on the Supreme Court during the Johnson years occurred in 1967 when, following the appointment of Ramsey Clark as Attorney General, his father, Associate Justice Tom Clark, felt that it would be inappropriate for him to continue to serve on this body and announced that he would retire at the end of the current Court session. For his successor, President Johnson made a most unusual move. He appointed the first black in American history to the High Court. Thurgood Marshall had served as Solicitor General from 1965 to 1967, and for four years before that as a U.S. Circuit Court judge. However, Marshall was best known for his work as the longtime (1940–1961) director-counsel of the NAACP Legal Defense and Educational Fund, and some years earlier had successfully argued this organization's case in the famous school segregation dispute of *Brown* v. *Board of Education of Topeka*. Since Marshall was an avowed liberal on both economic and social matters, his appointment helped maintain a balance on the Court in favor of such interests.

In part because of its makeup, the Court continued during the Kennedy-Johnson years to break new ground in the field of public law. In 1962, for example, it reversed a previous ruling regarding its right to intervene in legislative apportionment matters. In 1946 the Court had declared that the representative nature of a state legislature was not a justiciable issue and that the judicial branch of government should not "... enter the political thicket." But sixteen years later a more equalitarian Court, when presented with increasing evidence of the failure of many states to equitably reapportion their often outdated legislative bodies, did an almost complete about-face and decreed in the epic case of *Baker* v. *Carr* that this matter now fell within its purview. However, the Court did not indicate what standards should be employed in this regard. This question was resolved two years later when in *Reynolds* v. *Sims* the Court ruled, following the dictum of "one man, one vote," that population was the only permissible basis of representation in the bicameral (state) legislatures throughout the country. This decision soon led to a marked shift away from the longstanding favoritism of rural interests in state government to a more equitable representation of the nation's urban and suburban electorate.

The Warren Court also wrought profound changes in the realm of criminal law during the Kennedy and Johnson years. For instance, in *Gideon* v. *Wainwright* it ruled that any criminal defendant who was too poor to pay for a lawyer had the constitutional right to be provided one at government expense. With this decision the Court cast aside the notion that the equal protection clause merely required equal laws and that the state was not obliged to consider gross economic disparities in criminal proceedings. Furthermore, in two other cases decided shortly thereafter (*Escobedo* v. *Illinois* and *Miranda* v. *Arizona*), the Court declared that the right to counsel must become effective as soon as an individual is subjected to police interrogation. In other words, to make use of any confession, the police had to give full warning to the defendant that he had a right to remain silent and to have a lawyer, either retained by the suspect or court-appointed. Thus the coercive tactics that have been employed at times by police, particularly against poorly informed ethnics and indigents, were ruled illegal by these decrees.

During the Kennedy and Johnson years the Court also took some surprising steps in the realm of antitrust policy. Although, as already indicated, many corporate mergers went unopposed during this period, those that were challenged by either the Justice Department or the Federal Trade Commission were likely to be sustained by the Supreme Court. Moreover, the Court began to raise some new barriers, through its own interpretative rulings, against corporate acquisitions, particularly those involving the formation of joint ventures and those resulting in the elimination of even fairly small competitors, such as a company which controlled little more than 1 percent of the national market.[159] In short, the Supreme Court appeared to be telling the nation's corporate giants that most of their future growth must come from within rather than by merger. It is little wonder, then, that of the three major arms of the federal government, none roused more anxiety among big business leaders than the U.S. Supreme Court, a fear which may have stemmed indirectly from the fact that this body was manned largely by non-elite figures.[160]

To summarize, up to the end of the strife-torn 1960s the Supreme Court continued to be controlled (albeit at times by a close margin) by a bloc of fairly liberal jurists who had no noteworthy socio-economic ties, a pattern instituted by the judicial revolution wrought by New Deal President Franklin D. Roosevelt. However, the executive branch of government during the Kennedy and Johnson years was characterized by substantial representation of influential business interests. Well over half of the major Cabinet and ambassadorial posts in these two regimes were held by people who had key corporate or elite family links, most of them concentrated in the important Departments of State, Treasury, and Defense, as had been the case in the Truman administration. Yet, it should be noted, this was a significant reduction from the roughly 80 percent found under Eisenhower.[161] Perhaps the most striking difference in the economic recruitment patterns of the Eisenhower and Kennedy-Johnson regimes was that the former drew heavily from Establishment sources such as the Business Council, CED, and Council on Foreign Relations, whereas the latter picked relatively few people from these organizations (less than 10 percent of their total appointments).[162]

Although Johnson, in particular, was widely acclaimed as a liberal President because of his domestic policy, he would appear to have been, at heart, an extremely shrewd conservative who advocated a number of progressive programs largely to help secure his electoral base in the Northern urban areas.[163] That Johnson paid close heed to the views of big business leaders may be seen not only in his lax antitrust policy, but in the way in which he responded to their abrupt, post-Tet turnaround on the war in Vietnam. In retrospect, neither the Kennedy nor the Johnson administration represented another New Deal. The times and the pressures were quite different, and there was more major corporate influence at work in their regimes than in the Depression-ridden government of Franklin D. Roosevelt.

Notes

1. For an incisive analysis of this development, along with a list of the recent big corporate mergers, see Phillip L. Blumberg, *The Megacorporation in American Society* (Englewood Cliffs, N.J.: Prentice-Hall, 1975), pp. 47–53, especially Table 3-2.

2. There were a number of other noteworthy changes in the much troubled railroad industry. Two of the most important were the Pennsylvania Railroad's divestiture of its large holdings in the Norfolk & Western Railway and certain other lesser lines (which was a condition for the federal government's approval of its merger with the New York Central Railroad), and the de facto takeover of the Baltimore & Ohio Railroad by the (Cyrus Eaton–controlled) Chesapeake & Ohio Railway.

3. If America's major non-financial enterprises were ranked on the basis of 1968 income, not a single railroad would have made the "top 50."

4. These two corporations were, however, still viewed by *Moody's* as primarily public utilities. In the 1960s *Fortune* and *Moody's* treated the highly diversified ITT as an industrial concern.

5. If sales were used to rank America's largest non-financial enterprises in 1968, the Boeing (Airplane) Co. and the McDonnell Douglas Corp. would both have attained "top 30" status.

6. For a list of the top twenty-five Defense Department, NASA, and AEC contractors, see Steven Rosen (ed.), *Testing the Theory of the Military-Industrial Complex* (Lexington, Mass.: Heath, 1973), pp. 90–91.

7. Moreover, a number of these huge firms had recently begun to expand their operations abroad. For example, in 1962 the Chase Manhattan Bank secured a 49 percent stake in the Banco Mercantil y Agricola, Venezuela's third largest bank, and in 1966 bought a 51 percent interest in the Banco Atlantida, S.A., of Honduras, which was the biggest private commercial bank in Central America. See *Time* (September 7, 1962), p. 70, and the *New York Times* (December 28, 1966), p. 59.

8. For two studies that deal with this long-neglected topic, see David M. Kotz, *Bank Control of Large Corporations in the United States* (Berkeley: University of California Press, 1978), and Daniel J. Baum and Ned B. Stiles, *The Silent Partners: Institutional Investors and Corporate Control* (Syracuse, N.Y.: Syracuse University Press, 1965).

9. For an illuminating account of three of these concerns, see the following articles by T. A. Wise: "The Bustling House of Lehman," *Fortune* (December 1957), pp. 157–60 and 185–92; "Wherever You Look, There's Loeb Rhoades," *Fortune* (April 1963), pp. 128–32 and 145–57; and "Lazard: In Trinity There is Strength," *Fortune* (August 1968), pp. 100–03 and 156–65. The above statement, however, does not apply to such large brokerage concerns as Merrill, Lynch, Pierce, Fenner & Smith, which has generally been regarded as something of a maverick or "outsider" by financial leaders.

10. Up to 1960 the membership of the BAC was listed in the *Annual Report* of the Department of Commerce. However, since then there has been no regularly published source of such information.

11. For an incisive analysis of this dispute, see Hobart Rowen, *The Free Enterprisers: Kennedy, Johnson and the Business Establishment* (New York: Putnam, 1964), pp. 61–79. According to this source (p. 70), the administration's original intent "... was to let the Business Council wither on the vine. Hodges drew plans for a new BAC, one that would be a broad cross section of American business—big, medium, and small-sized. It would include representatives as well of labor, agriculture and education. But these plans were soon set aside and never revived."

12. See Rowen, *op. cit.*, p. 71. By 1965 the Business Council had established liaison groups with the White House, Council of Economic Advisers, and the Departments of State, Treasury, Defense, Commerce, Labor, and HEW. The White House liaison group was headed by William B. Murphy, president of the Campbell Soup Co., and included Texas businessman George R. Brown, who was a close friend of President Johnson, Henry Ford II, William A. Hewitt (board chairman of Deere & Co.), Frederick R. Kappel (board chairman of AT&T), and Frank Stanton (president of CBS). The heads of the Business Council's other liaison groups were as follows: Department of State, Thomas J. Watson, Jr. (board chairman of IBM); Treasury, Harold Boeschenstein (board chairman of the Owens-Corning Fiberglas Corp.); Defense, Crawford H.

Greenewalt (board chairman of E. I. du Pont de Nemours & Co.); Commerce, Stuart Saunders (board chairman of the Pennsylvania Railroad); Labor, J. Ward Keener (president of the B.F. Goodrich Co.); HEW, J. Irwin Miller (board chairman of the Cummins Engine Co.); and the Council of Economic Advisers, Donald K. David (vice-chairman of the Ford Foundation).

13. See Rowen, *op. cit.*, p. 77.

14. The reader may get a graphic idea of the deep-seated elitist prejudice at work from the following excerpt from one of Cleveland Amory's books: "There is a story in Boston that in the palmy days of the twenties a Chicago banking house asked the Boston [Brahmin] investment firm of Lee, Higginson & Co. for a letter of recommendation about a young Bostonian they were considering employing. Lee, Higginson could not say enough about the young man. His father, they wrote, was a Cabot, his mother a Lowell; farther back his background was a happy blend of Saltonstalls, Appletons, Peabodys, and others of Boston's First Families. The recommendation was given without hesitation. Several days later came a curt acknowledgment from Chicago. Lee, Higginson was thanked for its trouble. Unfortunately, however, the material supplied on the young man was not exactly of the type the Chicago firm was seeking. 'We were not,' their letter declared, 'contemplating using Mr. _____ for breeding purposes.'" See Cleveland Amory, *The Proper Bostonians* (New York: Dutton, 1947), p. 11.

15. For example, in 1945 Kennedy bought the world's biggest commercial building, Chicago's Merchandise Mart, which structure was alone worth, by the early 1960s, about $75 million. See Richard J. Whelan, "Joseph P. Kennedy: A Portrait of the Founder," *Fortune* (January 1963), pp. 162 and 167, and also his book, *The Founding Father: The Story of Joseph P. Kennedy* (New York: New American Library, 1964), p. 406.

16. See *Fortune* (January 1963), p. 111. At least $100 million of this was reported, in the postwar period, to be in real estate holdings, with another substantial amount in tax-exempt securities. There never has been any one major Kennedy family enterprise.

17. As one later example of such supportive efforts, when newspaperman Robert Donovan's book *PT-109* was published, Joseph P. Kennedy is reported to have decided that his son's wartime exploits "...would make a splendid movie. Renewing old Hollywood friendships, he proposed the idea to Jack Warner [of Warner Brothers Pictures]. From start to finish, *PT-109* was, according to Richard Whelan, "a Kennedy-supervised production, the latter-day equivalent of an 'authorized' biography." See Whelan, *The Founding Father*, p. 468.

18. For a brief account of the lavish pre-convention spending on the part of the Kennedy family, which helped overwhelm Hubert Humphrey in the critical West Virginia primary, see George Thayer, *Who Shakes the Money Tree?*, pp. 15–17. In all, this author estimated (see p. 158) that the Kennedys spent about $3 million to win the Democratic nomination and the presidential election in 1960.

19. For a brief account of this intriguing struggle, see Theodore H. White, *The Making of the President, 1960* (New York: Atheneum, 1961), pp. 70–75. Most of Rockefeller's chief aides and advisors in this drive were reportedly men who were closely associated with the family's major economic interests, such as his brother David, head of the Chase Manhattan Bank. The failure of Nelson Rockefeller to win the 1960 Republican presidential nomination shows that this very rich and influential family clearly did not dominate the American business establishment. Most of the nation's corporate executives preferred Richard Nixon, who, they believed, would be more amenable to their views or dictates. See Peter Collier and David Horowitz, *The Rockefellers*, p. 340.

20. To get some idea of Weinberg's status in the business community, one need only note that he was a vice-chairman of the BAC, a trustee of the CED, and a director of such large concerns as the Ford Motor Co., GE, and B.F. Goodrich. According to *Fortune*, six of the most important Republican fundraisers in this campaign were the above three financiers and three other corporate figures: Carter L. Burgess, president of the American Car & Foundry Co. (and a director of the Morgan Guaranty Trust Co.); David Mahoney, Jr., head of the fairly small Good Humor Corp., and Charles H. Percy, president of the Midwestern-based Bell & Howell Co. (who was a director of the Burroughs Corp., Chase Manhattan Bank, and Harris Trust &

Savings Bank of Chicago, and an active member of the BAC). The six key (non-family) fundraisers for the Kennedy campaign were August A. Busch, Jr., head of Anheuser-Busch, Inc., of St. Louis; Earl Dickerson, a black lawyer and president of the Supreme Life Insurance Co. of Chicago; Claude Jessup of the National Trailways Bus System; Chicago real estate developer Philip Klutznick; J. Howard Marshall, a high-ranking executive of the California-based Signal Oil & Gas Co.; and Richard Reynolds, president of Virginia's Reynolds Metals Co. Only one of these officials, Southern Democrat Richard Reynolds, Jr., had any nationally important links, the most important of which were with the BAC and CED. See *Fortune* (October 1960), pp. 88 and 93.

21. For an analysis of Johnson's politico-economic relations with the rising oil and natural gas interests of Texas in the postwar years, see Rowland Evans and Robert Novak, *Lyndon Baines Johnson: The Exercise of Power* (New York: New American Library, 1966), pp. 5–25. According to these observers, by 1948 Johnson was no longer a New Dealer, but a strong defender of the petroleum industry, which now carried a great deal of weight in both the executive and legislative branches of American government. In fact, they claim (p. 29) that a political entente had been forged in the 1950s between Johnson, Oklahoma Senator Robert Kerr (head of the Kerr-McGee Oil Industries), and Texas oilman and entrepreneur Clint Murchison.

22. See David Halberstam, *The Best and the Brightest* (New York: Random House, 1969), p. 40, and Stan Opotowsky, *The Kennedy Government* (New York: Dutton, 1961), pp. 14–15. Kennedy also consulted with former Secretary of State Dean Acheson, although not apparently to the same extent as with Lovett. The latter was actually asked to take any of the three top posts in Kennedy's Cabinet, but declined because of age and ill health.

23. See Halberstam, *op. cit.*, pp. 4–6.

24. Kennedy could not afford to exclude the illustrious liberal Adlai Stevenson from his administration, so he offered him the prestigious, but relatively unimportant, post of Ambassador to the United Nations. Stevenson was reportedly appalled, but finally agreed to accept. Stevenson was also a director of the Council on Foreign Relations and the (privately owned) Encyclopaedia Britannica, Inc., but the former elitist link was not enough to counter Dean Rusk's backing. For more on the revealing treatment meted out to two other well-known liberals, former Michigan Governor G. Mennen Williams and Harvard professor John Kenneth Galbraith, see Hobart Rowen, *The Free Enterprisers*, p. 22.

25. Although some of its trustees were not closely associated with the Rockefellers or other business interests, the Rockefeller Foundation had, in economic linkage, close to half of its assets invested in the Standard Oil Co. of N.J.

26. See the *New York Times* (November 28, 1961), p. 20, and Bauer, Pool, and Dexter, *op. cit.*, p. 328.

27. McGhee had also served from 1953 to 1958 as director of the Middle East Institute, a Washington-based organization devoted ostensibly to the promotion of knowledge concerning this oil-rich region. In addition, McGhee's father-in-law, E. L. DeGolyer (who was considered the "dean" of the Texas oil men), served up to his death in late 1956 as a director of Dresser Industries, Inc. (an oil industry supplier), the Great Plains Development Co. of Canada, Ltd., Louisiana Land & Exploration Co., Republic Natural Gas Co., Southern Pacific (Railroad) Co., and Texas Eastern Transmission Corp. (a big concern controlled by George and Herman Brown, two wealthy Texas contractors who were close friends of Lyndon Johnson).

28. McGhee was replaced by the even wealthier W. Averell Harriman, who was still listed as a limited partner in the New York investment banking firm of Brown Brothers Harriman & Co. and board chairman of the Merchant-Sterling Corp. (a family-dominated investment concern). Harriman's younger brother, Roland, was a senior partner in Brown Brothers Harriman & Co., board chairman of the Union Pacific Railroad, and a director of such large corporations as the Anaconda Co. and Mutual Life Insurance Co.

29. Dillon's father had, through his Wall Street activities, amassed a fortune estimated at more than $100 million. See *Fortune* (November 1957), p. 177, and the *New York Times* (March 14, 1971), Sect. III, p. 5.

30. See Peter Collier and David Horowitz, *op. cit.*, pp. 295–98.

31. Dillon's Under Secretary of the Treasury, Henry H. Fowler, was a member of a Washington, D.C. law firm known as Fowler, Leva, Hawes & Symington, which apparently had no major formal corporate ties. However, Fowler had been retained by the BAC in the mid-1950s to represent one of its officials called to testify in a Congressional investigation of this elitist body. In addition, Fowler was appointed in 1958 to a National Commission on Money and Credit, a body established by the CED to appraise the nation's overall financial structure. The majority of the members of this group were affiliated with either the CED, BAC, or some other major economic interest, such as the Bank of America or the Chase Manhattan Bank. Hence it seems safe to assume that Fowler was highly regarded by the leaders of America's powerful economic establishment. See the *New York Times* (May 29, 1958), p. 14.

32. See Lester Tanzer (ed.), *The Kennedy Circle* (Washington, D.C.: Robert B. Luce, 1961), p. 165. McNamara had also served in the last year as a director of the Pennsylvania-based Scott Paper Co. But perhaps of more importance in his Cabinet appointment was the fact that five high-ranking (or recently retired) Ford officials sat on the board of the One William Street Fund, a big mutual fund recently established by New York's influential investment banking house of Lehman Brothers, many of whose partners carried great weight in the Democratic party.

33. See the appropriate entries in the 1960 *Moody's Industrial Manual* and also Paul Hoffman, *Lions in the Street*, p. 16. Gilpatric himself apparently did not serve on any major corporate boards at this time, probably because he was still a relatively junior figure in the firm, although he was a director of the Foreign Policy Association, a second-tier civic group.

34. See *Fortune* (January 1953), p. 118, and for more on Connally's lobbying activities for Richardson, see *Fortune* (July 31, 1978), p. 90.

35. See *Fortune* (October 1954), p. 52, and *Forbes* (March 1, 1956), p. 19. Zuckert's predecessor as board chairman of the Nuclear Science and Engineering Corp. was former AEC Commissioner Gordon Dean, who up to his death in 1958 was both a partner in Lehman Brothers and a senior vice-president of the General Dynamics Corp.

36. See Stan Opotowsky, *op. cit.*, p. 81.

37. See Paul Hoffman, *Lions in the Street*, p. 25, and *Fortune* (December 1957), p. 191.

38. Actually, this job was first offered to Abraham Ribicoff, who was an early supporter of the President, but he apparently preferred the more challenging HEW post. It was at this point that strong parental pressure may have been exerted in Robert's behalf. See Arthur M. Schlesinger, Jr., *Robert Kennedy and His Times* (Boston: Houghton Mifflin, 1978), pp. 227 and 230.

39. Up to recently, very little has been known about the activities of these enterprises, because, being privately owned, they do not have to make their records public. The first overall accounts of their operations were apparently published in *Forbes* (February 1, 1965), pp. 33–35, and *Fortune* (July 15, 1966), pp. 224–25 and 327–48.

40. As his initial top aide in the department, Robert Kennedy chose a former Denver lawyer, Byron R. White, who had been a vigorous early supporter of his brother's presidential drive. When White was appointed to the Supreme Court in 1962, his place as Assistant Attorney General was taken by a former law professor at Yale and the University of Chicago, Nicholas Katzenbach.

41. Michigan Governor G. Mennen Williams reportedly coveted this Cabinet post, but was considered too liberal by the Kennedy administration and was therefore shunted over to the relatively new and much less important post of Assistant Secretary of State for African Affairs.

42. See, for instance, Paul Hoffman, *Lions in the Street*, pp. 112–121.

43. For example, the most prominent boards on which senior partner Simon Rifkind served were Revlon, Inc., and the Emerson Radio & Phonograph Corp., neither of which ranked among the nation's "top 200." The only sizable concern of which Adlai Stevenson was a director was Encyclopaedia Britannica, Inc.

44. Hodges also served as a director of the medium-sized (probably New York-controlled) American Thread Co. from 1952 to 1955. But neither this concern nor Marshall Field & Co. was ever associated with either the BAC or CED. Hodges' top aide in the department was actually a more important economic figure, for this executive, Edward Gudeman, had served through most of the 1950s as a vice-president of Sears, Roebuck & Co., before becoming a partner (in 1960–1961) in Lehman Brothers.

45. See Alexander Heard, *The Costs of Democracy* (Chapel Hill: University of North Carolina Press, 1960), pp. 84n and 264n.

46. See Lester Tanzer, *The Kennedy Circle*, pp. 35 and 37. Indeed, Bundy had worked for Dewey in 1948 as a part of a high-powered foreign policy team headed by John Foster Dulles, his brother, Allen, C. Douglas Dillon, and Christian Herter.

47. See David Halberstam, *The Best and the Brightest*, p. 44.

48. Halberstam stressed the fact (p. 62) that John Amory Lowell, the great-great-grandfather of McGeorge Bundy, was a towering civic figure in his day, "having picked no fewer than six presidents of Harvard." Bundy's maternal grandfather, William Lowell Putnam, also had key economic links, for as a Boston lawyer he had served, up to his death in 1924, as a director of such major concerns as AT&T, State Street Trust Co., and Suffolk Savings Bank of Boston, and as a vice-president of the Brahmin-dominated Massachusetts Hospital Life Insurance Co.

49. Choate, Hall & Stewart may have also served as counsel to the United Fruit Co., judging by the make-up of its board of directors. The Bundy family, moreover, controlled the nation's oldest fish company, Gorton's of Gloucester, Inc., which had sales of about $20 million a year in the early 1960s.

50. The Auchincloss family never had a great fortune of its own, but as Stephen Birmingham has pointed out, in each generation "... there has been at least one brilliant marriage to carry the family upward onto new plateaux of prestige and privilege." As he went on to emphasize, "through marriage, the Auchinclosses are now kin, in addition to Rockefellers, Sloans, Winthrops, Jenningses, Saltonstalls, and Smedbergs, to such other redoubtable families as the Frelinghuysens, the van Rensselaers, the Cuttings, the Reids, the du Ponts, the Grosvenors, the Truslows, the Tiffanys... the Adamses, the Ingrahams, the Burdens, the Vanderbilts, and, of course, the Kennedys." See *The Right People*, pp. 281–302, especially 284 and 288.

51. McGeorge Bundy co-authored Stimson's governmental memoirs shortly after World War II. He also worked briefly (in 1948–1949) as a political analyst for the Council on Foreign Relations, which body may have carried considerable weight with Bundy during his years as President Kennedy's chief White House diplomatic advisor. On this latter point, see David Halberstam, *op. cit.*, p. 77.

52. It is interesting to note that Dulles's former law firm, Sullivan & Cromwell, served, up to the early 1960s, as general counsel for two of the large American-owned sugar companies in Cuba—the Francisco Sugar Co. and Manati Sugar Co.—and that one of the outside directors of these two closely allied firms was Gerald F. Beal, who was president of the J. Henry Schroder Banking Corp. (of which Allen Dulles had once been a board member), until recently the head of the International Railways of Central America (which had long been linked with United Fruit), as well as the treasurer of the Foreign Policy Association (the board chairman of which organization was a partner in Sullivan & Cromwell). Moreover, some of the other recently seized sugar companies in Cuba had been controlled by American interests that carried a great deal of weight in the Democratic party. For instance, New York financier John L. Loeb and his business associates owned a big block of stock in the Compania Azucarera Atlantica del Golfo, which produced a substantial amount of that nation's raw sugar. Up to 1961 one of the outside directors of this company was Harold F. Linder, the vice-chairman of the Lehman-Lazard Frères–dominated General American Investors Co., who was appointed head of the Export-Import Bank of Washington by President Kennedy. For more on Bissell's elitist (financial and railroad) family background, see Peter Wyden, *Bay of Pigs*, p. 14.

53. Another affair in which the CIA was heavily involved about this time was the foreign-supported Katangan secessionist movement in the Belgian Congo, a long-exploited former colony that produced 69 percent of the free world's industrial diamonds and 49 percent of its cobalt (most of which was sold to the United States). Various American concerns had major holdings in this country. Among the largest of these was American Metal Climax, Inc., and the Anglo-American Corp. of South Africa, Ltd., one of whose economic partners was mining magnate Charles W. Engelhard (the reported prototype for James Bond's "Goldfinger"). Some of these interests had very close ties to high officials in the Kennedy administration, such as C. Douglas Dillon, whose family firm served as Engelhard's banker. For a recent study which places considerable weight on the economic links of many of Kennedy's chief advisors in this affair, see Stephen R. Weissman, *American Foreign Policy in the Congo, 1960–1964* (Ithaca, N.Y.: Cornell University Press, 1974), passim; for more on Engelhard, see *Forbes* (August 1, 1965), pp. 20–22.

54. Over the years the links between the CIA and the American business community have been intimate and of rather surprising scope, with a number of executives quietly serving as CIA agents and, conversely, CIA men posing as corporate officials. However, these connections have rarely come to light, and then only under unusual circumstances. For example, when Robert Kennedy's wife's brother, George Skakel, Jr., was killed in a 1966 airplane crash, the *New York Times* noted that one of the others killed in this tragedy was Lewis Werner II, who had been director of the St. Louis regional office of the CIA for the last fifteen years. Yet Werner was an active partner in a local investment banking house and a director of the fairly sizable Mercantile Trust Co. of St. Louis when he was killed. One might also wonder whether the CIA's subsidization of political parties abroad was informally integrated with that of certain major oil companies, such as Standard Oil of N.J., which contributed more than $45 million to various political parties in Italy between 1963 and 1972. In this latter regard, see the *New York Times* (July 17, 1975), p. 1, and (January 7, 1976), p. 4.

55. President Kennedy picked a similar figure, Wall Street lawyer Arthur H. Dean, to act as head of the American delegation to the nuclear test ban negotiations, which were held in Geneva in the early 1960s. Dean had labored in a like capacity to help bring the Korean War to a formal close in the early 1950s. He had spent most of his professional life as a partner in Sullivan & Cromwell and had served, often as a successor to one of the Dulles brothers, as a director of the Bank of New York, the American Agricultural Chemical Co., American Bank Note Co., American Metal Climax, Inc., El Paso Natural Gas Co., Lazard Fund, Mexican Light & Power Co., Ltd., and the Council on Foreign Relations.

56. In the first part of 1961 two of the seven "outside" directors of the United Nuclear Corp. were direct representatives of the Rockefeller family, T. F. Walkowicz and Harper Woodward, both of whom served on the board of the Rockefeller-dominated Itek Corp. and Geophysics Corp. of America. Three other directors were apparently on friendly terms with these influential forces. They were James T. Hill, Jr., who was a partner in the investment firm of William A. M. Burden & Co. and a vice-president of Petroleum Reserves, Inc. (and a director of the Itek Corp. and the Geophysics Corp. of America); James McCormack, a vice-president of MIT (and a director of Geophysics and two other enterprises); and Nathan R. Owen, who was a partner in J. H. Whitney & Co.

57. With the Democratic assumption of power in 1961, the International Cooperation Administration (an organizational descendant of the Economic Cooperation Administration and the Mutual Security Agency) was transformed into the Agency for International Development. The first head of this agency was New York attorney Fowler Hamilton, who was a partner in the probably second-tier law firm of Cleary, Gottlieb, Steen & Hamilton (with whose Washington office George Ball was associated), and a director of the New York Telephone Co., an AT&T subsidiary, and the Foreign Policy Association. Hamilton served in this capacity only until November 1962, when the post was taken over by David Bell, a man whose background was entirely in academic and governmental affairs.

58. Since Webb maintained a Washington law office throughout this period, he may have served mainly as a legislative agent for this company.

59. Interestingly, control of the Atomic Energy Commission had, following the departure of chairman John McCone in 1960, fallen increasingly to non-elite figures who had scientific, academic, and governmental backgrounds. McCone himself was replaced by a highly regarded University of California scientist, Glenn T. Seaborg, whose only known economic tie was as a director of the comparatively small Nuclear Science and Engineering Corp.

60. See Hobart Rowen, *The Free Enterprisers*, p. 153.

61. As Hobart Rowen has rightly noted, "in terms of 'dangerous radicals,' there weren't any. Pointedly, Leon Keyserling, who had been chairman of the Council of Economic Advisers (under Truman), was not invited onto the team at all, primarily because he was considered a 'spender' by some Kennedy men. For 'bêtes noirs,' the Republicans were reduced to heckling Arthur Schlesinger, Jr., noted historian and author who was taken on the White House staff for miscellaneous speech assignments; and Heller, who as a prolific writer, lecturer, and Congressional witness had made the correct liberal, academic record on all economic issues. But Schlesinger had virtually nothing to do with policymaking in the White House. And Heller yielded principles gracefully to the pressures of the feasible, proving that even a professor can learn the political ropes." See Hobart Rowen, *op. cit.*, p. 22.

62. In this spectacular clash between big business and government, President Kennedy managed to get the U.S. Steel Corp. to rescind its announced price hike. However, within about a year's time, after political tempers had cooled, the steel industry quietly boosted its prices in a more selective fashion, thus making the initial stand of the Kennedy administration seem, in retrospect, to be a largely symbolic action. For more on this affair and Kennedy's overall relations with business interests, see Grant McConnell, *Steel and the Presidency* (New York: Norton, 1973), and Jim F. Heath, *John F. Kennedy and the Business Community* (Chicago: University of Chicago Press, 1969). The latter account indicates that, the steel conflict aside, Kennedy was not viewed with great hostility by major corporate executives, particularly during the last year of his administration.

63. According to Bernard Nossiter, under the tax "reform" plan initiated by John F. Kennedy in his last year as chief executive (formally approved by President Johnson shortly after he took office), "some 2.4 percent of all taxpayers, those with taxable incomes of $20,000 or more, stood to pick up $2.3 billion. But the 39.6 percent with taxable incomes of $5,000 or less would gain only $1.5 billion." Put it more graphic terms, the 200,000 wealthiest taxpayers got an average tax cut of $4,600 and the lowest 20 million about $75 apiece. See Bernard D. Nossiter, *The Mythmakers* (Boston: Houghton Mifflin, 1964), pp. 24–42, especially 35–36, and Hobart Rowen, *op. cit.*, pp. 46–60 and 231–52.

64. See the *New York Times* (May 4, 1963), p. 34.

65. It should also be noted that the Kennedy administration introduced no new labor legislation in the early 1960s, preferring to stick with the status quo, to the dismay of the nation's top union leaders, almost all of whom were strong Democratic party backers.

66. See Robert J. Art, *The TFX Decision: McNamara and the Military* (Boston: Little, Brown, 1968), p. 77.

67. According to a later in-depth investigation of the matter, no member of the Pentagon's evaluation team was consulted at this critical stage, and no written or verbal inquiries were made of armed forces experts on any technical points. In fact, only one brief (five-page) memorandum could be found in the departmental files to justify the reversal of the recommendation of the appraisal panel, and this contained a number of errors and statements taken out of context. See the U.S. Senate Committee on Government Operations, *TFX Contract Investigation* (Washington, D.C.: Government Printing Office, 1970), pp. 14–16 and 18–21. Also, for more on the fiscal plight of General Dynamics, see Richard A. Smith, "How a Great Corporation Got Out of Control," *Fortune* (January 1962), pp. 64–69 and 178–84; for a more general analysis which argues that financial bailouts and other economic imperatives play an important part in the award of defense contracts, see James E. Kurth, "Aerospace Production Lines and American

68. See the U.S. Senate, Committee on Government Operations, *TFX Contract Investigation*, pp. 1–4 and 53–89, and the *New York Times* (December 19, 1970), p. 1. According to one authority, of the limited number of F-111's produced by the late 1960s, at least fifteen had crashed while operating under normal flight conditions, with the result that these planes remained grounded throughout most of 1970 while emergency efforts were made to locate and correct the trouble. See Richard F. Kaufman, *The War Profiteers* (Garden City, N.Y.: Doubleday, 1972), p. 73.

69. For instance, John Jay Hopkins, the recently deceased kingpin of General Dynamics, once freely admitted that he had hired former Secretary of the Army Frank Pace, Jr., to, as he cynically put it, "... answer the telephone" and "... take care of the Washington end of the business." See *Fortune* (January 1962), pp. 67 and 180.

70. See *TFX Contract Investigation* (especially p. 44) for some examples of Gilpatric's various efforts on behalf of General Dynamics. Gilpatric's advice to this concern even extended to political considerations involved in the location and concentration of facilities in states such as Texas, which had influential Senators and Congressmen. See the *New York Times* (October 20, 1963), p. 18.

71. As for Boeing, Gilpatric merely acted as a witness for the company in a single proceeding in early 1958, which effort involved one entire day and portions of eleven others, and generated no income other than Gilpatric's expenses. In short, it was a vastly different relationship. See the *TFX Contract Investigation*, p. 42.

72. See the *TFX Contract Investigation*, p. 51. According to one authority, Gilpatric even had an office in General Dynamics' headquarters in Rockefeller Center to facilitate his work. See Paul Hoffman, *Lions in the Street*, p. 14.

73. See *TFX Contract Investigation*, p. 47. Despite the damning evidence assembled in this report, a recent study by one researcher has, in a footnote, minimized Gilpatric's role in this dispute. See Robert F. Coulam, *Illusions of Choice: The F-111 and the Problem of Weapons Acquisition Reform* (Princeton, N.J.: Princeton University Press, 1977), p. 63. This book focuses almost exclusively on the bureaucratic forces at work in the TFX controversy, and simply does not look at any other kind of influence.

74. See the *TFX Contract Investigation*, pp. 47 and 49. A little over a year later Gilpatric resigned from the Defense Department and rejoined his old concern, moving up ahead of six other senior partners to the fourth-ranking position in the firm.

75. Of the other three key civilian officials involved in this controversial case, only one had a significant stake in the decision. Secretary of the Navy Fred Korth was a former high executive of the Continental National Bank of Fort Worth, where General Dynamics had one of its largest plants—the one ticketed to do most of the TFX work. The Continental National Bank had extended two loans to this big local unit, and Korth was a good friend of Frank Davis, the head of the Fort Worth division of General Dynamics. Korth's log as Secretary of the Navy showed that he had sixteen contacts with officials of General Dynamics (which covered a total of 391 minutes) and that he had just two meetings with representatives of Boeing (which took approximately 35 minutes). However, Korth did not play as prominent a role in these proceedings as Gilpatric, and was not even present at the final meeting in which it was decided to give the contract to General Dynamics. See the *TFX Contract Investigation*, pp. 37–38 and 51.

76. See Michael E. Kinsley, *Outer Space and Inner Sanctums: Government, Business and Satellite Communication* (New York: Wiley, 1976), pp. 1–25.

77. Some of the more prominent persons initially elected to the board of the Communications Satellite Corp. in 1963 were John T. Connor, president of Merck & Co. (and a trustee of the CED); Edgar F. Kaiser, president of the giant Kaiser Industries Corp. of California (and a director of the Bank of America); David M. Kennedy, board chairman of the big Continental Illinois National Bank & Trust Co.; George L. Killion, president of the California-based American President Lines, board chairman of Metro-Goldwyn-Mayer, Inc., and onetime

treasurer of the Democratic National Committee; Sidney J. Weinberg, a senior partner in the New York investment banking firm of Goldman, Sachs & Co. (and a member or trustee of both the Business Council and the CED); and Leonard Woodcock, vice-president of the United Auto Workers.

78. As its first president, the Comsat board chose Joseph V. Charyk, a highly regarded scientific and administrative figure who had served recently as Under Secretary of the Air Force, and before that had been a Ford Motor Co. executive and Princeton University aeronautics professor.

79. Another major diplomatic issue in the early 1960s was the Cuban missile crisis, in which the Kennedy administration, at the apparent risk of nuclear war, forced the Soviet Union to remove the missile-launching facilities it had helped build in this Communist-controlled nation. According to Graham Allison's analysis, President Kennedy's inner circle of advisors on this issue was an ad hoc group called ExCom, which consisted of key Cabinet officers and defense and diplomatic officials, presidential aide Theodore Sorensen, and several "outside" figures—namely, former Secretary of State Dean Acheson, former Defense Secretary Robert Lovett (a longtime senior partner in Brown Brothers Harriman), and New York banker, recent disarmament negotiator, and onetime High Commissioner to West Germany, John J. McCloy— whom Allison blandly described as surrogates of America's "bipartisan foreign policy establishment." However, as John Donovan has pointed out, Allison glossed over the elitist background of these last three leaders and failed to stress the fact that no member of Congress participated in these important proceedings. See Graham Allison, *Essence of Decision: Explaining the Cuban Missile Crisis* (Boston: Little, Brown, 1971), pp. 185 and 215, and John C. Donovan, *The Cold Warriors*, p. 50.

80. Not all high officials in the Kennedy administration fully agreed with this policy. Under Secretary of State George Ball (a former Washington partner in a second-tier New York law firm) and longtime diplomat (and major businessman) W. Averell Harriman both had grave doubts about the strength of the South Vietnamese regime and the wisdom of massive American military involvement.

81. According to David Halberstam, Kennedy picked Lodge largely at the insistence of Secretary of State Dean Rusk. One of the major reasons for Lodge's appointment was that if our Vietnam policy turned out to be a disaster, it would help to have a well-known Republican associated with it. See Halberstam, *op. cit.*, p. 319.

82. See Rowland Evans and Robert Novak, *Lyndon B. Johnson: The Exercise of Power* (New York: New American Library, 1966), p. 30. Johnson not only became a fierce defender of the oil and gas industry in his home state, as might be expected, but he also supported a number of clearly conservative measures such as the Taft-Hartley Act.

83. Evans and Novak claim that Connally was, in effect, the political agent for "cotton" Texas. "But he failed to make an accommodation with the state's new political elite. The result of this lack of foresight came, quite literally, in a Texas back room one day early in 1952. Displaying the cash they had collected to beat him in the Democratic primary, oil's political operatives told Connally the harsh facts of postwar life and simply bludgeoned him out of running." *Ibid.*, pp. 17-18.

84. In the latter part of 1962 Brown and Root was merged into the almost equally large Halliburton Co., an oil supply company. This transaction probably reduced their interest in the construction industry and heightened it in other areas, especially in the Texas Eastern Transmission Corp. For more on Johnson's relations with the Brown brothers, see Alfred Steinberg, *Sam Johnson's Boy: A Close-up of the President from Texas* (New York: Macmillan, 1968), p. 200.

85. See, for instance, T. Harry Williams, "Huey, Lyndon, and Southern Radicalism," *Journal of American History* (September 1973), pp. 267-93. In making this comparison, Williams was willing to concede that Johnson was not as radical as Huey Long, for as this historian noted (on p. 280), Long made the redistribution of wealth in this country his primary political issue, whereas although Johnson "...launched an imaginative program to alleviate

poverty, he did not attempt to redistribute wealth or to alter seriously the power relationship between the government and business."

86. See *Fortune* (September 1964), p. 132. No doubt this judgment stemmed partly from Johnson's extraordinary wooing of the business community during the 1964 presidential election campaign. And, of course, the outlook of the nation's economic leaders had changed considerably since the late nineteenth century. But *Fortune's* claim is still quite revealing. Indeed, as one prominent industrialist put it, "Johnson has perhaps the best understanding of business needs in the country of anyone we have had in there in a long time, including Ike."

87. Some sources have placed great weight on the fact that, thanks largely to his Austin radio, television, and banking interests, Johnson was one of the richest men ever to act as President of the United States, with an estimated family fortune of about $14 million (see *Life*, August 14, 1964, p. 80, and the *New York Times*, December 1, 1968, p. 74). However, in the author's estimation, this personal wealth was not as important as Johnson's overall pattern of economic associations. Even the entrepreneurial activities of Johnson's legislative aide, Bobby Baker, revealed much about the oil (Murchison) interests that were closely allied with LBJ. See the *New York Times* (November 14, 1963), p. 1 and (February 5, 1964), p. 34.

88. See Charles Roberts, *LBJ's Inner Circle* (New York: Delacorte, 1965), pp. 166–81, and the *New York Times* (February 28, 1965), Sect. VI, pp. 1, 18, and 78–84.

89. See the *New York Times* (November 28, 1963), p. 18.

90. See *Fortune* (December 1957), p. 191, and Paul Hoffman, *Lions in the Street*, p. 25.

91. See *Fortune* (December 1957), p. 91. Weisl occasionally sat in on the partners' meetings and had great influence in the firm. Weisl was also reported to be the wealthy Robert Lehman's closest friend and sat on the board of the One William Street Fund, which was controlled by Lehman Brothers. See also Paul Hoffman, *op. cit.*, p. 89.

92. In July 1965, just a few months before he was appointed to the Supreme Court, Fortas was made a vice-president of the Federated Department Stores.

93. The only two non-Texas outside directors of the Greatamerica Corp. were William H. Osborn, Jr., of Lehman Brothers and Gustave L. Levy, a partner in the closely allied Goldman, Sachs & Co., who was the chief banking advisor for the Murchison interests. Also, Fred Lazarus, Jr., the top official of Federated Department Stores, sat on the board of the One William Street Fund, along with Edwin Weisl. For more on Levy, see the *New York Times* (June 4, 1961), Sect. III, p. 3.

94. See Joseph C. Goulden, *The Superlawyers* (New York: Weybright & Talley, 1971), pp. 146 and 161–72.

95. See *Fortune* (September 1969), p. 197. In the latter part of 1966 Rowe was also appointed to the board of Metro-Goldwyn-Mayer.

96. See the *New York Times* (January 28, 1968), Sect. VI, p. 20. According to both this source and journalist Joseph Goulden, Clifford was also retained on certain occasions by such other mammoth concerns as the Pennsylvania Railroad, Phillips Petroleum Co., and Standard Oil Co. of California. In addition, Clifford sat on the board of the medium-sized National Bank of Washington from the mid-1950s to the late 1960s, most likely as a representative of one of this institution's chief secondary stockholders (rather than the United Mine Workers, which held close to 40 percent of the shares).

97. In his belated bid to stem the Goldwater tide, Scranton was backed by such influential businessmen as Thomas B. McCabe, the head of the Scott Paper Co. (who was a director of the Campbell Soup Co., General Electric Co., and a trustee of the CED); Thomas S. Gates, Jr., the Philadelphia-born president of the Morgan Guaranty Trust Co. of New York (who was a director of Campbell Soup, Scott Paper, and various other large concerns); and Walter N. Thayer, the president of the Whitney Communications Corp. (who was a director of the Bankers Trust Co. of New York and a trustee of the CED). Prior to his appointment to a State Department post in 1959, Scranton had served on the board of the Delaware, Lackawanna & Western Railroad, and his brother-in-law, James A. Linen, was president of Time, Inc., and a

trustee of the CED. For more on Scranton's elitist support, see Theodore H. White, *The Making of the President, 1964* (New York: Atheneum, 1965), pp. 86–87, and Robert D. Novak, *The Agony of the GOP: 1964* (New York: Macmillan, 1965), pp. 272–73.

98. The major financial forces behind the Goldwater movement were the more reactionary interests in the business community, many of whom were associated with family-controlled concerns. Goldwater's top fundraisers were Roger Milliken, head of the big privately-owned Deering Milliken textile empire (and a trustee of the rightist Foundation for Economic Education); Jeremiah Milbank, Jr., the dominant figure in the Commercial Solvents Corp. (and heir to a sizable Borden milk and Southern Railway fortune); George M. Humphrey, a high official of the Hanna-controlled National Steel Corp.; Lammot du Pont Copeland, Jr., who was a director of the American Conservative Union; John G. Pew, a senior vice-president of the family-dominated Sun Oil Co. (whose kinsman J. Howard Pew was apparently a substantial financial supporter of the John Birch Society); Henry Salvatori, a well-known reactionary California oilman; J. William Middendorf II, a minor New York and Baltimore financier who served on the board of the Oklahoma Natural Gas Co. (and whose father was a longtime trustee of the rightist American Enterprise Association); and a few other less prominent persons. Indeed, after the 1962 sale of his family's department store, Goldwater's most important economic link was probably, through his wife, with the big Borg-Warner Corp. of Chicago. See Philip H. Burch, Jr., "The NAM as an Interest Group," *Politics and Society* (Fall 1973), pp. 118–121, *Business Week* (August 1, 1964), pp. 19–20, *Wall Street Journal* (May 31, 1966), pp. 1 and 16, and the *New York Times* (October 10, 1971), Sect. 3, p. 9.

99. See Theodore H. White, *op. cit.*, pp. 351–52, and the *New York Times* (September 1, 1964), p. 25 and (September 4, 1964), p. 13. Minnesota's Senator Hubert Humphrey, who was once viewed in a negative light by major businessmen because of his marked liberal views, made a concerted effort to build up support for his vice-presidential candidacy by securing the backing of various key corporate executives through meetings arranged by such figures as Robert Anderson, Sidney Weinberg, and Herman Nolen, the board chairman of McKesson & Robbins, Inc., who was a director of the Bankers Trust Co. of New York and a trustee of the CED. See *Fortune* (August 1965), p. 142.

100. See Herbert E. Alexander and Harold B. Meyers, "The Switch in Campaign Giving," *Fortune* (November 1965), pp. 170–72 and 211–16.

101. That the CFR strongly favored Johnson's military escalation in Vietnam can be seen from the fact that in 1965 when a special civic group was created to support this marked shift in American foreign policy, a number of its top figures were CFR leaders, such as John J. McCloy, Arthur Dean (of Sullivan & Cromwell), David Rockefeller, and New York banker Gabriel Hauge. (See the *New York Times*, September 9, 1965, pp. 30.) William P. Bundy was also appointed as a trustee of the American Assembly about this time.

102. In the 1960s the first four "name" partners of this well-established firm served as directors of the General American Investors Co., American Sugar Co., Liggett & Myers Tobacco Co., American Airlines, and Equitable Life Assurance Society.

103. The influence of business interests extended into other areas of American diplomacy as well. For instance, following Christian Herter's death in December 1966, President Johnson nominated this patrician Republican leader's top aide, William M. Roth, to serve as his Special Representative for Trade Negotiation. Roth was a wealthy San Francisco businessman who had been both a trustee of the CED and a director of the Matson Navigation Co.

104. Since no definitive study has yet been written about Harriman's involvement in this dispute, one can only speculate as to the reasons for his independent role in these proceedings. It is interesting to note, however, that Harriman had not served as a director of the Council on Foreign Relations since the mid-1950s, whereas the more hawkish William P. Bundy had recently been elevated to this body's prestigious board.

105. When Rostow was first elected to this board in 1962, its top official was Charles S. Payson, who was John Hay Whitney's brother-in-law. However, this wealthy businessman

apparently disposed of his interest shortly thereafter, and the rest of the people involved in this concern were Texans.

106. For more on why Dillon left the Johnson administration, see David Halberstam, *op. cit.*, p. 528.

107. This law firm was not mentioned in Joseph Goulden's recent book, *The Superlawyers*, which describes the operation of Washington's top law firms. Johnson first offered the post to his close friend, Donald Cook, president of the big American Electric Power Co., who had served in the early 1950s as an SEC commissioner and before that as special counsel to the House Naval Affairs Committee. When Cook could not be persuaded to accept this post, Johnson turned to Kermit Gordon, the director of the Bureau of the Budget. However, because he was basically an academic, Gordon also declined the offer, for as he put it, the job "...required a man of somewhat conservative background, one who would have the confidence of the business and banking communities," which comment would indicate that Treasury was as much a "clientele" agency as many other arms of the federal government. See the *New York Times* (March 27, 1967), p. 16, and Evans and Novak, *op. cit.*, p. 506.

108. According to the *New York Times* (November 16, 1967), p. 73, Henry Fowler was one of the two persons (John T. Connor was the other) recommended for Cabinet office to President Johnson by New York City financier Sidney Weinberg, who was a longtime member of the BAC and a still active trustee of the CED.

109. See *Time* (April 23, 1965), p. 88.

110. Fowler's Under Secretary of the Treasury, Joseph Barr, was a relatively minor Indiana businessman, who had previously served briefly as a Congressman (1959–1960), a lesser Treasury Department executive (early 1960s), and most recently as Chairman of the Federal Deposit Insurance Corp. The Under Secretary of the Treasury for Monetary Affairs, Frederick Deming, was a well-regarded fiscal expert who had worked his way up through various Federal Reserve Bank posts.

111. As a graceful "exit," McNamara was appointed as George Woods' successor as president of the World Bank. His selection brought to an end the longtime executive domination of this institution by men closely associated with the Rockefeller interests.

112. See Jim F. Heath, *Decade of Disillusionment: The Kennedy-Johnson Years* (Bloomington: Indiana University Press, 1975), p. 269.

113. Similarly, up to late 1968 the National Aeronautics and Space Administration was headed by Kennedy appointee James Webb, who during most or all of the Eisenhower years had been a second-tier official of the Kerr-McGee Oil Industries, a director of the McDonnell Aircraft Corp., and a trustee of the CED. On the other hand, the Atomic Energy Commission came, under Johnson, to be increasingly controlled by people with scientific and academic backgrounds.

114. Vance had, moreover, married into the wealthy (W & J) Sloane family of New York, and his father-in-law served on the board of the big United States Trust Co. from 1923 to 1961 and the considerably smaller Atlantic Mutual Insurance Co. from 1921 to 1966.

115. In 1967 Nitze was succeeded as Secretary of the Navy by Paul R. Ignatius, who had held a series of second-echelon Defense Department posts since 1961. Prior to his entry into the Kennedy administration, Ignatius had been a vice-president of a relatively small Massachusetts management consulting firm, Harbridge House, Inc., which specialized in defense matters.

116. Moreover, Nitze's sister's son-in-law, Stephen M. DuBrul, Jr., was a partner in New York's Lehman Brothers and had served since 1962 as a director of the big May Department Stores Co.

117. This firm was co-founded by one of Truman's Defense Secretaries, Louis A. Johnson. Although it never achieved the status of a number of Washington's more important law firms, it was apparently retained by Pan-American World Airways in the early 1960s. See Joseph C. Goulden, *The Superlawyers*, p. 146.

118. To get some idea of the general standing and economic orientation of this law firm, one need only note that one of its senior partners, Eli W. Debevoise, served in the mid-1960s as a director of the Bank of New York, St. Joseph Lead Co., and West Virginia Pulp & Paper Co., while another partner, Francis T. P. Plimpton, sat on the board of the Bowery Savings Bank and the United States Trust Co. of New York.

119. Resor was also a close friend of Deputy Secretary of Defense Cyrus Vance; in fact, they had been roommates at Yale.

120. See Jim F. Heath, *Decade of Disillusionment*, p. 269.

121. The influential Business Council was very much opposed to the prospect of Robert Kennedy as LBJ's 1964 running mate, apparently primarily because some of the Justice Department's recent antitrust actions were viewed with grave misgivings by many major corporate executives. See the *New York Times* (May 17, 1964), Sect. 4, p. 12.

122. Two new Cabinet-level agencies were also created in the late 1960s as part of President Johnson's drive to provide improved public service in critical domestic areas. The first of these, the Department of Housing and Urban Development, was headed from its inception by Robert Weaver, who had spent most of the preceding decade as a state or federal housing official. (Weaver was the first black to be appointed to a Cabinet post in the United States.) The second agency was the Department of Transportation. It was established a year later and placed under the direction of another able non-elite figure, Alan Boyd, who had served for the last eleven years on various regulatory bodies which were concerned with air and railroad transportation policy.

123. Gardner had also recently served briefly as a director of the (foreign-controlled) Shell Oil Co. and the New York Telephone Co., a subsidiary of AT&T. But these associations may have been largely of a public relations nature and of less importance than Gardner's expertise in the realm of education. Gardner, however, resigned toward the end of the Johnson administration to return to a leadership role in the civic world, at which point he was replaced by his much-experienced top aide (and onetime university professor) Wilbur J. Cohen.

124. At first glance, the selection of Trowbridge would appear to be an exception, for he came from a series of second-echelon managerial positions with two major oil companies. However, he was a member of a wealthy family which had long been active in Detroit economic and civic affairs. For more on the elitist background of this official, see Lynda Ann Ewen, *Corporate Power and Urban Crisis in Detroit* (Princeton, N.J.: Princeton University Press, 1978), p. 163 and Chart 1.

125. Hodges, for example, had served on the board of the medium-sized American Thread Co., while Sawyer had been a director of the American Thermos Bottle Co. and Kemper-Thomas Co., neither of which could be considered a large concern.

126. When Kohler relinquished this post in November 1966, he was replaced by another longtime foreign service officer, Llewellyn Thompson, who had already served in this capacity once before (1957–1962). Bohlen was Ambassador to France until the first part of 1968, when he was succeeded by Kennedy kinsman R. Sargent Shriver, who had toiled loyally under Johnson as director of the Peace Corps and of the much heralded anti-poverty program. Shriver was a moderately wealthy Maryland figure who, after marrying one of Joseph P. Kennedy's daughters, had become assistant general manager of the family's big Merchandise Mart, a Chicago office building.

127. Like Bruce, McGhee was independently wealthy, in large part because of his marriage to the daughter of the former "dean" of the Texas oilmen, E. L. DeGolyer. McGhee, who served as Ambassador until May 1968 (when he was replaced by Henry Cabot Lodge), also owned a small oil production company in his home state of Texas.

128. Our initial Ambassador to NATO during the Johnson years was Kennedy incumbent Thomas K. Finletter, a former New York lawyer and a longtime director of the Council on Foreign Relations. Finletter was succeeded in the latter part of 1965 by a non-elite figure, Harlan Cleveland, who had primarily a governmental and academic background. But it is also

interesting to note that when a major crisis developed over NATO in 1966, Secretary of State Dean Rusk appointed Establishment leader John J. McCloy (who was still a director of the Chase Manhattan Bank, Metropolitan Life, and several other large concerns) to serve as a special aide and advisor on the matter. See the *New York Times* (April 12, 1966), p. 8.

129. Bunker served on the board of his former firm, the National Sugar Refining Co., up to early 1966, which tie would appear to have been a conflict of interest, for during this period Bunker was not only our Ambassador to the Organization of American States, but also acted in late 1965 as President Johnson's key de facto emissary to the Dominican Republic immediately after our military intervention in that country. He reportedly played a crucial role in the selection of conservative elitist leader Hector Garcia-Godoy as the new Washington-approved president of this strife-torn nation. Two recent studies of this controversial episode have erroneously portrayed Bunker as a former (presumably pre-1951) director of the National Sugar Refining Co. See Abraham F. Lowenthal, *The Dominican Intervention* (Cambridge, Mass.: Harvard University Press, 1972), p. 189, and Jerome Slater, *Intervention and Negotiation: The United States and the Dominican Revolution* (New York: Harper & Row, 1970), pp. 46–47, 54, 97, and 119–21. For a useful corrective, see the account of this affair presented by Fred Goff and Michael Locker in Irving Louis Horowitz, Josue de Castro, and John Gerassi (eds.), *Latin American Radicalism* (New York: Random House, 1969).

130. In addition, Bunker's younger brother, Arthur, had served as a director of the Lehman Corp. and the One William Street Fund (Lehman's mutual fund) up to his death in late 1964.

131. Bunker served on these two boards up through the end of the Johnson administration. Moreover, Lehman kinsman John L. Loeb, who had been a key "behind-the-scenes" figure in the shake-up of the Curtis Publishing Co., also bought a controlling (40 percent) interest in the Colorado-based Holly Sugar Corp. in early 1967, and installed Bunker's son, John, as president of this concern. See *Forbes* (July 15, 1962), p. 34, *Forbes* (May 15, 1968), p. 79, and *Fortune* (March 1969), p. 46.

132. Interestingly, in May 1967 President Johnson appointed Dallas lawyer Eugene Locke, who was a director of the fairly small Trinity Steel Co. and a political ally of Texas Governor John Connally, to serve in the newly created post of Deputy Ambassador to South Vietnam. See the *New York Times* (May 13, 1967), p. 13.

133. This company, in which McCone had a substantial interest, had, along with its Texaco partner, major oil reserves and operations in Indonesia, the scene of a bloody (perhaps CIA-supported) coup that overthrew the leftish government of President Sukarno shortly after McCone stepped down as head of the CIA. Although there is no direct evidence of CIA involvement in this affair, the agency did make one such attempt back in 1958. That such backing was quite possible may be seen from the recent revelation that President Johnson, apparently acting on the counsel of the CIA and certain other officials, was prepared to intervene with naval and airborne units in Brazil in 1964 if the business-supported military coup there failed to oust leftish President Goulart. See Jan K. Black, *United States Penetration of Brazil* (Philadelphia: University of Pennsylvania Press, 1977), passim, the *New York Times* (December 30, 1976), p. 7, *Fortune* (September 1964), pp. 147–49 and 210–21, and Norman Blume, "Pressure Groups and Decision-Making in Brazil," *Studies in Comparative International Organization* (1968), pp. 209–220.

134. See, for example, the *New York Times* (September 1, 1973), Sect. VI, p. 35, and Stewart Alsop, *The Center*, pp. 204–205. Given this highly elitist pattern of agency leadership, one might well suspect that the CIA was involved in the extraordinary course of events which led up to the ouster of democratically elected, somewhat leftist Papandreou government in Greece in the mid-1960s and the army-imposed installation a short time later of a strongly authoritarian regime headed by junta leader Colonel George Papadopoulos, who had been one of the key liaison figures between the CIA and the Greek secret police for many years. One top CIA agent, Richard Barnum, reportedly operated through the Esso-Pappas oil complex, which had been in considerable jeopardy until the requisite contracts were signed with the newly established military dictatorship. The Boston-based Pappas Foundation had also been a conduit for CIA

money destined for Greece, and it was perhaps no accident that after the coup a Pappas employee, Pavlos Totomis, was entrusted with the crucial Ministry of Public Order. See Constantine Tsoucalas, *The Greek Tragedy* (London: Penguin, 1969), p. 206, and *Fortune* (February 1966), pp. 69–70.

135. In like fashion, the Council of Economic Advisers was run by well-regarded economics professors, most of whom were, like its chairmen, Gardner Ackley and Arthur Okum, of a fairly liberal persuasion. Most of the special assistants to the President were also non-elite figures, chosen apparently because of their abilities or close personal ties to LBJ.

136. According to one recent study, the three "public" directors have exerted relatively little influence on the affairs of this important concern. See Michael E. Kinsley, *Outer Space and Inner Sanctums*, pp. 207–210 in particular.

137. In addition, McCormack was elected to the board of the (possibly Rockefeller-dominated) Eastern Airlines in 1965, which link he maintained throughout his years as head of the Communications Satellite Corp.

138. It is interesting to note that Johnson's antipoverty program received strong support initially from many now more socially conscious business executives, such as Stuart Saunders, head of the Pennsylvania Railroad, who lobbied actively for this controversial measure. Unlike the mid and late 1930s when Roosevelt was virtually at war with a host of arch-conservative business leaders, Johnson remained on very good terms with most major corporate executives, even when he was promoting the passage of welfare legislation. See Rowland Evans and Robert Novak, *op. cit.*, pp. 429, 432, and 433.

139. These totals include only those mergers involving manufacturing and mining concerns, and not those in other areas of activity, such as banking and transportation. All told, there were 1,950 mergers in 1964; 2,125 in 1965; 2,377 in 1966; 2,975 in 1967; and a striking 4,462 in 1968.

140. Largely because of merger activity, the nation's "top 200" manufacturing firms increased their share of America's industrial assets from roughly 45 percent in 1947 to a little over 60 percent by 1968, a proportion roughly equal to that held by the 1,000 biggest companies in 1941. In fact, between 1962 and 1968, 110 of the 500 largest industrial concerns in the country disappeared through mergers.

141. See *Forbes* (July 17, 1966), p. 43. The head of the Antitrust Division at this time was former Harvard professor Donald Turner, who had co-authored a book which took a hard line against large mergers. See Carl Kaysen and Donald F. Turner, *Antitrust Policy: An Economic and Legal Analysis* (Cambridge, Mass.: Harvard University Press, 1965), p. 98. For a critical analysis of Turner's surprisingly compliant role as an antitrust official, see Mark J. Green et al., *The Closed Enterprise System* (New York: Grossman, 1972), pp. 82–93, 287–91, and 305–06.

142. This compilation, based on FTC data, was taken from Phillip Blumberg's book, *The Megacorporation in American Society*, p. 49. Eleven mergers were not included here in the interest of space, all but two of which were approved in Johnson's last years in office. There was only one such giant merger in the 1950s, that involving the General Telephone & Electronics Corp. and Sylvania Electric, and there was also a significant tapering off of such activity after 1970. The above list does not include major bank mergers, of which there were three during this period, all in the early 1960s. By far the biggest of these was that linking two huge New York City institutions, the Hanover Bank and Manufacturers Trust Co., which action was belatedly and ineffectively challenged by the Justice Department under the Kennedy administration.

143. Around the end of 1968 the Justice Department did file an antitrust suit against IBM, which controlled about 74 percent of the $3 billion digital computer market. But this case was instituted by Turner's lame-duck successor, Edwin Zimmerman, with perhaps Ramsey Clark's tacit approval, just two days before Richard Nixon took office, and must therefore be viewed in a rather skeptical light. Just a few weeks earlier one of IBM's distant rivals, the Control Data Corp., had initiated antitrust proceedings, as permitted by federal law, against this corporate giant. See Mark J. Green et al., *op. cit.*, p. 307, and the *New York Times* (December 12, 1968), p. 1.

144. Antitrust chief Donald Turner reportedly decided not to contest the Union-Pure Oil merger because these two firms did not compete in the sale of their primary products in the same geographic area. But, as Mark Green and his Nader research group have pointed out, these two firms were direct competitors in the exploration for crude oil and natural gas and, perhaps less importantly, in the marketing of automotive oil and petrochemicals. See Mark J. Green et al., *op. cit.*, p. 287.

145. Much of the credit for this achievement should apparently be given to Pennsylvania Railroad executive Stuart Saunders, who, because of the strong early opposition of the Justice Department, spent many hours lobbying vigorously for this union with various high federal officials, especially President Johnson. As Saunders himself later told the press, "I could not have gotten the merger through without help from [influential] members of the Administration"; as he put it, in what was later described as a masterpiece of understatement, "they got the Justice Department to change its thinking." See *Time* (January 26, 1968), p. 71A, and Joseph R. Daughen and Peter Binzen, *The Wreck of the Penn Central* (Boston: Little, Brown, 1971), pp. 66–77.

146. See the President's Commission on Postal Organization, *Towards Postal Excellence* (Washington, D.C.: U.S. Government Printing Office, 1968).

147. America's economic stake in South Vietnam was probably not an important factor in our decision to shore up Saigon's sagging military regime. American oil companies, for example, did not begin to invest in exploration activities in this particular area until the summer of 1973, and the industry's total capital outlay reportedly never exceeded $100 million, whereas the French holdings in Vietnam were, despite its (1954) military withdrawal, roughly three times this size (see the *New York Times*, April 27, 1975, p. 26, and May 3, 1975, p. 15). However, certain major corporations may have had a substantial interest in the future development of the area close to Vietnam and Cambodia, for such concerns as the Continental Oil Co., Esso (Jersey Standard), and Tenneco were apparently about to procure the rights to large reserves off the nearby coasts of Malaysia and Indonesia (see *Forbes*, March 15, 1971, p. 19). Other American companies, such as Standard Oil of California, had long had large-scale operations in the latter country. Also, some other concerns had benefited handsomely from work which stemmed from our increasingly military involvement in Vietnam. For example, as Albert Steinberg has observed, Brown & Root, Inc. (which was run by men friendly to Johnson) secured a sizable share of the military construction program in South Vietnam, which grew from a modest $21 million in 1962 to about $1.3 billion a few years later. See Alfred Steinberg, *op. cit.*, p. 577.

148. See the *New York Times* (July 23, 1965), pp. 1 and 3. For more on the highly supportive role played by the nation's business and civic leaders during the early years of the war, see Godfrey Hodgson, "The Establishment," *Foreign Policy* (Spring 1973), pp. 19–22, Laurence H. Shoup and William Minter, *Imperial Brain Trust*, pp. 238–45, Laurence Shoup, "The Council on Foreign Relations and American Policy in Southeast Asia, 1940–1973," *The Insurgent Sociologist* (Winter 1977), pp. 19–30, and Thomas R. Dye, "Oligarchic Tendencies in National Policy-Making: The Role of the Private Policy-Planning Organizations," *Journal of Politics* (May 1978), p. 316.

149. See the *New York Times* (September 9, 1965), p. 30. All told, of the 46 members of this committee, 19 were prominent businessmen or corporate lawyers, ten were former high government officials (almost all of whom were now holding major economic posts), eleven were academic figures (some of whom had noteworthy directorship ties), three were newspaper people, two were foundation executives, and one was a writer of light fiction.

150. See *Dun's Review* (January 1970), p. 40. According to this account, Johnson spent more time in private meetings with Business Council leaders than any other President, including Eisenhower.

151. See Jim F. Heath, *Decade of Disillusionment*, p. 269.

152. See Townsend Hoopes, *The Limits of Intervention* (New York: David McKay, 1969), pp. 214–15. According to this onetime high Defense Department official, Dean, Lodge, McCloy, and former Army General Omar Bradley occupied something of a middle ground in

this debate, being deeply disturbed by the recent adverse events, but not quite ready for a drastic shift in policy.

153. As David Halberstam put it, these elitist leaders "... let him know that the Establishment—yes, Wall Street—had turned on the war.... It was hurting the economy, dividing the country, turning the youth [of the nation] against the country's best traditions." See David Halberstam, *op. cit.*, p. 653; see also Thomas R. Dye, *op. cit.*, pp. 316–17.

154. Apparently many prominent pro-Democratic businessmen feared or did not fully trust Robert Kennedy, for a strong "stop Kennedy" movement soon developed among the party's major financial forces. This drive was reportedly led by such influential figures as John L. Loeb, a senior partner in Loeb, Rhoades & Co. (who was a director of the Allied Chemical Corp. and the Distillers Corp.–Seagrams, Ltd., and had married into the Lehman family); John T. Connor, Johnson's former Secretary of Commerce who was now board chairman of Allied Chemical (and a director or trustee of the Business Council, CED, Chase Manhattan Bank, and General Motors); Edgar Bronfman, a major executive of the Distillers–Seagrams (who had married John L. Loeb's daughter and was a director of the Bank of New York and MGM); Leon Hess, head of the Hess Oil & Chemical Corp.; Edgar Kaiser, the board chairman of the Kaiser Industries Corp. (and a member of the Business Council); Armand Erpf, a partner in Loeb, Rhoades & Co. (and a director of the Seaboard Coast Line Railroad); and Crowdus Baker, the vice-chairman of Sears, Roebuck & Co. (and a director of the Chemical Bank New York Trust Co.). See *Finance* (July 1968), p. 12, and also Lewis Chester, Godfrey Hodgson, and Bruce Page, *An American Melodrama: The Presidential Campaign of 1968* (New York: Viking, 1969), pp. 143–44.

155. Laurence Shoup, *op. cit.*, p. 26.

156. According to one recent study, during the many years in which Johnson had held high federal office, he seldom made a major move without consulting this canny Washington lawyer. "Even from the bench Fortas did odd jobs for Johnson: advising on Vietnam, writing the speech in which Johnson ordered Federal troops into Detroit during the August, 1967 riots, helping the White House settle a steel price dispute." See Joseph C. Goulden, *The Superlawyers*, p. 127.

157. In addition, he had served for almost twenty years as a director of the much smaller Sucrest Corp. (and its pre-1961 corporate predecessor, the American Molasses Co.). For more on the Fortas law firm, see Joseph C. Goulden, *op. cit.*, pp. 110–143.

158. See the *New York Times* (June 4, 1967), Sect. 6, p. 86. According to this article, Fortas, as a jurist, expressed a sympathy for the problems of business that had not been reflected on the Court since the pre-New Deal days. In June 1968, when Chief Justice Earl Warren wrote the President informing him of his desire to retire in the near future, Johnson tried to appoint Fortas to this key post. But the nomination ran into a storm of protest, part of which stemmed from Fortas's various judicial improprieties (such as his acceptance of certain large outside fees), and the idea was soon dropped, with Warren continuing to hold office up through the first months of the Nixon administration.

159. See *Time* (June 24, 1966), p. 85.

160. See *Time* (July 3, 1964), p. 77.

161. Both Kennedy and Johnson relied more on people who had considerable governmental experience than did President Eisenhower, many of whose top choices came directly from the business world. However, while there was comparatively little difference in the proportion of high officials who had college degrees (as one might expect, it remained high), there was, under Kennedy in particular, a noteworthy drop in the percentage drawn from Ivy League institutions.

162. Although President Johnson was reported to be on close terms with the Business Council, this was apparently more of a personal relationship than an institutional one, and was not reflected to any significant extent in the recruitment pattern of his regime.

163. Given more time, President Kennedy might have developed into a more liberal leader, despite his wealthy family background. Yet despite Kennedy's initial brief split with the BAC and one much publicized clash with the steel industry, various actions promoted or sanctioned under his administration indicate pro-business influence, e.g., the Bay of Pigs invasion, the TFX scandal, and the initiation of the Tax Reform Act of 1963.

CHAPTER 6

The Nixon-Ford Regime

According to some recent studies, the rise of Richard Nixon to the Presidency in 1969 represented a major shift in the distribution of power in the United States, from a system long dominated by the Eastern establishment (a coalition of influential economic and political leaders with impressive ties to both parties, particularly the Republican) to one in which control passed to the more conservative emerging forces of the nation's "Southern Rim." This rim has been defined by the primary exponent of this thesis, Kirkpatrick Sale, to include thirteen Southern and Southwestern states—North and South Carolina, Georgia, Florida, Tennessee, Alabama, Mississippi, Arkansas, Louisiana, Oklahoma, Texas, New Mexico, and Arizona—plus the lower, more populous parts of California and Nevada. Sale maintained that one of the primary reasons for the emergence of this region as a major force in national affairs was its tremendous economic development in the postwar period, which was centered in six areas—agriculture (particularly "agribusiness"), defense, oil, technology, real estate, and leisure time activities.[1]

However, although during the Nixon-Ford years the Southern Rim produced a good deal of the nation's food, did a thriving tourist business, and probably had the sharpest rise in real estate values of any section of the country, its overall economic importance should not be exaggerated. For example, most of America's big oil companies were still Northeastern controlled. In the realm of defense, only three of the top ten firms in 1970—Lockheed, Litton Industries, and Hughes Aircraft—were purely Southern Rim enterprises. And although three other concerns—General Dynamics, McDonnell-Douglas, and Rockwell International (or North American Rockwell, as it was known up to 1973)—had major operations in this region, their locus of control lay in Chicago, St. Louis, and Pittsburgh. That the Southern Rim had not achieved true economic supremacy may be further seen in the fact that it still accounted for only about 30 percent of the nation's industrial employment and production by the mid-1970s. The Southern Rim's secondary position among the top non-financial firms is revealed by a look at Table 9.

231

TABLE 9
America's Top 30 Non-financial Firms in 1976

1976 Rank	Non-financial Firm (and location of its corporate headquarters)	1968 Assets ($ billions)	1976 Assets ($ billions)
1.	AT&T (New York)	40.2	86.7
2.	Exxon Corp. (formerly Standard Oil Co. of N.J., a New York-based concern)	16.8	36.3
3.	General Motors Corp. (Mich.)	14.0	24.3
4.	Mobil Corp. (N.Y.C.)	6.9	18.8
5.	Texaco, Inc. (New York)	8.7	18.2
6.	IBM (New York)	6.7	17.7
7.	ITT (New York)	4.0	17.5
8.	Ford Motor Co. (Mich.)	9.0	15.7
9.	Standard Oil Co. of Cal. (San Francisco)	5.8	13.8
10.	General Telephone & Electronics Corp. (Conn.)	6.2	13.6
11.	Gulf Oil Corp. (Pa.)	7.5	13.4
12.	Sears, Roebuck & Co. (Chicago)	6.5	12.7
13.	General Electric Co. (New York)	5.7	12.1
14.	Standard Oil Co. of Ind. (Chicago)	4.7	11.2
15.	U.S. Steel Corp. (Pittsburgh)	6.4	9.2
16.	Atlantic Richfield Co. (N.Y.C. up to 1972, Los Angeles thereafter)	2.5	8.9
17.	Southern Co. (a Georgia-based public utility holding company)	2.5	8.1
18.	Shell Oil Co. (a Texas-based subsidiary of the foreign-controlled Shell Petroleum N.V.)	4.2	7.8
19.	Pacific Gas & Electric Co. (San Francisco)	3.8	7.4
20.	Tenneco, Inc. (Texas)	3.9	7.2
21.	Chrysler Corp. (Mich.)	4.4	7.1
22.	E. I. du Pont de Nemours & Co. (Del.)	3.3	7.0
23.	American Electric Power Co. (N.Y.C.)	2.4	6.9
24.	Dow Chemical Co. (Mich.)	2.3	6.8
25.	Union Carbide Corp. (New York)	3.2	6.6
26.	Consolidated Edison Co. (New York)	3.8	6.6
27.	Standard Oil Co., Ohio (Cleveland)	0.8	6.3
28.	Loew's, Inc. (New York)	0.3	6.2
29.	Continental Oil Co. (Conn.)	2.5	6.0
30.	Commonwealth Edison Co. (Ill.)	2.6	5.9

In short, as late as 1976 only a small proportion of the nation's top thirty industrial concerns were run by Southern Rim interests.

Most claims about the size and power of financial institutions in the Southern Rim have also been grossly exaggerated, for they generally ignore the huge trust holdings of the big Northeastern banks.[2] This can readily be seen by a glance at Table 10.

TABLE 10
America's Top 30 Financial Institutions in 1976

1976 Rank	Financial Institution (and location)	1968 Assets* ($ billions)	1976 Assets* ($ billions)
1.	Citicorp. (up to early 1976 the First National City Bank of N.Y.C.)	28.4	90.9
2.	BankAmerica (San Francisco)	25.2	85.0
3.	Chase Manhattan Bank (N.Y.C.)	31.7	60.6
4.	Morgan Guaranty Trust Co. (N.Y.C.)	26.0	54.4
5.	Bankers Trust Co. (N.Y.C.)	17.9	45.9
6.	Prudential Insurance Co. of America (N.J.)	25.1	43.7
7.	Manufacturers Hanover Trust Co. (N.Y.C.)	16.5	43.0
8.	Metropolitan Life Insurance Co. (N.Y.C.)	24.6	37.5
9.	Chemical Bank (N.Y.C.)	13.0	34.3
10.	Continental Illinois National Bank & Trust Co. (Chicago)	11.3	29.9
11.	First National Bank of Chicago	11.4	28.7
12.	Mellon Bank (Pittsburgh)	11.5	23.8
13.	Western Bancorporation (Cal.)	8.5	23.8
14.	Equitable Life Assurance Society (N.Y.C.)	13.1	22.4
15.	Security Pacific National Bank (Los Angeles)	7.8	20.7
16.	Aetna Life & Casualty Co. (Conn.)	8.0	18.2
17.	Wells Fargo Bank (San Francisco)	6.6	17.8
18.	National Bank of Detroit	6.9	17.1
19.	First National Bank of Boston	9.0	15.3
20.	Crocker National Bank (San Francisco)	6.4	15.2
21.	New York Life Insurance Co. (N.Y.C.)	9.6	14.9
22.	Charter New York Corp. (parent company of Irving Trust Co.)	5.7	14.8
23.	Harris Trust & Savings Bank (Chicago)	5.6	14.7
24.	Marine Midland Banks, Inc. (Buffalo, N.Y.)	4.9	14.7
25.	First Bank System, Inc. (Minn.)	4.8	14.2
26.	John Hancock Mutual Life Insurance Co. (Boston)	8.9	14.0
27.	Travelers Corp. (Conn.-based insurance co.)	6.1	13.4
28.	United States Trust Co. (N.Y.C.)	8.8	13.2
29.	Northern Trust Co. (Chicago)	5.8	12.6
30.	Northwest Bancorporation (Minn.)	5.6	12.6

*Including commercial bank trust funds.

According to these rarely published totals, only five of the commercial banks located along the Southern Rim ranked among the nation's top thirty financial institutions in 1976.[3]

Also, in assessing the relative power of the Southern Rim vis-a-vis the Eastern establishment, one must take into account the influence of such groups as the Business Council, the CED, and the Council of Foreign Relations, which have long played a prominent role in national affairs. These elitist bodies remained active and relatively unchanged in their composition during the Nixon-Ford years. In addition, in the early 1970s two other important groups were formed, the Business Roundtable and the Trilateral Commission.

The Business Roundtable was organized in late 1972 through the merger of three lesser-known groups: the Labor Law Study Committee, the Construction Users Anti-Inflation Roundtable, and the so-called March group. The Labor Law Study Committee was set up in 1965 after labor's first major attempt to repeal Section 14(b) of the Taft-Hartley Act, and was reportedly led by Virgil Day and Douglas Soutar, the vice-presidents for industrial relations of GE and the American Smelting and Refining Co. The Construction Users Anti-Inflation Roundtable was created in 1969 under the leadership of U.S. Steel's recently retired board chairman, Roger Blough, to help combat rising construction costs, particularly those generated by labor. And the March group was formed in March 1971 (hence the name), mainly through the efforts of GE president Fred Borch, to improve the public image of business through the use of the mass media and, perhaps more importantly, to increase the political influence of the nation's major corporate interests, who had apparently become increasingly dissatisfied with the lobbying activities of the U.S. Chamber of Commerce and the NAM.[4] There was an extraordinary amount of overlap between the governing body of the Business Roundtable and the membership of the Business Council and CED in particular, on the order of 75 percent or more during the mid-1970s.[5] Judging from all accounts, the Business Roundtable soon emerged as the overt lobbying arm of America's potent economic establishment, apparently taking over or expanding on the politico-economic role previously (albeit quietly) played, primarily with regard to the executive branch of government, by the Business Council and the CED.[6]

The other influential body which was created about this time was the Trilateral Commission. This organization was formed in July 1973, reportedly largely at the urging of New York banker David Rockefeller, in an effort to deal more effectively with the problems besetting the free world's three key industrial regions—North America, Western Europe, and Japan. Hence its name. It was composed of around 225 members, drawn about equally from each of these three economically advanced regions. In the mid-1970s, its United States membership consisted of about 65 persons, of whom nearly 30 were major business executives or corporate lawyers, 15 were important government officials (or former officials), 12 were prominent academicians (mostly foreign policy experts), and a few were civic and labor leaders. Perhaps the most striking thing about the United States representation on this body is the extent to which its members have been linked to such elite groups as the Business Council, CED, and the Council on Foreign Relations. This new organization's first research or staff director was Zbigniew Brzezinski, a Columbia University professor who was also a recently appointed director of the Council on Foreign Relations. And the North American secretary of the Trilateral Commission was George S. Franklin, a David Rockefeller kinsman who had served, up to the early 1970s, as the executive director of the CFR. Thus, like the Business Roundtable, this organization, though different in form, was clearly an Establishment-oriented body.

NIXON'S ELECTION AND INFORMAL INNER CIRCLE

Thus it is clear that while the economic and political power of the Southern Rim has grown substantially during the postwar period, its relative influence has been considerably overstated by such commentators as Kirkpatrick Sale, who apparently do not know which organizations are an integral part of America's economic establishment. Yet in some respects Sale is quite right in saying that the rise of Richard Nixon to the Presidency in 1969 represented a distinct challenge to the Eastern establishment because Nixon clearly had strong ties to the Southern Rim. But Nixon was not simply a Southern Rimster, for he also had a number of noteworthy links to major business interests around the country, particularly to entrepreneurs and executives who were strong conservatives. Still, for a Republican President, Nixon had a rather unusual relationship with the nation's true economic establishment (which, despite what many have claimed, is not strictly Eastern or Northeastern). While many of these big business leaders did support Nixon in 1968, at least after he won the Republican nomination, and especially in 1972 (when even many pro-Democratic business figures and major party fundraisers were badly frightened by the specter of George McGovern's "radicalism"), these corporate chieftains apparently felt some antipathy toward and distrust of Nixon, which he probably sensed and returned in kind.[7]

That this is true may be seen from an analysis of the chief financial backers of Nixon's sharpest critic and most formidable opponent within the Republican party, Nelson Rockefeller. The story began in April 1968, when Robert Kennedy posed a strong threat to capture the Democratic party nomination and perhaps even the Presidency. At that time Nelson Rockefeller's candidacy was, in effect, announced through the creation of a special committee designed to promote his cause. Roughly half of this group was composed of prominent political leaders and the rest of influential business executives. All of the latter were elite figures, as shown in the following summary analysis of its two top officials and other twelve economic members:[8]

Chairman	J. Irwin Miller, board chairman, Cummins Engine Co., Ind.	Director of AT&T, Chemical Bank New York Trust Co., and Equitable Life Assurance Society (of N.Y.C.); member of executive committee of the Business Council; trustee of the CED (up to 1966)
Treasurer	Eugene Black, board chairman, Brookings Institution (former longtime head of World Bank)	Director of the Chase Manhattan Bank, Equitable Life Assurance Society, ITT, and Cummins Engine Co.
Other economic members	W. Harold Brenton, board chairman, Brenton Banks, Inc., Iowa	Trustee of the CED
	C. Douglas Dillon, president, U.S. & Foreign Securities Corp. (former high federal official)	Vice-chairman of the CED; director of AT&T and the Chase Manhattan Bank; active member of the Business Council
	Thomas S. Gates, chairman of the exec. comm. of Morgan Guaranty Trust Co. (former high federal official)	Active member of the Business Council; director of the Cities Service Co., GE, Scott Paper Co., and various other concerns
	H. J. Heinz, II, board chairman, H. J. Heinz Co., Pittsburgh	Director of the Mellon National Bank & Trust Co.; trustee of the CED
	Robert S. Ingersoll, board chairman, Borg-Warner Corp., Chicago	Director of the First National Bank of Chicago; active member of the Business Council
	Ralph Lazarus, board chairman, Federated Department Stores, Ohio	Vice-chairman of the Business Council; director of the Chase Manhattan Bank, GE, and Scott Paper Co.; trustee of the CED
	Stanley Marcus, president, Neiman-Marcus Co., Dallas	Trustee of the New York Life Insurance Co.; trustee of the CED
	Joseph A. Martino, honorary board chairman (and longtime head), National Lead Co.	Director of the Chase Manhattan Bank and the Continental Insurance Co.

John A. McCone, board chairman, Joshua Hendy Corp., Cal.	Director of the Standard Oil Co. of Cal., Western Bancorp. and ITT; trustee of the CED
Robert S. Oelman, board chairman, National Cash Register Co., Ohio	Director of the Ohio Bell Telephone Co. (subsidiary of AT&T) and the First National City Bank of N.Y.C.; trustee of the CED; active member of the Business Council
Walter N. Thayer, president, Whitney Communications Corp., N.Y.C.	Director of the Bankers Trust Co.; trustee of the CED
John Hay Whitney, board chairman, Whitney Communications Corp.; senior partner in J. H. Whitney & Co.	Active member of the Business Council (up to late 1960s)

In other words, Nelson Rockefeller's bid for the Republican presidential nomination in 1968 was strongly supported at the outset by a sizable number of important figures in America's business establishment, who may have felt that Rockefeller, although too liberal for their taste, was the only person capable of beating Robert Kennedy.[9] However, shortly after Kennedy's assassination in June, an interesting development took place. A major bloc of corporate executives closely associated with the BC-CED complex—men such as Russell DeYoung, board chairman of the Goodyear Tire and Rubber Co., George S. Moore, board chairman of the First National City Bank of New York, and Gwilyn A. Price, board chairman of the Westinghouse Electric Corp.—came out firmly in favor of Richard Nixon's candidacy.[10] Although the timing of this event may have been fortuitous, one cannot help but think that it had much to do with the sudden removal of Robert Kennedy from the 1968 presidential race.

Another insight into Richard Nixon's relations with the business community can be gained from an examination of his role as a lawyer, particularly after he left California in 1963, following his ignominious defeat in the gubernatorial race, to take up a much more important and lucrative practice in New York City. The firm Nixon joined—Mudge, Stern, Baldwin & Todd—was certainly not one of the city's top-tier concerns; indeed, it has been described by one authority as at that time a "legal backwater," a "Wall Street wallflower."[11] Nixon was apparently brought in not so much to practice law as to shore up the sagging economic fortunes of this rather marginal firm by attracting new clients and cases. For this reason, the firm's name was promptly changed to Nixon, Mudge, Rose, Guthrie & Alexander.[12] In this endeavor Nixon was apparently only moderately successful, for although the firm grew in size from 22 to 32 partners by the late 1960s, his only really prime catch among American corporations was the Pepsi-Cola Co., which since 1963 had been headed by Nixon's close friend, Donald M. Kendall.[13] The firm actually experienced a greater increase in its volume of business after Nixon entered the White House, even though he (like Attorney General John Mitchell) had severed all formal ties with it, either because of its now added prestige or its politico-economic influence.[14]

That Nixon was not closely associated with the nation's true business establishment may also be seen from a look at the three corporate boards on which this transplanted Californian served shortly before he was elected President of the United States. One of these was a relatively unknown, though fairly sizable, manufacturing firm known as the Harsco Corp. of Harrisburg, Pennsylvania, which had no important ties to any major metropolitan interests. Another of Nixon's directorships was with a Minnesota-based mutual fund known as Investors Mutual, Inc., which was indirectly controlled by the Alleghany Corp., one of the chief stockholders (up to 1968) in the New York Central Railroad. Although this was the largest mutual fund complex in the country, one cannot infer from this link that Nixon was closely tied to America's top economic interests, for mutual funds have never ranked very high in the world of finance. Nixon's third board tie was with the Mutual Life Insurance Co. of New York, an over $3-billion enterprise which had once been one of the nation's five biggest insurance companies, but which had slipped badly over the years until, by the mid-1960s, it might even be considered a second-tier firm.[15] Moreover, this once Morgan-dominated concern had shown a marked tendency toward the selection of more conservative trustees than most major New York City institutions in the postwar period, another sign that Nixon did not really fit into the mainstream of American business. Also, it should be noted that none of the companies with which Nixon was affiliated as a director were Southern Rim enterprises.

Further evidence that Nixon was not closely linked to America's powerful business establishment may be found through an analysis of the economic affiliations of his close friends. One of Nixon's earliest and most influential backers was San Diego entrepreneur and financier C. Arnholt Smith, who had contributed much needed money to Nixon's first Congressional campaign in the late 1940s and had reportedly capped his efforts in Nixon's behalf by raising more than $1 million for his 1968 presidential race.[16] Smith could well afford to engage in such endeavors, for starting from a relatively modest investment in a local bank in the early 1930s he had built up a large business empire over the years. By the late 1960s it included the U.S. National Bank of San Diego (which had assets of about $500 million), various hotels and real estate interests in this metropolis, and a big conglomerate concern, the Westgate-California Corp., which controlled the nation's third largest tuna packer and the taxicabs in almost all of California's major cities.[17] Yet despite these large local holdings, Smith was never associated with any of the organizations or business enterprises which made up America's economic elite. Instead he was, up to his financial collapse in the mid-1970s, a wealthy "lone wolf" who gave substantial support to various conservative Republicans, such as Richard Nixon.[18]

Another very close friend of Richard Nixon was Northeastern industrialist Elmer Bobst, who was considerably older than Nixon and had taken an almost parental interest in his political career.[19] Like many of Nixon's inner circle of informal advisors and financial supporters, Bobst was a self-made man who, through a combination of managerial drive and astute mergers, had managed to transform a drug company known as Warner-Hudnut, Inc., from an, at best, medium-sized concern into the large (over $320 million) Warner-Lambert Pharmaceutical Co. by the time he retired in 1967. However, despite his obvious success as a business executive, the New Jersey-based Bobst had never been affiliated with any real Establishment group or served on any key corporate boards.

A third member of Nixon's inner circle was another Northeastern executive, Donald Kendall, who had climbed up the corporate ladder to become president of the Pepsi-Cola Co. in 1963 (known after 1965 as Pepsico, Inc.). Unlike most of Nixon's other close associates, Kendall did maintain some important ties to major business interests. For instance, he served on the board of the Sinclair Oil Corp. up to March 1969, when it was merged into the Atlantic Richfield Co., at which time he was made a director of the latter concern. But even more significantly, Kendall apparently took Nixon's place on the board of Investors Mutual, Inc. (which position he held through 1974), and in the early 1970s he was elected a director of Pan-American World Airways. Furthermore, about 1970 Kendall was made a member of the Business Council and a trustee of the CED in what seemed to be an effort on the part of the nation's top business leaders to establish better ties with the Nixon administration.[20] Kendall probably served as an intermediary between the Nixon entourage and the country's economic elite.

Another intimate of Nixon was a Yonkers, New York, industrialist named Robert Abplanalp, who had started out as a poor man and through hard work and inventiveness had built up a fairly substantial privately owned concern known as the Precision Valve Corp., which by the early 1970s made about half of the aerosol valves in the world. Though this was not a large company by contemporary standards, it was nonetheless a highly lucrative enterprise. From its receipts Abplanalp managed to accumulate a fortune of about $100 million, some of which he used to aid Richard Nixon, both personally and politically.[21] But, his great wealth notwithstanding, Abplanalp was no more closely linked to the nation's business establishment than was San Diego entrepreneur C. Arnholt Smith or most of Nixon's other nouveau riche friends. In fact, unlike most CED-Business Council leaders, Abplanalp was an arch-conservative and contributed considerable money to the campaigns of such rightist figures as former Senator James Buckley of New York.[22]

The last member of Nixon's inner circle was a small businessman from Florida, Charles G. (Bebe) Rebozo. This man also had very humble origins, but riding the crest of his state's enormous postwar growth, he had managed to assemble a set of minor holdings, the most notable of which was the Key Biscayne Bank (and Trust Co.), of which enterprise Robert Abplanalp served, after 1970, as a director. Rebozo also had a significant interest in local real estate, a title search company, and a chain of coin-operated laundries.[23] Although an entrepreneurial figure, Rebozo was the only member of Nixon's coterie who did not have vast wealth.[24] And perhaps even more important, of these five members of Nixon's inner circle, only two—Smith and Rebozo—were from the nation's Southern Rim.

NIXON'S MAJOR ADMINISTRATIVE AND DIPLOMATIC APPOINTMENTS

As President of the United States, Richard Nixon had a number of important positions to fill at the outset of his administration. These appointments reveal much about his relations with America's potent economic establishment, which had wielded great influence under Eisenhower.[25] For example, after considerable negotiation and maneuver, President Nixon chose a rather unusual figure, former New York lawyer and onetime high federal official William P. Rogers, to serve as his Secretary of State.[26] Rogers had acted as Deputy Attorney General during the first part of the Eisenhower administration, and then upon the resignation of Herbert Brownell in 1958 had taken over the top post in the Justice Department. However, he had relatively little experience in or knowledge of foreign affairs. Moreover, unlike Eisenhower's first Secretary of State, John Foster Dulles, Rogers did not come from one of New York's top law firms, but from a second-tier concern (Royall, Koegel and Rogers).[27] Also, unlike Dulles, Rogers did not serve on any key corporate or civic boards, but had been a director of such less important enterprises as the Dreyfus Fund (one of the nation's larger mutual funds), the Gannett Co. (a big newspaper chain), the Twentieth Century-Fox Film Corp., and, ironically in the wake of later events, the Washington Post Co.[28] Rogers, then, was not the kind of elite figure who had generally held this post in the postwar period.

Though one of America's least effective Secretaries of State, Rogers held office until a year after Nixon's reelection in 1972, when, shortly after the Watergate scandal began to unfold, he decided to return to the less demanding regimen of his Wall Street law practice. He was replaced by a much more able and ambitious man, Henry Kissinger, who had served since the outset of the Nixon administration as Special Assistant to the President for National Security Affairs. Kissinger had a very different background from that of Rogers. He was essentially an academic figure, who as a professor of government at Harvard University had written a number of books and articles on international relations that had received considerable acclaim.

Yet Henry Kissinger was hardly a detached, ivory-tower figure. Shortly after securing his Ph.D. from Harvard, he was appointed the study director of an important panel which had been assembled by the Council on Foreign Relations to explore ways, short of all-out war, of coping with the Soviet challenge in a nuclear age. Kissinger apparently did well in this capacity, and gained many influential friends and supporters.[29] Having established himself as a politically safe and sound scholar in the eyes of many of America's most powerful business and civic leaders, he was soon asked to act as the (part-time) director of the Rockefeller Brothers Fund's special studies project. Kissinger emerged from these endeavors as Nelson Rockefeller's chief foreign policy advisor, which role he played for more than a decade (while retaining his Harvard professorship). In fact, he spent a great deal of time in 1968 working as a key staff aide in support of Nelson Rockefeller's presidential candidacy, an effort that proved abortive.[30] Hence it came as a distinct surprise when Kissinger was asked, despite the bitter feeling which had long existed between Rockefeller and Nixon, to enter the latter's administration as Special Assistant to the President for National Security Affairs. Whatever the reasons for his selection (and these still remain unclear), Kissinger was, to the Nixon forces, a rank outsider when he assumed this important post in early 1969.[31] It was most likely only because of his extraordinary ability and subsequently demonstrated loyalty to Nixon that he was asked to take over as Secretary of State when William Rogers resigned in September of 1973.

Although it took the Establishment considerable time to secure the top slot in the State Department, it had much better luck with the second-ranking post in this important agency. Note, for example, the backgrounds of the four people who served as Under (after 1972, Deputy) Secretary of State in the Nixon administration:[32]

Elliot L. Richardson (1969–1970)	Attorney General, Mass. (1967–1969); Lieutenant-Governor, Mass. (1965–1967); U.S. attorney, Mass. (1959–1961); Assistant Secretary of HEW (1957–1959); partner or assoc., Boston law firm of Ropes, Gray, Best, Coolidge & Rugg (1949–1953, 1954–1956, and 1961–1964); director of New England Trust Co. (1953–1957); uncle, Henry L. Shattuck, was a director of the Mutual Life Insurance Co. of New York (1933–1968) and the New England Merchants National Bank and one of its predecessor concerns (1922–1968)
John N. Irwin II (1970–1973)	Assistant Secretary of State for International Security Affairs (1958–1961); partner, New York City law firm of Patterson, Belknap & Webb (1950–1957 and 1961–1970); director of IBM World Trade Corp. (1962–1970), U.S. Trust Co. of N.Y.C. (1962–1970), Dominick Fund

Irwin (cont.)	(1963–1970), and Seamen's Bank for Savings, New York (1952–1970); married member of the Watson family of IBM
Kenneth Rush (1973–1974)	Deputy Secretary of Defense (1972–1973); Ambassador to West Germany (1969–1972); president, Union Carbide Corp. (1966–1969); lesser company official (1937–1966) director of the Bankers Trust Co. of New York (1967–1969) and American Sugar Co. (1962–1969); trustee of the Foreign Policy Association (1963–1969)
Robert S. Ingersoll (late spring 1974 on)	Ambassador to Japan (1972–1974); president or board chairman, Borg-Warner Corp., Chicago (1956–1971); lesser company official (1939–1956); director of the First National Bank of Chicago (1958–1971), Marcor, Inc., and one of its major predecessor concerns (1958–1971), and Burlington Northern, Inc. (1970–1971); active member of the Business Council (1965–1971)

All four of these officials were clearly Establishment figures. For example, while Richardson had held a number of fairly important state and federal posts since the late 1950s, he had also been a partner in one of Boston's most prestigious corporate law firms, and his uncle had, up to 1968, been a member of the board of the Mutual Life Insurance Co. of New York (along with Richard Nixon) and of a major Boston bank. His successor as Under Secretary of State, John N. Irwin II, had been a partner in a well-connected New York law firm (which was closely associated with the Rockefeller interests), a director of several large business enterprises, and had married a member of one of America's most influential families. The third person to hold this post under the Nixon administration, Kenneth Rush, was the former chief executive officer of the nation's 25th largest non-financial firm, and had several other key corporate or civic ties. And the last man to serve in this second-echelon capacity, Robert Ingersoll, had been the longtime head of another big concern and a recent active member of the Establishment-dominated Business Council. These men's backgrounds are in marked contrast to William Rogers'; even Kissinger's ties were much less impressive.[33]

A somewhat more Establishment-oriented pattern of appointments prevailed in the Treasury Department, perhaps because it had long been considered one of the most crucial federal agencies by the nation's major business and financial interests. After much negotiation and maneuver (during which Nixon fundraiser Maurice Stans was, in effect, vetoed by powerful pro-Establishment forces), President Nixon chose, at the suggestion of Chase Manhattan Bank board chairman George Champion and New York financier Robert B. Anderson, a prominent Midwestern banker,

David M. Kennedy, who had virtually no governmental experience.[34] Kennedy was the head of the country's eighth largest commercial bank, the Continental Illinois National Bank and Trust Co. He had also served on the boards of such big, mostly Midwestern, concerns as the International Harvester Co., Swift and Co., Federal Reserve Bank of Chicago, and Communications Satellite Corp. In addition, he had been a trustee of the CED and the Brookings Institution since the early 1960s. Kennedy's selection was therefore warmly endorsed by the nation's top financial leaders.[35]

Kennedy did not turn out to be a very successful Secretary of the Treasury and, in an unusual political move, he was replaced in late 1970 by former Texas governor and conservative Democrat John B. Connally. The ambitious Connally had a mixed background. A longtime friend and political advisor of Lyndon Johnson, he had also become, in the early 1950s, the principal attorney for Texas oil magnate Sid Richardson, and in this capacity had served from 1959 to 1961 on the board of the (then Murchison-Richardson-Kirby-controlled) New York Central Railroad. At Lyndon Johnson's request, he had been appointed Secretary of the Navy at the outset of the Kennedy administration, but he resigned this post in December of 1961 to run for governor of Texas. He won this and two later races, and served a total of six years in office, all reportedly with the support of the state's wealthy power structure.[36] Upon stepping down as governor, Connally became a partner in one of Houston's largest corporate law firms, Vinson, Elkins, Searls & Connally (as it was now known), a concern with enormous politico-economic influence.[37] Connally was soon appointed to the boards of a number of major Texas business concerns, such as the Halliburton Co. (assets of over $600 million), Texas Instruments (assets of more than $500 million), and the First City National Bank of Houston (assets of about $1.8 billion). But his ties were not solely with Southern Rim concerns, for he was also made a trustee of the United States Trust Co. of New York (which, including its trust funds, then had assets of almost $9 billion).

In May 1972 Connally resigned as Secretary of the Treasury, ostensibly to return to private life, but actually to take command of the recently organized Democrats for Nixon reelection drive. He was replaced at Treasury by an able ex-academician, George P. Shultz, who had served briefly as Nixon's first Secretary of Labor before he was asked to take over as director of the Office of Management and Budget (the expanded organizational successor of the Bureau of the Budget). Shultz had a rather unusual background for a high federal official. He had served for a number of years as the dean of the Graduate School of Business at the University of Chicago. Yet he had also sat on the board of such big Midwestern concerns as the Borg-Warner Corp., J. I. Case Co., and General American Transportation Corp. Perhaps even more important, he had served from 1965 to 1968 as a member of the CED's research advisory board or as one of its special subcommittee advisors. Presumably, he was viewed in a favorable light by the nation's major economic leaders.

Shultz headed the Treasury Department until May 1974 when, most likely distressed by the increasingly odious Watergate scandal, he resigned to take a lucrative post in the business world. His position was quickly filled by William E. Simon, who had been brought into the federal government as Deputy Secretary of the Treasury in late 1972, reportedly at the suggestion of Nixon's 1972 presidential campaign manager, former Attorney General John Mitchell.[38] Like Mitchell, Simon was a New York figure—to be precise, a partner in the investment banking and securities firm of Salomon Brothers. But although Simon reputedly made between $2 million and $3 million a year as the head of his firm's lucrative bond department, he was not a member of the Establishment. Indeed, Salomon Brothers was a relative newcomer in the New York financial community, and not one of the accepted inner circle.[39] In this sense, Simon, whose loyalty to Nixon never wavered during the Watergate crisis, had something in common with many Southern Rim leaders.

The now mammoth Defense Department was headed during most of the Nixon administration by a former Wisconsin Congressman, Melvin R. Laird.[40] From an economic standpoint, his selection stood in marked contrast to most of his predecessors in the postwar period—James V. Forrestal (of Dillon Read), Louis A. Johnson (who had graced the board of a big defense contractor), retired General George C. Marshall (who had developed some elite links), Robert A. Lovett (of Brown Brothers Harriman), Charles E. Wilson (of General Motors), Neil McElroy (of Procter and Gamble), Robert McNamara (of the Ford Motor Co.), and Clark Clifford (a well-established Washington lawyer frequently retained by major corporate interests). Laird had no such connections. He was, however, a wealthy man, in part because of his wife's money.[41]

To speculate, Nixon may have picked Laird for two reasons: first, to deprive the Establishment of the top slot in this department, and second, to have someone in this position who shared his own highly conservative views. Laird's rightist stance can be seen not only in his voting record in Congress, but also in the choice of his chief staff aide, William J. Baroody, Jr., who had worked for Laird for eight years in the House of Representatives and then served in a similar capacity for four years in the Pentagon. Baroody had long been on friendly terms with conservative interests, and his father, who had been one of Barry Goldwater's key advisors in 1964, had served since 1954 as the head of the rightist American Enterprise Institute for Public Policy Research (known up to 1962 as the American Enterprise Association).[42] Laird was also a longtime close friend of the arch-conservative Southern magnate, Edward Ball, who headed the $1-billion Alfred I. du Pont estate in Florida, which included the big St. Joe Paper Co., Florida East Coast Railway, and a sizable string of banks in the northern part of the state.[43] In short, Laird was probably more conservative than Nixon himself.

Despite his lack of administrative experience, Laird served as Secretary of Defense until shortly after Nixon's reelection when he decided to leave the government to accept a well-paid position with the *Reader's Digest*. He was replaced by Under Secretary of State Elliot Richardson. This well-connected Brahmin served in this capacity for only a few months before he was asked to take over the post of Attorney General, filling the vacancy created by the resignation of the scandal-tainted Richard Kleindienst. At this juncture Nixon turned to another man who, like Melvin Laird, had no overt links with major corporate interests, former Rand Corp. analyst and onetime University of Virginia economics professor James R. Schlesinger. The highly intelligent and opinionated Schlesinger had come into the administration in a rather subordinate position, as an assistant director of the Bureau of the Budget, but had quickly demonstrated his abilities and was soon appointed Chairman of the Atomic Energy Commission, a post he held until early 1973 when he was asked to take over, briefly, as director of the CIA. There were probably a number of reasons why Schlesinger was appointed to so many important positions in such a short period of time, not the least of which was his conservative politico-economic outlook. He was, by his own admission, a "Taft Republican" and thus fit nicely into the ideological mold of the Nixon regime.

This primarily non-Establishment recruitment pattern, however, contrasted rather sharply with that which prevailed for the second-ranking post in the Pentagon.[44] The three men to serve as Deputy Secretary of Defense under the Nixon administration were as follows:

David Packard (1969–1972)	No prior governmental experience; president or board president or board chairman, Hewlett-Packard Co., Cal. (1947–1969); director of the United States Steel Corp. (1965–1969), General Dynamics Corp. (1965–1969), Pacific Gas & Electric Co. (1959–1969), and Crocker-Citizens National Bank of Cal. (1958–1969); active member of the Business Council (1963–1969); trustee of the CED (1964–1969); member, board of the Hoover Institution (1958–1969)
Kenneth Rush (1972–1973)	Ambassador to West Germany (1969–1972); president, Union Carbide Corp. (1966–1969); lesser company official (1937–1966); director of the Bankers Trust Co., N.Y.C. (1967–1969) and the American Sugar Co. (1962–1969)
William P. Clements, Jr. (1973–1974)	No prior governmental experience; president, Southeastern Drilling Co. (SEDCO, (1947–1973); director of the Keebler Co., an Illinois-based biscuit company (1969–1972), and the First National Bank of Dallas (1965–1972)

The first two officials to hold this important post were clearly influential Establishment figures, and the one who did not have such ties, Southern

Rimster William Clements, was appointed toward the end of the Nixon regime, apparently as a reward for his labors as chairman of Nixon's reelection campaign in Texas in 1972.[45]

As his Attorney General, President Nixon chose a man to whom he felt particularly close, his former New York law partner John N. Mitchell. The rather dour Mitchell had no governmental experience, not even in municipal office. He had spent his entire career working as a bond attorney, first with a very small and obscure firm known as Caldwell, Trimble & Mitchell, and then, following its merger with the Nixon (Mudge, Rose) law firm in 1966, as a name partner in this concern. But even this now much expanded firm did not rank in Wall Street's top tier, but rather was a concern on the rise. Thus while Mitchell had derived a substantial income from his legal bond practice, he was not on close terms with the nation's major corporate interests; most of his work was, on the contrary, with state and local governmental agencies. His selection as Attorney General stemmed largely from the fact that he had become a friend and law partner of Richard Nixon and had served as the latter's presidential campaign manager in 1968.

When Mitchell stepped down from office in 1972 to assume command of Nixon's reelection campaign, his place was taken by another non-Establishment figure, former Phoenix lawyer Richard Kleindienst, who, though rated only a class "B" attorney, had served for the last three years as Mitchell's top aide in the Justice Department.[46] Kleindienst was obviously a Southern Rimster. However, he apparently had no significant corporate links, not even in his economically thriving home state, although he had been associated with a fairly sizable firm, Shimmel, Hill, Kleindienst & Bishop.[47] Indeed, it would appear that he was appointed to these two important posts in the Nixon administration largely for political and ideological reasons, for Kleindienst was an ally of Arizona's Senator Barry Goldwater and had held one of the top positions in the latter's 1964 presidential campaign. He was, to use Clifton White's term, a member of Goldwater's "Arizona Mafia."[48]

Kleindienst served as Attorney General for only a little over a year when he was forced to resign because of his highly dubious, if not illicit, actions in the growing Watergate scandal and the controversial ITT antitrust proceeding.[49] He was quickly replaced by Elliot Richardson. With his poise and patrician background, Richardson appeared to be a man of great ability and integrity, two qualities which the Nixon administration desperately needed to convey to a doubting nation. As pointed out earlier, Richardson had held a series of (mostly state) governmental posts over the years, and had also been at times a member of one of Boston's largest corporate law firms, which was now known as Ropes & Gray. In addition, he had, in the past, various direct or indirect ties with such major business enterprises as the Allied Chemical Corp., New England Merchants National Bank, New England Telephone & Telegraph Co., and the Mutual Life Insurance Co. of New York.[50] In contrast to his predecessors, Richardson was, then, a thoroughly Establishment figure.

However, he held this post for only a very short time, for upon President Nixon's sudden dramatic dismissal of the Attorney General's recently appointed special Watergate prosecutor, Archibald Cox, in October 1973, both Richardson and his chief deputy, William Ruckelshaus, resigned in protest against the so-called Saturday night massacre. As Richardson's replacement, Nixon chose a much more plebeian (and probably more amenable) figure, Ohio's Senator William Saxbe. Saxbe had served as the attorney general of his home state from 1963 to 1969. But other than that, he had no special qualities to commend him; indeed, like Richard Kleindienst, he was a "B"-rated lawyer.[51] Also, like Mitchell and Kleindienst, he had no major socio-economic links. Prior to becoming Ohio's attorney general, he had been a partner in two Columbus law firms—Saxbe, Boyd & Prime (in the mid-1950s) and Dargusch, Saxbe & Dargusch (in the early 1960s), but neither of these was a prominent concern. In fact, the only board on which he served was a distinctly minor enterprise, the Columbus Savings & Loan Association.

For his Secretary of the Interior, President Nixon bowed somewhat reluctantly to purely sectional pressures and chose Alaska's Governor Walter Hickel. Hickel's selection initially raised a storm of protest from the increasingly vocal environmental groups in the country, which felt that because of his reputed pro-oil background, he would not give proper consideration to preserving the nation's vast natural resources. Before entering Alaskan state politics, Hickel had been the longtime head of the (probably small or medium-sized) Hickel Construction Co. and more recently had served as board chairman of the Anchorage Natural Gas Co., two lines of activity which might well have made him insensitive to major environmental concerns. As it turned out, Hickel proved to be a fairly steady supporter of the naturalist cause, perhaps because of the charges leveled against him at the outset.[52] But in late 1970 when he criticized the White House for its callous, if not hostile, attitude toward the nation's youth, Hickel so irritated President Nixon that he was summarily dismissed from office.

At this juncture Nixon made a rather unusual move; he selected the first Easterner to occupy the Interior post in well over a half a century. This was Maryland Congressman Rogers C. B. Morton, who had actually been Nixon's first choice for this position, but had not been put forward because of strong opposition in Western circles, which had long viewed the department as their preserve.[53] Morton was a prominent political figure, for he had served, at Nixon's request, as the chairman of the Republican National Committee, and in this capacity had presumably forged good working relations with party leaders throughout the country. However, Morton clearly did not represent Western interests. In fact, he had certain noteworthy links with major business enterprises, at least one of which was located in the East. He had served up to 1970 as a director of the big Delaware-based Atlas Chemical Industries (where he mixed with such influential executives as Thornton Bradshaw, the president of Atlantic Richfield), and as a board member of the Minnesota-based Pillsbury Co., which in 1952 had absorbed a milling concern controlled by the Morton family.[54] Not surprisingly, given this background, Morton had frequently taken pro-oil positions as a Congressman.[55] This outlook carried over into his decisions as Secretary of the Interior, for he reportedly showed a marked tendency, particularly during the latter part of his term of office, to favor corporate interests in his rulings on such vital matters as Alaskan lands and oil leasing along the Continental Shelf.[56]

As his Secretary of Agriculture, President Nixon chose a man who, like many of his predecessors, came from the Midwest, Nebraska's Clifford Hardin. This official, however, did not have a great deal of first-hand experience in agricultural affairs, for he had served for the preceding fifteen years as chancellor of the University of Nebraska, and before that had acted briefly (from 1949 to 1953) as director of the agricultural experiment station at Michigan State University. Perhaps more important, Hardin had certain prominent business and civic ties since he had recently served as chairman of the Omaha branch of the Federal Reserve Bank of Kansas City, and had for some time graced the board of the fairly sizable Bankers Life Insurance Co. of Nebraska and the much more prestigious Rockefeller Foundation.[57] Hence Hardin would certainly seem to have been an Establishment-oriented figure.

Hardin held office until the latter part of 1971 when, perhaps because of his firm opposition to a proposed partial dismemberment of his department, he was replaced by another Midwesterner, Earl Butz, who had served since the late 1950s as head of the Purdue Research Foundation and as dean of the university's school of agriculture. Unlike Hardin, Butz had previously held a high post in the Department of Agriculture (in the mid-1950s) and was thus very astute about bureaucratic matters. But even more significant, Butz clearly represented what by now was the most potent set of forces in American agriculture—agribusiness, the big, efficient farmers and the nation's major food processing concerns.[58] That Butz was closely allied with the latter interests in particular may be seen from the fact that he had recently served as a director of four large food processing or farm supply companies— the J.I. Case Co. (farm equipment), the International Minerals and Chemical Corp. (fertilizers), Ralston-Purina Co. (livestock feed, poultry and cereal products), and Stokely-Van Camp, Inc. (canned goods).[59] Butz had also sat on the board of both the Farm Foundation (as had Ezra Taft Benson twenty years before him) and the Foundation for American Agriculture, two organizations which were set up to help promote an alliance between the big food processing and farm supply companies and the nation's larger farmers.[60] As Secretary of Agriculture, Butz pursued policies designed primarily to benefit these interests. Indeed, rather than trying to help America's many hard-pressed small farmers, Butz reportedly acted more like "... their funeral director."[61]

To the position of Secretary of Commerce, President Nixon appointed a longtime friend and major political fundraiser, Maurice Stans. As previously noted, Stans had desperately wanted to be Secretary of the Treasury, but had been strongly opposed by the nation's top economic interests, who reportedly felt that he was, curiously, too conservative and lacked sufficient stature and knowledge for this key fiscal post.[62] Hence Stans was relegated to the Commerce position. This decision was pretty much in keeping with his second-echelon status in the financial community, for while he had recently been a high official of a New York investment securities firm known as Glore, Forgan, William R. Staats, Inc., this company was clearly not a top-tier concern.[63] Moreover, Stans had not served, since the early 1960s, on the board of any nationally prominent firms, but rather had been a director of such lesser enterprises as the Fluor Corp., Ltd. (of California), the Oglebay-Norton Co. (of Ohio), the Pike Corp. of America (another California company), and Wean Industries, Inc. (of Ohio)—all four of which were no more than medium-sized concerns.[64] Thus it is rather surprising that Stans was chosen to serve as Nixon's chief fundraiser both in 1968 and 1972, for his economic ties were not very impressive. In addition, Stans was clearly more conservative than most major corporate executives and was allied with the rightist forces in the business community, as may be seen by the fact that he had recently been appointed to the board of the still fairly extremist NAM, and had served for an even longer period of time as a trustee of the conservative Tax Foundation.[65] In short, though a New York-based financier since the mid-1960s, Maurice Stans was far from an Establishment figure.

Stans held office for approximately three years, then resigned to resume his role as Nixon's chief political fundraiser. His place was taken by a Chicago executive, Peter G. Peterson, who had served briefly (in 1971–1972) as Special Assistant to the President for International Economic Affairs. Up to the early 1970s Peterson had been an important businessman, who had served as a high official of the Bell and Howell Co., a big Chicago-based camera company. Moreover, he had served recently as a trustee of the CED and the Brookings Institution and as a director of such major concerns as the Illinois Bell Telephone Co. (an AT&T subsidiary) and the First National Bank of Chicago, a near "top 10" financial enterprise. In other words, he was a much better-connected figure than Maurice Stans.

Peterson held this Cabinet post for only a short period. After a sharp clash with some influential White House aides, he left the administration to take a key position with New York's investment banking house of Lehman Brothers. As his successor, President Nixon picked a man whom many observers would classify as a Southern Rimster, South Carolina textile executive Frederick B. Dent. The fairly wealthy Dent had served during most of the postwar period as a key officer of a rather small family-owned enterprise known as Mayfair Mills, and he was a close friend of South Carolina's arch-conservative Senator, J. Strom Thurmond.[66] However, Dent also had a number of noteworthy Northern or national economic ties. In recent years he had been a member of the Business Council (one of the few small businessmen to be so affiliated), a trustee of the CED, and a director of both GE and the Scott Paper Co.[67] Thus Dent could be described either as a Southern Rim leader with certain key "outside" links, or as one of the more conservative members of America's economic establishment.

President Nixon chose a rather unusual figure to be his first Secretary of Labor, the dean of the University of Chicago graduate school of business, George P. Shultz, a man of marked ability who was to play a major role in various other arms of the administration. However, it should not be inferred from Shultz's primarily academic background that he was a totally objective official with regard to labor-management relations. As pointed out earlier, he had served on the board of a number of large Midwestern corporations in the years immediately preceding his appointment to Cabinet office, the most important of which were Borg-Warner, J. I. Case, and General American Transportation. In addition, he had served from 1965 to 1968 as a member of the CED's research advisory board or as one of its special subcommittee advisors. Hence Shultz was probably inclined to take a pro-business position in most industrial relations disputes.

Shultz held this Cabinet post for about a year and a half when he was asked to take over the direction of another key agency, the former Bureau of the Budget, which under the Nixon administration had been overhauled and transformed into the Office of Management and Budget. Shultz was thereupon replaced as Secretary of Labor by his chief aide, James D. Hodgson. This person had a business background too, for he had served for many years as a high official of the California-based Lockheed Aircraft Corp., most recently as vice-president for industrial (or labor-management) relations. Thus, although Hodgson was reportedly well regarded by union leaders (at least for a corporate figure), he most likely had a pro-business outlook.[68] It should also be noted that Hodgson was only the second former corporate executive to be named Secretary of Labor since the start of the New Deal (the other was Eisenhower's James P. Mitchell).

Hodgson served in this capacity until early 1973 when, after Nixon's reelection, he left the administration. President Nixon made a somewhat unusual move for a rightist Republican in that he chose a Northeastern labor leader, Peter J. Brennan, as Hodgson's successor. Brennan was the longtime head of the New York City Building and Construction Trades Council, a group primarily interested in preserving its members' rather comfortable economic status. In short, for a high-ranking union official, Brennan was a fairly conservative figure. While this was probably the primary reason for his appointment, it is also true that by this time, as the Watergate scandal was beginning to unfold, the Nixon regime was searching for support in many quarters.

For the politically sensitive post of Secretary of Health, Education and Welfare, Nixon initially chose a man in whom he had great confidence, his longtime California confidant and able party lieutenant, Robert Finch. However, Finch, who was widely regarded as one of Nixon's more liberal advisors, had comparatively little formal experience in governmental office, having recently served briefly as lieutenant-governor of California. He had spent most of his time in the postwar period working as a member of a Los Angeles law firm which apparently did not have a very large practice. Finch reportedly had a net worth of only $200,000 (most of which was in his two homes, other real estate, and cash savings), a rather modest sum compared to the holdings of most of the other members of Nixon's Cabinet.[69] He had a very difficult time coping as Secretary of HEW, caught as he was between the conservative fiscal policies of the Nixon regime and his department's many needy clients and traditionally liberal supporters. After about a year and a half in office, Finch felt so torn by these conflicting pressures that he asked to be relieved of his duties, and was given, by way of a graceful exit, the much less demanding post of Counselor to the President.

He was replaced by Elliot Richardson, a Boston Brahmin who had become one of the President's most reliable troubleshooters. Richardson had held a number of governmental posts over the years, including a brief stint as Assistant Secretary of HEW in the latter part of the Eisenhower administration. Because of his ability and experience, Richardson managed to effectively oversee this now vast agency up to February of 1973, when he was asked to take over the reins of the Pentagon from the retiring Melvin Laird.

He was thereupon succeeded by another of Nixon's California supporters, Casper Weinberger, who, up to the late 1960s, had been a San Francisco lawyer. However, his firm had apparently not been closely linked to any major economic interests. Weinberger, like Richardson, was a much more experienced administrator than Robert Finch. He had held several state government posts in the 1960s. In addition, he had been appointed chairman of the Federal Trade Commission in 1970, and then, six months later, was made a high official in the revamped OMB. Hence Weinberger was better prepared to cope with the complex task of directing the sprawling HEW department.

For the comparatively new post of Secretary of Housing and Urban Development (HUD), President Nixon initially selected a well-known Northerner, former Michigan Governor George Romney, who had established a fairly liberal political record as chief executive of his state, and thus appeared to be a good choice for this important office. Before he entered politics in the early 1960s, Romney had been head of the American Motors Co., where he had received considerable acclaim for lifting this company out of a precarious position and transforming it into a rather prosperous concern. Yet despite his success in this endeavor, Romney was not a part of the Eastern establishment.[70] He had never been associated with either the BAC or CED, and had served briefly on only one major corporate board, that of the California-based Douglas Aircraft Co. However, the often idealistic Romney did not get along well with the Nixon administration, in part because he strongly favored additional federal aid for the hard-pressed cities, more moderate- and low-cost housing, and the racial integration of the nation's predominantly white suburbs. But, having already sacked Secretary of the Interior Walter Hickel, Nixon felt he could not act against Romney until after the 1972 presidential election.

Almost immediately after that important race had been won, Romney was replaced by someone more acceptable, Cleveland lawyer James T. Lynn, whose only governmental experience had been gained through his recent (1969–1972) work as a high-level official in the business-oriented Department of Commerce. Unlike most high HEW officials, Lynn's background was that of a corporate lawyer. He had been associated since the early 1950s with one of Cleveland's largest law firms, Jones, Day, Cockley & Reavis, which included such potent interests as the Hanna Mining Co. among its many clients. Lynn himself apparently had not served on any major business boards, most likely because he was not yet one of the very top partners in the firm. But its most influential partner, John W. Reavis, had been a longtime director of such nationally prominent concerns as the Westinghouse Electric Corp. and Anchor Hocking Glass Corp. Lynn himself was much more conservative than Romney.

For his last Cabinet post—that of Secretary of Transportation—President Nixon picked, largely for geopolitical reasons, a well-known New Englander, John A. Volpe, who had been elected governor of Massachusetts three times in the 1960s. Volpe had also served briefly in the mid-1950s as President Eisenhower's Federal Highway Administrator, a special position created to oversee the construction of the massive Interstate Highway program. In private life Volpe had been a wealthy contractor and therefore knew a great deal about building matters. But his extensive involvement in this type of activity probably also caused him to favor governmental aid for highway construction over that for badly needed mass transit. When Volpe decided to step down from office shortly after Nixon's reelection, he was replaced by another strongly pro-highway figure, Claude S. Brinegar, who was a longtime high official of the big Union Oil Co. of California, which clearly had a major stake in the promotion of highway travel. So far as the highway lobby was concerned, the Department of Transportation was in safe hands under the Nixon administration.

In his major ambassadorial selections, President Nixon made one move which contrasted sharply with the practice of the Eisenhower administration and most other modern presidential regimes, and which cast some interesting light on his links with various segments of the business world. For the traditionally premier post of Ambassador to Great Britain, Nixon picked the first Philadelphian to occupy this office since the early post-Civil War years. This man was Walter Annenberg, the wealthy president of a large privately-owned concern known as Triangle Publications, Inc., which put out the *Philadelphia Inquirer*, *TV Guide*, and *Seventeen* magazine.[71] Annenberg, it should be emphasized, was not a member of America's powerful economic establishment. Indeed, until recently, he apparently had not even been accepted by his predominantly WASP peers in Philadelphia. Although his company had been operating in the city since the early 1940s, it was not until 1964 that he was appointed to the board of a major local enterprise, the Girard Trust (Corn Exchange) Bank. And although he was later made a director of the Campbell Soup Co. and the financially troubled Pennsylvania Railroad and its successor Penn-Central Co., he served on these boards for such brief periods that he may not have been able to shed his "outsider" status.[72] That Annenberg represented a marked deviation from the postwar Republican norm can also be seen from a comparison of his background with that of Eisenhower's two Ambassadors to Great Britain, Winthrop W. Aldrich and John Hay Whitney. Both of these men were well-connected patricians, closely tied to influential New York financial and industrial interests.

In contrast, President Nixon chose, after considerable delay (during which Democratic incumbent R. Sargent Shriver continued to hold office), a much more typical figure, IBM executive Arthur K. Watson, to serve in the somewhat less prestigious capacity of American Ambassador to France.[73] This wealthy executive had a number of other important economic links, for he had served in recent years as a director of the Continental Insurance Co. (of New York), Pan-American World Airways, and the Federal Reserve Bank of New York.[74] In addition, his brother, Thomas J. Watson, Jr., who was the board chairman of IBM, sat on the board of both the Bankers Trust Co. and (up to 1971) the Rockefeller Foundation, and was also a member of the Business Council from the mid-1960s to the early 1970s. Thus the Watson family was obviously an integral part of the nation's economic establishment. When Watson stepped down from office in the latter part of 1972, he was succeeded by John N. Irwin II, who had served as a high State Department official for the last few years, but was primarily a wealthy Wall Street lawyer (with the firm of Patterson, Belknap & Webb).[75] Actually, this diplomatic shift could be described as "all in the family," for Irwin was a brother-in-law of the Watson brothers, and probably for this reason served (up to 1970) on the board of the IBM World Trade Corp.[76]

Another key diplomatic post during the Nixon administration was, of course, that of Ambassador to South Vietnam. Ellsworth Bunker had been appointed by Lyndon Johnson, but he so impressed President Nixon that he was retained in this capacity until after the end of the Vietnamese war. Although Bunker had, by the late 1960s, severed all ties with the National Sugar Refining Co., with which he was once affiliated as a top official, he nonetheless continued to sit on the board of New York's fairly small but prestigious Atlantic Mutual Insurance Co. and the Lambert International Corp. (a New York-based investment company controlled by wealthy Belgian interests).[77] Moreover, his son, John Bunker, served through the early 1970s as the president of the Colorado-based Holly Sugar Corp.— apparently as the managerial agent of the economically dominant Loeb,

Rhoades interests of New York. Hence it would certainly seem that Ellsworth Bunker remained on good terms with various influential economic forces throughout his years of diplomatic service in Vietnam.

A major diplomatic post was also created shortly before President Nixon was compelled to resign from office. Following extensive high-level negotiations undertaken with the active backing of major American business interests, formal governmental relations were established between the United States and Communist China.[78] As our first representative (originally liaison officer) to the People's Republic of China, Nixon chose the seasoned diplomat David K. E. Bruce, who served in this capacity from 1972 to 1974, when he was appointed Ambassador to NATO. He was replaced by a former Texas business and political figure, George H. W. Bush, who had relatively little pertinent experience, having served only briefly as our chief emissary to the United Nations in the early 1970s. Prior to his entry into politics in 1966, Bush had been the head of a medium-sized domestic oil company known as the Zapata Off-Shore Co. But Bush was something more than the ordinary Texas oilman, for he had been born into a wealthy Northeastern family. His father, Prescott Bush, had been a New York financier (Brown Brothers Harriman) and onetime United States Senator. Thus the well-connected Bush was probably favorably disposed to the creation of good economic relations with Communist China, a potential supplier of valuable oil and a likely buyer of American goods.[79]

A number of important, primarily domestic, posts also had to be filled by the Nixon administration. Many of these were key White House staff positions, such as the one held for several years by Henry Kissinger. Initially, the most influential of these was the newly created office of Counselor to the President. The man whom Nixon tapped to serve in this capacity was a well-known Columbia University economist named Arthur F. Burns, who had acted as Eisenhower's first chairman of the Council of Economic Advisers, and who also had a longtime close association with the prestigious National Bureau of Economic Research.[80] Burns had first met Nixon through his work with the CEA, and they apparently established friendly relations. Subsequently, Burns had served for over a decade on the board of two major financial concerns, Dividend Shares, Inc., and the Mutual Life Insurance Co. (along, in the late 1960s, with Richard Nixon). That Burns was a dedicated conservative may be deduced from the fact that he served throughout much of the 1960s as a trustee of the rightist Tax Foundation, which organization counted among its board members such anti-public spending figures as nationally syndicated columnist Raymond Moley, Virginia Senator Harry F. Byrd, Jr., and Nixon Cabinet officer-elect Maurice Stans. In brief, Burns, who served as White House Counselor until early 1970 (at which time he took over the chairmanship of the Federal Reserve System), blended in well with the anti-welfare-state outlook of the Nixon administration.

An ultimately much more important figure in the new Republican regime was H. R. (Bob) Haldeman, who was appointed an Assistant to the President, charged with the responsibility of running the Oval Office and acting, in effect, as Nixon's "gate-keeper." Haldeman had served as Nixon's political chief-of-staff in a number of campaigns over the years, which efforts were finally capped by the presidential victory of 1968. In private life he had been a longtime second-tier official in one of the nation's largest advertising agencies, the New York-based J. Walter Thompson Co. However, Haldeman, who had been born and raised in Southern California, had worked for the last eight years in its Los Angeles office. In short, Haldeman was a Southern Rimster who, like many of Nixon's "inner core," had no major corporate or elite links. Furthermore, he was reportedly an extremely conservative figure, which may have been one reason why Nixon placed a great deal of trust in him.[81]

Another key member of Nixon's White House staff was Haldeman's longtime close friend and former UCLA classmate John Ehrlichman, who was brought into the administration because of his ties to Haldeman, but who soon emerged as a major force in his own right. By late 1969 he had virtually taken over Daniel Patrick Moynihan's role as, it was now entitled, Assistant to the President for Domestic Affairs.[82] Up to 1969 Ehrlichman had been a member of a Seattle law firm known most recently as Hullin, Ehrlichman, Carroll & Roberts, a medium-sized concern not linked to any large economic interests. Yet Ehrlichman came from a family which had some wealth and noteworthy business connections. For instance, his uncle, Ben B. Ehrlichman, was, up to his retirement in 1967, the head of a comparatively small financial firm known as the Equity Fund, Inc., and served, until the mid-1960s, on the board of a number of fairly prominent business enterprises, the most important of which was the Pacific Northwest Bell Telephone Co., an AT&T subsidiary. However, judging from all accounts, these links had little to do with Ehrlichman's appointment to a key White House post; that was primarily the product of his close tie with Haldeman.

Another important person on Nixon's White House staff was New York financier Peter Flanigan. At first glance, his appointment would appear to have been a rather unusual move, for while Flanigan had long worked for one of Wall Street's most influential investment banking firms, Dillon, Read & Co., he was merely a vice-president, not one of its very top officials.[83] But Flanigan had other, more crucial connections. His father, Horace C. Flanigan, who had been a Nixon fundraiser in 1960, was the head of the Manufacturers Trust Co. of New York up to the time of its merger (1961) with the Hanover Bank, and continued to serve as a director of this giant enterprise up to 1969; he was also a longtime board member of such sizable corporations as Anchor Hocking Glass and Hilton Hotels. Flanigan's mother was a member of the Busch family of Anheuser-Busch, Inc., the big St. Louis-based beer company.[84] And Peter Flanigan had himself served as a director of the large (Louisiana-based) United Gas Corp. up to 1965, when there was a marked shift in its locus of control. Hence it is not surprising that as an Assistant to the President, Peter Flanigan quickly became the principal intermediary between the business world and the White House. Indeed, Flanigan is reported to have recruited more than three hundred high officials for the administration in its first few years of operation, a sign that he wielded immense influence.[85]

A key agency in the Nixon administration was the Bureau of the Budget, or as it was known after a major reorganization implemented in 1970, the Office of Management and Budget.[86] In sharp contrast to the Kennedy-Johnson years when this important unit was directed largely by federal careerists and academics, the OMB was dominated in the Nixon regime by business-oriented officials, as may be seen in the following brief biographical descriptions of the men who served as its top officials:

Robert Mayo (1969–1970)	Vice-president, Continental Illinois National Bank & Trust Co. (1960–1969); various second- and third-tier Treasury Department posts (1941–1960)
George P. Shultz (1970–1972)	Secretary of Labor (1969–1970); dean, University of Chicago Graduate School of Business (1962–1968); recent director of the Borg-Warner Corp., J. I. Case Co., General American Transportation Corp., and Stein, Roe & Farnham Balanced Fund; member of the research advisory board of the CED (1965–1967)
Casper Weinberger (1972–1973)	Deputy director, OMB (1970–1972); chairman, Federal Trade Commission (Jan.–June 1970); director of finance, California state government (1968–1969); partner, San Francisco law firm of Heller, Ehrman, White & McAuliffe (1959–1968)
Roy L. Ash (1973–1974)	President, California's Litton Industries (1961–1972, lesser company official 1953–1961); director or trustee of the Bank of America (1968–1972), Pacific Mutual Life Insurance Co. (1965–1973), and the California-based Global Marine, Inc., a medium-sized offshore oil-drilling concern (1965–1973); trustee of the CED (1970–1973)

In sum, all but one of the directors of the Bureau of the Budget and its successor organization, the OMB, had either long-term ties or important recent links with big business interests, and that man, California's Casper Weinberger, served for less than a year. For instance, although Robert Mayo had held a variety of second- and third-tier posts in the federal government over a nineteen-year span (during which period he undoubtedly gained much valuable experience), he also spent the last nine years working as a vice-president of the Continental Illinois National Bank and Trust Co., and was brought into the administration by his former boss, Treasury Secretary-elect

David M. Kennedy, who had been a trustee of both the CED and the Brookings Institution, to mention just two of his major links. When Mayo resigned in 1970, his place was taken by the able former Secretary of Labor and dean of the University of Chicago Graduate School of Business, George P. Shultz, who had served on the board of several big Midwestern companies in the mid and late 1960s and had been a recent member of the CED's research advisory board. The last head of OMB under Nixon was a California executive, Roy Ash, who had been the president of Litton Industries, a large defense-oriented conglomerate. He had also directed a major organizational study of the federal government during the first part of the Nixon administration, and hence had considerable expertise in this area.[87] Though a Southern Rimster, Ash had become closely linked with the nation's powerful economic establishment, particularly through his affiliation with the CED.

Yet another important governmental unit which was run by an elite figure during most of the Nixon years was the CIA. The top post in this agency was held for several years by a highly regarded holdover from the Johnson administration, Richard Helms. The urbane Helms had been with the CIA since its inception and was generally viewed as a dedicated career official with no noteworthy socio-economic ties. However, Helms's grandfather had been a wealthy New York banker and had served, up to his death in 1940, on the boards of various large corporate enterprises, the most prominent of which was probably Bankers Trust. Hence Helms may have had a pro-business outlook on many politico-economic matters. He later became ensnared in a serious political conflict when he gave grossly misleading testimony to a Senate committee investigating the attempts of ITT and the CIA to overthrow the leftist Allende government in Chile, and in early 1973 he was given an easy exit by being appointed Ambassador to Iran.

His replacement was a rather unusual choice, James R. Schlesinger, who had no experience in governmental intelligence or any related area. Schlesinger was a former University of Virginia economics professor turned Rand analyst, who had entered the Nixon administration as a second-tier official in the Bureau of the Budget and was soon appointed, because of his quickly demonstrated ability, chairman of the Atomic Energy Commission. For a variety of reasons (some of which may have stemmed from his, at times, abrasive personality), Schlesinger proved to be an unfortunate selection and was replaced within a matter of months by a more seasoned and restrained figure, William E. Colby, who had spent the last eleven years working as a CIA official (before that he was a State Department executive). In Colby the CIA had a director who had basically a bureaucratic background.

Another set of appointments which revealed much about the Nixon administration were those made to the President's Council of Economic Advisers. The first person whom Nixon chose to head this body was a well-known professor of business administration at the University of Michigan,

Paul W. McCracken, who had served as a member of the Council back in the late 1950s. Since then McCracken had devoted himself mainly to academic affairs. But, it should be noted, he had found time to serve, from 1960 to 1968, as a director of the fairly large Group Securities, Inc., and shortly before his appointment to the CEA he had been elected to the board of the Hoover Ball and Bearing Co. of Michigan and the Lincoln National Corp. (a holding company which controlled the $2 billion-plus Lincoln National Life Insurance Co.). Thus McCracken clearly had a strong pro-business orientation. He was, in fact, widely regarded as an academic disciple of the arch-conservative economist Milton Friedman.[88] Also, because of his rightist outlook, he served in the mid and late 1960s as a trustee of the Tax Foundation, along with Maurice Stans and Arthur Burns, and as chairman of the advisory board of the American Enterprise Institute for Public Policy Research.

McCracken acted as Nixon's chief economic advisor until the early 1970s when he was replaced by one of his colleagues on the Council, Herbert Stein.[89] This rather pragmatic individual had a very different background from that of McCracken. Stein had served for 22 years (1945 to 1967) as an economist for the generally moderate CED, and then in the late 1960s had taken a position as a research fellow at the fairly liberal Brookings Institution. Thus it would appear that during Stein's tenure as chairman of the Council of Economic Advisers, the President was exposed to some less doctrinaire thinking.

Just before the end of the Nixon administration, Herbert Stein resigned as head of the CEA. The President made an unusual move in selecting his successor, for he chose a man, Alan Greenspan, who, unlike any of his predecessors, did not have a Ph.D. in economics and, furthermore, had not been a member of the academic profession. Instead, he had been the longtime chief executive of a New York-based business consulting firm known as Townsend-Greenspan & Co.[90] Not unexpectedly, given this background, Greenspan had served on the boards of a number of sizable business concerns, the most important of which were the Trans-World Financial Corp. (a California savings and loan holding company with assets of over $600 million) and the Dreyfus Fund (which had assets of more than $1.25 billion). But neither of these enterprises was an Establishment firm.[91] Moreover, Greenspan was an arch-conservative in his economic thinking. In fact, he was an avowed disciple of Ayn Rand, a once popular writer and founder of a rightist cult called Objectivism.[92] Greenspan's appointment was thus in line with the general social and economic orientation of the Nixon administration.

IMPORTANT POLICY ACTIONS OF THE NIXON ADMINISTRATION

Many of the Nixon administration's actions were of tremendous significance and will undoubtedly be the subject of much heated debate and searching analysis for years to come. None was more important than Nixon's startling decision in May 1970 to, contrary to President Johnson's "post-Tet" curtailment policy, reescalate the war in Southeast Asia by suddenly invading Cambodia in an attempt to destroy Communist sanctuaries and supply lines in that hitherto neutral and largely defenseless country. Up to recently, little was known about the origins of this ultimately disastrous action. But according to a new lengthy study, this step, which stunned the nation, was taken, following much secrecy and duplicity, largely at the initiative of a militarily-minded President Nixon and his politically ambitious special assistant, Henry Kissinger.[93] This extraordinary decision once again demonstrated that Nixon was not closely allied with the nation's economic establishment, for these interests were reportedly outraged by his wanton action and not only spoke out against it, but also sent a group of trusted academics to Washington to register a bitter protest, all apparently to no avail.[94]

The Nixon administration was extremely conservative on domestic economic matters too. This was readily demonstrated in the way in which the President continued to push defense spending to ever-higher levels, the badly skewed federal farm price support program, which mainly benefited the big farmers, and Nixon's reaction to various social welfare measures. For instance, he frequently raised the specter of inflation when he was presented with Congressional bills which called for the expenditure of more money for the nation's needy citizens.[95] Indeed, three times in his first four years in office, Nixon vetoed appropriation bills for the Department of Health, Education and Welfare on the grounds that the funds provided were excessive and would add to the inflationary spiral.[96] In fact, President Nixon's economic values and cynical political tactics were clearly revealed during the great controversy about hunger in America when, after telling Secretary of Agriculture Clifford Hardin that he could publicly proclaim that this administration would mount "...the first complete, far-reaching attack on the problem of hunger in history," he turned to this official and said, "Use all the rhetoric you want, so long as it doesn't cost any money."[97]

Nixon's strong pro-business bias was one of the major reasons why, to the surprise of many, he chose to employ the authority granted him under the Economic Stabilization Act of 1970 and imposed wage and price controls on the nation in late 1971. According to one economic journal, Nixon took this extraordinary step primarily at the urging of the influential Business Council in an effort to blunt or curb the wage demands of organized labor.[98] To achieve this objective, Nixon first established a Cost of Living Council, which was headed by Secretary of the Treasury George P. Shultz and was composed of other key Cabinet officers (most of whom had pro-business backgrounds) and certain lesser federal officials, such as Special Assistant to the President for Consumer Affairs Virginia Knauer.[99] This body was charged with the responsibility of formulating the nation's basic economic stabilization goals, coordinating this complex operation, and recommending any policies it deemed necessary or desirable to the President. To implement one part of this important program, a special seven-person Price Commission was established to set specific price standards and criteria. Its makeup was as follows:[100]

Chairman	C. Jackson Grayson, Jr.	Dean, School of Business Administration, Southern Methodist University since 1968 (before that dean and professor of business administration, Tulane University)
Other members	William T. Coleman, Jr.	Black Philadelphia corporate lawyer; trustee of the Penn Mutual Life Insurance Co. and Western Savings Fund Society; director of Pan-American World Airways
	Robert F. Lanzillotti	Dean, College of Business Administration, University of Florida
	J. Wilson Newman	Former chief executive, Dun & Bradstreet, Inc.; director of the Atlantic Mutual Insurance Co., Chemical Bank, Consolidated Edison Co., General Foods Corp., and Mutual Life Insurance Co.; trustee of the CED
	John W. Queenan	Former partner, Haskins & Sells, a large international accounting firm
	William W. Scranton	Former governor of Pennsylvania; director of the IBM World Trade Corp., Pan American World Airways, and Scott Paper Co.; recent trustee of the CED
	Marina vonN. Whitman	Professor of economics, University of Pittsburgh

As this list reveals, labor and consumer interests had little, even indirect representation on this commission.

At the same time Nixon created a fifteen-man Pay Board to perform much the same regulatory role with regard to wages. It was composed of five business executives, five labor representatives (by far the most important of whom was George Meany), and five public figures, one of whom, former federal judge George Boldt, served as chairman.[101] The background of the five business members and the other four public representatives was as follows:

Business members	Robert C. Bassett	President, Vertical Marketing, Inc., a small Chicago publishing company
	Benjamin F. Biaggini	President, Southern Pacific (Railroad) Co.; an active member of the Business Council; trustee of the Conference Board
	Virgil B. Day	Vice-president for industrial relations, GE; a prime mover in the Labor Law Study Committee, one of the groups that was shortly merged into the Business Roundtable
	Leonard F. McCollum	Board chairman, Continental Oil Co.; director of the Morgan Guaranty Trust Co.; graduate member of the Business Council
	Rocco C. Siciliano	Recently appointed president of TI Corp., a big California title insurance company; a former (1969–1971) Under Secretary of Commerce and onetime (1953–1957) Assistant Secretary of Labor; made a trustee of the CED some time in 1972
Public members	William G. Caples	President, Kenyon College; a former (1953–68) vice-president for industrial relations, Inland Steel Co.; director of Buckeye International, Inc., a medium-sized Ohio manufacturing firm
	Kermit Gordon	President, Brookings Institution; former director of Bureau of the Budget; former member of CEA; trustee of CED
	Neil H. Jacoby	Professor of business economics, Graduate School of Management of UCLA; longtime director of the Occidental Petroleum Corp.

Public members *(cont.)*	Arnold R. Weber	Former deputy director of OMB; Assistant Secretary of Labor (earlier in Nixon administration); before that a University of Chicago professor who was a close friend and colleague of George Shultz

Probably because of this marked skew in its membership and a general sense of frustration with the operation of the board, George Meany and three of the other labor representatives resigned from this body in March 1972, just five months after it was created.[102] Perhaps as a result, shortly after the 1972 election President Nixon abolished both the (now pared-down) Pay Board and the Price Commission and directed that their functions be taken over by the Cabinet-dominated Cost of Living Council. In mid-1974 this antiinflation agency was eliminated too.

The pro-business orientation of the Nixon administration was also pointed up by the way it manipulated the federal milk price support program in 1971. In early March of that year Secretary of Agriculture Clifford Hardin announced, after a careful review of the law and related economic conditions, that the federal subsidy for milk for the coming marketing year would be pegged at $4.66 a hundred pounds, the same amount set for the preceding year. However, the nation's big dairy farmers, who had begun to contribute handsomely to the Nixon cause, complained bitterly about this decision. Within two weeks' time the leaders of the dairy industry were able to secure a meeting with the President and some of his chief advisors, including Secretary of the Treasury John Connally. At this session the representatives of the big dairy groups agreed, speaking for the industry as a whole, to raise a total of $2 million for Nixon's upcoming presidential campaign in exchange for a more favorable ruling on milk price supports.[103] Two days later the Secretary of Agriculture dutifully announced that the federal government's milk subsidy was going to be raised by 27 cents (to $4.93 per hundred pounds). This action reportedly cost the American consumer at least $500 million a year in higher milk prices.[104]

Another area which received considerable attention during the early years of the Nixon administration was that of health and safety conditions in the nation's mines. These hazardous workplaces had long been ignored by the federal government, despite the fact that various mine disasters had claimed the lives of over 100,000 men since the turn of the century. In 1969, however, after an unusually severe explosion had taken the lives of 78 miners in a shaft in West Virginia, a wave of outrage surged through the Congress and resulted in the passage of one of the most comprehensive safety measures ever enacted. For the first time the Department of the Interior was given sufficient power to cope with this problem. In signing the bill, President Nixon acclaimed it an historic achievement. Furthermore, he appointed a longtime federal official who was widely regarded as a vigorous advocate of mine safety, John O'Leary, to serve as the director of the rejuvenated Bureau of Mines.

When O'Leary demonstrated that he meant to vigorously enforce the provisions of the act, the coal industry quickly launched an aggressive campaign to get him out of office. And, given the highly conservative and political nature of the Nixon regime, it did not take long—indeed only a matter of months—before the President decided to sack this intrepid official and replace him with a more amenable figure.[105]

A controversial issue which came up periodically during the Nixon administration was the oil import system. This rather arbitrary scheme had been adopted by presidential decree during the last years of the Eisenhower regime, largely because of heavy pressure from two major segments of the oil industry. By the end of the first decade of its operation, this system, which limited the import of the much cheaper foreign crude oil to 21 percent of the country's domestic production, was estimated to have cost the American consumer between $4 billion and $5 billion a year in higher oil and gas prices.[106] There was, consequently, considerable demand for change in America's oil quota system.[107]

Shortly after he took office, President Nixon, acting reportedly on the advice of certain prominent oil and business leaders, appointed a special seven-man Cabinet task force, headed by Secretary of Labor George Shultz, a professional economist, to look into the problem. With this action the White House hoped to defuse the issue.[108] But much to the President's surprise, about a year later the group submitted a report in which a majority of its members called for the gradual phase-out of the existing program and the establishment of a preferential tariff policy which would lower the price of foreign oil by 30 cents a barrel and eliminate many of the other deficiencies of the oil import quota system.[109] At the urging of various key oil executives such as Michael Haider, the recently retired board chairman of the Standard Oil Co. of New Jersey, President Nixon simply chose to ignore this document. He instead created another committee, which was composed of the same set of Cabinet members, except that the "overly academic" George Shultz was replaced by Nixon's more politically reliable Attorney General and former law partner John N. Mitchell (although he did not serve as chairman of this body). This group met briefly, with White House aide (and former natural gas company director) Peter Flanigan always present to keep it "on course."[110] As Robert Engler observed, it "...wasted little time on scholarly analysis."[111] Instead it quickly concluded that the costly oil import system should be retained, much to the delight of the President and most of the leaders of America's oil industry. And so this scheme remained in effect until early 1973, when a growing (pre-OPEC) oil shortage became a matter of considerable concern to many leaders in the petroleum industry and finally induced the President to abolish it.

A closely related issue which confronted the Nixon administration was how to handle the trans-Alaskan oil pipeline controversy. This dispute grew out of the discovery in 1968 of huge oil reserves at Prudhoe Bay along the northern slope of Alaska. These oil (and natural gas) resources were estimated to be worth at least $64 billion.[112] Three companies—Atlantic Richfield, British Petroleum, and the big Humble subsidiary of Standard Oil of New Jersey—controlled about 95 percent of the leased land in the Prudhoe Bay oilfield.[113] They needed some means of getting the valuable fuel out of this remote region down to the more populous parts of the United States. To accomplish this objective, the three concerns banded together to form a joint venture (later officially known as the Alyeska Pipeline Service Co.) which proposed to build an 800-mile pipeline across this vast pristine territory to a port at the southern end of Alaska, from whence the oil would be transported by ship to its ultimate destination in various parts of the United States.

However, considerable opposition soon arose to the proposed construction of the pipeline. Much of this was led by environmental groups, which claimed that the plans prepared by the tripartite company and their formal assessment by the Department of the Interior were inadequate. They also asserted that the proposal violated two federal statutes, the Mineral Leasing Act of 1920 and the more recently enacted National Environmental Policy Act. The latter law required that all such projects be approved only after the preparation of a soundly conceived environmental impact statement which appraised the ecological damage that would be inflicted by such construction and weighed all other alternatives. Three groups—the Wilderness Society, Environmental Defense Fund, and Friends of the Earth—filed suit in federal court under both statutes in an effort to block the pipeline. When Judge George L. Hart, Jr., ruled in favor of the environmentalists on grounds provided by the (perhaps outmoded) Mineral Leasing Act of 1920, the Alaskan oil interests became extremely concerned, not about this particular judgment, which they felt could be overturned, but about the prospect of even more adverse rulings.[114]

With the strong support of the Nixon administration and its chief energy-environmental spokesman, Secretary of the Interior Rogers C. B. Morton, a staunch ally of the oil industry, a major lobbying drive was mounted in the Congress to secure an exemption from the National Environmental Policy Act for the proposed Alaskan pipeline.[115] In this endeavor the oil industry was, after much travail, successful. In July 1973 the United States Senate narrowly passed a measure which provided for just such an exemption, with the Lower House soon following suit. Thus, with the aid of the pro-oil Nixon forces, the Alaskan pipeline issue was taken out of the courts and placed well on the road to construction.[116]

Antitrust matters were also of considerable concern to the Nixon administration. Although the number of big mergers began to taper off during this period, an increasing proportion of the corporate acquisitions were being made by giant conglomerates, many of which were headed by highly aggressive executives or free-wheeling entrepreneurs. Perhaps the most famous example of such activity in the late 1960s was that provided by the International Telephone and Telegraph Corp. Under the leadership of Harold S. Geneen, ITT had been transformed from a public utility built around big operations abroad into a huge, widely diversified firm involved in all sorts of unrelated enterprises, such as Avis (rent-a-car), Levitt and Sons (a major home builder), and the Sheraton (hotel) Corp. of America.[117] In May 1970, after a series of extensive negotiations and maneuvers, Geneen consummated his greatest corporate coup when he acquired the Hartford Fire Insurance Co., a concern with assets of over $1.9 billion. Overall, ITT's assets grew from about $2 billion in 1965 to $5.2 billion in 1969, and by 1974 it had reached a total of over $10 billion, most of which increase came from Geneen's many corporate acquisitions.

Given the magnitude of this merger activity, it is not surprising that when the Nixon administration's newly appointed head of the Antitrust Division of the Justice Department, Richard McLaren, assumed office, he devoted much of his time to contesting some of the conglomerate acquisitions made in recent years.[118] In fact, three of the four cases which McLaren instituted in 1969 were directed against ITT—the first against its acquisition of the Canteen Corp. (a big food-vending company), the second against its absorption of the Grinnell Corp. (which made 87 percent of the nation's fire alarm systems), and the third against its proposed purchase of the Hartford Fire Insurance Co. ITT responded by taking the position that it would be prepared to divest itself of the Canteen Corp., most of the Grinnell Corp., and, as a further lure, the apparently unprofitable Levitt and Sons, provided it could keep the extremely valuable Hartford Fire Insurance Co. At first McLaren stood firm. He would agree to an out-of-court settlement of these cases only if the Hartford Fire Insurance Co. were relinquished too.

McLaren's stand created a great deal of concern in the top ranks of ITT. For one thing, there was a judicial appeal pending in the Grinnell case, which ITT felt it would probably lose in the Supreme Court, much to the detriment of the company's overall position in the divestiture proceedings. However, if the appeal could be delayed or prevented, ITT believed it had a good chance to work out an economically favorable settlement with the administration. Hence on April 16, 1971, New York attorney Lawrence Walsh, who was a close friend of Richard Nixon and whose firm was "outside" counsel for ITT, and Felix Rohatyn, who was a partner in the investment banking firm of Lazard Frères, which served as the chief financial advisor of ITT, telephoned Richard Kleindienst, the Deputy Attorney General, urging him to delay any appeal of the Grinnell case. On the same day ITT president Harold Geneen and one of his vice-presidents, William R. Merriam, called on Treasury Secretary John Connally and White House aide Peter Peterson to ask them to throw their weight behind ITT's cause. As a result, President Nixon expressly directed Kleindienst (who initially denied this charge under oath), not to appeal the Grinnell decision and, in effect, to work out a "satisfactory" settlement of the matter.[119]

In fact, there were many meetings, both before and after this date, between high-ranking ITT officials and important administration figures in an attempt to resolve this issue on terms acceptable to the company. For example, Harold Geneen himself talked to John Ehrlichman, Charles Colson (H. R. Haldeman's special counsel), White House aide Peter Flanigan, Attorney General John Mitchell, and Secretary of Commerce Maurice Stans.[120] In addition, Geneen's influential financial advisor, Felix Rohatyn, met frequently with Nixon's chief business intermediary, Peter Flanigan, and Deputy Attorney General Richard Kleindienst (six times with the latter).[121] In the end, McLaren was persuaded, allegedly on the basis of the so-called Ramsden report, which had been prepared at the request of Peter Flanigan and stressed the grave impact which the divestiture of the Hartford Fire Insurance Co. would have on ITT's stockholders, to reverse himself and withdraw his opposition to a negotiated settlement of this dispute.[122] Interestingly, nine days after ITT reportedly pledged to contribute $400,000 to the 1972 Republican national convention, which was then scheduled to be held in San Diego, an out-of-court agreement was reached which permitted ITT to retain the coveted Hartford Fire Insurance Co. in exchange for its sale of the Canteen Corp., Avis, Levitt and Sons, a major arm of the Grinnell Corp., and two small insurance companies—almost exactly the offer which ITT had proposed in the first place.[123]

Another matter that tied ITT to the Nixon administration was the American government's abortive attempt to block the installation of Chile's recently elected Socialist President, Salvador Allende, in 1970, and its later successful effort to help bring down this left-wing regime. Despite many official denials in the early 1970s, it has since been revealed that powerful American political and economic interests had long played a prominent, though generally clandestine, role in Chilean affairs, largely because certain United States concerns had a huge stake (about $1.1 billion) in mining and other business enterprises in that country.[124] These activities intensified when the avowed Marxist, Salvador Allende, was elected, by a plurality vote, president of Chile.[125] Confronted with this deeply disturbing development, which certainly boded ill for business in that country, the Nixon administration decided that it would try to prevent Allende from assuming office. After meeting with certain key advisors, the President ordered CIA director Richard Helms, who came from a wealthy pro-business background, to try to promote a military coup in Chile to block Allende's imminent accession to power. As a result, the CIA did make some (probably ill-conceived) efforts to carry out this directive.[126] These proved to be abortive, and Allende was duly sworn into office as the first democratically elected socialist president of any state in the Western hemisphere.

President Allende proceeded to nationalize many major business enterprises in Chile, particularly those owned by large foreign interests. This sweeping action led to the loss of the vast mining properties of the Anaconda Co. and Kennecott Copper, and the Chile Telephone Co. subsidiary of

ITT, which utility had a market value of more than $150 million. Some of these concerns reacted sharply to this turn of events. Indeed, just two days after the Allende government had taken over the operation of its Chilean telephone subsidiary, ITT officials submitted an elaborate eighteen-point plan to bring down this leftist regime to White House aide (and former Bell and Howell executive) Peter Peterson.[127] Although this particular proposal was not officially accepted, ITT remained in close touch with influential figures in the Nixon administration. This was especially true with regard to the CIA, in part because ITT had some years earlier elected former CIA head John A. McCone to its board of directors, and he proved to be extremely useful to the company in its contacts with the agency.[128]

Provoked by the Chilean government's expropriation of American property, and extremely concerned about Allende's socialism, the Nixon administration, acting on the advice of Henry Kissinger and the high-level special 40 Committee, decided to intensify its efforts to topple this ideologically dangerous regime. Public and private financial aid to Chile were drastically reduced as part of a carefully contrived program of economic strangulation.[129] Moreover, between 1970 and 1973 about $8 million was covertly pumped into Chile, primarily through the CIA, to support influential anti-Allende newspapers, hostile right-wing paramilitary organizations, various private opposition groups, and perhaps most important, to back widespread strikes in Chile.[130] In addition, close contact was maintained during this crucial period, both through the CIA and the American military attachés in Chile, with high-ranking anti-Allende army officers.[131] Having done so much to promote such an act, the Nixon administration was hardly surprised when in September 1973 the rightist military leaders in Chile staged a bloody armed coup in which President Allende was killed and his government destroyed.[132] In this brutal manner, Chile was transformed, as Peter Winn has put it, into "...the Spain of the 1970s—a socialist dream transformed into a fascist nightmare...."[133]

The most famous—or infamous—event of the Nixon administration was, of course, the Watergate scandal. This affair started innocently enough with the creation in the early 1970s of a group known as the Committee for the Re-Election of the President (or as it is generally abbreviated, CREEP).[134] In early 1972 President Nixon's chief political advisor and former law partner, John N. Mitchell, resigned as Attorney General to become campaign director of CREEP. At about the same time Secretary of Commerce Maurice Stans also resigned from the Cabinet to become chairman of the closely affiliated Finance Committee for the Re-Election of the President, a key fundraising post similar to the one he held in 1968.[135] Despite the fact that he was not an Establishment figure and did not have very important corporate ties, Stans was extraordinarily sucessful in this endeavor, in considerable part because wealthy interests were afraid of the alleged radicalism of Nixon's Democratic opponent, South Dakota's Senator George McGovern, particularly in the areas of public welfare and tax reform. In all, Stans' forces were able to raise at least $75 million for Nixon's reelection campaign, more than twice the sum collected by his heavily underdog Democratic rival. However, a significant amount of this money was generated by illegal means, as was later revealed in the exhaustive Watergate investigation.[136]

As presidential campaign director, Mitchell selected for his top aides a set of highly conservative men from the nation's Southern Rim who had become part of the Nixon and Mitchell political team in the late 1960s. One of these was Mississippi oil heir Fred LaRue, who had been an ardent backer of Barry Goldwater in 1964, but later became a close friend and political lieutenant of John Mitchell.[137] Another was Jeb Stuart Magruder, an ambitious, opportunistic Californian, who had caught the eye of Nixon's chief aide, H. R. Haldeman. Mitchell's third assistant was a wealthy Arizona businessman named Robert Mardian, who had been a longtime Goldwater supporter and was reportedly the closest friend of the newly appointed Attorney General, Richard Kleindienst.[138] Mitchell also hired a tough undercover operator, former Poughkeepsie (New York) Assistant District Attorney and onetime FBI agent G. Gordon Liddy, ostensibly to act as CREEP's general counsel. But because of certain personality conflicts, he was soon given another formal position, that of counsel to Maurice Stans' finance committee, although he continued to report to Jeb Magruder as CREEP's de facto intelligence chief.

In the spring of 1972 CREEP decided to try to obtain some inside information about Democratic National Chairman Lawrence O'Brien's reputed political and financial relations with industrialist Howard Hughes. It also wanted to find out if the Democrats had any damaging data about Nixon's own dealings with Hughes or other influential figures.[139] To achieve this objective, Liddy brazenly proposed to break into the Watergate-based headquarters of the Democratic National Committee. His illicit plan was approved, with some modifications, by John Mitchell and other high officials of CREEP, with the full knowledge of such key White House aides as John Ehrlichman and H. R. Haldeman. This attempt at political espionage and burglary failed dismally because Liddy's small crew of specially employed thieves was accidentally discovered and apprehended by the Washington police. This, of course, created great consternation among both the top officials of CREEP and important White House leaders. It was now feared that although these men were sworn to secrecy and had been promised that they would be "taken care of" if they were caught, the police and FBI would be able to trace the break-in through various records or "laundered" funds to Liddy, then to CREEP, and ultimately to the White House.[140] This, it was felt, could be politically disastrous in a presidential election year. Hence tremendous efforts were made to cover up this nefarious affair by certain high (or former high) officials of the Nixon administration.

The cover-up, which included the payment of substantial hush money, succeeded through all of 1972, during which period the Watergate burglars were found guilty and Nixon was elected to his second term of office by a record margin of votes, carrying every state in the Union but one. However, in early 1973 there was a major break in the case, for as the time for sentencing drew near, one of the Watergate burglars, James McCord, grew increasingly rebellious at the thought of enduring a long jail term to protect some influential higher-ups, who apparently were going to get off scot-free. In an effort to secure a reduced sentence, he sent a letter to Judge John J. Sirica stating that political pressure had been applied to the burglars to keep silent, that perjury had been committed at their trial, and that other, as yet unidentified, figures had been involved in the Watergate plot.

The letter touched off a series of important events and disclosures. A number of men who had been associated with the distribution of the hush money and various other aspects of the scandal now felt threatened, and feared they were about to be made scapegoats by such high and equally culpable officials as John Ehrlichman, H. R. Haldeman, and President Nixon himself. At this point, White House counsel John W. Dean, an ambitious non-elite figure, decided to cooperate with the federal investigators and tell everything he knew about the scandal.[141]

As the cover-up unraveled, President Nixon felt compelled to get rid of his now tainted top aides, Ehrlichman and Haldeman.[142] Attorney General Richard Kleindienst, who had long played a dubious role in these proceedings because of his close ties to Mardian and Mitchell, finally came to realize that he too should resign. Now, with the Watergate scandal apparently linked to the White House, the President needed to demonstrate to the public that he was determined to bring all wrongdoers to justice. Hence Nixon appointed as Attorney General Elliot Richardson, his able Secretary of Defense, who projected an image of unquestioned integrity.

If by this maneuver Nixon hoped to head off the appointment of an independent investigator outside the range of White House control, however, he was badly mistaken, for by this time the Justice Department's efforts in the case had come under considerable criticism and suspicion.[143] In fact, both houses of Congress quickly passed bipartisan resolutions calling for the appointment of just such a person. As a result, Richardson had virtually no choice, if he wanted to secure Senate confirmation, but to pick a completely independent Watergate prosecutor. After several unsuccessful recruitment efforts, he selected his old Harvard constitutional law professor, Archibald Cox, a man who had spent 23 years in the academic ranks. He had also served as Solicitor General, a purely legal post, in the Kennedy and early Johnson years, but had few significant outside ties.[144]

During his first few months on the job, Cox proceeded with his investigation, but was often thwarted by an uncooperative White House. However, in July 1973 there was an unexpected break in the case when in the course of some routine questioning about White House procedures, Cox's staff learned that since 1971 the President had been taping all of his office conversations. This disclosure led both the Special Prosecutor's Office and the recently created Senate Select Committee on Presidential Campaign Activities (the so-called Ervin Committee), to issue subpoenas for a number of important tapes. In the latter part of July the President, fearful about what the tapes would reveal, rejected the subpoenas, thereby forcing both the Ervin Committee and the Special Prosecutor's Office to take this issue to the courts. After the presentation of arguments by both sides, Judge Sirica ruled that the President could not, under the cloak of executive privilege, withhold crucial evidence from a grand jury, but that he must turn this material over to him for examination. This decision was promptly taken by the administration to the U.S. Court of Appeals, which ruled about a month later that the President must deliver the tapes to Judge Sirica in a week's time, thus setting the stage for one of the most surprising political events in the nation's history.

For President Nixon decided not to appeal the tapes decision to the Supreme Court; this, he felt, would probably be futile and would risk a confrontation with the most prestigious tribunal in the country. Instead, after a series of last-minute maneuvers aimed at working out a compromise between Cox and the White House had failed, the President decided that he would fire the Special Prosecutor and thus render the case moot (since there would be nobody occupying that particular office who could subpoena the tapes). Nixon therefore ordered Attorney General Elliot Richardson, who was one of the last real Establishment figures to hold a high post in his administration, to dismiss the doughty Special Prosecutor. Richardson, however, true to his pledge to Cox and to Congress, refused to do so, and forthwith resigned from office. Nixon turned next to Richardson's top aide, Deputy Attorney General William D. Ruckelshaus, but he too refused to remove Cox and was, as a consequence, summarily dismissed from office. Finally, Nixon found a more pliable figure in the highly conservative Solicitor General (and former Yale University law professor), Robert Bork, who, having indicated his willingness to carry out the President's order, was quickly designated acting Attorney General so that he could fire Cox.[145] And this he did, thereby completing what came to be called the "Saturday night massacre."

The reaction to this sequence of events was both swift and stunning. The American people were plainly outraged by Nixon's action, and a giant wave of protest descended on the nation's capital. Within a matter of days, over 400,000 telegrams poured into Washington. Calls for President Nixon's impeachment were raised in many quarters. The administration had clearly made a monumental mistake. A new special prosecutor simply had to be appointed.

The man chosen to fill Cox's shoes was a very different sort of person from his predecessor. Leon Jaworski was a highly successful Texas corporate lawyer.[146] In sharp contrast to Cox, the relatively insulated Ivy League professor, Jaworski had worked for almost forty years as a partner in one of Houston's largest law firms, Fulbright, Crooker & Jaworski, a concern closely linked with major banking and business interests in the Lone Star

State.¹⁴⁷ Jaworski had served for over a decade as a director of the nation's largest cotton wholesaler, Anderson, Clayton & Co. (which had 1973 assets of about $380 million) and the Houston-based Bank of the Southwest (which had assets of $1 billion), and in the early 1970s he was appointed to the board of the Coastal States Gas Corp. (a new economic giant with assets of about $1.25 billion). All these were essentially Southern-tier concerns. Yet it should be noted that Jaworski had also served in 1971–1972 as president of the influential American Bar Association, which had long been dominated by pro-business interests, and he thus might well be regarded as an Establishment figure.

Shortly after assuming office, Jaworski was stunned, along with the rest of the nation, when he was informed by White House counsel Fred Buzhardt that two of the nine subpoenaed tapes were missing, and that there was an important eighteen-minute gap in one other. Jaworski nevertheless plunged into his work with a determination which no doubt distressed the Nixon administration and came as a surprise to many of Cox's initially skeptical staff members. By the middle of December Jaworski had requested some 25 additional tapes of presidential conversations, and in the early spring of 1974 he asked for an even larger number, as did the House Judiciary Committee, which had now embarked on its own investigation of the matter.¹⁴⁸ Not surprisingly, given its untenable position (that the President was above the law), the administration rebelled at Jaworski's first fairly modest request and merely sent over typewritten transcripts of the "edited" tapes, which upon inspection were found to contain numerous gaps and discrepancies, but which were still sufficiently incriminating to cast much doubt on Nixon's famous claim that he was "not a crook." Moreover, the President had still not complied with Jaworski's most recent subpoena for a total of 64 tapes, and he was not about to do so.

Instead, Nixon went to court to try to block Jaworski's subpoena.¹⁴⁹ He met with no success, for after a series of judicial moves, the U.S. Supreme Court ruled unanimously in Jaworski's favor.¹⁵⁰ This was a tremendous blow to the President's position. Then just a few days later, before the controversial tapes were turned over to Judge Sirica, the House Judiciary Committee's impeachment proceedings were brought to a close with a formal, highly dramatic vote accusing the President of (1) obstruction of justice in the Watergate case, (2) grave abuse of executive power, and (3) unconstitutionally defying the Committee's subpoena of pertinent evidence. Shortly thereafter, the White House complied with the Court ruling and released the disputed tapes, the net effect of which was devastating for the administration. One tape, for instance, revealed that six days after the Watergate burglary the President, contrary to all previous claims, knew a great deal about the major phases of the Watergate cover-up. Even Nixon's staunchest defenders now shifted over to the other side. In short, the President had no choice but to resign or be formally removed from power by a thoroughly aroused Congress.

And so on August 8, 1974, Richard Nixon resigned from office in total disgrace, thus ending what must be ranked as the greatest political scandal in American history.[151]

Leon Jaworski received considerable acclaim at this time for his work as Special Prosecutor, and a good deal of it was surely merited. On short notice, he had plunged into a tumultuous situation and led the Watergate investigation to an expeditious and seemingly satisfactory conclusion, bringing most of the major culprits to justice.

But there are certain disturbing questions that can be raised about Jaworski's performance in this important proceeding. First, although no fewer than eight separate kinds of crimes were described in a report prepared by his staff outlining Nixon's complicity in the Watergate cover-up, Jaworski did not seek an indictment of Nixon either while he was President or after he had resigned from office, even though he was strongly urged to do so by his own legal staff.[152] And there is good reason to think that the grand jury would have done so had it received any encouragement from the Special Prosecutor, who simply never presented this as one of its alternatives.[153] Jaworski later claimed that he did not do so because of the possibility that such an indictment would be struck down by the Supreme Court, that Nixon might not have been able to get a fair trial (a concern he didn't feel for the other major indicted parties), and that it would have produced months of delay in disposing of this case, during which, he claimed, "...the country would be suffering from the trauma of an indicted President" (a consideration which apparently loomed larger in Jaworski's mind than the concept of justice). He also chose not to appeal or protest President Ford's quickly dispensed unconditional pardon of Nixon, although as New York Law School dean Anthony Davis has pointed out, this presidential act was "...no more sacrosanct [or less subject to challenge] than any other executive action."[154]

Kirkpatrick Sale claims that Jaworski acted in this compliant fashion because he was "...a man who had a rough identity with Richard Nixon and a lifelong attachment to exactly the same interests (particularly Texas oil, banking, real estate, and agribusiness) and who could be expected to be as minimal a prosecutor as possible."[155] The author, however, is not convinced that this is the right or sole explanation, for, it must be remembered, Jaworski did pursue the most glaring criminal aspects of this case with considerable vigor, and this action ultimately resulted in the imprisonment of some of Nixon's most trusted Southern Rim aides. Rather it would seem that although Jaworski was from the nation's conservative sunbelt, he was in this instance most likely acting as a representative of the country's powerful politico-economic establishment, which, while it was in no way involved in this sordid scandal, was nevertheless appalled at the awful impression which the affair was making both at home and abroad. Thus in much the same manner that Owen J. Roberts managed to wrap up the Teapot Dome scandal in the 1920s without delving into the possible involvement of influential business interests in other aspects of this case, so Leon Jaworski was probably intent on bringing the infamous Watergate affair to an expeditious close, without further damaging, by the indictment of Richard Nixon, the nation's already badly tarnished public image.[156]

TOP OFFICIALS OF THE FORD ADMINISTRATION

With the resignation of Richard Nixon, America was presented with its first appointed President, Gerald R. Ford. This amiable but not especially able man had been made Vice-President by his predecessor about ten months earlier to fill the vacancy created by the enforced departure of Spiro Agnew. Like Nixon, Ford was primarily a politician. He had been a Michigan Congressman for 24 years, during the last one-third of which he had served as the Republican minority leader in the House. As one might expect, given Nixon's own orientation, Ford was a highly conservative figure. In 1973, for instance, he was given a zero rating on 25 key issues by the liberal Americans for Democratic Action. But unlike Nixon, who up to the late 1960s had three noteworthy directorship ties, Ford had no major formal socio-economic links.[157] He had been essentially a small-time lawyer who had practiced for many years in his hometown of Grand Rapids, first as a member of a firm known at the time of its dissolution in 1961 as Amberg, Law & Buchen, and thereafter as an independent attorney. Thus, contrary to what some writers have claimed, Ford was not an integral part of the American Establishment, but a man who had generally been associated with second-tier business figures or the political agents of key interests.[158]

However, over the years Ford, as a Republican leader, had developed a number of close informal ties with the Washington legislative representatives of various major American business concerns. When he took over the reins of executive leadership, Gerald Ford counted among his intimate friends such important lobbyists as William G. Whyte, the Washington vice-president of the United States Steel Corp., Rodney W. Markley, Jr., the chief national lobbyist for the Ford Motor Co., and Bryce Harlow, the longtime political agent of the Procter and Gamble Co. (who was a board member of the arch-conservative Hoover Institution).[159] Also, while in the House of Representatives, Ford frequently played golf in Washington and other places around the country with the legislative representatives or lesser officials of these and other corporate enterprises, usually at the latter's expense, which practice certainly provided these businesses with easy access to a key federal official, who, even as President, probably could not dissociate himself from these interests and their general economic views.[160]

Upon taking over as the nation's chief executive in August 1974, President Ford chose, quite understandably under the circumstances, to retain a number of Nixon's Cabinet officials. For example, he kept on Henry Kissinger as Secretary of State, perhaps because, despite his breach with Establishment interests over the Cambodian incursion, Kissinger had managed to maintain close ties with the Rockefeller forces.[161] Similarly, Ford continued to rely on the services of William E. Simon as head of the Treasury, in part because this former New York (non-Establishment) financier was a staunch conservative.[162] Ford also retained Secretary of Agriculture Earl Butz, who clearly had the backing of agribusiness, a strong force in American politics.[162]

There were other Nixon carryovers in Ford's Cabinet. The able, conservative technocrat James R. Schlesinger, who had held several important posts in the Nixon administration, continued to act as Secretary of Defense until the fall of 1975, when he was dismissed from office because President Ford reportedly could no longer abide his supercilious manner. His successor, Donald Rumsfeld, was basically a political figure who had served in various prominent administrative and diplomatic capacities during the six preceding Republican years. Like Schlesinger, he had no elitist links.[164]

Similarly, when Frederick B. Dent stepped down as Secretary of Commerce in March 1975 to become the President's Special Representative for Trade Negotiations, he was replaced by Rogers C. B. Morton, a former Maryland Congressman and Kentucky businessman (with two recent major corporate ties), who had been serving since 1970 as Secretary of the Interior. But Morton held office for only a short period (until December 1975), when, apparently because of ill health, he was replaced by Elliot Richardson, who had emerged as one of the few "heroes" of the Watergate scandal and, after a brief stint as American Ambassador to Great Britain, now assumed his third Cabinet post in less than six years—a modern record.[165]

Ford's other Cabinet appointments involved the recruitment of new people. Three, curiously, considering Ford's non-intellectual image, were academics. After the diplomatic dispatch of the rather mediocre Attorney General, William Saxbe, in early 1975, President Ford selected the more able president of the University of Chicago (and onetime dean of its prestigious law school), Edward H. Levi, to serve as his replacement. Levi had also been one of the eight public members of the National Commission on Productivity and Work Quality, a special advisory body created in the early 1970s as part of Nixon's economic stabilization program. This board included such figures as Arch Moore, governor of West Virginia; William Kuhfuss, president of the American Farm Bureau Federation; Arjay Miller, dean of the Stanford Graduate School of Business (and a director of the Ford Motor Co., Wells Fargo Bank of California, and Levi Strauss and Co.); and W. Allen Wallis, chancellor of the University of Rochester (who was a director or trustee of the Eastman Kodak Co., Esmark, Inc., Metropolitan Life Insurance Co., and the Hoover Institution, and was chairman of the rightist Tax Foundation). Levi had also served recently as a trustee of the Urban Institute and the (Colorado-based) Aspen Institute for Humanistic Studies, two research groups whose boards were heavily weighted with elite figures. Thus, while Levi apparently had no formal corporate ties, he had some other important links which did much to promote his prospects for high federal office.

Shortly thereafter, with the resignation of Nixon's last Secretary of Labor, Peter Brennan, President Ford picked Harvard University dean (and long-time economics professor) John T. Dunlop to serve as his successor. Dunlop had also acted, in its later stages, as director of the now defunct Cost of Living Council (an ad hoc agency created by the Nixon administration to deal with the problem of inflation), and had been a public member of various other governmental bodies over the years. However, unlike most persons with this background, Dunlop had managed to forge fairly close ties with some of the top labor leaders in the country and was, in fact, financially involved, along with AFL-CIO president George Meany and various other figures, in an 11,000-acre resort development in the Dominican Republic.[166] But Dunlop served as Secretary of Labor only until the first part of 1976, when he resigned in protest over President Ford's failure to fulfill a major pledge he had made to support organized labor's Congressionally approved bill on common-site picketing (Ford vetoed the measure apparently because of a late corporate drive, capped by a White House meeting with various key leaders of the Business Roundtable). Most likely in an effort to mollify labor, President Ford chose as Dunlop's successor a former AFL-CIO official, Willie J. Usery, Jr., who had served under the Nixon administration as director of the Federal Mediation and Conciliation Service and later as Assistant Secretary of Labor.[167]

The last academic to be appointed to Ford's Cabinet was drawn, probably for geo-political reasons, from the deep South, a region which would otherwise have been without any high-level representation in the administration. F. David Mathews, the youthful president of the University of Alabama, was selected in mid-1975 to take over as Secretary of Health, Education and Welfare for California's recently resigned Casper Weinberger. However, unlike the other two academic officials chosen by Ford (who were economic moderates), Mathews was a distinctly conservative figure and was apparently on good terms with business interests in his home state. As evidence of this orientation, he served on the board of the Birmingham branch of the Federal Reserve Bank of Atlanta in the early 1970s. Also, in line with the thinking of the Ford regime, Mathews reportedly felt that the federal government was doing too much to cure the nation's social ills, and directed his department accordingly.[168]

As for the Department of the Interior, President Ford made two rather conventional moves when Rogers C. B. Morton stepped down in the spring of 1975 to become Secretary of Commerce. Ford's first selection for the vacated post was Wyoming Governor Stanley K. Hathaway, a man who, as a former (Torrington) lawyer, had been closely linked up to the late 1960s with various oil interests in the West.[169] But because of unusual personal and political pressures, Hathaway held office for only about six weeks—one of the shortest Cabinet careers on record.[170] He was replaced by another Westerner, North Dakota's Thomas Kleppe, who had recently served as the head of the U.S. Small Business Administration, a post awarded him as a reward for his futile sacrificial effort to win a U.S. Senate seat in 1970. Kleppe had served until the mid-1960s as president of the Gold Seal Co., a little-known household products company, and as a high official of a medium-sized Minneapolis investment banking firm known as J. M. Dain & Co. In addition, up to the early 1970s he had sat on the board of the Dakota National Bank of Bismarck, which was an affiliate of the big Northwest Bancorporation, and the small Montana-based Cardinal Petroleum Co. (this second link raised considerable protest about his nomination from various environmental groups). Kleppe was also a wealthy man, with a net worth of about $3.5 million.[171] Thus, by North Dakota (but not national) standards, Kleppe was an elite figure, and one probably disposed to favor private oil interests.

Another new face in President Ford's Cabinet was that of California's Carla Hills who, upon her appointment in 1975 as Secretary of Housing and Urban Development, became the third woman in American history to hold such a high-level post, and the first to do so since Eisenhower's selection of Oveta Culp Hobby to be the original head of HEW. Mrs. Hills had served briefly (in 1974–1975) as an Assistant Attorney General, her only other federal office. However, there is some question as to how dedicated Mrs. Hills was to the cause of the urban poor, for she had been a longtime member of a fairly prominent Los Angeles corporate law firm (Munger, Tolles, Hills & Rickershauer). Her husband was a senior partner in this firm too, and in 1972 he also became board chairman of a big manufacturing and service company known as the Republic Corp.[172] With this kind of background, it is rather doubtful that Mrs. Hills had much empathy with the underprivileged.

Another new member of Ford's Cabinet was Philadelphia lawyer William T. Coleman, Jr., who, although he had little experience in government, was appointed Secretary of Transportation when Nixon incumbent Claude Brinegar resigned in the first part of 1975 to return to the Union Oil Co. of California. Coleman had many corporate links, such as his directorships with the Philadelphia Electric Co., First Pennsylvania Corp. (a big bank holding company), Penn Mutual Life Insurance Co., and Pan-American World Airways.[173] Moreover, he had recently served both as a director of the Council on Foreign Relations and as a member of the Trilateral Commission. These two ties undoubtedly did much to enhance his chances for appointment to high federal office.[174]

President Ford, like many of his predecessors, relied mainly on a mixture of wealthy elite figures and longtime career officials to serve as America's chief diplomatic emissaries.[175] For example, as his first Ambassador to Great Britain, he chose the widely respected Elliot Richardson, who was by now a director of both the elitist-dominated Council on Foreign Relations and the closely linked Trilateral Commission.[176] But Richardson held office for only about a year before he was summoned back to Washington to take over as Secretary of Commerce.[177] At this juncture he was replaced by the first woman ever to occupy this post, Anne L. Armstrong. Mrs. Armstrong had been a prominent Republican leader in Texas in recent years, but was without any significant diplomatic experience, having merely served briefly as a member of Nixon's White House staff during his last year in office. However, she was a wealthy, well-connected figure. Her husband owned a big (18-square mile) ranch in Texas, and perhaps even more importantly, the Armstrongs were related to the rich Klebergs of the famous King Ranch interests.[178] In the brief span of time between her White House service and ambassadorial appointment, Mrs. Armstrong had been elected to the board of such nationally known concerns as American Express, Union Carbide, First City Bancorporation of Texas (a major bank holding company with which John B. Connally was associated), and also apparently the Boise Cascade Corp. (a big Northwestern paper company) and International Harvester.[179] These directorships clearly indicate that Mrs. Armstrong was, like Elliot Richardson, on close terms with America's major corporate interests.

President Ford chose another Establishment figure, former Union Carbide executive Kenneth Rush, to serve as America's chief emissary to France. By this time Rush had acquired a good deal of diplomatic experience, for since entering the federal government in 1969 he had acted as Ambassador to West Germany, and then from 1972 to 1974 as Deputy Secretary of State. But like other presidents before him, Ford relied on two longtime foreign service officers, Martin Hillenbrand and Walter J. Stoessel, Jr. (both of whom had been appointed by Nixon) to represent the United States in West Germany and the Soviet Union.[180]

In choosing our emissary to the People's Republic of China, President Ford adhered to a rather familiar pattern. He retained former Republican party leader, UN Ambassador, and wealthy Texas oilman George Bush up to early 1976, when the latter was appointed director of the CIA. This important diplomatic position was then filled by an even more elite figure, a Philadelphia patrician turned New York executive, Thomas S. Gates, Jr. Gates had held a number of key posts in the Defense Department during the Eisenhower years. But he was primarily a big busines figure. Since leaving the federal government, he had served as a high official of the Morgan Guaranty Trust Co. and as a director of such giant concerns as Bethlehem Steel, Campbell Soup, Cities Service, GE, and Scott Paper. If the underlying purpose of the establishment of diplomatic relations with Red China was, as many contend, to increase trade between the two counties, then Gates would seem to have been a good choice for this position.

Thus, although there was certainly a good deal of business influence in the Ford administration, it was not really dominated by Establishment forces, as was, for example, the Eisenhower administration. Other economic interests were strongly represented in Ford's regime. And these were generally of a highly conservative nature, as was perhaps best revealed by the continued, if not increasingly important, presence of the rightist chairman of the Council of Economic Advisers, Alan Greenspan, the first non-academic to hold this post since the CEA was created.[181]

MAJOR ISSUES AND ACTIONS OF THE FORD ADMINISTRATION

One area in which the Ford administration was, of necessity, heavily embroiled was the energy crisis, which, because of the 1973-1974 OPEC-decreed oil embargo and various later price hikes, plunged this nation into confusion and tumult. A number of critics have charged that the abrupt rise in prices was due primarily to the oil industry's domination of various key arms of the federal government, such as the Department of the Interior and the newly created Federal Energy Administration. For example, Robert Engler has recently argued that such was the case during the late Nixon and early Ford years. But his work is not especially convincing, in part because it does not delve adequately into the backgrounds of some of the top figures involved in the oil and energy decision-making process in the federal government. For instance, Engler presents no information on the (pre-1970) non-governmental links and activities of Secretary of the Interior Rogers C. B. Morton, who held this important post for five years.[182] Yet, as indicated earlier, Morton not only had two major corporate links himself (albeit neither with an oil company) before he assumed Cabinet office, but his brother, former Kentucky Senator Thruston B. Morton, served from 1969 through 1975 as a director of the big Texas Gas Transmission Corp. and the almost equally large Pittston Co., a highly diversified, New York-based enterprise which included oil distribution among its many activities.[183] There may have been more than just normal industry pressure at work during Morton's years as Secretary of the Interior.

Another person who played an important role in shaping the Ford administration's energy (and fiscal) policies was former New York bond executive William E. Simon, who had come into the federal government reportedly as the Treasury Department protégé of Attorney General John N. Mitchell. Shortly after imposition of the OPEC oil embargo, Simon was made head of the newly created Federal Energy Office, and six months later, upon the resignation of George P. Shultz, he was appointed Secretary of the Treasury. Simon apparently got along well, both personally and ideologically, with the President, for he continued to serve in this capacity throughout the remainder of Ford's term. However, as indicated earlier, Simon was not really an Establishment figure, for his old firm, Salomon Brothers, was a fairly new force on Wall Street. Yet it should be noted that he had at least one noteworthy link with the oil industry, for his uncle, William R. Stott, had been a longtime high official of Standard Oil of New Jersey (up to this retirement in the late 1960s) and had been this company's top negotiator in working out an important deal with his close friend and influential Nixon supporter, Thomas A. Pappas, for the giant ($200 million) Esso Pappas oil complex in Greece in the early 1960s.[184] Hence it seems reasonable to assume that although Simon had no directorship links with the oil industry, he was at least sympathetic to its interests.[185]

A third set of figures dealing with the nation's largely OPEC-induced oil crisis were the top officials of the newly spawned Federal Energy Administration (or as it was first known, the Federal Energy Office).[186] The first head of this agency was, as just noted, William E. Simon. But after six rather hectic months Simon left this post to become Secretary of the Treasury, a more prestigious and powerful position. His successor as energy czar was the second-ranking official in the agency (and a recent OMB officer), John C. Sawhill, who had been a senior vice-president of Baltimore's big Commercial Credit Co. from 1968 to 1973, a New York management consultant (with McKinsey and Co.) from 1965 to 1968, and in the early 1960s an associate professor and dean of New York University's School of Business Administration—none of which activities could be construed as making Sawhill into a pliant Establishment figure. In fact, Sawhill did not get along well, particularly from a policy standpoint, with either President Ford, Secretary of the Interior Rogers Morton, or the oil industry, and was soon replaced as head of the Federal Energy Administration.[187] He was succeeded in late 1974 by a relatively obscure person, Frank Zarb, who had recently served briefly as a high OMB official and earlier in the 1970s as an Assistant Secretary of Labor.[188] Zarb was primarily a businessman who had worked for seven years in the 1960s with a medium-sized brokerage concern known as Goodbody & Co., and then for short periods as a fairly high official of Hayden, Stone, Inc., a New York financial firm. While he probably had a pro-business outlook, and a number of his chief aides and advisors were drawn from the oil industry, there is no evidence that he was a spokesman for these economic interests.

Another important issue in the Ford years was antitrust legislation. Distressed by the growing trend toward corporate bigness and various illicit price-fixing schemes by large companies, a number of Congressmen managed to get considerable support for the adoption of certain controls. The proposed legislation would have given the federal government additional power to obtain evidence in its antitrust investigations, required all companies above a specified size to notify the government well in advance of any anticipated mergers (so that it would be easier to block such acquisitions), and, most important of all, authorized the attorneys-general of the fifty states to bring class-action suits seeking treble damages on behalf of consumers against alleged price-fixers. Thoroughly alarmed by the prospect of such a measure, America's large corporations, acting primarily through the influential Business Roundtable, succeeded in blocking this bill during the 1975 session of Congress.[189] This proposal was reintroduced the following year, with much the same support and opposition. Yet such are the vagaries of politics that this time the measure was approved (1976 was a presidential election year and President Ford, who was behind in the polls, probably felt he could not afford to veto such popular legislation).[190]

SUPREME COURT APPOINTMENTS AND ACTIONS

The Nixon and Ford administrations also had a profound effect on the make-up and general outlook of the Supreme Court, for there were during this period no less than five openings on this influential body, four of which occurred in the first three years Nixon was in office. The first vacancy was of an especially critical nature, because it was created by the departure of the Court's progressive Chief Justice, Earl Warren, who felt compelled to resign in early 1969 because of his advancing age and increasingly poor health. President Nixon now had a chance to put someone of his own ideological mold in this pivotal position. And he chose his man well. After consulting only with Attorney General John N. Mitchell, Nixon selected a longtime (1956–1969) judge of the U.S. Court of Appeals, Warren E. Burger, to serve as Warren's successor. Burger was picked because he had amply demonstrated that he was a highly conservative judge and a "strict constructionist," in contrast to many of the justices who had been appointed since the late New Deal days. He had a strong following among the more conservative members of Congress, and he was also much admired and cited by various rightist news commentators as a strong "law and order" man. It is possible that Burger's pronounced conservatism may have stemmed in part from the fact that he had served for many years, up to his 1953 appointment to a post in the Eisenhower administration, as a name partner in a medium-sized St. Paul law firm, then known as Faricy, Burger, Moore & Costello, which did a good deal of work for a variety of business concerns in the Midwest, the most prominent of which was the Cudahy Packing Co.[191]

As for the other members of the Supreme Court, four previously appointed justices served throughout the Nixon-Ford years. Two of these jurists, Thurgood Marshall and William J. Brennan, were, probably largely because of their socio-economic origins, distinctly liberal figures, although Brennan was an Eisenhower appointee and had once been a member of a Newark, New Jersey, corporate law firm. But Potter Stewart and Byron ("Whizzer") White generally took a rather conservative position on economic issues, although White had been selected by Kennedy. Consequently, these four jurists often split evenly on major cases.

President Nixon's first opportunity to pick another member of the Supreme Court came shortly after his appointment of Warren Burger. It occurred under most unusual circumstances; Associate Justice Abe Fortas was forced in 1969 to resign under fire as a result of the revelation that in 1966 he had accepted a dubious $20,000 fee (which he later returned) from the family-controlled foundation of Florida entrepreneur Louis Wolfson, who had been imprisoned for stock manipulation. The President, in line with his much publicized strategy of expanding the electoral base of the Republican party by wooing rightist support in the South, made two abortive attempts to fill this vacancy with Southern jurists.[192] After being thwarted in this political endeavor by strong public and Congressional opposition, Nixon turned to a Northerner, Minnesota's Harry A. Blackmun, who had served for the last eleven years as a judge of the U.S. Court of Appeals. Prior to his appointment to the federal bench, Blackmun had acted from 1950 to 1959 as the resident counsel for the famous Mayo Clinic, and before that had been a member of a fairly large Minneapolis law firm then known as Dorsey, Owen, Barker, Scott & Barber, which represented a number of major business enterprises in the Midwest, such as the Minneapolis-Honeywell Regulator Co., Cargill, Inc. (a big privately owned grain dealer), and the First National Bank of Minneapolis. Given this background, it is not surprising that Blackmun was initially an ideological ally of Chief Justice Warren Burger, who was also his close friend.[193]

In September 1971 the strongly New Dealish Hugo Black and the able conservative John Marshall Harlan were forced to resign because of illness, thereby giving President Nixon two more openings to fill. After a search which initially centered on three distinctly mediocre candidates, Nixon chose as his replacement for Black a man from the same section of the country, but one of a very different economic and ideological mold, Virginia lawyer Lewis F. Powell, Jr.[194] Unlike Black, Powell had no significant experience in government, although he had been a member of several federal commissions. Instead, he had been a longtime senior partner in one of Virginia's most prominent corporate law firms (Hunter, Williams, Gay, Powell & Gibson), and he had been elected president of the American Bar Association in the mid-1960s. Powell also had a number of noteworthy business links, for he had served on the board of the (now Southern-dominated) Ethyl Corp., (New York-controlled) Philip Morris, Inc., Chesapeake and Potomac Telephone Co. of Virginia (an AT&T subsidiary), Commonwealth Natural Gas Corp. (a big Virginia-based public utility), United Virginia Bankshares, Inc. (a major bank holding company), and the Richmond Corp. (a large insurance enterprise).[195] Thus, not unexpectedly, upon his elevation to the Supreme Court, Lewis Powell assumed a very active role in the economic area and proceeded to lead this increasingly conservative body in a series of rulings which generally favored corporate interests. In short, as the *New York Times* recently pointed out, for American business Justice Powell was indeed "...a friend in Court."[196]

As the replacement for Harlan, Nixon chose a former Phoenix lawyer, William H. Rehnquist, who had served briefly (from 1969 to 1971) as an Assistant U.S. Attorney General. Although widely acknowledged to be an able figure, Rehnquist was not elevated to the High Court solely because of his legal qualifications. Another important reason was that he was a zealous arch-conservative who had been an ardent supporter of Arizona Senator Barry Goldwater in the 1960s and had been brought into the Justice

Department by his close friend and ideological ally, Richard Kleindienst.[197] Rehnquist's conservatism, however, did not stem primarily from an association with major business interests in Arizona (his fairly small Phoenix law firm represented few large corporations), but apparently from the pro-entrepreneurial wave of economic growth and prosperity which had taken place in the Southwest in the postwar period.[198] Whatever the origins of his ideology, Rehnquist soon demonstrated that he was a very able judicial spokesman for America's renascent right wing.

In brief, it was through such pivotal appointments as Rehnquist, Powell, and the "Minnesota twins," as Burger and Blackmun were often initially described, that Nixon managed within a few short years to transform the Supreme Court from a staunchly liberal body into an essentially conservative one.

The last Supreme Court justice to be picked during this period was not appointed until four years later when, upon the incapacitation of the progressive William O. Douglas, President Ford chose a man of a very different mold, former Chicago lawyer and recent (1970–1975) U.S. Circuit Court judge John Paul Stevens as his successor. Stevens' conservatism apparently stemmed from two sources: first, his family's affluence, derived largely from hotel and insurance interests; and second, his lengthy (1952–1970) association with a medium-sized law firm known as Rothschild, Hart, Stevens & Barry, which, although none of its partners served on any major business boards, did a great deal of corporate and antitrust work.[199] Unlike some of Nixon's appointees (and proposed appointees), Stevens was generally conceded to be both able and independent. But as President Ford was no doubt well aware, he was also a fairly conservative jurist.

As a result of these important changes, the Supreme Court began to reverse or pull back from a number of positions it had taken on various key socio-economic issues since the late 1930s. For instance, in 1976 the Court ruled, by a narrow (5–4) margin, to invalidate a recently adopted Congressional act which would have extended the provisions of the federal minimum wage and maximum hours program to state and municipal employees. This was a rather strange ruling, for the Court declared, in effect, that non-federal public employees do not enjoy the same type of protection provided by national law to workers in the private sector. Moreover, as Anthony Lewis has pointed out, this was the first time in forty years that the Court had struck down an act that "...was an exercise of Congress' plenary constitutional power to regulate interstate commerce."[200] Also in 1976 the Supreme Court removed a number of the constraints which had been placed on political contributions by the Campaign Finance Act of 1974 in a post-Watergate attempt to reduce the pernicious effect of gross economic inequalities in contests for high federal office. The Court eliminated most of the spending limits that had been imposed by this law, thereby allowing wealthy candidates to spend as much of their own or their family's money in Congressional races as they wished. In addition, although the Court upheld the limit of $1,000 on individual contributions made *directly* to a candidate, it probably rendered this provision a nullity by permitting a contributor to spend unlimited amounts of money on behalf of a candidate so long as the donor did not "coordinate" the expenditures with the candidate's own campaign committee.[201] In short, while some salutary financial provisions still apply to presidential races, the Supreme Court removed many of the controls that were originally imposed on Congressional campaigns.

Clearly Nixon and Ford headed highly conservative administrations, as demonstrated by their appointments to high federal office and various major policy actions. There was little difference in the educational levels of their top administrative and diplomatic officials (except that Nixon drew less from prestigious colleges) and in the prior government experience of these officials (both were in the 60–70 percent range). But considering the fact that these were Republican regimes, they did not rely as much on economic elite figures as one might expect, certainly not as much as the Eisenhower administration. In fact, only about two-thirds of the Nixon-Ford officials had important business links, and an even smaller percentage had what might be called Establishment ties. Indeed, one might argue that the Watergate scandal would never have occurred if the Nixon administration had not relied so heavily on ambitious, if not amoral, "outsiders." And contrary to Kirkpatrick Sale's claim, there was no "Yankee counterattack" in the Ford administration. In point of fact, Ford had fewer Establishment officials (19 percent) than Nixon (35 percent). But whatever their similarities and differences, neither government contributed much to American life.

Notes

1. See Kirkpatrick Sale, *Power Shift* (New York: Random House, 1975), pp. 11 and 17–53. Sale extended the scope of the Southern Rim upward to include San Francisco, although many critics would argue that this city does not belong in the category because it has a more liberal tradition than such centers as Los Angeles, Phoenix, and San Diego.

2. For a recent (1976) list of trust fund holdings, see *Forbes* (July 1, 1977), pp. 63–64.

3. In addition, almost all of the nation's big investment banks and brokerage houses, which handle billions of dollars each year, were based in the Northeast. And California's big savings and loan associations were probably offset roughly in size by the large savings banks found in the Northeast.

4. See Peter Slavin, "The Business Roundtable: New Lobbying Arm of Big Business," *Business and Society Review* (Winter 1975–76), pp. 28–32. Although the precise reasons for the creation of the Business Roundtable are still unclear, some well-informed observers believe that it stemmed largely from the fact that many big companies had come under increasing fire

from various anti-corporate or pro-consumer groups such as those led by Ralph Nader, and were often delayed or thwarted in their building or expansion plans by environmentalists (or having added operating costs imposed upon them by demands generated by these civic interests).

5. See Philip H. Burch, Jr., "An Organizational Analysis of the Business Roundtable" (unpublished manuscript, 1979).

6. Another increasingly influential body which should be noted here is the American Enterprise Institute for Public Policy Research, the more refined organizational and ideological successor of the onetime arch-conservative American Enterprise Association. Because of its former extremist stance, this organization did not begin to attract the more moderate major corporate executives to serve on its board until the mid-1970s.

7. Though one would not ordinarily expect such funding of a Democratic candidate, almost all of Hubert Humphrey's campaign money in 1968 came from large contributors in important business and labor circles. And much of his financial support within the business community was centered in New York, where various "our crowd" investment bankers worked hard in his behalf. As evidence of this, one need only note the make-up of a special committee created in the fall of 1968 to promote Humphrey's candidacy. The chairman of this group was John L. Loeb and the treasurer was Armand Erpf (both of Loeb, Rhoades & Co.), and at least five of the fifteen (non-officer) members were associated with Lazard Frères, Loeb Rhoades, or Kuhn, Loeb & Co. Two other important figures in this Democratic drive were New York financier Sidney Weinberg, a senior partner in Goldman, Sachs & Co., and Humphrey's close friend and financial benefactor, Dwayne Andreas, whose family controlled the Archer Daniels Midland Co., a Minnesota "agribusiness." Conversely, when George McGovern captured his party's presidential nomination in 1972, his ultra-liberal economic views so upset leading Democrats on Wall Street that most of these people either simply withdrew their financial support or threw it to Nixon. As a result, the McGovern forces were, with a few exceptions, compelled to rely to an unprecedented extent on small donors. See Herbert E. Alexander, *Financing the 1968 Election* (Lexington, Mass.: Heath, 1971), pp. 63-65 and 152, Lewis Chester, Godfrey Hodgson, and Bruce Page, *An American Melodrama*, pp. 143-44, 404, and 715, the *New York Times* (October 28, 1968), p. 42 and (July 3, 1972), p. 1, and for more on Humphrey's relations with certain influential business interests, see the *New York Times* (July 11, 1978), p. A2 and (July 26, 1978), p. D1.

8. See the *New York Times* (April 12, 1968), p. 22.

9. See, for instance, Chester, Hodgson, and Page, *An American Melodrama*, p. 144.

10. See the *New York Times* (July 3, 1965), p. 12 and also (July 30, 1968), p. 24 for a more extensive list. Of the 51-man economic advisory and support committee created in early July, only six came from the nation's Southern Rim, and the percentage among Nixon's second group of backers was not much larger.

11. See Hoffman, *Lions in the Street*, p. 108.

12. As part of its rebuilding program, this concern absorbed a number of other lesser firms in the mid-1960s, the most important of which was probably that of Caldwell, Trimble & Mitchell, a small lucrative enterprise which brought in, as a partner, municipal bond attorney John N. Mitchell.

13. At the time of Nixon's entry into the Mudge, Stern law firm, its principal clients were apparently the General Precision Equipment Corp. (which was merged into the Singer Co. in 1968), the Studebaker Corp., and the Warner-Lambert Pharmaceutical Co., which had been run for many years by one of Nixon's most intimate associates, Elmer Bobst, who was reportedly responsible for the former Vice President's transcontinental shift to this particular New York City law firm. Another large (foreign-controlled) concern which Nixon brought into his firm's fold was the American arm of Japan's giant Mitsui Co. See John G. Roberts, *Mitsui: Three Centuries of Japanese Business* (New York: Weatherhill, 1973), p. 476.

14. The firm continued to expand in size throughout Nixon's years in executive office, ultimately attaining a total of 42 partners. It counted among its clients the big Penn-Central Co.,

which now-bankrupt enterprise retained the firm to, among other things, help secure a $225 million loan guarantee from the federal government. The Nixon administration initially approved the request, but was soon forced to rescind its action under heavy fire. See Goulden, *The Superlawyers*, pp. 219–221, and the *New York Times* (June 23, 1970), p. 1 (September 26, 1970), p. 12, (May 7, 1972), Sect. III, p. 1, and (May 11, 1973), p. 18.

15. For example, the most important nonfinancial concern with which its board chairman, Roger Hull, was connected as a director was Hart, Schaffner & Marx, the Chicago-headquartered men's clothing store. In the late 1930s, on the other hand, Mutual Life's chief executive, David F. Houston, sat on the board of the United States Steel Corp., AT&T, and the Guaranty Trust Co. of New York.

16. See *Forbes* (August 15, 1971), p. 26. Another more recently acquired friend and substantial supporter of Nixon was self-made Chicago businessman W. Clement Stone, who, together with his family, controlled the Combined Insurance Co. of America, a fairly sizable concern, but far from one of the giants of the industry. Stone is reported to have given about $1 million to Nixon's 1968 campaign and a total of $2 million to his 1972 cause. See *Newsweek* (December 13, 1971), p. 24, and Alexander, *op. cit.*, p. 72.

17. See the *New York Times* (May 14, 1972), Sect. III, p. 1, (September 10, 1973), p. 1, and (November 10, 1973), p. 39. According to the last article, C. Arnholt Smith, who was frequently referred to as "Mr. San Diego," had some significant ties, through various friends and business associates, to a number of Mafia figures in Southern California.

18. In late 1973 Smith's $1-billion U.S. National Bank collapsed, largely because Smith had systematically looted this institution of at least $170 million, which he channeled into his own personal or corporate coffers. *Forbes* magazine, in fact, described Smith as perhaps the greatest swindler of the century. Smith subsequently pleaded *nolo contendere* to charges of conspiracy, misapplication of funds, and the issuance of false statements and records. In what *Forbes* described as a "mockery of justice," the 76-year-old Smith received (from a Nixon-appointed judge) a "penalty" of five years' probation and a fine of $30,000, to be paid conveniently at a rate of $100 a month over the next 25 years, by which time Smith, if he lived, would be 101. See *Forbes* (August 15, 1975), pp. 4 and 17–20.

19. For more on this relationship, see the *New York Times* (November 17, 1970), pp. 1 and 17. Another less influential member of the inner circle was New York's Hobart Lewis, the editor of *Readers' Digest*. Other New York business or legal figures reputed to be fairly close to Nixon were Elliott V. Bell, the former editor of *Business Week*, George Champion, a longtime high official of the Chase Manhattan Bank, Gabriel Hauge, the president of the Manufacturers Hanover Trust Co., George Murphy, board chairman of the Irving Trust Co., and Thomas E. Dewey.

20. Shortly after Nixon's election Kendall was made a member of the Business Council's White House liaison committee, which was headed by GE president Fred Borch. Its other members included Russell De Young, board chairman of the Goodyear Tire & Rubber Co.; Robert V. Hansberger, board chairman of the Boise Cascade Corp.; Jack V. Horton, board chairman of the Southern California Edison Co.; Frederick R. Kappel, board chairman of AT&T; Barry T. Leithead, board chairman of Cluett, Peabody & Co. (Arrow shirts); Thomas F. Patton, board chairman of the Republic Steel Corp.; and Lynn A. Townsend, board chairman of the Chrysler Corp. The 1970 chairmen of the other major governmental liaison committees of the Business Council were as follows: Department of State, Patrick Haggerty (board chairman of Texas Instruments, Inc. and a trustee of the CED); Defense, Roger Blough (the recently retired head of the U.S. Steel Corp., who was a trustee of the Equitable Life Assurance Society); Treasury, Thomas S. Gates, Jr. (board chairman of the Morgan Guaranty Trust Co.); Commerce, Roger Milliken (president of Deering-Milliken, Inc. and a director of the First National City Bank of New York); Labor, J. Ward Keener (board chairman of the B. F. Goodrich Co., who had been a trustee of the CED up to 1969); Interior, Charles A. Thomas (former head of the Monsanto Co. and a trustee of Metropolitan Life); HUD, Edgar F. Kaiser (board chairman of the Kaiser Industries Corp. and a director of BankAmerica); Trans-

portation, Elisha Gray (board chairman of the Whirlpool Corp.); and the Council of Economic Advisers, Birny Mason (board chairman of the Union Carbide Corp., who served on the board of both Manufacturers Hanover Trust Co. and Metropolitan Life).

21. See the *New York Times* (August 12, 1973), Sect. III, p. 1. For example, Abplanalp loaned the President more than $1 million to buy and fix up his estate at San Clemente, California, and then paid a substantially higher price to buy most of this land back from Mr. Nixon a few years later.

22. See the *New York Times* (May 26, 1973), p. 10.

23. See the *New York Times* (December 23, 1968), p. 34, and (January 21, 1974), p. 1. According to the latter source, Rebozo also had some questionable connections with various Caribbean gambling interests, such as Resorts International.

24. Actually, Rebozo was worth only about $675,000 when Nixon entered the White House, but by late 1973 his holdings had jumped to a total of $4.5 million.

25. Nixon's Vice President, Spiro T. Agnew, proved to be an execrable choice and was later forced to resign in disgrace after he had been charged in a 50-count indictment with taking kickbacks and bribes while he had been a Maryland state official in the mid-1960s. As a look at his politico-economic record revealed even in 1968, Agnew had been involved in a number of dubious, if not improper, ventures, such as sitting on the board of a Towson, Maryland, bank while serving both as Baltimore County chief executive and Maryland's governor, and being a participant in real estate speculation near the terminus of a proposed Chesapeake Bay bridge. Such activities should have given ample warning as to his character. For more on this topic, see the *New York Times* (October 22, 1968), p. 29, (October 26, 1968), p. 36, and (September 7, 1973), p. 21.

26. Evans and Novak claim that Nixon's first choice for this position was former Pennsylvania Governor William W. Scranton, a wealthy patrician who was a director of the Scott Paper Co. and a trustee of the CED. Having failed dismally in his last-minute anti-Goldwater bid for the 1964 Republican presidential nomination, Scranton had left elective politics, vowing never to return. He apparently would not even permit the subject of his possible appointment to be brought up. The CFR-led foreign policy establishment then turned to onetime high federal official C. Douglas Dillon, who in 1965 had returned to the world of finance. But, as Evans and Novak put it, "...he never had a chance. He had been entered twice on that invisible ledger of past wrongs kept so meticulously by Richard Nixon. First, Dillon had failed to ask Nixon's approval in advance before becoming the resident Republican in John F. Kennedy's Cabinet as Secretary of the Treasury in 1961. Second, and perhaps more important, Nixon felt that Dillon had joined the Republican elite of Manhattan in snubbing him at the (then) low point of his life when he moved to New York following his defeat in the race for governor of California in 1962. Instead of inviting Nixon into their clubs and homes, the rich Republicans who had never liked him anyway, now ignored him as a has-been beneath their notice." At this juncture, Thomas E. Dewey and Herbert Brownell are reported to have suggested William Rogers, who, ever since his service in the Eisenhower administration, had been on friendly terms with Nixon. See Rowland Evans, Jr., and Robert D. Novak, *Nixon in the White House* (New York: Random House, 1971), pp. 22–23.

27. None of the other partners in this concern (which was an offshoot of Charles Evans Hughes's old firm) served on any major corporate boards. However, while Nixon may have felt that the selection of Rogers constituted a rebuff to the business establishment, it is interesting to note that one of Rogers's partners, John A. Wells, was a longtime political aide of New York's Nelson Rockefeller. In fact, Wells had served as the latter's presidential campaign manager in 1964 and later helped to arrange for the publication of a scurrilous biography of Rockefeller's 1970 Democratic gubernatorial opponent, Arthur Goldberg. See Hoffman, *Lions in the Street*, p. 31, and the *New York Times* (October 12, 1974), p. 1.

28. Though not a top-tier figure, Rogers managed to derive a very substantial income—about $300,000 a year—from his law practice and directorship fees. See *Time* (January 3, 1969), p. 21.

29. See Marvin Kalb and Bernard Kalb, *Kissinger* (Boston: Little, Brown, 1974), pp. 51–56. One product of Kissinger's work on this panel was the publication of his book, *Nuclear Weapons and Foreign Policy*, which was put out under the auspices of the Council on Foreign Relations. Later, from 1965 to 1973, Kissinger served on the editorial advisory board of the CFR's influential organ, *Foreign Affairs*.

30. See Kalb and Kalb, *op. cit.*, pp. 16–21.

31. That Kissinger was still strongly tied to Nelson Rockefeller may be seen from the fact that the latter gave Kissinger $50,000 just three days before he entered the Nixon administration, reportedly to ease the fiscal burden he would soon encounter as a high federal official. This gift would seem to raise some question as to Kissinger's ethics. Indeed, Richard Nixon almost had to withdraw from the presidential ticket in 1952 when it was found that a number of businessmen (some of whom may have had different points of view) had contributed to a fund to supplement his public salary. As Anthony Lewis has noted, "it...is surely much more dangerous, and a clearer violation of principle, to have a single immensely rich man giving large sums of money to key officials," such as Henry Kissinger. See the *New York Times* (October 7, 1974), p. 35.

32. However, it should be noted that most of the other major posts in this department were occupied by career officials. Only a few non-professional appointees were picked by the Nixon administration. One such selection was Deputy Under Secretary of State for Economic Affairs Nathaniel Samuels, a former partner in the New York investment banking firm of Kuhn, Loeb & Co. (and a recent director of the Rockefeller-dominated International Basic Economy Corp., Harvey Aluminum, Inc., Industria Electrica de Mexico, S.A., and Societe Financière de Transport et d'Enterprise Industrielles, a Belgian concern commonly referred to as Sofina). Samuels was succeeded in 1972 by a former New York City lawyer and 1971–1972 SEC chairman, William J. Casey, who had served on the board of the Capital Cities Broadcasting Co., a relatively unimportant concern. Of the other upper-echelon officials in the State Department, only one, Assistant Secretary of State for Inter-American Affairs Charles A. Meyer, was a prominent business executive. Meyer, who was a grandson of William Howard Taft's Secretary of the Navy, was a vice-president of Sears, Roebuck & Co. and a director, through much or all of the 1960s, of the Boston-based Gillette Co. and United Fruit Co. The latter tie might raise some question about his serving in this governmental capacity.

33. Another important White House post filled in 1969 was that of the United States Special Representative for Trade Negotiations. The first person to occupy this office during the Nixon administration was an obvious Establishment figure, New England industrialist Carl J. Gilbert, who was a major executive of the Gillette Co. (and, up to 1969, a member of the Business Council, a trustee of the CED, and a director of the Morgan Guaranty Trust Co. and the Raytheon Manufacturing Co.). When he stepped down from this post in late 1971, he was replaced by William D. Eberle, who had served in recent years as a high official of American Standard, Inc. (a big New York–based concern), a board member of the smaller Atlantic Mutual Insurance Co., and through the mid-1970s as a trustee of the CED. Both men were advocates of a liberal trade policy.

34. According to Evans and Novak, Maurice Stans, who was a high-ranking figure in one of New York's second-tier investment banks, desperately wanted this position, but arrayed against him were the most influential forces in the financial community, including important officials in the American Bankers Association. See Evans and Novak, *Nixon in the White House*, pp. 25–26.

35. The two second-ranking posts in the department were initially held by men of the same general mold, Under Secretary of the Treasury Charls E. Walker, who had been executive vice-president of the American Bankers Association, and Under Secretary of the Treasury for Monetary Affairs Paul A. Volcker, a former vice-president of the Chase Manhattan Bank and onetime Treasury Department official.

36. Connally was reportedly paid, while serving as governor of Texas, at least $225,000 by the Richardson interests for work performed by December 1961 in settling the estate of this rich

oilman, who died in 1959. Apparently Connally's fee was spread out over this period for tax reasons. See the *New York Times* (February 1, 1977), p. 1.

37. In most cities big financial interests dominate the major law firms, but in Houston, which claims three of the ten largest law firms in the country, the law firms are reported to dominate industry and the banks. See the *New York Times* (March 5, 1973), p. 21. For more on the above firm's extraordinary political role, see Neal R. Peirce, *The Megastates of America* (New York: Norton, 1972), p. 508, and George Thayer, *Who Shakes the Money Tree?*, p. 188.

38. See the *New York Times* (November 7, 1976), Sect. III, p. 1. Because of his ability and strong political backing, Simon was asked about a year later to take over as head of the newly created Federal Energy Office, an agency established on short notice to deal with the OPEC-generated oil crisis in the United States.

39. See the *New York Times* (December 30, 1974), Sect. III, p. 11.

40. In a rather surprising move, Nixon first offered this post to Washington's hawkish Democratic Senator, Henry Jackson, in an attempt to build some bipartisan support for his defense policy. However, Jackson was forced to refuse because of party pressure. See Evans and Novak, *Nixon in the White House*, p. 24.

41. The Lairds owned a substantial interest in a Wisconsin lumber company (apparently the Connor Building Supply Co.), and had an overall fortune of almost $1 million. See *Time* (January 3, 1969), p. 21.

42. See *Business Week* (August 4, 1973), p. 28 and (March 19, 1974), pp. 114–16, *Dun's Review* (April 1976), p. 43, and Philip H. Burch, Jr., "The NAM as an Interest Group," *Politics and Society* (Fall 1973), pp. 115–130.

43. See *Business Week* (August 4, 1973), p. 28 and (March 19, 1974), pp. 114–16, *Dun's Money Tree?*, p. 105, and for more on Ball himself, *Business Week* (August 27, 1960), p. 6, and *Finance* (May 1967), pp. 23–25 and (June 1967), p. 30.

44. By the time of the Nixon administration the status of the three service (Army, Navy, and Air Force) secretaries had dropped a few notches. Only Stanley R. Resor, who served as Secretary of the Army until 1971, was really a prominent figure in either the economic or political world, and he was a carryover from the preceding Democratic regime of Lyndon B. Johnson, kept on probably because he was the brother-in-law of New York banker and Nixon advisor Gabriel Hauge. Resor was succeeded by Robert F. Froehlke, who was a vice-president of the small Sentry Insurance Co. of Wisconsin and the manager of Laird's eight Republican Congressional campaigns. When he resigned two years later, his place was taken by a former Georgia Congressman, Howard H. Callaway, whose family had a $40 million textile fortune and various key politico-economic ties, particularly in the South. Callaway was a staunch conservative, as evidenced by the fact that he had been board chairman of the Freedoms Foundation and his uncle, Fuller E. Callaway, had been a longtime trustee of the American Enterprise Institute for Public Policy Research (and its organizational predecessor, the AEA). The position of Secretary of the Navy was filled during the first part of the Nixon administration by former Rhode Island governor and Providence lawyer John H. Chaffee, another relatively obscure figure. When he resigned in 1973 to reenter state politics, this post was taken by his top aide, John W. Warner, a Washington lawyer and strong Nixon supporter, who had married into the Mellon family, which had contributed more than $1 million to Nixon's 1972 reelection campaign. When Warner stepped down about a year later to take a prestigious civic post, he was succeeded by a major Republican party fundraiser (and recent American Ambassador to the Netherlands), J. William Middendorf II, a board member of the rightist Hoover Institution. The position of Secretary of the Air Force, however, was held throughout these years by two men who had no such financial or political credentials, but were essentially able technocrats, Robert C. Seamans, Jr., and John L. McLucas.

45. The wealthy Clements served on the board of the Illinois-based Keebler Co. from 1969 to 1972. This concern had been controlled since 1966 by certain Texas entrepreneurs.

46. See the 1968 *Martindale-Hubbell Law Directory* (Summit, N.J.: Martindale-Hubbell), Vol. I, p. 79.

47. Judging from *Poor's Register of Corporations, Directors and Executives* and other similar sources, none of his partners had important ties either.

48. See F. Clifton White, *Suite 3505: The Story of the Draft Goldwater Movement* (New Rochelle, N.Y.: Arlington House, 1967), pp. 263-79, and also Stephen Shadegg, *What Happened to Goldwater?* (New York: Holt, Rinehart & Winston, 1965), pp. 86-120, 137-44, and 164-73. Apparently for much the same reason, Nixon picked former Arizona lawyer and ardent Goldwater supporter Dean Burch to serve as chairman of the Federal Communications Commission in 1969, even though he had no special qualifications for this post.

49. In his confirmation hearings before the Senate Judiciary Committee in early 1972, Kleindienst apparently lied under oath about White House pressure exerted on him to arrive at a "friendly" out-of-court settlement of the ITT antitrust case. He had also withheld information from Watergate investigators about some significant aspects of the Watergate scandal concerning the role of his former boss, John N. Mitchell. Yet the second, more conservative Watergate prosecutor, Leon Jaworski, a wealthy Texas corporate lawyer, later permitted Kleindienst to plead guilty to one relatively minor misdemeanor charge involving the refusal of a witness to testify, a clause which didn't even apply in Kleindienst's case, and escape with a token penalty instead of being tried for perjury. Three attorneys who had been handling the ITT matter for the federal government resigned in protest over Jaworski's perverted application of the law in this proceeding. See the *New York Times* (October 30, 1973), p. 1, (May 30, 1974), p. 19, and (June 21, 1974), p. 37, and Richard Ben-Veniste and George Frampton, Jr., *Stonewall: The Real Story of the Watergate Prosecution* (New York: Simon & Schuster, 1977), p. 378, and Robert M. Goolrick, *Public Policy Toward Corporate Growth: The ITT Merger Cases* (Port Washington, N.Y.: Kennikat Press, 1978), p. 162.

50. Most of Richardson's ties were indirect. To illustrate, he had married the daughter of Rhode Island financier Thomas P. Hazard, who had served up to 1962 as a director of the Allied Chemical Corp.; Hazard's nephew, Robert H. I. Goddard, sat up to the early 1970s on the board of the New England Telephone & Telegraph Co., an AT&T subsidiary. But perhaps even more important, Richardson's uncle, Henry L. Shattuck, had served until recently as the longtime treasurer of well-endowed Harvard University, as a director or trustee of the big New England Merchants National Bank and the Mutual Life Insurance Co. of New York (with which latter institution Richard Nixon had also been associated), and had played a major behind-the-scenes role in Boston politics over the years. For example, he was reportedly the person on whom Edwin O'Connor based his strongly anti-Curley character, Nathaniel Gardiner, in *The Last Hurrah*. On this last point, see the *New York Times* (May 20, 1973), Sect. VI, p. 97.

51. See the 1968 *Martindale-Hubbell Law Directory*, Vol. III, p. 987.

52. Further evidence that Hickel was willing to back the environmental movement may be seen in the fact that he picked California's Russell Train to be Under Secretary of the Interior. Train had served since 1965 as president of the Conservation Foundation, a pro-ecology group.

53. See Evans and Novak, *Nixon in the White House*, p. 25.

54. When Secretary of the Interior Morton belatedly stepped down from the latter post, his place was quickly taken by his brother, former Kentucky Senator Thruston Morton, who also served throughout this period on the board of the big Texas Gas Transmission Corp. and the New York-based Pittston Co., a highly diversified company which included oil distribution among its many major activities.

55. See Bruce I. Oppenheimer, *Oil and the Congressional Process* (Lexington, Mass.: Heath, 1974), p. 28.

56. See the *New York Times* (March 30, 1975), Sect. IV, p. 14.

57. Hardin had also been a director of the considerably smaller Behlen Mfg. Co. of Nebraska (a farm equipment company).

58. The marked increase in the influence of large corporate interests in this area was pointed up in 1963 by Edward Higbee in a Twentieth Century Fund study entitled *Farms and Farmers in an Urban Age* (New York: Twentieth Century Fund, 1963). Three companies—Purex, United Brands, and Bud Antle, Inc.—now produce a substantial amount of all the lettuce eaten in the United States. And by the early 1970s about twenty companies, the most prominent of which were probably the Ralston-Purina Co. and the Pillsbury Co., had come to dominate the broiler industry. In fact, out of every dollar spent on food in the United States, only 38 cents went to the American farmer, and the other 62 cents was taken by processing, wholesaling, and retailing interests.

59. At about the same time that Butz stepped down from the board of the Ralston-Purina Co., his departmental predecessor, Clifford Hardin, was made vice-chairman of this concern, indicating that he too was on close terms with these interests. The dangers inherent in these kinds of ties were vividly pointed up by the grain scandal of 1971 in which certain huge trading companies negotiated a $750 million sale of wheat to the Soviet Union, through which, because they apparently had advance information about the deal, they reaped well over $100 million in profit. One official involved in these proceedings was Assistant Secretary of Agriculture Clarence Palmby who, after handling much of the required governmental negotiations, left his high federal post to become a vice-president of the giant Continental Grain Co., one of the principal parties in this transaction, just one month before public announcement of the deal. That this concern probably had advance knowledge both of Russia's vast need for grain and the Department of Agriculture's position in this affair may also be inferred from the fact that Continental had long maintained an extraordinary private intelligence network around the world. As one business journal put it, "gathering intelligence on the daily goings-on around the world is a key to successful grain trading, and Continental is plugged into virtually every major foreign government. Its listening network is like a vast news agency that never publishes a word. It is so good, in fact, that members of the U.S. Central Intelligence Agency often wine and dine the company's traders to pick their brains." See the *New York Times* (September 9, 1972), p. 10, *Business Week* (March 11, 1972), p. 85, and Dan Morgan, *Merchants of Grain* (New York: Viking, 1979), passim.

60. See the *New York Times* (April 16, 1972), Section VI, p. 91, and also for an earlier analysis of these organizations, Wesley McCune, *Who's Behind Our Farm Policy?*, pp. 140-55.

61. See the *New York Times* (June 13, 1976), Sect. VI, p. 51.

62. See *Newsweek* (December 23, 1968), p. 18.

63. Actually, in the early 1960s Stans had been president of the California-based Western Bancorporation, which ranked among the "top 10" financial institutions in the country. But he held this crucial post for only a short period of time before he, for some reason, accepted a much less prestigious partnership with the relatively small William R. Staats, Inc.

64. Stans had also served briefly, in the early 1960s, on the board of the Southern California Edison Co., which had assets of over $1.5 billion. Yet for some reason, this relationship was not maintained for any length of time, not even for the duration of Stans's economic career in Los Angeles.

65. For more on these and similar groups, see Philip H. Burch, Jr., "The NAM as an Interest Group," *Politics and Society* (Fall 1973), pp. 115-30. Another conservative member of Nixon's Cabinet was Postmaster-General Winston Blount, who was a wealthy Alabama contractor and former ardent Goldwater supporter. Although Blount served on the boards of several local business enterprises, his only national ties were as a director of the NAM and the less extremist U.S. Chamber of Commerce, of which he had recently been elected president. Blount, however, held office only until 1971, when, because of the recent passage of a law conceived and backed by major business interests, the Post Office Department was transformed into a public corporation.

66. See the *New York Times* (December 7, 1972), p. 69.

67. Dent had grown up in the Northeast, where his father had some major business connections, and had attended the exclusive St. Paul's prep school and Yale University.

68. On the first point, see the *New York Times* (June 11, 1970), p. 37.

69. See *Time* (January 3, 1969), p. 21.

70. Romney, it is true, was strongly supported by Nelson Rockefeller in the early stages of the Republican presidential race in 1968, but this was basically a maneuver designed to thwart other more formidable rivals and pave the way for the later nomination of New York's ever-ambitious Governor.

71. In 1969 Triangle Publications was estimated to have about $200 million in sales, which, if it had been a publicly-owned enterprise, would rank it among the "top 500" industrials. See *Forbes* (May 15, 1969), p. 191.

72. Annenberg was appointed to the latter board just before the merger of the Pennsylvania Railroad and the Kirby-controlled New York Central system because he had recently procured a substantial block of voting stock in the PRR.

73. Although the fundraising records for the 1968 presidential race are grossly inadequate, Annenberg probably contributed a great deal of money to the Nixon cause, perhaps more than Arthur Watson. Yet, interestingly, in 1972 Watson gave a larger sum ($303,000) to Nixon's reelection campaign than did Walter Annenberg, who donated a mere $254,000. On this latter point, see Herbert E. Alexander, *Financing the 1972 Election*, p. 387.

74. Just before his appointment to this high post, Watson had also been president of the International Chamber of Commerce, a largely ignored and probably underrated, organization.

75. This firm had long been closely associated with the Rockefeller interests. One of its original partners, Vanderbilt Webb, served up to his death in 1956 as a vice-president of Rockefeller Center, Inc., and as a director of the probably Harkness-dominated New York Trust Co. Irwin also sat on the board of several other major business and civic enterprises, the most important of which was the United States Trust Co. For more on Irwin's law firm, see Paul Hoffman, *Lions in the Street*, pp. 27 and 80.

76. As indicated earlier, the position of Ambassador to West Germany was filled initially by a thoroughly Establishment figure, Kenneth Rush, who was the president of the Union Carbide Corp. (and a director of the Bankers Trust Co. and the American Sugar Co.). His 1972 successor was an able career diplomat, Martin J. Hillenbrand. And, following a well-established pattern, two longtime foreign service officers, Jacob Beam and Walter Stoessel, were chosen to act as chief emissary to the Soviet Union. Our Ambassadors to NATO, on the other hand, were a rather mixed lot. Two (Robert Ellsworth and Donald Rumsfeld) were Republican party leaders, and the other (David M. Kennedy) was Nixon's first Secretary of the Treasury and a former nationally prominent banker.

77. Bunker also served as a director of the financially troubled Curtis Publishing Co. of Philadelphia up to 1969, when the New York-based group with which he was apparently affiliated abandoned its stake in this concern. In addition, until the early 1970s Bunker sat on the board of the Foreign Policy Association, a less important, though more representative body than the Council on Foreign Relations.

78. In the early 1970s this long overdue move was given a substantial boost by a group of influential executives interested in promoting increased trade with China, a country which was believed to have vast offshore oil resources (recently estimated to be as much as thirty billion barrels, a total close to that of the United States). This specially constituted committee was made up of David Rockefeller, chairman of the Chase Manhattan Bank; Gabriel Hauge, chairman of the Manufacturers Hanover Trust Co.; Donald C. Burnham, chief executive officer of the Westinghouse Electric Corp.; William A. Hewitt, chairman of Deere & Co.; Thornton A. Wilson, president of the Boeing Co.; John W. Hanley, president of the Monsanto Co.; Robert H. Malott, chairman of the FMC Corp.; David Packard, chairman of the Hewlett-Packard Co.; Donald Kendall, chairman of Pepsico; Joseph Kenneally, chairman of the International Systems & Controls Corp. (a Texas company with major oil interests); Anthony Bryan,

president of the Cameron Iron Works of Texas; Charles Robinson, president of the Marcona Corp., a joint subsidiary of the Cyprus Mines Corp. and Utah International; Fred Seed, chairman of the Cargill Corp., a giant grain trading company; Edward W. Cook, president of Cook Industries (another big grain trader); Albert Artieres, a high West Coast official of R. H. Macy & Co.; Andrew Gibson, president of the small Interstate Oil Transport Co., a concern which was half owned by the Cities Service Co.; and Walter Surrey, a Washington tax lawyer and onetime Treasury Department official. A majority of these figures were affiliated with one or more of the following elite groups: the Business Council, Business Roundtable, and CED. See the *New York Times* (March 27, 1973), p. 1; for the recent estimate of China's offshore oil reserves, see *Business Week* (November 6, 1978), p. 76.

79. After Bush stepped down from this post, some Texas oil interests, particularly Pennzoil, were able to make good use of the ties that this pro-business official had established in Peking to help promote their economic position in China. See *Forbes* (September 4, 1978), p. 90.

80. Another fairly well-known figure who was initially appointed to an important post in Nixon's executive office was former Harvard professor and longtime Democratic party advisor Daniel Patrick Moynihan, who became Assistant to the President for Urban Affairs. However, Moynihan's role as the White House's one avowed liberal was rather frustrating and relatively brief. He was often opposed by such influential operators as Arthur Burns, H.R. Haldeman, and John Ehrlichman. As the latter two figures grew in power and importance, Moynihan was eased out of his position and given another seemingly prestigious assignment, but one which carried little weight.

81. See Rowland Evans, Jr., and Robert D. Novak, *Nixon in the White House*, pp. 45–49, and J. Anthony Lukas, *Nightmare: The Underside of the Nixon Years* (New York: Viking, 1976), pp. 224–25.

82. See Evans and Novak, *Nixon in the White House*, pp. 49–51, and the *New York Times* (November 6, 1969), p. 23. There were, of course, a number of other fairly important White House aides such as John W. Dean III, who later became a key figure in the malodorous Watergate proceedings. But none were as influential as Haldeman and Ehrlichman.

83. From an institutional standpoint, Flanigan's selection would seem contradictory, for, as pointed out earlier, Nixon had summarily rejected the idea of appointing C. Douglas Dillon, who had once headed this family-dominated firm, as Secretary of State, in large measure because the President felt he had been snubbed by such elite leaders.

84. Peter Flanigan also served up to 1969 as a director of a family financial trust known as the Augustus Busch Estate, Inc.

85. See the *New York Times* (March 20, 1972), p. 24.

86. Other major agencies, such as the Atomic Energy Commission and the National Aeronautics and Space Administration, were controlled during this period by able technocrats rather than by elite figures.

87. From 1969 to 1971 Ash served as chairman of the President's Advisory Council on Executive Organization, which made a comprehensive study of the overall structure and operation of the federal government. Some of these recommendations were implemented in the early 1970s. Although Ash himself was from the Southern Rim, this special ad hoc group was dominated by Establishment interests. The other five members of this body were as follows: George P. Baker, dean of the famous Harvard Business School (and a director of Lockheed, Mobil Oil, and First National Bank of Boston); Texas lawyer and political leader John B. Connally (a director of the First City National Bank of Houston, Halliburton Co., Texas Instruments, and United States Trust Co. of New York); Frederick R. Kappel, the former longtime head of AT&T and recent board chairman of the International Paper Co. (and a director of the Chase Manhattan Bank, Metropolitan Life, General Foods, Standard Oil of New Jersey, and an executive committee member of the Business Council): New York management consultant Richard M. Paget (a director of the United States Trust Co., Union Dime Savings Bank, and Atlas Chemical Industries); and Walter N. Thayer, a high official of the Whitney

Communications Corp. (and a board member of the Bankers Trust Co., National Dairy Products Corp., and CED).

88. See Hugh S. Norton, *The Employment Act and the Council of Economic Advisers*, p. 220.

89. The other initial Nixon appointee to the CEA was Harvard professor Hendrik S. Houthakker, who apparently took little interest in these proceedings. Later replacements as Council members included Stanford economist Ezra Solomon, University of Pittsburgh professor Marina Whitman, and Yale University professor William J. Fellner, who had served as a research scholar at the conservative American Enterprise Institute shortly before being appointed to the CEA.

90. Actually, Greenspan had served as Nixon's top domestic economic advisor during his 1968 campaign, and had frequently been consulted informally by the President thereafter.

91. Greenspan also served, in the last year or two before his appointment to the CEA, as a director of New York's big Bowery Savings Bank, the General Cable Corp., and the Sun Chemical Corp.

92. See the *New York Times* (July 24, 1974), p. 57, and (July 28, 1974), Sect. III, p. 1.

93. William Shawcross, *Sideshow: Kissinger, Nixon, and the Destruction of Cambodia* (New York: Simon & Schuster, 1979), passim, especially pp. 140–42. According to this incisive account, Secretary of State William Rogers and Secretary of Defense Melvin Laird, who had been firmly opposed to such a venture, were kept largely in the dark about this proposed operation up until the time it was launched, and the advice of such people as Attorney General John Mitchell and Nixon crony Bebe Rebozo apparently carried more weight in these proceedings.

94. See Godfrey Hodgson, "The Establishment," *Foreign Policy* (Spring 1973), pp. 3–40, especially pp. 25–28. Kissinger's role in this affair is an intriguing one. Shawcross, for instance, claims (see p. 157) that Kissinger may have backed the ill-conceived "anti-Establishment" policy primarily because he wanted "...to demonstrate to men like Mitchell, Rebozo, Haldeman and Ehrlichman that his loyalty, as well as his intellect, had been transferred with other baggage from Harvard to the White House...." Yet upon his retirement from high federal office in 1977, Kissinger quickly became a director of the Council on Foreign Relations, a member of the Trilateral Commission, a trustee of the Rockefeller Brothers Fund, vice-chairman of the international advisory committee of the Chase Manhattan Bank, and a well-paid (over $250,000 a year) part-time advisor for Goldman, Sachs & Co., the last tie being his only apparent non-Rockefeller connection. Thus one does not know how much to make of Kissinger's reported split with the Establishment. See the *New York Times* (March 22, 1977), p. 51 and (April 16, 1978), Sect. VI, p. 29, and *Time* (September 11, 1978), p. 52.

95. On the other hand, when the Lockheed Aircraft Corp. fell into serious financial difficulties in the early 1970s (largely because of bad management), the Nixon administration was quick to come to its rescue with a $250 million loan package which, when approved by a narrow margin in Congress, saved this giant corporation from bankruptcy. The Nixon regime also tried in 1969 to push a plan through Congress to bail out the sorely distressed Penn Central, but this economic effort failed because of legislative opposition generated by some conflict-of-interest revelations.

96. Nixon's much-heralded welfare reform program was not a very liberal measure. It provided only moderately increased benefits for the average poor family in the South, and no additional aid for the needy in most Northern cities. And, although more people would have been eligible to participate under Nixon's plan, the payments would have fallen far short of what was considered necessary for mere subsistence in most sections of the country. This controversial measure was subsequently killed in Congress by a coalition of liberal and conservative interests. See the *New York Times* (April 19, 1970), Sect. IV, p. 4; for a more sanguine account of this ill-fated Republican proposal, see Vincent J. and Vee Burke, *Nixon's Good Deed: Welfare Reform* (New York: Columbia University Press, 1974), passim.

97. See Nick Kotz, *Let Them Eat Promises: The Politics of Hunger in America* (Englewood Cliffs, N.J.: Prentice-Hall, 1969), p. 200.

98. See *Dun's Review* (December 1976), p. 94.

99. Mrs. Knauer was a former Philadelphia Republican leader and municipal official who had taken an active interest in consumer affairs at the local level of government. However, she did not play as prominent a role in this area as her two Democratic predecessors, Esther Peterson and Betty Furness, in part because the Nixon administration had little sympathy for the consumer cause. Another possible reason for Mrs. Knauer's rather ineffective performance in office may have stemmed from the fact that her daughter, Mrs. I. Townsend Burden III, had married into a rich family whose fortuné had been founded by former Pennsylvania industrialist Henry Clay Frick.

100. See the *New York Times* (October 23, 1971), p. 14.

101. Though seemingly a neutral figure, Boldt was, according to one recent study, a personal friend of some relatives of White House aide John Ehrlichman. See Arnold R. Weber and Daniel J. B. Mitchell, *The Pay Board's Progress: Wage Controls in Phase II* (Washington, D.C.: Brookings Institution, 1978), p. 25.

102. According to a recent Brookings study, the Pay Board gave scant attention to the question of corporate executive compensation, which rose at roughly twice the rate of salaried employees' pay in 1972—13.5 percent as contrasted with a little over 6 percent (the latter figure was more in consonance with the administration's prescribed goal of 5.5 percent). See Arnold R. Weber and Daniel J. B. Mitchell, *op. cit.*, pp. 107, 326–331, and 391–92.

103. Much of this money was to be channeled through a couple of President Nixon's longtime close associates, Murray Chotiner and Herbert Kalmbach, a California lawyer who reportedly had already acted as the conduit for other funds given by these same parties to help kill an antitrust suit that had been instituted against some of the big milk co-ops.

104. See the *New York Times* (September 28, 1971), p. 38, (August 26, 1972), p. 24, and (May 3, 1974), pp. 1 and 28.

105. See the *New York Times* (February 24, 1970), p. 20, (March 1, 1970), p. 30, and (August 19, 1970), p. 38. Additional evidence of Nixon's strong pro-business orientation can be found in the types of persons he appointed to many of the independent regulatory commissions. For example, he selected former Goldwater aide Dean Burch to serve as chairman of the Federal Communications Commission. He chose a conservative New Hampshire lawyer, John Nassikas, to be head of the Federal Power Commission, although the latter's law firm had been general counsel to a local gas company. Moreover, in early 1973, after New York lawyer William Casey stepped down as chairman of the Securities and Exchange Commission, he was succeeded by a former Chicago attorney, G. Bradford Cook, who, prior to joining the SEC staff in 1971, had been a partner in the big corporate law firm of Winston & Strawn. Cook had also married into the wealthy Armour (meat-packing) family, and his father was president of the Bankers Life Insurance Co. of Nebraska and a director of the Keebler Co. and Philadelphia Suburban Water Co. When Cook was forced to resign from office later in 1973 because of his illicit action in behalf of financier Robert Vesco, he was replaced by another well-connected Chicago attorney, Ray Garrett. This official had been a partner in the influential law firm of Gardner, Carton & Douglas, and had served briefly in the early 1970s on the board of the big Chicago, Milwaukee, St. Paul & Pacific Railroad, which, according to one business journal, had engaged in some financially deceptive practices which the SEC, perhaps because of its new chairman, chose not to investigate. See *Forbes* (June 15, 1975), pp. 19–20.

106. At that time Middle Eastern oil cost about $2.00 per barrel as compared to $3.30 for that produced in America. See *Time* (January 26, 1970), p. 69. For an analysis of the way in which this system was operating in the early 1970s, much to the satisfaction of America's biggest international oil companies and to the general detriment of various lesser (crude oil-short) concerns, see Fred C. Allvine and James M. Patterson, *Highway Robbery: An Analysis of the Gasoline Crisis* (Bloomington: Indiana University Press, 1974), pp. 119–122 and 132–133, in particular.

107. Another program in which there was some change even earlier in the Nixon administration was that of the hotly disputed oil depletion allowance which, thanks apparently to industry pressure, had been pegged at a rather arbitrary 27.5 percent back in 1926. In the late 1960s, after the voting public had become aroused by some startling revelations concerning certain other major tax loopholes, the oil depletion allowance became the target of various reformers in Congress, who wanted to drastically reduce, if not eliminate, this dubious provision. After much negotiation and maneuver, a bill was passed in 1969 which pushed the oil depletion allowance down to 22 percent. But this act was not a very impressive achievement, for by this time the politically astute oil industry was reportedly ready to accept some "reasonable" decrease in this lucrative federal subsidy. For more on this matter, see Bruce I. Oppenheimer, *Oil and the Congressional Process*, pp. 124–30.

108. See Robert Engler, *The Brotherhood of Oil* (Chicago: University of Chicago Press, 1977), p. 90.

109. Shultz was firmly backed in this affair by Secretary of the Treasury David M. Kennedy and George A. Lincoln, the director of the Office of Emergency Preparedness. Two other members of the task force's majority, William Rogers and Melvin Laird, recommended consultation with other countries before any new policy was instituted. The two Cabinet officials opposed to the abolition of the existing oil import quota system were Walter Hickel and Maurice Stans. (See the *New York Times*, February 21, 1970, p. 1.) While Shultz and Kennedy were Establishment figures, neither had any overt ties with oil interests. Hickel and Stans did have such connections, although the latter's were indirect.

110. See Morton Mintz and Jerry S. Cohen, *America, Inc.* (New York: Dial, 1971), pp. 247–49.

111. See Engler, *op. cit.*, p. 94.

112. See the *New York Times* (October 14, 1973), Sect. VI, p. 102.

113. By the early 1970s British Petroleum owned or indirectly controlled about 55 percent of the oil land in the Prudhoe Bay area, and Atlantic Richfield and Standard Oil of New Jersey (or Exxon, as it has been known since November 1972) each had 20 percent. The remaining 5 percent was held by several other large companies, such as Amerada Hess, Mobil Oil, Phillips Petroleum, and the Union Oil Co. of California.

114. As the *New York Times* put it, "fearing what the courts might do if they looked behind the inadequate environmental impact statement issued in behalf of the pipelines by Secretary of the Interior Morton, the oil industry fought hard for the amendment offered by Senator Gravel of Alaska to forbid any judicial review..." of this issue. See the *New York Times* (July 18, 1973), p. 36.

115. As previously noted, Morton had served for many years prior to his appointment as Secretary of the Interior as a director of the fairly large Atlas Chemical Industries, along with Thornton Bradshaw, the president of the Atlantic Richfield Co. Hence one might assume that these two men were on good terms. For more on Morton's pro-oil voting record in the House of Representatives, see Oppenheimer, *Oil and the Congressional Process*, pp. 28 and 124.

116. Shortly thereafter, as a result of the energy crisis precipitated by the OPEC oil embargo, the Nixon administration created a special Federal Energy Office in the White House. The agency was headed, for brief spans, by a number of rather diverse figures, of whom the most prominent was former Deputy Secretary of the Treasury (and New York bond executive) William E. Simon. Though it was in operation for only a relatively short period before Nixon was forced to resign from office, this agency recruited over 100 figures from the oil industry to serve in various important capacities. This rather striking number is a reflection of both the expertise and influence possessed by this sector of the economy. For an overall list and description of these ex-oil company officials, see Norman Medvin, et al., *The Energy Cartel: Big Oil vs. the Public Interest* (New York: Marine Engineers' Beneficial Association, 1975), pp. 60–72.

117. For an interesting account of the overall development of this concern, see Anthony

Sampson, *The Sovereign State of ITT* (Greenwich, Conn.: Fawcett, 1974), pp. 13–151.

118. McLaren had been a partner in the fairly sizable Chicago law firm of Chadwick, Keck, Kayser, Ruggles & McLaren, which specialized in defending large corporations in antitrust suits, and may therefore have leaned toward a pro-Establishment point of view in this area. That is to say, he may have had grave doubts about the recent rise of conglomerate concerns, most of which were headed by economic "outsiders" such as Harold Geneen, who, though a New York executive, did not serve on any major corporate boards. For more on this subject, see Anthony Sampson, *op. cit.*, pp 153 and 167.

119. For a detailed account of this revealing exchange, see Robert M. Goolrick, *Public Policy Toward Corporate Growth: The ITT Merger Cases*, pp. 120–121.

120. Mitchell later claimed that when he met with Geneen in late 1970 they merely talked about antitrust policy in general terms, but as Anthony Sampson has pointed out, since three of the four major cases pending involved ITT, "... it would have been hard *not* to refer to them...." (*op. cit.,* pp. 238–39). An even more dubious merger involving two directly competitive companies—the Warner-Lambert Pharmaceutical Co. (which had long been headed by President Nixon's close friend, Elmer Bobst), and Parke, Davis & Co.—was permitted to go through without a formal challenge by the Nixon administration in 1970, despite the fact that the Antitrust Division of the Justice Department had strongly recommended filing suit against such action. See the *New York Times* (November 26, 1970), p. 1.

121. See Anthony Sampson, *op. cit.,* p. 209, and the *New York Times* (October 30, 1973), pp. 1 and 33. Perhaps more than anything else, Sampson's intriguing account of the many contacts between ITT and the Nixon administration demonstrates the importance of political "access," a concept first stressed in David Truman's much-cited book, *The Governmental Process.*

122. The Ramdsen report was hardly an in-depth analysis of the subject since it was written in just two days for a fee of $242. See Anthony Sampson, *op. cit.*, p. 232, and Leonard Lurie, *The Running of Richard Nixon* (New York: Coward, McCann & Geoghegan, 1972), p. 378. Furthermore, Ramdsen had worked for Dillon, Read & Co. when Flanigan was affiliated with this Wall Street firm, and Ramsden's present employer, an almost unknown concern, depended on ITT for a good deal of its business.

123. This convention aid arrangement was reputedly made through one of ITT's Washington lobbyists, Dita Beard, who, once word of the deal leaked out, suddenly disappeared from the nation's capital, only to turn up later in a Denver hospital, suffering, according to her physician, from "impending coronary thrombosis." Interestingly, it was G. Gordon Liddy who, according to former White House aide Robert Mardian, whisked "...Dita Beard out of Washington to a Denver hospital." See Anthony Sampson, *op. cit.*, pp. 207–08 and 288.

124. In 1970, when Chile came under Allende's rule, America's private investment in that mineral-rich state represented roughly two-thirds of the overall total of $1.67 billion owned by outside interests. In all, United States firms controlled about 80 percent of Chile's copper production, which, in turn, accounted for a like percentage of that country's foreign trade revenue. See the U.S. Senate, Select Committee to Study Governmental Operations with Respect to Intelligence Activities, *Covert Action in Chile, 1963–1973* (Washington, D.C.: Government Printing Office, 1975), p. 32

125. In 1970 the CIA had spent nearly $1 million covertly in an effort to secure the election of a more conservative candidate. ITT contributed about $350,000 to the cause of Allende's major opponent, Jorge Allessandri, and a similar sum was donated by other American concerns with substantial operations in Chile. During this campaign ITT representatives met frequently with CIA officials both in Chile and in the United States to discuss how ITT might discreetly channel its funds into Alessandri's hands. In addition, the Anaconda Co., which had huge holdings in Chile, offered to funnel at least $500,000 through the State Department in support of such endeavors. However, this agency refused to go along with the idea. See the U.S. Senate Select Committee, *Covert Action in Chile*, pp. 13 and 20–21, and the *New York Times* (December 24, 1976), p. A3.

126. Some idea as to the nature of the CIA's activities in 1970 can be derived from the fact that between October 5 and October 20 its operatives made 21 contacts with key military and *Carabinero* (police) officials in Chile. See the U.S. Senate Select Committee, *op. cit.*, p. 26.

127. See the *New York Times* (July 3, 1972), p. 3.

128. McCone reportedly continued to act, allegedly unknown even to Harold Geneen, as a consultant to the CIA while he served as a director of ITT. For a summary description of many of the contacts between ITT and the CIA, see Anthony Sampson, *op. cit.*, pp. 259–83.

129. See the U.S. Senate Select Committee, *op. cit.*, pp. 32–33. In another somewhat similar action, ITT was also able to get the Nixon administration to withhold $21 million in loans for Ecuador in 1971 and 1972, after it had seized this company's All American Cables and Radio subsidiary in that country. Indeed, according to one high federal official, ITT's lobbyist Jack Neal didn't even "...ask us to hold stuff up—he'd order us to do it." See *Business Week* (August 11, 1973), pp. 102–103, and the *New York Times* (August 10, 1973), p. 37.

130. For example, the 40 Committee authorized the allocation of more than $1.5 million to Chile's largest opposition newspaper, *El Mercurio*, which was published by a wealthy Santiago businessman named Augustin Edwards, who also served, interestingly, as a vice-president of Pepsico in the early 1970s. This transaction was apparently arranged at a quiet breakfast meeting in Washington between Edwards, Henry Kissinger, and Attorney General John Mitchell, which was reportedly set up by President Nixon's close friend Donald Kendall, who was the head of Pepsico. Some of the funds to support striking truck owners, shopkeepers, and professional groups in Chile also came from wealthy local businessmen. See the *New York Times* (December 5, 1975), p. 10, (September 20, 1974), p. 1, and (October 16, 1974), p. 8.

131. See the U.S. Senate Select Committee, *op. cit.*, pp. 1, 28, and 37.

132. The pro-business orientation of Chile's junta-dominated government may be seen not only in its reliance on the advice of Milton Friedmanite economists, but in the appointment of its first Minister of Economy, Development, and Reconstruction, Fernando Leniz, who had been a high official of the Edwards-owned newspaper, *El Mercurio*, and also served on the board of the Chilean subsidiary of the Rockefeller-controlled International Basic Economy Corp. Moreover, by the late 1970s the junta leaders had sold off all but 15 of the almost 500 companies that had been nationalized by the Allende government and had attracted at least $2.5 billion in foreign investments, a good deal of which was provided by such American concerns as Exxon, Atlantic Richfield, General Motors, and the Goodyear Tire & Rubber Co. See Richard E. Ratcliff, "Capitalists in Crisis: The Chilean Upper Class and the September 11 Coup," *Latin American Perspectives* (Summer 1974), pp. 79–81; *Forbes* (October 30, 1978), p. 148; *Business Week* (May 21, 1979), p. 55; Orlando Letelier, "Economic Freedom's Awful Toll: The 'Chicago Boys' in Chile," *Review of Radical Political Economics* (Fall 1976), pp. 44–52; Maurice Zeitlin, Lynda Ann Ewen, and Richard E. Ratcliff, "'New Princes' for Old? The Large Corporation and the Capitalist Class in Chile," *American Journal of Sociology* (July 1974), pp. 87–121; Robert J. Alexander, *The Tragedy of Chile* (Westport, Conn.; Greenwood Press, 1978), pp. 396–413; and the *New York Times* (October 14, 1979), p. A7.

133. See the *New York Times* (May 9, 1976), Sect. 7, p. 7.

134. Initially this committee was composed of eight business or civic figures—its chairman, Francis Dale, who was a Cincinnati newspaper publisher (and a director of the First National Bank of Cincinnati); Frank Borman, an ex-astronaut who now served as a senior vice-president of Eastern Airlines; Max M. Fisher, a Detroit real estate magnate (who was a director of the Fruehauf Corp., Owens-Illinois, Inc., Michigan Consolidated Gas Co., Manufacturers National Bank of Detroit, and Michigan Bell Telephone Co.); Rita Hauser, a New York City lawyer, Republican party activist, and U.S. delegate to the United Nations; J. Erik Jonsson, the former longtime head of Texas Instruments (who still served on the board of the New York-based Equitable Life Assurance Society and the Republic National Bank of Dallas); Thomas A. Pappas, an influential Greek-American entrepreneur; Donald Schollander, a former famous Olympic swimmer who now worked as a college administrator; and Robert H. Volk, the president of Unionamerica, Inc. (a big Los Angeles–based bank holding company), who had

been a member of the same law firm as Nixon in the early 1960s. Only two of these individuals, Fisher and Jonsson, could be classified as Establishment figures.

135. The make-up of the latter group is, unfortunately, not readily available. However, according to the *New York Times* (see its September 8, 1973 issue, p. 27), the initial vice chairman of this body was Daniel S. Parker, the head of the medium-sized Parker Pen Co., who had been closely linked with the arch-conservative NAM, and to a lesser extent with the CED. The long-constituted Republican National Finance Committee had relatively few Establishment-oriented figures on its executive committee at this time. Its most prominent members were Max Fisher; Nixon's close friend, Donald Kendall, the president of Pepsico; Richard M. Scaife, who was a member of the rich, highly conservative Mellon family, a director of the Mellon National Bank & Trust Co., and a board member of the Hoover Institution; and Jeremiah Milbank, Jr., who was the head of the Commercial Solvents Corp., a director of the Chase Manhattan Bank (an ideologically curious link), and a former avid Goldwater supporter. Some of its lesser-known members were Greek junta backer Thomas A. Pappas; William C. Leidtke, Jr., the president of the big Texas-based Pennzoil Co.; W. Clement Stone, the chief executive of Chicago's Combined Insurance Co. of America; and Kenneth H. Dahlberg, the head of a probably small, Minnesota-based concern known as Dahlberg Electronics, Inc.

136. For a list of the (thus far revealed) illicit corporate contributions in the 1972 presidential campaign, see Herbert E. Alexander, *Financing the 1972 Election*, pp. 708–710. During one part of this period, the Nixon campaign was taking in an average of $100,000 a day. Numerous excesses reportedly occurred in the course of this drive. Both Mitchell and Stans were later tried in federal court for accepting a $250,000 contribution from American international financier Robert Vesco in a covert attempt to quash an SEC investigation of some of his piratical business practices. Both men were acquitted for want of sufficient evidence. A year later Stans did plead guilty to five charges of violating the nation's campaign finance laws and was fined $5,000, a modest sum for a man of his wealth.

137. LaRue's long-deceased father was a first cousin of Texas oil magnate Sid Richardson, and, apparently with some help from the latter source, the family had been able to build up a fortune of about $30 million by the late 1960s. See the *New York Times* (June 28, 1973), p. 37.

138. See the *New York Times* (July 20, 1973), p. 10. Although Mardian himself was a former lawyer and savings and loan association official, his family had made its fortune primarily through a contracting business which generally grossed over $20 million a year.

139. See Donald L. Bartlett and James B. Steele, *Empire: The Life, Legend, and Madness of Howard Hughes* (New York: Norton, 1979), pp. 460–62.

140. G. Gordon Liddy rushed out to the Burning Tree Golf Club to tell Attorney General Richard Kleindienst that John Mitchell wanted the Watergate burglars to be released from jail because some of them might be connected with either the White House or CREEP. Kleindienst apparently did not believe Liddy and did not accede to his request. Yet, although he was the chief law enforcement officer in the land, Kleindienst did not reveal this important piece of information to the Watergate prosecutors until under pressure at a much later date, thereby impeding the investigation.

141. Although Leonard Garment, one of Nixon's former New York law partners, formally replaced John Dean as counsel to the President, the real legal problems relating to Watergate were entrusted to J. Fred Buzhardt, who, like many of Nixon's loyal supporters, was a conservative Southern Rim figure. His father had been a close friend and former law partner of South Carolina Senator J. Strom Thurmond, and he himself had worked for eight years on the Senator's staff (see the *New York Times*, June 29, 1973, p. 27). As Haldeman's successor, Nixon shrewdly chose a man who, as a Kissinger deputy, had demonstrated his administrative and political loyalty, General Alexander Haig. Former Cabinet member Melvin Laird was appointed to take over Ehrlichman's position.

142. According to one account, President Nixon actually offered his two departing aides "... between $200,000 and $300,000 in cash, nominally for legal fees and family support, but

presumably also to guarantee their continued silence on matters which could damage him." They rejected the offer. See J. Anthony Lukas, *op. cit.*, p. 336.

143. Henry Peterson, a longtime career official who now served as Assistant Attorney General in charge of the Criminal Division, had, for example, worked to ensure that the Watergate investigation would be confined to extremely narrow limits, and had kept President Nixon fully informed of all major developments in the case, thereby helping the administration to stay one step ahead of the probe. See J. Anthony Lukas, *op. cit.*, pp. 246–47 and 321–34.

144. Although Cox had gone to the elitist St. Paul's prep school and had once worked briefly (before World War II) for a Boston Brahmin law firm, he had spent the bulk of his adult life working in a purely academic capacity. His only noteworthy socio-economic tie was that forged through the recent marriage of his son, Archibald Cox, Jr., to the daughter of Dale E. Sharp, a former high official of the Morgan Guaranty Trust Co., and an active director of the big American Smelting and Refining Co. and the Continental Corp. His son became a partner in the investment banking firm of Morgan, Stanley & Co. just a few months before Cox was appointed Watergate special prosecutor. However, unlike some writers, the author is not inclined to place much weight on this set of links because he believes that Cox's university affiliation was of a much more important and enduring nature.

145. In the early 1970s, shortly before his appointment as Solicitor General, Bork was an adjunct scholar at the American Enterprise Institute for Public Policy Research, to which rightist organization he returned in 1977, upon the completion of his federal service.

146. Though Jaworski was formally chosen by Bork, the President clearly exercised great influence in the matter. Indeed, as Anthony Lukas put it, "...the White House wanted Jaworski very badly," despite the fact that Jaworski was a well-known Democrat and acknowledged ally of Lyndon Johnson. See J. Anthony Lukas, *op. cit.*, pp. 445–46.

147. Jaworski also served, apparently on a part-time basis, as a special assistant to the U.S. Attorney General from 1962 to 1965, but this was his only significant experience in the federal government.

148. On March 1, 1974, the grand jury, convened by the Special Prosecutor's Office, handed down its long-awaited indictments of seven men—White House special counsel Charles Colson, John Ehrlichman, H. R. Haldeman, Robert Mardian, John Mitchell, CREEP's recently retained attorney Kenneth Parkinson, and Nixon aide Gordon Strachan. They were charged with various counts of conspiracy, perjury, and obstruction of justice. On January 1, 1975, after a long trial, all but three were found guilty of the offenses with which they had been charged (the case against Colson was dropped when he pleaded guilty to obstructing justice in the so-called Daniel Ellsberg–Pentagon Papers case). The three principal defendants—Ehrlichman, Haldeman, and Mitchell—were each sentenced to prison terms of two and a half to eight years. Thus John Mitchell became the second Cabinet member and first Attorney General in American history to be sent to prison.

149. By this time President Nixon had retained Boston attorney James D. St. Clair to take the place of the rather inept Fred Buzhardt as his special Watergate counsel. The steely St. Clair was a member of a fairly prominent firm known as Hale & Dorr, some of whose partners had major corporate connections. However, St. Clair himself had no such links, and he was apparently hired because he was generally considered to be one of the best trial lawyers in the country.

150. Justice William Rehnquist abstained from this decision because of his recent association with the Nixon administration.

151. The first three great scandals in American political history were, unlike Watergate, all related to the opening or expansion of some highly profitable or potentially valuable segment of the nation's economy, be it land (the famous Yazoo title fraud), railroads (the Crédit Mobilier affair), or oil (the Teapot Dome scandal). Watergate was the first major political scandal to involve essentially a gross abuse of governmental power, an ultimately more serious matter.

152. One member of Jaworski's staff had prepared a lengthy memorandum which concluded that there was no constitutional or legal precedent which explicitly barred a grand jury from indicting a sitting President, although there was a serious question about the institutional "propriety" of such a move. Jaworski ruled out the idea of naming Nixon as an unindicted co-conspirator, of making a "presentment" naming Nixon (a statement which is similar to an indictment in that it exposes wrongdoing, but does not initiate a criminal prosecution against the accused), or even of issuing a report to the grand jury summarizing the evidence that had been collected. This decision created a furor within the Special Prosecutor's Office. For more on this matter and the rather weak compromise that was worked out, indirectly indicating Nixon's obvious guilt, see Richard Ben-Veniste and George Frampton, Jr.; *Stonewall: The Real Story of the Watergate Prosecution* (New York: Simon & Schuster, 1977), pp. 211–254.

153. See Ben-Veniste and Frampton, *op. cit.*, p. 250, and Leon Jaworski, *The Right and the Power* (New York: Readers' Digest Press, 1976), p. 224. Jaworski also permitted Attorney General Richard Kleindienst to plead guilty to a relatively minor misdemeanor charge, which clearly did not apply to his obvious act of perjury, and thereby escape with a miniscule penalty of a $100 fine and 30 days in jail, both of which were suspended. In addition, at one point Jaworski agreed "in principle" to permit John Ehrlichman to plead guilty to a single charge in the Ellsberg case (although, ironically, Ehrlichman himself later broke off these negotiations). See Ben-Veniste and Frampton, *op. cit.*, p. 234.

154. See the *New York Times* (October 16, 1974), p. 43, and also Richard Ben-Veniste and George Frampton, Jr., *op. cit.*, pp. 291–315.

155. See Kirkpatrick Sale, *Power Shift*, p. 287.

156. For more on Owen Roberts' role in the Teapot Dome investigation, see Volume II of *Elites in American History*.

157. Most of the people Ford appointed to serve as his chief White House aides did not have elitist links either. However, there were a few exceptions. For instance, one of Ford's most important advisors was his close friend and onetime law partner, Philip Buchen, who, in addition to serving on the board of a couple of local business concerns, had been a (non-public) director of the Communications Satellite Corp. from 1969 to 1974, when he became chief counsel to the President. Though only a Grand Rapids attorney, Buchen's firm (of Law, Buchen, Weathers, Richardson & Dutcher) managed to attract as clients such big concerns as the Ford Motor Co., U.S. Steel Corp., and Chesapeake & Ohio Railway. Another influential White House aide was L. William Seidman, who was a wealthy Grand Rapids accountant (his firm ranked in the top fifteen in the country) and longtime intimate friend of President Ford. See the *New York Times* (August 19, 1974), p. 38 and (September 2, 1976), p. 1.

158. Kirkpatrick Sale, for example, contends (see *Power Shift* pp. 109 and 294–304) that Ford was a major cog in the "Yankee [Establishment] counterattack" on the "cowboy"-dominated Nixon administration, both because of his various legal and personal ties and because he chose New York's Nelson A. Rockefeller as his Vice President. Though he was an able man, Rockefeller's power as Vice President was distinctly limited, and he was dropped from the Republican ticket in 1976 because it was felt that his liberal image and the threat posed to Ford's candidacy by his arch-conservative rival Ronald Reagan would make him a liability to Ford's reelection campaign. That Ford himself was not really an anti-Southern Rim figure may be seen from the fact that the three men who served as manager of his 1976 presidential primary and general election campaign were drawn from the nation's lower tier. They were the recently resigned Secretary of the Army Howard H. Callaway (a rich Georgia textile heir), former Cabinet member Rogers C. B. Morton (a onetime Maryland Congressman and Kentucky businessman who, up to his entry into the Nixon administration, had two major directorship ties outside the Southern tier), and Under Secretary of Commerce James A. Baker III (who prior to his assumption of this federal post had been a partner in the big Houston corporate law firm of Andrews, Kurth, Campbell & Jones).

159. See the *New York Times* (August 19, 1974), p. 1 and (November 17, 1974), Sect. 3,

p. 1. There was reportedly one exception to this pattern of second-tier ties, and that was California industrialist David Packard, who became a close friend of Ford when he served as Deputy Secretary of Defense during the early years of the Nixon administration. By the time Ford became President, Packard was chairman of the Business Council, a member of the policy committee of the Business Roundtable, a trustee of the CED, and a member of the Trilateral Commission. However, Packard also served on the board of the highly conservative Hoover Institution. See *Dun's Review* (December 1976), p. 94.

160. One of the most serious questions raised by this practice is that of favorable access to governmental power. Indeed, as the Ford's Rodney Markley himself admitted, "I have talked to him [Gerald Ford] about legislative matters of general interest on the golf course and elsewhere. For example, he would say to me, 'Rod, how is the Clean Air Act coming?' " Yet, as many critics have observed, Ford did not play golf with Ralph Nader and, between strokes, casually discuss consumer affairs. Nor did he so associate with the head of the Sierra Club when environmental legislation was under consideration. See the *New York Times* (October 12, 1976), p. 21.

161. A number of Kissinger's major State Department appointments would appear to have been made with an eye to closing this gap with the nation's chief economic leaders. For example, Kissinger's top aide during most of the Ford years was a former big businessman, Robert S. Ingersoll, who had served from 1972 to 1974 as the American Ambassador to Japan. Prior to his assumption of this diplomatic post, Ingersoll had been the head of the Borg-Warner Corp., a longtime board member of several big Chicago-based concerns, a recently elected director of the Atlantic Richfield Co., and (until 1972) an active member of the Business Council. When he stepped down as Deputy Secretary of State, he was replaced by another elitist figure, Charles W. Robinson, who had served briefly (in the mid-1970s) as Under Secretary of State for Economic Affairs, but had spent most of his career as a major executive of the Marcona Corp., which was jointly controlled by two big concerns, the Cyprus Mines Corp. and Utah International, Inc. However, the primary reason Robinson was appointed to these State Department posts was probably that he had been a member of the Trilateral Commission. Most of the other high officials in the State Department were career diplomats, such as Under Secretary of State for Political Affairs Joseph Sisco (although this official's wife served on the board of such big concerns as Textron in the mid-1970s).

162. Shortly after Simon returned to private life, he was asked by *Reader's Digest* to write a book about his views on business and government. With the hired help of one of Ayn Rand's economic disciples, Edith Efron, he soon completed this work, which was entitled *A Time for Truth*, and contained a preface by Milton Friedman and a foreword by Friedrich A. Hayek. (See the *New York Times*, November 19, 1978, Sect. VII, p. 88.) By the late 1970s Simon not only held a number of major corporate directorships, but also served on the board of the Hoover Institution.

163. Shortly before the end of his term of office, Butz was forced to resign because of an off-the-cuff racist remark.

164. Two men served as Deputy Secretary of Defense during this period. The first was Texas oilman William P. Clements, Jr., a Nixon appointee. When he resigned in the first part of 1976, he was replaced by Assistant Secretary of Defense for International Security Affairs Robert Ellsworth, who was a former (1969–1971) Ambassador to NATO and onetime (1961–1967) Kansas Congressman. However, it should be noted that upon his return from his NATO assignment, Ellsworth had become the president of the Lazard Frères International Corp., and a director of the Allied Chemical Corp. and Kinney National Services, Inc. (a rapidly growing conglomerate).

165. Since his abrupt exit from the Nixon administration, Richardson had bolstered his elite links by becoming a member of the newly formed Trilateral Commission and a director of the Establishment-dominated Council on Foreign Relations.

166. This concern, which was known as the Compania de Desarollo Turistico, Residencial

e Industrial, S.A., was headed by New York lawyer and labor mediator Theodore Kheel. Both Dunlop and Meany had reportedly only a minor stake in this enterprise. See the *Newark Star-Ledger* (February 13, 1975), p. 9.

167. Although it apparently went unnoticed, in mid-1975 President Ford appointed someone essentially from the ranks of big business to serve as Under Secretary of Labor, namely Robert O. Aders, who, up to the preceding year (when he became a member of a fairly small Washington law firm), had been board chairman of the Kroger Co., an Ohio-based merchandising concern which had assets of a little over $1 billion.

168. See the *Newark Star-Ledger* (August 9, 1975), p. 1.

169. Up to his election as governor in 1967, Hathaway had been a member of a small Torrington law firm which, according to the *Martindale-Hubbell Law Directory*, included among its "representative clients" such economic interests as the Champlin Oil & Refining Co., Skiles Oil Corp., and Southern Petroleum Exploration, Inc. (the last two of which were fairly small concerns).

170. One of the factors which reportedly had much to do with Hathaway's extremely brief stay in office was the pressure exerted by the White House to have him appoint Dr. William S. Banowsky, who was a fundamentalist minister, the president of a small college, and a reputed fundraiser for California's rightist Governor Ronald Reagan, as Under Secretary of the Interior, a post for which he was clearly unqualified. See the *New York Times* (July 26, 1975), p. 10.

171. See the *New York Times* (September 4, 1975), p. 28.

172. About eight months after Mrs. Hills's appointment, her husband was appointed chairman of the Securities and Exchange Commission where, according to one newspaper account, he did much to "defang" this important agency. See the *New York Times* (April 18, 1976), Sect. III, p. 1.

173. As indicated earlier, Coleman had also served as a member of Nixon's specially constituted Price Commission and an ancillary advisory body, the National Commission on Productivity and Work Quality, in the early 1970s, which put him in contact with various important people.

174. While apparently an able man, Coleman was also a black man, another consideration which may have influenced his Cabinet selection.

175. An important figure in foreign (and at times domestic) affairs was William E. Colby, who was appointed director of the CIA in early 1973 after Richard Helms stepped down from office under a cloud of suspicion. Colby was a longtime federal official, having served with the CIA for more than a decade and for nearly as long before that as a diplomatic aide. When Colby relinquished the CIA directorship in 1975 after a highly critical Congressional investigation of the agency's activity, he was replaced by America's recent emissary to Red China, former Texas oilman George Bush.

176. The President first offered this prestigious post to Arkansas' wealthy Democratic Senator J. William Fulbright, who had long taken a very active role in foreign affairs in the Upper House. However, because of his wife's poor health, Fulbright could not accept the position. See the *New York Times* (December 14, 1974), p. 1.

177. The World Bank was still headed during the 1970s by former Secretary of Defense and onetime Ford Motor Co. executive Robert McNamara, a primarily technocratic figure. The Export-Import Bank of the United States was directed up to the mid-1970s by William J. Casey, a former politically oriented New York City lawyer who had recently acted as chairman of the SEC and as Under Secretary of State for Economic Affairs. In December 1975 Casey was replaced by a more elite figure, Stephen M. DuBrul, Jr., who had been a partner in both Lazard Frères and Lehman Brothers and a director of the General Dynamics Corp., Jewel Companies, Inc. (a big merchandising concern), RCA Corp., and Signal Companies, Inc. (a major oil enterprise).

178. See *Fortune* (August 1, 1969), p. 113.

179. Mrs. Armstrong was evidently elected to the last two boards at too late a point in 1975 to be included as a director of these companies in *Moody's Industrial Manual*, and resigned too early in 1976, because of her ambassadorial appointment, to be listed in the 1976 volume. For confirmation of these corporate ties, see the *New York Times* (January 6, 1976), p. 6.

180. As his first Ambassador to NATO, President Ford picked a very able and experienced figure, David K. E. Bruce, who had held a number of major diplomatic posts over the years, the most recent of which were as U.S. representative to the Vietnam peace talks in 1971–1972 and as the American (pre-recognition) liaison officer to Communist China in 1972–1974. Like many such officials, Bruce was a wealthy patrician whose family had many important ties. He was succeeded in this position in early 1976 by former University of Pennsylvania political science professor (and recent diplomatic emissary) Robert Strausz-Hupe, a staunch conservative, perhaps in part because his wife came from a rich and well-established Philadelphia family. In fact, up to his death in the early 1920s, her father, T. DeWitt Cuyler, had been the general counsel of the Pennsylvania Railroad and a director of the Bankers Trust Co. (of New York), Equitable Life Assurance Society, Equitable Trust Co. (of New York), Girard Trust Co. (of Philadelphia), Guaranty Trust Co. (of New York), Western Union Telegraph Co., and Atchison, Topeka & Santa Fe Railway.

181. According to one source (see the *New York Times*, August 22, 1976, Sect. 3, p. 1), Greenspan probably exerted more influence in the White House than any CEA chairman in the postwar period. A number of other important non-Cabinet posts in the Ford administration were also filled by men who had a pro-business orientation. For example, the director of the Office of Management and Budget was, after the resignation of Roy Ash in December 1974, a relatively young Cleveland attorney named James T. Lynn, who had served for a little over two years as Secretary of Housing and Urban Development, and before that as a high official in the Department of Commerce. However, Lynn had spent most of his adult life working as a member of a major Cleveland corporate law firm—Jones, Day, Cockley & Reavis—which represented many big business concerns in northern Ohio, one of the most prominent of which was the Hanna Mining Co.

182. See Robert Engler, *The Brotherhood of Oil*, passim, especially p. 197, and for general background, his earlier work, *The Politics of Oil* (Chicago: University of Chicago Press, 1961), passim. For a somewhat different, less polemical line of analysis by a respected economist, see John M. Blair, *The Control of Oil*, passim.

183. In case there is any doubt that the Morton brothers were on fairly close terms, one need only note that when Rogers C. B. Morton entered Nixon's Cabinet in 1970, his place as a director of the Pillsbury Co. was quickly taken by his brother.

184. See the *New York Times* (April 26, 1974), p. 16, and *Fortune* (February 1966), p. 70. Upon retirement, Stott formed his own business concern, the Stott Capital Development Corp., and through this firm continued to take an active part in various oil enterprises. Stott also served as a director of the Foreign Policy Association up to the early 1970s. Pappas was reportedly an important backer of the then powerful Greek junta and a close friend of America's ambassador to that country. For more on Thomas Pappas's ties, see the *New York Times* (April 26, 1974), p. 16, (August 2, 1974), p. 2, and (December 19, 1975), p. 27, *Business Week* (July 28, 1973), p. 72, *Time* (February 14, 1969), p. 86, and Constantine Tsoucalas, *The Greek Tragedy*, p. 206.

185. Simon later admitted that he had extensive economic (presumably stockownership) interests in the oil and gas industry when he entered the Nixon administration; these were apparently placed in a blind trust. See the *New York Times* (May 27, 1979), Sect. 3, p. 11.

186. Thanks largely to the creation of OPEC, there was another important action taken in this area, for in 1975 the oil depletion allowance was repealed for the nation's major oil companies. In addition, limits were imposed on the amount which smaller firms could claim, with the depletion allowance for these concerns being gradually phased down to 15 percent. However, by the mid-1970s, oil industry opposition to such steps had lessened considerably.

See Robert Engler, *The Brotherhood of Oil*, p. 211.

187. See Robert Engler, *op. cit.*, pp. 206–07, and the *New York Times* (October 31, 1974), p. 33.

188. President Ford originally planned to replace Sawhill with Andrew E. Gibson, who, prior to his recent appointment as federal Maritime Administrator, had been the president of the fairly small Interstate Oil Transport Co. But this nomination had to be withdrawn when it was discovered that this concern was half-owned by the giant Cities Service Co., and that Gibson had an unusually lucrative severance agreement with his former company, which assured him of $100,000 a year for the next decade.

189. See the *New York Times* (November 16, 1975), p. 1, and (March 7, 1976), Sect. III, p. 3. This group has also been given credit for playing a major role in keeping a bill calling for an audit of the Federal Reserve System bottled up in the House Rules Committee, securing alterations in the recommendations of a national commission dealing with the government's water pollution control programs, and in persuading President Ford to announce in advance that he would veto any legislation which called for the establishment of a national consumer protection agency, thus effectively extinguishing all hopes for its adoption during his last years in office. For more on the work of this potent economic body and its recent employment of former Watergate Special Prosecutor Leon Jaworski as one of its legislative agents, see *Business Week* (December 20, 1976), pp. 60–63, and *Time* (July 4, 1977), p. 63.

190. This law, however, was soon substantially weakened by a Supreme Court ruling which allowed multiple damage suits only if the consumers had bought directly from the manufacturing concern, and not if they had purchased the company's goods from a middleman, such as a wholesaler or retailer. Since most transactions are handled in the latter fashion, this decree greatly reduced the effect of the law.

191. In 1953 Burger was made an Assistant Attorney General in the Justice Department, primarily because, as Harold E. Stassen's politically astute floor manager at the 1952 Republican National Convention, he had played a decisive role in the shift of the latter's Minnesota's favorite son delegation to Eisenhower at a critical point in his battle with Ohio Senator Robert A. Taft.

192. Nixon first attempted to appoint U.S. Circuit Court Judge Clement F. Haynsworth, Jr., who, since his appointment to this post in 1957, was generally considered to be a moderately able, though hardly distinguished, jurist. But this highly conservative South Carolinian ran into severe opposition, particularly in labor and liberal circles, because of an apparent conflict-of-interest in the early 1960s when as a federal judge he had participated in a case involving a subsidiary of a big anti-union textile enterprise known as Deering, Milliken, Inc. This concern, along with J. P. Stevens & Co. (another labor-hostile firm), provided considerable business for a small company, the Carolina Vend-a-Matic Co., with which Haynsworth himself was associated as an officer, director, and stockholder up to 1963, when because of a recent ruling by the U.S. Judicial Conference he was compelled to sever this connection. Haynsworth's former law firm had long represented a number of textile concerns, insurance companies, and other interests in the South, the most important of which were the big Daniel Construction Co. and J. P. Stevens & Co. Haynsworth also served on the board of the fairly large Liberty Life Insurance Co. and the much smaller Southern Weaving Co. up to around 1960. After a bitter protracted battle, Haynsworth was rejected by the Senate by a vote of 55 to 45. Stung by this rebuff, Nixon turned to U.S. District Court Judge G. Harrold Carswell of Florida, who, it was soon discovered, had a background which included a number of racist incidents. In addition, Carswell, who had married into an economically prominent Tallahassee family, was a mediocre jurist; indeed, he had one of the highest rates of appellate court reversals of any federal judge in the nation. As a result, Carswell's nomination was rejected too. See the *New York Times* (August 16, 1969), p. 10 and (September 17, 1969), p. 26, and U.S. Senate, Committee on the Judiciary, 91st Congress, 1st Session, *Hearings on the Nomination of Clement F. Haynsworth, Jr.* (Washington, D.C.: U.S. Government Printing Office, 1969), pp. 65–128 and 334–36.

193. These two jurists had been friends since childhood. They had attended the same elementary school and Sunday school in St. Paul, and Blackmun had been Burger's best man at the latter's wedding in 1933. See Louis M. Kohlmeier, Jr., *God Save This Honorable Court* (New York: Scribner's, 1972), p. 169.

194. For an incisive, though depressing account of the search proceedings, see James F. Simon, *In His Own Image: The Supreme Court in Richard Nixon's America* (New York: McKay, 1973), pp. 216–228.

195. Powell also served as a director of some smaller companies and as a trustee of the (Rockefeller-backed) Colonial Williamsburg Foundation. In fact, he maintained his affiliation with this prestigious civic enterprise after his appointment to the High Court, and in 1974 he was elected board chairman of Colonial Williamsburg.

196. See the *New York Times* (March 14, 1976), Sect. 3, p. 5.

197. See Abraham, *Justices and Presidents*, p. 11, and the *New York Times* (October 18, 1971), p. 26.

198. Rehnquist's financial assets were rather modest, for even in the late 1970s his savings (excluding real estate) reportedly totaled less than $15,000. See *Time* (May 23, 1979), p. 16.

199. See the *New York Times* (November 19, 1975), p. 1, and (June 28, 1979), p. A1. One of the companies for which Stevens worked as an attorney was the big Kaiser Aluminum and Chemical Corp. of California.

200. See the *New York Times* (June 2, 1977), p. A21.

201. See the *New York Times* (January 30, 1976), p. 1, (January 31, 1976), p. 24, (February 1, 1976), p. 1, and (February 4, 1976), p. 32.

CHAPTER 7

The Carter Administration

In 1976 there was a marked shift in the political control of the nation when former Georgia Governor James E. (Jimmy) Carter, Jr., was elected President of the United States. But there was comparatively little change in the makeup of America's giant industrial and financial enterprises in the late 1970s. For instance, by 1978 (the latest date for which such figures were available) the only noteworthy development was that ITT had dropped out of the "top 10" industrial category, primarily as a result of the divestitures it had been forced to make in its recent antitrust settlement with the federal government.

Similarly, there was relatively little change in the makeup of the organizations representing the American business community. For example, the NAM remained a body which, judging from its board of directors, was composed mostly of the heads of small or medium-sized concerns and second-tier officials of various large companies, strong evidence that this group was not controlled by big business. The U.S. Chamber of Commerce also continued to reflect primarily the views of small and medium-sized concerns, although perhaps not to the same extent as the NAM, for some of its more important special committees were apparently dominated by major corporate executives.

The CED, on the other hand, remained very much under the influence of big business interests. Unlike most other such groups, however, it continued to include a number of important academic figures among its roughly 200 trustees, such as Derek Bok, the president of Harvard. And the even more elitist (65-man) Business Council, which may well represent the inner core of America's economic establishment, was thoroughly dominated by key corporate interests. This can be seen in the following analysis of the primary affiliations of its top leaders in the mid and late 1970s:

Business Council Post	1975	1977	1979
Chairman	Board chairman, Utah International, Inc. (a big Western construction and mining company)	Board chairman, AT&T	Board chairman, GE
Vice-Chairmen	Board chairman, AT&T	Board chairman, GM	Board chairman, Exxon Corp.
	Board chairman, GE	Board chairman, E.I. du Pont de Nemours & Co.	Board chairman, Bethlehem Steel Corp.
	Board chairman, General Mills, Inc.	Board chairman, Continental Group, Inc. (the former Continental Can Co.)	Board chairman, Sperry Rand Corp.
	Board chairman, Sears, Roebuck & Co.	Board chairman, Southern Pacific (Railroad) Co.	Board chairman, Bechtel Group (a big privately owned California-based construction company)

High officials of such giant enterprises as Citicorp, (Deering) Milliken and Co., Eaton Corp., Hanna Mining Co., Mobil Oil Corp., and Hewlett-Packard Co. also served as members of the Business Council's 19-man executive committee in every year throughout this period.

As indicated in the preceding chapter, a new economic group known as the Business Roundtable emerged in the early 1970s, and by the latter part of the decade this organization had developed into a potent body, engaging in a great deal of overt lobbying in both the executive branch of government and Congress. Even before the end of the Ford administration, this group was acclaimed by at least one well-informed conservative source as the most powerful business lobby in Washington, its influence far eclipsing that wielded by such long-established interests as the NAM and the U.S. Chamber of Commerce.[1] Also, interestingly, its top leadership structure bore a remarkable resemblance to that of the Business Council, although it had fairly close ties to certain other groups too. Note, for example, the chief corporate links of the occupants of the most important posts in the Business

Roundtable in the last half of the 1970s:

Business Roundtable Post	1975	1977	1979
Chairman	Board chairman, Alcoa	Board chairman, E.I. du Pont de Nemours & Co.	Board chairman, GM
Co-chairmen	Board chairman, AT&T	Board chairman, GM	Board chairman, Exxon Corp.
	Chief of exec. comm., Procter & Gamble Co.	Board chairman, GE	Board chairman, GE
			Board chairman, Goodyear Tire & Rubber Co.

In addition, the heads of such big companies as Citicorp, Hewlett-Packard, IBM, Mobil Oil, National Steel, Union Carbide, and U.S. Steel served on the governing body of the Business Roundtable in each of these years. Indeed, such was the overlap between the Business Roundtable and the Business Council that in the late 1970s approximately 70 percent of the members of the policy committee of the former were actively associated with the latter. Thus it might be said that the Business Roundtable was almost an organizational affiliate of the Business Council.

A different kind of business-oriented body which has undergone enormous development in recent years is the Washington-based American Enterprise Institute for Public Policy Research. Up to the early 1960s this group was known simply as the American Enterprise Association. It had a small staff, an extremely conservative outlook, and conducted little research of any consequence. Its board of trustees was made up largely of rightist corporate officials, many of whom were strictly second-tier figures. However, under the leadership of William J. Baroody, Sr., the AEI, as it is now popularly known, has vastly expanded its staff and substantially improved both the scope and quality of much of its work, although it still has a distinctly conservative tinge.[2] As a result, the AEI has been able, since the early 1970s, to recruit a number of top-tier corporate executives for its board of trustees, men such as Robert Hatfield of the Continental Group, Mark Shepherd, Jr., of Texas Instruments, and more recently, David Packard of Hewlett-Packard—all members of America's big business establishment. Also, of probably greater importance in the long run, the AEI launched in 1978 a three-year development drive to raise a total of $60 million, a goal that, if realized, would enable it to far overshadow the operations of the more moderate Brookings Institution, a body often described as a kind of Democratic "think tank." Some idea of the extraordinary backing now provided the AEI may be gained from the fact that the chairman and five co-chairmen of this key financial drive were:[3]

Chairman— William J. Baroody, Sr.	Recently retired president of AEI
Co-chairmen— Reginald H. Jones	Head of GE; co-chairman of the Business Roundtable; member of the executive committee of the Business Council
Thomas A. Murphy	Head of GM; chairman of the Business Roundtable; vice-chairman of the Business Council
Walter B. Wriston	Head of the Citicorp; member of the policy committee of the Business Roundtable; member of the executive committee of the Business Council; director of GE
Irving Kristol	Henry R. Luce Professor of Human Values, New York University; co-editor of *The Public Interest*; senior fellow at the AEI; director of the Warner-Lambert Co. (a big pharmaceutical company) and the Lincoln National Corp. (a large life and casualty insurance holding company)
Paul W. McCracken	Professor of business administration, University of Michigan; chairman of the AEI's Council of Academic Advisers; chairman of President Nixon's Council of Economic Advisers (1969–1971); director of the Consolidated Foods Corp., K Mart Corp., Lincoln National Corp., and Texas Instruments; member of the Trilateral Commission

In the foreign policy area one organization has long exercised unusual influence in American affairs, and that is the Council on Foreign Relations. As noted earlier, the CFR has been firmly allied with the Rockefeller interests throughout most of the postwar period.[4] That the latter forces still carried great weight in the CFR may be seen from the fact that in late 1976, on the eve of the Carter presidency, its top three officials were:

Chairman— David Rockefeller	Board chairman of the Chase Manhattan Bank (took over post in 1970 upon the retirement of his predecessor and longtime banking associate, John J. McCloy)
Vice-chairman— C. Douglas Dillon	Head of the Dillon family-controlled U.S. & Foreign Securities Corp.; member of the boards of the Chase International Investment Corp. and the Rockefeller Foundation (up to 1975)

President— Bayless Manning	Former dean of the Stanford University law school; now a director of the Aetna Life & Casualty Co., Scovill Manufacturing Co., and the New York-based J. Henry Schroder Banking Corp. (a concern long allied with one branch of the Rockefeller family)

A significant number of other directors of the Council on Foreign Relations had close ties to these economic interests, men such as Robert O. Anderson, the head of the Atlantic Richfield Corp. (who was, up to 1975, a director of the Chase Manhattan Bank); W. Michael Blumenthal, the chief executive officer of the Bendix Corp. (and a trustee of the Rockefeller Foundation); George S. Franklin, David Rockefeller's college roommate and later his kinsman; the Reverend Theodore Hesburgh, the president of the University of Notre Dame (who served on the board of the Chase Manhattan Bank and the Rockefeller Foundation); Robert Roosa, a partner in Brown Brothers Harriman & Co. (and a trustee of the Rockefeller Foundation); and, some might say, Lane Kirkland, the secretary-treasurer of the AFL-CIO (who was also a trustee of the Rockefeller Foundation).[5] Thus, although there was a brief internal upheaval in the Council on Foreign Relations in the early 1970s over the appointment of William P. Bundy to serve as the editor of *Foreign Affairs*, it would appear that the Rockefeller forces still played a prominent role in the proceedings of this group.

Another important organization, the Trilateral Commission, was created in 1973, largely at the initiative of David Rockefeller, in an attempt to deal more effectively with the many pressing problems confronting the free world's three key regions—North America, Western Europe, and Japan.[6] By 1976 it was composed of about 230 members, drawn in roughly equal numbers from each of the three regions. At that time its United States membership consisted of approximately 65 people, of whom nearly 30 were top-tier business executives or corporate lawyers (a number of whom had considerable diplomatic experience), 15 were high-level governmental officials (or former officials), 12 were prominent academicians (mostly foreign policy experts), 4 were civic figures, and 3 were labor leaders. By 1979 the (non-Canadian) American membership had increased to a little more than 75 persons, with roughly the same proportions selected from various major sectors of the population. Perhaps the most striking thing about the United States representation on this body is the extent to which its economic members in particular have been affiliated with such influential groups as the Business Council, Business Roundtable, CED, and especially the Council on Foreign Relations.

It should also be noted that by the late 1970s the American labor movement, which had constituted a fairly important force in political affairs since the New Deal years, was showing serious signs of slippage, both in terms of general public support and its overall share of the nation's work force.[7] Even the once highly cohesive AFL-CIO was beginning to display a significant amount of internal dissension, with such leaders as Sol Chaikin of the International Ladies' Garment Workers and Glenn Watts of the Communications Workers of America openly voicing opposition to some of the policies advocated by their aging, at times imperious, chieftain, George Meany.[8] In short, labor was no longer as formidable a force as it had been.

CARTER'S POLITICAL RISE AND MAJOR TIES

Without a doubt, the most surprising aspect of the 1976 presidential election was the emergence of a virtually unknown figure, former Georgia Governor Jimmy Carter, to capture the Democratic nomination through a series of hard-fought primary battles waged in many states, and then to score a close win over the conservative Republican incumbent, Gerald Ford. Up to 1976 Carter's governmental experience had been rather limited, being confined to four years of service as a state legislator in the mid-1960s and one term (a constitutional restriction) as governor of Georgia in the early 1970s, in which capacity he had established a record as a civil rights liberal, an organizational reformer, and a fiscal conservative. The rest of the time he had devoted to running his family's fairly sizable (3,000-acre) peanut farm business in Plains, Georgia, which he had taken over after he left the Navy upon the death of his prosperous father in 1953. Indeed, Carter proved to be so successful as a small businessman that by 1976 he was reportedly worth nearly $1 million, with his family's various agricultural enterprises grossing more than $2 million a year.[9]

Although he held no important governmental office in the mid-1970s, Jimmy Carter was nevertheless a man with great political ambition. Bolstered by the help of a small set of primarily Georgia-based aides and advisors, Carter set out in early 1976 to capture the Democratic presidential nomination. His competition for this position consisted mainly of a number of much better-known liberal leaders from other parts of the country, men such as Henry Jackson, Morris Udall, and Birch Bayh, and also Alabama Governor George Wallace, who through his many conservative and segregationist speeches in recent years had built up a substantial following among like-minded citizens in the South and blue-collar groups in the North. As basically an outsider, Carter entered a large number of Democratic state primary contests in many sections of the country. One of the most important of these battles in the critical early stages was in Florida, where, because it was a conservative Southern state, most liberal and moderate observers feared that Alabama's George Wallace would score a smashing victory. As a result, all but one of the liberal aspirants for the Democratic nomination eschewed the Florida primary, leaving the field largely to two Southerners, Carter and Wallace. In this confrontation Carter acquired some crucial support from a number of black and liberal leaders, such as Martin Luther

King, Sr., Georgia's black Congressman Andrew Young, and Leonard Woodcock, the president of the United Auto Workers (the only major labor union to back Carter in the Democratic primaries), many of whom viewed the Carter candidacy mainly as a vehicle for defeating George Wallace.[10] In this endeavor Carter scored a major surprise, registering a narrow win over Wallace, thereby putting an end to the latter's long-simmering presidential hopes. •

Although he suffered some distressing setbacks along the way, Carter went on to post a number of well-financed primary victories over his more liberal non-Southern contenders, the most decisive of which was his triumph in Pennsylvania where, to the surprise of many, he bested Washington's strongly labor-backed Senator, Henry Jackson.[11] Carter also managed to beat back a belated challenge from California's young governor, Edmund G. (Jerry) Brown, Jr., and went on to wrap up his party's presidential nomination considerably before the Democratic national convention. Because of his winsome personality and his image as a man untainted by Watergate-tarnished Washington, Carter entered the presidential race with a huge popular lead over the rater pedestrian Gerry Ford. The contest, however, turned out to be much closer than most person had anticipated, primarily because Carter, in sharp contrast to his earlier political effectiveness, conducted a rather inept campaign, and President Ford a very astute one. But in the end Carter managed to eke out a narrow victory, becoming the first (non-incumbent) Southerner to be elected to this high office since before the Civil War.

In both the primary and general elections Carter projected a rather confusing image to the American people. At times he sounded like a Southern populist, calling strongly for major tax reform and other liberal measures. More often, he adopted the role of the anti-Establishment or anti-Washington outsider, pledged to bring new ideas and new faces to the federal government. In fact, Carter and his advisors led the country to believe they would eschew Establishment figures in creating a new Democratic administration.[12] Carter also avoided taking a clear-cut stand on many key issues, and, judging from most accounts, won mostly on the basis of his personality. In short, upon assuming office in 1977, Carter was something of a puzzle to the general public and many respected political observers.

However, some revealing clues as to Carter's real politico-economic leanings may be obtained through an analysis of his close friends and political associates in Georgia, where he got his start as a governmental leader. According to most accounts, three men played important roles in aiding and advising Carter in his rise to power—Hamilton Jordan, Joseph L. (Jody) Powell, and Charles Kirbo. The first two joined Carter's political team in the late 1960s, both basically fresh out of college. The former served as Carter's chief campaign manager, the latter as his press secretary. In part because of their youth, neither aide had any significant socio-economic ties.

Charles Kirbo was a much older man (almost 60), who, as an Atlanta attorney, had become involved with Carter in the early 1960s when he was called in by Carter to serve as his lawyer in his first close (legally disputed) race for state legislative office. The two became fast friends, with Kirbo acting primarily as an influential behind-the-scenes advisor on various major issues. But Kirbo was no ordinary Atlanta attorney; rather he was a senior partner in one of the city's (and state's) most important corporate law firms, King & Spalding. This concern had long served as general counsel to the Coca-Cola Co., which, with 1976 assets of $1.9 billion, was by far the largest manufacturing firm in the state and reportedly represented the very center of Atlanta's powerful politico-economic establishment.[13] It also represented the closely allied Trust Co. of Georgia, which had, counting its trust funds, about $4.6 billion in assets in 1976. Kirbo, then, provided Carter with a crucial link to Georgia's key corporate interests.[14] And although this business tie has been largely overlooked or underestimated, it warrants close attention, for Kirbo himself had only a limited number of contacts outside the state of Georgia.[15]

Up to 1976, Carter was a largely unknown quantity to most of America's chief corporate executives who, because of their conservative leanings, may have been uneasy about many of his stated political and economic views. Part of the task of promoting Carter's candidacy and providing proper assurances to key business figures was undertaken by Coca-Cola's board chairman, J. Paul Austin, who was a member of the policy committee of the Business Roundtable, a graduate member of the Business Council, a charter member of the Trilateral Commission, and a director of the Morgan Guaranty Trust Co., GE, and (as a result of a mid-1976 merger), the Federated Department Stores.[16] In fact, according to one source, before the 1976 election the influential Austin spent the better part of a year, a sizable block of time for any major corporate executive, allaying big businessmen's fears about Jimmy Carter and his alleged populist tendencies.[17]

In addition to his Georgia links, Jimmy Carter had forged some crucial ties with influential national interests, which, though not apparent at the time, did much to help his cause in major business and civic circles. Without question, the most important of these was with the little-known Trilateral Commission. Initially, the United States membership on this tripartite body was made up of about 60 people, of whom nearly half were business executives or corporate lawyers, ten high-level government officials, ten prominent academicians, and a few civic figures and labor leaders. Most of the governmental members of the commission were federal officials, such as Representative Wilbur Mills, the then influential chairman of the House Ways and Means Committee, and U.S. Senator William V. Roth, Jr., of Delaware. Only two of the ten governmental figures—Carter and Washington's Governor Daniel Evans—were state officials, so Carter was clearly one of a very select group.

It was primarily through this organization that Carter, with the help of fellow Trilateralist J. Paul Austin, gained access and exposure to many key business and academic leaders, such as Alden W. Clausen, president of the

Bank of America, Peter G. Peterson, the recently appointed head of Lehman Brothers, and Columbia University professor Zbigniew Brzezinski.[18] The ambitious but relatively inexperienced Carter was a very active member of this body, which did much to help mold his thinking about governmental affairs, especially in the realm of foreign policy.[19] Perhaps not coincidentally, Carter chose another member of the Trilateral Commission, Minnesota's Senator Walter Mondale, to serve as his running mate on the Democratic national ticket in 1976. Thus as Laurence Shoup has observed, Carter was an "... 'insider' [who] campaigned as an 'outsider.' "[20] Or as Dye and Ziegler have put it in the fourth edition of *The Irony of Democracy*, Jimmy Carter represents, in essence, "a new smile on the face of the Establishment."[21]

Indeed, such was Carter's relationship with the nation's corporate interests that by early 1978 big business reportedly had greater access to the White House than it had under either of his two Republican predecessors. According to a *New York Times* account, there were about a dozen men who had especially effective entree to the President.[22] These executives (and their major organizational affiliations) were:

J. Paul Austin	Head of the Coca-Cola Co.; active member of the Business Council, Business Roundtable, and the Trilateral Commission
William M. Batten	Chairman of the New York Stock Exchange; member of the executive committee of the Business Council
Alden W. Clausen	President of the Bank of America; active member of the Business Council; recent member of the Trilateral Commission
John D. deButts	Head of AT&T; chairman of the Business Council; vice-chairman of the Conference Board; member of the executive committee of the Business Roundtable
Henry Ford II	Head of the Ford Motor Co.; graduate member of the Business Council
Ben W. Heineman	President of Northwest Industries, Inc.; longtime trustee of the Rockefeller Foundation
Reginald H. Jones	Head of GE; a co-chairman of the Business Roundtable; member of the executive committee of the Business Council
Donald M. Kendall	Head of Pepsico (and longtime Nixon friend); an active member of the Business Council; director of the U.S. Chamber of Commerce (a possibly erroneous entry on this list of Carter advisors)
R. Heath Larry	President of the NAM; former longtime high official, U.S. Steel Corp.
Richard L. Lesher	President of the U.S. Chamber of Commerce
Thomas A. Murphy	Head of GM; co-chairman of the Business Roundtable; vice-chairman of the Business Council

Irving S. Shapiro	Head of the du Pont Co.; chairman of the Business Roundtable; vice-chairman of the Business Council; trustee of the Conference Board
Walter B. Wriston	Head of the Citicorp; member of the executive committee of the Business Council; policy committee member of the Business Roundtable

Moreover, a few months later the *Times* went even further and claimed that some of the top figures in this group—namely, deButts, Jones, Larry, and Shapiro—were, in effect, members of President Carter's informal corporate "brain trust," although this was a far different sort of body from that which advised FDR during his early years in office.[23]

EARLY MAJOR ADMINISTRATIVE AND DIPLOMATIC APPOINTMENTS

Yet, a skeptic may ask, how much truth is there to these assertions about Carter's influential business and civic backers? How do they square with the fact that, according to various other accounts, the Carter administration engaged in a widespread talent search designed to find the most qualified people to serve as its top officials?[24] One way to get at these questions, and also to analyze the extent to which Carter did bring new people into the federal government, is to take a close look at the socio-economic background of the persons tapped to fill the key posts in his administration.

To start with foreign affairs, Carter chose as his Secretary of State an able, thoroughly Establishment figure, Cyrus Vance.[25] Like many occupants of this office, Vance had a substantial amount of experience in the federal government. But most of it had been in the Defense Department under the Kennedy and Johnson administrations, although he had also served briefly at times as a special diplomatic troubleshooter. However, it would appear that Vance's non-governmental links were probably of greater importance in his appointment to this premier Cabinet post. For instance, his influential law firm of Simpson, Thacher & Bartlett had long acted as general counsel for Lehman Brothers, the Manufacturers Hanover Trust Co., and a host of other large business enterprises.[26] And Vance himself served up to 1977 as a director of IBM, the Aetna Life and Casualty Co., New York Times Co., Pan-American World Airways, and One William Street Fund (a mutual fund controlled by Lehman Brothers). Vance's most critical ties, though, may have been with certain other elite groups, since he served in the mid-1970s as board chairman of the Rockefeller Foundation, vice-chairman of the Council on Foreign Relations, and a member of the Trilateral Commission. In short, Vance could hardly have had better socio-economic links.[27]

The marked Establishment orientation of many of Carter's appointments to high-level State Department posts can be seen in the selection of Los

Angeles lawyer Warren Christopher to serve as Vance's Deputy Secretary, the second-ranking official in this important agency. Curiously, Christopher had no experience in diplomatic affairs and had spent only two years in the federal government, having served as Deputy Attorney General in the latter part of the Johnson administration, during which stint he apparently got to know Vance through the latter's involvement in the investigation of the great urban riots of the late 1960s. But Christopher had devoted the bulk of his professional life to working for one of Los Angeles's most prominent corporate law firms, O'Melveny & Myers. He had also been a director of such large regional concerns as the Pacific Mutual Life Insurance Co. and the Southern California Edison Co., and had reportedly acted as the Los Angeles lawyer for IBM.[28] And Christopher had an even more crucial tie, for he was a member of the influential Trilateral Commission; indeed, he was the only lawyer from the western half of the United States to grace this body.

The rather striking extent to which the Trilateral Commission played a vital role in the high-level staffing of the State Department was evinced in still other ways. For example, two of this agency's next most important officials, Under Secretary of State for Economic Affairs, Richard Cooper, and Under Secretary of State for Security Assistance, Science and Technology, Lucy Wilson Benson, were both former members of the Trilateral Commission.[29] Moreover, although it has rarely been noted, these two officials had significant economic links. Although Richard Cooper was best known as a Yale University professor of international economics, he had recently been appointed to the boards of the big Phoenix Mutual Life Insurance Co. (of Connecticut), and the J. Henry Schroder Banking Corp., a fairly sizable (roughly $450 million) concern that had long been allied with the Rockefeller interests.[30] Lucy Benson was generally viewed as a nationally prominent civic leader, having served from 1968 to 1974 as president of the U.S. League of Women Voters and then as a trustee of the prestigious Brookings Institution. Yet she also graced the boards of the giant Continental Group (a part of America's economic establishment) and Northeast Utilities (a big New England-based enterprise).[31] In brief, Lucy Benson was clearly a pro-business civic figure, whose appointment to a high State Department post probably stemmed largely from her Trilateral connection.[32]

Still other evidence of what might be described as the Trilateral takeover of American foreign affairs under the Carter administration may be found in the fact that several of the nation's newly appointed special ambassadors-at-large were drawn from this same set of politico-economic interests.[33] For the position of Ambassador-at-Large for Non-Proliferation Matters (i.e., nuclear weapons negotiations), the President chose a Washington attorney, Gerald C. Smith, who had considerable experience in this area, having been head of America's delegation at the Strategic Arms Limitation Talks (SALT) in the first part of the Nixon administration. He had since been associated, in the somewhat restricted role of counsel, with a firm known as Wilmer, Cutler & Pickering, which had long represented a number of the nation's large corporations. More important, Smith had been the North American chairman of the Trilateral Commission and a trustee of the Brookings Institution.[34]

Yet, interestingly, the influence of the Trilateral Commission did not extend in any marked way to the selection of America's major ambassadors under the Carter administration, perhaps because of a new screening and review procedure adopted by the President shortly after he took office.[35] In fact, Carter's initial top emissaries were drawn entirely from non-corporate sources, although two had important civic links. They were as follows:

Ambassador to Great Britain (1977 on)	Kingman Brewster, Jr.	No prior government experience; president, Yale University (1963–1977); professor and later provost at Yale (1950–1963); trustee of the Carnegie Endowment for International Peace (mid-1970s) and the Urban Institute (1976–1977)
Ambassador to France (1977 on)	Arthur A. Hartman	Career diplomat since 1952
Ambassador to West Germany (September 1976 on)	William J. Stoessel, Jr.	Career diplomat since 1942 (most recent major assignment, Ambassador to the Soviet Union, 1974–1976)
Ambassador to the Soviet Union (September 1976 on)	Malcolm Toon	Career diplomat since 1946
Ambassador (or liaison officer) to Communist China (1977 on)	Leonard Woodcock	No prior governmental experience, but one of Carter's early political backers; president, United Auto Workers (1970–1977; lesser union official, 1940–1970); member of the Trilateral Commission (1973–1977)
Ambassador to NATO	W. Tapley Bennett, Jr.	Career diplomat since 1941

Thus, four of President Carter's first six appointments in this area were longtime career diplomats, and two of these were carryovers from the last part of the Ford administration. The other two selections (Brewster and Woodcock) would appear to have been picked in part because of their prominent civic ties, particularly with such organizations as the Trilateral Commission and the Carnegie Endowment for International Peace.[36]

The influence of the Trilateral Commission extended even to important posts outside of the State Department. For instance, as his Special Assistant to the President for National Security Affairs (the post made famous first by McGeorge Bundy and later Henry Kissinger), Carter picked a Columbia

University professor, Zbigniew Brzezinski, who was a knowledgeable but highly "hawkish" authority on international relations. As indicated earlier, Brzezinski had been intimately involved with the operation of the Trilateral Commission.[37] Indeed, he had been its chief staff director since it was created in 1973. Furthermore, Brzezinski took an early interest in Carter as a presidential hopeful and, assuming something of a tutor's role, sent him a series of articles on foreign policy over the next few years. In addition, in 1976 Brzezinski acted as the head of the Carter campaign's 28-man task force on defense and foreign affairs. Hence Brzezinski clearly had the inside track for this key position. And if there is any doubt as to his ties, it need only be noted that he had served as a director of the Council on Foreign Relations for five years prior to his appointment to this high federal post.[38]

In one last hotly disputed appointment in the realm of foreign relations, President Carter chose as his chief disarmament negotiator Paul C. Warnke, a former Defense Department official under the Johnson administration, who, because of his "dovish" views on the war in Vietnam, was initially attacked by many conservatives as being too "soft" or weak for this position.[39] Ironically enough, Warnke was an Establishment figure. Since leaving the federal government in the late 1960s, he had been a senior partner in the large Washington law firm headed by the influential Clark Clifford, who by the mid-1970s sat on the board of the big Phillips Petroleum Co. Even more important, Warnke was both a member of the Trilateral Commission and a director of the Council on Foreign Relations. In short, this was one more in a rather remarkable string of such appointments made from a select recruitment base which may well be unrivaled in American history.[40]

For the key post of Secretary of the Treasury, President Carter chose, after an extensive search, a prominent Michigan executive, W. Michael Blumenthal, who had previously secured some significant governmental experience under the Kennedy and Johnson administrations, primarily as an international trade negotiator.[41] He also had earned a Ph.D. in economics, the first such official to have a doctorate. However, Blumenthal had made his mark mainly as a businessman. After leaving the federal government in 1967 he had quickly risen to become the chief executive officer of the Bendix Corp., a major industrial concern. Blumenthal had many other more important ties. He had served in recent years as a director of the big (New York-based) Equitable Life Assurance Society, a trustee of the Rockefeller Foundation, a director of the Council on Foreign Relations, and, up to 1975, a member of the Trilateral Commission. So Blumenthal had virtually the same set of civic links as Secretary of State Cyrus Vance.

For the second-ranking post in the department, that of Deputy Secretary of the Treasury, Blumenthal chose a Wall Street lawyer, Robert Carswell, who had been a middle-tier partner in the huge firm of Shearman & Sterling, which had long acted as general counsel for Citicorp (the former First National City Bank of New York) and many other potent interests, such as the United Technologies Corp. (the former United Aircraft Corp.) and apparently the wealthy (C. Douglas) Dillon family.[42] Carswell himself had served on the board of only one fairly sizable concern, the Graniteville Co., a $135 million Southern textile company—not an especially important link given the size of many modern business enterprises.

The third-ranking official in the Treasury Department, Under Secretary for Monetary Affairs Anthony M. Solomon, was a more unusual choice in that he had never held a truly prominent post in the business world. Instead, he had spent a considerable amount of time in his younger years working for the federal government, and then in 1969, at the request of World Bank president Robert McNamara, he became head of the International Investment Corp. for Yugoslavia, a specially constituted concern created to promote the financing of joint ventures between this dissident Communist country and Western business interests. But this enterprise had only a fairly short existence, and from 1972 to 1974, Solomon was employed mainly as a governmental consultant, practicing largely on his own—hardly the kind of position that usually catapults a person into high federal office.[43] Yet Solomon did have one key link which might help explain why he was picked to be Under Secretary of the Treasury for Monetary Affairs; he too was a member of the Trilateral Commission.

The next three most important posts in the Treasury Department were filled by people with somewhat similar backgrounds. The Assistant Secretary of the Treasury for Domestic Finance, Roger Altman, was a high official in the investment banking firm of Lehman Brothers. Judging from various newspaper accounts, he was probably appointed because he had served, along with two other members of his firm, as a major fundraiser for Carter's crucial pre-convention drive. The Assistant Secretary for Economic Policy was apparently a less important person, Daniel H. Brill, the executive vice-president of Baltimore's Commercial Credit Co., which, despite its size (over $4 billion in assets), was not really an Establishment concern, most likely because this city had fallen out of the nation's high financial ranks long ago. The Assistant Secretary of the Treasury for International Affairs, C. Fred Bergsten, was not a businessman, but instead had held a series of second-tier government jobs up to the early 1970s, when he accepted a position as a senior research fellow at the Brookings Institution. He had also been associated with a number of influential civic interests.[44] Thus most of the key Assistant Secretaries of the Treasury under the Carter administration had corporate or Establishment ties.[45]

As Secretary of Defense, President Carter appointed a man who might be said to represent the rise of the "meritocracy." Harold Brown had both considerable high-level experience in the federal government and special advanced training in the scientific field. He had served as Secretary of the Air Force from 1965 to 1969 (during which period he was a strong supporter of the war in Vietnam), and for four years before that he had held other lesser posts in the Pentagon. In addition, he had been a University of California (Berkeley) physicist for eleven years prior to entering the Defense Department, and upon his departure from the federal government he became president of the California Institute of Technology, a post he held up to 1977. In short, Brown's appointment could hardly be faulted on meritocratic grounds.

However, Brown had certain other ties which may have played an important role in his selection. Like Vance and Blumenthal, he was a member of the influential Trilateral Commission. In fact, he was the only college president in the country to serve on this body. Furthermore, he sat on the board of several large corporations, such as IBM, the Times-Mirror Co., and Schroders, Ltd., a British banking concern which was the parent company of the J. Henry Schroder Banking Corp. of New York. Hence, although primarily a technocrat, Brown had close ties to certain major economic interests.

The second-ranking post in the Pentagon, that of Deputy Secretary of Defense, was filled by a relatively unknown businessman, Charles W. Duncan, Jr., who had no experience in the federal government.[46] Duncan, who was a native of Texas, had been president of the medium-sized, family-owned Duncan Foods Co. up to 1964, when it was acquired by the Coca-Cola Co., of which concern he then became a high official. In fact, Duncan served from 1971 to 1974 as president of the Coca-Cola Co., after which he returned to Texas to become head of a fairly small firm known as the Rotan Mosle Financial Corp. However, Duncan still maintained a number of economic ties of considerable importance. For instance, not only did he continue to serve on the board of Coca-Cola, but he was a director of several other large corporations, the most prominent of which was the Southern Railway.[47] On the basis of this evidence, it would appear that Duncan was not a national Establishment figure, but a man who owed his appointment primarily to his Coca-Cola connections.[48]

The pro-business orientation of the Defense Department under Carter is also evident when one examines the backgrounds of the men chosen to serve as this agency's three major service secretaries:

Secretary of the Army	Clifford L. Alexander, Jr.	White House aide (mid-1960s); partner, Washington law firm of Arnold & Porter, Abe Fortas's old firm (1969–1975); thereafter, a partner in the lesser-known Washington firm of Verner, Liipfert, Bernhard, McPherson & Alexander; director of the Pennsylvania Power & Light Co. (1972–1976)
Secretary of the Navy	W. Graham Claytor, Jr.	No prior governmental experience; president, Southern Railway Co. (1967–76); director of the Morgan Guaranty Trust Co. (1969–1977); trustee of the CED (1972–1976)

Secretary of the Air Force	John C. Stetson	No prior governmental experience; president, A.B. Dick Co., Ill. (1970–1977); president, Houston Post Co. (1963–1970); director of the Houston Post Co. (1970–1976), the big Lumbermens Mutual Casualty Co. (1973–1976), and two lesser concerns

Clearly, all these officials had significant economic links. But only one, Claytor, could be said to be an integral part of America's powerful business establishment.

To head the Justice Department, President Carter chose a native of his home state, Griffin Bell, whose most conspicuous activity in recent years had been as a judge of the U.S. Circuit Court of Appeals, a position he held from the early 1960s to just before his appointment as Attorney General. Bell's nomination raised a storm of protests from liberal and civil rights groups around the country. And it would appear that these critics had good reason to be concerned, for on the bench Bell had demonstrated that he was no crusader in the bitter struggle to enforce the Supreme Court's mandate to integrate the public schools in America; in fact, he seemed sympathetic toward the segregationist forces in the South.[49] On other matters Bell had proved to be a rather pedestrian jurist, with staunchly conservative views.[51] For example, in 1969 he firmly backed the proposed appointment of President Nixon's second Southern nominee for the Supreme Court, Florida's mediocre G. Harrold Carswell.[51]

Why, then, did President Carter pick Griffin Bell to be his Attorney General? One possible reason for his selection may be that both before and briefly after his fifteen-year period of service as a federal judge, Bell had been a member of Atlanta's economically elite law firm of King & Spalding, which represented many important business interests in the South and the nation. It also counted Jimmy Carter's longtime friend and political counselor, Charles Kirbo, among its senior partners.[52] Although Bell had only recently returned to his old firm, he had quickly resumed his largely corporate practice and by early 1977 was described by no less a source than *Forbes* as Coca-Cola's Atlanta lawyer.[53]

President Carter followed a long-established political tradition in choosing a man from the western section of the country, Idaho's Governor Cecil Andrus, as Secretary of the Interior. Andrus, who was reportedly a close personal friend of the President, was a rather unusual appointee in that he had been primarily a political leader and had no noteworthy business ties.[54] In fact, he had been the first Democrat to be elected governor of Idaho in 26 years, and in this role he had frequently opposed the economic development plans of the state's powerful mining and utility interests. In his first years on the job in Washington, Andrus retained the confidence of environmental groups by taking positions which incurred the wrath of a large number of influential farmers, ranchers, oilmen, mining firms, and land-hungry developers in the West.⁵⁵ For these reasons, many environmental leaders in the nation's capital have acclaimed Andrus to be the best Secretary of the Interior in the postwar period.⁵⁶

For his Secretary of Agriculture, President Carter chose a person who, as customary, came from the agrarian heartland of the country, Minnesota Congressman Robert Bergland. Actually, this selection was reportedly made largely at the urging of Bergland's state Democratic colleague and personal friend, Vice President Walter Mondale.⁵⁷ Bergland was well-suited to this post, for in his six years (1971–1977) in Congress he had been an active member of the House Agricultural Committee, and for five years in the mid-1960s he had worked in Minnesota as an employee of the U.S. Department of Agriculture. In addition to this governmental experience, he had long operated a 600-acre family farm near Roseau, Minnesota. Bergland was a liberal on most major issues confronting the American farmer. It is not surprising, therefore, that his nomination was warmly supported by the progressive National Farmers Union and strongly opposed by the more conservative and commercially-oriented American Farm Bureau Federation.⁵⁸ Thus Bergland, like Andrus, did not fit into the general Establishment pattern of the Carter Cabinet.⁵⁹ Even more important, his outlook on the nation's farm problems was certainly far different from that of his agribusiness-oriented predecessor, Earl Butz.

When he came to fill the post of Secretary of Commerce, President Carter took an unprecedented step, for he picked a woman to hold this pro-business office. After an extensive search, he appointed Juanita Kreps, who had been a longtime professor of economics at Duke University and had more recently served as a vice-president of this institution.⁶⁰ In fact, she was the first professionally trained economist to hold this clientele-dominated post. However, Professor Kreps was no ivory-towered academic, but one who in recent years had developed a number of noteworthy corporate ties. For instance, in the mid-1970s she served on the board of such giant enterprises as the Eastman Kodak Co., North Carolina National Bank (a $4.4 billion concern), J.C. Penney, R.J. Reynolds Industries, and Western Electric Co. (the manufacturing subsidiary of AT&T).⁶¹

In his efforts to select a Secretary of Labor, President Carter ran into unexpected trouble. For this so-called clientele position, the AFL-CIO's George Meany strongly supported President Ford's first Secretary of Labor, former Harvard professor John T. Dunlop, as one of his two candidates for Cabinet office (Leonard Woodcock was Meany's choice to be Secretary of HEW).⁶² Meany had developed very close personal and economic ties with Dunlop over the years, and pushed hard for his appointment. But many feminist and civil rights groups were opposed to his selection because of what they contended was his poor record during his recent Cabinet stint in combating job discrimination by certain unions. Disregarding the pressure from organized labor (which, with the exception of the UAW, had not backed Carter in his arduous pre-convention campaign), the President passed over the controversial Dunlop and instead chose a relatively unknown University of Texas professor of economics and labor relations, F. Ray Marshall, who, although he had no prior government experience, was well regarded by most of the union movement and was also favorably viewed by many black and feminist leaders.[63] Moreover, unlike some of his Republican predecessors, Marshall had no corporate links. In fact, he proved to be one of the more liberal members of Carter's Cabinet.[64]

For the highly demanding post of Secretary of Health, Education and Welfare, President Carter chose a man with considerable experience in Washington affairs, Joseph A. Califano, Jr. The Brooklyn-born Califano had served as a special assistant to President Johnson from 1965 to 1969, and for four years before that he had held a series of less important posts in the federal government. During this period Califano had demonstrated that he was an extremely able man, and had acquired extensive knowledge about the internal operations of the legislative and executive branches of government. Upon leaving the Johnson administration Califano stayed on in Washington and took a position with the pro-Democratic law firm of Arnold and Porter (the longtime kingpin of which was LBJ's close friend and political counselor Abe Fortas). Then in 1971 he became a name partner in another fairly large but less prominent concern known as Williams, Connolly & Califano. Unlike many other former government officials, Califano apparently did not serve on any major corporate boards. Thus it would seem that he was selected solely on the basis of his ability and knowledge of federal affairs. Yet such may not have been entirely the case, for his firm had a number of important corporate clients.[65] And Califano's prospects for appointment to high office were clearly enhanced by the fact that he was Coca-Cola's Washington lawyer.[66]

In selecting his Secretary of Housing and Urban Development, President Carter paid particular attention to his avowed goal of bringing more blacks and women into the upper echelons of the federal government. After two abortive efforts to appoint a black man to this Cabinet post, the President found a person who filled the recruitment bill from both a racial and sexual standpoint in Washington attorney Patricia Roberts Harris.[67] This appointee, whose father had been a railroad dining-car waiter, had only a limited amount of government experience, and that had been confined to the relatively unimportant post of Ambassador to Luxembourg in the mid-1960s. Mrs. Harris had spent a considerable amount of time in her earlier years serving as a professor, and later briefly as a dean, at the Howard University law school. She left the academic profession in 1970 to become a partner in a fairly prominent, though not top-tier, Washington law firm known as Fried, Frank, Harris, Shriver & Kampelman, which actually had its main office and base of operations in New York City.[68] Hence it would appear that in Mrs. Harris President Carter had found someone who could be counted on to promote and defend the interests of the nation's many poor urban blacks.

Yet some critics would contend that Carter's choice was not as progressive as it seemed, for in recent years Mrs. Harris had served, perhaps largely as a result of changing corporate (public relations) policies, as a director of such giant concerns as the Chase Manhattan Bank, IBM, and Scott Paper Co.[69] In fact, she was the third person in Carter's Cabinet who had been a member of the board of IBM, a sign that it probably exercised a great deal of influence in his administration.[70]

For the fairly new position of Secretary of Transportation, President Carter picked a man who, unlike most other members of his Cabinet, had no formal corporate ties, but was instead primarily a governmental leader, Washington Congressman Brockman Adams. He had long practiced law in his home state, originally as an associate of a fairly large Seattle firm, but since entering political life in the mid-1960s he had chosen to practice on his own. However, it was as a Congressman that Adams made his mark in national affairs, especially in the area of transportation. For instance, in 1973 he was a major force behind the legislation which was adopted, with considerable business support, to consolidate the bankrupt Penn-Central system and other financially ailing Northeast railroads into a federally backed network known as Conrail.[71] Hence, from a substantive standpoint, Adams would appear to have been a sound choice for this Cabinet post.[72]

Because of the nation's growing oil and energy crisis, President Carter was forced to create, shortly after he took office, a new Cabinet-level agency called the Department of Energy (which incorporated the old FEA, among other units). To head this vital agency, the President chose a man who had an impressive technical background and had held several prominent posts in the Nixon and Ford regimes, James R. Schlesinger. Schlesinger had received a Ph.D. in economics from Harvard University, then taught in this field at the University of Virginia; later, in the 1960s, he took a research staff position at the Rand Corp., which did a great deal of work for the federal government, particularly the Defense Department. In 1969, when Nixon entered the White House, Schlesinger was given a second-tier job in the Bureau of the Budget, but because of his demonstrated ability he was asked within a short time to assume a series of other more important government posts—chairman of the Atomic Energy Commission, then briefly director of the CIA, and finally Secretary of Defense. In fact, he held this key Cabinet office through the first year of the Ford administration when he was suddenly fired by the President, reportedly because of his imperious manner.

At this juncture Schlesinger took an academic position as director of a special project that was jointly supported by the Johns Hopkins School for Advanced International Studies and the Center for Strategic and International Studies at Georgetown University.[73] The Georgetown Center is of particular interest as an indicator of Schlesinger's politico-economic outlook because of its conservative orientation.[74] Given its origins, this rightist slant is hardly surprising, for the people who helped found the center in 1962 included William Baroody, Sr., president of the AEI, and former chief of naval operations Arleigh Burke, who by this time sat on the board of such large enterprises as the Chrysler Corp. and Texaco. Indeed, the center's director, David Abshire, had briefly been head of the special projects division of the AEI (he also later became a member of the Trilateral Commission). During the half-year prior to the 1976 Republican national convention, Schlesinger provided further evidence of his rightist views by serving as Ronald Reagan's principal foreign policy advisor in the latter's hard-fought quest for the GOP presidential nomination against the incumbent Gerald Ford.[75] Also, although it is rarely noted, Schlesinger had established one major corporate link during this brief period, for he sat on the board of the big Corning Glass Works, a family-owned concern that had long been on friendly terms with the Rockefeller interests.[76] Many found it strange that President Carter would choose a man of this kind (by his own admission a "Taft Republican") to serve as his Secretary of Energy, perhaps the most critical post in his entire administration.[77]

What assessment should one make, then, of Carter's Cabinet-level appointments? Were they really the product of an extensive search for the best talent available, as some have claimed? Or were these people picked in some other more select fashion? Judging from the evidence assembled here, the answer would certainly seem to be the latter.[78] While many of Carter's appointees were undoubtedly able persons, one cannot help but think that the influence of such civic and corporate entities as the Trilateral Commission, Coca-Cola, and IBM had much to do with their recruitment. That this is probably true may also be seen from the fact that the Carter administration reportedly checked out many of its proposed appointees with the leaders of another potent group, the Business Roundtable.[79] Its top figures have been in close touch with the President; as *Fortune* noted in 1978, "one chief executive or another is almost always in contact with Secretary of the Treasury Michael Blumenthal, Secretary of Commerce Juanita Kreps, Energy Secretary James Schlesinger, and Charles Schultze, chairman of the Council of Economic Advisers."[81]

Curiously, this skewed appointment pattern did not prevail in Carter's other choices for important federal office. For instance, in selecting his White House staff, he relied heavily on his Georgia friends and associates. Not only did he retain both his youthful campaign manager and his press secretary, Hamilton Jordan and Jody Powell, as high-level aides, but Carter chose a junior partner in Atlanta's elite firm of King & Spalding, Jack H. Watson, Jr., to head his presidential transition team, and later to serve as Special Assistant to the President. As his general counsel, Carter picked another Atlanta attorney, Robert Lipshutz, who was the senior partner in a medium-sized concern which had a less impressive list of corporate clients than King & Spalding. However, Lipshutz had reportedly been one of Carter's chief fundraisers during the presidential campaign and had long served as one of his major political advisors. Carter selected still another Atlanta attorney, Stuart Eizenstat, who had been a partner in the big firm of Powell, Goldstein, Frazer & Murphy, to act as his chief aide on domestic matters, a critical post almost equivalent to that held by Zbigniew Brzezinski in foreign affairs. Eizenstat's concern did not represent many large Georgia companies, although it did serve as local or regional counsel for a number of the country's top-tier enterprises. Unlike Carter's other high-level White House aides, Eizenstat had some experience in national politics, having served briefly as a speech writer for LBJ and later as research director for Hubert Humphrey's 1968 presidential campaign. In sum, Carter's White House staff was composed primarily of political neophytes at the federal level.

Carter's tendency to favor Georgians for certain posts was also reflected in the President's choice of his longtime friend and financial ally, T. Bertram Lance, to be director of the Office of Management and Budget (OMB).[81] The folksy and flamboyant Lance had originally been a small-town (Calhoun, Georgia) banker, but, because of his close ties to Carter, had been made head of the Georgia highway department in the early 1970s when Carter was elected governor of the state. In 1974 when Lance stepped down from office, he joined with two other business associates to obtain control of one of Atlanta's large banks, the National Bank of Georgia, which had 1976 assets of about $400 million. By the mid-1970s Lance had become a wealthy man, with a net worth of nearly $3 million.[82] Yet he was not part of the Coca-Cola "crowd." Nor did he have any major national corporate ties, although, apparently because of his political or economic position, he had managed to secure some questionable loans from a few big banks in the North.[83] As director of OMB, Lance proved to be a rigid fiscal conservative who clearly took a dim view of high government spending and social reform measures. However, because of revelations about the apparently improper way in which he manipulated bank funds under his control in Georgia in the early and mid 1970s, Bert Lance was forced to resign from office in late 1977.[84] He was replaced by his young top aide in OMB, James McIntyre, Jr., another Georgian, but one whose background was primarily in state government affairs. In fact, McIntyre had never held a major position in either the legal or business world, but had held a number of public posts, the most recent and prominent of which had been as head of the Georgia equivalent of OMB.

For the somewhat less important position of chairman of the Council of Economic Advisers, President Carter chose a very different sort of person. Charles L. Schultze had spent many years in both the federal government and in various academic and research capacities. He had been employed for six years in the mid-1950s as a staff member of the CEA, then served briefly as a professor of economics at the University of Maryland. In 1961 he reentered the federal government as a high official of the Bureau of the Budget, becoming its director by 1965. In the course of this activity, Schultze had established a fairly liberal record. At the end of the Johnson administration he was appointed a research fellow at the Brookings Institution, which position he held until 1977. Schultze had also forged some other noteworthy links in recent years, for he served in the mid-1970s as a member of the research advisory board of the CED and as a trustee (board chairman in 1976) of the less prestigious Urban Institute, another Washington-based research unit.[85] While these ties were of considerable importance, they were not of sufficient weight to help win him the post he really wanted in the Carter administration, Secretary of the Treasury. To many, this was a source of disappointment and concern, for although Schultze's views had shifted somewhat to the right by the late 1970s, he was one of the more liberal high-level members of the Carter regime.[86]

As director of the CIA, President Carter initially nominated former Kennedy advisor and now New York lawyer Theodore Sorensen.[87] But many conservatives in the country strongly opposed his appointment for several reasons, the most critical of which were Sorensen's pacifist leanings, his ties to the Kennedy family, and the fact that he had submitted affidavits in the famous Pentagon Papers case which revealed that he had used classified White House documents in writing a book about the Kennedy administration. These criticisms had a telling effect, and Sorensen soon asked that his name be withdrawn from consideration. Carter then selected a longtime military man, Admiral Stansfield Turner, whom he had known while the two were classmates at Annapolis. Turner did not have much experience in intelligence work, and, perhaps as a consequence, he appointed a Harvard University professor of international affairs, Robert Bowie, as one of his top aides. Bowie was the sixteenth member of the Trilateral Commission to be awarded a high federal post at the start of the Carter administration.[88]

Because of America's mounting problems in the realm of international economics and foreign exchange, President Carter created a new position in the late 1970s, that of an ambassador who would serve as his special trade negotiator. To fill this new post, he chose a rather unusual figure, Texas lawyer-businessman Robert Strauss,[89] a man with little experience in this crucial area.[90] Instead, Strauss had been primarily a political leader, having served in the early 1970s as the treasurer of the Democratic National Committee, and then after the 1972 presidential election debacle, as the Democratic chairman who helped stitch the party back together, giving Carter some kind of cohesive unit with which to work after he won the nomination in 1976.

Though not widely noted, Robert Strauss had also accumulated considerable wealth through his various business and legal endeavors. He was a senior partner in one of Dallas's larger law firms, Akin, Gump, Strauss, Hauer & Feld.[91] But most of his wealth apparently came from his investments in banking, radio stations, and real estate, although the companies he controlled in the first two areas were extremely small enterprises. The Strauss Broadcasting Co., for instance, had only thirty employees in the late 1970s, and his Valley View State Bank of Dallas (which he founded in 1971) had assets of under $30 million in 1977, a piddling sum compared to the resources of the big banks in Texas.[92]

However, in recent years Strauss had developed other more important economic ties. From 1974 to 1977 he served as a director of the New York–based Columbia Pictures Industries, Inc., an enterprise dominated by Wall

Street's influential Allen interests, a group with close financial links to the Democratic party.[93] In addition, in 1976, shortly before he was appointed the President's special trade negotiator, Strauss was elected to the boards of the Xerox Corp. and Braniff Airways. The latter, largely Texas-controlled airline included among its outside directors such weighty figures as Perry R. Bass (a nephew of the deceased Texas oilman Sid Richardson, who had taken over the management of his business affairs), Leonard F. McCollum, Jr. (a vice-president of the Federated Capital Corp. and the son of the longtime head of the Continental Oil Co.), and Robert H. Stewart III (the chairman of a big holding company known as the First International Bankshares, Inc., whose board included John D. Murchison and various other wealthy Texans).[94] Hence it is clear that although Strauss was primarily a political figure, he also had close ties to certain important business interests, though only one (Xerox) was of an Establishment nature.

In late 1978 President Carter decided to upgrade his administration's badly lagging fight against inflation, which, in theory, had been conducted largely by the Council on Wage and Price Stability (a Cabinet-dominated advisory body created by his predecessor), but initially had really been directed on a part-time basis by Robert Strauss. Spiraling prices had made it imperative to appoint a full-time official. As his chief inflation fighter, President Carter chose Alfred Kahn, a recently appointed federal official who had been a professor of economics at Cornell University during most of the postwar period and had written widely on the subject of governmental regulation. In 1974 Kahn was appointed head of the New York State Public Utility Commission, in which position he exhibited considerable ability and drive. Three years later he was appointed chairman of the Civil Aeronautics Board, in which role he proved to be an ardent exponent of less governmental control of and more competition in the airlines industry. Thus from the standpoint of business, labor, and consumers, he would appear to have been a good choice to lead President Carter's fight to control inflation, for he seemed beholden to no special interest.

MAJOR ISSUES AND ACTIONS

Despite the President's lack of experience in diplomatic affairs, he has been fairly successful in the foreign policy area, perhaps because of the aid provided him by his many Trilateralist advisors. For instance, the Carter administration played a key role in helping bring about, after much trial and effort, the negotiation of a peace treaty between Egypt and Israel in the politically explosive Middle East, no mean achievement.[95]

Another area in which President Carter secured a notable victory was in reaching an agreement with the Republic of Panama over the long-simmering issue of American control of the Canal Zone, which strip of land and its vital waterway had long been viewed by the majority of Panamanians as an affront to their political sovereignty. Since the mid-1960s there had been a number of sharp anti-American outbursts and riots in Panama over our possession of this facility, the control of which had been granted, thanks to Theodore Roosevelt's aggressive action, to the American government in perpetuity. Most American business and government leaders could plainly see that the trend toward Panamanian nationalism could only lead to a permanent impairment of relations between the two countries, and perhaps between Washington and Latin America generally. Yet up to the Carter administration no significant progress had been made toward a resolution of this matter, largely because of adverse pressure generated in the United States, most recently by such men as California's arch-conservative former Governor, Ronald Reagan, who effectively exploited this issue in his 1976 Republican presidential bid against Gerald Ford.[96]

Shortly after assuming office, President Carter acted decisively to try to settle this dispute. To direct the accelerated efforts, he appointed a special two-man team which consisted of Ellsworth Bunker and Sol M. Linowitz. Bunker had a great deal of experience in diplomatic affairs, Linowitz considerably less. Both men had served, one after the other, as Ambassador to the Organization of American States under the Johnson administration. Since 1974 Bunker had been acting as head of the United States delegation which had been negotiating, albeit with modest results, with the Panamanian government over this pressing issue.

Neither of these men could be described as a career diplomat, as a public official without important outside links. For instance, although the elderly Bunker had long ago retired as a major business (sugar company) executive and had devoted much of his life since the early 1950s to diplomatic affairs, he had retained a number of corporate directorship ties. He still served as a trustee of the New York–based Atlantic Mutual Insurance Co., a medium-sized concern whose prestigious board included such important figures as Cleveland E. Dodge, a former high official of the Phelps Dodge Corp., and J. Peter Grace, the head of W. R. Grace and Co.[97] Similarly, since the late 1960s Linowitz had been one of the Washington partners of a fairly large Wall Street law firm known as Coudert Brothers, and served as a director of such giant enterprises as Pan-American World Airways, Time, and the Mutual Life Insurance Co.[98] Linowitz was also a member of the Trilateral Commission. In short, both of the men Carter picked to serve as co-negotiators of the Panama Canal treaty were economically elite figures.

These two officials were soon able to arrive at an agreement with Panamanian authorities which seemed acceptable to both parties. This accord provided that, upon approval by the two countries, Panama would immediately assume territorial jurisdiction over the Canal and within three years secure control over all the land in the American-held zone around this key waterway. However, the treaty also specified that the United States government would continue to operate and defend the Canal until the year 2000 (when Panama would take over this function), in return for which concession Panama would receive nearly $300 million in economic loans and guarantees, a $50 million military assistance package, and, in lieu of toll revenue, a sum of between $40 and $50 million a year until the end of the century, when it would automatically obtain all such shipping levies. From an American standpoint, the key provision in this treaty was the one which guaranteed that even after the year 2000 the United States government would have the irrevocable right to defend the neutrality of the Canal from any threat posed to its operations.

Despite certain clauses which displeased some nationalists, the Republic of Panama quickly adopted the treaty, largely because of the support of its ruler, General Omar Torrijos.[99] Yet its generally favorable nature notwithstanding, the proposed treaty ran into a great deal of opposition in the United States, particularly in the Senate, which would have to ratify or reject the document. A bitter battle was waged in this body, both openly and behind the scenes, before it finally voted, by a very narrow margin, to approve the accord in early 1978. Although many conservative interests worked hard to defeat the treaty, certain influential economic groups, such as the Business Roundtable, threw their weight behind the measure in what might be termed an act of enlightened self-interest. As du Pont's Irving Shapiro put it, apparently speaking mainly for this elite body, "we all worked on the Panama Canal treaties.... We all helped round up votes. We talked to everybody we knew, and urged their support."[100] Given the politico-economic connections of the Business Roundtable, its backing may have been a crucial factor in the adoption of the Canal pact.

It was in the domestic realm that President Carter came in for his heaviest criticism. For unlike most Democratic chief executives in recent decades, Jimmy Carter, in his professed efforts to fight inflation and balance the federal budget by 1981, adopted a distinctly conservative stance with regard to spending for social welfare measures and, aside from his veto of the extraordinarily costly B-1 bomber program, was, in part because of a pledge to NATO, more supportive of a fairly high level of defense expenditures.[101] In fact, the Carter administration took its toughest fiscal stand against three agencies that had long been strongly backed by the liberal forces in the Democratic party—HUD, HEW, and the Department of Labor.[102]

When Jimmy Carter campaigned for office in 1976, he vigorously supported a comprehensive national health insurance program for all segments of the population, which promise drew warm applause from liberal and labor groups around the country. But once ensconced in the White House, Carter adopted a much more cautious position on this important issue. His administration delayed for a considerable period before it formulated any major plan in this area. When revealed, it proved to be a rather timid proposal, which was severely criticized by progressive spokesmen such as Massachusetts Senator Edward Kennedy, who had developed a much broader (and more costly) program for national health care. Apparently largely because of mounting pressure, President Carter revised his plan substantially upward in 1979 to provide for insurance of all family medical costs above $2,500 a year, although it was to be implemented on a fiscally prudent ten-year "phase-in" basis and fell far short of what Senator Kennedy and other liberals strongly advocated.

In the realm of taxation, President Carter's record was likewise rather mixed or modest. In his first nationally televised debate with Gerald Ford during the 1976 presidential campaign, Carter had claimed that "the present tax structure is a disgrace to this country. It is just a welfare program for the rich."[103] Yet Carter's initial fiscal proposals were ones which primarily stressed tax relief for business and the general population, rather than progressive tax reform, which, Secretary of the Treasury Blumenthal persuaded the President, could wait till a later date.[104] After securing the adoption of a rather moderate tax reduction measure in 1977, Carter came forward with a more substantial plan in 1978 which called for some significant cuts in the income tax rates imposed on low- and middle-income groups (and slightly higher levies on those in the upper brackets).[105] Furthermore, the President recommended that corporate income taxes be decreased by about 10 percent, although he also called for a modest increase in the taxation of capital gains and a tightening or curtailment of expense-account deductions, two much-criticized sections of America's tax code.[106] By the time his bill got through both houses of Congress, much had changed, primarily for the worse. The most drastic shift was the adoption of a Republican-led measure to slash the maximum tax on capital gains from 49 percent to 28 percent, thereby largely undoing nearly a decade of financial reform in this area.[107] As a result of such maneuvering and a lack of progressive White House leadership, the 1978 revenue law provided for a $19 billion tax cut, of which at least 60 percent went to businesses and people with incomes of over $30,000 a year, while the bulk of the population got little more than 35 percent of the total tax relief.

Still another area in which the Carter administration chose to act—many would argue, belatedly—was in inflation. After initially relying on the part-time efforts of Robert Strauss, President Carter appointed former Cornell University professor and CAB head Alfred Kahn to take over the inflation control drive in late 1978. Because of inadequate statutory backing, however, this was essentially a voluntary program which depended largely on the persuasive powers of its top official and the force of public opinion.

Kahn plunged into his job with vigor and gusto. But comparatively little was accomplished, even when one makes due allowance for the short time he held office as chairman of the Council on Wage and Price Stability. For one thing, this agency was badly understaffed, with only about 200 people on its March 1979 payroll (in contrast to over 4,500 employed to administer the wage-price control program adopted by the Nixon regime in the early 1970s).[108] And a few months later the Council still employed only 25 persons to monitor wage increases around the nation and about 90 persons to check into price increases.[109] How could 25 people possibly oversee all, or even a substantial portion, of the wage boosts granted in the United States each year? At best, they could concentrate on the limited number of large-scale labor negotiations involving major unions.[110] Similarly, how could 90 persons properly monitor the prices imposed upon the myriad products manufactured in America? It was not even until the spring of 1979 that the first requirement for the periodic reporting of price increases was promulgated by the Council on Wage and Price Stability. Moreover, this body has not employed a consistent set of standards, for in mid-1979 it excused the United States Steel Corp. and eleven oil and chemical companies from complying with its test for price deceleration, and allowed them to use the (for them) less restrictive profit-margin approach.[111] The general unevenness and inequity of the program was even further revealed by the fact that in 1979 the overall compensation (including bonuses) of high corporate executives in the United States increased by almost 15 percent, while that of union workers rose by 8.3 percent, and that of non-union employees by only 7.2 percent.[112] Scant wonder that many people, particularly those in the middle- and low-income brackets, began to take a dim view of President Carter's anti-inflation program.[113]

For many reasons, President Carter's relations with organized labor were strained from the outset of his administration, although the union movement had strongly backed Carter *after* he won the Democratic nomination. Labor had also reportedly spent over $8 million to help elect a heavily Democratic Congress in 1976.[114] Yet perhaps because most union leaders had much preferred either Hubert Humphrey or Henry Jackson as the party's nominee, President Carter did not choose to appoint any of labor's top candidates to high federal office.

Moreover, shortly after he entered the White House, Carter rejected one of labor's first major requests, that the minimum wage be raised from $2.30 to a flat $3.00 an hour and that it be pegged thereafter at 60 percent of the average hourly wage in manufacturing. Instead, he agreed to a relatively modest increase of twenty cents an hour. Later, in July 1977, Carter finally acquiesced to a somewhat higher figure ($2.65) and a corollary provision that the minimum would, by an incremental process, be lifted to a level of 53 percent of the average manufacturing wage (roughly $3.10) by 1980.[115] But this fell far short of labor's original goal, and even the prescribed 1979 minimum wage standard was a little below the federally computed "poverty" line of $2.95 an hour.[116]

At about the same time organized labor received a sharp setback when its attempt to secure the passage of the common-site picketing bill, which would have allowed a striking union to picket (and, in effect, close down) an entire construction site, failed to pass in the House of Representatives, where its prospects for support had seemed very good. Such a measure had almost been adopted a year earlier (it came a cropper because of an unexpected Ford veto), and labor had felt fairly sure that, with the addition of a number of new Democratic members in Congress following the 1976 election, it could get this bill through with relative ease. However, the newly installed

President took a lukewarm position toward this measure, saying that he would sign it if Congress approved, but that he would not work actively to round up votes for its support.[117] Also strongly arrayed in opposition to this proposal was a potent ad hoc coalition of important economic interests, spearheaded by the Associated General Contractors of America, Associated Builders and Contractors, Inc., the reactionary National Right to Work Committee, the U.S. Chamber of Commerce, the National Association of Manufacturers, the Business Roundtable, and several large individual companies.[118] This alliance was able to build up a great deal of grassroots pressure, which organized labor simply failed to match, with the result that the common-site picketing bill was defeated in the House of Representatives.

In 1978 the AFL-CIO and its union allies received yet another stunning blow when its vigorously backed Labor Law Reform Act was killed by a filibuster in the United States Senate after it had been passed in the Lower House. This measure, which was widely viewed as one of the most important pieces of labor legislation to come before the Congress in recent decades, was aimed at shoring up the sagging fortunes of the union movement in America. Particularly disturbing was the increasing ineffectiveness of labor's organizational drives, which were frequently being foiled by the shrewd, at times questionable, tactics of many non-union employers. This bill would have set time limits for holding representation elections (thereby speeding up this often slow process), increased the penalties for businesses that violated the law, expanded the size of the National Labor Relations Board, and granted this body additional power to deal with "refusal to bargain" cases. The AFL-CIO and its affiliated unions reportedly spent about $2.5 million in a concerted effort to secure passage of this measure.[119] But after some initial division among America's large corporations, the various major business groups in the United States again closed ranks and, though perhaps not as well mobilized as in the common-site picketing battle, managed to generate enough support to make the filibuster in the Senate an effective one.[120] In the end labor was forced to give up this struggle, reluctantly conceding that it could not get such an act adopted in the foreseeable future. Thus organized labor suffered its second grievous defeat within a span of two years, thereby raising considerable question about its political power, particularly in the Carter administration.[121]

Another important field in which pro-business forces have prevailed in recent years is that of consumer protection, which has become a subject of increasing interest and concern. Although considerable progress has been made in this area at the state level of government, usually through the creation of well-staffed consumer protection agencies, no such gains have been registered in Washington. Instead the President has simply had a small office headed by a consumer affairs advisor. Several major attempts had been made in the early and mid 1970s to create a more effective unit, but without success. In the last try (in 1975) a consumer protection agency bill was approved by a fairly narrow margin by both houses of Congress, only to die in the face of a threatened veto by President Ford.

In late 1977 another concerted effort was made to enact a law calling for a somewhat diluted version of a consumer protection agency. It was strongly backed by Esther Peterson, President Carter's special advisor in this area, and various major consumer groups and liberal interests around the country.[122] But this bill was beaten back in the Lower House by a powerful coalition of nearly 400 business organizations and large companies, which was reportedly led by the Business Roundtable, the U.S. Chamber of Commerce, the Grocery Manufacturers of America, and such concerns as Procter and Gamble and the Armstrong Cork Co.[123] With this setback the consumer movement would appear to have been dealt a serious blow at the federal level, from which it may not recover for some time.

Overall, the most important problem which faced President Carter was the nation's rapidly escalating energy crisis. So seriously did Carter view this problem that when he introduced his first energy program in Congress in 1977, he described it as the "moral equivalent of war." This legislative package was a combination of energy conservation, taxation, and development measures ranging from a stiff levy on gas-guzzling cars to certain incentives for business, particularly public utilities, to convert from the use of gas and oil to coal, of which the country had enormous reserves. Yet for various reasons, one of which was an apparent lack of effective leadership on the part of the President himself (or his White House staff), over a year and a half elapsed before any action was taken in this area by Congress. Moreover, the measure that was adopted was a much altered and reduced version of the President's original plan. It provided for the construction of a pipeline to help bring natural gas from the northern slope of Alaska to the lower 48 states and, contrary to the President's initial request, for the gradual removal of governmental controls over the price of natural gas by 1985, much to the delight of many producers.[124] But Congress also failed to enact Carter's proposed tax on industrial users of oil and natural gas, one of the reputed cornerstones of his first energy plan.[125] In part because of this mixed legislative response, which clearly benefited the nation's natural gas interests, many other more effective steps were still needed by late 1978.[126]

Apparently to correct this state of affairs, President Carter presented, in early 1979, a major two-part oil program. This proposal stunned many people, for it represented a complete reversal of the position that Carter had taken during the 1976 presidential campaign when he proclaimed his strong support for continuation of oil price controls, which had been imposed in 1971, for a ten-year period, in an effort to help curb inflation.

The most important part of Carter's plan was his decision to let the existing control system expire, on a two-step "phase-out" basis, by October 1981, at which time all domestic oil would be allowed to float with the prevailing world price, however high that might be. In making this decision President

Carter chose essentially to follow the advice of the oil industry and many of his conservative Cabinet members, especially Secretary of Energy Schlesinger, who ardently espoused a "free market" solution to the nation's growing energy problem. The President was apparently convinced that a substantial boost in oil prices would significantly curtail oil consumption and at the same time provide a much needed incentive to the nation's major petroleum producers to expand their oil exploration and development efforts. However, as various critics pointed out, the use of higher prices to curtail gasoline consumption was, in essence, a rationing plan which would simply favor the well-to-do, who could better afford such prices. Furthermore, there was no evidence, judging from the higher price of gasoline and auto use in Europe, that prices of as much as $1.50 or even $2.00 a gallon would have much effect on the motoring public.

With regard to the argument that new corporate funds would do much to spur additional oil exploration and development, there was also considerable reason to doubt that all of this money would be so used. Indeed, as President Carter once noted, in the midst of the nation's first (1973–1974) great oil crisis, when gas prices and corporate profits were increasing at a striking rate, one major concern, Mobil, invested about $800 million in the acquisition of another large business enterprise, Marcor, Inc., which had nothing to do with oil or any other form of energy. Yet there was no requirement in President Carter's new program that the additional corporate funds generated through decontrol be employed in oil exploration and development. Moreover, in May 1979, just a few weeks after Carter put forward his decontrol plan, Exxon announced that it had made a bid of $1.2 billion for Cleveland's Reliance Electric Co., only 12 percent of which company's business had anything to do with energy. President Carter, curiously, did not raise any objection to this proposed merger, although even so conservative a source as *Fortune* magazine expressed considerable doubt about the matter.[127]

The other major part of President Carter's oil program was one which seemed to have much appeal, for it called for the imposition of a 50 percent "windfall" profits tax on the additional revenue the oil companies would gain from his decontrol program. This money would be channeled into a newly created governmental trust fund to aid the poor (who would be particularly hard hit by decontrol), to subsidize mass transportation, and to help develop other energy sources for the American people. However, Carter did not make decontrol conditional upon Congressional approval of an effective windfall profits tax. Instead, he had decided to proceed forthwith with decontrol (it would require negative votes in both the House and Senate to block his expiration decree), and then in a separate later action asked Congress to adopt his proposed windfall profits tax. Thus, by pushing decontrol through first, President Carter threw away whatever leverage he might have had to keep the oil industry from either blocking or seriously weakening a later tax act.

Various opponents of Carter's plan also pointed out that his windfall profits tax was not really as stiff a measure as it seemed, its 50 percent figure notwithstanding, for because of certain special clauses in the original proposal the bulk of the additional revenue generated through decontrol would still be retained by the oil companies.[128] Indeed, Orin Atkins, the head of the Ashland Oil Co., the nation's largest independent oil company (which had no great reserves of its own), calculated that if OPEC oil were selling, in real dollar terms, at $16 a barrel in 1982, the eight largest oil companies in the United States would end up with about $1.8 billion in additional after-tax profits from President Carter's decontrol program. As this knowledgeable authority put it, "... if Congress enacts decontrol and the windfall tax, the majors will cry all the way to the bank."[129]

In June and early July 1979, while the President was largely preoccupied by foreign policy, another major energy crisis erupted. Suddenly the Northeastern section of the country found itself seriously short of fuel, with the result that thousands of motorists were forced to wait in long lines to get what gas they could. To many citizens, there appeared to be no excuse for this situation (government data later showed that oil imports into the United States were actually higher in the first half of 1979 than in the same part of the preceding year). A substantial number of people were now compelled to get up at daybreak to have a reasonable chance of purchasing gas when the service stations opened. As a result, a great deal of suspicion and anger was directed at the oil companies, whose profits continued to rise spectacularly during this period, and at the Department of Energy, which appeared unable to handle the problem. In addition, reports soon began to indicate that this particular shortage had been created, in part, by the Department of Energy's faulty gas allocation system, and that much of the gas being sold was priced at a level higher than that permitted by law.[130] In short, although it was now a 20,000-man agency, the Department of Energy had been slow to react to this mounting crisis. Indeed, many critics contended that the agency was an administrative shambles.[131]

When President Carter returned to the United States from a Far Eastern diplomatic trip, he was immediately briefed about these grievous problems. At the very least, they posed a serious threat to his possible reelection in 1980 and even conceivably to his renomination as the Democratic party's candidate, for the polls now indicated that his public opinion rating had dropped to an all-time low, below that of Richard Nixon shortly before he was forced to resign from office. At the urging of some members of his White House staff, Carter hastily announced that he would make a major policy address to the nation. But within 48 hours he abruptly canceled his proposed speech, without explanation. He then went to his Camp David retreat for about ten days during which period he called in nearly 140 persons from diverse segments of the population to get the benefit of their counsel.[132]

On July 15 the President made his long-awaited address to the nation. It was, at heart, a highly political speech, and he again reverted to one of his favorite 1976 campaign themes, that of Americans feeling increasingly isolated from their government and of himself as an outsider.[133] The major part of his speech, in fact, did not deal with America's mammoth energy problem, but with what the President called that nation's "crisis in confidence," a general spiritual malaise and lack of faith in America's future.

However, the President did present a number of specific plans and programs. He promised that the United States would never import more oil in a single year than it had in 1977, a dramatic but hardly helpful proclamation since 1977 represented an all-time import high. Also, he renewed his plea for standby authority for gasoline rationing. And, much to the unease of many environmentalists, particularly those concerned about the dangers of nuclear power, he called for the creation of an Energy Mobilization Board to cut through red tape, the delays and the endless roadblocks to completing key energy projects. Most important of all, Carter urged that a government-backed Energy Security Corp. be established to spur the development of synthetic fuels in the United States, which sources, such as shale oil, had not yet been tapped because of the extraordinary expense involved. As initially conceived, this quasi-public agency, which would be granted a twelve-year Congressional charter and would be governed by a seven-member board (consisting of three Cabinet officers and four other members, appointed by the President with the advice and consent of the Senate), would receive, in the course of its existence, at least $88 billion, a colossal sum which, according to Carter's plan, would be generated through the proposed windfall profits tax.[134]

LATER MAJOR ADMINISTRATIVE AND DIPLOMATIC APPOINTMENTS

Shortly after presenting his new energy plan, President Carter announced that, as a result of his Camp David deliberations, he was making some major changes in his Cabinet and, to a lesser extent, in his personal staff. He then accepted the formally tendered resignations of two of his Cabinet officers, Griffin Bell and the heavily criticized James Schlesinger, and fired two others, Blumenthal and Califano, both of whom had strained relations with certain members of the Georgia-dominated White House staff. A fifth Cabinet member, Brock Adams, quit, stating that he would not submit to executive interference with the operation of his department. At the same time, the President's longtime top aide and campaign manager, Hamilton Jordan, was elevated to the position of White House chief of staff. The net effect of this massive shake-up was to create much consternation and confusion. Both Blumenthal and Califano were widely acknowledged to be very capable men (indeed, Califano was probably the best Secretary HEW ever had). Some critics contended that they were merely scapegoats for a politically troubled administration or possibly the victims of the dubious influence of Carter's Georgia coterie of White House advisors.[135] Conversely, Hamilton Jordan was viewed in many quarters as a relatively inexperienced, if not inept, figure who was probably incapable of effectively administering the White House staff or coordinating the reins of government.[136]

Yet despite President Carter's talk about the need for change, most of his new Cabinet officers did not really represent new blood in his administration.[137] For instance, as the successor to Attorney General Griffin Bell (who had long wanted to return to his Atlanta law practice and was the only Cabinet member who left on friendly terms), the President picked Bell's top aide in the Justice Department, former Baltimore lawyer Benjamin Civiletti. Until 1977 Civiletti had relatively litle experience in the federal government, having merely served briefly as an Assistant U.S. Attorney for Maryland in the early 1960s while a fairly young lawyer. He was reportedly made an Assistant Attorney General in 1977 primarily on the advice of President Carter's close friend and political counselor, Charles Kirbo, who, as a member of Atlanta's most influential law firm, had worked with Civiletti on several cases.[138] In May 1978 Civiletti was promoted to Deputy Attorney General when Pennsylvania's Peter Flaherty resigned to run for governor of his home state. But Civiletti had spent the bulk of his professional life as a member and then a full partner in one of Baltimore's largest law firms, Venable, Baetjer & Howard. Like many other top-tier concerns, this firm has not chosen to list any of its clients in either the *Martindale-Hubbell Law Directory* or the more prestigious *Bar Register*. However, two of its senior partners, H. Norman Baetjer, Jr., and H. Vernon Eney, had long served as directors of (and probably general counsel for) the Mercantile Bankshares Corp. of Baltimore, which had, counting its trust funds, total assets of well over $3 billion and had a substantial stake in many important business enterprises in the East, the most prominent of which was the Seaboard Coastline Industries, Inc., a big railroad.[139] Thus, although Civiletti had apparently never served on a major corporate board himself, he was, in effect, an elite figure.

As indicated, another of President Carter's changes involved the forced ouster of HEW Secretary Joseph A. Califano, a former well-connected Washington lawyer and onetime high staff aide to LBJ. As Califano's replacement, the President, perhaps because of the press of time, simply reached into his Cabinet and transferred his Secretary of Housing and Urban Development, Patricia Roberts Harris, a black lawyer with several former corporate ties, over to this more critical and complex post.

About a week later, after one rebuff, President Carter appointed former New Orleans mayor Moon Landrieu to serve as Mrs. Harris's successor at HUD.[140] Landrieu was a onetime (1958–1969) New Orleans lawyer whose fairly small firm apparently had no major corporate clients. He had made his reputation primarily by serving as mayor of this Southern metropolis from 1970 to 1978 (the maximum time permitted by law), during which period he had been very supportive of the civil rights movement and had done much to provide jobs for blacks in the city's government. During his two terms in office he had also played a prominent role in both the U.S. Conference of Mayors and the National Urban Coalition. Upon stepping down from municipal office in 1978, Landrieu became a high official of a local real estate concern which was, up to recently, in partnership with the (now deposed) Iranian dictator, Shah Mohammad Reza Pahlavi.[141] But regardless of Landrieu's recent economic connections, it would appear that he was appointed as Mrs. Harris's successor primarily for political reasons, to build up President Carter's shaky base of support in the South and among the nation's black population.

As his replacement for the deposed Secretary of the Treasury, W. Michael Blumenthal, President Carter chose a man of a very similar mold in G. William Miller, who only eighteen months earlier had been appointed to the post of Chairman of the Board of Governors of the Federal Reserve System.[142] Up to early 1978 Miller had been the head of a big (roughly $2 billion) New England–based conglomerate known as Textron, Inc., and had served in more recent years as a director of such other important enterprises as Allied Chemical, Federated Department Stores, and the Federal Reserve Bank of Boston. Yet, impressive as this set of connections may seem, Miller had other even more influential ties, for he had, up to 1978, been an active member of the Business Council and the chairman of the (National Industrial) Conference Board, which had become closely linked in recent years to both the Business Council and the Business Roundtable. Indeed, according to the *New York Times*, there were two men who played extremely important roles in Miller's selection as Chairman of the Federal Reserve Board (and one might assume, as Secretary of the Treasury), both of whom were members of President Carter's informal corporate "brain trust."[143] They were Irving Shapiro, the head of the du Pont Co., who was the (1977–1978) chairman of the Business Roundtable, a vice-chairman of the Business Council, and a trustee of the Conference Board, and Reginald Jones, the chief executive officer of GE, who was a co-chairman of the Business Roundtable and a member of the executive committee of the Business Council.[144] Thus there would appear to be very little difference in the economic background and organizational affiliations of the recently deposed Secretary of the Treasury, W. Michael Blumenthal, and his successor, G. William Miller, which fact lends credence to the charge that Blumenthal was fired primarily because of his strained personal relations with Carter's White House Staff.[145]

To take the place of Secretary of Transportation Brock Adams, President Carter chose, after a brief delay, a man from the same part of the country, Portland's mayor Neil Goldschmidt. Goldschmidt did not have as much experience as Adams in the transportation area, especially at the federal level. But, like Adams, he was a non-elite figure. In fact, he had been elected mayor of Portland in 1973 at the age of 32, and before that had been a local attorney practicing on his own, often as a legal aid lawyer. Perhaps the most unusual thing about this appointment is that it represented Carter's second Cabinet selection of a person who was (or had recently been) a mayor of one of the nation's big cities, for such people have, curiously, rarely been placed in the Cabinet (the only other mayor to be so chosen in the entire post-1933 period was John F. Kennedy's second Secretary of HEW, Anthony Celebrezze). Hence this action might be viewed as an attempt on President Carter's part to boost his political stock in America's urban areas.

As the much-criticized James R. Schlesinger's successor as Secretary of Energy, the President chose Charles W. Duncan, Jr., a man who became acquainted with Carter as president of the Coca-Cola Co. in the early 1970s and, because of this connection, was later appointed Deputy Secretary of Defense.[146] As indicated earlier, Duncan was originally a Texas businessman whose family-dominated food company had been merged into the Coca-Cola Co. in 1964. Duncan then accepted a second-tier position with this big Georgia-based company and apparently did very well, for in 1971 he became its president. However, Duncan only held this key post until 1974, when he returned to Texas to become head of a fairly small, privately owned concern known as the Rotan Mosle Financial Corp. (which in the mid-1970s had only a few hundred employees and sales of a little over $20 million a year).[147] During this period Duncan continued to sit on the board of Coca-Cola (he was one of its largest stockholders), and he also served, up to 1977, as a director of the Great Southern Corp. (a big Texas-based financial holding company), the Southern Railway, and the A.P.S. subsidiary of the giant conglomerate, Gulf and Western Industries, Inc.

Yet there is another side to Duncan's business background which should be emphasized at this point, for, apparently unknown to the press and many government officials, the Duncan family had long been closely associated with various oil and natural gas interests in the Lone Star State. The new Energy Secretary's brother, John H. Duncan, had been a board member of the big Houston Natural Gas Corp. since 1968, and also served as a director of the Bank of the Southwest from 1968 to 1974 and thereafter as a director of an ever larger bank holding company known as Texas Commerce Bankshares, Inc.[148] Moreover, although a Georgia-based executive for a decade after 1964, Charles W. Duncan, Jr., acted as an advisory director of the Bank of the Southwest up to 1967, and his father maintained a similar affiliation up to 1978. What made these financial links so important was the fact that the boards of these two Houston banks have been dominated by oil and natural gas figures. For example, in 1979 the board of Texas Commerce Bankshares, Inc., included a high official of the Exxon Corp., the president of Scurlock Oil Co. (a big privately owned concern), the head of the El Paso (Natural Gas) Co., the chief executive of the Houston Natural Gas Corp., the board chairman of the Hughes Tool Co. (which makes most of the oil-drilling equipment in the United States), a vice-president of the Getty Oil Co., the president of the General Crude Oil Co., and a number of other such interests.[149] In short, as Duncan himself recently said, "I have friends in the Texas oil industry."[150] Thus, many might question whether Duncan could act as an objective public official, particularly in an area in which potent business forces have long wielded great influence in American government.[151]

Shortly after his mid-1979 Cabinet shake-up, President Carter also decided, reacting a bit belatedly to many negative comments about his largely Georgia-recruited White House staff, to make a number of changes in this area, with a view apparently to transforming it into a more effective and broadly based operation.[152] His first step in this direction was to appoint Hedley Donovan, the recently retired editor-in-chief of *Time* magazine, to serve as a special advisor who would report directly to him, rather than to press secretary Jody Powell, a now much overshadowed figure. This move was obviously made in an effort to improve the President's public image. But what is most interesting about this appointment is that Donovan had a number of key civic ties, for he was both a member of the influential Trilateral Commission and a director of the Council on Foreign Relations.[153] In short, Donovan was, unlike Powell, an elite figure.

In another change made about the same time, President Carter picked Alonzo L. McDonald, Jr., a former New York management consultant who had served recently as Robert Strauss's deputy special trade negotiator, to act as director of the White House staff under Hamilton Jordan. This appointment was apparently made because of the harsh criticism directed at Jordan by many well-informed Washington observers, who felt that this relatively youthful political operative, to whom the President was strongly attached, was simply incapable of effectively administering the White House staff or coordinating the reins of government in the critical months ahead. Yet McDonald was something more than the ordinary management executive, for prior to his entry into the federal government he had been a high-ranking official of McKinsey & Co., one of the nation's leading business consultants and, even more important, he had been one of the three people in his profession to grace the 208-person board of the Establishment-dominated CED.

Finally, in yet another striking move, the President persuaded his rather ineffectual general counsel, Robert Lipshutz, to resign, so that he might be replaced by a more able figure. As his successor, Carter chose Washington lawyer Lloyd Cutler, who had much experience in dealing with the federal government. Indeed, judging from various accounts, there was no one in the nation's capital who ranked above Cutler as a political and legal operative, not even the legendary Clark Clifford.[154] In addition, Cutler had, unlike Lipshutz, numerous crucial links, for he was a member of the Trilateral Commission, a director of the American Cyanamid Co. and the Council on Foreign Relations, and a trustee of the Brookings Institution, all elite organizations.[155] Thus it would certainly appear that with Cutler's appointment as White House general counsel, and the selection of Donovan and McDonald, the nation's economic establishment had taken over a significant part of the operations of this vital center of American government.

In retrospect, it may be said that the Carter administration was, for a post–New Deal Democratic regime, rather remarkable for its representation of elite interests.[156] This is especially true when one considers the fact that Carter campaigned as an anti-Establishment figure who would bring fresh blood and new thinking to Washington. However, he had actually forged, fairly early in his career, major ties with important forces in Georgia's business community, particularly the Atlanta-based Coca-Cola Co. and its law firm, King & Spalding. Carter had also become closely associated through the Trilateral Commission with a number of influential corporate executives and academics, primarily in the Northeast, and these contacts were of great value to him at various points in his uphill battle to win the nation's highest office. Hence it is not surprising that when he took over as President in January 1977, he turned to an extraordinary extent to those select circles for his top government officials. They clearly served as key recruitment channels. In fact, over 65 percent of the Cabinet and major diplomatic positions were filled, under Carter, by elite figures. This was one of the two highest percentages for any Democratic administration since the turn of the century, and was by far highest when computed in terms of Cabinet officials alone.

As one might expect, given its essentially conservative makeup, the Carter administration followed a rather cautious line of action in many areas, though there were some significant exceptions. Most of the latter were in the realm of foreign policy, where Carter tackled a series of difficult problems, such as the long-seething Panama Canal dispute, the bitter conflict between Israel and the Arab states, and the SALT (strategic arms limitation treaty) talks, and achieved at least two notable successes, in the first case with the help of major American business interests eager to reach an enduring accord on the status of this vital waterway.

On the domestic front, Carter's record was largely negative. Although he talked much about the need for reform in many areas during his 1976 presidential campaign, there have been few major accomplishments during his administration, in part because of the inexperience of some high officials and in part because of the clearly conservative nature of the regime. For instance, little was achieved in the realm of tax reform or national health care. Also, Carter took a rather lukewarm position on the first two pieces of labor legislation that the AFL-CIO strongly backed during the first part of his administration, the common-site picketing bill and the Labor Law Reform Act, both of which were effectively thwarted by pro-business interests in Congress.

However, there was one area in which the Carter administration moved with considerable vigor, particularly in 1979, and that was with regard to the nation's growing energy crisis. But the crucial part of Carter's program to resolve this problem, to spur oil exploration and production through the two-staged removal of governmental control over prices, was one which, despite the President's claims about the merits of his windfall profits tax, would be of tremendous benefit to the petroleum industry, as some high oil company executives now readily concede. Furthermore, after his great Cabinet purge, Carter replaced his first, administratively inept Secretary of Energy, who had basically an academic and governmental background, with an official who was on friendly terms with important oil and natural gas interests in Texas. This was a revealing commentary on a man who, in running for President, claimed to be an anti-Establishment "outsider."

Notes

1. See *Business Week* (October 20, 1976), p. 60. The influence of the Business Roundtable clearly did not stem from the size of its staff or operating budget, which were quite small compared to those of such groups as the NAM, U.S. Chamber of Commerce, American Bankers Association, and American Petroleum Institute, but rather from the collective power exerted by its roughly 200 members, the vast majority of whom were the chief executive officers of firms found in either *Fortune's* "top 200" industrial ranking or one of its other "top 50" lists.

2. A significant amount of the AEI's research is now undertaken in conjunction with the Stanford-based Hoover Institution, an even more rightist body whose board includes William Baroody, Sr.; Gertrude Himmelfarb, the wife of New York publicist Irving Kristol; J. Howard Wood, a longtime high official of the Chicago *Tribune*; former Secretary of the Treasury William Simon; and the recent chairman of the Council of Economic Advisers, Alan Greenspan.

3. See American Enterprise Institute for Public Policy Research, *Memorandum* (September–October, 1978), p. 3, and the *New York Times* (July 16, 1978), Sect. III, p. 1.

4. For an extended treatment of this group, see Laurence H. Shoup and William Minter, *Imperial Brain Trust*.

5. Kirkland's CFR tie could be interpreted in a number of ways, but whatever the case, he was the first union official to be appointed to the board of this civic body.

6. For more on the origins of the Trilateral Commission, see Jeremiah Novak, "The Trilateral Commission," *Atlantic* (July 1977), pp. 57–58.

7. See Thomas Ferguson and Joel Rogers, "The Political Economy: The State of the Unions," *The Nation* (April 28, 1979), pp. 462–65.

8. See, for instance, *Business Week* (March 5, 1979), p. 24.

9. The overall financial holdings of the Carter family were estimated to be worth about $5 million in the mid-1970s. See Laurence H. Shoup, *The Carter Presidency—and Beyond* (Palo Alto, Cal.: Ramparts Press, 1980), p. 22.

10. See Robert Shogan, *Promises to Keep: Carter's First Hundred Days* (New York: Crowell, 1977), p. 44. Interestingly, both Young and Woodcock were members of the Trilateral Commission, Woodcock being one of the three union officials in the country to be affiliated with this influential group.

11. Despite the image conveyed by his small-town, peanut-growing background, Carter was reportedly the most successful Democratic fundraiser and biggest spender in the race for his party's presidential nomination—the Carter total being $11.4 million, about 50 percent more than that of George Wallace and almost twice that of Morris Udall. See Laurence H. Shoup, *op. cit.*, p. 30.

12. For instance, Carter's young campaign manager, Hamilton Jordan, told Robert Sheer of *Playboy* magazine that if Cyrus Vance were named Secretary of State and Zbigniew Brzezinski head of national security in the Carter administration, "then I would say we failed, and I'd quit." Shortly before the general election *Los Angeles Times*' Robert Shogan queried Jordan further about this matter, and the latter said that he should not have singled out these two men for exclusion. But he remained firm on his basic point, stating that "if you look at the top twenty people in the Carter administration, whether they're Cabinet officials or White House advisers or whatever, fifteen of them will be people you've never heard of before, people that are not big names nationally." See Robert Shogan, *op. cit.*, p. 84; and for similar statements, see Bruce Adams and Kathryn Kavanagh-Baran, *Promise and Performance: Carter Builds a New Administration* (Lexington, Mass.: Heath, 1979), p. 35.

13. According to one reliable source, E. J. Kahn, Jr., the Trust Co. of Georgia has long been informally referred to as "the Coca-Cola bank." The only other larger financial enterprise in Georgia was the Citizens & Southern National Bank, which was more of a statewide banking empire than one rooted in Atlanta. Two other big Atlanta-based concerns, the Georgia Power Co. and Delta Air Lines, were both apparently on friendly terms with the Coca-Cola Co. This famous beverage company has been dominated, since 1919, by Atlanta's wealthy Woodruff family, the longtime head of which, Robert Woodruff, was reportedly the best friend of both Georgia's onetime influential U.S. Senator Walter George and Atlanta's former mayor, Fred Hartsfield, two ties which would indicate that Coca-Cola carried great weight in governmental affairs. See. E. J. Kahn, Jr., *The Big Drink: The Story of Coca-Cola* (New York: Random House, 1950), pp. 52, 62–63, 77, and 140.

14. For two books which deal with Atlanta's power structure, but reach much different conclusions, see Floyd Hunter, *Community Power Structure* (Chapel Hill: University of North Carolina Press, 1953), and M. Kent Jennings, *Community Influentials: The Elites of Atlanta* (Glencoe, Ill.: Free Press, 1964). For one business article which indirectly supports Hunter's findings, see *Fortune* (September 1961), pp. 108–112 and 180–190.

15. Kirbo has apparently never served on any major corporate boards. However, two of his senior law partners, James M. Sibley and Hughes Spalding, Jr., had important business connections. Both served on the board of the Trust Co. of Georgia, along with J. Paul Austin, the present head of Coca-Cola; Charles H. Candler, Jr., a large stockholder in Coca-Cola and a grandson of its founder; Charles H. Dolson, a high official of Delta Air Lines; and Robert W. Scherer, the chief executive officer of the Georgia Power Co. Sibley's father, John A. Sibley, and Spalding's brother-in-law, George S. Craft, both of whom were former heads of the Trust Co. of Georgia, were directors of Coca-Cola, together with Robert Woodruff and his brother, George. Up to his death in 1969 Spalding's father, who helped build up this elite law firm, graced the board of both the Coca-Cola Co. and the Trust Co. of Georgia. It should also be noted that Hughes Spalding's brother, Jack, served as the editor of the *Atlanta Journal*, one of the two major newspapers owned by the wealthy Cox family.

16. Up to 1976 Austin had also been a director of the Continental Oil Co. Coca-Cola had maintained these kinds of crucial national links for many years. For instance, although some years past the normal point of retirement, this company's long-dominant chief executive, Robert Woodruff, served on the board of the Morgan Guaranty Trust Co. up to 1960, the Metropolitan Life Insurance Co. up to 1965, and the Southern Railway up to 1971. In addition, in his earlier years Woodruff had been an active member of the Business Council.

17. See *Dun's Review* (December 1976), p. 94. Though sheer chance, it is rather ironic, from a politico-economic standpoint, that Carter's single most important corporate link is with the Coca-Cola Co., and that of President Nixon was with its arch-rival, Pepsico. Perhaps not coincidentally, less than one week after President Carter announced the establishment of formal diplomatic relations with Communist China, the Coca-Cola Co. signed an agreement with this government to begin selling its products there. It was the first American food or beverage company to reach such an accord with China.

18. It should also be noted that a considerable amount of Carter's pre-convention campaign money was raised by New York interests. Of the six national finance directors of Carter's costly nomination race, three were high officials in Lehman Brothers, one was a vice-president of Paine, Webber, Jackson & Curtis, another was a vice-president of Kidder, Peabody & Co., and the sixth was apparently John L. Loeb, Sr., the senior partner in Loeb, Rhoades & Co. (who had married into the Lehman family). Other prominent businessmen who were involved in fundraising efforts for Carter's general election campaign included Henry Ford II, Edgar M. Bronfman, president of the Canadian-controlled Seagram Co., Ltd., former New York department store executive Walter Rothschild (who had married a member of the Warburg family of Kuhn, Loeb & Co.), and Felix Rohatyn, a partner in Lazard Frères & Co. See the *New York Times* (August 26, 1976), p. 49, and (November 26, 1976), Sect. 4, p. 1.

19. For the best available account to date of Carter's involvement with the Trilateral Commission, see Laurence H. Shoup, *op. cit.*, pp. 39–62, and for two briefer analyses of this relationship, see Christopher Lydon, "Jimmy Carter Revealed: He's a Rockefeller Republican," *Atlantic* (July 1977), pp. 50–57, and Jeremiah Novak, *op. cit.*, pp. 57–59.

20. See Laurence H. Shoup, *op. cit.*, p. 52.

21. See Thomas R. Dye and L. Harmon Zeigler, *The Irony of Democracy* (North Scituate, Mass.: Duxbury Press, 1978), p. 253.

22. See the *New York Times* (February 5, 1978), Sect. 3, p. 1.

23. See the *New York Times* (July 24, 1978), p. D1.

24. For an analysis of this special recruitment process, generally described as the talent inventory program, see Bruce Adams and Kathryn Kavanagh-Baran, *Promise and Performance*, passim.

25. Vance, interestingly, had not been one of Carter's early supporters, but had been a backer of R. Sargent Shriver, one of the first casualties in the Democratic presidential campaign. See Jules Witcover, *Marathon: The Pursuit of the Presidency, 1972–1976* (New York: Viking, 1977), p. 151.

26. See Paul Hoffman, *Lions in the Street*, p. 25.

27. As for elite family connections, Vance had married the daughter of a wealthy New York businessman, John Sloane, and in 1974 his daughter married the son of James H. Higgins, the board chairman of the Mellon Bank and a director of the Gulf Oil Corp.

28. On this last point, see the *New York Times* (February 4, 1977), p. A10.

29. The other two Under Secretaries of State for Political Affairs and for Management were longtime career diplomats David Newsom and Benjamin Read.

30. In 1976 Cooper was also a member of the CED's research advisory board, another sign that he was favorably perceived by Establishment leaders.

31. Mrs. Benson had also been extremely active in Common Cause, and had served briefly (in 1974–1975) as a director of the large Federated Department Stores.

32. Of the six Assistant Secretaries of State for major area affairs, only one could be described as an Establishment-oriented figure, and that was Assistant Secretary of State for East Asian and Pacific Affairs Richard Holbrooke, who had been managing editor of *Foreign Policy* magazine and was a member of the Trilateral Commission. The other Assistant Secretaries were either longtime career diplomats or such experienced persons as Richard Moose, who had served since the late 1960s as a staff aide for the Senate Foreign Relations Committee.

33. President Carter appointed three other ambassadors-at-large: Alfred L. Atherton, a longtime career diplomat, Henry Owen, a Brookings Institution researcher, and Elliot Richardson. Both Owen and Richardson were members of the Trilateral Commission.

34. When Smith stepped down from this Trilateral post to enter the Carter administration, he was replaced by New York banker David Rockefeller.

35. Although the purpose of this new procedure was to help the President make diplomatic

appointments primarily on the basis of merit, Carter nevertheless selected a few wealthy Atlanta figures, such as attorney Philip H. Alston, Jr., and Anne Cox Chambers, head of the family-owned Atlanta Newspapers, Inc., to serve as ambassadors to certain second-tier countries. For a description of this screening process, see Bruce Adams and Kathryn Kavanagh-Baran, *Promise and Performance*, pp. 131-39, and the *New York Times* (May 18, 1979), p. 15.

36. Former Georgia Congressman Andrew Young, whom Carter picked to serve as our Ambassador to the United Nations, had also been a member of the Trilateral Commission, although the author has not been able to determine just when in 1976 he joined its prestigious ranks.

37. By way of emphasizing the centrality of this set of "civic" ties, Roger Morris has somewhat uncharitably asserted that "... it was far more important... that Zbigniew Brzezinski was a protege of David Rockefeller's and a guest at Averell Harriman's Georgetown house than that he was the author of an unbroken succession of misguided mediocre books." See Roger Morris, "Jimmy Carter's Ruling Class," *Harper's* (October 1977), p. 41.

38. That Brzezinski and Vance had similar civic links does not mean that they had identical views on American foreign policy, for the former frequently took a harder line toward Russia and Red China than Vance, perhaps because of Brzezinski's European (Polish-Czechoslovakian) background.

39. Perhaps because of these unwarranted charges and the many frustrations encountered in this job, Warnke resigned as director of the U.S. Arms Control and Disarmament Agency in late 1978, and was replaced by a more hawkish figure, former Army General George Seignious II, who was now president of a military college (the Citadel) and a director of the Southern Bancorporation, a fairly big South Carolina bank holding company.

40. No doubt for these reasons *Time* magazine ran a special feature in late 1976 on the Trilateral Commission and Brookings Institution, two fairly closely linked groups which it described as Carter's "brain trusts" (see *Time*, December 20, 1976, p. 19). It is difficult to estimate the extent to which this recruitment pattern was a product of the influence exerted by these institutions, as contrasted with the lack of knowledge and naïvete of the relatively inexperienced Jimmy Carter.

41. Three other major executives had originally been viewed as strong candidates for this position—Alden W. Clausen, president of the Bank of America, Irving Shapiro, the head of the du Pont Co., and Robert Roosa of Brown Brothers Harriman & Co. All were clearly Establishment figures. Clausen and Roosa were, for instance, Trilateralists, and Roosa was also chairman of the Brookings Institution. Shapiro was chairman of the Business Roundtable, an active member of the Business Council, and a director of the Citicorp. and IBM. However, for various reasons each asked that his name be withdrawn from consideration at some point in the proceedings. This left only Charles Schultze, a onetime high federal official, in the final running, but perhaps because of his largely academic background, he was ultimately given a less prominent post.

42. See Paul Hoffman, *Lions in the Street*, p. 21. This Treasury position was first offered to New York executive Kenneth Axelson, a longtime high official of the J. C. Penney Co., and a director of the Grumman (Aircraft) Corp., who had recently served briefly as a deputy mayor of New York City. But because of a recently initiated investigation of his previous conduct as a corporate official, Axelson removed himself from consideration for this post.

43. According to the biographical sketch he prepared for his nomination hearings before the Senate Finance Committee in 1977, Solomon had worked primarily as a sculptor during 1975 and early 1976—not a common pre-appointment occupation for a high Treasury Department official.

44. Since 1973 Bergsten had served as a member of the editorial advisory board of the CFR's prestigious journal, *Foreign Affairs*, and as a consultant to the Rockefeller Foundation. In the mid-1970s he worked briefly for the Trilateral Commission and was elected a director of the Consumers Union.

45. Similarly, although the Treasury Department's general counsel, Robert Mundheim, had

been a University of Pennsylvania law professor, he too had at least one significant corporate link. In fact, judging from various business manuals, he served as a director of the big ($1.5 billion) securities concern known as the Weeden Holding Corp. (originally Weeden & Co.) from 1972 to 1979, which post-1976 tie would appear to constitute a gross conflict of interest.

46. Two other important offices were created in the Defense Department under Harold Brown. One was Under Secretary of Defense for Research and Engineering, a position filled by William J. Perry, who had been head of a medium-sized scientific enterprise known as ESL, Inc. The other post, established in 1978, was Under Secretary for Policy, the primary purpose of which was to integrate the activities of this vast, often unwieldy department. This office was assumed by former Wall Street lawyer and Defense Department executive Stanley Resor, who had been serving since 1973 as head of the American delegation to the European talks on mutual and balanced armed force reductions. Resor was a well-connected figure, for he had married into the Pillsbury family and his brother-in-law, Gabriel Hauge, was the recently retired head of the Manufacturers Hanover Trust Co., and the longtime treasurer of the Council on Foreign Relations. However, Resor soon found this job to be extremely frustrating, and resigned in despair in early 1979.

47. Duncan also served as a director of the Trust Co. of Georgia ("Coca-Cola's bank") from 1972 to 1975, about which time he shifted his primary base of economic operations to Houston.

48. For more on Duncan, see Richard J. Walton, "Why Things Go Better With Coke," *The Nation* (March 31, 1979), pp. 335-36.

49. As many critics pointed out, Bell belonged to several segregated social clubs in Atlanta up to 1976.

50. See, for instance, the *New York Times* (December 30, 1976), p. 23.

51. See Robert Shogan, *op. cit.*, p. 89.

52. For a brief but incisive analysis of King & Spalding as the Establishment law firm of Atlanta, see the *New York Times* (December 24, 1976), p. A10.

53. See *Forbes* (January 15, 1977), p. 28. As his first Deputy Attorney General, Bell picked a non-elite figure from the North, Peter Flaherty, who had spent most of his adult life engaged in local politics and had most recently served as mayor of Pittsburgh. Flaherty had been a strong early backer of Carter's candidacy in the critical Pennsylvania primary. However, the ambitious Flaherty stepped down from office in early 1978 to run for governor of his home state. He was replaced at this juncture by a recently appointed Assistant Attorney General, Benjamin Civiletti, who, unlike Bell and Flaherty, had comparatively little experience in government. He had instead been a longtime member of a large Baltimore law firm known as Venable, Baetjer & Howard.

54. See Robert Shogan, *op. cit.*, p. 85.

55. The next two most important posts in the department, Under Secretary of the Interior and Solicitor, were curiously filled by second-tier officials recruited from the same set of corporate interests, the Cummins Engine Co. of Indiana and its allied enterprises. These two people were James A. Joseph, who was a (black) vice-president for corporate action for the above concern, and Leo Krulitz, who was a vice-president and treasurer of the Irwin Management Co., which controls and invests the assets of the J. Irwin Miller family, which has long controlled the big Cummins Engine Co., which makes most of the diesel engines in America.

56. See the *New York Times* (February 20, 1978), Sect. 4, p. 3 and (May 23, 1978), p. 16.

57. See Robert Shogan, *op. cit.*, p. 86.

58. See the *New York Times* (December 21, 1976), p. 24. Bergland had once served as a state official and organizer for the National Farmers Union.

59. The man first picked to be Deputy Secretary of Agriculture, John C. White, had an even longer record of activity in this area, for he had served for 17 years (1950-1977) as the

Commissioner of Agriculture in Texas, which remarkable tenure of office would indicate that he got along well with major farm interests in the Lone Star State. That White was also probably an influential political figure may be inferred from the fact that when former Texas lawyer and businessman Robert Strauss stepped down as chairman of the Democratic National Committee in late 1977, he was replaced by White. The latter's post in the Department of Agriculture was later taken by Jim Williams, the Lieutenant-Governor of Florida.

60. President Carter first offered this position to Jane Cahill Pfeiffer, one of about thirty vice-presidents of IBM. Mrs. Pfeiffer was also a director of Bache & Co. (a big brokerage firm) and Chesebrough-Pond's, Inc. (a large cosmetics and household products company). In addition, she was, like Vance and Blumenthal, a trustee of the Rockefeller Foundation. However, Mrs. Pfeiffer turned down Carter's offer for personal reasons.

61. As her top aide in the department, Professor Kreps made a somewhat unusual choice in that she picked a relatively obscure New York businessman named Sidney Harman. This person had no prior governmental experience, but had been the longtime head of a concern known as Harman International Industries, Inc., a fairly sizable, family-owned sound and auto equipment company. Harman held this post until the first part of 1979 when he was succeeded as Deputy Secretary of Commerce by another North Carolina figure, Luther Hodges, Jr., the son of President Kennedy's Secretary of Commerce. Hodges had been head of the big North Carolina National Bank before he resigned to make an unsuccessful bid in 1978 to capture one of his state's two U.S. Senate seats.

62. See Bruce Adams and Kathryn Kavanagh-Baran, *Promise and Performance*, pp. 38–39, and *Time* (November 22, 1976), p. 14.

63. Apparently unknown to many leaders of the labor movement, Dunlop had recently been elected to the board of the big General Telephone & Electronics Corp., a tie that might have made him less pro-union than Meany anticipated.

64. Almost all the other major executives of this department were former government officials, such as Under Secretary of Labor Robert Brown, who had held a number of lesser posts in this area since 1964. Contrary to its reputation for being a clientele agency, only two of Labor's second-tier officials, Robert Burkhardt and Howard Samuel, had been connected with the union movement. Actually, it was not until April 1977 that Carter finally threw labor what *Time* magazine has described as its only significant "sop" in the appointment process when he picked John Fanning, a longtime federal official who was friendly to the union cause, to be chairman of the National Labor Relations Board. See *Time* (April 11, 1977), p. 55.

65. That Califano probably had numerous wealthy corporate clients can be inferred from the fact that he made over $500,000 a year prior to his appointment to Cabinet office. See the *New York Times* (February 26, 1977), p. 9.

66. See *Forbes* (January 15, 1977), p. 28, and also the *New York Times* (February 14, 1977), p. A10. Most of the other high officials in HEW, however, were drawn from various academic sources, a now widely accepted practice.

67. Initially, President Carter offered this post to New York civic leader Franklin A. Thomas, who was the longtime head of the Bedford-Stuyvesant redevelopment project and, thanks to a recent trend, a director of at least six large corporations—the Allied Stores Corp., CBS, Cummins Engine Co., Citicorp, New York Life Insurance Co., and New York Telephone Co. (an AT&T subsidiary). However, Thomas, who was later appointed president of the Ford Foundation, turned down the job. Carter then asked Georgia Congressman Andrew Young, who was one of his early presidential supporters and a member of the Trilateral Commission, to assume this position, but he too declined.

68. The best known partner in this concern was former high federal official R. Sargent Shriver, a Kennedy in-law. But its most influential economic figure was clearly New York attorney Sam Harris, who served on the board of the huge Rio Tinto Zinc Corp., Ltd. (which was dominated by the French Rothschild interests), Brinco, Ltd. (a Canadian minerals company probably controlled by Rio Tinto), and the American-based GAF Corp. Sam Harris was not, by

the way, related to Patricia.

69. A possible counterbalance may have been created through Mrs. Harris's service on the board of trustees of the Twentieth Century Fund, one of the more liberal major civic groups in the country.

70. Most of the other high posts in HUD were filled by people who represented a wide variety of backgrounds, which appeared to blend in with the overall goal and operation of this department.

71. For an analysis of the legislative origins and development of the Conrail system, which apparently was strongly backed by certain major banking interests in the East and a number of the big railroads in the West which depended heavily on the traffic generated by the Penn Central, see Richard Saunders, *The Railroad Mergers and the Coming of Conrail* (Westport, Conn.: Greenwood Press, 1978), pp. 307–09.

72. None of the other high officials in this department had any significant socio-economic links. The Deputy Secretary of Transportation was Adams's longtime Congressional aide, Alan Butchman, and the major assistant secretaries were men who had largely governmental backgrounds.

73. The chairman of the advisory council of the Johns Hopkins School for Advanced International Studies was Paul Nitze, a former Defense Department official, who probably shared Schlesinger's strongly hawkish views.

74. For a brief analysis of the Center for Strategic and International Studies, Morton Kondrake "Georgetown's Think Tank on the Potomac," *Change* (September 1978), pp. 44–45.

75. See *Time* (February 19, 1979), p. 16.

76. Prior to his appointment as Secretary of Energy, Schlesinger also owned a modest amount of stock in a California concern known as the Newhall Land and Farming Co., which had assets of about $140 million and included gas and oil operations among its various activities. Schlesinger reportedly relied very little on the advice of other high-level officials in the Department of Energy, most of whom had governmental or technical backgrounds. In fact, initially, only one major officer in DOE had any important corporate ties, and that was its general counsel, Lynn R. Coleman, who was a Washington partner in the big Houston law firm of Vinson & Elkins, which had long represented influential oil interests such as the Occidental Petroleum Co. and the Texas Eastern Transmission Corp. Coleman had also been a registered lobbyist for the Houston Natural Gas Corp., although he pledged in his nomination hearings to disqualify himself on any matters that involved his former law firm's clients. See the *New York Times* (February 7, 1978), p. 6.

77. See the *New York Times* (December 24, 1976), p. 11.

78. In fact, one study recently concluded that Carter's much heralded talent search was, in the end, "little more than a charade," although for different reasons than advanced here. It claimed that Carter's talent inventory program came a cropper because of the dubious influence of the President's chief political advisor, Hamilton Jordan, a rather weak argument. See Bruce Adams and Kathryn Kavanagh-Baran, *Promise and Performance*, pp. 28–29.

79. See the *New York Times* (February 5, 1978), Sect. 3, p. 1.

80. See *Fortune* (March 27, 1978), pp. 53–54.

81. Though little noted at the time, Carter is reported to have first offered this post (without success) to one of his most influential informal advisors, GE boss Reginald Jones, who was a co-chairman of the Business Roundtable and a member of the executive committee of the Business Council. See the *New York Times* (September 16, 1979), Sect. 6, p. 34.

82. See *Time* (December 6, 1976), p. 20 and (May 23, 1977), p. 38. According to these accounts, Lance owned a forty-room Gatsby-like mansion in Atlanta, a $100,000 house in Calhoun, and a vacation home in exclusive Sea Island, Georgia.

83. The only boards on which Lance served as an outside director at the time of his appointment to federal office were the Atlantic American Corp. (a fairly small Georgia financial holding company) and Crown Crafts, Inc. (a medium-sized Calhoun-based concern).

84. It was later revealed that Lance had granted financial favors to various kinsmen and close friends, one of whom was President Carter, whose peanut business received substantial loans from the National Bank of Georgia at preferred interest rates and without adequate collateral. See the *New York Times* (November 19, 1978), p. 1, and (January 19, 1979), p. 1.

85. In addition, Schultze had served as a director of a large textile concern known as Indian Head, Inc., from 1968 to 1974, when this company was taken over by foreign economic interests. This was Schultze's only recent corporate link, and its effect was probably outweighed by his other affiliations.

86. The other two members of the CEA under Schultze were William Nordhaus, a Yale University professor, and Lyle Gramley, a senior economist with the Federal Reserve Board, both of whom were technocrats.

87. Since his departure from the federal government following President Kennedy's assassination, Sorensen had been associated with a major New York law firm that had a strongly Democratic orientation, Paul, Weiss, Rifkind, Wharton & Garrison. For more on this firm and its many politically influential partners, see Paul Hoffman, *Lions in the Street*, pp. 112–121.

88. President Carter's record of appointments to the nation's independent regulatory agencies has been a rather mixed one. For example, as chairman of the Securities and Exchange Commission, he chose a Californian, Harold M. Williams, who since 1970 had been dean of UCLA's rapidly growing Graduate School of Management. But before that Williams had been a high official of Hunt Foods & Industries, Inc., and of its successor, Norton Simon, Inc. Moreover, up to 1977 Williams served on the boards of the last named concern, the CNA Financial Corp., Phillips Petroleum Co., and the Signal Companies, Inc. (a California-based conglomerate). As SEC chairman, Williams has thus far followed a fairly conservative course of action, which has been welcomed by the securities industry. (See the *New York Times*, April 3, 1977, Sect. 3, p. 7, and May 14, 1979, p. D1.) Some of Carter's other appointments to such regulatory agencies have been of a more moderate or liberal nature. For example, as chairman of the Federal Trade Commission, he picked the former chief counsel of the Senate Commerce Committee, Michael Pertschuk, who had no corporate ties. Similarly, Carter appointed Joan Claybrook, who had been director of one of Ralph Nader's governmental "watchdog" groups, to be head of the Highway Traffic Safety Administration, much to the dismay of the auto industry.

89. For a brief period early in the Carter administration, the energetic Strauss had acted as the President's Special Counselor on Inflation, a post later taken over and built into a much larger operation by Cornell professor Alfred Kahn. For six months in 1979 Strass also served as a special diplomatic troubleshooter in the Middle East, before he was asked to become head of Carter's reelection campaign.

90. However, Strauss's lack of knowledge and expertise about international business were probably compensated for by the fact that he chose as his top aide in these negotiations a man with better organizational connections and more suitable experience, Alonzo L. McDonald, Jr., who was a longtime high official of McKinsey & Co., a big management consulting firm, and a trustee of the CED. That America's economic establishment was firmly behind the "free trade" drive can be seen from the full-page ad which was placed in the July 9, 1979, issue of the *New York Times* (p. A18). It showed clearly that the Business Roundtable strongly endorsed the recently introduced international trade bill, which would gradually, over an eight-year period, reduce industrial tariffs by about 35 percent.

91. This firm, which does not list its major clients in any directory, also had a fairly sizable Washington office, of which Strauss himself was the head, from which relationship one might assume that his political ties were probably put to good use.

92. Although the Valley View State Bank was a small operation which one would not expect to attract important people, one of its original outside directors was Mrs. John D. Murchison, whose husband had, through oil and other interests, great wealth and influence. Since Mrs. Murchison could easily have graced the board of many larger financial enterprises, one can only assume that she served as a director of this small Dallas bank primarily because she and her husband were close friends of Robert Strauss.

352 *Elites in American History*

93. See the *New York Times* (July 18, 1973), p. 47 (November 28, 1976), Sect. 3, pp. 1 and 9, and (November 22, 1978), p. D1.

94. Because Strauss served on the Braniff board for only a short time (apparently a matter of months), he is not recorded as a director of this company in any of the major business directories. But he is so listed in the 1976 annual report of the Braniff Airways, and there is reference to this fact in a late 1977 *New York Times* editorial concerning the White House's recent award of the much coveted Dallas-to-London route to Braniff rather than to Pan-Am. See the *New York Times* (December 31, 1977), p. 16.

95. Since this chapter was written in the fall of 1979, no attempt will be made to appraise the Carter administration's handling of the SALT negotiations or of a number of other major issues which have yet to be resolved.

96. For an incisive historical analysis of this controversy, see Walter LaFeber, *The Panama Canal: The Crisis in Historical Perspective* (New York: Oxford University Press, 1978).

97. In addition, Bunker had served until 1973 as a director of the Lambert International Corp., an investment company apparently controlled by Belgian capitalists, and his son, John B. Bunker, had, been the chief executive officer of the Holly Sugar Corp.

98. Though a Washington-based lawyer, Linowitz had also graced the board of New York's Marine Midland Banks, Inc. from 1974 to 1976.

99. There were undoubtedly a variety of reasons why Torrijos insisted upon adoption of this treaty, one of which was that it would help still nationalistic unrest about this longstanding territorial grievance. But it should also be noted that the Torrijos regime had begun to develop fairly close ties to the growing American banking interests in Panama. For more on this latter point, see Walter LaFeber, *op. cit.,* pp. 117 and 197-99.

100. See the *New York Times* (July 24, 1978), p. D1. There were two important reasons why the nation's major corporate interests strongly backed the pact. First, they were uneasy about the probably widespread adverse consequences of the rejection of this treaty in the rest of Central and South America. Second, they believed that a politically quiescent Panama would be conducive to the growing foreign, particularly U.S., investment in this country, which they envisaged as becoming "the Hong Kong of the West." For a recent article describing the escalating business development in Panama, see *Business Week* (June 18, 1979), pp. 62-63.

101. For a study which attributes Carter's decision to drop the proposed B-1 bomber program to a report prepared by the prestigious Brookings Institution, see Thomas R. Dye, "Oligarchic Tendencies in National Policy-Making: The Role of the Private Policy-Planning Organizations," *Journal of Politics* (May 1978), p. 321.

102. See *Business Week* (August 15, 1977), p. 36, and *Time* (December 4, 1978), p. 33. It is true that, apparently because of his 1976 campaign pledge, President Carter did submit the following year a massive welfare reform package to Congress that would have added about $20 billion in federal welfare costs. But this plan ran into a wall of conservative protests and was, in effect, declared "dead on arrival." In any case, the President did not fight hard for his reform package. And about eighteen months later he presented a much scaled-down measure which would require only about one-third of the new money he had originally requested and would also do comparatively little to aid the financially hard-pressed cities of the Northeast.

103. See the *Congressional Quarterly Weekly Report,* Vol. 34 (September 25, 1976), p. 2584.

104. See the *New York Times* (November 12, 1977), p. 1.

105. Originally, Charles Schultze, the head of the Council of Economic Advisers, suggested that a $50 rebate be given each person in the country, but this progressive measure was strongly opposed by many conservatives such as Federal Reserve Board chairman Arthur Burns, and was ultimately dropped from the overall tax package. An adjustment of the tax rates was made instead. Carter's plan also called for the imposition of substantially higher Social Security taxes on upper and middle income groups.

106. In its early deliberations the Carter administration drafted a proposal to tax capital gains at the same rate as ordinary income, which would have resulted in a doubling of this levy in many cases. This idea encountered stiff opposition, and in the end a smaller rise was recommended, though to no avail.

107. Up to 1969 the maximum tax on capital gains was 25 percent. Then Congressional liberals, who felt that this figure represented a gross favor for the wealthy, raised the rate 49.1 percent.

108. See *Time* (March 5, 1979), p. 51. As this article put it, "even a cast of thousands seems barely adequate. Every day more than 1,200 phone calls come in from corporate controllers and finance officers anxious to learn what the regulations actually mean. Tidal waves of paper work arrive in the mail from companies disgorging themselves of pricing data in an effort to prove compliance or plead for exemptions, or just beat back the bureaucrats with a statistical deluge."

109. See the *New York Times* (May 29, 1979), p. 11.

110. Even here the Carter administration was forced to bend considerably from its much publicized 7 percent wage increase standard, for in the 1979 Teamsters union settlement the overall figure finally arrived at was closer to 9 percent.

111. See the *New York Times* (June 13, 1979), p. D4.

112. See *Business Week* (November 5, 1979), p. 158, and *Time* (November 12, 1979) p. 105. In 1978 the median rate of return for stockholders in the nation's 500 largest industrial concerns was 14.3 percent, the highest figure recorded since *Fortune* began collecting such data in 1955. See *Fortune* (May 7, 1979), p. 268.

113. Because of increasing criticism, the President in late 1979 created a new tripartite Pay Advisory Committee. This move was reportedly made, in the face of much business opposition, to mollify union leaders, who were unhappy about the conduct of Carter's anti-inflation program. Yet, interestingly, of the six public members appointed to this body, four had corporate ties. They were: its chairman, Harvard professor (and former Labor Secretary) John T. Dunlop, who was now a director of the General Telephone & Electronics Corp.; Robben W. Fleming, president of the University of Michigan and a director of the Chrysler Corp.; Washington economist Robert Nathan, a trustee of the CED and director of two small companies; and MIT professor Phyllis Wallace, a director of Boston's State Street Bank & Trust Co. and a trustee of the Brookings Institution.

114. See *Time* (April 11, 1977), p. 55.

115. The primary resistance to this increase in the nation's minimum wage came not from big corporations, which generally paid wages far in excess of that amount, but from various special trade associations (such as hotels and motels), and the U.S. Chamber of Commerce, which drew much of its support from the ranks of small business. See *Fortune* (March 27, 1978), p. 57.

116. See the *New York Times* (July 13, 1977), pp. A1 and A12.

117. See Norman J. Ornstein, *Interest Groups, Lobbying, and Policymaking* (Washington, D.C.: Congressional Quarterly Press, 1978), p. 124.

118. The number of groups reportedly involved in this coalition varies considerably, ranging from a low of 40, according to one source, to a high of 100, according to another. See Norman J. Ornstein, *op. cit.*, p. 125, and *Fortune* (March 27, 1978), p. 57.

119. See *Business Week* (May 22, 1978), p. 64. President Carter is reported to have backed the Labor Law Reform Act, but, given his conservative orientation and strained relations with the union movement, there is some question as to how strongly he supported this measure.

120. The economic alliance forged to fight the Labor Law Reform Act was virtually the same as that created to oppose the common-site picketing bill, except that the National Federation of Independent Business (a small employers group) apparently played a more prominent role in the second major struggle. The Business Roundtable was initially beset by a sharp division of opinion among its key members, but soon decided to throw its weight against

this measure. See Thomas Ferguson and Joel Rogers, "Labor Law Reform and its Enemies," *The Nation* (January 6–13, 1979), pp. 18–20.

121. Organized labor suffered a lesser setback in its attempt to get Congress to enact, in its original form, the so-called Humphrey-Hawkins bill, which was designed to strengthen the Employment Act of 1946 by providing more specific goals for reducing unemployment in the United States and requiring that, if necessary, certain steps be taken to achieve that objective. But many objections were raised to this proposal by pro-business forces in Congress, which ultimately succeeded in adding a partially offsetting inflation-control section and, more importantly, further diluted this measure by removing any provision which called for firm action by the federal government. In short, the Humphrey-Hawkins bill was reduced, by the time of its passage in late 1978, to what even such a conservative spokesman as U.S. Chamber of Commerce president Richard Lesher described as "a toothless alligator." See *Fortune* (3/27/78), p. 57.

122. It is difficult to assess the effect of the support which the White House gave to this drive because of the increasingly conservative temper of the times and the rather inept lobbying efforts of the Carter administration during its early years in office.

123. For an article which sheds much light on the way in which the Business Roundtable operated, with its many contacts, in this Congressional fight, see *Fortune* (May 27, 1978), pp. 53–58. Because of its recent origins, the Business Roundtable has not been subjected to much study. But an examination of its leadership structure reveals that it is a very close-knit group with many overlapping ties among its members, which linkage, contrary to what David Truman once claimed, probably vastly strengthens rather than weakens the influence of this elite body.

124. Although Carter called for the deregulation of interstate natural gas prices during his 1976 presidential campaign, his original energy plan nevertheless recommended the continuation of such controls. However, during the 18-month battle to get his program through Congress, Carter apparently agreed to go along with decontrol.

125. According to one report, the proposed tax on industrial users of oil, which would have provided for close to 50 percent of the energy savings in President Carter's original oil program, was effectively killed through the efforts of a coalition of influential economic interests, spearheaded by Washington lobbyist Charls E. Walker (who was a director of the Texas-based Tracor, Inc.) and the Business Roundtable. See the *New York Times* (August 9, 1979), p. D14.

126. *Business Week*, for instance, recently reported that Arkansas entrepreneur Jackson T. Stephens, who was a Naval Academy classmate of Jimmy Carter's and a close friend and economic ally of OMB's first director, Bert Lance, would, along with his brother, Wilton Stephens, reap a great fortune from the federal government's decontrol of natural gas prices, since they owned the Stephens Production Co., which had reserves, as of 1977, of nearly one trillion cubic feet of natural gas. Jackson T. Stephens was one of Carter's early major financial backers in 1976, and in 1977 he was involved in helping Texas businessman Jess Hay, Robert Strauss's successor as chairman of the Democratic National Committee, in forging a new fundraising arm for the party. For more on the Stephens brothers' many economic holdings and relationship with Bert Lance's National Bank of Georgia, see *Business Week* (April 11, 1977), p. 88, and the *New York Times* (July 24, 1977), p. 30, (July 29, 1977), p. A9, and (May 17, 1978), pp. D1 and D19.

127. See *Fortune* (June 18, 1979), p. 23. Indeed, many might ask, why could not Exxon have chosen to buy the electric motor division of the Reliance Electric Co. (a not uncommon practice in today's business world), or even enter into a joint venture with this company? Interestingly, it was not until the last part of July 1979 that any attempt was made to block this proposed merger, and that action was taken by the Federal Trade Commission, and not by the Carter administration's Justice Department.

128. It is interesting to note that by 1974 even such business groups as the CED had accepted the idea that some sort of windfall profits tax was probably necessary. (See the Committee for Economic Development, *Achieving Energy Independence*, p. 47.) At the time

this study went to press, the windfall profits tax had still not been enacted, primarily because the Senate was advocating an even milder version.

129. See *Fortune* (June 18, 1979), p. 63. Not only have the profits of the major oil companies begun to soar (by 66 percent in the second quarter of 1979 over the same period in 1978), but huge sums are now being expended for the acquisition of little-known, privately owned concerns which happen to have substantial reserves. For instance, in late 1979 the International Paper Co. paid $805 million for the Bodcaw Co., and Shell spent a total of $3.6 billion for the Belridge Oil Co.

130. *Time* magazine noted that although as much as half of the gas sold was pegged illegally at too high a price, the Department of Energy had only about 400 inspectors to police the 225,000 gasoline retail outlets in the country. Many informed observers were also highly critical of the DOE's ability to police the energy industry and complained that it relied too much on oil companies and other parties in the private sector for its basic data. See *Time* (July 23, 1979), p. 29, and the *New York Times* (July 16, 1979), p. A12.

131. For a brief account of this agency's many failings, see "What's Wrong at DOE?" *Dun's Review* (July 1979), pp. 38–40.

132. Typical of the people invited were Washington lawyer (and onetime Secretary of Defense) Clark Clifford, GE boss Reginald Jones, Lane Kirkland, secretary-treasurer of the AFL-CIO, John Sawhill, president of New York University (and a former high official in DOE's predecessor agency), Harvard economist John Kenneth Galbraith, New York's Terence Cardinal Cooke, Vernon Jordan, the executive director of the National Urban League, and, of course, President Carter's close friend and political advisor, Atlanta attorney Charles Kirbo. For a list of most of those who came, by presidential request to Camp David, see *Time* (July 23, 1979), p. 30.

133. The *New York Times* found much fault with Carter's claim that "Washington, D.C. has become an island. The gap between our citizens and our Government has never been so wide." Its editors rightly pointed out that, as chief executive, he could no longer play the role of outsider divorced from all governmental responsibility. As they put it, "having found much merit in the ideas and works of the Carter administration over the past thirty months, we are not quite sure what to make of Jimmy Carter's sudden assault upon it." See the *New York Times* (July 19, 1979), p. A18.

134. In addition, President Carter proposed to pump an additional $10 billion into improving the nation's mass transit system over the next ten years, and an even larger sum into aid to the low-income groups, who would be particularly hard hit by the rapidly rising price of fuel. But neither sum would apparently go very far toward meeting these two economic needs.

135. Clearly, no economic analysis can account for the fall of Blumenthal and Califano, for the former had been a member of the Trilateral Commission and had other important civic and corporate ties, and while Califano had incurred the wrath of the tobacco interests because of his strong anti-smoking campaign, he had previously been a Washington lawyer with many influential clients (one of which was the Coca-Cola Co.). The only explanation the author can offer is a psychological one, namely that since such people as Hamilton Jordan and Jody Powell had worked with Carter early in his political career when he was very much an outsider, he had developed an almost blind loyalty to them.

136. At Camp David Clark Clifford is reported to have told Carter that his White House staff was amateurish and that Hamilton Jordan was probably his chief liability and should be replaced. See the *New York Times* (July 20, 1979), p. A10.

137. President Carter also made a few changes in the diplomatic area in the latter half of 1979, but most of the new appointees were elite figures. For instance, he appointed former IBM chief executive Thomas J. Watson, Jr. to serve as Ambassador to the Soviet Union, a post long held by career diplomats. And a few months later Carter picked New York lawyer Sol Linowitz to replace Robert Strauss as the nation's special Middle East negotiator. Linowitz was a member of the Trilateral Commission and a director of the Mutual Life Insurance Co., Pan-

American World Airways, and Time, Inc. (Watson had also been a board member of the last two concerns up to the late 1970s).

138. See the *New York Times* (July 20, 1979), p. A8.

139. For the most recent report on the Mercantile Bankshares' vast trust funds and a revealing earlier account of its many economic links and large stockownership interests, one of which was R. J. Reynolds Industries, Inc., see *Forbes* (April 16, 1979), p. 135 and (February 1, 1970), p. 44. It is also interesting to note, particularly in light of the cigarette industry's opposition to HEW Secretary Califano, that one of the directors of the Mercantile Bankshares Corp. was Reynolds tobacco heir W. Smith Bagley, who was a close friend of President Carter.

140. According to one report, this job was initially offered (actually for the second time) to UN Ambassador Andrew Young. But Young preferred to keep, albeit briefly, his diplomatic post. See *Newsweek* (July 30, 1979), p. 26.

141. It was revealed during his confirmation hearings that Landrieu had become a business partner of real estate developer Joseph Canizaro, an economic outsider, while he was still serving as mayor of New Orleans, although he claimed this did not pose a conflict of interest. Because of a lack of information about Landrieu's post-mayoralty ties, his elite (or non-elite) status remains a question mark. See the *New York Times* (July 27, 1979), p. A9 and (September 7, 1979), p. A12, and *Time* (November 5, 1979), p. 87.

142. About a week after Miller agreed to take over as Secretary of the Treasury, President Carter picked Paul Volcker to be his successor as head of the Federal Reserve System, apparently at the suggestion of the Chase Manhattan Bank's David Rockefeller. Volcker was a former high Treasury Department official and onetime Chase Manhattan Bank executive, who since 1975 had been serving as president of the Federal Reserve Bank of New York. In the late 1970s Volcker had also been a member of the Trilateral Commission, a trustee of the Rockefeller Foundation, and a director of the Council on Foreign Relations, all organizations closely allied with the Rockefeller interests. Actually, this post was first offered to three other even more influential figures—David Rockefeller, A.W. Clausen, president of the Bank of America, and Robert Roosa, a partner in Brown Brothers Harriman & Co.—all of whom turned it down. See *Time* (August 6, 1979), p. 19.

143. See the *New York Times* (December 29, 1977), p. D3.

144. It is revealing to note that this Cabinet post was first offered to David Rockefeller, head of the Chase Manhattan Bank (who was also the North American chairman of the Trilateral Commission, an active member of the Business Council, and a member of the policy committee of the Business Roundtable) and Reginald Jones, the chief executive officer of GE (who was chairman of the Business Council and a co-chairman of the Business Roundtable). See *Fortune* (September 10, 1979), p. 62.

145. The only significant difference between Blumenthal and Miller was that the former had, through his civic and corporate links, a greater Rockefeller orientation, while Miller was obviously an integral part of the organizational nexus (the Business Council and Business Roundtable) of America's economic establishment.

146. As Duncan's successor as the second-ranking official in the Defense Department, President Carter picked Secretary of the Navy W. Graham Claytor, Jr. Like his predecessor in the Pentagon, Claytor was an elite figure, for up to 1977 he had been the president of the big Southern Railway, a trustee of the CED, and a director of the Morgan Guaranty Trust Co.

147. It is not clear whether Duncan's decision to resign as Coca-Cola's chief executive was due to a personality clash, some major policy differences, or his overall administrative performance. In any case, he served as president for a remarkably short period of time, 2½ years.

148. John H. Duncan, who in recent years had been head of a large subsidiary of the Mead Corp., was also a longtime board member of Tracor, Inc. (along with the president of the Rotan Mosle Financial Corp. and Washington lobbyist Charles Walker, who helped scuttle a key part

of Carter's original energy program) and the New York-based conglomerate, Gulf & Western Industries, Inc.

149. It is interesting to note that in 1978 Garner Anthony, who was a member of a wealthy Atlanta family which had been strong supporters of President Carter (his sister-in-law was appointed Ambassador to Belgium in 1977) and a major executive of the Cox Broadcasting Corp., was elected a director of Texas Commerce Bankshares, Inc., and that Ben Love, the president of this Houston-based bank, was made a board member of the Cox Broadcasting Corp. a year earlier. Furthermore, Garner Anthony's wife, Barbara Cox Anthony, was placed on the board of Tenneco, Inc. (a huge conglomerate once known as the Tennessee Gas Transmission Corp.) in either late 1976 or early 1977. Because of their timing and geographically distant nature, these associations would appear to be of a dubious, if not highly suspicious, nature. Also, Cox Enterprises owned about 80 percent of the stock in the recently formed Hampton Roads Energy Co., which planned to build a $650 million oil refinery on Virginia's east coast. See the *New York Times* (August 7, 1979), p. A1.

150. See *Newsweek* (July 30, 1979), p. 31. Duncan's last corporate concern, the Rotan Mosle Financial Corp., specialized, as befits a Texas firm, in oil and gas (and related service) securities. For more on this point, see Alexander Stuart, "Rotan Mosle: It's Up on Oil," *Fortune* (March 24, 1980), pp. 122–128.

151. As for his Deputy Secretary of Energy, Duncan made a choice that was also very revealing, for he picked New York University president John Sawhill, a man with some governmental experience in this area. This able individual had held the two top posts in DOE's organizational predecessor, the Federal Energy Administration, in 1973–1975, although he was eased out as this agency's boss because of an as yet unexplained major policy dispute. However, by mid-1979 Sawhill had become a well-connected Establishment figure, as seen by the fact that he was a member of the Trilateral Commission, a trustee of the CED, and a director of the Rockefeller-oriented J. Henry Schroder Banking Corp. (which had assets of over $1.5 billion), Consolidated Edison Co., Crane Co., General American Investors Co., North American Coal Corp., Philip Morris, Inc., RCA, and the American International Group (which was a subsidiary of the big American International Reinsurance Co.).

152. In the late fall of 1979 Secretary of Commerce Juanita Kreps was compelled to resign for personal reasons. As her successor, President Carter picked (after receiving many rebuffs) former Chicago developer Philip Klutznick, who was a longtime trustee of the CED, a director of the big MGIC Investment Corp., and more recently a limited partner in the investment banking firm of Salomon Brothers. Around the same time a new Cabinet-level Department of Education was created as a spin-off from HEW. To fill the top post in this department, Carter selected, to the surprise of many, California's Shirley Hufstedler, who since the early 1960s had served, in order, as a municipal, state, and federal judge. Mrs. Hufstedler also had some key civic ties, for she was a trustee of the Aspen Institute (for Humanistic Studies) and the more prestigious Colonial Williamsburg Foundation.

153. Donovan also served on the boards of the Ford Foundation and the Carnegie Endowment for International Peace, but these ties were probably of less importance.

154. A few years ago Mark Green devoted a substantial part of an entire book to the work of Lloyd Cutler. See Mark J. Green, *The Other Government: The Unseen Power of Washington Lawyers* (New York: Norton, 1978), pp. 45–64 and passim.

155. Cutler also served as a director of Florida's Southeast Banking Corp. (which had assets of over $4 billion) and had been a board member of the big California-based Kaiser Industries Corp. up to its liquidation in 1977 following a major reorganization of the vast Kaiser economic complex. For more on Cutler's other large corporate clients, see Mark J. Green, *op. cit.*, p. 56.

156. Since President Carter has not had an opportunity to make an appointment to the Supreme Court, only a few observations will be made here concerning the role of this now fairly conservative, largely Nixon-molded body. In the late 1970s the Supreme Court gave two substantial boosts to the nuclear power industry in the so-called Vermont Yankee and Duke

Power cases. And in another recent decision (*First National Bank* v. *Bellotti*) it struck down a Massachusetts statute which was designed to prohibit corporations from using their funds to influence any referendum that did not notably affect their business or property, totally oblivious of the immense financial advantages that most companies have over the vast majority of civic groups and people. Also, in the area of social policy the Supreme Court made another noteworthy ruling in 1977 which revealed much about its general line of thinking when it declared that neither existing law nor the equal protection clause of the Constitution compelled state governments to appropriate funds for non-therapeutic abortions. In this case (*Maher* v. *Roe*) the Court, in effect, took the position, despite Justice Brennan's ringing dissent, that women with ample or moderate means could continue to secure safe abortions, while poor women would be forced to either undergo "kitchen-table" operations or have unwanted children, thereby fueling the cycle of poverty. While not a party to these proceedings, it was with reference to this case that President Carter made his widely quoted remark that "there are many things in life that are not fair."

CHAPTER 8

Conclusion

This three-volume work, which consists of a detailed historical analysis of the recruitment pattern and selected governmental actions of the nation's chief Cabinet and diplomatic officials and Supreme Court justices, was undertaken primarily as a means of assessing the distribution of power in the country at different points in time. This research involved the compilation and organization of a great mass of data on which other scholars can, and hopefully will, build in the years ahead. At this stage, however, it is essential to summarize the material and place it in its proper perspective. In short, what are the major findings of this study of roughly 190 years of American history? Are there any recurrent themes or important trends which merit special emphasis?

GEOGRAPHIC BACKGROUND OF APPOINTEES

It is clear that in the primarily agrarian and mercantile pre-Civil War period certain states were, from a statistical standpoint, heavily over-represented in almost every presidential administration up to 1861. Three states in particular—Massachusetts, Pennsylvania, and Virginia—secured a disproportionate share of the key Cabinet and diplomatic posts during these early years (see Table 11). In all, these states had between 36 and 40 percent of the nation's population in the last decade of the 18th century, and only about 25 percent of the total by the late 1820s. Yet they received about 50 percent of the most important federal posts during this period, one long span of which was known as the reign of the "Virginia dynasty" because all of the presidents between 1801 and 1825 came from this important state.[1] And though these three states had, by 1860, less than 20 percent of the population, they still managed, thanks partly to the power of the Richmond Junto, to obtain nearly 40 percent of the major Cabinet and diplomatic posts between the outset of the Jackson administration and the start of the Civil War, in contrast to New York, which fell significantly behind during this

359

TABLE 11
Percentage of High Federal Posts Held by People from Different States or Regions: 1789–1980

Major Cabinet and Diplomatic Posts

Period	Mass.	Other New England States	N.J.	N.Y.	Pa.	Va.	Other Southern States	East North Central States	Mid-western States	Rocky Mountain States	Pacific Coast States	District of Columbia
1789–1801	15.4%	7.2%	—	11.5%	15.4%	26.9%	23.1%	—				
1801–1829	12.7	1.8	3.6	14.5	20.0	14.5	32.7	—				
1829–1841	—	9.1	6.1	15.1	9.1	9.1	42.4	9.1%				
1841–1861	14.5	3.9	—	6.6	17.1	17.1	34.2	6.6				
Pre-Civil War Totals	11.6	4.7	2.1	11.1	16.3	16.3	33.7	4.2				
1861–1877	10.4	6.9	3.4	19.0	8.6	—	8.6	29.3	5.2	—	1.7	6.9
1877–1897	9.9	7.0	2.8	18.3	5.6	—	16.9	22.5	14.2	1.4	1.4	—
1897–1913	7.9	—	1.6	34.9	7.9	—	4.8	25.4	11.1	—	6.3	—
1913–1921	—	—	4.0	20.0	8.0	4.0	16.0	16.0	20.0	—	8.0	4.0
1921–1933	7.4	1.9	1.9	20.4	13.0	—	5.6	22.2	14.9	5.6	7.4	—
Civil War to New Deal Totals	8.1	3.7	2.6	22.9	8.5	0.4	10.0	24.0	12.2	1.5	4.4	1.8

1933–1940	—	5.0	5.0	30.0	5.0	—	15.0	15.0	10.0	5.0	—	10.0
1940–1953	1.5	6.1	—	33.3	3.0	—	15.2	9.1	7.6	4.5	3.0	16.7
1953–1961	7.1	—	—	42.9	4.8	—	7.1	19.0	2.4	2.4	4.8	9.5
1961–1969	10.4	1.5	1.5	23.9	—	—	13.4	13.4	3.0	3.0	1.5	28.4
1969–1977	12.9	—	—	17.1	4.3	—	14.3	20.0	4.3	2.9	12.9	11.4
1977–1980	—	7.4	—	7.4	—	—	22.2	11.1	3.7	3.7	11.1	33.3
1933–1980 Totals	6.8	2.7	0.7	26.0	2.7	0.0	14.0	14.7	4.8	3.4	5.8	18.1
1789–1980 Totals	8.5	3.6	1.7	21.1	8.2	4.2	17.3	15.4	6.2	1.9	3.9	7.7
Supreme Court Posts*												
Pre-Civil War	8.6%	8.6%	2.9%	11.4%	8.6%	14.3%	42.9%	2.9%				
Civil War–New Deal	9.3	—	4.7	16.2	7.0	—	23.2	23.2	7.0	4.7	4.7	—
Post-New Deal	3.7	3.7	3.7	14.8	—	3.7	18.5	22.2	14.8	7.4	3.7	3.7
1789–1980 Totals	7.6	3.8	3.8	14.3	5.7	5.7	28.6	16.2	6.7	3.8	2.9	1.0

*In this analysis William O. Douglas has been treated as a representative of the other New England states because prior to his appointment to federal (regulatory) office he had been a resident of Connecticut.

period.² Indeed, it was the marked edge that Virginia enjoyed in the recruitment process which enabled the South to maintain a small but decisive margin in high administrative circles in the critical two pre-Civil War decades, although by 1860 it had only about 35 percent of the nation's population. Moreover, as may be seen by a glance at the second part of Table 11, the South was able, largely because most of America's presidents came from this section of the country, to obtain a majority on the Supreme Court (albeit often by a one-vote margin) up to the time of the "war between the states." This control was buttressed even further by the fact that the critical position of Chief Justice was held from early 1801 up through 1861 by two very able and forceful Southerners, John Marshall and Roger B. Taney.

There were, as one might expect, a number of important changes in the federal recruitment pattern between the Civil War, which is generally thought to have marked the beginning of the Industrial Revolution in America, and the New Deal, during which watershed period the country underwent a series of major shifts that ushered in a new era in politico-economic relations. One of the most striking developments was the emergence of New York City as a key source of high administrative and diplomatic officials. For example, in contrast to the pre-Civil War period when New York state supplied about 10 percent of such governmental figures (one-third of whom were upstate leaders), close to 23 percent were drawn from the Empire State between 1861 and 1933, and the vast majority of these were from New York City.³ However, at no time after about 1870 did New York state constitute more than roughly 10 percent of the nation's population (with New York City providing about half of that total). In short, this shift in federal recruitment was not basically a demographic development, but one related primarily to New York City's rapidly rising economic influence.⁴

Conversely, certain other states experienced a sharp decline in their geopolitical power during this period, at least as measured by their ability to have their leaders appointed to high federal office. For instance, Virginia, as one of the key states in the Confederacy, suffered a disastrous drop after the Civil War in its (non-legislative) representation in the upper echelons of the federal government. Only one of its leaders, Congressman Carter Glass, was appointed to an important Cabinet or diplomatic post during this 72-year period, and that was during the latter part of the perhaps atypical Wilson administration.⁵ Indeed, the heavily Democratic South fell sharply out of favor during these largely Republican-dominated years (actually, if it had not been for the efforts of the Cleveland and Wilson regimes to build up party support in the South, this region's rather modest total would have been reduced even further).⁶ Thus the Civil War not only broke the political power of the South, but dealt it such a devastating blow that it did not recover for generations.

Another state which suffered a serious decline in its ability to secure key federal positions after the Civil War was, somewhat surprisingly, Pennsylvania. This state has, of course, long been looked upon as perhaps the very heart of American industry—the home, for example, of both Bethlehem Steel and (in terms of its major base of operations) the United States Steel Corp. Yet it did not fare well in its high-level (non-legislative) representation, dropping from an average of about 16 percent of all key Cabinet and diplomatic posts in the pre-Civil War years to little more than 8 percent between 1861 and 1933. This was due chiefly to the fact that Philadelphia, which was once the financial center of the country, fell precipitously in both economic and political influence following Andrew Jackson's destruction of the Biddle-dominated Second Bank of the United States, and then the collapse of the financial house of Jay Cooke & Co. in the early post-Civil War years.[7] Of Pennsylvania's total of 23 major Cabinet and diplomatic appointments between 1861 and 1933, four represented two men (one of whom was a three-time carryover) selected to serve, because of their union backgrounds, as Secretary of Labor, and thus, from the standpoint of business–government relations, they should be deleted from these calculations. Of the remaining 19, ten were Pittsburgh appointees (seven of which were accounted for by Andrew Mellon and his attorney, Philander C. Knox, each of whom served under three administrations); one was from northeastern Pennsylvania; and four, all chosen well before the turn of the century, were either relatives of, or lawyers for, the state Republican party boss, Simon Cameron, who was a central Pennsylvania leader. Hence, although it was one of the nation's very largest cities, Philadelphia—unlike Boston, Cleveland, and Chicago—obviously carried little weight in high Washington circles in the post–Civil War period.

There was a similar shift in the pattern of appointments to the Supreme Court between 1861 and 1933. Again, the greatest drop was in the South, which declined from 57 to 23 percent in its share of Supreme Court seats (although this loss was not quite as sharp as that which it experienced in the administrative and diplomatic area, where it fell off from about 50 percent to a little under 10 percent). On the positive side, the biggest gain was registered by the north central section of the country, which jumped from about 3 to 23 percent in its representation on the High Court. And perhaps equally important, of the six Chief Justices picked during this period, four were from this region, with Ohio faring particularly well, receiving three of these selections.

After 1933 the geographic pattern of appointments to the Supreme Court did not change markedly, despite a general westward shift in the nation's population.[8] But this was not true of America's top Cabinet and diplomatic posts, for while some parts of the country continued to secure roughly the same share of such offices as they had in the 1861–1933 period, many others did not. For instance, New York state managed to obtain, after the beginning of the New Deal, a major increase in such appointments—from nearly 23 to 26 percent. However, these figures are somewhat misleading, for the gain was registered entirely by New York City, which, because of its growing economic power, rose from about 19 to nearly 25 percent in its representation in high level administrative and diplomatic circles, although this city claimed less than 5 percent of the nation's population by 1950 and no more than 3.5 percent of the total by 1970.⁹ Also, Texas finally began to receive a significant share of the government's top posts during this period, a policy initiated under the Eisenhower administration and later expanded by Nixon. Yet certain other states and regions have obviously lost power in recent times. Ohio, for example, fell off—now that it was no longer the chief "breeding ground" of America's presidents—from 8 percent to a little over 3 percent of the nation's major executive and diplomatic officials. The Midwest suffered an almost equally grievous decline, slipping from roughly 12 to 5 percent of the government's key (non-judicial) appointees. Indeed, it was now able to secure little more than the two "geo-political" positions of Secretary of the Interior and of Agriculture.

A new type of federal official emerged in the post-1933 period, and that was the Washington-based figure who, because of his background and expertise, came to be relied upon increasingly by the nation's presidents. Most of these officials (26 out of 41) were longtime foreign service officers, some of whom even began to assume diplomatic posts traditionally reserved for wealthy influential business leaders, such as those of Ambassador to Britain or France. Seven were former military men who in the course of their careers had proved to be unusually able executives, capable of dealing with various difficult problems or special missions.¹⁰ And an equal number were well-established Washington lawyers, such as Dean Acheson and Clark Clifford, who, because of their unusual ability or unrivaled knowledge of the increasingly complex Washington scene, were called upon, despite their often pro-corporate ties, to help direct governmental affairs.¹¹

EDUCATIONAL BACKGROUND OF APPOINTEES

In the early, predominantly Federalist period the nation's top officials were—perhaps of necessity, given the economic and educational state of the country—a very select group indeed. For at a time when only an extremely small, wealthy segment of the population (about 0.2 percent) had the benefit of a higher education, 87 percent of the (23) major Cabinet and diplomatic officers appointed by the Washington and John Adams regimes had attended college (see Table 12), and all but three of these had graduated. In part because there were then relatively few well-established schools, most of these officials went to one of four colleges—Columbia, Harvard, Yale, or Princeton (as the last school has been known since 1896). And a majority of those who did not attend what are now referred to as Ivy League colleges were educated abroad, still further evidence that it was basically only the rich, particularly the urban elite, who went to college in colonial times and in the early days of the Republic.¹²

With the rise of the agrarian-dominated Jeffersonian Republican forces, there were some noteworthy changes in the educational characteristics of the government's chief administrative and diplomatic officials. For one thing, there was a marked increase (from 13 to 28 percent) in the proportion of men who, for financial or other reasons, had no college education at all. In all, about 60 percent of the major Cabinet and diplomatic officers from 1801 to 1829 graduated from college—mostly from Ivy League institutions—in contrast to nearly 75 percent for the preceding Federalist years.[13] In other words, though still highly elitist, these more agrarian-oriented regimes were less educationally skewed than the commercially and financially dominated Washington and Adams administrations.

This trend was accelerated during the tumultuous "age of Jackson." Close to 35 percent of the major Cabinet and diplomatic officers appointed between 1829 and 1841 had never attended college, but were largely self-made men. This recruitment pattern could be construed as lending considerable support to the argument, advanced earlier in Volume I of this study and in certain other works, that this was a period which witnessed the rise of new entrepreneurial interests in American politics.[14] Since most of the key Jacksonian leaders had lower socio-economic origins than their predecessors, it is not surprising that a fairly small proportion, only a little over a third, had graduated from an Ivy League institution.

In the two pre-Civil War decades, however, there were some notable shifts back to the practice of recruiting better-educated Cabinet and diplomatic officials. Only about 20 percent of the men appointed in these years had not attended college, and the vast majority of those who had entered such institutions graduated. But because of the growing power of the so-called "slavocracy" during this period, there was a marked movement away from the appointment of men who had gone to Ivy League colleges to those who had attended one of two essentially Southern schools, the College of William and Mary and the University of North Carolina. These two institutions alone had almost as many graduates holding high federal office between 1841 and 1861 as all of the Ivy League colleges combined. An even larger percentage of these governmental leaders had graduated from other lesser known institutions, both public and private, a pattern which would indicate that there was a somewhat less elitist recruitment trend during these two decades.

As might be expected, there was a marked similarity in the educational characteristics of the Supreme Court justices who were appointed between 1789 and 1861. A little over 28 percent of these important figures had never gone to college, but they had in every instance made up for this deficiency through either extensive self-education or professional tutelage. Close to two-thirds graduated from college, while another 6 percent had the benefit of some higher education. And as was the case with the nation's top administrative and diplomatic officials during the pre-Civil War period, roughly 35 percent of the justices attended an Ivy League institution, while another 11 percent went to college abroad—two signs of substantial family wealth. However, one difference between the appointment pattern of Supreme Court

TABLE 12

Educational Background of High Federal Officials: 1789–1980

Cabinet and Diplomatic Officials

Period	No College Education	Some College Education	Total Number College Education	Harvard, Yale, Princeton	Other Ivy League College	Other Private College	Public College	College Education Abroad
1789–1801	13.1%	13.1%	73.8%	43.5%	4.3%	4.3%	—	21.7%
1801–1829	27.7	12.8	59.5	40.3	6.4	4.3	—	8.5
1829–1841	34.6	11.5	52.9	23.2	11.5	15.4	3.8%	—
1841–1861	20.8	5.6	73.6	15.3	9.7	29.2	19.4	—
Pre-Civil War Totals	23.8	9.5	66.7	27.4	8.3	16.7	8.9	5.4
1861–1877	21.8	12.7	65.5	27.3	7.3	23.6	7.3	—
1877–1897	30.0	12.9	57.1	25.6	4.3	18.6	8.6	—
1897–1913	19.0	8.6	72.4	27.6	5.2	34.4	5.2	—
1913–1921	20.8	25.0	54.2	—	4.2	41.6	8.4	—
1921–1933	16.0	14.0	70.0	12.0	6.0	20.0	28.0	4.0
Civil War–New Deal Totals	22.2	13.2	64.6	21.4	5.4	25.7	11.3	0.8

1933–1940	—	20.0	80.0	25.0	—	45.0	10.0	—
1940–1953	10.4	17.2	72.4	19.0	5.2	25.8	22.4	—
1953–1961	10.0	5.0	85.0	42.5	5.0	15.0	22.5	—
1961–1969	—	3.1	96.9	35.4	4.6	16.9	40.0	—
1969–1977	4.7	4.7	90.6	34.4	4.7	34.4	17.1	—
1977–1980	—	19.2	80.8	15.4	7.7	30.8	26.9	—
1933–1980 Totals	4.8	9.2	86.0	30.1	4.8	26.1	25.0	0.0
1789–1980 Totals	15.8	10.8	73.4	26.2	5.9	23.6	16.1	1.6

Supreme Court Justices

1789–1861	28.6%	5.7%	65.7%	28.6%	5.7%	17.1%	2.9%	11.4%
1861–1933	4.7	9.3	86.0	25.6	14.0	41.9	4.7	—
1933–1980	14.8	3.7	81.5	11.1	3.7	45.0	29.6	—
1789–1980 Totals	15.2	6.7	78.1	22.9	8.6	32.3	10.5	3.8

judges and that of major Cabinet and diplomatic officers lay in the fact that only one justice (out of 35) had graduated from a public college, whereas about 10 percent of the latter had done so.

As America emerged from its pre-industrial state to become a major economic power in the Civil War-to-New Deal period, the educational trends at work in the high-level federal recruitment process continued. For instance, after holding firm for a number of years, there was a gradual, albeit uneven, decrease in the percentage of major Cabinet and diplomatic officers who had never attended college, while the proportion of men who had secured at least some college education held almost constant. But there was a substantial increase over the two pre-Civil War decades in the percentage of Ivy League graduates who were appointed to high office up to the Wilson regime (although there was a marked fall-off thereafter).[15] However, this trend was offset to a considerable extent by the recruitment of men who had gone to other prestigious schools such as Stanford and Amherst, and the proportion provided by other lesser-known private colleges climbed even more sharply. Perhaps equally significant was the emergence toward the end of this era of the publicly supported institutions of higher education as a noteworthy source of executive and diplomatic talent. Although only about 3 percent of the male population went to college during the first third of the century, the proportion of men with college degrees who were appointed to major Cabinet and diplomatic posts remained about the same as it had been in the pre-Civil War period, around 67 percent.

The Supreme Court justices who were chosen between 1861 and 1933 were, interestingly, of an even higher educational status than the men picked to hold key administrative and diplomatic posts. Over 85 percent were college graduates (see Table 12), and those who were not had either secured some college education or engaged in a good deal of other closely supervised study, so as to meet professional standards. Close to 40 percent had gone to an Ivy League college (in contrast to a little under 35 percent in the pre-Civil War years), and another nearly 14 percent had attended other fairly prestigious private schools. In short, from an educational standpoint, the recruitment pattern of Supreme Court justices between 1861 and 1933 was of a highly elitist nature. In fact, only one of the 43 justices appointed during this period (Ohio's William R. Day) went to a state university or other public college—a rather revealing commentary on the nation's still badly skewed socio-economic opportunity structure.[16]

Since the early 1930s, however, there have been a number of notable changes in the educational characteristics of America's top (non-legislative) governmental leaders. For instance, the proportion of major Cabinet and diplomatic officials with college degrees has risen from around 75 percent during the Roosevelt and Truman years to (excepting the Carter administration) somewhere between 85 and 95 percent in more recent times.[17] In other words, it has now reached the point where the appointment of a high federal official who does not have such schooling has become something of a rarity. Yet, to many, one of the most surprising aspects of the appointment process in the post-New Deal period has been the continued reliance of presidential administrations on men who graduated from the (up to recently, elitist) Ivy League colleges. In fact, a higher proportion (35 percent) of Ivy League graduates was appointed to key federal posts during these years (reaching a peak under Eisenhower) than at any time since the early days of the Republic, a phenomenon which would indicate that, despite various countervailing pressures, a great deal of elite influence was still at work in American government and society.[18] In addition, there continued to be a significant number of appointees who had graduated from other almost equally prestigious schools, so that, overall, close to half of the top administrative and diplomatic officers in the post-1933 years had attended what might be termed elite institutions. However, aside from a lapse during the recent Nixon-Ford regime, there has been a growing trend toward the appointment of people who have graduated from publicly supported colleges, which have traditionally drawn largely from the nation's middle and lower classes.

Finally, while there has been no major change since 1933 in the proportion of Supreme Court judges with college degrees (it has, quite understandably, remained high), there were some marked shifts in the types of schools these men had attended. For example, there was a profound drop in the proportion of Ivy League graduates who were appointed to the High Court during this period, from about 40 percent to less than 15 percent, a decline which was only partially countered by a relative increase in the number of appointees who had gone to other fairly prestigious schools. Conversely, there was a substantial jump of from 2 to almost 30 percent in the proportion of justices who had graduated from state universities and other public institutions.[19] While not all of these persons proved to be progressive judges, this shift does indicate that the Supreme Court recruitment pattern had become less elitist—or to put it another way, more pluralistic—in the post-1933 period, and it certainly differed significantly from that which prevailed in the administrative and diplomatic areas.

PRIOR GOVERNMENTAL EXPERIENCE OF APPOINTEES

Other important aspects of the federal recruitment process warrant close attention and study. One of these involves the amount of governmental experience America's top (non-legislative) officials have had prior to their appointment to high federal office. In the pre-Civil War years it was almost a tradition that a person have a record of longtime government service before being named to an important Cabinet or diplomatic post. Over 90 percent of the people appointed to such positions in this period had a considerable amount of significant government experience, and there were only two persons out of this total who had never held at least one public office.[20]

TABLE 13
Amount of Prior Governmental Experience of High Federal Officials: 1789–1980

Period	Major Cabinet and Diplomatic Officials				Supreme Court Justices			
	Total No. of Officials	% No Experience	% Relatively Little Experience	% Considerable Experience	Total No. of Officials	% No Experience	% Relatively Little Experience	% Considerable Experience
1789–1801	23	4.3%	4.3%	91.4%				
1801–1829	47	4.2	6.4	89.4				
1829–1841	26	—	7.7	92.3				
1841–1861	71	—	9.9	90.1				
Pre-Civil War Totals	167	1.2%	7.2%	91.6%	35	2.9%	28.6%	68.6%
1861–1877	55	12.7	29.1	58.2				
1877–1897	70	8.6	31.4	60.0				
1897–1913	58	12.1	27.6	60.3				
1913–1921	24	25.0	25.0	50.0				
1921–1933	49	26.5	18.4	55.1				
Civil War-to-New Deal Totals	256	15.2%	27.0%	57.8%	43	11.6%	27.9%	60.5%

1933–1940	20	20.0	30.0	50.0			
1940–1945	15	6.7	27.6	66.7			
1945–1953	43	7.0	9.3	83.7	13*	7.7*	7.7*	84.6*
1953–1961	41	36.6	24.4	39.0			
1961–1969	65	9.2	13.8	77.0			
1969–1977	64	18.8	18.8	62.4	14†	7.1†	42.9†	50.0†
1977–1980	26	23.1	11.5	65.4			
Post-1933 Totals	274	17.1%	15.6%	67.3%	27	7.4%	25.2%	68.0%

*1933–1953 figures
†1953–1980 figures

NOTE: Four early New Deal officials (Hull, Ickes, Morgenthau, and Perkins) have been excluded from the computations of the figures for the first half of the 1940s because it would otherwise have produced some misleading totals in terms of prior governmental service. With the exception of the post-1933 period, which was marked by a striking difference between the Supreme Court recruitment pattern of the FDR-Truman years and that of later administrations, judicial totals have been aggregated according to this study's three basic time eras, so as to provide a more reliable statistical base.

Indeed, this was a better record than that achieved overall by the Supreme Court appointees up to 1861, for only two-thirds of these influential figures had extensive experience in any area of major governmental affairs.[21]

But this practice changed noticeably after the Civil War, particularly with regard to Cabinet and high diplomatic officials (see Table 13). After 1861 the nation's chief executives relied to a significant extent on men who had either little or no governmental experience, but were drawn directly (or almost directly) from outside sources, usually from the worlds of business, corporate law, or finance. In surprisingly consistent fashion, more than 40 percent of the men appointed to high office in both the late 19th and early 20th centuries came in as virtual political neophytes, having been most likely selected for reasons of geography, economic influence, or other essentially non-governmental factors.[22] This practice continued to be employed on a somewhat reduced scale and in a more uneven manner in the post-1933 period, especially during the Eisenhower regime.[23]

In the post-Civil War era there was some increase in the proportion of Supreme Court justices with little or no judicial or governmental experience, to roughly the same proportion of people (about 40 percent) appointed without much significant prior service to important Cabinet or diplomatic posts. However, this pattern did not hold after the early 1930s.[24] In fact, only two of the thirteen Supreme Court justices who were chosen during the FDR and Truman years did not have much experience in either governmental or judicial affairs, and both of these men, Felix Frankfurter and Wiley Rutledge, were longtime college law professors who had no pro-corporate views.[25] In contrast, of the 14 Supreme Court justices picked since that time, seven had little or no experience in American government, and five of these—Harlan, Whittaker, Fortas, Powell, and Goldberg—had significant economic links (four pro-business and one pro-labor) prior to their appointments. Thus the New and Fair Deal years presented a very different picture from that which prevailed in most other periods.

ECONOMIC AND OCCUPATIONAL BACKGROUNDS OF APPOINTEES

Although often overlooked or underestimated, the economic and occupational backgrounds of high federal officials have long had a profound effect on the operation of the preceding geo-political, educational, and experience factors generally considered to be so important by American political and social scientists. Even more significant from a philosophical standpoint, the economic background of these federal officials tells much about the nature of American society, particularly in terms of whether it has been a relatively open or closed society at the top, or to put it another way, whether there has been much real equality of political opportunity in the country over the years. Many people believe that for a nation to be truly democratic, its upper political structure must be pluralistic—that is, its leaders should be recruited to a substantial extent from different economic levels (and some would add, occupational categories), mainly on the basis of merit.[26]

A look at the prior occupations of the nation's chief administrative and diplomatic officials reveals that during the early pre-Civil War years the bulk of these appointees were lawyers, most of whom had either large landholdings, primarily in the South, or major business interests, usually of a mercantile or financial nature.[27] As time wore on, however, there was, as Table 14 indicates, a marked fall-off in the percentage of officials with substantial landholdings.[28] And there was, conversely, a significant increase in the proportion of lawyers who had key entrepreneurial and corporate links, such as Benjamin Butler, Martin Van Buren's influential aide in the Albany Regency (who served as a director of at least two New York banks), and Roger B. Taney, the former general counsel of the Baltimore and Ohio Railroad (who also sat on the board of several financial enterprises in Maryland). Thus while the percentage of attorneys appointed to high posts in the federal government remained fairly steady during this period, there was a noticeable shift in the type of lawyers selected, from those whose families had large landholdings to those with strong business ties.

After 1861, as America began to emerge as a great economic state, there was a decided change in the recruitment pattern of the nation's top administrative and diplomatic officials. For one thing, with the defeat of the South, there were, understandably, very few appointees, be they lawyers or other leaders, who derived a substantial part of their wealth and income from plantation or other landholding interests. In addition, there was, around the turn of the century, a significant decrease in the proportion of lawyers tapped for such important posts, especially after the Wilson regime. Yet there was also, paradoxically, a sharp rise in the percentage of corporate (or pro-business) lawyers recruited for key positions.[29] This pattern is most clearly seen with reference to the office of Secretary of State, which was occupied at various times in the pre-Civil War period by such essentially non-corporate leaders as James Monroe (a member of the Virginia dynasty), John Quincy Adams (an ex-Federalist political outcast), John Forsyth (an Augusta, Georgia, lawyer), and James Buchanan (a onetime Lancaster, Pennsylvania, lawyer); in the late 19th and early 20th centuries, however, this post was held by such business-oriented attorneys as Hamilton Fish, William M. Evarts, Frederick T. Frelinghuysen, Richard Olney, Elihu Root, Philander C. Knox, and Henry L. Stimson, all of whom had previously served on one or more major corporate boards.[30]

There was also a marked increase in the appointment of important business executives during this period, which trend reached its pre-World War II peak during the Harding, Coolidge, and Hoover regimes, when close to half of the high federal officials were recruited from such sources.[31] Furthermore, for the first time in American history a significant number (19) of newspapermen were appointed to high administrative or diplomatic office.

TABLE 14
General Occupational Background and Elite (or Non-Elite) Status of Major Cabinet and Diplomatic Officers: 1789–1980

Presidency	Large Land-owner, Farmer, or Land Specu-lator	Lawyer and Large Land-owner	Lawyer	Big Busi-ness	Small Busi-ness	Govern-ment Service	Other	No. of Elite Appoin-tees	% of Elite Appoin-tees	No. of Non-Elite Appoin-tees	Indeter-minate Status
Washington	2	5	4	2	—	—	1	14	100.0%	—	—
J. Adams	—	3	3	2	—	—	1	9	100.0	—	—
Jefferson	2	3	5	1	—	—	1	9	81.8	2	1
Madison	2	3	6	3	—	—	2	18	100.0	—	4
Monroe	—	2	6	2	—	—	—	9	100.0	—	2
J. Q. Adams	—	2	5	2	—	—	—	9	100.0	—	1
Jackson	1	3	11	—	1	—	—	22	95.7	1	—
Van Buren	1	1	7	—	—	—	1	8	88.9	1	1
W. H. Harrison	—	—	5	—	—	—	—	4	100.0	—	1
Tyler	1	2	9	1	—	—	2	12	100.0	—	6
Polk	—	2	6	1	—	—	1	9	100.0	—	3
Taylor	—	1	6	1	—	—	—	7	100.0	—	1
Fillmore	—	1	8	1	—	—	1	11	100.0	—	—
Pierce	1	1	7	—	—	—	—	8	100.0	—	1
Buchanan	—	2	10	1	—	—	—	9	75.0	3	2
Pre-Civil War Totals	10	31	98	17	1	0	10	158	95.8	7	23
Lincoln	—	—	10	1	—	—	2	12	92.3	1	—
A. Johnson	—	—	9	1	—	4	4	11	68.7	5	2
Grant	—	—	17	4	—	1	2	20	83.4	4	3
Hayes	—	—	8	1	—	—	2	9	75.0	3	1
Garfield	—	—	5	—	—	1	4	6	100.0	—	—
Arthur	—	—	8	3	—	—	1	9	81.8	2	1
Cleveland	—	—	11	1	—	—	—	11	91.7	1	—

374

B. Harrison	—	—	—	—	6	5	—	1	—	1	11	91.7	1	2
Cleveland	—	—	—	—	9	2	—	—	—	2	11	84.6	2	1
McKinley	—	—	—	—	8	5	—	—	—	3	15	93.8	1	1
T. Roosevelt	—	—	—	—	10	8	—	—	3	5	24	88.9	3	4
Taft	—	—	—	—	7	5	—	—	—	3	13	92.9	1	1
Wilson	—	—	—	—	12	6	—	—	—	6	12	57.1	9	4
Harding	—	—	—	—	3	7	—	—	—	3	9	81.8	2	2
Coolidge	—	—	—	—	7	8	—	1	1	4	16	80.0	4	2
Hoover	—	—	—	—	5	8	—	—	—	4	13	81.2	3	2
Civil War–New Deal Totals	—	—	—	—	135	65	1	11	44	202	83.5	40	26
New Deal years of F. D. Roosevelt	—	—	—	—	6	5	1	1	7	9	47.4	10	1
WWII years of F. D. Roosevelt	—	1	—	—	6	5	—	4	3	11	57.9	8	—
Truman	—	—	—	—	18	11	1	11	2	25	55.6	20	2
Eisenhower	—	—	—	—	5	20	4	4	7	30	81.1	7	5
Kennedy	—	—	—	—	11	4	—	9	3	14	58.3	10	3
L. B. Johnson	—	—	—	—	14	6	—	9	8	23	65.7	12	5
Nixon	—	—	—	—	10	13	2	8	7	30	69.8	13	5
Ford	1	—	—	—	5	5	1	4	8	18	66.7	9	1
Carter	1	—	—	—	5	5	1	8	6	17	65.4	9	1
Post-New Deal Totals	2	1			80 (28.7%)	74	10	58	51	177	64.4	98	18
Overall 1789–1980 Totals	12	32			313 (44.8%)	156	12	69	105	537	78.7	145	67

NOTE: The first (occupational) part of this table has been compiled according to the number of people who held high federal office, while the second part, dealing with economic elite (or non-elite) status, has been compiled on the basis of the number of appointments made, because the status of some multiple officeholders changed between their periods of government service. The "other" occupational column includes academic figures, newspapermen, and various other types of persons. The last category was established because there was not enough background data to classify some officials. Although not new appointees, four New Deal officials were counted again as World War II entries since these two periods were treated separately.

But a majority of these were really wealthy business (or pro-business) figures, such as John Hay (who served, up to 1899, as a director of the Western Union Telegraph Co.), Whitelaw Reid (who had married into the enormously rich Mills family), and Walter Evans Edge (who was the best friend of the president of the Standard Oil Co. of New Jersey), and thus should probably be included in the corporate category.[32] And as part of a modest trend, there was an almost equal number of academic and literary figures appointed to high office during these years, some of whom also had strong elitist ties.[33]

Since 1933 many of these trends have continued to work, albeit in uneven fashion. For example, with the exception of the (perhaps atypical) Eisenhower administration, an average of between 20 and 40 percent of the nation's top administrative and diplomatic officials have been drawn from the ranks of the legal profession, with the less business-oriented Democratic regimes frequently relying more heavily than the Republicans on this long important source.[34] As in the past, a substantial percentage of these appointees have been wealthy, well-connected corporate lawyers, who have, no doubt, been chosen in part because of their ability and professional affinity for such positions. But a sizable number were apparently selected because they served as very useful (and not readily identified) politico-economic intermediaries.[35]

The proportion of businessmen appointed to key Cabinet and diplomatic posts remained fairly high during this period, certainly higher than their share of the nation's workforce.[36] This was due in considerable measure to the heavily pro-corporate recruitment policy of the Eisenhower administration, which more than made up for the lesser use of such figures by the Kennedy and Johnson regimes. In fact, largely because of Eisenhower's marked preference for major executives, the business sector secured almost as much representation in the federal government in the post-1933 period as did the legal profession. But this statement masks some important differences, for certain types of figures, such as those involved in manufacturing and finance, received more high federal posts than any other kind of businessmen.[37] For instance, there was an almost complete absence of officials drawn from the railroads or other large public utilities, a gap that can be explained only in part by the fact that most of these concerns fall under the jurisdiction of specially constituted state and federal regulatory commissions. And although much has been written in recent years about America as a great "post-industrial" state in which the service and trade sectors have assumed immense importance (along with the technocrats), there has been remarkably little representation of these interests in high-level federal posts, even in the 1970s.[38] There has also been a rather curious pattern of appointment within the financial realm, for by far the greatest number of officials recruited from this area have been major bankers, particularly investment bankers, and not savings and loan officials, mutual fund managers, or even high-ranking executives of the big insurance companies.[39] In short, as various other authorities have pointed out, the vast majority of the legal and economic figures who have been recruited into the federal government in the post-1933 period, if not even earlier, have been drawn from the worlds of "big law" and "big business."[40] In fact, only about ten people appointed to major Cabinet or diplomatic office during this period could be classified as small or medium-sized businessmen, a small fraction of the number drawn from the ranks of the nation's large corporations.[41]

However, there have been some other significant developments in the federal recruitment process since the early 1930s. Perhaps the most striking of these was the sudden emergence of a marked trend on the part of American presidents to appoint to high posts persons who had spent the bulk of their adult lives working for the federal government, so that this sector now became a third major source of top-tier officials. Some of these were former high-ranking military men, whose knowledge and expertise in time of national crisis, such as World War II and the early cold war years, were deemed extremely valuable by presidential policymakers. But most of these appointees were longtime career diplomats whose training and ability were being increasingly recognized and utilized by the American government. There was likewise a sharp increase in the government's reliance on academic figures (the Carter administration had, for instance, five such officials), although some of these appointees also had major economic links.[42] This growing recruitment pattern might even be described as the belated rise of a special kind of "meritocracy."

Some major segments of American society, however, have never been well represented in the upper echelons of the federal government. For instance, unlike certain large farm groups, which since at least the early 1920s have secured many appointive posts in the Department of Agriculture, organized labor has not received the kind of treatment one might expect of such a large and presumably potent politico-economic body. Since 1913 there have been only six officials—five of them Secretaries of Labor—who were in any important way directly linked with the union movement, and only one of these (William B. Wilson) served for a lengthy period.[43] In few other highly industrialized countries, one suspects, have union leaders received such a meager share of the key governmental posts.

Since 1789 there have been various shifts of less striking scope in the economic backgrounds of Supreme Court justices, even though all of these men have necessarily been lawyers. In the pre-Civil War years a substantial number of judges, such as Virginia's John Blair, came from families that had large landholdings, particularly in the South. Several others, such as John Marshall and Henry Brockholst Livingston, had both major land and business interests. However, after 1861 there was a marked change in the type of lawyer appointed to the High Court, for at least half of these men now had strong pro-business ties, as seen, for instance, in the former corporate practices of two key Chief Justices, Morrison R. Waite and Melville W. Fuller. And as one might expect, given the results of the Civil War, only a handful of appointees had sizable landholdings. Yet during the New and Fair Deal period, there was a complete turn away from the pro-business appointment policies of the preceding, primarily Republican, regimes. Not one of the thirteen justices who were picked during these pivotal years had been affiliated with large corporate interests. Since then, the record has been somewhat mixed, with most of the more conservative appointments being made by Republican presidents.

ELITE OR NON-ELITE STATUS OF APPOINTEES

The last important aspect of the federal recruitment process which must be examined from a broad historical standpoint is that of the economic status of the various people who have been appointed to high office over the years.[44] This raises the question as to what, if any, relationship there has been between political and economic elite groups in American history, or to put it another way, between the nation's governmental and economic structure.[45]

In this study the term *economic elite* has been used to describe someone who held an important (executive or directorship) post in a major business enterprise or corporate law firm and/or whose family had considerable wealth or like executive or directorship ties at or around the time of his (or her) appointment to high federal office.[46] In terms of numbers, this rich and/or well-connected segment of the population has probably never constituted more than about 0.5 or 1 percent of the people in the country, and has clearly represented the core of the American upper class.[47]

In its early years America was, as Table 14 plainly shows, an elite-dominated nation. This is not surprising given an undeveloped economy that bound the vast majority of people to a life of arduous toil, particularly in the rural areas where the bulk of the population lived. In fact, during the Federalist period there was not a single high official, administrative, diplomatic, or judicial, who was not a member of one of the nation's economic elites.[48] Indeed, about the only difference between the Federalist Supreme Court justices and key Cabinet and diplomatic officials was that the latter had more multiple elite links, such as Alexander Hamilton, who was a prominent pro-corporate lawyer, a director of the Bank of New York, and the son-in-law of the wealthy Philip Schuyler.

During the Jeffersonian Republican years there was some, almost inevitable, reduction in the amount of elite influence in the nation's top governmental circles and, concomitantly, a modest increase in the number of non-elite appointees. Actually, so far as administrative and diplomatic posts are concerned, all of this occurred during Thomas Jefferson's presidency, in which 18 percent (2 out of 11) of the appointments went, perhaps largely for geo-political reasons, to non-elite figures.[49] However, the next three administrations adhered to a highly elitist recruitment pattern; in fact, all of the Cabinet and diplomatic officials, about whom such an assessment can be made, had major socio-economic links.⁵⁰ Although the numbers involved are too small to form a reliable base, there was a lesser proportion (83 percent) of elite leaders appointed to the Supreme Court during this period.

The next period, the Jacksonian era, has been described by many authorities as an age in which more equalitarian democratic forces seized power for the first time in American history. But there was, revealingly, only a slight rise (of a few percentage points) in the representation of non-elite figures in the upper ranks of the federal government during these stormy years.⁵¹ In fact, all of the Supreme Court appointees during this period were elite leaders, the most prominent of these being Chief Justice Roger B. Taney, who had been closely linked with Maryland railroad and banking interests. Hence it would certainly appear that Bray Hammond and Edward Pessen were quite right in contending that the Jacksonian movement represented, not the rise of the "common man," but rather the emergence of a new set of elite forces which wrested power away from long-established economic interests, particularly those associated with the patrician-dominated Second Bank of the United States.⁵²

During the two pre-Civil War decades this pattern of elite appointment continued to prevail. Aside from the Buchanan administration, all of the major Cabinet and diplomatic officers (about whom there is much pertinent background data) were drawn from elite sources.⁵³ As a rule, these men represented either large landholding (pro-slavery) interests in the South, or the nation's growing business forces, especially banking and railroads, most of which were located in the North. Since only six Supreme Court justices were picked during this 20-year period, it is difficult to draw any inferences from this set of selections, except to note that five were apparently elite figures. Because of this pattern and the previous Jacksonian record of appointing elitist leaders, the Court remained firmly in the hands of conservative upper-class interests.

During the Civil War and Reconstruction years there were some interesting shifts in the proportions of elite and non-elite figures appointed to high office in the United States. After the highly elitist (and pro-railroad) Lincoln administration, there was a significant increase in the relative number of non-elite persons named to important executive and diplomatic posts during the presidential regime of Andrew Johnson, perhaps because Johnson himself was a man of modest means and humble origins. However, this pattern did not continue during the administration of former General Ulysses S. Grant, probably because his national fame had brought him into close contact with influential economic and political leaders. Similarly, in the judicial realm nearly 90 percent of the men who were elevated to the Supreme Court during this critical period were elite figures.

In the course of the next 20 years, from the administration of Rutherford B. Hayes through Grover Cleveland's second term, there was little change in the relative amount of elite and non-elite representation in the upper ranks of the federal government. Although there was some variation, all of these administrations were dominated by wealthy or well-connected (mostly railroad and/or banking) elite figures, who made up an average of 88 percent of the key executive and diplomatic appointees—a higher percentage than that of the Civil War and Reconstruction years. Excluding the brief, ill-fated Garfield regime, the greatest proportion of economically elite officials was picked by New York Democrat Grover Cleveland (during his first presidency) and Benjamin Harrison, while the largest number of non-elite selections was made during the administration of Rutherford B. Hayes and, curiously, during the second term of Grover Cleveland. One possible reason for Cleveland's less overt reliance on elite figures during his second term may be that upon relinquishing office in 1889, this conservative leader became affiliated with the "Morgan" law firm of Bangs, Stetson, Tracy, and MacVeagh (as it was then known) in New York City, and with this informal tie did not have as great a need for economically elite Cabinet and diplomatic officials. A highly elitist pattern was also maintained in the selection of Supreme Court justices throughout this 20-year period, for 83 percent of these men had important corporate (usually railroad) ties or pro-business backgrounds.

The practice of making elitist Cabinet and diplomatic appointments reached its post–Civil War peak between 1897 and 1913. Ironically, this was an era in which there was a great deal of populist and progressive sentiment in the country. According to many historians, this movement found much support in the administration of Theodore Roosevelt, an ambitious patrician turned civic reformer. Yet there was not much difference between the percentage of elitist appointments of the Roosevelt regime and that of either the McKinley or Taft administration (see Table 14 again). Thus Gabriel Kolko and various other authorities were apparently right when they described Theodore Roosevelt as essentially a conservative who, through his often colorful rhetoric and occasional reformist actions, did more to defuse than to advance the progressive movement in America.[54] Similarly, during this period all of the men appointed to the High Court (about whom sufficient information exists) were elite leaders.

During the Wilson regime, on the other hand, the number of non-elite people appointed to major Cabinet and diplomatic posts increased markedly, from about 8 percent in the McKinley-through-Taft period to a high of 43 percent under New Jersey Democrat Woodrow Wilson.[55] This was, as Table 14 makes clear, by far the highest level reached in the recruitment of such officials since the founding of the Republic, and it would seem to have signified a major shift in American politico-economic relations. However, the overall impact of this appointment policy was muted considerably by the fact that both President Wilson and his chief informal advisor, Colonel House, were essentially conservative figures. As one might expect, there was a similar pattern in the selection of Supreme Court justices during this period, though the number of such officials picked was extremely small—only three.

In the Republican-dominated 1920s and early 1930s there was a sharp increase in the proportion of elitists appointed to important office. But for all their conservatism, Harding, Coolidge, and Hoover did not match the high levels of elite appointments set by many previous Republican presidents, such as Roosevelt and Taft. Overall, the proportion of elite leaders appointed to high executive and diplomatic posts during these years averaged about 80 percent.[56] In addition, a higher percentage of economically elite figures were elevated to the High Court under Harding, Coolidge, and Hoover than were appointed to major Cabinet and diplomatic posts, which policy was in marked contrast to that followed by many later administrations.[57]

The New Deal years ushered in a very different type of appointment practice, for most of the people who were picked to hold high office during this stormy period were, for the first time in American history, non-elite figures. A little over half of the people who were appointed to key Cabinet and diplomatic posts between 1933 and 1940 did not have wealthy backgrounds or important corporate links, but were drawn from diverse sources and even included two former social workers.[58] And a substantial proportion of those who did have major business or elitist ties, such as Joseph P. Kennedy and New York retailer Jesse Straus, were awarded diplomatic posts—this at a time when the nation's most pressing problems were of a domestic economic nature. Moreover, none of the five men appointed to the Supreme Court during the (late) New Deal period had any significant economic links, perhaps because all were chosen after FDR's many frustrating attempts to pull the nation out of the Depression had been thwarted, prior to his famous "Court-packing" threat, by this long arch-conservative body. Given this general appointment pattern and the critical problems and temper of the times, it is not surprising that the New Deal led to a number of major changes in governmental policy and politico-economic relations.[60]

In the World War II and Truman years there was a noticeable shift back toward a more elitist recruitment practice, at least with regard to key Cabinet and diplomatic posts. This was particularly true during the war when many able executives and corporate lawyers, such as James V. Forrestal and Henry L. Stimson, were asked to assume important positions in the federal goverment to aid in the direction of the nation's war effort. However, as Table 14 reveals, the Truman administration was not able to reestablish the primarily non-elitist pattern of the New Deal, for America's major corporate interests, which had lost considerable influence in the late 1930s, had managed during the war to secure a firm grip on certain key federal agencies, especially the Departments of State, Treasury, and Defense.[61] Yet a very different policy was followed in the judicial realm. Probably because of Roosevelt's effort to liberalize the Supreme Court in the late 1930s, none of the appointees to this august body was an elitist leader.

The Eisenhower administration, on the other hand, was heavily dominated, so far as major Cabinet and diplomatic positions were concerned, by wealthy corporate—in fact, largely Establishment—interests. About 81 percent of the top administrative and ambassadorial posts were occupied by elite figures, a total unmatched since the 1920s. Indeed the Eisenhower government was, in one sense, the most staunchly elitist regime since the early days of the Republic, for it had a higher proportion of Cabinet and diplomatic officials with multiple (i.e., both primary and secondary) elite ties than any administration since George Washington's. And although they comprised a much smaller number, most of Eisenhower's (five) Supreme Court appointments were of the same pro-corporate character. However, they did not have the same marked Establishment orientation as the President's chief Cabinet and diplomatic officers, and it should be emphasized that one of his non-elitist selections, Chief Justice Earl Warren, turned out to be a crucial miscalculation.

Since the Eisenhower administration, the economic pattern of major executive and diplomatic appointments would appear to have stabilized to a considerable extent, regardless of which party was in power. About 60 to 70 percent of these high officials were drawn from America's wealthy, pro-corporate ranks, while the other 30 to 40 percent were recruited from non-elite sources.[62] This general finding disguises the fact that a significant number of the people picked by the Nixon regime represented a relatively new, highly conservative set of politico-economic forces rather than the more moderate Establishment interests which had played a prominent role in most postwar governments, especially that of Dwight D. Eisenhower. Moreover, the Carter administration, although it initially claimed to represent political "outsiders," turned out to have one of the two highest percentages of elite figures holding major Cabinet and diplomatic posts of any Democratic regime since the turn of the century, in part because of President Carter's close ties to the Trilateral Commission.[63] This skewed appointment pattern was in sharp contrast to that which prevailed with reference to Supreme Court appointments in recent years, even under the Nixon and Ford administrations.

A clear picture of the nation's overall recruitment policy can be gained from the summary analysis of the elite status of America's top government officials presented in Table 15.[64]

These figures show that, in terms of the top appointive posts, the United States has certainly not been a land of equality of political opportunity.[65] Rather, it has been an elitist-dominated nation, except for certain brief periods such as the New Deal years, the earlier Wilson regime, and the post-1937 Supreme Court.[66] Since 1789 about 79 percent of America's top (non-judicial) officeholders have been economically elite figures, a considerably higher percentage than the proportion of Presidents with such ties (58 percent, by best estimate).[67] However, the former total has varied over time, ranging for broad periods from a high of about 96 percent in the pre–Civil War era to roughly 64 percent since 1933—a much reduced sum, but one which still stands much at odds with the democratic ideal of a (high-level) representative bureaucracy.[68]

Similarly, about 74 percent of the appointments made to the Supreme

TABLE 15

1789–1980 Summary Analysis of Elite Status of America's Major Cabinet, Diplomatic, and Supreme Court Officers

	Elite Cabinet and Diplomatic Appointees (%)	Elite Supreme Court Appointees (%)
Federalist period (1789–1801)	100.0	
Jeffersonian Republican years (1801–1829)	95.7	
Jacksonian era (1829–1841)	93.8	
Two pre-Civil War decades	95.2	
Pre-Civil War period (1789–1861)	**95.8**	**94.1**
Civil War and Reconstruction years (1861–77)	81.1	
1877–1897 period	86.8	
McKinley-Taft years (1897–1913)	91.7	
Wilson regime (1913–1921)	57.1	
Harding-Hoover years (1921–1933)	80.9	
1861–1933 period	**83.5**	**87.2**
New Deal years (1933–1940)	47.4	
World War II years (1940–1945)	57.9	
Truman administration (1945–1953)	55.6	
Eisenhower administration (1953–1961)	81.1	
Kennedy-Johnson years (1961–1969)	62.7	
Nixon-Ford regime (1969–1977)	68.6	
Carter administration (1977–1980)	65.4	
Post-1933 period	**64.4**	**25.0**
Overall 1978–1980 period	**78.7**	**74.2**

Court between 1789 and 1980 have been of an elitist nature. Yet it should be emphasized that there has been a tremendous shift in judicial recruitment practice, thanks primarily to the New Deal, for the proportion of non-elite figures elevated to this body rose, following Roosevelt's first term in office, from an average of about 13 percent to 75 percent, truly one of the most remarkable turnabouts in American politico-economic history.

At this point it is appropriate to ask, how do these findings relate to those of other works in the field? This is an important question, for this topic has been marked by much debate and sharply divided opinion. In fact, it has been a source of considerable controversy ever since C. Wright Mills published his provocative book, *The Power Elite*. Over the years two major schools have developed, the pluralist and the elitist, and to judge from the political science literature, the former has gained greater acceptance.[69] Elitist works have generally come under heavy attack, although the pluralists themselves have, curiously, done relatively little research in the area. But the evidence assembled here clearly shows that such elitist scholars as G. William Domhoff have been much closer to the mark than their many bitter critics.[70]

This study's basic data run completely counter to those of Thomas Dye who, in a recent book entitled *Who's Running America?*, has, in effect, refuted some of his own (and Harmon Zeigler's) earlier findings and now claims, on the basis of a survey made in the early 1970s of the nation's most important institutions and officeholders, that "...there is very little overlap among people at the top of the corporate, governmental, and military sectors of society."[71] Or as Dye and one of his later associates asserted in another closely related study, "...governmental leadership is not interlocked with the corporate world."[72] More precisely, Dye maintained that business concerns supplied only 16.6 percent of the nation's high federal officials, who were recruited instead primarily from the legal profession (a body treated as completely apart from the corporate community) and secondarily from such areas as education and the government itself.[73]

However, Dye and his associates made certain gross errors in their recent analysis of America's overall leadership structure which renders their findings, at a minimum, suspect. For instance, they chose to classify all lawyers, even those associated with large corporate law firms, as part of the nation's "civic establishment" or "public interest" sector. At one point they even claimed that the "senior partners in top Wall Street law firms are not interlocked in directorships of major corporations and banks."[74] This treatment of corporate lawyers is simply contrary to the facts.[75]

Another defect in Dye's study is that although he and his colleagues were aware that many people holding high federal office in the early 1970's had major directorship ties, they nevertheless chose, in their key aggregate analysis, to ignore such associations and to classify all figures solely on the basis of their primary occupational affiliations.[76] Thus such recent Cabinet officials as William P. Rogers and George P. Shultz were merely treated as former legal and academic figures, even though they had various prominent corporate links. With these kinds of crucial flaws, it is not surprising that Dye (and company) came to the erroneous conclusion that America's corporate interests supplied only a small fraction of the nation's high federal officials.

CIRCULATION AND TRANSFORMATION OF ELITES

There is, moreover, only one book in this area which provides much of a historical dimension to the analysis of political (or politico-economic) elites in American life, and that is *The Irony of Democracy*.[77] Yet even in this work (which is primarily a political science text), the authors, Dye and Zeigler, devoted only abut 70 pages to the historical development of major elite forces, half of which described the nation's "founding fathers." This left relatively little space for the treatment of various elite interests in the pre–Civil War era, "the rise of the new industrial elite," "the political dominance of the industrial elite" (their phrases employed to describe two briefly etched periods), and the emergence of what the authors call the "liberal establishment" (a section which focuses heavily on the New Deal).[78] But this sketchy discussion leaves a good deal to be desired and simply does not do justice to the changing nature or "circulation of elites," to use Pareto's term, in American history, particularly in the post–Civil War period.[79]

The data presented in this study of the federal recruitment and policy-making process do permit such an analysis (although it is one that will undoubtedly require much modification and elaboration in the years ahead).

As Volume I shows, the nation was dominated at the outset, during the Federalist years of the Washington regime and, to a lesser extent, the John Adams administration, by a small wealthy group of primarily commercially or entrepreneurially oriented urban forces. With the rise of the Jeffersonian Republicans to power in 1801, the governmental balance quickly shifted to upper-class agrarians, many of whom were major Virginia landholders, while the party's minority mercantile wing was made up largely of certain dissident elements, such as the wealthy Smith brothers of Baltimore.

After many years in power, during which it too became a vested interest, this coalition, generally described as the "Virginia dynasty," was challenged and bested by a new set of politico-economic forces led by Andrew Jackson in the late 1820s. Most of the major figures associated with this movement were of a very different breed than their patrician predecessors, for they represented not, as has often been claimed, the emergence of more democratic or equalitarian forces, but the rise of new entrepreneurial interests, particularly those associated with state banks, which found political expression in such groups as Jackson's "Nashville Junto" and Martin Van Buren's "Albany Regency." Their crowning achievement (though some would not call it that) was the destruction of the Second Bank of the United States, a quasi-public institution that had been controlled by Philadelphia's able, aristocratic Nicholas Biddle and his allies.

During the 1840s control of the government shifted back and forth between the newly formed (but short-lived) Whig party and the better-entrenched Democrats, who claimed the mantle of Andrew Jackson. But regardless of which party was in power, various elite forces were firmly in control, for there was substantial representation of wealthy landed and entrepreneurial (primarily banking, though also some railroad and textile) interests. As a result of the eruption of the long-suppressed slavery issue in the 1850s, the conservative, commercially oriented Democrats, led by Franklin Pierce (who had married into a branch of the rich and well-connected Appleton family) and Pennsylvania's "doughface" James Buchanan, emerged briefly as the nation's dominant political body, in large measure because they were extremely solicitous of Southern interests and anxious to maintain normal trade relations with that region. The Whig forces, on the other hand, fell into increasing disarray over the slavery issue and were unable to contend with the growing, mostly non-elitist, abolitionist sentiment in the country. This agitation soon led to the creation of a new third (initially fairly weak) party, known as the Republicans, and later, after much angry exchange and travail, to that "irrepressible conflict, the Civil War.

With the advent of the Lincoln administration, there was not only a bitter military struggle which finally broke the back of the South, but a marked change in the economic makeup of America's top governmental officials. For after 1861 railroad forces (not manufacturing, which was still a small-scale operation) assumed a very important place in the economic and political life of the nation. Indeed, this was symbolized by the rise of Lincoln himself, for although he was elected largely for other reasons, he had the backing of influential railroadmen in the West and was the first lawyer with such support to be elected President. In one administration after another between 1861 and the late 1890s, railroad interests were very strongly represented in key Cabinet, diplomatic, and judicial posts, almost always by lawyers and other leaders closely associated with such enterprises. However, these forces did not usually constitute a cohesive bloc, but were often rival (and when need be, ruthless) entrepreneurs, each jockeying for economic position and governmental favor. It made little difference, aside perhaps from the tariff issue, which party was in power. In fact, the most pro-railroad figure ever to run for President of the United States was a Democrat, Samuel J. Tilden. And with regard to governmental action, it was another Democrat, Grover Cleveland, who, acting on the advice of his Attorney General (and still active railroad director), Richard Olney, used federal troops to break the Pullman strike in 1894.

From shortly before the turn of the century to the New Deal, the most significant development in the business sector was the emergence around 1900 of many big manufacturing firms, partly through expanded natural growth and partly through the consummation of various giant mergers, the most spectacular being that creating the great United States Steel Corp. This was followed by the formation of a number of large public utilities and, after World War I, several huge public utility holding companies. Yet the nation's major railroads continued to play an important role in American business affairs. In addition, certain financial interests emerged as crucial forces in all of the above areas. The most influential of these (though it had some potent rivals) was the so-called House of Morgan, which first achieved economic prominence in the railroad sector, particularly as the agent or ally of the Vanderbilt lines, but soon extended its activities into the manufacturing and public utility fields.[80] Morgan leaders also exerted considerable power in the political realm, not so much at the outset of this period (for McKinley was Mark Hanna's "man"), but during various later regimes, especially those of Theodore Roosevelt, Calvin Coolidge, and Herbert Hoover.[81] In these administrations Morgan interests were clearly at their politico-economic peak.

After 1933, however, there were a number of enormous changes in the political and economic life of the nation. Largely because of the Depression, a new, more pragmatic (and later liberally oriented) Democratic regime was installed in Washington. This was composed of a very different, less elitist type of high-level executive (and, after 1937, judicial official) than had served under previous administrations. After a brief, fairly conservative phase these New Deal leaders adopted, with the aid of Congress, a series of critical remedial measures, some of which enhanced the position of certain major segments of the population, such as organized labor (a hitherto ineffective force), while others had enormous impact in the business world. For instance, the Public Utility Anti-Holding Company Act of 1935 not only broke up most of these great chains, but also struck a vital blow at the House of Morgan, which was intimately involved in at least two of them. As a result of this and other events, the power of the House of Morgan was seriously diminished, and it entered into an economic decline from which it never really recovered.[82] At the same time, a number of other financial concerns emerged as extremely potent national forces, chief of which were the Rockefeller interests (now more in banking than in oil) and a well-knit group of Jewish investment bankers led by Lehman Brothers and Goldman, Sachs & Co., which latter complex had close ties with the Democratic party.[83]

Even more important was the fact that during the New Deal and World War II years there evolved a more stable and institutionalized alignment of economic forces in America, primarily through the creation in 1933 of the Business Advisory Council (known after 1961 as the Business Council), and in 1942 of the Committee for Economic Development. These two closely related groups provided—along with certain other organizations, such as the Council on Foreign Relations—the core of what soon came to be recognized as the nation's "business establishment."[84] This powerful set of interests exercised a great deal of influence in the federal government in the postwar period, not only, most obviously, in the Eisenhower regime, but also to a rather surprising extent (in the areas of defense, finance, and foreign affairs) in the administrations of most Democratic presidents, especially, through two new organizations (the Business Roundtable and the Trilateral Commission), that of Jimmy Carter. Indeed, the only period in which the business establishment did not exert as much influence as one might expect was, ironically, during the administrations of Nixon and Ford. This was largely because of Nixon's ties to fairly new, highly conservative economic forces, many of which were located in the nation's fast-growing Southern Rim.

There has, then, been a good deal of change in the nature of the elites which have, with a few exceptions, dominated American government over the years. In summary, these elites have taken the following major forms: first, those based on large landholdings and mercantile pursuits; second, along with the former, those closely linked, beginning with the age of Jackson, with state banking and other budding entrepreneurial interests; third, with the Civil War, various powerful railroad forces; fourth, starting shortly before the turn of the century, big industry and finance, with the latter being led by the great J. P. Morgan; and finally, after the New Deal, the institutionalization of America's top economic leadership, primarily through such groups as the Business (Advisory) Council, the CED, and more recently the Business Roundtable and Trilateral Commission.[85]

Most of these developments have represented the rise of new interests, such as the railroad-rich Vanderbilts in the post-Civil War years and, about a half-century later, New York's influential Jewish investment bankers. However, in a number of cases, particularly after the growth of America's first great fortunes, families which achieved vast wealth and power in one period were able, through the retention or expansion of their economic interests, to continue to wield substantial influence in national affairs in later eras.[86] Indeed, one of the most striking findings to emerge from this study of American politico-economic history is the extent to which elite family ties have, contrary to our democratic precepts, played an important role in the federal recruitment and policymaking process. This is not to say that any rich family can readily obtain almost any high-level federal post or dictate governmental policy, let alone establish a powerful political dynasty (the postwar rise of the ambitious Kennedy clan notwithstanding). Rather, it is to assert that great family wealth, as well as corporate wealth, has long exercised more influence in American government than has generally been realized. In fact, if anything, this is an understatement. For, judging from the evidence assembled here, it would be more accurate to say that, regardless of its changing form, America has almost always been dominated by some kind of wealth.

Notes

1. New York state was also fairly well represented during this period, but not grossly out of its proportion of the nation's population.

2. This recruitment pattern stemmed partly from the fact that Pennsylvania and Virginia were two of the three largest states in the Union in the pre-Civil War period. But Massachusetts' favored position is not so easily explained (except perhaps in terms of its marked economic influence), since there were a number of states that were about as big, such as North Carolina. Although New York had, by 1820, passed every other state in population, it nevertheless fared worse in the post-1840 era than it had in preceding times, claiming only 6.6 percent of the top governmental positions between 1841 and 1861, in contrast to 14 percent during earlier years.

3. Of the New York (1861–1933) appointment total of 58, eight were from the northern half of the state. Half of this aggregate represented two prestigious ex-college presidents, Andrew D.

White and David J. Hill, each of whom held two diplomatic offices. The other half was made up by Auburn lawyer William H. Seward (who served as Secretary of State in two administrations) and Corning Glass Works owner Alanson B. Houghton (who held diplomatic posts under both Harding and Coolidge). Yet even these two latter men had ties to New York City—Houghton through his directorship with the Metropolitan Life Insurance Co., and Seward through his longtime legal and political association with the entrepreneurially-oriented Richard M. Blatchford.

4. The major Cabinet and diplomatic representation of the rapidly growing (and increasingly industrialized) north central section of the country—Ohio, Illinois, Indiana, Michigan, and Wisconsin—jumped sharply during this period, more or less in line with its share of the nation's population and overall economic output. On the other hand, although New England's proportion of high-level federal appointments fell off somewhat after the Civil War, the decline was not as severe as one might have expected, in large measure because Boston itself continued, as a major financial hub, to wield considerable influence in American politics.

5. The first Virginia Supreme Court justice to be appointed in the post-Civil War period was Richmond lawyer Lewis F. Powell, Jr., who was selected in the early 1970s.

6. Even though Texas had become by far the largest state in the South shortly before the turn of the century, it did not receive its first Cabinet seat (or diplomatic post) until the Wilson administration. And that no doubt stemmed from the influence of the President's intimate informal advisor, Colonel House.

7. In like manner, the city of Baltimore, which once claimed a significant number of major Cabinet and diplomatic posts (a total of ten in the pre-Civil War era), fell off sharply thereafter, obtaining only two between 1861 and 1900, and the same small number in the first third of the 20th century. Both of the latter were held by the same person, the patrician reformer Charles J. Bonaparte, who was probably picked primarily because he was a member of the executive committee of the then influential National Civil Federation.

8. The Pacific Coast area has consistently received considerably less than its demographic due on the Supreme Court, perhaps because of the time lag often involved in such appointment proceedings. Ohio fell off markedly in its representation on the Court during this period, primarily because it had gotten more than its share of seats under earlier regimes, while Pennsylvania has not received a Supreme Court appointment since the Hoover administration, and only one since the turn of the century. The substantial rise in the Midwest's percentage is, it should be emphasized, based on a deceptively small number of selections, and may simply be a reflection of Nixon's rather unusual appointment of two Minnesota justices, Blackmun and Burger.

9. Actually, New York City probably reached its peak of politico-economic power under Eisenhower and carried much less weight under Nixon and Ford, particularly the latter. Pennsylvania, on the other hand, continued to drop sharply in both Cabinet and diplomatic appointments, falling from 8.5 percent between the Civil War and the New Deal to a mere 2.7 percent in the post-1933 years.

10. In the early post-Civil War years there were, as Table 11 shows, some Army officers who, because of their general reputations, the pro-military temper of the times, or their close ties to President Grant, were elevated (usually briefly) to Cabinet office. But this was a special set of circumstances, not really comparable to that of the post-New Deal period. For another, albeit much inflated, assessment of the influence of military leaders in American government, see C. Wright Mills, *The Power Elite* (New York: Oxford University Press, 1956), pp. 171–224.

11. For one recent journalistic analysis of both the public and private (primarily lobbying) role played by some of these figures, see Joseph C. Goulden, *The Superlawyers*, passim. However, important as some of these lawyers may be, most of the real "superlawyers" in the country are not in Washington, but in Wall Street and, to a lesser extent, in the corporate law firms of certain other large cities.

12. If those educated abroad were considered to have secured the equivalent of an Ivy

League education, the proportion of college graduates receiving such prestigious degrees would rise from about 65 to 94 percent, almost the same total found for the following Jeffersonian Republican years. In this section all people who graduated from law school have been treated as having the equivalent of a college education, even though in some cases they did not.

13. Overall, roughly 70 percent of the high federal officials in the Washington and Adams administrations graduated from Ivy League institutions (or their European equivalents), whereas only about 55 percent of the Jeffersonian Republican leaders did so. Sidney Aronson's findings point in the same general direction, although they are of a lesser magnitude, probably becaue he worked with a different time frame and governmental elite sample. See Sidney H. Aronson, *Status and Kinship in the Higher Civil Service* (Cambridge, Mass.: Harvard University Press, 1964), p. 124.

14. There was a somewhat lesser percentage of high federal officials who had either attended or graduated from college in the administrations of Andrew Jackson and Martin Van Buren than in the preceding Republican regimes.

15. Some may find it rather curious that Woodrow Wilson, who was a former Ivy League college president, did not recruit more heavily from such institutions, but he may not have felt free to do so because of strong party and other pressures.

16. Although a number of other justices (such as Harlan, McKenna, Miller, and Van Devanter) attended relatively unknown private colleges (such as De Pauw and Transylvania), they still represented a fairly small percentage of the total number of Supreme Court justices appointed during this period.

17. One might add that within the last decade there has been a marked increase in the number of men with doctorates holding high administrative office. This trend began with the Nixon administration, which employed five Ph.D.s in Cabinet positions (two of whom were in the field of agriculture). The Ford regime had about the same number, although three of these were carryovers. Similarly, President Carter appointed four people with Ph.D.s to his initial Cabinet. Some scholars—following the lead of Harold Lasswell, who heralded the arrival of a major "skills revolution" back in 1948—have placed great emphasis on the increased educational attainments of recent high federal office holders. This "revolution," however, has certainly been a long time coming. In addition, some of the Ph.D. holders may have been picked in considerable part because of their key economic ties (such as Earl Butz and George Shultz, each of whom graced several major corporate boards), or because of their important civic connections (such as Harold Brown, who was a member of the Trilateral Commission, and Michael Blumenthal, who was a trustee of the CED and the Rockefeller Foundation and a recent member of the Trilateral Commission). See Harold D. Lasswell, *The Analysis of Political Behavior* (New York: Oxford University Press, 1948), pp. 133–145, and for a later study, see Kenneth Prewitt and William McAllister, "Changes in the American Executive Elite, 1930–1970," in Heinz Eulau and Moshe M. Czudnowski (eds.), *Elite Recruitment in Democratic Politics* (New York: Sage, 1976), pp. 105–132.

18. Another study, which surveyed more than 1,000 first- and second-echelon executives (including commissioners of the independent regulatory agencies) between 1933 and 1965, found that one-quarter of these officials were Ivy League men, that nearly half had gone to one of 18 exclusive Eastern prep schools, and that these elitist figures were heavily concentrated in the most important arms of the federal government—the Departments of State, Treasury, and Defense. (See David T. Stanley et al., *Men Who Govern* [Washington, D.C.: The Brookings Institution, 1967], pp. 20–22, and 123–28.) The author has not attempted to make any analysis on the basis of religion, because such data are difficult to obtain and also because, prior to the first part of the century, almost all high federal officials were WASPs. In fact, the great ethnic breakthrough did not occur until after the early 1930s. And women did not begin to be represented until the mid-1970s, when they made a few gains, though they have not yet received a seat on the Supreme Court.

19. Felix Frankfurter was the only Supreme Court justice (or for that matter, other high appointive official), to have graduated from New York's City College, an excellent school that has long drawn its students from the middle and lower classes.

20. In the absence of any well-established standard as to what constitutes a "considerable" amount of "significant" governmental experience, this study has relied on the following guideline: anything over four years as either a prominent federal official or a major state executive.

21. This study differs from that of Henry Abraham who, in *Justices and Presidents*, has categorized the Supreme Court justices on the basis of the position they held immediately prior to their appointment to the High Court, even if this post was occupied for only a short time. The most important difference in the pre-Civil War period is in the treatment of John Marshall, who, because he served as Secretary of State and as a Virginia Congressman for only about two years, is considered here to have been previously engaged primarily in private practice.

22. C. Wright Mills was one of the first observers to point out (in *The Power Elite*, pp. 229–30) this marked shift in recruiting practice, emphasizing especially the decline of any kind of state and local government experience and the increased importance of direct (often corporate-based) high-level entry into the federal government. In another study which dealt only with Cabinet recruitment, John Witte has calculated that the mean number of prior elective offices per Cabinet member was 1.71 in the 19th century, while in the 20th century it was only 0.49. See John F. Witte, "Theories of Elite Change: The United States Cabinet from 1789–1976," *Journal of Politics*, forthcoming.

23. Despite much academic effusion about the so-called skills revolution in American government in recent years, very little reliable data are available (other than the award of a formal college degree, which is not always a very good indicator) as to the relative ability of the different types of Cabinet and diplomatic officials appointed over time, particularly in the pre-1933 period. However, it is interesting to note that in a recent Brookings study (covering the 1933–1961 period) the evaluation of the performance of federal executives indicated that long-time career officials served more effectively than did those recruited from either the business or legal worlds. See Dean E. Mann and Jameson W. Doig, *The Assistant Secretaries*, p. 300. For a presumably well-informed, though essentially negative judgment as to the overall quality of Cabinet officers between 1913 and the late 1950s, see Richard F. Fenno, *The President's Cabinet* (Cambridge: Harvard University Press, 1959), p. 77.

24. From an economic class standpoint, the pre-New Deal data are misleading too, for many experienced men were appointed to the High Court in both the pre-Civil War period and the 1861–1933 years—e.g., John Jay, Brockholst Livingston, and Smith Thompson in the first era, and Horace Gray, Samuel Blatchford, and Mahlon Pitney in the second—who came from wealthy families and clearly shared the conservative views of their close kinsmen.

25. Only four previously appointed Supreme Court justices—Horace H. Lurton, Owen J. Roberts, Harlan Fiske Stone, and William Howard Taft—had served for any significant period of time as law school professors, and at least two of these (Roberts and Taft) had key corporate, family, or civic links.

26. See, for instance, T. B. Bottomore, *Elites and Society*, pp. 17 and 112, and Heinz Eulau and Moshe M. Czudnowski (eds.), *op. cit.*, p. 23.

27. Initially, as pointed out in Volume I of this study, there was a good deal of business influence in the operation of the Washington administration, particularly through the presence of New York lawyer Alexander Hamilton and his various politico-economic lieutenants. But this balance of power shifted markedly, actually more than the statistical data indicate, with the rise of the Jeffersonian Republican forces, which, while they included certain (essentially dissident) mercantile leaders, were basically agrarian in orientation.

28. Lest the reader gain the wrong impression from the meager percentage of overt corporate figures appointed to high office during the Jacksonian era (as shown in Table 14), it should be noted that the emergence of entrepreneurial forces in national affairs was reflected primarily through the appointment of business-oriented lawyers rather than of influential economic leaders.

29. Although various authorities have aptly described the period from the 1860s to roughly the turn of the century as "the great age of American railroads," remarkably few entrepreneurs

or executives associated with this industry were appointed to high federal office during these years. Instead, this influential sector made its weight felt in governmental affairs through the selection of lawyers and political leaders who were closely linked with the railroads, usually through directorship ties.

30. Some staunchly pro-business figures had served as Secretary of State in the pre-industrial era (e.g., Daniel Webster and William L. Marcy), but these were the exception rather than the rule. After the 1860s, on the other hand, even such statesmen as John Hay and James G. Blaine (both of whom were former newspapermen rather than attorneys) were closely linked with influential economic interests. And the same may be said of Delaware's patrician Senator Thomas F. Bayard, who was a longtime friend of New York financier August Belmont.

31. The 25 percent business recruitment figure for the Wilson administration may be somewhat deceptive because two-thirds of these officials served in a diplomatic capacity rather than in a Cabinet post. This appointment pattern was not maintained in either the preceding or succeeding Republican regimes.

32. Not all newspapermen appointed to high office during this period were pro-business. Two of those selected by the Wilson administration, William Jennings Bryan and Josephus Daniels, were clearly progressive leaders.

33. In addition, a small number of men appointed to important Cabinet and diplomatic posts during this (1861–1933) period had spent most of their lives in some form of government service. But the majority of these were former Army generals who were appointed shortly after the Civil War when such figures were still extremely popular.

34. Since the start of the New Deal an average of about 29 percent of the top federal officials have been attorneys, in contrast to a little over 40 percent for the post-Civil War period, and an overall (1789–1980) average of almost 45 percent. Because the legal profession makes up only about 0.1 percent of the nation's total workforce, Donald R. Matthews has rightly referred to lawyers as the "high priests of American politics." See his analysis of *The Social Background of Political Decision-Makers* (Garden City, N.Y.: Doubleday, 1954), p. 30.

35. The author is obviously taking issue here with the incredibly sanguine view of Thomas Dye, who, in his recent book *Who's Running America?* (see pp. 97–101 of the first edition), has treated all attorneys, whatever their economic status, as essentially "civic" figures. For a more accurate assessment of the role of influential corporate lawyers, see Louis Auchincloss, *Powers of Attorney*, p. 148 (a non-fictional passage), Adolf Berle's pre-World War II appraisal in the *Encyclopedia of the Social Sciences* (Vol. IX, pp. 341–42), and Paul Hoffman's *Lions in the Street*, passim.

36. There is no way in which the author's findings as to the proportion of high federal officials with (direct) business backgrounds can be reconciled with the extraordinarily large (1889–1949) totals arrived at by Harold Lasswell and his associates in their early post-World War II studies of governmental elites (see Harold D. Lasswell, Daniel Lerner, and C. E. Rothwell, *The Comparative Study of Elites*, p. 30). John Witte's more recently compiled figures are much closer to the mark.

37. Manufacturing and financial executives obtained two-thirds of all the important posts awarded to businessmen in the post-1933 period.

38. For the most widely known treatment of this topic, see Daniel Bell, *The Coming of Post-Industrial Society* (New York: Basic Books, 1973), passim. Actually, the only administration which had a significant number of such figures holding high federal office was that of Dwight D. Eisenhower, and half of these served in posts that were not of great importance to the business community (such as Secretary of the Interior Douglas McKay, who was appointed primarily as a political representative of the West, rather than as an Oregon automobile dealer).

39. The only large insurance company officer to be appointed to a high federal post in American history was one of our post-World War II Ambassadors to Great Britain, Lewis Douglas, and one cannot be sure whether he was recruited because of this affiliation or because he was a trustee of the Rockefeller Foundation, a director of the Council on Foreign

Relations, or as a result of his other elite corporate and family ties.

40. See, for instance, David T. Stanley, Dean E. Mann, and Jameson W. Doig, *Men Who Govern* (a 1933–1965 study), p. 79.

41. Relying on certain generally accepted economic benchmarks, and to some extent, his own judgment, the author would classify the following ten officials as former small or medium-sized businessmen: Harry Woodring, Clinton P. Anderson, Douglas McKay, Frederick Mueller, Fred Seaton, Dudley C. Sharp, Walter Hickel, Melvin Laird, Thomas S. Kleppe, and Cecil Andrus.

42. A noteworthy trend in the opposite direction was the gradual disappearance, especially after the Eisenhower administration, of the practice of appointing able or influential newspapermen to high federal office. Indeed, the only person to be so appointed since the early 1950s was Philadelphia publisher Walter Annenberg, who was apparently picked largely because he had been a substantial contributor to the Nixon campaign in 1968 and was a close friend of the President.

43. In years past, labor apparently did show a lack of interest in other Cabinet offices. Yet there is no reason to believe now that able union executives would not like to be appointed to such key posts as Secretary of Health, Education and Welfare, or Housing and Urban Development. In fact, the AFL-CIO proposed a number of candidates for many second-tier posts in the Carter administration, but apparently only a few were accepted. See Bruce Adams and Kathryn Kavanagh-Baran, *Promise and Performance*, p. 54.

44. This study is concerned primarily with the socio-economic background of America's governmental elite, and not whether these officials constitute some sort of intellectual, technocratic, or other less important elites, as was stressed by Suzanne Keller in her book, *Beyond the Ruling Class*.

45. From the outset, the author has taken as his primary line of analysis a systematic study of the economic aspects of the political recruitment process over time. This type of research can be carried out with considerable rigor, accuracy, and detail, whereas, as many scholars have learned to their sorrow, it is very difficult to ascertain the relative impact of all of the public and private parties involved in even a fairly small set of decisions (for more on this point, see the introduction to Volume I of this work). No attempt will be made to summarize this study's analysis of major issues and events in American history because they were chosen selectively, primarily for illustrative purposes.

46. This definition has not always been easy to apply, in part because of the usual "boundary-line" problems, and has of necessity been employed on a relative scale over time, pitched to fit the level of economic development in various periods.

47. The author suspects that G. William Domhoff was close to the mark when he claimed that America's upper class has represented less than 1 percent of the population. Suzanne Keller also noted in her broad survey of the subject that few estimates of elites have placed them in excess of 3 percent of any given population, and a number of authorities have set the figure as low as 0.1 percent. See Suzanne Keller, *op. cit.*, p. 78, and G. William Domhoff, *Who Rules America?*, p. 7, and also his *The Powers That Be* (New York: Random House, 1979), p. 3.

48. Again, it should be emphasized that the author is not taking the position that all economic elite figures were close-knit and unified in their views and actions, for, as pointed out in this study's first volume, Thomas Jefferson and Edmund Randolph had a strictly agrarian orientation, whereas many other members of Washington's administration had a more mercantile or entrepreneurial outlook. And although John Adams and Alexander Hamilton were both urban, Northeastern-based leaders, they differed sharply on matters of governmental policy. John Adams himself was probably more of a non-elite figure than any of the other early leaders, but he was not included in these computations because he never held one of the specified major Cabinet, diplomatic, or Supreme Court posts. See Appendix A and Appendix B of Volume I of this study for a breakdown of the elite (or non-elite) status and socio-economic background of all high federal officials in the pre-Civil War period.

49. These two appointees, Levi Lincoln and Henry Dearborn, were New Englanders who were probably picked by the Southern agrarian-oriented Jefferson to give some sectional balance to the Cabinet.

50. As Table 14 indicates, there were eight Cabinet and diplomatic officials appointed between 1809 and 1829 who, because of a lack of pertinent data, could not be classified as to their socio-economic status. Later research may show that some were non-elite leaders and thus alter this finding.

51. Although Sideny Aronson analyzed a larger (and less influential) set of government leaders of just three administrations (John Adams, Jefferson, and Jackson), his findings are in rough agreement with those of the author as to the elite domination of the federal government. See his *Status and Kinship in the Higher Civil Service*, pp. 26–28, 62, 68, 88, 96, and 124.

52. See Bray Hammond, *Banks and Politics in America*, pp. 326–450, and Edward Pessen, *Jacksonian America* (Homewood, Ill.: Dorsey Press, 1969), passim.

53. In the Tyler and Polk administrations there were, again, a significant number of officials about whom little is known; they were, as a result, placed in the indeterminate status category in Table 14.

54. See Gabriel Kolko, *The Triumph of Conservatism* (Glencoe, Ill.: Free Press, 1963), passim.

55. There were four Wilson appointees who, either because of a mixed background or a lack of sufficient biographical data, have been placed in the indeterminate status category (see Table 14). If most of these men were, in fact, non-elite figures, the total of such appointments under Wilson would, of course, be even larger.

56. If these (1921–1933) non-elite figures were analyzed on the basis of length of time served in office (another perhaps equally important yardstick), the above totals would in each case be reduced by about 5 percentage points.

57. Only the last of the Supreme Court justices appointed during this period, New York's Benjamin Cardozo, was clearly a non-elite figure. Overall, if one excludes four "indeterminate status" cases, about 87 percent of the Supreme Court appointees between 1861 and 1933 could be classified as elite, compared to about 84 percent of the major Cabinet and diplomatic officers. The latter total represented a 12 percent drop from the pre–Civil War period.

58. As Appendix A shows, Harry Woodring, FDR's second Secretary of War, has not been classified as an economic elite figure because the concern with which he was affiliated was a very small enterprise. New Jersey industrialist Charles Edison has been placed in the indeterminate status category, primarily because, though his company was of considerable size, he had no major corporate links in the New York metropolitan area and may thus have been an independent or "maverick" operator. In any case, Edison did not serve long as a Cabinet official.

59. Of the five elitist leaders in the domestic realm, only three served for a considerable period, and two of these—Henry Morgenthau, Jr., and Daniel C. Roper—held posts traditionally reserved for business spokesmen. Furthermore, their economic ties were of an indirect (family) nature.

60. It is hard to know how much weight should be assigned to the pressures generated by the Great Depression as contrasted with the New Deal's recruitment policy, in part because the latter was itself affected by the compelling need for change. But the Depression obviously created a public climate for sweeping reform, which did not exist, at least on the same scale, back in Wilson's time. Another factor which may have contributed to the more liberal flavor of the New Deal regime was that Roosevelt himself, though a wealthy patrician, was apparently less closely linked to influential corporate interests than was former Princeton University president Woodrow Wilson, who had served briefly, prior to entering political life, on the board of the Mutual Life Insurance Co.

61. As in the past, most of the top diplomatic posts in the Truman administration were awarded to economically elite figures. If these officials were deleted from this tally, there would

be roughly the same number of elite as non-elite leaders in the Truman regime. In all these tabulations each appointment is counted as a separate entry, even though some individuals held several high offices in a particular administration. One reason for adhering to this mode of computation is that some people forged important economic links between tours of government duty, as in the case of former Army General George C. Marshall, who became a member of the Business Advisory Council and a director of Pan-American World Airways between the time he served as Secretary of State and as Secretary of Defense under Truman.

62. These totals exclude persons who were brief (under six months) holdovers from preceding regimes, for some of these people were on either cool or distant terms with the newly installed president. However, all holdover officials who served more than six months under another administration have been counted as new appointees, since they were presumably deliberately retained in their high posts.

63. Perhaps even more revealingly, Carter had by far the largest percentage of elite Cabinet officials of any Democratic president in the 20th century, with a proportion (about 75 percent) which came close to that of Eisenhower and Nixon.

64. For a somewhat narrower study of the economic links of Cabinet members between 1897 and 1973, see Peter J. Freitag, "The Cabinet and Big Business: A Study of Interlocks," *Social Problems* (December 1975), pp. 137–51. The elitist percentages arrived at in this analysis differ substantially from those of the author (they are even higher), in part because Freitag considered only Cabinet officers and counted directorship ties which were established after a person left the federal government. However, Freitag did not examine elite family links.

65. In his 1954 study of *The Social Background and Political Decision-Makers*, Donald Matthews asserted that there seemed to be "...a sort of class ranking of public offices in the United States—that is, as a rule, the more important the office, the higher the social status of the incumbent" (p. 32). This skew cannot be facilely explained by claiming that only a minority of the American people have the time and money necessary for sustained political activity, for the less important, though often equally time-consuming, posts have been held, to a much greater extent, by non-elite figures.

66. One scholar has recently taken a very different, extremely naive, view of this matter, claiming that in the United States (and certain other industrialized countries) "...many cabinet members and national administrators have been coopted from the ranks of the economic elite...." See William A. Welsh, *Leaders and Elites* (New York: Holt, Rinehart & Winston, 1979), p. 84.

67. From these figures it seems fair to conclude that elite influence has manifested itself more through the appointment of high administrative and diplomatic officials than through the selection of the nation's chief executives (although this differential has been reduced somewhat in recent years). Moreover, many of America's "elitist" presidents have been of a much less elitist character than their major Cabinet and diplomatic officers. That is to say, the latter generally have more key corporate or family ties. For the author's assessment of the elite (or non-elite) status of America's 39 presidents, see Apprendix A at the end of each volume in this study.

68. John Witte has similarly found that the upper-class origin of American Cabinet members (but not key diplomatic officials or Supreme Court justices) has ranged from a high of about 80 percent during the nation's first two decades to a remarkably stable 40 to 45 percent since 1850. This part of Witte's analysis focuses on the class origins of Cabinet officers, which may reveal much about social mobility. But, as pointed out earlier, the author is not so interested in this topic as he is in the economic status of people when they were appointed to high federal office. See John F. Witte, "Theories of Elite Change: The United States Cabinet, 1789–1976," *Journal of Politics* (forthcoming).

69. See, for example, Arnold Rose, *The Power Structure* (New York: Oxford University Press, 1967), passim. While the author in some ways agrees with Rose's "multi-influence" hypothesis (at least in recognizing that there have always been a number of fairly powerful, often rival elite groups in the country), he nevertheless takes strong issue with the latter's use of this

term and the overall anti-elitist argument which runs through this book, which apparently was written in an attempt to refute the controversial claims of C. Wright Mills. As indicated earlier, Mills's book, *The Power Elite*, has many flaws, the most serious of which are his depiction of an extraordinarily powerful single politico-economic elite, his relative ignorance of the structure and operation of the American economy, and his overemphasis on the importance of the military (the "warlords") in governmental affairs. For a lesser known work which was published about the same time and has much more information and insight, albeit from a Marxist perspective, see Victor Perlo's *The Empire of High Finance* (New York: International Publishers, 1957).

70. Domhoff's best-known book, *Who Rules America?*, is an analysis of America's political economy from the standpoint of the nation's influential upper class, which places greater weight on the overall cohesiveness of such interests than is probably warranted. Yet it is a work which has much merit and deserves more favorable recognition than it has received.

71. See Thomas R. Dye, *Who's Running America?—Institutional Leadership in the United States* (Englewood Cliffs, N. J.: Prentice-Hall, 1976), pp. 145-56. As late as 1972 Dye and Zeigler had a very different point of view, for they claimed in *The Irony of Democracy* that the nation's economic and political systems were inextricably associated, asserting that "often there is no clear line of division between government and business enterprise, or between government elites and business elites" (p. 112). And at another point they observed that our "top governmental executives—Cabinet members, presidential advisors, department officers, special ambassadors—are generally men who have occupied key posts in private industry and finance or who have sat in influential positions in education, in the arts and sciences, or in social, civic, and charitable associations" (p. 97). Dye and Zeigler deleted the first set of statements from later editions of *The Irony of Democracy*.

72. See Thomas R. Dye and John W. Pickering, "Governmental and Corporate Elites: Convergence and Differentiation," *Journal of Politics* (November 1974), p. 906; and Thomas R. Dye, Eugene R. DeClercq, and John W. Pickering, "Concentration, Specialization, and Interlocking among Institutional Elites," *Social Science Quarterly* (June 1973), pp. 22 and 27.

73. See Dye, *Who's Running America?*, p. 160, and the two closely related articles cited in note 72.

74. See Dye, DeClercq, and Pickering, *op. cit.*, p. 20.

75. See, for instance, William L. Hudson, Jr. (comp.), *Outside Counsel: Inside Director—Lawyers on the Boards of American Industry* (New York: Law Journal Press, 1973), passim, and for more insight into these relationships, see Paul Hoffman, *Lions in the Street*, passim.

76. In their two earlier related articles Dye and his associates actually stated, in almost identical language, that "...top government officials have not held many corporate directorships" (although much of their data, and that found elsewhere, clearly indicates the contrary). See Dye and Pickering, *op. cit.*, p. 912, and Dye, et al., *op. cit.*, p. 24.

77. At one point (in a long, easily overlooked footnote), Mills, it is true, did make a summary analysis of the social origins of the 513 men who had served as President, Vice President, Cabinet officer, Supreme Court justice, and Speaker of the House of Representatives between 1789 and 1953, in which he found that 58 percent came from well-to-do families, 24 percent from the middle class, and 18 percent from the lower class. But these figures were not broken down by major time periods, and Mills, like many other men in his profession, was concerned primarily with a leader's social origins rather than his status at the time he attained high federal office. See C. Wright Mills, *The Power Elite*, pp. 400-01.

78. As Robert Putnam pointed out in *The Comparative Study of Political Elites* (p. 185), there has been remarkably little evidence compiled by researchers as to the overall historical development or transformation of elites in the United States, so that Dye and Zeigler should not be judged too harshly in this regard. In fact, the only detailed analysis of this nature to be made in any economically advanced country in recent years is W. L. Guttsman's study of *The British Political Elite*, and that, perhaps because of the longtime influence exerted by England's landed aristocracy, does not pay much attention to the rise and fall of various forces within that nation's industrial and financial sector.

79. There are two ways in which this term was employed in Pareto's works, as the movement (or circulation) of *individuals* between the elite and non-elite, and as the process by which *one elite* is replaced by another over time. While the former usage predominated in Pareto's writings, it is the more important latter concept that has been emphasized here. For sake of clarity, it is described as the *transformation of elites*.

80. In addition to J. P. Morgan & Co., this vast complex included as its "core" concerns the Bankers Trust Co., Chase National Bank (up to 1930), First National Bank of New York, Guaranty Trust Co., National Bank of Commerce (until 1929 when it was absorbed by the last-named company), Mutual Life Insurance Co., and several major law firms. There was no comparable financial force in America, following the collapse of Jay Cooke & Co., from 1873 to the early 1890s.

81. Morgan's influence in the Taft administration was of a more limited nature. Moreover, there was ultimately a major break between Taft and the great "J.P.," mainly over antitrust matters, so that the 1912 split in the Republican ranks and subsequent election of Woodrow Wilson was probably much to Morgan's liking. Wilson, however, had to contend with certain powerful liberal and progressive interests within his own party, which made him take a moderate reformist stance on a number of important issues. While business-dominated, the Harding regime was, curiously, one which apparently did not have much Morgan influence.

82. Perhaps not coincidentally, the last of the relatively few "Morgan" candidates for President of the United States was a man who had a very different image, Morgan utility executive Wendell Willkie.

83. The first firm in this financial cluster (described in Stephen Birmingham's *Our Crowd*) to achieve true national importance was Kuhn, Loeb & Co., which was led for many years by the able Jacob Schiff and was closely allied with the Harriman railroad interests. In fact, there has been some circulation of elites within this economic circle, as seen by the fact that in recent years Lehman Brothers and Goldman, Sachs & Co. have apparently relinquished the top leadership role in the investment banking world to such comparative newcomers as Lazard Frères and (Carl M.) Loeb, Rhoades & Co.

84. Although the Council on Foreign Relations was formed in 1921, it apparently did not become an influential politico-economic body until about 1940 when, with America's impending immersion in the Second World War, the federal government found its support and advice very useful. By this time the leaders of the BAC and CED had begun to take a more moderate stance on most public policy issues (in effect, accepting many of the reforms instituted by the New Deal), unlike the NAM and certain other such non-Establishment interests, which continued to adhere to an extremely conservative line.

85. These organizations have been of much greater significance, from a governmental recruitment and policymaking standpoint, than the less overtly business-dominated National Civic Federation in the first part of the century.

86. For instance, Grover Cleveland's chief aide and advisor, William C. Whitney, had made his fortune primarily through railroad and transit enterprises and a marriage into one of the original Standard Oil families; the most famous later member of this rich family, John Hay Whitney, had, at the time of his appointment as Eisenhower's (second) Ambassador to Great Britain, a host of large holdings, ranging from the Freeport Sulphur Co. to the Minute Maid Corp. For more on the latter figure, see "Jock Whitney: Unclassified Capitalist," *Fortune* (October 1964), pp. 114-20 and 184-94.

Appendix A

Primary Background Data of Major Cabinet and Diplomatic Officials: 1933–1980

ABBREVIATIONS

BD	board of directors
BT	board of trustees
BC	board chairman
VC	vice-chairman
CEC	chairman of executive committee
P	president
VP	vice-president
GC	general counsel
Sec.	secretary
ptr.	partner
off.	official
dir.	director
adm.	administrator
E	elite status
NE	non-elite status
?	indeterminate status

Note: Because of a lack of sufficient data, a number of officials have been classified with less certainty, as probably elite (E?) or probably non-elite (NE?). A few carryover officials served so briefly that they were not counted in the concluding chapter's summary analysis and are indicated by n/c in the last column of the tables. Persons holding office at the start of an administration (or time period), or serving into another, are indicated by an italicized date.

NEW DEAL YEARS OF THE FRANKLIN D. ROOSEVELT ADMINISTRATION (1933–1940)

Officeholder	College Education	Prior Governmental Experience	Primary Non-governmental Occupation	Important Secondary Economic Affiliations	Family and Other Socio-Economic Ties	Other Pertinent Information	Elite or Non-Elite Status
President Franklin D. Roosevelt, N.Y. (1933 through 1940)	Harvard Univ.	Governor of New York (1929–1933); Democratic Vice Presidential candidate (1920); Asst. Sec. of Navy (1913–1920); New York legislator (1911–1913)	Ptr., N.Y.C. law firm of Roosevelt & O'Connor (1924–1928); N.Y. VP of Fidelity & Deposit Co. of Md. (1920–1928); ptr., New York law firm of Emmett, Marvin & Roosevelt and predecessor firm of Marvin, Hooker & Roosevelt (1910–1913 and 1920–1924)	No major corporate boards	Member of old wealthy (Hudson Valley) N.Y. family; uncle, Frederic A. Delano, dep. chrm. or chrm. Federal Reserve Bank of Richmond (1931–1936; also a dir., 1922–1931), BT, Carnegie Endowment for International Peace (1920 through 1940), and off. or trustee, Brookings Institution (up to mid-1930s); first cousin, Lyman Delano, P or BC, Louisville & Nashville RR (1920 through 1940), BC of parent company, Atlantic Coast Line RR (1932 through 1940), and BD, Pan-American Airways Corp. (1929 through 1940) and Safe Deposit & Trust Co., Baltimore (1933 through 1940)	Member of executive committee of National Civic Federation (early 1920s); Board of Overseers, Harvard Univ. (1918–1924)	E

400

Secretary of State				
Cordell Hull, Tenn. (1933 through 1940)	—— (Cumberland Univ. Law School)	U.S. Senator, Tenn. (1931–1933); Tenn. Congressman (1907–1921, 1923–1931); Tenn. judge (1903–1907); state legislator (1893–1897)	Longtime Tenn. lawyer (first at Celina, then Gainsboro, and later Carthage)	Chairman, Democratic National Committee (1921–1924) NE
Secretary of Treasury				
William H. Woodin, N.Y. (Mar.–Dec., 1933)	Columbia Univ. (not complete)	N.Y. fuel adm. (briefly in early 1920s); head of N.Y. comm. to study state banking laws (late 1920s)	P or BC, American Car & Foundry Co. (1916–1933, lesser off. before that); P or BC, American Locomotive Co. (1925–1932)	BD, American Ship & Commerce Corp. (1926–1933), Cuba Co. (1921–1933), General Steel Castings Co. (1929–33), Remington Arms Co. (1927–33), Federal Reserve Bank of N.Y. (1926–33), General Motors Corp. (1921–27), and American Locomotive Co. (up to 1926) E

401

NEW DEAL YEARS OF THE FRANKLIN D. ROOSEVELT ADMINISTRATION (1933–1940) (continued)

Officeholder	College Education	Prior Governmental Experience	Primary Non-governmental Occupation	Important Secondary Economic Affiliations	Family and Other Socio-Economic Ties	Other Pertinent Information	Elite or Non-Elite Status
Henry Morgenthau, Jr., N.Y. (Jan. 1934 through 1940)	Cornell Univ. (not complete)	Under Sec. of Treasury (Nov. 1933–Jan 1934); head, U.S. Farm Credit Administration (1933); member, N.Y. Conservation Com. (1931–1933); member and then chrm., Taconic State Park Com. (1929–1931); chrm., N.Y. Agricultural Advisory Com. (1929)	P and publisher, *American Agriculturalist* (1922–1933)	No major corporate boards	Father, Henry Morgenthau, on BD of Underwood Elliott Fisher Co. and predecessor concern (1904 through 1940); wife's mother a member of Lehman family; cousin, Jules Ehrich, also wed member of Lehman family		E
Attorney General							
Homer S. Cummings, Conn. (1933–Jan. 1939)	Yale Univ.	Mayor of Stamford, Conn. (early 1900s)	Ptr., Cummings & Lockwood, Stamford, Conn., law firm (1909–1933); also P., some local real estate concerns	BD, First Stamford National Bank & Trust Co. (1918–1933)		Democratic National Committeeman, Conn. (1900–1925; Chrm., Democratic National Committee (1919–1920)	NE?

402

Name	Education	Career	Business affiliations	Notes	
Frank Murphy, Mich. (Jan. 1939–Jan. 1940)	Univ of Michigan	Governor of Michigan (1936–1938); gov.-gen. of Philippine Islands (1933–1936); mayor of Detroit (1930–1933); Detroit judge (1923–1930)	Detroit lawyer (1914–1917, 1920–1923)		NE
Secretary of War					
George H. Dern, Utah (1933–Aug 1936)	Freemont Normal Coll., Neb.	Governor of Utah (1924–1932); state legislator (1914–1923)	High off., Consolidated Mercur Gold Mine Co. (1901–1914); gen. mgr., Tintic Milling Co. (1915–1919); VP, Dixie Power Co. (1923–1929); VP, Consolidated Wagon & Machine Co. (1926–1933); P, Park City Consolidated Mining Co. (up to 1933); P, Eureka Banking Co. (up to 1932)	BD, First Security Trust Co. and one of its predecessor concerns (1923–1936) and National Copper Bank and its successor institution, the Security National Bank (1922–1932)	Father, P of Consolidated Mercur Gold Mine Co., Utah (1894–1914) and of Uncle Sam Consolidated Mining Co. (1915–at least 1918)	E?
Harry H. Woodring, Kansas (Sept 1936–Jan. 1940)	1 year at Lebanon Univ., Ind.	Asst. Sec. of War (1933–1936); Governor of Kansas (1931–1933)	VP, First National Bank, Neodesha, Kans. (1922–29; lesser off. before that)		NE

403

NEW DEAL YEARS OF THE FRANKLIN D. ROOSEVELT ADMINISTRATION (1933–1940) (continued)

Officeholder	College Education	Prior Governmental Experience	Primary Non-governmental Occupation	Important Secondary Economic Affiliations	Family and Other Socio-Economic Ties	Other Pertinent Information	Elite or Non-Elite Status
Secretary of Navy							
Claude A. Swanson, Va. (1933–July 1939)	Randolph-Macon Coll.	U.S. Senator, Va. (1910–33); Governor of Va. (1906–1910); Va. Congressman (1893–1906)	Chatham, Va., lawyer (1886 on)				NE
Charles Edison, N.J. (Dec. 1939–July 1940)	MIT	Asst. Sec. of Navy (1936–1939); NRA off. (1933–1935)	P, Thomas A. Edison, Inc. (1926–1936; lesser exec. before that)				?
Secretary of Interior							
Harold L. Ickes, Ill. (1933 through 1940)	Univ. of Chicago		Longtime (1907–1932) Chicago lawyer (first with Richberg, Ickes, Davies & Lord; later Ickes, Lord, Wise & Cobb)			Longtime Progressive party leader in Ill.; led Ill. Progressives for FDR in 1932	NE

404

Secretary of Agriculture				
Henry A. Wallace, Iowa (1933–Sept. 1940)	Iowa State Coll.		Editor or other high off., *Wallace's Farmer* (1910–1933)	E?: Late father, Henry C. Wallace, Sec. of Agriculture under Harding; uncle, John P. Wallace, on BD of National Bank & Trust Co. and its predecessor concern in Des Moines (1925–1934)
Secretary of Commerce				
Daniel C. Roper, Wash., D.C., orig. S.C. (1933–Dec. 1938)	Trinity Coll., S.C.	Comr., Internal Revenue (1917–1920); First Asst. Post-Gen. (1913–1916); special agent, U.S. Bureau of Census (1900–1911)	Ptr., Roper, Hurrey & Dudley, Wash., D.C. law firm, and predecessor concern (1921–1932)	BD, Marlin-Rockwell Corp. (1921–1923, P of company, 1920–1921)	E?: Son-in-law of David R. Coker, P, J.L. Coker & Co., Hartsville, S.C. (1918–1938), member of BAC (1933–1938), BD of Federal Reserve Bank of Richmond (1918–1934), and Charlotte, Munroe & Columbia RR, subsidiary of Seaboard Air Line Rwy. (1918–1938)

NEW DEAL YEARS OF THE FRANKLIN D. ROOSEVELT ADMINISTRATION (1933–1940) (continued)

Officeholder	College Education	Prior Governmental Experience	Primary Non-governmental Occupation	Important Secondary Economic Affiliations	Family and Other Socio-Economic Ties	Other Pertinent Information	Elite or Non-Elite Status
Harry L. Hopkins, N.Y. (Jan. 1939–Sept. 1940)	Grinnell Coll., Iowa	Head, WPA (1935–1938); adm., Fed. Emergency Relief Adm. (1933–1935); chrm. or dep. chrm., N.Y. Temporary Emer. Relief Adm. (1931–1934); exec. sec., Board of Child Welfare, N.Y.C. (1914–17)	Asst. dir., N.Y. Tuberculosis Assn. (1924–1931); gen. mgr., American Red Cross, Washington, D.C. (1918–1922); asst. dir., Assn. for Improving Conditions of the Poor, N.Y.C. (1922–1924)				NE
Secretary of Labor							
Frances Perkins, N.Y., orig. Mass. (1933 through 1940)	Mt. Holyoke Coll.	N.Y. State Industrial Comr. (1929–1933); member, N.Y. State Industrial Board (1923–1929, chrm., 1926–1929); Comr., N.Y. State Industrial Com. (1919–1921)	Exec. sec., Committee of Safety, N.Y. (1912–1917); exec. sec., Maternity Center Assn., N.Y. (1918–1919); exec. sec., Council on Immigrant Education (1921–1923)				NE

406

Ambassador to Great Britain					
Robert W. Bingham, Ky. (May 1933–Nov. 1937)	Univ. of Va. (not complete)	Several local governmental posts (pre-WWI)	Publisher, *Louisville Courier-Journal* and *Louisville Times* (1918–1933); Louisville lawyer (1897–1918); ptr., Louisville law firm of Kohn, Bingham, Sloss & Spindle (1912–1918)	BD, Louisville and Nashville RR (1931–1932), American Creosoting Co. (1919–1933), and Liberty Bank & Trust Co., Louisville (1931–1933)	Wed wealthy widow of H. M. Flagler in 1916	Sizable donor to 1932 Democratic presidential campaign	E
Joseph P. Kennedy, N.Y., orig. Mass. (Mar. 1938–Oct. 1940)	Harvard Univ.	Chrm., SEC (1934–1935); chrm., U.S. Maritime Com. (1937–1938)	N.Y.C. financier (early 1930s); BC, Pathé Exchange, Inc. (1928–1930) and Keith-Albee-Orpheum Corp. (5 mos., 1928); P and BC, Film Booking Offices of America (1926–1929); mgr., Boston branch, Hayden, Stone & Co. (1919–1924)			Prominent Democratic party fundraiser (1930s)	E

NEW DEAL YEARS OF THE FRANKLIN D. ROOSEVELT ADMINISTRATION (1933–1940) (continued)

Officeholder	College Education	Prior Governmental Experience	Primary Non-governmental Occupation	Important Secondary Economic Affiliations	Family and Other Socio-Economic Ties	Other Pertinent Information	Elite or Non-Elite Status
Ambassador to France							
Jesse I. Straus, N.Y. (June 1933– Aug. 1936)	Harvard Univ.		P, R. H. Macy & Co., N.Y.C. (1919–1933); lesser posts in company (1896–1919)	BD, New York Life Insurance Co. (1927–1934) and Bowery Savings Bank (1927–1933)	Brother, P. S. Straus, on BD of New York Life Insurance Co. (1934–1936); many family ties to New York Jewish business and financial figures	Family a big contributor to 1932 Democratic presidential campaign	E
William C. Bullitt, Pa. (Oct. 1936– July 1940)	Yale Univ.	Ambass. to Soviet Union (1933–1936); various lesser foreign policy posts (1917–1919)	Spent most of 1920s abroad as wealthy man of leisure		Brother, O. H. Bullitt, on BD of Muskogee Co. (1925–1940) and Central-Penn National Bank, Philadelphia (1928–1934); father former P of Pocahontas Coal Co., and grandfather, J. C. Bullitt, on BD of many railroads (including Northern Pacific RR)		E
Ambassador to Germany							
William E. Dodd, Ill.	Va. Polytech. Inst.		Professor of history, Univ. of				NE

408

Officeholder	College Education	Prior Governmental Experience	Primary Nongovernmental Occupation	Important Secondary Economic Affiliations	Family and Other Socio-Economic Ties	Other Pertinent Information	Elite or Non-Elite Status
(Aug. 1933–Dec. 1937)	(later Ph.D., Univ. of Leipzig)					Chicago (1909–1933)	NE
Hugh R. Wilson, Wash., D.C. (Mar.–Nov. 1938)	Yale Univ.	Longtime career diplomat; Asst. Sec. of State (1937–1938); Min. to Switzerland (1927–1937)					

WORLD WAR II YEARS OF FRANKLIN D. ROOSEVELT ADMINISTRATION

Officeholder	College Education	Prior Governmental Experience	Primary Nongovernmental Occupation	Important Secondary Economic Affiliations	Family and Other Socio-Economic Ties	Other Pertinent Information	Elite or Non-Elite Status
President							
Franklin D. Roosevelt, N.Y. Univ. (*1940*–Apr. 1945)	Harvard	President of U.S. (1933–1940)	SEE NEW DEAL ENTRY				E
Secretary of State							
Cordell Hull, Tenn. (*1940*–Nov. 1944)	—— (but did graduate from law school)	U.S. Sec. of State (1933–1940)	SEE NEW DEAL ENTRY				NE

WORLD WAR II YEARS OF THE FRANKLIN D. ROOSEVELT ADMINISTRATION (continued)

Officeholder	College Education	Prior Governmental Experience	Primary Non-governmental Occupation	Important Secondary Economic Affiliations	Family and Other Socio-Economic Ties	Other Pertinent Information	Elite or Non-Elite Status
Edward R. Stettinius, Jr., N.Y. (Nov. 1944–July 1945)	Univ. of Va. (not complete)	Under Sec. of State (1943–1944); Spec. Asst. to President of U.S. (1941–1943); dir., Office of Production Management (Jan.–Sept. 1941); chrm., War Resources Board (May 1940–Jan. 1941)	High off, U.S. Steel Corp. (1934–1940; BC, 1938–1940); off., General Motors Corp. (1926–1934; VP, 1931–1934)	BD of Metropolitan Life Insurance Co. (1938–1940)	Brother-in-law of Juan Trippe, P, Pan-American Airways; brother, William Stettinius, dir., Worthington Pump & Machinery Corp. (up to his death in 1937)	Member, BAC (1937–1941); BT, Brookings Institution (1940–1945)	E
Secretary of Treasury							
Henry Morgenthau, Jr., N.Y. (1940–July 1945)	Cornell Univ. (not complete)	Sec. of Treasury (1934 through 1940)	SEE NEW DEAL ENTRY				E
Attorney General							
Robert H. Jackson, N.Y. (Jan.		U.S. Solicitor General (1938–1940); Asst. Attorney	Longtime Jamestown, N.Y., lawyer (1913 on); ptr., law	BD, Bank of Jamestown (1919–1941)		BT of Twentieth Century Fund (1938–1941)	NE?

1940–July 1941)		General (1936–1938); gen. counsel, Bureau of Internal Revenue (1934–1936)	firm of Jackson, Herrick, Durkin & Lest (1928–1934); VP and GC of Jamestown Street Rwy. and Jamestown, Westfield & Northwestern RR (1930–1938)	and Jamestown Telephone Co. (at least 1926–1940)	
Francis Biddle, Pa. (Sept. 1941–June 1945)	Harvard Univ.	U.S. Solicitor General (1940–41); judge, U.S. Circuit Court of Appeals (1939–40); Chrm., Natl. Labor Relations Board (1934–1935)	Ptr., Phila. law firm of Barnes, Biddle & Myers (1917–1939)	BD of Philadelphia Contributionship for the Insurance of Houses from Loss by Fire (1931–1945)	Many elite Philadelphia family ties	BT of Twentieth Century Fund (1938–1945)	E

Secretary of War

Henry L. Stimson, N.Y. (June 1940–Sept. 1945)	Yale Univ.	Secretary of State (1929–33); Secretary of War (1911–1913); gov. gen. of Philippine Islands (1927–1929)	Longtime ptr., Winthrop, Stimson, Putnam & Roberts (1901–1911, 1913–1927); "counsel" to firm (1933–1940)	BD of American Superpower Corp., N.Y.C. (1925–1927)	Cousin, L. K. Thorne, on BD of First Natl. Bank of N.Y.C. (1933–1945), Federal Insurance Co. (1930–1945), and Southern Pacific Co. (1943 on)	E

WORLD WAR II YEARS OF THE FRANKLIN D. ROOSEVELT ADMINISTRATION (continued)

Officeholder	College Education	Prior Governmental Experience	Primary Non-governmental Occupation	Important Secondary Economic Affiliations	Family and Other Socio-Economic Ties	Other Pertinent Information	Elite or Non-Elite Status
Secretary of Navy							
Frank Knox, Ill. (July, 1940–April, 1944)	Alma College, Mich.		Publisher, *Chicago Daily News* (1931–1940); former newspaper exec., N.H. (1912–1931) and Boston (1927–1931)	BD of City National Bank & Trust Co., Chicago (1933–1940)		Republican Vice Presidential candidate (1936); longtime Ill. Republican leader	E
James V. Forrestal, N.Y. (May 1944–1945)	Princeton Univ. (not complete)	Under Secretary of Navy (1940–44); adm. asst. to President (briefly in 1940)	Longtime high off., Dillon, Read & Co., N.Y.C. (1919–1940; P from 1938–1940)				E
Secretary of Interior							
Harold L. Ickes, Ill. (1940–1945)	Univ. of Chicago	Secretary of the Interior (1933–1940)	SEE NEW DEAL ENTRY				NE

Secretary of Agriculture				
Claude R. Wickard, Ind. (Sept. 1940–June 1945)	Purdue Univ.	Under Secretary of Agriculture (Feb.–August 1940); off., Dept. of Agriculture (1933–1940)	Longtime Ind. farmer (1915–1933)	NE
Secretary of Commerce				
Jesse H. Jones, Texas (Sept. 1940–Feb. 1945)		Chrm, Reconstruction Finance Corp. (1932–1939); Federal Loan Adm. (1939–1940); CEC, Export-Import Bank (1936–1943)	BC or P, National Bank of Commerce, Houston (1922 through 1945); BC, Bankers Mortgage Co. (and its predecessor concern), Houston (1920–1932); P, *Houston Chronicle* (1926–1945); owner of much commercial real estate in Houston, Dallas, Ft. Worth, and N.Y.C.	BD, American General Insurance Co., Houston (1936–42) E
Henry A. Wallace, Iowa (Mar. 1945 on)	Iowa St. Coll.	Vice-President of U.S. (1941–1945); Sec. of Agriculture (1933–1940)	SEE NEW DEAL ENTRY	NE

413

WORLD WAR II YEARS OF THE FRANKLIN D. ROOSEVELT ADMINISTRATION (continued)

Officeholder	College Education	Prior Governmental Experience	Primary Non-governmental Occupation	Important Secondary Economic Affiliations	Family and Other Socio-Economic Ties	Other Pertinent Information	Elite or Non-Elite Status
Secretary of Labor							
Frances Perkins, N.Y. (*1940–May 1945*)	Mt. Holyoke Coll.	Sec. of Labor (1933–1940)	SEE NEW DEAL ENTRY				NE
Ambassador to Great Britain							
John G. Winant, N.H., orig. N.Y. (Mar. 1941 through 1945)	Princeton Univ. (not complete)	Dep. dir. or dir., International Labor Organization (1937–1941); Chrm., Social Security Bd. (1935–1937); Governor of N.H. (1925–1927 and 1931–1935)	Longtime owner and publisher, *Concord Monitor* and *New Hampshire Patriot*; one-time owner of Concord Oil Co.		Married into Russell and Pyne families of N.Y.C.	BT, Brookings Institution (1935–1945)	E

Ambassador to France				
William D. Leahy, Wash., D.C., orig. Iowa (Jan. 1941–May 1942)	U.S. Naval Academy	Governor of Puerto Rico (1939–1940); longtime naval officer (1897–1939, last rank, admiral)		NE
Jefferson Caffrey, Wash., D.C., orig. La. (Dec. 1944 through 1945)	Tulane Univ.	Longtime career diplomat (1911 on)		NE?
Ambassador to Soviet Union				
Lawrence A. Steinhardt, N.Y. (Aug. 1939–Nov. 1941)	Columbia Univ.	Ambassador to Peru (1937–1939) and to Sweden (1933–1937)	Member, N.Y.C. law firm of Guggenheimer, Untermyer & Marshall (1920–1933)	BD, G. R. Kenney Co. and Affiliated Products, Inc. (1930–1933)	Nephew of Samuel Untermyer, longtime civic figure and attorney for Guggenheim interests; cousin (and former law partner), Alvin Untermyer on BD of Consolidated Oil Corp. (1932 through 1941)	E

WORLD WAR II YEARS OF THE FRANKLIN D. ROOSEVELT ADMINISTRATION (continued)

Officeholder	College Education	Prior Governmental Experience	Primary Non-governmental Occupation	Important Secondary Economic Affiliations	Family and Other Socio-Economic Ties	Other Pertinent Information	Elite or Non-Elite Status
William H. Standley, Wash., D.C., orig. Cal. (Aug. 1942– Sept. 1943)	U.S. Naval Academy	Longtime naval officer (1895–1937, last rank admiral); recalled to active duty (1941 on)		BD, Pan-American Airways (1940 through 1943)		Member of Century Group, which was closely linked with the Council on Foreign Relations	E
W. Averell Harriman, N.Y. (Oct. 1943 through 1945)	Yale Univ.	Various defense and foreign policy posts (1941–1943); NRA off. (1934–1935)	Ptr, Brown Brothers Harriman & Co., and predecessor co., N.Y.C. (1920–1945); BC, Union Pacific RR (1932–1945); CEC, Illinois Central RR (1931–1942); BC, American Ship & Commerce Corp. (1921–1931)	BD of Western Union Telegraph Co. (1929–1940), Guaranty Trust Co., N.Y.C. (1916–1940), Union Pacific RR (1913–1932), American Ship & Commerce Corp. (1933–1940), and Illinois Central RR (1942–46)	Brother, E. Roland Harriman, on BD of Union Pacific RR and Anaconda Copper Mining Co. (through 1945)	Member, BAC (1933 through 1945), actually chrm. or vice-chrm. of this body (1934–1939)	E

416

TRUMAN ADMINISTRATION (1945–1953)

Officeholder	College Education	Prior Governmental Experience	Primary Non-governmental Occupation	Important Secondary Economic Affiliations	Family and Other Socio-Economic Ties	Other Pertinent Information	Elite or Non-Elite Status
President							
Harry S. Truman, Mo. (Apr. 1945–Jan. 1953)		Vice-President of U.S. (Jan.–April 1945); U.S. Senator, Mo. (1935–45); U.S. re-employment dir., Mo. (1933–1934); Mo. county judge (a nonjudicial post, 1923–25 and 1927–1934)	Salesman, Kansas City Auto Club and P of Community Savings & Loan Assn., Independence, Mo. (1924–1926); ptr., Truman & Jacobson haberdashery store, Kansas City (1919–1922)				NE
Secretary of State							
James F. Byrnes, S.C. (July 1945–Jan. 1947)		Various high federal defense posts (1942–1945); Justice, U.S. Supreme Court (1941–1942); U.S. Senator, S.C. (1931–1941); S.C. Congressman (1911–1925)	Longtime S.C. lawyer, first at Aiken, then Spartanburg (1903–1941)				NE?

417

TRUMAN ADMINISTRATION (1945–1953) (continued)

Officeholder	College Education	Prior Governmental Experience	Primary Non-governmental Occupation	Important Secondary Economic Affiliations	Family and Other Socio-Economic Ties	Other Pertinent Information	Elite or Non-Elite Status
Secretary of State							
George C. Marshall, Wash., D.C., orig. Pa. (Jan. 1947–Jan 1949)	VMI	Longtime high-ranking U.S. Army officer (1902–1945)					NE
Dean G. Acheson, Wash., D.C., orig. Conn. (Jan. 1949–Jan. 1953)	Yale Univ.	Under Sec., State (1945–1947); Asst. Sec. of State (1941–1945); Under Sec. of Treasury (May–Nov. 1933)	Ptr, Washington law firm of Covington, Burling, Rublee, Acheson & Shorb, and predecessor concerns (1926–1941 and 1947–1949; member of firm, 1921–1926)		Mother a member of the Gooderham family (of Hiram Walker-Gooderham & Worts, Ltd.)	VC, Brookings Institution (1940–1948); pre-1941 member of the pro-Allied "Century Group" (an organization closely linked with the Council on Foreign Relations)	E
Secretary of Treasury							
Fred M. Vinson, Ky. (July 1945–June 1946)	Centre Coll., Ky.	Various high special federal defense posts (1943–1945);	Former longtime Ashland, Ky., lawyer				NE

418

		judge, U.S. Court of Appeals (1938–1943); Ky. Congressman (1924–1929, 1931–1938)		
Secretary of Treasury				
John W. Snyder, Mo. (June 1946–Jan. 1953)	Vanderbilt Univ. (not complete)	Dir., Office of War Mobilization and Reconstruction (1945–1946); various lesser federal posts (1930–1943)	VP, First National Bank of St. Louis (1943–1945); off., various small-town banks in Mo. (1919–1930)	Member, BAC (1945 through 1953) E
Secretary of War (post abolished 1947)				
			SEE WORLD WAR II ENTRY	
Henry L. Stimson, N.Y. (*1940*–Sept. 1945)	Yale Univ.	Sec. of War (1940–1945)		E
Robert P. Patterson, N.Y. (Sept. 1945–July 1949)	Union Coll., N.Y.	Under Sec. of War (1940–1945); Asst. Sec. of War (late 1940); federal judge (1930–1940)	Ptr., N.Y.C. law firm of Webb, Patterson & Hadley (1922–1929) and Murray, Aldrich & Webb (1929–30)	?

TRUMAN ADMINISTRATION (1945–1953) (continued)

Officeholder	College Education	Prior Governmental Experience	Primary Non-governmental Occupation	Important Secondary Economic Affiliations	Family and Other Socio-Economic Ties	Other Pertinent Information	Elite or Non-Elite Status
Secretary of Defense (new post)							
James V. Forrestal, N.Y. (July 1947–Mar. 1949)	Princeton Univ. (not complete)	Sec. of Navy (1944–1947); Under Sec. of Navy (1940–1944)	High off., N.Y.C. investment banking firm of Dillon, Read & Co. (1916–1940; P, 1938–1940)	BD, Chase Securities Corp., affiliate of Chase National Bank (1930–1931)			E
Louis A. Johnson, W.Va. (Mar. 1949–Sept. 1950)	Univ. of Va.	Spec. rep. of President to India (1942); Asst. Sec. of War (1937–1940); onetime state legislator	Longtime ptr., Steptoe & Johnson, Clarksburg and Charleston, W.Va. law firm; later a ptr. in Washington law firm of same name	BD, Consolidated Vultee Aircraft Corp., Cal. (1942–1949); General Aniline & Film Corp. (1944–1949), and Union National Bank, Clarksburg (1930 through 1950)		Major Democratic party fundraiser (1936, 1940, 1948)	E

420

George C. Marshall, Wash., D.C., orig. Pa. (Sept. 1950–Sept. 1951)	VMI	Sec. of State (1947–1949); long-time high-ranking U.S. Army officer (retired)		BD of Pan-American World Airways, Inc. (1949–1950)	Member, BAC (1949 through 1951)	E
Robert A. Lovett, N.Y. (Sept. 1951–Jan. 1953)	Yale Univ.	Dep. Sec. of Defense (1950–1951); Under Sec. of State (1947–1949); Asst. Sec. of War for Air (1941–1945)	Ptr., N.Y.C. investment banking house of Brown Bros. Harriman (1926–1941, 1946–1947, 1949–1950)	BD, Union Pacific RR (1926–1940, 1946–1947, 1949–1950), New York Life Insurance Co. (1949 through 1953), and New York Trust Co. (1926–1940)	BT of CED (1949 through 1953) and Rockefeller Foundation (1949–1953)	E
Secretary of Army (new non-Cabinet post)						
Kenneth C. Royall, N.C. (July 1947–Apr. 1949)	Univ. of N.C.	Under Sec. of War (1945–1947); spec. asst. to Sec. of War (1944–1945); U.S. Army officer (1942–1944)	Ptr., law firm of Ehringhaus, Royall, Gosney & Smith (and predecessor concerns), Raleigh and Goldsboro, N.C. (1937–1942); Goldsboro and Raleigh, N.C. lawyer (1930–1936); Goldsboro lawyer (1919–1930)			NE?

421

TRUMAN ADMINISTRATION (1945–1953) (continued)

Officeholder	College Education	Prior Governmental Experience	Primary Non-governmental Occupation	Important Secondary Economic Affiliations	Family and Other Socio-Economic Ties	Other Pertinent Information	Elite or Non-Elite Status
Gordon Gray, N.C. (June 1949–Apr. 1950)	Univ of N.C.	Asst. Sec. of the Army (1947–1949); former N.C. state legislator (1940–1941, 1946–1947)	P, Piedmont Publishing Co., Winston-Salem, N.C. (1937–1947); Winston-Salem lawyer (1935–1937)		Brother, Bowman Gray, a VP of R. J. Reynolds Tobacco. Co. and dir. of Wachovia Bank & Trust Co; uncle, James A. Gray, BC, R. J. Reynolds Tobacco Co. and dir. of Wachovia Bank & Trust Co.		E
Frank Pace, Jr., Ark. (Apr. 1950–Jan. 1953)	Princeton Univ.	Dir. and asst. dir., Bureau of the Budget (1948–1950); other lesser federal posts (1946–1948); U.S. Air Force off. (1942–1946)	Little Rock, Ark., lawyer (1936–1942)		Married daughter of Walter S. Janney, Philadelphia investment banker		NE?
Secretary of Navy (non-Cabinet post after 1947)							

422

Name		SEE	TRUMAN ADMINISTRATION ENTRY			
James V. Forrestal, N.Y. (*1945–Sept. 1947*)						E
John L. Sullivan, N.H. (Sept. 1947–May, 1949)	Dartmouth Coll.		Under Sec. of Navy (1946–1947); various other high federal posts (1939–1946)	Ptr., Sullivan & Sullivan, Manchester, N.H., law firm (1930–1939)	Friend of Frank Knox	NE
Franklin P. Matthews, Neb. (May 1949–July 1951)	Creighton Univ.			Ptr., Matthews, Kelley, Matthews & Delehant, Omaha law firm (1949–1951); longtime Omaha lawyer before that; P or BC, Securities Acceptance Corp. (1933–1951); P, First Federal Savings & Loan Assn., Omaha (at least 1937–1949)	BD, Northwestern Bell Telephone Co., subsidiary of AT&T (1939 through 1951)	Dir., U.S. Chamber of Commerce (1941–1951); longtime Nebraska Democratic leader	E
Dan A. Kimball, Cal. (July 1951–Jan. 1953)			Under Sec. of Navy (1949–1951)	High off., Aerojet General Corp. or other subsidiary of the General Tire & Rubber Co. (1920–1949)		E

TRUMAN ADMINISTRATION (continued)

Officeholder	College Education	Prior Governmental Experience	Primary Non-governmental Occupation	Important Secondary Economic Affiliations	Family and Other Socio-Economic Ties	Other Pertinent Information	Elite or Non-Elite Status
Secretary of Air Force							
W. Stuart Symington, Mo. (Aug. 1947–Apr. 1950)	Yale Univ. (not complete)	Asst. Sec. of War for Air (1946–1947); chrm., Surplus Property Board (1945–1946)	P or BC, Emerson Electric Mfg. Co., St. Louis (1938–1945); P, Rustless Iron & Steel Co., Baltimore (1935–1938); P, Colonial Radio Co., Rochester (1930–1935)	BD, Mississippi Valley Trust Co., St. Louis (1943 through 1950)	Married daughter of James W. Wadsworth (who had married a daughter of John Hay)		E
Thomas K. Finletter, N.Y.C., orig. Pa. (Apr. 1950–Jan. 1953)	Univ of Pa.	Chief, British mission, ECA (1948–1949); dir., office of Foreign Economic Coordinator (1943–1944); special asst. to Sec. of State (1941–1943)	Ptr., Coudert Brothers, N.Y.C., law firm (1926–1950, except for WW II years and 1948–1949); law lecturer, Univ. of Pa. (1931–1941)	BD, American Machine & Metals, Inc. (1932–1948), Reynal & Hitchcock, Inc. (1947), and Coty, Inc. (1949–1950)		BD, Council on Foreign Relations (1944 through 1953)	E

Attorney General					
Thomas C. Clark, Texas (June 1945–Aug. 1949)	Univ. of Texas	Justice Dept. posts (1937–1945; Asst. Attorney General, 1942–1945); civil district attorney, Dallas Co. (1927–1932)	Dallas lawyer, both individual practice and small firm (1922–1937)		NE?
J. Howard McGrath, R.I. (Aug. 1949–Apr. 1952)	Providence Coll.	U.S. Senator, R.I. (1946–1949); U.S. Solicitor General (1945–1946); Governor of R.I. (1940–1945); U.S. attorney for R.I. (1934–1940)	Off., J. J. McGrath & Sons, Providence real estate and insurance firm (1936–1949); P, First Federal Savings & Loan Assn., Providence (at least 1938–1949); former Providence lawyer	BD, small Lincoln Trust Co., Providence (mid-1940s), Mortgage & Trust Co. (up to 1948), and Pawtucket Broadcasting Co. (up to at least 1948)	Chrm., Democratic National Committee (1947–1949)	?
James P. McGranery, Pa. (May 1952–Jan. 1953)	Temple Univ. (not complete, but finished its law school)	Federal judge (1946–1952); Asst. to U.S. Attorney General (1943–46); Pa. Congressman (1937–1943)	Philadelphia lawyer (1928–1943)		Longtime local Democratic leader	NE

TRUMAN ADMINISTRATION (1945–1953) (continued)

Officeholder	College Education	Prior Governmental Experience	Primary Non-governmental Occupation	Important Secondary Economic Affiliations	Family and Other Socio-Economic Ties	Other Pertinent Information	Elite or Non-Elite Status
Secretary of Interior							
Harold Ickes, Ill. (1945– Mar. 1946)	\multicolumn{7}{l}{SEE TRUMAN AND ROOSEVELT ADMINISTRATION ENTRIES}						NE
Julius A. Krug, Wis. (Mar. 1946– Nov. 1949)	Univ. of Wisconsin	Off., War Production Board and predecessor agencies (1941–1945); off., TVA (1938–1941); off., FCC (1935–1937); off., Wis. Public Utility Comm. (1932–1935)	Engineering (business) consultant, Washington (1945–1946)				NE?
Oscar L. Chapman, Colo. (Jan 1950–Jan. 1953)	Univ. of N.M. and Univ. of Denver	Under Sec. of the Interior (1946–1949); Asst. Sec. of the Interior (1933–1946)	Denver lawyer, individual practice (1929–1933)				NE

426

Secretary of Agriculture				
Clinton P. Anderson, N.M. (June–May 1945–May 1948)	Dakota Wesleyan Univ. and Univ. of Michigan (not complete)	U.S. Congressman, N.M. (1941–1945); various state posts (1936–1940)	P, Mountain States Mutual Casualty Co., N.M. (1937 on); owner, Albuquerque insurance agency (1927–1937)	NE
Charles F. Brannan, Colo. (May 1948–Jan. 1953)	Regis Coll. (not complete)	Asst. Sec. of Agriculture (1944–1948); regional dir., Farm Security Adm. (1941–1944); lesser federal posts (1935–1941)	Denver lawyer, individual practice (1929–1935); half owner, cattle ranch (1940–1948)	NE
Secretary of Commerce				
Henry A. Wallace, Iowa (Mar. 1945–Sept. 1946)	Iowa St. Coll.	Vice-President of U.S. (1941–1945); Sec. of Agriculture (1933–1940)	Former publisher, *Wallace's Farmer*	NE
W. Averell Harriman, N.Y (Sept. 1946–May 1948)	Yale Univ.	U.S. Ambassador to Great Britain (Mar.–Oct., 1946); Ambassador to Russia (1943–	Ptr., Brown Brothers Harriman & Co., N.Y.C. (1920–1946, limited ptr. since	BD, Merchant-Sterling Corp. (1945–1948), Illinois Central RR	Active member, BAC (1933–1945); graduate member thereafter	E

Brother, E. Roland Harriman, a longtime ptr. in Brown Bros. Harriman & Co.; also BC, Union Pacific RR (1946 on) and

427

TRUMAN ADMINISTRATION (continued)

Officeholder	College Education	Prior Governmental Experience	Primary Non-governmental Occupation	Important Secondary Economic Affiliations	Family and Other Socio-Economic Ties	Other Pertinent Information	Elite or Non-Elite Status
Harriman (continued)		1946); various defense and foreign policy posts (1941–1943)	1946); BC, Union Pacific RR (1932–1946); CEC, Illinois Central RR (1931–1942)	(1942–1946), Guaranty Trust Co., N.Y.C. (up to 1940), Western Union Telegraph Co. (up to 1940), and American Ship & Commerce Corp. (up to 1940)	BC and P, Merchant-Sterling Corp., N.Y.C. (at least 1936 through 1948); also BD, Anaconda Copper Mining Co. and Mutual Life Insurance Co. (through 1948)		
Charles Sawyer, Ohio (May 1948– Jan. 1953)	Oberlin Coll.	U.S. Ambassador to Belgium (1944–1946); Lt.-Gov., Ohio (1933–1934)	Ptr., Cincinnati law firm of Dinsmore, Shohl, Sawyer & Dinsmore (1921–1948)	BD, American Thermos Bottle Co. (1926 through 1953); Kemper-Thomas Co. (1928 through 1953), Crosley Corp. (1929–1946), and Cincinnati Baseball Club, Inc. (1938 through 1953)		Democratic National Committeeman, Ohio (1936–1944)	E

Secretary of Labor				
Lewis B. Schwellenbach, Wash. (July 1945–June 1948)	Univ. of Wash. (not complete, but finished its law school)	Federal judge (1940–1945); U.S. Senator, Wash. (1935–1940)	Dean, Gonzaga Law School, Spokane, Wash. (1944–1945); Seattle lawyer (1919–1940)	NE
Maurice J. Tobin, Mass. (Aug. 1948–Jan. 1953)	Boston Coll. (not complete)	Governor of Mass. (1945–1948); Mayor of Boston (1937–1945); former state legislator (late 1920s)	District traffic mgr., New England Telephone & Telegraph Co., subsidiary of AT&T (1928–1937)	NE
Ambassador to Great Britain				
John G. Winant, N.H., orig. N.Y. (1945–Apr. 1946)	SEE ENTRY FOR WORLD WAR II YEARS			E
W. Averell Harriman, N.Y. (Apr.–Sept. 1946)	SEE SECRETARY OF COMMERCE ENTRY			E

TRUMAN ADMINISTRATION (continued)

Officeholder	College Education	Prior Governmental Experience	Primary Nongovernmental Occupation	Important Secondary Economic Affiliations	Family and Other Socio-Economic Ties	Other Pertinent Information	Elite or Non-Elite Status
Lewis W. Douglas, N.Y., orig. Ariz. (Mar. 1947–Nov. 1950)	Amherst College	Dir., Bureau of the Budget (1933–1934); Arizona Congressman (1927–1933)	P, Mutual Life Insurance Co., N.Y. (1940–1947); vice-chancellor, McGill Univ., Canada (1938–1939); VP, American Cyanamid Co. (1934–1938)	BD, General Motors Corp. (1945 through 1950) and Homestake Mining Co., SF (1946 through 1950)	Brother-in-law, John Zinsser (a Philadelphia industrialist) on BD of J. P. Morgan & Co.; another brother-in-law, John J. McCloy (a Wall St. lawyer), on BD of Union Pacific RR and Empire Trust Co., N.Y.C. (1947); uncle, Walter Douglas, on BD of Phelps Dodge Corp. (up to death in 1946)	BT, Rockefeller Foundation (1935–1947) and BD, Council on Foreign Relations (1940 through 1950)	E
Walter S. Gifford, N.Y. (Dec. 1950–Jan. 1953)	Harvard Univ.		BC or P, AT&T (1925–1949, VP 1919–1925)	BD, U.S. Steel Corp. (1928–1950) and First National Bank of N.Y.C. (1924–1950)		BT, Rockefeller Foundation (1936–1950)	E
Ambassador to France							
Jefferson Caffrey, Wash., D.C., orig. La. (1945–May 1949)	Tulane Univ.	Longtime career diplomat (1911 on)					NE?

430

David K. E. Bruce, Md. (May 1949–Mar. 1952)	Princeton Univ. (not complete, but law degree, Univ. of Md.)	ECA off. (1948–1949); Asst. Sec. of Commerce (1947–1948); U.S. Army off. (1941–1945); foreign service off. (1925–1928)	Baltimore and Pittsburgh businessman (1928–1940); Baltimore lawyer (1921–1925)	BD, Aluminum Co. of America, Pittsburgh (1931–1940) and Pan-American World Airways (1935–1939)	Brother, James Bruce (a businessman turned diplomat) on BD of Avco Mfg. Corp., American Airlines, Chemical Bank & Trust Co. of N.Y.C. Commercial Credit Co. of Baltimore, Congoleum-Nairn, Inc., Equity Corp. of N.Y.C., General American Investors Corp. of N.Y.C., National Dairy Products Corp., and Republic Steel Corp.	BT, Brookings Institution (1943–1952)	E
James C. Dunn, Wash., D.C., orig. N.J. (Mar. 1952–Mar. 1953)	Educated privately	Longtime career diplomat (1920 on)			Married a member of the Armour (meat packing) family of Chicago		E
Ambassador to Soviet Union							
W. Averell Harriman, N.Y. (1945–Jan. 1946)	SEE ENTRY FOR WORLD WAR II YEARS						E

TRUMAN ADMINISTRATION (continued)

Officeholder	College Education	Prior Governmental Experience	Primary Non-governmental Occupation	Important Secondary Economic Affiliations	Family and Other Socio-Economic Ties	Other Pertinent Information	Elite or Non-Elite Status
Walter B. Smith, Wash., D.C., orig. Ind. (Apr. 1946–Dec. 1948)	——	Former longtime high-ranking Army off. (1917–1945)					NE
Alan G. Kirk, Wash., D.C., orig. Pa. (July 1949–Oct. 1951)	U.S. Naval Academy	Former longtime high-ranking naval off. (1911–1946)					NE
George F. Kennan, Wash., D.C., orig. Wis. (May–Sept. 1952)	Princeton Univ.	Longtime career diplomat (1926 on)					NE

U.S. High Commissioner to Germany					
John J. McCloy, N.Y. (May 1949–July, 1952)	Amherst Coll.	P, World Bank (1947–1949); Asst. Sec. of War (1941–1945)	Ptr., N.Y.C. law firm of Milbank, Tweed, Hope, Hadley & McCloy (1946–1947); ptr., Cravath, deGersdorff & Wood (1929–1940)	BD, Union Pacific RR (1946–1949) and Empire Trust Co., N.Y.C. (1946–1947)	Brother-in-law, John S. Zinsser, on BD of J. P. Morgan & Co. (1943 through 1952)	BT, Rockefeller Foundation (1946–1949)	E
Ambassador to NATO					
Charles M. Spofford, N.Y. (June 1950–Jan. 1952)	Yale Univ.		Ptr., N.Y.C. law firm of Davis, Polk, Wardwell, Sunderland & Kiendl (1940–1950; associate, 1930–1940)			E
William H. Draper, Jr., N.Y. (Apr. 1952–May 1953)	New York Univ.	Under Sec. of the Army (1947–1949); various federal economic posts (1944–1947); U.S. Army (1940–1944)	VP, N.Y.C. banking firm of Dillon, Read & Co. (1937–1941, 1949–1952; lesser company off., 1927–1937)	BD, German Credit & Investment Corp. (1929–1941)		E

EISENHOWER ADMINISTRATION (1953–1961)

Officeholder	College Education	Prior Governmental Experience	Primary Non-governmental Occupation	Important Secondary Economic Affiliations	Family and Other Socio-Economic Ties	Other Pertinent Information	Elite or Non-Elite Status
President							
Dwight D. Eisenhower, Kansas, orig. (1953–1961)	U.S. Military Academy	Supreme Commander of NATO forces in Europe (1950–1952); longtime (1915–1948) high-ranking Army off. (two posts as commander of Allied forces in Europe in WWII and early postwar years)	President of Columbia University, N.Y.C. (1948–1950)	BD, Central Savings Bank, N.Y.C. (1950–1951)	Brother, Milton Eisenhower, on BT of CED (1945–1949); another brother, Edgar, on BD of St. Regis Paper Co. (1954 through 1961); another brother, Arthur, on BD of TWA (1947–57)	BT, CED (1950–1952) and Carnegie Endowment for International Peace (1948–early 1950s)	E
Secretary of State							
John Foster Dulles, N.Y. (1953–Apr. 1959)	Princeton Univ.	U.S. Senator, N.Y. (July–Nov. 1949); various special diplomatic posts in post-WWII period	Ptr., N.Y.C. law firm of Sullivan & Cromwell (1920–1949)	BD, Bank of New York (1930–1953), American Agricultural Chemical Co. (1927–1950), American Bank Note Co. (1925–49),	Brother, Allen W. Dulles, longtime high off. of Council on Foreign Relations (P, 1947–1951)	BC, Rockefeller Foundation (1950–1952, BT 1935–1950) and Carnegie Endowment for International Peace (1948–52)	E

434

Name	Education	Government positions	Business positions		Other
Christian A. Herter, Mass. (Apr. 1959–Jan. 1961)	Harvard Univ.	Under Sec. of State (1957–1959); Governor of Mass. (1953–1957); longtime (1943–1953) Mass. Congressman; state legislator (1931–1943)	Mass. newspaper editor, *The Independent* (1924–1928) and *The Sportsman* (1927–1936)	Babcock & Wilcox Co. (1933–1949), and International Nickel Co. of Canada, Ltd. (1926–1949)	Married member of wealthy Pratt family of N.Y.C. (long associated with Standard Oil interests)	E Son, C. A. Herter, Jr. (a Boston lawyer) on BD of Foreign Policy Association, N.Y. (1959 through 1961)

Secretary of Treasury

Name	Education	Government positions	Business positions	Other	
George M. Humphrey, Ohio (1953–June 1957)	Univ. of Michigan		P, M. A. Hanna Co., Cleveland (1929–1952); CEC, National Steel Corp. (1930–1952); BC, Pittsburgh Consolidation Coal Co. (1947–1952); CEC, Industrial Rayon Corp. (1942–1952, dir. many years before that)	BD, Phelps Dodge Corp. (1938–1952) and National City Bank of Cleveland (1934–1952)	Son, G. W. Humphrey, on BD of Industrial Rayon Corp. (1953 through 1957)	E BT, CED (1950–1952); member, BAC (1942–1952), member, BAC executive committee, 1943–1952

EISENHOWER ADMINISTRATION (continued)

Officeholder	College Education	Prior Governmental Experience	Primary Non-governmental Occupation	Important Secondary Economic Affiliations	Family and Other Socio-Economic Ties	Other Pertinent Information	Elite or Non-Elite Status
Robert B. Anderson, Texas originally, later N.Y. (July 1957–Jan. 1961)	Southwestern Univ., Texas	Dep. Sec. of Defense (1954–1955); Sec. of Navy (1953–1954); former Texas state off.	P, Ventures, Ltd. of Canada (1956–1957); CEC and VP, Dresser Industries, Inc. (1957); GC or gen. mgr., Waggoner estate, Tex. (1937–1953); Dep. Chrm., Federal Reserve Bank of Dallas (1946–1952); P, Mid-Continent Oil and Gas Assn. (1947–1951)	BD, Dresser Industries (1956); Hanover Bank, N.Y.C. (1957), American Overseas Investing Co. (1957), Missouri-Pacific RR (1956–1957), and Southwestern Bell Telephone Co., subsidiary of AT&T (just before 1953 entry into federal government)		BT, CED (1956–1957), and member of the BAC (1956 through 1961); BT, Ford Foundation (1956–1957)	E
Secretary of Defense							
Charles E. Wilson, Mich. (1953–Oct. 1957)	MIT		P, General Motors Corp. (1941–1953, VP, 1929–1940)	BD, National Bank of Detroit (1942–1953)		Member, BAC (1947–1951); GM BC, A. P. Sloan, Jr., on BD of J. P. Morgan & Co. (1943 through 1957)	E

Name	Education	Government	Business	
Neil H. McElroy, Ohio (Oct. 1957–Dec. 1959)	Harvard Univ.		P, Procter & Gamble Co., Cincinnati (1948–1957), lesser official 1929–1947	BD, General Electric Co. (1950–1957) and Chrysler Corp. (1953–1957)	Member, BAC (1957–1959); BC of Procter & Gamble, R.R. Deupree, trustee, CED (1951–1956), member, BAC (1935–55), and dir., J. P. Morgan & Co. (1953 through 1959)	E
Thomas S. Gates, Jr., Pa. (Dec. 1959–Jan. 1961)	Univ. of Pa.	Sec. of Navy (1957–1959); Under Sec. of Navy (1953–1957)	Longtime off., Philadelphia investment banking firm of Drexel & Co. (ptr. 1940–1953; limited ptr., 1953 through 1961)	BD, Scott Paper Co., Pa. (1937–1959) and International Basic Economy Corp., N.Y.C. (1947–1954)		E
Secretary of Army					
Robert T. Stevens, N.Y. (1953–July 1955)	Yale Univ.		P or BC, J. P. Stevens & Co., N.Y.C. (1929–1953); Chrm., Federal Reserve Bank of N.Y. (1949–1952)	BD, Mutual Life Insurance Co. (1938–52), General Foods Corp. (1946–1952), General Electric Co. (1947–1952), Alexander Smith & Sons	Brother, J. P. Stevens, Jr., trustee, CED (1948 through 1955) and BD, New York Life Insurance Co. (1948 through 1955) and Hanover Bank (1945 through 1955)	Member, BAC (1941–1955; chrm, 1951–1952)	E

EISENHOWER ADMINISTRATION (continued)

Officeholder	College Education	Prior Governmental Experience	Primary Non-governmental Occupation	Important Secondary Economic Affiliations	Family and Other Socio-Economic Ties	Other Pertinent Information	Elite or Non-Elite Status
Stevens (continued)				Carpet Co. (1948–1952), New York Telephone Co., subsidiary of AT&T (1946–1952), and Owens-Corning Fiberglas Corp. and Pan-American World Airways (both 1952–1953)			
Wilbur M. Brucker, Mich. (July 1955–Jan. 1961)	Univ. of Mich.	Gen. counsel, Defense Dept (1954–1955)	Ptr., Clark, Brucker & Waples, Detroit law firm (1937–1954)	BD, First Federal Savings & Loan Assn., Detroit (1938–1954)			?
Secretary of Navy							
Robert B. Anderson, Texas (1953–Apr. 1954)		SEE SEC. OF TREASURY ENTRY					E
Charles S. Thomas, Cal. (May 1954–Feb. 1957)	Cornell Univ. (not complete)	Asst. Sec. of Defense for Supply and Logistics (1953–1954)	VP or P, Foreman & Clark, Inc. a small L.A. department store (1932–1953)	BD, Broadway-Hale Stores, Inc., L.A. (1947–1952), Lockheed Air-			E

438

Thomas S. Gates, Jr., Pa. (Apr. 1957–June 1959)	SEE SEC. OF DEFENSE ENTRY	(1946–1952), and Pacific Finance Corp. (1948–1952)	E
William B. Franke, N.Y. (June 1959–Jan. 1961)	Under Sec. of Navy (1957–1959); Asst. Sec. of Navy (1954–1957); special asst. to Sec. of Defense (1951–1952)	Ptr., Franke, North, Hannon & Withey, N.Y.C. accounting firm (1928–1954); BC, John Simmons Co., N.J. (1938–1954); BC, General Shale Products Corp., N.Y.C. (at least 1950–1952); VP, Carolina, Clinchfield & Ohio Rwy. (1953–1957)	BD of Julius Kayser & Co., N.Y.C. (1945–1953) and Carolina, Clinchfield & Ohio Rwy. (1946–1952)	?

Secretary of Air Force

Harold E. Talbott, N.Y. (1953–Aug 1955)	Yale Univ.	VP, Talbott Co., N.Y.C. realty firm (1942–1952); BC, Standard Cap & Seal Corp., N.Y.C. (1934–1952)	BD, Chrysler Corp. (1928–1952), Mead Corp. (at least 1921–1952), Electric Autolite Co. (1935–1952), Madison Square Garden Corp. (1936–1952), Baldwin-Lima-	Prominent Republican party fundraiser	E

EISENHOWER ADMINISTRATION (continued)

Officeholder	College Education	Prior Governmental Experience	Primary Non-governmental Occupation	Important Secondary Economic Affiliations	Family and Other Socio-Economic Ties	Other Pertinent Information	Elite or Non-Elite Status
Talbott *(continued)*				Hamilton Corp. (1951–1952), and Commercial National Bank & Trust Co., N.Y.C. (1929–1951)			
Donald A. Quarles, N.Y. (Aug. 1955–May 1957)	Yale Univ.	Asst. Sec. of Defense for Research and Development (1953–1955)	Exec., Western Electric Co., subsidiary of AT&T (1919–1953)				E
James H. Douglas, Jr., Ill. (May 1957–Dec. 1959)	Princeton Univ.	Under Sec. of the Air Force (1953–1957)	Ptr., Gardner, Carton & Douglas, Chicago law firm (1943–1953)	BD, Metropolitan Life Insurance Co., N.Y.C. (1942–1953), American Airlines (1951–1952), and Chicago Title & Trust Co. (1939–53)			E
Dudley C. Sharp, Texas (Dec. 1959–Jan. 1961)	Princeton Univ.	Under Sec. of the Air Force (1959); other Defense Dept. post (1955–1959)	P, Texas Fund, Inc. (1950–1955); high off., Mission Mfg. Co. (1927–1955)				?

440

Attorney General					
Herbert Brownell, Jr., N.Y. (1953–Jan. 1958)	Univ. of Neb.	Former N.Y. state legislator (1933–1937)	Ptr., N.Y.C. law firm of Lord, Day & Lord (1932–1953)	BD, Commodore Hotel, Inc., N.Y.C. (1950–1953), National Retailers Mutual Insurance Co. (1949–1953), and World Trade Corp., N.Y. (1947–48)	Mgr., Dewey presidential campaigns in 1944 and 1948; Chrm., Republican National Committee (1944–1946)	E
William P. Rogers, N.Y. (Jan. 1958–Jan. 1961)	Colgate Univ.	Asst. U.S. Attorney General (1953–1958); counsel, Senate special committee to investigate national defense program (1947–1950); asst. district attorney of N.Y.C. (1938–1942 and 1946–1947)	Ptr., Dwight, Royall, Koegel, Harris & Caskey, N.Y.C. law firm (1950–1953)			?

EISENHOWER ADMINISTRATION (continued)

Officeholder	College Education	Prior Governmental Experience	Primary Non-governmental Occupation	Important Secondary Economic Affiliations	Family and Other Socio-Economic Ties	Other Pertinent Information	Elite or Non-Elite Status
Secretary of Interior							
Douglas J. McKay, Ore. (1953–June 1956)	Oregon State Coll.	Governor of Oregon (1949–1953); former state legislator (1934–1949, except WW II years)	Owner, Douglas McKay Chevrolet agency, Salem (1927–1955)				NE
Fred Seaton, Neb. (June 1956–Jan. 1961)	Kansas State Agricultural Coll.	Asst. Sec. of Defense for Legislative Affairs (1953–1955); U.S. Senator, Neb. (1951–1953); former state legislator (1945–1949)	P, Seaton Publishing Co. and a number of other newspaper, radio, and television companies in Neb. (1937–1953); publisher, *Daily Tribune*, Hastings, Neb.				NE?
Secretary of Agriculture							
Ezra Taft Benson,	Brigham Young		VC or BC, American Institute of Co-			BD, Farm Foundation	E?

442

Name	Education	Prior Gov't Position	Business (Principal)	Business (Other Directorships)	Family/Notes	Organizations	
Utah (1953–1961)	Univ.		operation, Salt Lake City (1942–1952); exec. sec., National Council of Farm Cooperatives (1939–1944); sec., Idaho Cooperative Council (1933–38)			(1946–1950); BT, Brigham Young Univ. (at least 1953–1961)	

Secretary of Commerce

Name	Education	Prior Gov't Position	Business (Principal)	Business (Other Directorships)	Family/Notes	Organizations	
Sinclair Weeks, Mass. (1953–Oct. 1958)	Harvard Univ.	U.S. Senator, Mass. (Feb.–Dec. 1944)	P or BC, United-Carr Fastener Corp., Boston (1930–1952); P or BC, Reed & Barton Corp. (1923–1953)	BD, First National Bank, Boston (1927–1952), Gillette Co. (1941–1952), West Point Mfg. Co. (1938–1950), Atlas Plywood Corp. (1939–1953), Pacific Mills (1940–1952), and Pullman Co. of Chicago (1948–1952)	Son of former (1921–1925) Sec. of War	Chrm., Republican National Finance Committee (1947–1952); BD, NAM (1938–1952; exec. committee, 1938–1948); BT, American Enterprise Assn. (1945–1952)	E

EISENHOWER ADMINISTRATION (continued)

Officeholder	College Education	Prior Governmental Experience	Primary Non-governmental Occupation	Important Secondary Economic Affiliations	Family and Other Socio-Economic Ties	Other Pertinent Information	Elite or Non-Elite Status
Lewis L. Strauss, N.Y. (Oct. 1958–June 1959)		Chrm., AEC (1953–1958); member, AEC (1946–1950)	Consultant and financial advisor to Rockefellers (1950–1953); ptr., Kuhn, Loeb & Co., N.Y.C. (1929–1947)		BD, General American Transportation Corp. (1932–1946, 1951–1952), Industrial Rayon Corp. (1951–1953), General Tire & Rubber Co. (1951–1952), Rockefeller Center, Inc. (1951–1953), and RCA (1953)		E
Frederick H. Mueller, Mich. (Aug. 1959–Jan. 1961)	Michigan State Univ.	Under Sec. of Commerce (1958–1959); Asst. Sec. of Commerce (1955–1958)	Ptr., Mueller Furniture Co., Grand Rapids (1914–1955); P, Furniture Mutual Insurance Co. (1941–1955)	BD, People's National Bank of Grand Rapids (1949–1958)			NE?
Secretary of Labor							
Martin P. Durkin, Ill. (Jan.–Oct. 1953)			P, United Assn. of Journeymen Plumbers and Steamfitters of U.S. and Canada (1943–1953); state director of labor for Ill. (1938–1941)	BD, Union Labor Life Insurance Co., an AFL-dominated concern (1944–1953)		Longtime Democrat	NE

Name	Education	Position	Business affiliations	
John P. Mitchell, N.J. & N.Y. (Jan. 1954–Jan. 1961)		Asst. Sec. of Army (1953); federal welfare and personnel posts (1936–1945)	VP, Bloomingdale's, subsidiary of Federated Dept. Stores, Inc. (1947–1953); dir., personnel and industrial relations, R. H. Macy & Co., N.Y. (1945–1947)	E?

Secretary of Health, Education and Welfare

Name	Education	Position	Business affiliations	
Mrs. Oveta Culp Hobby, Texas (1953–Aug 1955)	Mary Hardin-Baylor Coll. (not complete)	Federal Security Adm. (Feb.–Apr. 1953)	Exec. and editor, *Houston Post* (1938–1953)	Former Democrat; BT, American Assembly (1951–1953)	E
Marion B. Folsom, N.Y. (Aug 1955–Aug 1958)	Univ. of Georgia	Under Sec. of the Treasury (1953–1955)	Treas., Eastman Kodak Co., N.Y. (1935–1953); P, Eastman Savings & Loan Assn., Rochester (1947–1952)	BD, Federal Reserve Bank of New York (1949–1953), Rochester Savings Bank (1931–1949), and Lincoln Rochester Trust Co. (1946–1949)	VC or BC, CED (1945–1952, BT, 1943–1945); member, BAC (1936–1958, VC 1945–1949); BD, U.S. Chamber of Commerce (1942–1948)	E

EISENHOWER ADMINISTRATION (continued)

Officeholder	College Education	Prior Governmental Experience	Primary Nongovernmental Occupation	Important Secondary Economic Affiliations	Family and Other Socio-Economic Ties	Other Pertinent Information	Elite or Non-Elite Status
Arthur S. Flemming, Ohio (Aug. 1958–Jan. 1961)	Ohio Wesleyan Univ. (also M.A., American Univ.)	Dir., Office of Defense Mobilization (1953–1957); member, U.S. Civil Service Comm. (1939–1948)	P, Ohio Wesleyan Univ. (1948–1953, 1957–1958); dir., American Univ. school of public affairs (1934–1938)				NE
Ambassador to Great Britain							
Winthrop W. Aldrich, N.Y. (Feb. 1953–Feb. 1956)	Harvard Univ.		P or BC, Chase National Bank (1932–1953)	BD, Metropolitan Life Insurance Co. (1938–1952), Westinghouse Electric Corp. (1934–1952), International Paper Co. (1944–1952), New York Central RR (1948–1952), AT&T (1931–1952)	Nephew, David Rockefeller, VP, Chase National Bank and of Council on Foreign Relations; another nephew, John D. Rockefeller, Jr., on BT of Rockefeller Foundation (1932 through 1956) and N.Y. Life Insurance Co. (1950 through 1956); another nephew, Nelson A. Rockefeller, on BT of CED (1947–1953); another nephew, Laurence S. Rockefeller, on BD of Chase National Bank (1947–1956), Eastern Airlines (1938	BT, Rockefeller Foundation (1936–1951)	E

Name	Education	Business Positions	Other	
John Hay Whitney, N.Y. (Feb. 1956–Jan. 1961)	Yale Univ.	Ptr., J. H. Whitney & Co., N.Y.C. (1947 through 1961); BC, Freeport Sulphur Co. (1949–1956); also publisher, *New York Herald Tribune* (1958–1961)	BD, Great Northern Paper Co. (1951–1957)	Brother, C. V. Whitney, P and BC, Hudson Bay Mining & Smelting Co., Ltd. (1931 through 1961); ptr., James F. Brownlee, on BD of Chase Manhattan Bank (1956 on) and BT of CED (1947–1959); paternal grandfather, William C. Whitney, one-time N.Y.C. financier (and Cleveland Cabinet member); maternal grandfather, former Sec. of State John Hay; and granduncle, O. H. Payne, one of the founders of Standard Oil Co.	Member, BAC (1953 through 1961)	E
through 1956), and International Nickel Co. of Canada, Ltd. (1946 through 1956); son of the long-deceased Senator Nelson W. Aldrich						

Ambassador to France

Name	Education	Business Positions	Other	
C. Douglas Dillon, N.Y. (Mar. 1953–Mar. 1957)	Harvard Univ.	VP, P or BC, Dillon, Read & Co. (1938–1953); P, U.S. and Foreign Securities Corp. (1947–1953)	BD, Amerada Petroleum Corp. (1947–1953)		E

447

EISENHOWER ADMINISTRATION (continued)

Officeholder	College Education	Prior Governmental Experience	Primary Non-governmental Occupation	Important Secondary Economic Affiliations	Family and Other Socio-Economic Ties	Other Pertinent Information	Elite or Non-Elite Status
Amory Houghton, N.Y. (Apr. 1957–Jan. 1961)	Harvard Univ.	—	P or BC, Corning Glass Works, N.Y. (1930–1956)	BD, Metropolitan Life Insurance Co. (1940 through 1961), First National City Bank of N.Y.C. (1938–1957), Erie RR (1942–1956), and Investors Management Co. (1946–53)	Cousin, A. A. Houghton, Jr., on BD of U.S. Steel Corp. (1956–61), Delaware, Lackawanna & Western RR (1936 through 1961) and BT of Rockefeller Foundation (1958 through 1961); father, A. B. Houghton, onetime Ambassador to both France and Great Britain	BT, CED (1949–1956)	E

Ambassador to Soviet Union

Officeholder	College Education	Prior Governmental Experience	Primary Non-governmental Occupation	Important Secondary Economic Affiliations	Family and Other Socio-Economic Ties	Other Pertinent Information	Elite or Non-Elite Status
Charles E. Bohlen, Pa. orig. (Apr. 1953–Apr. 1957)	Harvard Univ.	Longtime State Dept. career diplomat (1929 through 1957)			Married a member of Philadelphia's long-wealthy Thayer and Wheeler families		?

Llewellyn E. Thompson, Colo. (July 1957 through *1961*)	Univ. of Colorado	Longtime State Dept. off. (1929 through 1961)		NE
Ambassador to West Germany				
James B. Conant, Mass. (Jan. 1953–Feb. 1957)	Harvard Univ.		P, Harvard Univ. (1933–1953)	BT, CED (1952 through 1957) E
David K. E. Bruce, Md. (Apr. 1957– Oct. 1959)	Princeton Univ. and Univ. of Va. (not complete)	Under Sec. of State (1952–1953); Ambassador to France (1949–1952); ECA official (1948–1949); Asst. Sec. of Commerce (1947–1948); other federal posts (1941–1947)	Baltimore and Pittsburgh businessman (1928–1940)	Brother, James Bruce, on BD of National Dairy Products Corp. (up to 1958), Republic Steel Co., U.S. Industries, American Airlines, Avco Mfg. Corp., Fruehauf Trailer Co., and Chemical Corn Exchange Bank, N.Y.C. (all but first firm up through 1959) E
Walter C. Dowling, Ga. (Dec. 1959 through *1961*)	Mercer Univ., Ga.	State Dept. off. (1931 through 1961)		NE

EISENHOWER ADMINISTRATION (continued)

Officeholder	College Education	Prior Governmental Experience	Primary Nongovernmental Occupation	Important Secondary Economic Affiliations	Family and Other Socio-Economic Ties	Other Pertinent Information	Elite or Non-Elite Status
Ambassador to NATO							
John C. Hughes, N.Y. (June 1953–Mar. 1955)	Princeton Univ.		P, McCampbell & Co., N.Y.C. textile sales concern (1947–1953, lesser off. before that)	BD, Graniteville Co., S.C. (1942–1953)			E?
George W. Perkins, N.J. & N.Y. (Mar. 1955–Oct. 1957)	Princeton Univ.	Asst. Sec. of State (1949–1953); ECA off. (1948–1949)	Treas., Merck & Co., N.J. (1929–1947)	BD, City Bank Farmers Trust Co., subsidiary of National City Bank of N.Y.C. (1935–1949)	Married a member of the Merck family; deceased father a onetime high official in J. P. Morgan & Co.	BT, Foreign Policy Association (up to at least 1955)	E
W. Randolph Burgess, N.Y. (Sept. 1957–Mar. 1961)	Brown Univ.	Under Sec. of Treasury (1953–1957)	VC or CEC, National City Bank of N.Y.C. (1938–1952)	BD, Mutual Life Insurance Co. (1941–1952), IT&T (1948–1953), and Union Pacific RR (1948–1952)			E

450

JOHN F. KENNEDY ADMINISTRATION

Officeholder	College Education	Prior Governmental Experience	Primary Non-governmental Occupation	Important Secondary Economic Affiliations	Family and Other Socio-Economic Ties	Other Pertinent Information	Elite or Non-Elite Status
President							
John F. Kennedy, Mass. (Jan. 1961– Nov. 1963)	Harvard Univ.	U.S. Senator, Mass. (1953– 1961); Mass. Congressman (1947– 1953)			Father a very rich former N.Y.C. and Hollywood businessman (much of fortune invested in real estate), and pre-WWII Ambassador to Great Britain		E
Secretary of State							
Dean Rusk, N.Y., orig. Ga. (1961 through 1963)	Davidson Coll.	Asst. Sec. of State (1950–1951); other lesser State Dept. posts (1947–1950); special asst. to Sec. of War (1946– 1947)	P, Rockefeller Foundation (1952– 1961); dean of faculty, Mills Coll. Cal. (1938–1940); professor of government and international relations, Mills Coll. (1934– 1938)				E

451

JOHN F. KENNEDY ADMINISTRATION (continued)

Officeholder	College Education	Prior Governmental Experience	Primary Non-governmental Occupation	Important Secondary Economic Affiliations	Family and Other Socio-Economic Ties	Other Pertinent Information	Elite of Non-Elite Status
Secretary of Treasury							
C. Douglas Dillon, N.Y. (1961 through 1963)	Harvard Univ.	Under Sec. of State (1959–1961); Under Sec. (or Dep. Under Sec.) of State for Economic Affairs (1957–1959); Ambassador to France (1953–1957)	High off., Dillon, Read & Co. (1938–1953, except WW II years); P, U.S. and Foreign Securities Corp. (1947–1953)	BD, Amerada Petroleum Corp. (1947–1953)		BT, Rockefeller Foundation (1960–1961)	E
Secretary of Defense							
Robert S. McNamara, Mich., orig. Cal. (1961 through 1963)	Univ. of Cal. at Berkeley		High off., Ford Motor Co. (1946–1961; P, late 1960–early 1961); asst. professor of business administration, Harvard Univ. (1940–1943)	BD, Scott Paper Co. (1960–1961)			E

452

Secretary of Army				
Elvis J. Stahr, Jr., W. Va. (1961–July 1962)	Univ. of Kentucky	Special asst to Sec. of Army (1951–1952); consultant, Dept. of the Army (1952–1953)	P, W. Va. Univ. (1959–1961); Vice-Chancellor, Univ. of Pittsburgh (1957–1959); law professor and academic off., Univ. of Ky. (1947–1957)	NE
Cyrus R. Vance, N.Y. (July 1962 through 1963)	Yale Univ.	Gen. counsel, Defense Dept. (1961–1962); special (PT) counsel, preparedness subcommittee of Senate Armed Services Committee (1957–1960)	Member, N.Y.C. law firm of Simpson, Thacher & Bartlett (1947–1961, ptr. 1956–1961)	Married member of W. & J. Sloane family of N.Y.; father-in-law, John Sloane, on BD of Atlantic Mutual Insurance Co. (1921 through 1963), U.S. Trust Co. of N.Y.C. (1923–1961), and Mutual Life Insurance Co. (1933–1959)	E
Secretary of Navy				
John B. Connally, Texas (Jan–Dec. 1961)	no college degree (but law degree, Univ. of Texas)	Administrative asst. to Senator Lyndon B. Johnson (1949)	Attorney for Sid W. Richardson and Perry R. Bass, Ft. Worth oil operators (1952–1961); ptr., Powell, Wirtz & Rauhut, Austin law	BD, New York Central RR (1959–1961)	E

453

JOHN F. KENNEDY ADMINISTRATION (continued)

Officeholder	College Education	Prior Governmental Experience	Primary Non-governmental Occupation	Important Secondary Economic Affiliations	Family and Other Socio-Economic Ties	Other Pertinent Information	Elite or Non-Elite Status
Connally *(continued)*			firm (1950–1952); gen. mgr., radio station KVET, Austin (1946–49)				
Fred Korth, Texas (Dec. 1961–Oct. 1963)	Univ. of Texas	Asst. Sec. of Army (1952–1953)	Exec. VP or P, Continental National Bank, Ft. Worth (1953–1961); Fort Worth lawyer (1935–1951, except WW II years)	BD, Bell Aerospace Corp., subsidiary of Textron, Inc. (1960–1961) and Texas & Pacific Rwy., subsidiary of Missouri-Pacific RR (1961)			E
Paul H. Nitze, N.Y. (Oct. 1963 on)	Harvard Univ.	Asst. Sec. of Defense for Intl. Security Affairs (1961–1963); dir., policy planning staff, State Dept. (1950–1953); other lesser federal posts (1944–1949)	P, Foreign Service Educational Foundation (1953–1961); VP, Dillon, Read & Co., N.Y. (1929–1938, 1939–1940)		Married member of wealthy Pratt family of N.Y.C.; wife's cousin, Richardson Pratt, on BD of U.S. Trust Co. of N.Y.C. (1951–1959), another cousin, J. T. Pratt, Jr., on same BD (1960 on)		E

454

Secretary of Air Force				
Eugene M. Zuckert, Washington D.C., orig. N.Y.C. (1961 through 1963)	Yale Univ.	Member, AEC (1952–1954); Asst. Sec. of Air Force (1947–1952)	BC, Nuclear Science and Engineering Corp., Pittsburgh (1960–1961); Washington lawyer, individual practice (1956–1960) and D.C. management consultant (1954-60)	?
Attorney General				
Robert F. Kennedy, Mass. (1961 through 1963)	Harvard Univ.	Chief counsel, Senate Comm. to Investigate Labor-Management Relations (1957–1959); other lesser federal and Congressional staff posts (1951–1953, 1955–1957)	Married member of the wealthy Skakel family (of the Great Lakes Carbon Corp.)	E Manager of John F. Kennedy's 1960 presidential campaign

JOHN F. KENNEDY ADMINISTRATION (continued)

Officeholder	College Education	Prior Governmental Experience	Primary Non-governmental Occupation	Important Secondary Economic Affiliations	Family and Other Socio-Economic Ties	Other Pertinent Information	Elite or Non-Elite Status
Secretary of Interior							
Stewart L. Udall, Ariz. (1961 through 1963)	Eastern Arizona Jr. Coll. (not complete, but law deg., Univ. of Arizona)	Arizona Congressman (1955–1961)	Ptr., Udall & Udall, Tucson law firm (1948–1954)			Member of Mormon Church	NE
Secretary of Agriculture							
Orville S. Freeman, Minn. (1961 through 1963)	Univ. of Minnesota	Governor of Minn. (1955–1961)	Ptr., Larson, Loevinger, Lindquist, Freeman & Fraser, Minneapolis law firm (1947–1955)				NE

Secretary of Commerce				
Luther H. Hodges, N.C. (1961 through 1963)	Univ. of N.C.	Governor of N.C. (1954–1961); Lt-Gov., N.C. (1952–1954)	Gen. mgr. or VP (N.C. area), Marshall Field & Co. (1939–1950, and lesser off., 1927–1938)	BD, American Thread Co. (1952–1955)	E?
Secretary of Labor				
Arthur J. Goldberg, Ill. (1961–Sept. 1962)	Crane Jr. Coll., and later Northwestern Univ.		Ptr., Goldberg, Devoe, Shadur & Mikva, Chicago law firm (1947–1961); ptr., Washington law firm of Goldberg, Feller & Bredhoff (1948–1961); gen. counsel, United Steelworkers of America (1948–1961); gen. counsel, CIO (1948–1955) and of industrial union dept, AFL-CIO (1955–1961); individual Chicago lawyer (1933–45)	BD, Amalgamated Trust & Savings Bank of Chicago (1948–1961)	NE BT, Carnegie Endowment for International Peace (1958 through 1962)

JOHN F. KENNEDY ADMINISTRATION (continued)

Officeholder	College Education	Prior Governmental Experience	Primary Non-governmental Occupation	Important Secondary Economic Affiliations	Family and Other Socio-Economic Ties	Other Pertinent Information	Elite or Non-Elite Status
W. Willard Wirtz, Ill. (Sept 1962 through 1963)	Beloit Coll.	Under Sec. of Labor (1961–1962)	Ptr., Stevenson, Rikfind, & Wirtz, Chicago law firm (1955–1961) and member of N.Y.C. law firm of Paul, Weiss, Rifkind, Wharton & Garrison (1958–1961); professor of law, Northwestern Univ. (1946–1954, 1939–1942)				?
Secretary of Health, Education and Welfare							
Abraham Ribicoff, Conn. (1961–July 1962)	N.Y.U. (not complete, but law degree Univ. of Chicago)	Governor of Conn. (1955–61); Conn. Congressman (1949–1953); municipal judge (1941–1943, 1945–1947); former state legislator	Ptr., Ribicoff, Ribicoff & Kotkin, Hartford law firm (1941–1954)				NE

Anthony J. Celebrezze, Ohio (July 1962 through 1963)	John Carroll Univ. (not complete)	Mayor of Cleveland (1953–1962); former state legislator (1951–1953)	Cleveland lawyer, individual practice (1939–1942, 1945–1952)	First Italian-born member of any Cabinet	NE
Ambassador to Great Britain					
David K. E. Bruce, Md. (Mar. 1961 through 1963)	Princeton Univ. and Univ. of Va. (not complete)	Ambassador to West Germany (1957–1959); Under Sec. of State (1952–1953); Ambassador to France (1949–1952); other lesser federal posts (1946–1949)	Onetime Baltimore and Pittsburgh businessman (1928–1940)	Brother, James Bruce, on BD of American Airlines (1939 through 1963), General American Investors Co. (1941 through 1963), Avco Mfg. Co. (1951 through 1963), Continental Insurance Co. (1955 through 1963), Fruehauf Trailer Co. (1955 through 1963), Republic Steel Corp. (1933 through 1963), Revlon, Inc. (1957–1963), U.S. Industries Inc., and its predecessor concern (1951 through 1963), and various lesser concerns	E

JOHN F. KENNEDY ADMINISTRATION (continued)

Officeholder	College Education	Prior Governmental Experience	Primary Non-governmental Occupation	Important Secondary Economic Affiliations	Family and Other Socio-Economic Ties	Other Pertinent Information	Elite or Non-Elite Status
Ambassador to France							
James M. Gavin, N.Y. orig. (Mar. 1961–Sept. 1962)	U.S. Military Academy	Longtime (1929–1958) U.S. Army officer (with rank of Lt.-General upon retirement)	Exec. VP or P, Arthur D. Little, Inc., Boston management consultant firm (1958–1961)	BD, Merchants National Bank of Boston (1960–1961) and American Electric Power Co. (late 1960 through 1962)			E
Charles E. Bohlen, Pa. (Oct. 1962 through 1963)	Harvard Univ.	Special asst. to Sec. of State for Soviet Affairs (1959–1961); Ambassador to Philippines (1957–1959) and to Soviet Union (1953–1957); career Foreign Service officer (1929 through 1963)			Married a member of Philadelphia's long-wealthy Thayer and Wheeler families		?

Ambassador to Germany				
Walter C. Dowling, Ga. orig. (*1961*–Apr. 1963)	Mercer Univ., Ga.	Ambassador to Germany (1959 on); State Dept. career diplomat (since 1929)		NE
George C. McGhee, Texas (May 1963 on)	Univ. of Oklahoma	Under Sec. of State for Political Affairs (1961–1963); Ambassador to Turkey (1951–1953); Asst. Sec. of State for Near Eastern Affairs (1949–1951)	Owner, McGhee Production Co., Tex. (since apparently mid-1950s); dir., Middle East Institute, Washington (1953–1958)	BD, Petroleum Reserves, Inc. (1956–1960)	BT, CED (1957–1961) and Brookings Institution (1955–1961)	E
Ambassador to Soviet Union				
Llewellyn Thompson, Colo. (*1961*–July 1962)	Univ. of Colorado	Ambassador to Soviet Union (1957 on); longtime State Dept. off. (1929 through 1963)		NE
Foy D. Kohler, Ohio (Sept. 1962 through 1963)	Ohio State Univ.	Longtime State Dept. official (1931 on); Asst. Sec. of State for European Affairs (1959–1962)		NE

JOHN F. KENNEDY ADMINISTRATION (continued)

Officeholder	College Education	Prior Governmental Experience	Primary Non-governmental Occupation	Important Secondary Economic Affiliations	Family and Other Socio-Economic Ties	Other Pertinent Information	Elite or Non-Elite Status
Ambassador to NATO							
Thomas K. Finletter, N.Y. (Mar. 1961 through 1963)	Univ. of Pa.	Sec. of Air Force (1950–1953); ECA off. (1948–1949)	Ptr., N.Y.C. law firm of Coudert Bros. (1926–1941, 1944–61)			BD, Council on Foreign Relations (1944 through 1963)	E
Ambassador to South Vietnam							
Frederick E. Nolting, Jr., Va. (May 1961–Aug. 1963)	Univ. of Va.	State Dept. off. (since 1946)	Member, Richmond, Va., investment banking firm (1934–1939)				NE
Henry Cabot Lodge, Mass. (Aug. 1963 on)	Harvard Univ.	Ambassador to UN (1953–1960); U.S. Senator, Mass. (1937–43, 1947–1953)	Dir. gen., Atlantic Institute (1961–1962); onetime Northeastern newspaperman	BT, John Hancock Mutual Life Insurance Co., Boston (1961 on)	Mother a member of Frelinghuysen family (of N.J.)	BT, Foreign Policy Association (1961–1964)	E

LYNDON B. JOHNSON ADMINISTRATION (1963–1969)

Officeholder	College Education	Prior Governmental Experience	Primary Non-governmental Occupation	Important Secondary Economic Affiliations	Family and Other Socio-Economic Ties	Other Pertinent Information	Elite or Non-Elite Status
President							
Lyndon B. Johnson, Texas (Nov. 1963–Jan. 1969)	Southwest Texas State Coll.	Vice President of U.S. (1961–1963); U.S. Senator, Texas (1949–1961); Texas Congressman (1937–1941, 1942–1948)	Owner (indirectly, through wife) of Texas Broadcasting Corp., Austin (1943 on)				E?
Secretary of State							
Dean Rusk, N.Y., orig., Ga. (1963–1969)	Davidson Coll.	Sec. of State (1961–1963)	SEE ENTRY UNDER KENNEDY ADMINISTRATION				E
Secretary of Treasury							
C. Douglas Dillon, N.Y. (1963–Mar. 1965)	Harvard Univ.	Sec. of the Treasury (1961–63)	SEE ENTRY UNDER KENNEDY ADMINISTRATION				E

LYNDON B. JOHNSON ADMINISTRATION (continued)

Officeholder	College Education	Prior Governmental Experience	Primary Non-governmental Occupation	Important Secondary Economic Affiliations	Family and Other Socio-Economic Ties	Other Pertinent Information	Elite or Non-Elite Status
Henry H. Fowler, Wash., D.C. (Mar. 1965–Jan. 1969)	Roanoke Coll.	Under Sec. of the Treasury (1961–1964); high off., National Production Authority and Office of Defense Mobilization (1952–1953)	Ptr., Washington law firm of Fowler, Leva, Hawes & Symington (1946–1951, 1953–1961, 1964–1965)			Member, National Independent Committee for President Johnson and Senator Humphrey (1964); member, National Commission on Money and Credit (1958–1961)	E?
Secretary of Defense							
Robert S. McNamara, Mich. (*1963*–Mar. 1968)	Univ. of California, Berkeley	Sec. of Defense (1961–1963)	SEE ENTRY UNDER KENNEDY ADMINISTRATION				E
Clark M. Clifford, Wash., D.C. (Mar. 1968–Jan. 1969)	—— (but law degree, Washington Univ., St. Louis)	Special counsel to President of U.S. (1946–1950)	Ptr., Washington law firm of Clifford & Miller (1950–1968); ptr., St. Louis law firm of	BD, National Bank of Washington (1954–1968)			E

Secretary of Army				
Cyrus R. Vance, N.Y. (*1963*–Jan. 1964)	Yale Univ.	Sec. of the Army (1962–1963); gen. counsel, Defense Dept. (1961–1962); special counsel, preparedness investigating subcommittee of Senate Armed Services Committee (1957–1960)	Member, N.Y.C. law firm of Simpson, Thacher & Bartlett (1947–1961, ptr. 1956–1961)	Lashly, Miller & Clifford and predecessor concern (1933–1941)
Stephen Ailes, Wash., D.C. (Jan. 1964–June 1965)	Princeton Univ.	Under Sec. of Army (1961–1964)	Ptr., Washington law firm of Steptoe & Johnson (1948–1961)	?
Stanley R. Resor, N.Y. (July 1965 through *1969*)	Yale Univ.	Under Sec. of the Army (briefly, 1965)	Ptr., N.Y.C. law firm of Debevoise, Plimpton, Lyons & Gates (1946–1965)	E Brother-in-law, Gabriel Hauge, P of Manufacturers Hanover Trust Co, N.Y.C. (P, 1963–1969, other posts, 1958–1963); treas. of Council on Foreign Relations (1964 through

The top-right cell (Vance row) reads: "E Married member of W. & J. Sloane family of N.Y.; father-in-law, John Sloane, on BD of Atlantic Mutual Insurance Co. (1921–1966) and U.S. Trust Co. of N.Y.C. (1923–1961)"

465

LYNDON B. JOHNSON ADMINISTRATION (continued)

Officeholder	College Education	Prior Governmental Experience	Primary Nongovernmental Occupation	Important Secondary Economic Affiliations	Family and Other Socio-Economic Ties	Other Pertinent Information	Elite or Non-Elite Status
Resor *(continued)*					1969), and BD of American Metal Climax, Inc. (1964 on); BT of CED (1962 through 1969); father-in-law, John S. Pillsbury, former longtime head of Pillsbury Co. and BD, Northwest Bancorp. (up to 1963, brother-in-law on BD thereafter); late father, Stanley Resor, on BD of Scott Paper Co. and Greenwich Savings Bank (up to 1962)		
Secretary of Navy							
Paul H. Nitze, N.Y. (Oct. 1963–June 1967)	Harvard Univ.	Asst. Sec. of Defense for International Security Affairs (1961–1963); dir., policy planning staff, State Dept. (1950–1953); other lesser federal posts (1944–1949)	P, Foreign Service Educational Foundation (1953–1960); VP, Dillon, Read & Co., N.Y. (1929–1938, 1939–1940)		Married member of wealthy Pratt family of N.Y.C.; wife's cousin, J. T. Pratt, Jr., on BD of U.S. Trust Co. of N.Y.C. (1960 through 1969)		E

Name	Education	Government positions	Other positions	Notes
Paul Ignatius, Mass., orig. Cal. (Aug. 1967–Jan. 1969)	Univ. of Southern California	Asst. Sec. of Defense for Installations and Logistics (1965–1967); Under Sec. of Army (1964–1965); lesser Defense Dept. posts (1961–1964)	VP, Harbridge House, Inc., Boston (1950–1961)	NE

Secretary of Air Force

Name	Education	Government positions	Other positions	Notes
Eugene Zuckert, Wash., D.C. (*1963*–Oct. 1965)	Yale Univ.	Sec. of Air Force (1961–1963); member, AEC (1952–1954); Asst. Sec. of Air Force (1947–1952)	BC, Nuclear Science and Engineering Corp., Pittsburgh (1960–1961); Washington lawyer, individual practice (1956–1960) and Washington management consultant (1954–1960)	?
Harold Brown, Cal. (Oct. 1965–Jan. 1969)	Columbia Univ. (B.S. and Ph.D.)	Dir., defense research and engineering, Defense Dept. (1961–1965)	Univ. of Cal. physicist (1950–1961)	NE BT of Aerospace Corp., a defense-oriented nonprofit corp. (1960)

LYNDON B. JOHNSON ADMINISTRATION (continued)

Officeholder	College Education	Prior Governmental Experience	Primary Non-governmental Occupation	Important Secondary Economic Affiliations	Family and Other Socio-Economic Ties	Other Pertinent Information	Elite or Non-Elite Status
Attorney General							
Robert F. Kennedy, Mass. (*1963*–Sept. 1964)	Harvard Univ.	U.S. Attorney General (1961–1963); chief counsel, Senate Comm. to Investigate Labor-Management Relations (1957–1959); other lesser congressional staff posts before that			Married member of wealthy Skakel family (of Great Lakes Carbon Corp.)		E
Nicholas Katzenbach, Ill., orig. N.J. (Feb. 1965–Oct. 1966)	Princeton Univ.	Dep. Attorney General (1962–1965); lesser Justice Dept. post (1961–1962)	Law professor, Univ. of Chicago (1956–1960); associate professor of law, Yale Univ. (1952–1956)		Married member of (Phelps) Stokes family once associated with Phelps, Dodge & Co.; wife's cousin, I. N. P. Stokes, ptr. in N.Y.C. law firm of Webster, Sheffield, Fleischmann, Hitchcock & Chrystie and predecessor firms (from mid-1950s on)		?

468

Ramsey Clark, Texas (Oct. 1966–Jan. 1969)	Univ. of Texas	Dep. Attorney General (1965–1966); other lesser Justice Dept. posts (1961–1965)	Ptr., Clark, Reed & Clark, Dallas law firm (1951–1961)	Son of U.S. Supreme Court Justice Thomas C. Clark	NE
Secretary of Interior					
Stewart L. Udall, Ariz. (*1963*–1969)	Eastern Arizona Jr. Coll. (not complete, but law degree, Univ. of Ariz.)	Sec. of Interior (1961–1963); Ariz. Congressman (1954–1961)	Ptr., Udall & Udall, Tucson law firm (1948–1954)		NE
Secretary of Agriculture					
Orville S. Freeman, Minn. (*1963*–1969)	Univ. of Minnesota	Sec. of Agriculture (1961–1963); Governor of Minn. (1955–1961)	Ptr., Larson, Loevinger, Lindquist, Freeman & Fraser, Minneapolis law firm (1947–1955)		NE
Secretary of Commerce					
Luther H. Hodges, N.C. (*1963*–Jan. 1965)	Univ. of N.C.	Sec. of Commerce (1961–1963); Governor of N.C. (1954–1960); Lt. Gov. of N.C. (1952–1954)	Gen. mgr. or VP (N.C. area) of Marshall Field & Co. (1938–1950; lesser company off., 1927–1938)	BD, American Thread Co. (1952–1955)	E?

LYNDON B. JOHNSON ADMINISTRATION (continued)

Officeholder	College Education	Prior Governmental Experience	Primary Non-governmental Occupation	Important Secondary Economic Affiliations	Family and Other Socio-Economic Ties	Other Pertinent Information	Elite or Non-Elite Status
John T. Connor, N.J. (Jan. 1965–Jan. 1967)	Syracuse Univ.		P, Merck & Co., N.J. (1955–1965, lesser off. 1947–1955)	BD, General Foods Corp. (1962–1965), Communications Satellite Corp. (1963–1964), and General Motors Corp. (1964–1965)		BT, CED (1956–1965) and member, Business Council (1962–1967)	E
Alexander B. Trowbridge, N.Y.(?) (June 1967–Feb. 1968)	Princeton Univ.	Asst. Sec. of Commerce (1965–1967)	High off., Standard Oil Co. of N.J., So. American subsidiary (1959–1965); off., CalTex Oil Co., joint subsidiary of Standard Oil Co. of Cal. and Texaco (1954–1958)				E
Cyrus R. Smith, N.Y., orig. Texas (Mar. 1968–Jan. 1969)	Univ. of Texas		P or BC, American Airlines (BC, 1934–1968, except WWII years)	BD, Chase Manhattan Bank (1954–1966)		Former long-time active member of BAC	E

Secretary of Labor				
W. Willard Wirtz, Ill. (*1963*–Jan. 1969)	Beloit Coll.	Sec. of Labor (1962–1963); Under Sec. of Labor (1961–1962)	Ptr., Stevenson, Rifkind & Wirtz, Chicago law firm (1955–1961) and a member of N.Y.C. law firm of Paul, Weiss, Rifkind, Wharton & Garrison (1958–1961); professor of law, Northwestern Univ. (1946–1954, 1939–1942)	?
Secretary of Health, Education and Welfare				
Anthony J. Celebrezze, Ohio (*1963*–Aug. 1965)	John Carroll Univ. (not complete)	Sec. of HEW (1962–1963); Mayor of Cleveland (1953–1962)	Cleveland lawyer, individual practice (1939–1942, 1945–1952)	NE
John W. Gardner, N.Y (Aug. 1965–Jan. 1968)	Stanford Univ.		P, Carnegie Corp. of N.Y. (1955–1965, VP 1949–1955)	E
			BD, Shell Oil Co. (1963–1965) and New York Telephone Co., subsidiary of AT&T (1962–1965)	

471

LYNDON B. JOHNSON ADMINISTRATION (continued)

Officeholder	College Education	Prior Governmental Experience	Primary Non-governmental Occupation	Important Secondary Economic Affiliations	Family and Other Socio-Economic Ties	Other Pertinent Information	Elite or Non-Elite Status
Wilbur J. Cohen, Mich. (May 1968–Jan. 1969)	Univ. of Wisconsin	Under Sec. of HEW (1965–1968); Asst. Sec. of HEW (1961–1965); off., U.S. Social Security Administration (1936–1956)	Professor, public welfare administration, Univ. of Mich. (1956–1961)				NE
Secretary of Housing and Urban Development							
Robert C. Weaver, N.Y. (Jan. 1966–Jan. 1969)	Harvard Univ. (B.S. and Ph.D.)	Adm., U.S. Housing and Home Finance Agency (1961–1966); off., N.Y. Rent Adm. (1955–1959) 1954); cons., Ford	Dir., opportunity funds program, J. H. Whitney Foundation (1949–1954) cons., Ford Fdtn. (1959–60)			First black appointed to Cabinet post	NE
Secretary of Transportation							
Alan S. Boyd, (Jan. Fla.	Univ. of Fla. (not	Und. Sec. of Commerce for Trans-	Member, Miami law firm of Mar-				NE

				E
1967–Jan. 1969)	complete, but law deg., Univ. of Va.)	portation (1965–1967); Chrm., Civil Aeronautics Board (1961–1965, member, 1959–1961); member, Fla. Railroad & Public Utilities Com. (1955–1959)	(1956–1957); individual Miami attorney (1954–1955); assoc., firm of Smathers, Thompson, Maxwell & Dyer (late 1940s–1953)	
Ambassador to Great Britain				
David K. E. Bruce, Md. (*1963*–Mar. 1969)	Princeton Univ. and Univ. of Va. (not complete)	Ambassador to Great Britain (1961–1963) and to West Germany (1957–1959); Under Sec. of State (1952–1953); Ambassador to France (1949–1952)	Onetime Baltimore and Pittsburgh businessman (1928–1940)	Brother, James Bruce, on BD of American Airlines (1939 through 1969), Avco (Mfg.) Corp. (1951 through 1969), Continental Insurance Co. (1955 through 1969), Fruehauf Trailer Co. (1955 through 1969), General American Investors Co. (1941 through 1969), Republic Steel Corp. (1933 through 1969), Revlon, Inc. (1957 through 1969), and U.S. Industries, Inc. (1951 through 1969)

LYNDON B. JOHNSON ADMINISTRATION (continued)

Officeholder	College Education	Prior Governmental Experience	Primary Non-governmental Occupation	Important Secondary Economic Affiliations	Family and Other Socio-Economic Ties	Other Pertinent Information	Elite or Non-Elite Status
Ambassador to France							
Charles E. Bohlen, Pa. *(1963–Feb. 1968)*	Harvard Univ.	Ambassador to France (1962 through 1963)	SEE KENNEDY ADMINISTRATION ENTRY				?
R. Sargent Shriver, Jr., Md. (May 1968–1969)	Yale Univ.	Dir., Peace Corps (1961–1966); dir., Office of Equal Opportunity (1964–1968)	Asst. gen. mgr., Merchandise Mart, Chicago (1948–1961)		Married daughter of Joseph P. Kennedy		E
Ambassador to West Germany							
George C. McGhee Texas *(1963–May 1968)*	Univ. of Oklahoma	Under Sec. of State for Political Affairs (1961–1963); Ambassador to Turkey (1951–1953); Asst. Sec. of State for Near Eastern affairs (1949–1951)	Owner, McGhee Production Co., Texas (since apparently mid-1950s); dir., Middle East Institute, Washington (1953–1958)	BD, Petroleum Reserves, Inc. (1956–1960)		BT, CED (1957–1961) and Brookings Institution (1955–1961)	E

474

Henry Cabot Lodge, Mass. (May 1968–Jan 1969)	Harvard Univ.	Ambassador to South Vietnam (1963–1964, 1965–1967); also see Kennedy administration entry	Dir. gen., Atlantic Inst. (1961–62); onetime Northeastern newspaperman	BD, John Hancock Mutual Life Insurance Co., Boston, (1961–68)	E

Ambassador to Soviet Union

Foy D. Kohler, Ohio orig. (1963–Nov. 1966)	Ohio State Univ.	Ambassador to Soviet Union (1962 through 1963); longtime career diplomat			NE
Llewellyn E. Thompson, Colo. orig. (Jan. 1967–Jan. 1969)	Univ. of Colorado	Former (1957–1962) Ambassador to Soviet Union; longtime career diplomat			NE

Ambassador to NATO

Thomas K. Finletter, N.Y. (1963–Sept. 1965)	Univ. of Pa.	Ambassador to NATO (1961 through 1963); Sec. of Air Force (1952–1953); ECA off. (1948–1949)	Ptr., N.Y.C. law firm of Coudert Bros. (1944–1961)	BD, Council on Foreign Relations (1944 through 1965)	E

475

LYNDON B. JOHNSON ADMINISTRATION (continued)

Officeholder	College Education	Prior Governmental Experience	Primary Non-governmental Occupation	Important Secondary Economic Affiliations	Family and Other Socio-Economic Ties	Other Pertinent Information	Elite or Non-Elite Status
Harlan Cleveland N.Y. (Sept. 1965–Jan. 1969)	Princeton Univ.	Asst. Sec. of State for International Affairs (1961–1965); many second-tier federal posts (1940–1953)	Dean, Maxwell school, Syracuse Univ. (1956–1961); editor or publisher, *Reporter* magazine (1953–1956)				NE
Ambassador to South Vietnam		SEE PRECEDING JOHNSON ENTRY					
Henry Cabot Lodge, Mass. (August 1963–June 1964 *and* July 1965–Mar. 1967)	Harvard Univ.						E
Maxwell D. Taylor, Mo., orig. (July 1964–July 1965)	U.S. Military Academy	Chrm., Joint Chiefs Staff (1962–1964); military representative of President of U.S. (1961–1962); U.S. Army officer (1922–1959)	BC, Mexican Light & Power Co., Ltd. (1959–1960)	BD, Bullock Fund and other affiliated financial concerns (1959–1961)			E

Officeholder	College Education	Prior Governmental Experience	Primary Non-governmental Occupation	Important Secondary Economic Affiliations	Family and Other Socio-Economic Ties	Other Pertinent Information	Elite or Non-Elite Status
Ellsworth Bunker, N.Y. (Apr. 1967 through 1969)	Yale Univ.	Ambassador at-large (1966–1967); Ambassador to Organization of American States (1964–1966); Ambassador to India (1956–1961) and Italy (1952–1953)	P or BC, National Sugar Refining Co. (1940–1951, lesser company official before that), also BD of company, (1951–early 1966); limited ptr., Wood, Walker & Co., N.Y.C. brokerage firm (1963–1964)	BD, Atlantic Mutual Insurance Co., N.Y. (1945–through 1969), Curtis Publishing Co. (1963–1969), and Lambert International Corp. (1962 through 1969)	Son, John Bunker, P, Holly Sugar Corp. (Feb. 1967 on)		E

NIXON ADMINISTRATION (1969–1974)

President

Officeholder	College Education	Prior Governmental Experience	Primary Non-governmental Occupation	Important Secondary Economic Affiliations	Family and Other Socio-Economic Ties	Other Pertinent Information	Elite or Non-Elite Status
Richard M. Nixon, N.Y., orig. Cal. (1969–Aug. 1974)	Whittier Coll., Cal.	Vice-President of U.S. (1953–1961); U.S. Senator, Cal. (1951–1953); Cal. Congressman (1947–1951)	Ptr., N.Y.C. law firm of Nixon, Mudge, Rose, Guthrie, Alexander & Mitchell (and predecessor firms, 1963–1968); counsel, L.A. law firm of Adams, Duque	BD, Mutual Life Insurance Co., N.Y.C. (1966–1968), Investors Mutual, Inc., Minn. (1964–1968), and Harsco	Brother, F. Donald Nixon, P, Ogden Foods, Inc. (1969–1970) and VP, Marriott Corp. (indeterminate period, early 1970s); another brother, Edward C. Nixon, on BD of Oceanographic Fund (1969–1971); nephew,		E

NIXON ADMINISTRATION (continued)

Officeholder	College Education	Prior Governmental Experience	Primary Non-governmental Occupation	Important Secondary Economic Affiliations	Family and Other Socio-Economic Ties	Other Pertinent Information	Elite or Non-Elite Status
Nixon (*continued*)			& Hazeltine (1961–1963); officer in U.S. Navy (1942–1946); Whittier, Cal. lawyer (1937–1942)	Corp., Pa. (1965–1968)	Donald A. Nixon, administrative asst. to international financier Robert Vesco (1971–1973)		
Secretary of State							
William P. Rogers, N.Y. (1969–Sept. 1973)	Colgate Univ.	U.S. Attorney General (1958–1961); Dep. Attorney General (1953–1958); various lesser federal posts (prior to 1950)	Ptr., N.Y.C. law firm of Royall, Koegel & Rogers (and predecessor firm, 1950–1953, 1961–1969)	BD, Dreyfus Fund (1964–1968), Washington Post Co. (1964–1968), Gannett Co. (1967–1968), and Twentieth Century-Fox Corp. (Feb.–Dec. 1968)			E
Henry Kissinger, Mass., orig. N.Y. (Sept. 1973 through 1974)	Harvard Univ.	Special Asst. to President of U.S. for National Security Affairs (1969–1973)	Professor or asst. professor of government, Harvard Univ. (1958–1969, lesser academic posts before that)			Member, editorial advisory board, *Foreign Affairs* (1965–1973)	E?

478

Name	Education	Government	Business/Other	
Secretary of Treasury				
David M. Kennedy, Ill. (1969–Dec. 1970)	Weber Coll. Utah	Special Asst. to Sec. of the Treasury (1953–1954)	P or BC, Continental Illinois National Bank & Trust Co., Chicago (1956–1969, lesser company posts over most of preceding decade)	BD, Abbott Laboratories (1958–1968), Commonwealth Edison Co., Ill. (1959–1968) International Harvester Co. (1959–1968), Pullman Co. (1961–1968), Swift & Co. (1962–1968), U.S. Gypsum Co. (1962–1968), Communications Satellite Corp. (1963–1968), and Federal Reserve Bank of Chicago (1961–1968)	BT, CED (1964–1968) and Brookings Institution (1962–1968) E
John B. Connally, Texas (Dec. 1970–May 1972)	Law degree, Univ. of Texas	Governor, Texas (1963–1969); Sec. of Navy (1961)	Ptr., Houston law firm of Vinson, Elkins, Searls & Connally (1969–1970); attorney, Sid W. Richardson oil and other economic interests and estate (1952–1961)	BD, First City Natl. Bank of Houston (1969–1970), Halliburton Co. (1969–1970), General Portland Cement Co. (1969–1970), Texas Instruments, Inc. (1969–1970), Gibralter Savings Assn, Houston (1969–1970), and U.S. Trust Co. of N.Y.C. (1969–1970); BD, N.Y. Central RR (1959–1961)	E
George P. Shultz, Ill. (May 1972–May 1974)	Princeton Univ. (also Ph.D. from MIT)	Dir., Office of Management and Budget (1970–1972); Sec. of Labor (1969–1970)	Dean, Univ. of Chicago Graduate School of Business (1962–1968); professor, industrial re-	BD, Borg-Warner Corp. (1964–1969), J. I. Case Co. (1964–1968), General American Transportation Corp. (1966–1969), and Stein,	Member, research advisory board, CED (1965–1967) E

NIXON ADMINISTRATION (continued)

Officeholder	College Education	Prior Governmental Experience	Primary Non-governmental Occupation	Important Secondary Economic Affiliations	Family and Other Socio-Economic Ties	Other Pertinent Information	Elite or Non-Elite Status
Shultz *(continued)*			lations, Univ. of Chicago (1957–1962); economics professor, MIT (1949–1957)	Roe & Farnham Balanced Fund (1966–1968)			
William E. Simon, N.Y. (May 1974–end of Nixon administration)	Lafayette Coll.	Dep. Sec. of Treasury (late 1972–Dec. 1973); head, Federal Energy Office (Dec. 1973–May 1974)	Ptr., N.Y.C. securities firm of Salomon Bros. (1964–1972); VP, Weeden & Co. (1957–1963)				E
Secretary of Defense							
Melvin R. Laird, Wis. (1969–Jan. 1973)	Carleton Coll.	Wis. Congressman (1953–1969); former state legislator	Off., Connor Building Supply Co., Wis. (indeterminate period)				NE?
Elliot L. Richardson, Mass. (Feb.–Apr. 1973)	Harvard Univ.	SEE ATTORNEY GENERAL ENTRY					E

480

James R. Schlesinger, Cal. (July 1973 through 1974)	Harvard Univ. (also Ph.D., Harvard)	Dir., CIA (Feb.–July 1973); chrm., AEC (1971–early 1973); asst. dir., Bureau of Budget and OMB (1969–1971)	Staff member, Rand Corp. (1963–1969); asst. and assoc. professor of economics, Univ. of Va. (1956–1963)	NE
Attorney General				
John N. Mitchell, N.Y. (1969–Feb. 1972)	Fordham Univ. (not complete, but later secured degree from Fordham Univ. Law School)		Ptr., N.Y.C. law firm of Nixon, Mudge, Rose, Guthrie, Alexander & Mitchell (1966–1968); ptr., N.Y.C. law firm of Caldwell, Trimble & Mitchell (1942–1966)	Manager of Nixon's 1968 and 1972 presidential campaigns E
Richard G. Kleindienst, Ariz. (Feb. 1972–Apr. 1973)	Harvard Univ.	Dep. Attorney General (1969–1972); former state legislator (1953–1954)	Ptr., Shimmel, Hill, Kleindienst & Bishop, Phoenix law firm (1958–1969); ptr., Jennings, Strous, Salmon & Trask, Phoenix law firm (1950–1957)	High-ranking figure in Goldwater's 1964 presidential campaign NE?

NIXON ADMINISTRATION (continued)

Officeholder	College Education	Prior Governmental Experience	Primary Non-governmental Occupation	Important Secondary Economic Affiliations	Family and Other Socio-Economic Ties	Other Pertinent Information	Elite or Non-Elite Status
Attorney General							
Elliot L. Richardson, Mass. (May–Oct. 1973)	Harvard Univ.	Sec. of Defense (Feb.–Apr. 1973); Sec. of HEW (1970–1973); Under Sec. of State (1969–1970); Attorney General of Mass. (1967–1969); Lt.-Gov. of Mass. (1965–1967); U.S. attorney, Mass. (1959–1961); Asst. Sec. of HEW (1957–1959)	Ptr., Boston law firm of Ropes & Gray (1961–1964); assoc. member of Ropes, Gray, Best, Coolidge & Rugg (1949–1953, 1954–1956)	BD, New England Trust Co. (1953–1957)	Uncle, Henry L. Shattuck, on BD of Mutual Life Insurance Co. of N.Y. (1933–1968), New England Merchants National Bank (and predecessor concern, 1922–1968); father-in-law, T. P. Hazard, on BD of Allied Chemical Corp. (1951–1962)		E
William B. Saxbe, Ohio 1973 through 1974)	Ohio State Univ.	U.S. Senator, Ohio (1969–1973); Attorney-General of Ohio (1957–1958, 1963–1969); state legislator (1947–1954)	Ptr., Columbus law firms Dargusch, Saxbe & Dargusch (1960–1962) and Saxbe, Boyd & Prime (1954–58)	BD, Columbus Savings & Loan Assn. (at least 1960–probably 1974)			NE?

482

Secretary of Interior				
Walter J. Hickel, Alaska (1969–Nov. 1970)		Governor of Alaska (1966–1969)	Head, Hickel Construction Co., Anchorage (1947 on); BC, Anchorage Natural Gas Co. (up to apparently 1966)	?
Rogers C. B. Morton, Md., orig. Ky. (Nov. 1970–summer of 1974)	Yale Univ.	Md. Congressman (1963–1970)	VP or P, Ballard & Ballard Co., Ky. (1920–1951)	BD, Atlas Chemical Industries and predecessor concern, Del. (1960–1970) and Pillsbury Co., Minn. (1952–1970)	Brother, Thruston Morton, on BD of Pillsbury Co. (1971 through 1975), Pittston Co. (1969 through 1975), and Texas Gas Transmission Corp. (1969 through 1975)	Chrm., Republican National Committee (1969–1971)	E
Secretary of Agriculture				
Clifford M. Hardin, Neb. (1969–Nov. 1971)	Purdue Univ. (B.S. and Ph.D.)	Chancellor, Univ. of Neb. (1954–1969); dean of agriculture, Michigan State Univ. (1953–1954); dir., agricultural experimental station,	Chrm., Omaha branch, Federal Reserve Bank, Kansas City (1962–1967); BD, Bankers Life Insurance Co., Omaha (1959–1968)		BT, Rockefeller Foundation (1961–1969)	E

NIXON ADMINISTRATION (continued)

Officeholder	College Education	Prior Governmental Experience	Primary Non-governmental Occupation	Important Secondary Economic Affiliations	Family and Other Socio-Economic Ties	Other Pertinent Information	Elite or Non-Elite Status
Earl L. **Butz**, Ind. (Nov. 1971 through 1974)	Purdue Univ. (B.S. and Ph.D.)	Asst. Sec. of Agriculture (1954–1957)	Michigan State Univ. (1949–1953); Dean, Purdue Research Foundation (1968–1971); dean, school of agriculture, Purdue Univ. (1946–1954, 1957–1967)	and Behlen Mfg. Co., Neb. (1964–1968) BD, J. I. Case Co. (1966–1970), International Minerals & Chemical Corp. (1960–1971), Ralston-Purina Co., (1958–1971), Stokely-Van Camp, Inc. (1971), and Standard Life Insurance Co., Ind. (1951–71)		BT, Farm Foundation (1960–1970) and Foundation for American Agriculture (1957–1971)	E
Secretary of Commerce							
Maurice H. **Stans**, N.Y., orig. Ill. (1969–Jan. 1972)	Northwestern and Columbia Univ. (not complete)	Dir., Bureau of the Budget (1958–1961); Dep. Postmaster General (1955–1957)	Senior ptr. or P, Glore, Forgan, Wm. R. Staats, Inc., N.Y.C. (1965–1969); senior ptr., William R. Staats, Inc., L.A. (1963–1965);	BD, Fluor Corp. Ltd., Cal. (1965–1968), Oglebay-Norton Co., Cleveland (1966–1968), Pike Corp. of America Cal. (1966–1968), Wean Industries, Inc., Ohio (1967–1968), W. W. Grainger, Inc., Ill. (1968–1969), and Southern		BT, Tax Foundation (1963–1969) and BD of NAM (1968–1969)	E

Peter G. Peterson, Ill. (Jan. 1972–Jan. 1973)	Northwestern Univ.	Spec. Asst. to the President for International Economic Affairs (1971–1972)	P, Western Bancorporation, Cal. (1961–1962) California Edison Co. (1962–1963)	P or BC, Bell & Howell Co., Chicago (1961–1971; lesser company off., 1958–1961)	BD, Illinois Bell Telephone Co. (1968–1970) and First National Bank of Chicago and its parent company, the First Chicago Corp. (1967–1970)	BT, CED (1966–1972) and Brookings Institution (1968–1972)	E
Frederick B. Dent, S.C. (Feb. 1973 through *1974*)	Yale Univ.		P, Mayfair Mills, Arcadia, S.C. (1958–1972; lesser company official, 1947–1958)	BD, GE (1967–1972) Scott Paper Co. (1972–1973), Mutual Life Insur. Co. (1972), and the S.C. National Bank (1965–1972)	Father, Magruder Dent, BC, Mayfair Mills (up to 1967) and BD, Bank of New York (1951–1966)	Member, Business Council (1970–1973) and BT of CED (1969–1973)	E

NIXON ADMINISTRATION (continued)

Officeholder	College Education	Prior Governmental Experience	Primary Non-governmental Occupation	Important Secondary Economic Affiliations	Family and Other Socio-Economic Ties	Other Pertinent Information	Elite or Non-Elite Status
Secretary of Labor							
George P. Shultz, Ill. (1969–July 1970)	Princeton Univ. (Ph.D., MIT)		Dean, Univ. of Chicago Graduate School of Business (1962–1968); professor of industrial relations or economics, Univ. of Chicago and MIT (1949–1962)	Dir. of several large corporations (see Sec. of Treasury entry)			E
James D. Hodgson, Cal., (July 1970–Feb. 1973)	Univ. of Minnesota	Under Sec. of Labor (1969–1970)	VP for industrial relations, Lockheed Aircraft Corp., Cal. (1968–1969; lesser company official, 1946–1968)				E
Peter J. Brennan, N.Y. (July 1973 through 1974)	City Coll. of N.Y. (not complete)		P, N.Y.C. Building & Construction Trades Council, AFL-CIO (1957–1973)				NE

Secretary of Health, Education and Welfare				
Robert H. Finch, Cal. (1969–June 1970)	Occidental Coll.	Lt.-Gov. of Cal. (1967–1969)	Ptr., L.A. law firm of Finch, Bell, Duitsman & Marguilis, and predecessor firm (1951–1966)	Longtime Nixon political aide	NE
Elliot L. Richardson, Mass. (June 1970–Feb. 1973)	Harvard Univ.	Under Sec. of State (1969–1970); Asst. Sec. of HEW (1957–1959)	Onetime Boston (Brahmin) lawyer	SEE ATTORNEY GENERAL ENTRY	E
Casper Weinberger, Cal. (Feb. 1973 through 1974)	Harvard Univ.	Dir. or dep. dir., OMB (1970–1973); chrm., FTC (Jan.–June 1970); dir. of finance, Cal. state govt. (1968–1969); former state legislator	Ptr., San Francisco law firm of Heller, Ehrman, White & McAuliffe (1959–1968); assoc. of firm, 1947–1959	Prominent Cal. Republican party leader	NE?
Secretary of Housing and Urban Development					
George Romney, Mich.	Univ. of Utah and George	Governor of Mich. (1963–1968)	P or BC, American Motors Co., Mich. (1954–1962);	BD, Douglas Aircraft Co., Cal. (1961–62)	E

NIXON ADMINISTRATION (continued)

Officeholder	College Education	Prior Governmental Experience	Primary Non-governmental Occupation	Important Secondary Economic Affiliations	Family and Other Socio-Economic Ties	Other Pertinent Information	Elite or Non-Elite Status
Romney (continued) (1969–Nov. 1972)	Washington Univ. (not complete)		exec., Nash-Kelvinator Co. (1950–1954)				
James T. Lynn, Ohio (Dec. 1972 through 1974)	Western Reserve Univ.	Under Sec. of Commerce (1971–1972); gen. counsel, Dept. of Commerce (1969–1971)	Ptr., Cleveland law firm of Jones, Day, Cockley & Reavis (1960–1969; assoc. member, 1951–1960)				E
Secretary of Transportation							
John A. Volpe, Mass. (1969–Dec. 1972)		Governor of Mass. (1965–1969, 1961–1963); Federal Highway Adm. (1956–1957)	P or BC, John A. Volpe Construction Co., Mass. (1933–1969)				E?
Claude S. Brinegar, Cal. (Dec. 1972 through 1974)	Stanford Univ. (B.A. and Ph.D.)		VP or senior VP, Union Oil Co. of Cal. (1965–1972; lesser company official, 1953–1965)	BD, Daytona International Speedway Corp., Fla. (1966–1973)			E?

488

Ambassador to Great Britain				
Walter H. Annenberg, Pa. (Apr. 1969 through *1974*)		P, Triangle Publications, Inc., Philadelphia (1942–1969)	BD, Girard Trust Bank, Philadelphia (1964–1969), Pa. RR and Penn-Central Co. (1967–1969), Campbell Soup Co. (1966–1969), and Times-Mirror Co., L.A. (1967–1969)	E
Ambassador to France				
R. Sargent Shriver, Md. and Ill. (*1969*–Mar. 1970)	Yale Univ.	SEE JOHNSON ADMINISTRATION ENTRY		
Arthur K. Watson, N.Y. (May 1970– Oct. 1972)	Yale Univ.	VC, IBM (1966– 1970; lesser company posts, 1947– 1966)	BD, Continental Insurance Co. (1959–1970), Pan American Brother, Thomas J. Watson, Jr. (BC of IBM), on BD of Bankers Trust Co. (1948 through 1972), Pan American World Airways	E P, International Chamber of Commerce (1969)

NIXON ADMINISTRATION (continued)

Officeholder	College Education	Prior Governmental Experience	Primary Non-governmental Occupation	Important Secondary Economic Affiliations	Family and Other Socio-Economic Ties	Other Pertinent Information	Elite or Non-Elite Status
Watson (continued)				World Airways (1969–1970), and Federal Reserve Bank of N.Y. (1965–1970)	(1971 on), BT of Rockefeller Foundation (1963–1971), and member of Business Council (mid-1960s–early 1970s)		
John N. Irwin II, N.Y. (Mar. 1973 through Aug. 1974)	Princeton Univ.	Dep. Sec. of State (1972–1973); Under Sec. of State (1970–1972); Asst. Sec. of State for International Security Affairs (1958–1961)	Ptr., N.Y.C. law firm of Patterson, Belknap & Webb (1950–1957, 1961–1970)	BD, IBM World Trade Corp. (1962–1970), U.S. Trust Co. of N.Y.C. (1962–1970), Dominick Fund, N.Y.C. (1963–1970), and Seamen's Bank for Savings, N.Y.C. (1952–70)	Brother-in-law of A. K. Watson and Thomas J. Watson, Jr.	BD, Foreign Bondholders Protective Council (late 1960s–early 1970s)	E

Ambassador to West Germany					
Kenneth Rush, N.Y. (July 1969–Feb. 1972)	Univ. of Tenn.		P, Union Carbide Corp. (1966–1969; lesser company off., 1937–1966)	BD, Bankers Trust Co, N.Y. (1967–1969) and American Sugar Co. (1962–1969)	BT, Foreign Policy Association (1963–1969)	E
Martin J. Hillenbrand, Ohio orig. (June 1972 through 1974)	Univ. of Dayton	Foreign service officer (1939 on)				NE
Ambassador to Soviet Union					
Jacob D. Beam, N.J. orig. (Apr. 1969–Jan. 1973)	Princeton Univ.	Foreign service officer (early 1930s on)				NE
Walter J. Stoessel, Jr., Kansas orig. (Jan. 1974 on)	Stanford Univ.	Foreign service officer (1942 on)				NE

NIXON ADMINISTRATION (continued)

Officeholder	College Education	Prior Governmental Experience	Primary Non-governmental Occupation	Important Secondary Economic Affiliations	Family and Other Socio-Economic Ties	Other Pertinent Information	Elite or Non-Elite Status
Chief, U.S. liaison office, China							
George H. W. Bush Texas, orig N.Y. and Conn. (June 1974 on) Ambassador to Vietnam	Yale Univ.	Ambassador to UN (1971–1972); Texas Congressman (1967–1971)	P or BC, Zapata Off-Shore Co., Texas (1956–1966)	BD, Zapata Off-Shore Co., (1966–1967) and Camco, Inc., Texas (1960–1966)	Father, Prescott Bush (died in Oct 1971), longtime partner in N.Y.C. banking firm of Brown Bros. Harriman and one-time U.S. Senator, Conn.	Chrm., Republican National Committee (1973–1974)	E
Ellsworth Bunker, N.Y. (1969–May 1973)	Yale Univ.	Ambassador to Vietnam (1967 on), to OAS (1964–1966), and to India (1956–1961)	P, National Sugar Refining Co. (up to 1951)	BD, Atlantic Mutual Insurance Co. (1945 through 1973), Lambert International Corp. (1962–1973), and Curtis Publishing Co. (1963–1969)	Son, John Bunker, P of Holly Sugar Corp., Colo. (1967 through 1973)		E

492

Ambassador to South Vietnam			
Graham A. Martin, N.C. orig. (July 1973 through 1974)	Wake Forest Univ.	Foreign Service officer (1947 on)	NE
Ambassador to NATO			
Robert Ellsworth, Kansas (May 1969–June 1971)	Univ. of Kansas	Special Asst. to President (early 1969); Kansas Congressman (1961–1967)	Lawrence, Kans., lawyer (1954–1969)	NE
David M. Kennedy, Ill. (Mar. 1972–Feb. 1973)	George Washington Univ.	Sec. of the Treasury (1969–1970); Ambassador at-large (1971–1972)	SEE SECRETARY OF TREASURY ENTRY	E
Donald Rumsfeld, Ill. (Feb. 1973 through Aug. 1974)	Princeton Univ.	Counsellor to President of U.S. (1971–1973); Special Asst. to President (1969–1970); Ill. Congressman (1963–1969)	Off., A. G. Becker & Co., Chicago investment banking firm (1960–1962)	NE

FORD ADMINISTRATION (1974–1977)

Officeholder	College Education	Prior Governmental Experience	Primary Non-governmental Occupation	Important Secondary Economic Affiliations	Family and Other Socio-Economic Ties	Other Pertinent Information	Elite or Non-Elite Status
President							
Gerald R. Ford, Mich. (Aug. 1974–Jan. 1977)	Univ. of Michigan	Vice-President of U.S. (Oct. 1973–Aug. 1974); Mich. Congressman (1949–1973); House minority leader (1965–1973)	Grand Rapids, Mich. lawyer (1941–1973); ptr., Amberg, Law & Fallon law firm (1951–1959; assoc. of predecessor concern, 1946–1951); independent practice thereafter				NE
Secretary of State							
Henry Kissinger, Mass., orig. N.Y. *(1974–Jan. 1977)*	Harvard Univ.	Sec. of State (1973 on); Special Asst. to the President for National Security Affairs (1969–1973)	Professor of government, Harvard Univ. (1959–1969)			Member, editorial advisory board, *Foreign Affairs* (1965–1973)	E?

494

Secretary of Treasury			
William E. Simon, N.Y. (*1974*–Jan. 1977)	Lafayette Coll.	Sec. of the Treasury (early 1974 on); head, Federal Energy Office (late 1973–May 1974); Dep. Sec. of the Treasury (1972–1973)	Ptr., N.Y.C. securities firm of Salomon Bros. (1964–1972); VP, Weeden & Co., N.Y.C. (1957–1964)	E
Secretary of Defense				
James R. Schlesinger, Cal. (*1974*–Nov. 1975)	Harvard Univ. (also Harvard Ph.D.)	Sec. of Defense (starting 1973); dir., CIA (Feb–July 1973); chrm., AEC (1971–1973); asst. dir., Bureau of Budget and OMB (1969–1971)	Staff member, Rand Corp. (1963–1969); asst. and assoc. professor of economics, Univ. of Va. (1956–1963)	NE
Donald Rumsfeld, Ill. (Nov. 1975–Jan. 1977)	Princeton Univ.	Counsellor to President (1971–1973, 1974–1975); Ambassador to NATO (1973–1974); Special Asst. to President (1969–1970); Ill. Congressman (1963–1969)	Off., A. G. Becker & Co., Chicago investment banking firm (1960–1962)	NE

FORD ADMINISTRATION (continued)

Officeholder	College Education	Prior Governmental Experience	Primary Non-governmental Occupation	Important Secondary Economic Affiliations	Family and Other Socio-Economic Ties	Other Pertinent Information	Elite or Non-Elite Status
Attorney General							
William B. Saxbe, Ohio (1974–Jan. 1975)	Ohio State Univ.	U.S. Attorney General (starting 1973); U.S. Sen., Ohio (1969–1973); Attorney General of Ohio (1957–1958, 1963–1969)	Ptr., Dargusch, Saxbe & Dargusch, Columbus law firm (1960–1962); ptr., Columbus law firm of Saxbe, Boyd & Prime (1954–1958)	BD, Columbus Savings & Loan Assn. (at least 1960–probably 1974)			NE (n/c)
Edward H. Levi, Ill. (Feb. 1975–Jan. 1977)	Univ. of Chicago (law degree, Yale Univ.)		P, Univ. of Chicago (1968–1975); provost, Univ. of Chicago (1962–1968); dean, Univ. of Chicago Law School (1950–1962); professor, Chicago Law School (1936–1940, 1945–1950)			BT, Urban Institute, Wash., D.C. (1968–1975), Aspen Institute for Humanistic Studies (1970–1975), and Russell Sage Foundation (1971–1975)	E?

Secretary of Interior					
Rogers C. B. Morton, Md. (1974–May 1975)	Yale Univ.	Sec. of the Interior (starting 1970); Md. Congressman (1963–1970)	VP or P, Ballard & Ballard Co., Ky. (1937–1951)	BD, Atlas Chemical Industries, Inc., and predecessor concern, Del. (1960–1970) and Pillsbury Co., Minn. (1952–1970)	Brother, Thruston Morton, on BD of Pillsbury Co. (1971 through 1975), Pittston Co. (1969 through 1975), and Texas Gas Transmission Corp. (1969 through 1975)	Chrm., Republican National Committee (1969–1971)	E
Stanley K. Hathaway, Wyo. (June–July 1975)	Univ. of Nebraska	Governor of Wyo. (1967–1975); local prosecuting attorney (part-time basis, 1954–1962)	Torrington, Wyo. lawyer (early 1950s–1967)			NE
Thomas S. Kleppe, N.D. (Oct 1975–Jan. 1977)	Valley City State Coll., N.D. (not complete)	Head, U.S. Small Business Administration (1971–1975); N.D. Congressman (1967–1971)	P, Gold Seal Co., N.D. (1958–1964, lesser off., 1946–1958); high off., J. M. Dain & Co., Minn. investment banking firm (1965–1966)	BD, Dakota National Bank of Bismarck, affiliate of Northwest Bancorp. (1949–1972) and off. or dir., Cardinal Petroleum Co. Mont. (1964–1971)		NE?

FORD ADMINISTRATION (continued)

Officeholder	College Education	Prior Governmental Experience	Primary Nongovernmental Occupation	Important Secondary Economic Affiliations	Family and Other Socio-Economic Ties	Other Pertinent Information	Elite or Non-Elite Status
Secretary of Agriculture							
Earl L. Butz, Ind. (*1974–Oct 1976*)	Purdue Univ. (B.S. and Ph.D.)	Secretary of Agriculture (starting 1971); Asst. Sec. of Agriculture (1954–1957)	Dean, Purdue Research Foundation (1968–1971); dean, school of agriculture, Purdue Univ. (1957–1967)	BD, J.I. Case Co. (1966–1970), International Minerals & Chemical Corp. (1960–1971), Ralston-Purina Co. (1958–1971), Stokely-Van Camp, Inc. (1971), and Standard Life Insurance Co., Ind. (1951–1971)		BT, Farm Foundation (1960–1970) and Foundation for American Agriculture (1957–1971)	E
Secretary of Commerce							
Frederick B. Dent, S.C. (*1974–Mar. 1975*)	Yale Univ.	Sec. of Commerce (starting 1973)	P, Mayfair Mills, S.C. (1958–1972; lesser company off., 1947–1958)	BD, GE (1967–1972), Scott Paper Co. (1972–1973), and South Carolina National Bank (1965–1972)		Member, Business Council (1970–1973) and BT, CED (1969–1973)	E

Name	Education	Prior position	Other affiliations	
Rogers C. B. Morton, Md. (May–Dec. 1975)	Yale Univ.	SEE SECRETARY OF INTERIOR ENTRY		E
Elliot L. Richardson, Mass. (Dec. 1975–Jan. 1977)	Harvard Univ.	Ambassador to Great Britain (1975–1976); U.S. Attorney General (May–Oct. 1973); Sec. of Defense (Feb.–Apr. 1973); Sec. of HEW (1970–1973); Under Sec. of State (1969–1970); various state govt. posts	Member of the Trilateral Commission (1974–1977) and BD, Council on Foreign Relations (1974–1975)	E
		SEE PRECEDING ENTRIES UNDER NIXON ADMINISTRATION		

Secretary of Labor

Name	Education	Prior position	Other affiliations	
Peter J. Brennan, N.Y. (1974–Feb. 1975)	City Coll., N.Y. (not complete)	Sec. of Labor (starting 1973)	P, N.Y.C. Building & Construction Trades Council, AFL-CIO (1957–1973)	NE (n/c)
John T. Dunlop, Mass. (Mar. 1975–Jan. 1976)	Univ. of California, Berkeley (Ph.D., Univ. of Chicago)	Dir., national Cost of Living Council (1973–1974)	Dean, Harvard Univ. (1970–1973); economics professor, Harvard Univ. (1945 on)	NE

FORD ADMINISTRATION (continued)

Officeholder	College Education	Prior Governmental Experience	Primary Non-governmental Occupation	Important Secondary Economic Affiliations	Family and Other Socio-Economic Ties	Other Pertinent Information	Elite or Non-Elite Status
Willie J. Usery, Jr., Wash., D.C., orig. Ga. (Jan. 1976–Jan. 1977)	Mercer College, Ga. (not complete)	Asst. Sec. of Labor (1969–1973); dir. Federal Mediation and Conciliation Service (1973–1976)	AFL-CIO off. (1956–1969)				NE
Secretary of Health, Education, and Welfare							
Casper Weinberger, Cal. (1974–July 1975)	Harvard Univ.	Sec. of HEW (starting early 1973)	SEE NIXON ADMINISTRATION ENTRY				NE?
F. David Mathews, Ala. (Aug. 1975–Jan. 1977)	Univ. of Alabama (also Columbia Univ., Ph.D.)		P, Univ. of Alabama (1969–1975); exec. asst. to P, Univ. of Alabama (1966–1968); dean, Univ. of Alabama (1960–1966)	BD of Birmingham branch of Federal Reserve Bank of Atlanta (1971–1975)			E

500

Secretary of Housing and Urban Development					
James T. Lynn, Ohio (*1974*–Jan. 1975)	Western Reserve Univ.	Sec. of HUD (starting late 1972); Under Sec. of Commerce (1971–1972); Gen. counsel, Dept. of Commerce (1969–71)	Ptr., Cleveland law firm of Jones, Day, Cockley & Reavis (1960–1969; assoc. member, 1951–1960)		E (n/c)
Carla A. Hills, Cal. (Mar. 1975–Jan. 1977)	Stanford Univ.	Asst. Attorney General (1974–1975)	Ptr., Munger, Tolles, Hills & Rickershauer, LA law firm (1962–1974)	Husband (and law ptr.), BC of Republic Corp. (1971–1975)	E
Secretary of Transportation					
Claude S. Brinegar, Cal. (*1974*–Feb. 1975)	Stanford Univ. (B.A. and Ph.D.)	Sec. of Transportation (starting late 1972)	Senior VP, Union Oil Co. of Cal. (1968–1972, lesser company off., 1953–1968)	BD, Daytona International Speedway Corp., Fla. (1966–1973)	E?
William T. Coleman, Jr., Pa.	Univ. of Pa.		Ptr., Philadelphia law firm of Dilworth, Paxson,	BD, Pan-American World Airways (1970–75), First Pa.	E BD, Council on Foreign Relations (1974–

FORD ADMINISTRATION (continued)

Officeholder	College Education	Prior Governmental Experience	Primary Non-governmental Occupation	Important Secondary Economic Affiliations	Family and Other Socio-Economic Ties	Other Pertinent Information	Elite or Non-Elite Status
(Mar. 1975–Jan. 1977)			Kalish, Levy & Coleman and predecessor concern (1956–1975)	Corp., bank holding co. (1972–74), Penn Mutual Life Insurance Co. (1969–74), Philadelphia Electric Co. (1973–74), and Western Savings Fund Society, Philadelphia (1971–74)		1975); BT, Brookings Institution (1972–1975); member, Trilateral Commission (1974 through 1976)	
Ambassador to Great Britain			SEE SECRETARY OF COMMERCE ENTRY				
Elliot L. Richardson, Mass. (Jan.–Dec. 1975)	Harvard Univ.						E
Anne L. Armstrong, Texas (Jan. 1976–early 1977)	Vassar Coll.	Counsellor to President of U.S. (1973–1974)		BD, First City Bancorp. of Texas (1975–1976), American Express Co., (Jan. 1975–Jan. 1976), Union Carbide Corp. Jan. 1975–	Related to Klebergs of the King Ranch interests	Republican National Committeewoman, Texas (1968–1973)	E

Ambassador to France					
Kenneth Rush, N.Y. (Nov. 1974–early 1977)	Univ. of Tenn.	Dep. Sec. of State (1972–1974); Ambassador to West Germany (1969–1972)	P, Union Carbide Corp. (1966–1969; lesser company posts, 1937–1966)	BD, Bankers Trust Co., N.Y. (1967–1969) and American Sugar Co. (1962–1969) Jan. 1976), and apparently for an even shorter time, the Boise Cascade Corp. and International Harvester Co.	BT, Foreign Policy Association (1963–1969)	E
Ambassador to West Germany					
Martin J. Hillenbrand (1972–early 1977)		SEE ENTRY UNDER NIXON ADMINISTRATION			NE
Ambassador to Soviet Union					
Walter J. Stoessel, Jr. (Jan. 1974–early 1977)		SEE ENTRY UNDER NIXON ADMINISTRATION			NE

FORD ADMINISTRATION (continued)

Officeholder	College Education	Prior Governmental Experience	Primary Non-governmental Occupation	Important Secondary Economic Affiliations	Family and Other Socio-Economic Ties	Other Pertinent Information	Elite or Non-Elite Status
Chief, U.S. liaison office, China							
George H. W. Bush, Texas (June 1974– Jan. 1976)	Yale Univ.	Ambassador to UN (1971–1972); Texas Congressman (1967–1971)	P or BC, Zapata Off-Shore Co., Texas (1956–1966)	BD, Zapata Off-Shore Co. (1966–1967) and Camco, Inc., Texas (1960–1966)		Chrm., Republican National Committee (1973–1974)	E
Thomas S. Gates, Jr., N.Y., orig. Pa. (Mar. 1976– early 1977)	Univ. of Pa.	Sec. of Defense (1959–1961); Sec. of the Navy (1957–1959); Under Sec. of Navy (1953–1957)	P, BC, or CEC, Morgan Guaranty Trust Co., N.Y.C. (1961–1971); ptr., Drexel & Co., Philadelphia investment banking firm (1940–1953)	BD, Scott Paper Co. (1961–1976), Campbell Soup Co. (1961–1976), GE (1963–1976), Cities Service Co. (1962–1976), Bethlehem Steel Corp. (1970–1976), Smith, Kline & French Laboratories, Pa. (1962–1976), Insurance Co. of North America, Philadelphia (1962–1976), and Morgan Guaranty Trust Co. (1971–1973)			E

504

Ambassador to NATO				
David K. E. Bruce, Md. (Oct. 1974–Jan. 1976)	Princeton Univ. and Univ. of Va. (not complete)	U.S. liaison off., Communist China (1972–1974); U.S. representative to Vietnam Peace Talks (1971–1972); Ambassador to Great Britain (1961–1969); other diplomatic posts in post-WWII period	Onetime Baltimore and Pittsburgh businessman (1928–1940)	Businessman brother, James Bruce, on many major boards of directors up to about 1970	E
Robert Strausz-Hupe, Pa. (Feb. 1976–early 1977)	Coll. educ. abroad (but Ph.D., Univ. of Pa.)	Ambassador to Sweden (1974–1976); Ambassador to Belgium (1972–1974); and Ambassador to Ceylon (1970–1972)	Professor of political science, Univ. of Pa. (1946 on)	Wed daughter of long-deceased T. DeWitt Cuyler, former gen. counsel of Pa. RR and BC of Commercial Trust Co. of Philadelphia, who also once served on many major corporate boards	E?

CARTER ADMINISTRATION (1977–1980)

Officeholder	College Education	Prior Governmental Experience	Primary Non-governmental Occupation	Important Secondary Economic Affiliations	Family and Other Socio-Economic Ties	Other Pertinent Information	Elite or Non-Elite Status
President							
James E. Carter, Jr., Ga. (Jan. 1979 on)	U.S. Naval Academy	Governor of Ga. (1971–1974); state senator (1962–1966); U.S. naval officer (1947–53)	Plains, Ga., peanut farmer and warehouseman (1953–1977)			Member, Trilateral Commission (1973–1976)	E
Secretary of State							
Cyrus R. Vance, N.Y. (Jan. 1977 on)	Yale Univ.	Dep. Sec. of Defense (1964–1967); Sec. of Army (1962–1964); gen. counsel, Defense Dept. (1961–1962)	Ptr., N.Y.C. law firm of Simpson, Thacher & Bartlett (1956–1961, 1967–1977)	BD, IBM, (1969–1977), Aetna Life & Casualty Co. (1968–1975), Pan-American World Airways (1969–1977), New York Times Co. (1974–1977), and One William Street Fund (1975–1976)	Married member of W. & J. Sloane family; father-in-law on BT of Atlantic Mutual Insurance Co. (until 1966 when he reached his early 80s); daughter married son of James H. Higgins, P or BC, Mellon Bank (since 1971) and dir. of Gulf Oil Corp. (since 1971)	Member, Trilateral Commission (1973–1976); VC, Council on Foreign Relations, (1973–1976); BT, director, 1968–1976); BT, Rockefeller Foundation (1970–1976; BC, 1975–76); BT, Urban Institute (mid-1970s)	E

506

					E
Secretary of Treasury					
W. Michael Blumenthal, Mich. (Jan. 1977–Aug. 1979)	Univ. of Cal. at Berkeley (Ph.D., Princeton Univ.)	President's Dep. Special Representative for Trade Negotiations (1963–1967); Dep. Asst. Sec. of State for Economic Affairs (1961–1963)	High off., Bendix Corp. (1967–1977; BC and P, 1972–1977); VP, Crown Cork International Corp. (1957–1961)	BD, Equitable Life Assurance Society (1972–1976)	Member, Trilateral Commission (1973–1975); dir., Council on Foreign Relations (1972–1976); trustee, Rockefeller Foundation (1973–1976); trustee, CED (1973–1976)
G. William Miller, R.I. (Aug. 1979 on)	U.S. Coast Guard Academy	Chrm., Board of Governors, Federal Reserve System (1978–1979)	P or BC, Textron, Inc. (1960–1978; lesser company official, 1956–1960)	BD, Federal Reserve Bank of Boston (1971–1978), Allied Chemical Corp. (1973–1978), and Federated Department Stores (1977–1978)	Chrm., Conference Board (1976–1978; BT, 1973–1976); active member, Business Council (1971–1978)

507

CARTER ADMINISTRATION (continued)

Officeholder	College Education	Prior Governmental Experience	Primary Non-governmental Occupation	Important Secondary Economic Affiliations	Family and Other Socio-Economic Ties	Other Pertinent Information	Elite or Non-Elite Status
Secretary of Defense							
Harold Brown, Cal. (Jan. 1977 on)	Columbia Univ. (also Ph.D., Columbia University)	Sec. of Air Force (1965–1969); lesser Defense Dept posts (1961–1965)	P, Cal. Institute of Technology (1969–1977); Univ. of Cal. (Berkeley) physicist (1951–1961)	BD, IBM (1972–1976), Times-Mirror Co. (1972–1976), Beekman Instruments, Inc., Cal. (1976), and Schroders, Ltd., of Great Britain (1970–1976)		Member, Trilateral Commission (1973–1976)	E
Attorney General							
Griffin B. Bell, Ga. (Jan. 1977–Aug. 1979)	Southwestern Coll., Ga. (not complete); LLB, Mercer Univ.	U.S. circuit court judge (1961–1976); high administrative aide to Governor of Ga. (1959–1961)	Ptr., Atlanta law firm of King & Spalding (1953–1961, Mar. 1976–Jan. 1977)				E

Benjamin R. Civiletti, Md. (Aug 1979 on)	Johns Hopkins Univ.	Asst. U.S. Attorney for Md. (1962–1964)	Ptr., Baltimore law firm of Venable, Baetjer & Howard (1970–1977; member of firm, 1964–1970)		E
Secretary of the Interior					
Cecil D. Andrus, Idaho (Jan. 1977 on)	Ore. State Univ. (not complete)	Governor of Idaho (1971–1977); state legislator (1961–1966, 1969–1970)	Gen. mgr., Paul Revere Life Insurance Co., Idaho (1969–1970)		NE
Secretary of Agriculture					
Robert S. Bergland, Minn. (Jan. 1977 on)	Univ. of Minn. (not complete)	Minn. Congressman (1971–1977); midwestern off., U.S. Dept. of Agriculture (1961–1968)	Minn. farmer (1950 on); field representative, Minnesota Farmers Union (1948–1950)		NE
Secretary of Commerce					
Juanita M. Kreps, N.C. (Jan. 1977– Nov. 1979)	Berea Coll., Ky. (also Ph.D., Duke Univ.)	VP, Duke Univ. (1973–1977); professor of economics, Duke Univ. (1948 on)		BD, North Carolina National Bank (1975–1976), Eastman Kodak Co. (1975–1976), J. C. Penney Co. (1972–1976), R. J. Reynolds Industries, Inc.	E

CARTER ADMINISTRATION (continued)

Officeholder	College Education	Prior Governmental Experience	Primary Non-governmental Occupation	Important Secondary Economic Affiliations	Family and Other Socio-Economic Ties	Other Pertinent Information	Elite or Non-Elite Status
Kreps (continued)				(1976), and Western Electric Co., sub. of AT&T (1974–76)			
Philip M. Klutznick, Ill. (Jan, 1980 on)	Univ. of Kansas and Univ. of Nebraska (not complete)	U.S. representative on Economic & Social Council of UN (1961–1963)	Limited ptr., Salomon Bros. (1974–1979); founder and head, Urban Investment & Development Co., Chicago real estate firm (late 1940s–early 1970s); BC, American Bank & Trust Co., N.Y.C. (1963–1974)	BD, MGIC Investment Corp. (1968–1979)	Son, Thomas J. Klutznick, chrm., Urban Investment & Development Co. since its merger into the Aetna Life & Casualty Co. in 1970	BD, CED (1964–1979, VC 1976–1979)	E
Secretary of Labor							
F. Ray Marshall, Texas (Jan. 1977 on)	Millsaps Coll., Miss. (also Ph.D., Univ. of Cal. at Berkeley)		Professor of economics, Univ. of Texas (1969–1977, 1962–1967), Univ. of Ky. (1967–1969), and La. State Univ. (1957–1962)				NE

Position	Name	Education	Career		Boards
Secretary of Health, Education, and Welfare	Joseph A. Califano, Jr., Wash, D.C. (Jan. 1977–Aug. 1979)	Holy Cross Coll.	Special Asst. to President Johnson (1965–1969); second-tier Defense Dept. off. (1961–1965)	Ptr., Washington law firm of Williams, Connally & Califano (1971–1977); ptr., Washington law firm of Arnold & Porter (1969–1971); assoc., Dewey, Ballantine, Bushby, Palmer & Wood, NYC (1958–61)	E
	Patricia Roberts Harris (Aug. 1979 on)		SEE FOLLOWING ENTRY		E
Secretary of Housing and Urban Development	Patricia Roberts Harris, Wash, D.C. (Jan. 1977–Aug. 1979)	Howard Univ.	Ambassador to Luxembourg (1965–1967)	Ptr., Washington law firm of Fried, Frank, Harris, Shriver & Kampelman (1970–1977); dean, Howard	E, BD, IBM (1971–1976), Scott Paper Co. (1972–1976), and Chase Manhattan BT, Twentieth Century Fund (1969–1977)

CARTER ADMINISTRATION (continued)

Officeholder	College Education	Prior Governmental Experience	Primary Non-governmental Occupation	Important Secondary Economic Affiliations	Family and Other Socio-Economic Ties	Other Pertinent Information	Elite or Non-Elite Status
Harris *(continued)*			Univ. (1969); law professor, Howard Univ. (1961–1965, 1967–1969)	Bank (1971–1976)			
Moon Landrieu, La. (Sept 1979 on)	Loyola Univ.	Mayor of New Orleans (1970–1978); city councilman (1966–1970); state legislator (1960–1965)	P, Joseph C. Canizaro Interests, Inc, New Orleans real estate firm (1978–1979); ptr., New Orleans law firm of Landrieu, Calogero & Kronlage (1958–1969); individual New Orleans lawyer (1954-1958)				?
Secretary of Transportation							
Brockman Adams, Wash. (Jan. 1977– July 1979)	Univ. of Wash.	Wash. Congressman (1965–1977); U.S. attorney, western district Washington (1961–1964)	Independent Seattle lawyer (1965–1977); member, Seattle law firm of LeSourd, Patton &				NE

512

Neil S. Goldschmidt, Wash., D.C. (Aug. 1979 on)	Univ. of Oregon	Mayor of Portland, Ore. (1973–1979); city councilman (1971–1972)	Portland attorney (1967–1972, apparently mostly legal aid practice) Adams and predecessor concern (1952–1961)	NE

Secretary of Energy

James R. Schlesinger, Wash., D.C. (Aug. 1977– Aug. 1979)	Harvard Univ. (also Ph.D., Harvard Univ.)	Asst. to President for energy affairs (Jan.–Aug. 1977); Sec. of Defense (1973–1975); dir., CIA (Feb.–July 1973); chrm., AEC (1971–1973); second-tier off., Bureau of Budget and OMB (1969–1971)	Visiting scholar, Johns Hopkins School for Advanced International Studies and Georgetown Univ. Center for Strategic and International Studies (1976–1977); staff member, Rand Corp. (1963–1967); professor of economics, Univ. of Va. (1956–63)	BD, Corning Glass Works (1976–1977)	E

CARTER ADMINISTRATION (continued)

Officeholder	College Education	Prior Governmental Experience	Primary Non-governmental Occupation	Important Secondary Economic Affiliations	Family and Other Socio-Economic Ties	Other Pertinent Information	Elite or Non-Elite Status
Charles W. Duncan, Jr., Texas (Aug. 1979 on)	Rice Univ.	Dep. Sec. of Defense (1977–1979)	Chrm, Rotan Mosle Financial Corp., Tex. (1974–1977); P, Coca-Cola Co., Ga. (1971–1974; lesser company off., 1964–1971); P or BC, Duncan Foods Co., Tex. (1958–1964; lesser company off, 1948–1958)	BD, Coca-Cola Co. (1974–1976), Southern Rwy. (1972–1976), Great Southern Corp. (1973–1976), and A.P.S. subsidiary of Gulf & Western Industries, Inc. (1977)	Brother, John H. Duncan, on BD of Gulf & Western Industries (1961–1979), Houston Natural Gas Corp. (1968–1979), Texas Commerce Bankshares, Inc. (1975–1979), and Tracor, Inc. (1973–1979)		E
Secretary of Education							
Shirley M. Hufstedler, Cal. (Dec. 1979 on)	Univ. of N.M.	Judge, U.S. Court of Appeals (1968–1979); judge, Cal. Court of Appeal (1966–1968); judge, L.A. Superior Court (1961–1966)	Member, L.A. law firm of Beardsley, Hufstedler & Kemble (1951–1961)		Husband a longtime partner in law firm of Beardsley, Hufstedler & Kemble	BT, Aspen Institute (1976–1979) and Colonial Williamsburg Foundation (1976–1979)	E?

Ambassador to Great Britain			
Kingman Brewster, Conn. (Apr. 1977 on)	Yale Univ.	P, Yale Univ. (1963–1977); provost, Yale Univ. (1961–1963); professor of law, Yale Univ. (1953–1960); asst. professor of law, Yale Univ. (1950–1953)	BT, Carnegie Endowment for International Peace (mid-1970s) and Urban Institute (1976–1977) E
Ambassador to France			
Arthur A. Hartman, Wash., D.C. (Apr. 1977)	Harvard Univ.	Career diplomat (1952–1977); ECA official (1948–1952)	NE
Ambassador to West Germany			
William J. Stoessel, Jr., Wash., D.C. (Sept 1976 on)	Stanford Univ.	Career diplomat (1942 on); Ambass. to Soviet Union (1974–1976); Asst. Sec. of State for European Affairs (1972–1974)	NE

CARTER ADMINISTRATION (continued)

Officeholder	College Education	Prior Governmental Experience	Primary Non-governmental Occupation	Important Secondary Economic Affiliations	Family and Other Socio-Economic Ties	Other Pertinent Information	Elite or Non-Elite Status
Ambassador to Soviet Union							
Malcolm Toon, Wash., D.C. (Sept. 1976–July 1979)	Tufts Univ.	Career diplomat (1946 on)					NE
Thomas J. Watson, Jr., N.Y. (Oct. 1979 on)	Brown Univ.		CEC, IBM (1971–1977); BC, IBM (1961–1971); P, IBM (1952–1961); lesser company off. (1937–1940, 1946–1952)	BD, Pan-American World Airways (1971–1977), Time, Inc. (1975–1977), and Bankers Trust Co. (1948–1975)	Brother-in-law, John N. Irwin II, on BD of IBM (1975 on)		E
Ambassador to NATO							
W. Tapley Bennett, Jr., Wash., D.C. (Apr. 1977 on)	Univ. of Georgia	Career diplomat (1941 on)					NE

516

Ambassador (or liaison officer) to China				
Leonard Woodcock, Mich. (May 1977 on)	Wayne State Univ. (not complete)	P, United Auto Workers (1970–1977); lesser union official (1940–1970)	Member, Trilateral Commission (1973–1976)	E

Appendix B

Primary Background Data of
Supreme Court Justices:
1933–1980

SUCCESSION OF U.S. SUPREME COURT JUSTICES (1933–1980)

Chief Justice	Associate Justices							
Charles Evans Hughes (*1930–1941*)	W. Van Devanter (*1910–1937*)	James McReynolds (*1914–1941*)	Louis D. Brandeis (*1916–1939*)	George Sutherland (*1922–1938*)	Pierce Butler (*1922–1939*)	Harlan F. Stone (*1925–1941*)	Owen J. Roberts (*1930–1945*)	Benjamin Cardozo (*1932–1938*)
	Hugo Black (1937–1971)			Stanley F. Reed (1938–1957)				Felix Frankfurter (1939–1962)
			William O. Douglas (1939–1975)		Frank Murphy (1940–1949)			
Harlan F. Stone (1941–1946)		James F. Byrnes (1941–1942)				Robert H. Jackson (1941–1954)		
		Wiley Rutledge (1943–1949)						
Fred M. Vinson (1946–1953)							Harold H. Burton (1945–1958)	
		Sherman Minton (1949–1956)			Tom C. Clark (1949–1967)			
Earl Warren (1953–1969)						John M. Harlan (1955–1971)		

William J.
Brennan
(*1956* through
1979)

Charles E.
Whittaker
(*1957*–1962)

Potter
Stewart
(*1959* through
1979)

Arthur J.
Goldberg
(*1962*–1965)

Abe Fortas
(*1965*–1969)

Harry
Blackmun
(*1970* through
1979)

Byron R.
White
(*1962* through
1979)

Thurgood
Marshall
(*1967* through
1979)

William H.
Rehnquist
(*1972* through
1979)

John Paul
Stevens
(*1975* through
1979)

Lewis F.
Powell, Jr.
(*1972* through
1979)

Warren E.
Burger
(*1969* through
1979)

Note: Incumbents are indicated by italicized initial date of appointment.

U.S. SUPREME COURT

Officeholder	College Education	Prior Governmental Experience	Primary Non-governmental Occupation	Important Secondary Economic Affiliations	Family and Other Socio-Economic Ties	Other Pertinent Information	Elite or Non-Elite status
Chief Justice							
Charles Evans Hughes, N.Y. (*1930*–June 1941)	Brown Univ.	Chief Justice, U.S. Supreme Court (1930 on); judge, Permanent Court of International Justice (1929–1930); U.S. Sec. of State (1921–1925); Assoc. Justice, U.S. Supreme Court (1910–1916); Governor of N.Y. (1907–1910)	Ptr., Hughes, Rounds, Schurman & Dwight, N.Y.C. law firm (1917–1921, 1925–1929)		Son, C. E. Hughes, Jr. (who was a member of the same law firm), on BD of New York Life Insurance Co. (1931–1934); former law ptr., R. E. Dwight, on BD of Merck & Co. (1929–1937) and various lesser concerns	BT, Rockefeller Foundation (1917–1921, 1926–1928); councillor, National Industrial Conference Board (late 1920s)	E
Assoc. Justice							
Willis Van Devanter, Wyo. (*1910*–June 1937)	DePauw Univ., Ind.	Judge, U.S. Circuit Court of Appeals (1903–1910); Asst. U.S. Attorney General (1897–1903)	Longtime Cheyenne, Wyo. lawyer; ptr., law firm of Lacey and Van Devanter (1891–1897)				?

522

James C. McReynolds, Tenn., later N.Y. (*1914*–Jan. 1941)	Vanderbilt Univ.	U.S. Attorney General (1913–1914); special asst., U.S. Attorney General (1907–1912); Asst. U.S. Attorney General (1903–1907)	Individual New York law practice (1912–1913); assoc. N.Y.C. law firm of Cravath, Henderson & deGersdorff (Jan. 1907); Nashville, Tenn. lawyer (1884–1903); VP, City Savings Bank, Nashville (1900–probably 1903)		?
Louis D. Brandeis, Mass. (*1916*–Feb. 1939)		Assoc. Justice, U.S. Supreme Court (1916 on)	Ptr., Boston law firm of Brandeis, Dunbar & Nutter (1897–1916)	BD, United Shoe Machinery Corp. (1899–1906)	Longtime advocate of liberal or progressive causes (1906–1916) NE?
George Sutherland, Utah (*1922*–Jan. 1938)	Brigham Young Univ.	U.S. Supreme Court Justice (1922 on); U.S. Senator, Utah (1905–1917); Utah Congressman (1901–1903)	Washington lawyer (1917–1922); Salt Lake City lawyer (1893–1917); VP, Home Trust & Savings Co., Salt Lake City (about 1910–1926)	BD, Deseret Savings Bank, Salt Lake City (at least 1911–1922) and Home Trust & Savings Co. (1927–1928)	BT, Carnegie Endowment for International Peace (1920–1925); P, American Bar Association (1917) E

523

Officeholder	College Education	Prior Governmental Experience	Primary Non-governmental Occupation	Important Secondary Economic Affiliations	Family and Other Socio-Economic Ties	Other Pertinent Information	Elite or Non-Elite Status
Pierce Butler, Minn. (1922–Nov. 1939)	Carleton Coll.	Special counsel, Food & Drug Administration and Justice Dept. (first few years of Taft administration)	Ptr., St. Paul law firm of Butler, Mitchell & Doherty (1893–1922)	BD, Capital National Bank, St. Paul (1917–1921) and St. Paul Gas Light Co., subsidiary of American Light & Traction Co. (at least 1921–1923)	Son, Francis D. Butler, member of father's former law firm, VP of Northern States Contracting Co. (1930 on) and BD, Northwestern Trust Co., St. Paul (1930 through 1939)		E
Harlan F. Stone, N.Y. (1925–July 1941)	Amherst Coll.	U.S. Attorney General (1924–1925)	Ptr., Sullivan & Cromwell, N.Y.C. law firm (1923–1924); ptr., N.Y.C. law firm of Satterlee, Canfield & Stone (up to 1923); dean, Columbia Univ. Law School (1910–1923)	Off. or dir., Atlanta & Charlotte Air Line Rwy. (1909–1924)			E?

524

Owen J. Roberts, Pa. (*1930*–July 1945)	Univ. of Pa.	Investigating and prosecuting off., Teapot Dome scandal (1924–1929)	Ptr., Philadelphia law firm of Roberts & Montgomery and predecessor firm (1902–1930); professor, Univ. of Pa. Law School (1898–1918)	BD, Equitable Life Assurance Society, N.Y. (1926–1930), Bell Telephone Co. of Pa. (1926–1929), AT&T (1929–1930), and Franklin Life Insurance Co., affiliate of Home Insurance Co. of N.Y.C. (1924–1930)	E Nephew's father, Thomas S. Gates, on BD of Pa. RR (1931–1945), United Gas Improvement Co. (1928–1943), and Penn Mutual Life Insurance Co. (1931 through 1945)
Benjamin N. Cardozo, N.Y. (*1932*–July 1938)	Columbia Univ.	Chief judge, N.Y. Court of Appeals (1928–1932); judge on same court (1914–1928)	N.Y.C. lawyer (1892–1914); ptr., Cardozo Brothers (up to 1903); then with Simpson, Werner & Cardozo		NE
Hugo L. Black, Ala. (Aug. 1937–Sept. 1971)	Univ. of Ala. (law school only)	U.S. Senator, Ala. (1927–1937)	Birmingham, Ala., lawyer (1907–1927, except WW II years)		NE
Stanley F. Reed, Ky. (Jan. 1938–Feb. 1957)	Kentucky Wesleyan Coll. and Yale Univ.	U.S. Solicitor General (1935–1938); gen. counsel, RFC (1932–1935);	Maysville and Ashland, Ky., lawyer (1910–1929)	BD, Bank of Maysville (1919–1932)	NE

Officeholder	College Education	Prior Governmental Experience	Primary Non-governmental Occupation	Important Secondary Economic Affiliations	Family and Other Socio-Economic Ties	Other Pertinent Information	Elite or Non-Elite Status
Reed *(continued)*		counsel, Federal Farm Board (1929–1932); state legislator (1912–1916)					
Felix Frankfurter, Mass., orig. N.Y. (Jan. 1939–Aug. 1962)	City College of N.Y.	No recent noteworthy governmental experience (although had served as a War Dept. off. [1911–1914], and was later an informal New Deal advisor); Asst. U.S. Attorney, southern district, N.Y. (1906–1910)	Harvard Univ. law professor (1914–1939)				NE?
William O. Douglas, Conn., orig. Wash. (Apr. 1939–Nov. 1975)	Whitman Coll., Wash.	Chrm. or member, SEC (1936–1939); member of staff, SEC (1934–1936)	Law professor, Yale Univ. (1929–1934) and Columbia Univ. (1927–1928); Yakima, Wash., lawyer (1926–1927);				NE

526

			assoc., N.Y.C. law firm of Cravath, Henderson & deGersdorff (1925–1926)		
Frank Murphy, Mich. (Jan. 1940–July 1949)	Univ. of Michigan	U.S. Attorney General (1939–1940); Governor of Mich. (1936–1938); gov.-gen. of Philippine Islands (1933–1936); Detroit mayor (1930–1933) and municipal judge (1923–1930)	Detroit lawyer (1914–1917, 1920–1923)		NE
James F. Byrnes, S.C. (June 1941–Oct. 1942)		U.S. Senator, S.C. (1931–1941); S.C. Congressman (1911–1925)	Longtime Aiken and Spartanburg, S.C. lawyer (1903–1941)		NE?
Chief Justice					
Harlan Fiske Stone, N.Y. (July 1941–Apr. 1946)	Amherst Coll.	Assoc. Justice, U.S. Supreme Court (1925–1941); U.S. Attorney General (1924–1925)	Ptr., Sullivan & Cromwell, N.Y.C. (1923–1924), and Satterlee, Canfield & Stone (up to 1923); dean, Columbia Law School (1910–1923)	Off. or dir., Atlanta & Charlotte Air Line Rwy. (1909–1924)	NE?

Officeholder	College Education	Prior Governmental Experience	Primary Nongovernmental Occupation	Important Secondary Economic Affiliations	Family and Other Socio-Economic Ties	Other Pertinent Information	Elite or Non-Elite Status
Associate Justice							
Robert H. Jackson, N.Y. (July 1941–Oct. 1954)		U.S. Attorney General (1940–1941); U.S. Solicitor General (1938–1940); other federal posts (1934–1938)	Longtime Jamestown, N.Y. lawyer (1913 on); VP and gen. counsel, Jamestown Street Rwy. and Jamestown, Westfield & Northwestern RR (1930–1938)	BD, Bank of Jamestown (1919–1941) and Jamestown Telephone Corp. (at least 1926–1940)		BT of Twentieth Century Fund (1938–41)	NE?
Wiley B. Rutledge, Iowa (Feb. 1943–Sept. 1949)	Univ. of Wisconsin	Judge, U.S. Court of Appeals (1939–1943)	Law school professor and dean, Univ. of Colorado, Washington Univ., St. Louis, and Univ. of Iowa (1924–1939)				NE
Harold H. Burton, Ohio (Sept. 1945–Oct 1958)	Bowdoin Coll.	U.S. Senator, Ohio (1941–1945); mayor of Cleveland (1935–1940); state legislator and municipal official	Former Cleveland lawyer; ptr., Andrews, Hadden & Burton (1932–1935), and Day, Day & Wilkins (1923–1929)	BD, Ohio Trust Co., a small Cleveland concern (1925–1926)			NE

528

Chief Justice				
Frederick M. Vinson, Ky. (June 1946–Sept. 1953)	Centre Coll., Ky.	Sec. of the Treasury (1945–1946); various high federal defense posts (1943–1945); judge, U.S. Court of Appeals (1938–1943); Ky. Congressman (1924–1929, 1931–1938)	Longtime Ashland, Ky., lawyer	NE
Associate Justice				
Tom C. Clark, Texas (Aug. 1949–June 1967)	Univ. of Texas	U.S. Attorney General (1945–1949); various Justice Dept. posts (1937–1945)	Dallas lawyer, both individual practice and small law firm (1922–1937)	NE?
Sherman Minton, Ind. (Oct. 1949–Oct. 1956)	Indiana Univ.	Judge, U.S. Court of Appeals (1941–1949); U.S. Senator, Ind. (1935–1941)	Onetime New Albany, Ind., ptr. in law firm of Stotensburg, Weathers, Minton & Phillips (1922–1925, 1928–1933); Miami law practice (1925–1928)	NE

Officeholder	College Education	Prior Governmental Experience	Primary Non-governmental Occupation	Important Secondary Economic Affiliations	Family and Other Socio-Economic Ties	Other Pertinent Information	Elite or Non-Elite status
Chief Justice							
Earl Warren, Cal. (Oct. 1953–June 1969)	Univ. of Cal., Berkeley	Governor of Cal. (1943–1953); Attorney General of Cal. (1939–1943); various local govt. posts (Alameda County district attorney, 1925–1939)	Oakland lawyer (1914–1917)				NE
Assoc. Justice							
John M. Harlan, N.Y. (Mar. 1955–Dec. 1971)	Princeton Univ.	U.S. Circuit Court judge (Mar. 1954–Mar. 1955); chief counsel, N.Y. Crime Commission (1951–1952)	Ptr., N.Y.C. law firm of Root, Ballantine, Harlan, Bushby & Palmer and predecessor concerns (1932–1954, except WW II years)	BD, United States Trust Co., N.Y.C. (1947–1954)			E
William J. Brennan, N.J. (Oct. 1956–1980)	Univ. of Pa.	Judge, N.J. Supreme Court (1952–1956); judge, N.J. Superior Court (1949–1952)	Ptr., Newark, N.J., law firm of Pitney, Hardin, Ward & Brennan (1937–49, except WW II years)			Roman Catholic and Democrat; deceased father one of Newark's top labor leaders	?

Name	Education	Position	Prior practice	Other	Rating
Charles Whittaker, Mo. (Mar. 1957–Apr. 1962)	(got law degree from night school)	U.S. federal district and appeals court judge (1954–1957)	Ptr., Kansas City law firm of Watson, Ess, Whittaker, Marshall & Enggas (1930–1954)	Law ptr., Harry N. Ess, BD, City National Bank & Trust Co., Kansas City (1941 through 1962)	E
Potter Stewart, Ohio (Oct. 1958–1980)	Yale Univ.	U.S. Circuit Court judge (1954–1958)	Ptr., Cincinnati law firm of Dinsmore, Shohl, Dinsmore & Todd (1947–1954); assoc., N.Y. law firm of Debevoise, Stevenson, Plimpton & Page (1941–1942, 1945–1947)		E
Byron R. White, Colo. (Apr. 1962–1980)—suc-	Univ. of Colorado	Dep. Attorney General (1961–1962)	Ptr., Denver law firm of Lewis, Grant & Davis (1950–1961)	Head, Citizens for Kennedy organization (1960); organizer of Colorado for Kennedy clubs (1959–1960)	NE
Arthur J. Goldberg, Ill. (Sept. 1962–July 1965)—	Crane Jr. Coll. and later Northwestern Univ.	Sec. of Labor (1961–1962)	Ptr., Goldberg, Devoe, Shadur & Mikva, Chicago law firm (1947–1961); gen. coun-	BD, Amalgamated Trust & Savings Bank, Chicago (1948–1961)	NE

BT, Carnegie Endowment for International Peace (1958 through 1965)

Officeholder	College Education	Prior Governmental Experience	Primary Non-governmental Occupation	Important Secondary Economic Affiliations	Family and Other Socio-Economic Ties	Other Pertinent Information	Elite or Non-Elite Status
Goldberg (continued)			sel, United Steelworkers of America (1948–1961), CIO (1948–1955), and industrial union dept., AFL-CIO (1955–1961)				
Abe Fortas, Wash., D.C., orig. Tenn. (Aug. 1965–May 1969)	Southwestern Coll., Tenn.	Under Sec. of the Interior (1942–46); lesser Interior Dept. posts (1931–1942)	Ptr., Washington law firm of Arnold, Fortas & Porter (1946–1965)	VP and BD, Great-America Corp., Texas (1962–65); BD, Federated Department Stores, Inc. (1961–65), VP, July–Aug. 1965), Sucrest Corp. and predecessor firm (1946–65) and Madison National Bank of Wash, D.C. (1964–65)			E
Thurgood Marshall, N.Y., orig. Md. (Sept.	Lincoln Univ., Pa.	U.S. Solicitor General (1965–1967); judge, U.S. Circuit Court of	Special counsel, NAACP (1938–1950); director-counsel, NAACP			First black appointed to U.S. Supreme Court	NE

1967–1980			Appeals (1961–1965)	Legal Defense and Education Fund (1940–1961)	?

Chief Justice

Warren E. Burger, Minn. (June 1969–1980)	Univ. of Minn. (not complete, but degree St Paul Univ. law-school)	Judge, U.S. Court of Appeals (1956–1969); Asst. U.S. Attorney General (1953–1956)	Ptr., Faricy, Burger, Moore & Costello and predecessor firm, St Paul (1935–1953)	

Assoc. Justice

Harry A. Blackmun, Minn. (June 1970–1980)	Harvard Univ.	Judge, U.S. Court of Appeals (1959–1970)	Resident counsel, Mayo Clinic, Minn. (1950–1959); ptr., Dorsey, Owen, Barker, Scott & Barber, Minneapolis law firm (1939–1950)	BD, Kahler Corp., in which Mayo Clinic apparently had a significant stake (1958–1964)	?
William H. Rehnquist, Ariz. (Dec. 1971–1980)	Stanford Univ.	Asst. U.S. Attorney General (1969–1971)	Ptr., Phoenix law firm of Powers & Rehnquist (1960–1969); member, other Phoenix law firms (1953–1960)		NE

533

Officeholder	College Education	Prior Governmental Experience	Primary Non-governmental Occupation	Important Secondary Economic Affiliations	Family and Other Socio-Economic Ties	Other Pertinent Information	Elite or Non-Elite Status
Lewis F. Powell, Jr., Va. (Dec. 1971–1980)	Washington & Lee Univ.		Ptr., Richmond, Va., law firm of Hunton, Williams, Gay, Powell & Gibson (1937–1971)	BD, Commonwealth Natural Gas Corp. (1954–1971), United Va. Bankshares, Inc., and predecessor concern (1961–1971), Richmond Corp. (1967–1971), Chesapeake & Potomac Telephone Co. of Va. (1964–1971), Ethyl Corp. and predecessor company (early 1950s–1971), and Philip Morris, Inc. (1965–1971)		BT, Colonial Williamsburg Foundation (1955–1978); also its BC (1974 to 1978)	E
John Paul Stevens, Ill. (Dec. 1975–1980)	Univ. of Chicago	U.S. Circuit Court judge (1970–1975)	Ptr., Chicago law firm of Rothschild, Hart, Stevens & Barry (1952–1970)				E?

534

Index

Abplanalp, Robert, 239, 286
Acheson, Dean, 57, 79, 81–82, 102–03, 107, 111, 114, 146, 197, 208, 209, 216, 222, 364, 418; his law partners, 82, 120
Adams, Brock, 325, 338, 340, 512–13
Adams, Charles F., 9, 28
Adams, Frederick B., 41, 55
Adams, John, 393
Adams, Sherman, 162
Agnew, Spiro, 286
Agribusiness, 136–37, 248, 290
Ailes, Stephen, 199–200, 465
Akers, Robert O., 302
Alaskan oil pipeline controversy, 263–64, 295
Albany Regency, 373
Aldrich, Winthrop W., 16, 63, 119, 140–42, 160, 162, 446–47
Alexander, Clifford L., 321
Allen, George E., 115
Allende, Salvador (overthrow), 266–67, 297
Alperovitz, Gar, 91, 117
Altman, Roger, 320
Altschul, Charles, 18
Altschul, Frank, 24, 125
America First Committee, 111
American Assembly, 126
American Association for Labor Legislation, 42, 43, 64
American Enterprise Association, 160, 161, 1963, 224, 284; *also see* American Enterprise Institute for Public Policy Research
American Enterprise Institute for Public Policy Research, 244, 258, 288, 293, 299, 309–10, 344
American Farm Bureau Federation, 29, 78, 88, 137, 160, 323
American Federation of Labor (AFL), 13, 43;
  AFL-CIO, 173, 311–12, 334, 343, 349, 393
American International Corp., 24
American Liberty League, 19, 45, 52, 54, 66
Amory, Cleveland, 215
Amory, Robert, Jr., 146

Anderson, Clinton P., 88, 166, 392, 427
Anderson, Dillon, 144, 145, 162, 166
Anderson, Robert B., 129, 131, 133, 152, 156, 159, 166, 196, 224, 242, 436
Andrus, Cecil, 322–23, 393, 509
Annenberg, Walter, 252–53, 291, 393, 489
Anti-poverty program (LBJ), 205, 228
Antitrust activity (U.S.), 205–06, 212–13, 228–29, 264–66
Arkes, Hadley, 101
Armstrong, Anne, 277, 303, 502–03
Ash, Roy, 256, 257, 292
Ashland Oil Co., 337
Astor family, 21, 26, 41, 57
Astor, Vincent, 21, 34, 41, 55, 60
Atlantic Fruit & Sugar Co., 41
Atomic bomb, development and use, 91–93, 117–18
Austin, J. Paul, 314, 315, 345
Austin, Warren, 116–17
Aviation Corp., 22, 31, 55, 57
Axelson, Kenneth, 347

Bacher, Robert, 105
Bailey, Stephen K., 104
Baker, James A., 300
Baker, Newton D., 54–55
Ball, George, 176, 197, 208, 209, 222
Bard, Ralph, 76, 117
Baroody, William J., 244, 309, 310, 325, 344
Barr, Joseph, 225
Barrows, Arthur S., 86
Baruch, Bernard M., 30, 32, 35–36, 55, 60, 61, 62, 81, 88, 107, 114, 117
Batt, William L., 80
Bay of Pigs episode, 185
Bayard, Thomas F., 392
Beam, Jacob, 491
Beard, Charles A., 1, 2
Beard, Dita, 296
Bechtel, Stephen D., 150
Beck, David, 150
Becker, Loftus, 119, 158
Bell, David, 187, 207, 219

535

Bell, Elliott V., 125, 285
Bell, Griffin, 322, 338, 339, 348, 508
Bellush, Bernard, 36
Belmont, August, 392
Bennett, W. Tapley, Jr., 318, 516
Benson, Ezra Taft, 136–37, 160, 442–43
Benson, Lucy Wilson, 317, 346
Benton, William, 110, 114
Bergland, Robert, 323, 348, 509
Bergsten, C. Fred, 320, 347
Berle, Adolf A., 34, 40, 41, 60–61
Bernstein, Barton, 67–68
Bernstein, Irving, 13
Biddle, Francis, 43, 65, 77, 112, 411
Biddle Nicholas, 5, 112
Bingham, Robert W., 31–32, 407
Birmingham, Stephen, 18, 218
Bissell, Richard M., Jr., 100, 120, 146, 185
Black, Eugene, 94, 119, 208, 236
Black, Hugo, 49, 61, 107, 210, 525
Black, Van Lear, 22
Blackmun, Harry, 281, 305, 533
Blaine, James G., 392
Blough, Roger, 234
Blount, Winston, 290
Blumenthal, W. Michael, 311, 319, 338, 340, 355, 356, 507
Bobst, Elmer, 239, 284, 296
Bohlen, Charles, 102, 142, 167, 183, 202, 226, 448, 460
Boldt, George, 261, 294
Bonaparte, Charles J., 389
Borch, Fred, 207, 234, 285
Bork, Robert, 270, 299
Bowie, Robert, 328
Bowles, Chester, 176
Boyd, Alan, 226, 472–73
Braden, Spruille, 114
"Brains trust," 33–35
Brandeis, Louis D., 47, 523
Brandt, Karl, 163, 187
Brannan, Charles F., 88, 427
Brennan, Peter J., 250, 486, 499
Brennan, William J., 153–54, 167, 210, 280, 358, 530
Brewster, Kingman, 318, 515
Brill, Daniel H., 320
Brinegar, Claude S., 252, 488, 501
Brookings Institution, 21, 64, 67, 78, 347, 352
Bross, John A., 146
Brown brothers, Texas (George and Herman), 193, 214, 222, 229
Brown, Edmund G. (Jerry), 313
Brown, Harold, 200, 208, 320–21, 390, 467, 508
Brownell, Herbert, Jr., 135, 153, 160, 286, 441
Brownlee, James F., 126
Bruce, David, K. E., 22, 23, 82, 90, 101, 114, 116, 142, 176, 182, 202, 254, 303, 431, 449, 459, 473, 505

Bruce, Howard, 120
Brucker, Wilbur M., 133, 167, 438
Bruere, Henry, 23, 31, 38, 59
Bruere, Robert, 38
Brundage, Percival, 145
Brush, Matthew C., 22, 24
Bryan, William Jennings, 8, 392
Brzezinski, Zbigniew, 235, 315, 319, 345, 347
Buchanan, James, 5
Buchen, Philip, 300
Bullitt, William C., 33, 60, 408
Bundy, Harvey H., 92, 118, 120, 146, 184
Bundy, McGeorge, 184–85, 218
Bundy, William P., 146, 184, 197, 224, 311
Bunker, Ellsworth, 203, 227, 253–54, 291, 330, 352, 477, 492
Burch, Dean, 289, 294
Bureau of the Budget. *See* U.S. Bureau of Management and Budget
Burger, Warren E., 280, 281, 304, 305, 533
Burgess, W. Randolph, 98, 143, 158–59, 450
Burnham, William H., 126
Burns, Arthur F., 163, 254, 292, 352
Burton, Harold, 108, 528
Bush, George H. W., 254, 277, 292, 302, 492, 504
Bush, Vannevar, 92, 117
Business Advisory Council (Business Council), 18–20, 31, 36–37, 42, 43, 51, 54, 59, 62, 72–73, 79–80, 83, 85, 98–101, 109, 110–111, 113, 114, 117, 132, 135, 149, 159, 165, 166, 173, 188–89, 198, 201, 207–208, 209, 214–15, 226, 229, 230, 234, 235, 236–37, 259, 285–86, 292, 301, 307–309, 314, 315, 340, 356, 387–388, 397
Business Roundtable, 233, 275, 279, 283–84, 292, 304, 308–09, 314, 315, 326, 331, 334–35, 340, 344, 352, 353–54, 356, 387–88
Businessmen's Committee for Tax Reform (1963), 183–84
Butler, Benjamin, 373
Butler, Pierce, 46–47, 66, 523
Butz, Earl, 248, 274, 290, 390, 484, 498
Buzhardt, J. Fred, 271, 298
Byrd, Harry F., 81, 160
Byrd, Harry F., Jr., 159, 254
Byrnes, James F., 60, 92, 107, 113, 417, 526

Cabell, Charles P., 146
Cabot, John M., 164–65
Caffrey, Jefferson, 113, 415, 430
Califano, Joseph A., Jr., 324, 338, 339, 349, 355, 356, 511
Callaway, Howard H., 288, 300
Cambodian invasion, 259; *also see* Vietnamese war
Cameron, Simon, 363
Cardozo, Benjamin, 12, 47, 394, 525
Carswell, G. Harrold, 304

Carswell, Robert, 319–20
Carter, James E., Jr. (Jimmy), 312–58, 382, 387, 506
Casey, William J., 287, 302
Celebrezze, Anthony, 180, 181, 201, 459, 471
Central Intelligence Agency (CIA). *See* U.S. Central Intelligence Agency
Century group, 73, 79, 111
Chadbourne, Thomas L., 30, 58–59, 64
Chaffee, John H., 288
Chapman, Oscar, 58, 88, 426
Charyk, Joseph V., 222
Chile. *See* Allende, Salvador
China-U.S. diplomatic and trade relations, 291–92
Christopher, Warren, 317
Civil rights litigation, 153, 212
Civiletti, Benjamin, 339, 348, 509
Clark, Grenville, 67, 111, 114
Clark, John, D., 104, 121
Clark, Ramsey, 200–01, 469
Clark, Thomas, 87, 108, 122, 211, 425, 529
Clausen, Alden, 314, 315, 347, 356
Clay, Lucius D., 103, 130, 135, 149–50, 156, 163
Claybrook, Joan, 351
Clayton, William, 98, 111, 112, 114, 118, 119, 120
Claytor, W. Graham, 321, 356
Clements, William P., 245–46, 288, 301
Cleveland, Grover, 7, 45, 194, 380, 386
Cleveland, Harlan, 226, 476
Clifford, Clark M., 121, 195, 199, 208, 209, 223, 319, 355, 364, 464
Coca-Cola Co., 314, 321, 322, 324, 343, 345
Cohen, Benjamin, 35, 40, 61
Cohen, Wilbur J., 226, 472
Coker, David, 30, 59
Colby, William, 257, 302
Coleman, Lynn R., 350
Coleman, William T., Jr., 260, 276, 302, 501–02
Colson, Charles, 266, 299
Colt, S. Sloan, 150
Committee for Economic Development (CED), 73, 85, 98–101, 104, 109, 110–111, 116, 121, 127, 135, 149, 159–60, 161, 165, 166, 188–89, 196, 198, 207–208, 217, 223, 233, 234, 236–37, 287, 292, 307, 342, 354, 387–88, 397
Communications Satellite Corp., 191, 204, 221–22, 228
Compton, Karl T., 92, 117
Conant, James B., 92, 142, 449
Conflict of interest, definition, 4
Congress of Industrial Organization (CIO), 65
Connally, John B., 11, 178, 193, 194, 227, 243, 262, 287–88, 453–54, 479
Connally, Tom, 222

Connor, John T., 196, 201, 221, 225, 230, 470
Consumer protection issue (Carter), 334–35
Continental Grain Co., 290
Cook, Donald, 225
Cook, G. Bradford, 294
Cooke, Jay, 363
Coolidge, Calvin, 9, 381
Coolidge, T. Jefferson, 57, 148, 164
Cooper, Richard, 317, 346
Corcoran, Thomas, 35, 40, 61, 84, 195
Cordiner, Ralph J., 80
Council on Foreign Relations, 55, 73–74, 97, 102, 111, 119, 125, 126, 146, 164, 183, 197, 218, 224, 235, 286, 301, 310–311, 319, 342, 387
County Trust Co. of N.Y., 21, 57
Cox, Archibald, 269–70, 299
Cox family (of Atlanta), 345, 347, 357
Cox, James M., 60
Cuban missile crisis, 222
Cullman, Howard S., 56
Cummings, Homer, 27, 58, 402
Cutler, Lloyd, 342, 357
Cutler, Robert, 143, 144, 148, 155
Cutting, Bronson, 29

Dahl, Robert A., 1, 10
Daniels, Josephus, 392
Davis, Chester C., 78, 98, 112
Davis, Donald, 80
Davis, Dwight F., 78, 114
Davis, John W., 12, 55, 56
Davis, Norman H., 55, 56
Dawes family, 74–75, 112
Day, William R., 368
Dean, Arthur H., 208, 209, 219, 224, 229
Dean, Gordon, 105, 217
Dean, John W., 269
Debs, Eugene V., 121
deButts, John D., 315, 316
DeGolyer, E. L., 83, 114, 216, 226
Delano, Frederic A., 21, 30
Delano, Lyman, 21, 32, 40, 41, 55
Dent, Frederick B., 249–50, 274, 291, 485, 498
Dern, George, 27–28, 58, 64, 402
Dewey, Thomas E., 83, 153, 285, 286
Dickinson, John, 40, 59
Dillon, C. Douglas, 140–41, 142, 158, 161, 177, 187, 198, 209, 219, 225, 236, 286, 291, 309, 447, 452
Dillon, Clarence, 157, 216
Dodd, William E., 60, 408–09
Dodge, Joseph M., 145, 163
Domhoff, G. William, 1, 42, 384, 393, 396
Dominican Republic (U.S. intervention), 227
Donovan, Hedley, 342, 357
Donovan, John C., 120, 222
Douglas, James H., Jr., 132, 133, 440
Douglas, Lewis W., 35, 75, 89–90, 98, 111, 118, 162, 164, 392, 430

Douglas, Stephen A., 6
Douglas, William O., 40, 50, 61, 67, 107, 115–16, 210, 526
Douglass, Kingman, 119
Dowling, Walter, 143, 167, 183, 449, 461
Draper, Ernest, 59
Draper, William H., Jr., 91, 433
Dred Scott decision, 6
DuBrul, Stephen M., 225, 302
Dulles, Allen W., 97, 111, 145–46, 147, 155, 164, 185
Dulles, John Foster, 119, 127–28, 135, 151, 155, 164, 166, 434–35
Duncan, Charles W., Jr., 321, 341–42, 348, 356–57, 514
Dunlop, John T., 275, 302, 323, 349, 353, 499
Dunn, James C., 90, 113, 431
du Pont interests, 15, 224, 244
du Pont, Pierre, 19, 25, 62, 167
Durkin Martin P., 137, 138, 160, 444
Dye, Thomas, 315, 384, 396

Early, Stephen, 85
Eberle, William B., 287
Eccles, Mariner S., 28, 40–41, 64
Economic elite, definition, 11
Edge, Walter Evans, 375
Edison, Charles, 28–29, 394, 404
Edwards, Augustin, 297
Ehrlichman, John, 255, 266, 268, 269, 292, 294, 299, 300
Eisenhower, Arthur, 154
Eisenhower, Dwight D., 126–67, 185, 213, 381–82, 387, 389, 392, 434
Eisenhower, Milton, 127
Eizenstat, Stuart, 326–27
Elliott, William Y., 100
Ellsworth, Robert, 301, 493
Energy issue (Carter), 335–38, 353–54
Engelhard, Charles W., 219
Engler, Robert, 263, 278

Fanning, John, 349
Farm Foundation, 136–37
Federal Energy Administration (or Office), 279, 295
Federal Reserve System, 40–41, 63, 121
Finch, Robert, 250–51, 487
Finch, T. Austin, 19, 62
Finletter, Thomas, 86, 101, 183, 226, 424, 462, 475
Flaherty, Peter, 348
Flanders, Ralph E., 111, 149
Flanigan, Horace, 175, 255
Flanigan, Peter, 255–56, 263, 266, 292, 296
Fleischmann, Manly, 120
Flemming, Arthur S., 161, 446
Folsom, Marion, 42, 111, 129, 140, 161, 445

Ford, Gerald R., 272, 273–80, 300–05, 313, 387, 390, 494
Ford, Henry II, 188, 196, 214, 315, 346
Foreign Policy Association, 157, 217
Forrestal, James V., 75, 84, 381, 412, 420
Fortas, Abe, 194–95, 209–210, 211, 223, 230, 280, 372, 532
Foster, William C., 85, 100, 116, 120, 150–51, 186
Fowler, Henry H., 196, 198–99, 217, 225, 464
Franke, William B., 132–33, 167, 439
Frankfurter, Felix, 35, 40, 49, 67, 107, 111, 114, 372, 390, 526
Franklin, George S., Jr., 125, 235, 311
Freeman, Orville S., 180, 181, 187, 200, 456, 469
Frick, Henry Clay, 294
Froehlke, Robert, 288
Fulbright, J. William, 176, 302

Gadsden, Philip H., 44
Gaither, H. Rowan, 150, 165
Galvin, Michael J., 116
Gardner, John, 201, 226, 471
Gardner, O. Max, 82, 116
Garrett, Ray, 294
Garrison, Lloyd D., 43, 64–65
Gates, Artemus L., 76
Gates, Thomas S., Jr., 132, 159, 223, 236, 277, 285, 437, 504
Gavin, James M., 182–83, 460
Geneen, Harold, 169, 265–66, 296
General Dynamics Corp., 189–90
General Motors Corp., 159, 155, 165, passim
Giannini interests, 18, 41
Gibson, Andrew E., 292, 304
Gifford, Walter S., 18, 90, 430
Gilbert, Carl J., 287
Gilpatric, Roswell, 86, 177–78, 190, 217, 221
Glass, Carter, 28, 57, 362
Glass-Steagell Act (1933), 39
Glennan, T. Keith, 121–22, 163
Goelet, Robert W., 23, 41
Goldberg, Arthur, 180, 181, 210–11, 372, 457, 531–32
Goldman, Sachs & Co., 18, 53, 387, 397
Goldschmidt, Neil S., 340–41, 513
Goldwater, Barry, 195–96, 224, 246, 281
Good neighbor policy (FDR), 41–42
Gordon, Kermit, 187, 204, 225, 261
Governmental elite, definition, 2, 11
Grant, Ulysses S., 379, 389
Gray, Gordon, 85, 144, 145, 422
Green, William, 38
Greenspan, Alan, 258, 278, 293, 303, 344
Grew, Joseph C., 92, 113, 117, 118
Guatemala (CIA intervention), 147–48
Gudeman, Edward, 218

Guggenheim interests, 53, 113

Hager, Eric, 158
Haig, Alexander, 298
Halberstam, David, 175, 197, 230
Haldeman, H. R. (Bob), 255, 268, 269, 292, 299
Hamilton, Alexander, 5, 378, 391, 393
Hamilton, Fowler, 219
Hammond, Bray, 5, 379
Hancock, John M., 16, 62, 113–14
Hanes, John W., 57, 63, 116
Hanes Robert M., 101
Hanna interests, 129, 130, 159, 252, 386
Hardin, Clifford, 248, 259, 262, 289, 290, 483–84
Harding, Warren G., 9, 381, 397
Harlan, John Marshall, 153, 167, 210, 372, 530
Harman, Sidney, 349
Harriman, E. H., 7, 8, 55, 397
Harriman, E. Roland, 23, 116, 216
Harriman, Henry I., 19, 35, 36
Harriman, W. Averell, 22–24, 30–31, 34, 36, 40, 54, 55, 56, 60, 62, 79, 89, 90, 92, 98, 101, 116, 119, 198, 216, 222, 416, 427–28
Harris, Patricia Roberts, 324–25, 339, 349–50, 511–12
Harrison, Benjamin, 380
Harrison, George L., 92–93, 117–18
Hartman, Arthur A., 318, 515
Harvey, George, 8
Hathaway, Stanley K., 275, 302, 497
Hauge, Gabriel, 200, 208, 285, 291
Hay, John, 375, 392
Hayes, Rutherford B., 380
Haynsworth, Clement F., 304
Heller, Walter W., 187, 220
Helms, Richard, 203–04, 257, 266
Hensel, H. Struve, 76
Herter, Christian A., 100, 128, 135, 158, 166, 224, 435
Hertz, John D., 30, 59
Hickel, Walter, 247, 295, 393, 483
Hillenbrand, Martin D., 277, 491
Hillenkoetter, Roscoe, 95
Hills, Carla, 276, 302, 501
Hilsman, Roger, 197
Hobby, Oveta Culp, 139–40, 445
Hodges, Luther, 173, 180, 182, 201, 202, 218, 226, 457, 469
Hodges, Luther, Jr., 349
Hodgson, James D., 250, 486
Hoffman, Paul G., 73, 99, 100, 127, 165
Hoover, Herbert C., 9–10, 381
Hoover, Herbert, Jr., 158
Hopkins, Harry, 30–31, 112, 406
Houghton, Alonson B., 389
Houghton, Amory, 141, 142, 448

House, Edward M., 8, 380, 389
Howe, Louis McH., 26
Hufstedler, Shirley M., 357, 514
Hughes, Charles Evans, 9–10, 46, 106, 522
Hughes, John C., 143, 450
Hughes, Rowland R., 145
Hull, Cordell, 25, 41, 56, 74, 128, 401
Humphrey, George M., 129, 159, 224, 435
Humphrey-Hawkins Act, 354
Humphrey, Hubert, 174, 196, 224, 284
Hunt, H. L., 149
Hutchinson, B. Edwin, 160
Hydrogen bomb, development, 105–06

Ickes, Harold, 29, 74, 87, 404
Ignatius, Paul R., 225, 467
Inflation control issue (Nixon and Carter), 259–62, 294, 332–33, 353
Ingersoll, Robert S., 236, 242, 301
Interstate highway program, 149–50
Iran (CIA intervention), 146–47
Irwin, John N. II, 241–42, 253, 291, 490
ITT, 169, 265–67, 296–97

Jackson, Andrew, 5, 363, 385
Jackson, Henry, 288, 312, 313
Jackson, Robert H., 77, 107–108, 112, 410–411, 528
Jackson, William, H., 97, 144, 145
Jacoby, Neil H., 163, 261
Jaworski, Leon, 270–72, 289, 299, 300
John Birch Society, 160, 224
Johnson, Andrew, 379
Johnson, Hiram, 29
Johnson, Hugh, 35–38, 60, 61–62
Johnson, Keen, 116
Johnson, Louis A., 84, 87, 102, 115, 225, 420
Johnson, Lyndon B., 174, 175, 179, 192–213, 222–30, 463
Jones, Jesse, 77, 112, 413
Jones, Reginald H., 310, 315, 340, 350, 354, 356
Jones, W. Alton, 127
Jordan, Hamilton, 313, 326, 338–39, 342, 345, 350, 355

Kahn, Alfred, 329, 332
Kaiser, Edgar, 196, 221, 230, 285
Kalmbach, Herbert, 294
Kappel, Frederick R., 188, 207, 214, 285, 292
Katzenbach, Nicholas, 197–98, 200, 217, 468
Kendall, Donald, 238, 239, 291, 297, 298, 315
Kennan, George F., 90, 101, 432
Kennedy, David M., 221, 243, 291, 295, 479

Kennedy, Edward, 331–32
Kennedy, John F., 174–92, 210–11, 215–222, 451
Kennedy, Joseph P., 32, 51, 59–60, 174, 215, 226, 381, 407
Kennedy, Robert F., 179, 181, 200, 210, 219, 226, 230, 235, 237, 455, 468
Kerr, Robert, 139, 166, 187, 191, 193, 216 225
Kestnbaum, Meyer, 162
Keyserling, Leon, 104, 220
Kimball, Dan, 85, 423
Kirbo, Charles, 313–14, 322, 345, 355
Kirby family, 156
Kirk, Alan, 90, 432
Kirkland, Lane, 311, 344, 355
Kirstein, Louis, 36, 38
Kissinger, Henry, 240–41, 254, 259, 267, 273, 287, 293, 297, 478, 494
Kleberg interests, 192, 277
Kleindienst, Richard, 246, 265–66, 268, 269, 282, 289, 298, 300, 481
Kleppe, Thomas S., 275–76, 393, 497
Klutznick, Philip, 216, 357, 510
Knauer, Virginia, 259, 294
Knox, Frank, 74–75, 412
Knox, Philander, 363
Kohler, Foy, 183, 202, 461, 475
Kolko, Gabriel, 120, 122, 380
Korth, Fred, 178, 190, 221, 454
Kreps, Juanita M., 323, 344, 509–10
Kristol, Irving, 310
Krug, Julius, 80, 88, 426
Kuhn-Loeb interests, 16, 18, 22–24, 34, 284, 397
Kyes, Roger, 131, 159

Labor legislation (Carter), 333–34, 353–54. *Also see* Wagner Act and Taft-Hartley Act
Laird, Melvin R., 244, 288, 293, 295, 393, 480
Lance, T. Bertram, 327, 350–51, 354
Landon, Alfred, 45, 66
Landrieu, Moon, 339–40, 356, 512
Lansing, Robert, 119, 127
Larry, R. Heath, 315, 316
Larson, Arthur, 161
LaRue, Fred, 268, 298
Lazard Frères, 18, 284, 397
Leahy, William D., 92, 113, 415
Leffingwell, Russell, 26, 157
Lehman, Herbert H., 21, 55, 57
Lehman interests, 18, 22, 25, 26–27, 32, 53, 57, 61, 178, 194, 196, 217, 218, 223, 227, 346, 387, 397
Leuchtenburg, William, 52
Levi, Edward H., 274, 496
Lewis, John L., 38
Lewisohn, Adolph, 18
Liddy, G. Gordon, 268, 296, 298

Lilienthal, David E., 105, 106
Lincoln, Abraham, 6–7, 386
Linder, Harold F., 218
Linowitz, Sol, 330, 352, 355–56
Lipshutz, Robert, 326, 342
Locke, Eugene, 227
Lodge, Henry Cabot, 174, 175, 184, 192, 202–03, 209, 222, 226, 229, 462, 474
Loeb, Rhoades interests, 196, 203, 218, 227, 230, 284, 346, 397
Long, Huey, 44, 194, 222
Lovett, Robert A., 75, 82, 85, 98, 151, 175–76, 177, 222, 421
Lowi, Theodore J., 101
Luce, Henry, 66, 178
Lynn, James T., 252, 303, 488, 501
Lyon, Peter, 126

MacVeagh, Charlton, 66
McAdoo, William G., 29, 30
McCabe, Thomas B., 111, 121, 223
McCarthy, Joseph R., 148–49, 156, 165
McClellan, John, 165
McCloy, John J., 75, 89, 90, 92, 94, 125, 151, 158, 162, 185–86, 208, 209, 222, 224, 227, 229, 433
McCone, John A., 86, 163, 185, 203, 220, 227, 237, 267, 297
McCord, James, 269
McCormack, James, 204, 219
McCracken, Paul, 163, 257–58, 310
McDonald, Alonzo, 342, 351
McElroy, Neil, 132, 437
McGhee, George C., 83, 114, 176–77, 183, 202, 216, 226, 461, 474
McGovern, George, 235, 267, 284
McGranery, James P., 87, 425
McGrath, J. Howard, 87, 425
McIntyre, James, Jr., 327
McKay, Douglas, 136, 155, 392, 393, 442
McLaren, Richard, 265–66, 296
McNamara, Robert, 119, 177, 189–90, 199, 208, 209, 217, 225, 302, 452
McQuaid, Kim, 36, 37
McReynolds, James C., 46, 523
Madden, J. Warren, 65
Magill, Roswell, 57
Magruder, Jeb Stuart, 268
Manion, Clarence, 160
Manning, Bayless, 311
Mardian, Robert, 268, 298
Markley, Rodney, 273, 301
Marshall, F. Ray, 324, 510
Marshall, George C., 81, 85, 92, 395, 418, 421
Marshall, John, 362, 377
Marshall Plan, 97–101, 120
Marshall, Thurgood, 211–12, 280, 532
Martin, Graham A., 493
Martin, William McC., Jr., 78, 114

Marvin, Langdon P., 54
Mason, Edward S., 93–94, 99, 118
Mathews, F. David, 275, 500
Matthews, Franklin P., 85, 115, 423
Mayo, Robert, 256
Mazur, Paul, 22, 38, 40
Meany, George, 99, 207, 261, 262, 275, 302, 312, 323
Mellon, Andrew W., 9, 363
Mellon interests, 159, 288, 298, 346
Meyer, Charles A., 287
Meyer, Eugene, 60, 63, 94, 188
Mid-Continental Oil & Gas Assn., 152
Middendorf, J. William II, 224, 288
Milbank, Jeremiah, Jr., 224, 298
Milk price support program (federal), 262
Miller, G. William, 340, 356, 507
Miller, J. Irwin, 207, 215, 236, 348
Miller, Edward G., Jr., 83
Milliken, Roger, 224, 285
Mills, C. Wright, 1, 383, 391, 396
Mine safety program (federal), 262–63
Minton, Sherman, 107, 529
Mitchell, John N., 244, 246, 263, 266, 267–269, 280, 284, 293, 296, 297, 298, 299, 481
Mitchell, John P., 137, 138, 445
Moley, Raymond, 34–35, 60, 61
Mondale, Walter, 315, 323
Morgan (J.P.) interests, 7, 8, 16, 19, 28–29, 39, 41, 44, 45, 53, 54, 55, 63, 65, 66, 72, 124–25, 150, 380, 386–87, 397
Morgenthau, Henry, Jr., 26–27, 29, 51, 54, 57, 74, 304, 402
Morgenthau, Henry, Sr., 26–27, 54, 55, 57
Morton, Rogers C. B., 247–48, 265, 274, 275, 278, 279, 289, 295, 300, 303, 483, 497
Morton, Thruston, 278, 289, 303
Moulton, Harold, 99, 100
Moynihan, Daniel P., 292
Mueller, Frederick H., 138, 139, 393, 444
Mundheim, Robert, 347–48
Murchison interests, 156, 165, 216, 223, 351
Murphy, Frank, 27, 50, 58, 107, 403, 527
Murphy, Thomas A., 310, 315
Murphy, William B., 207, 209, 214
Murray, Thomas E., 122
Myers, William I., 99, 160

Nassikas, John, 294
National Aeronautics & Space Administration. *See* U.S. National Aeronautics & Space Administration
National Association of Manufacturers (NAM), 13, 19, 42, 45, 51, 53, 64, 72, 104, 111, 121, 161, 234, 307, 308, 315, 334, 397
National Civic Federation, 54, 110, 397
National Farmers Union, 88, 104, 323

National Independent Committee for President Johnson and Senator Humphrey (1964), 196
National Industrial Conference Board, 42
National Planning Association, 104
National Recovery Administration (NRA), 35–39, 61–63
Nelson, Donald M., 79, 113
New York City bar association, 4
New York Stock Exchange, 40, 63
Nitze, Paul, 98, 102–03, 120, 199, 208, 350, 454, 466
Nixon, Richard M., 157, 174–75, 215, 235–273, 280–82, 284–300, 345, 387, 390, 477–78
Noble, Edward J., 31, 59
Nolting, Frank E., Jr., 183, 462
Nourse, Edwin G., 104

O'Brien, Lawrence, 184, 268
O'Connell, James T., 161
O'Connor, Basil, 20, 26
O'Leary, John, 263
Odlum, Floyd, 115
Oil Colony Trust Co., 144, 148
Oil depletion allowance, 9, 295, 303
Oil import quota system, 151–52, 166, 263, 295
Olney, Richard, 7, 373, 386
"Our crowd," 16, 18, 22, 26, 33, 51, 65, 397

Pace, Frank, Jr., 221, 422
Packard, David, 245, 291, 301, 309
Paepcke, Walter, 103, 199
Page, Arthur W., 93
Panama Canal treaty, 329–31, 352
Pappas, Thomas, 227–28, 279, 297, 298, 303
Patman, Wright, 171
Patterson, Richard C., Jr., 59
Patterson, Robert P., 75, 84, 114, 122, 419
Pauley, Edwin, 88, 113
Pecora, Ferdinand, 39, 63
Penn-Central (RR) merger, 170, 206, 229
Perkins, Frances, 31, 36, 38, 65, 74, 406
Perkins, George W., 83, 143, 162, 450
Pertschuck, Michael, 351
Pessen, Edward, 379
Peterson, Esther, 335
Peterson, Henry, 299
Peterson, Peter G., 249, 265, 267, 315, 485
Pew family, 224
Pfeiffer, Jane C., 349
Phillips, William, 26, 41, 56
Phleger, Herman, 158
Pierce, Franklin, 385
Pike, Sumner, 105
Postal Service, recent creation, 207–08

542 Index

Powell, Joseph F. (Jody), 313, 326, 342, 355
Powell, Lewis, F., Jr., 281, 305, 372, 389, 534
Pratt family, 100, 103, 128, 158, 199
Pryor, Samuel F., 22, 41
Pryor, Samuel F., Jr., 66
Public utility holding companies, 16, 44
Public Utility Holding Company Act, 44–45, 52
Pullman strike, 7

Quarles, Donald, 132, 159, 440

Raborn, William F., Jr., 203
Randall, Clarence, 162
Raskob, John J., 12, 19, 25
Reagan, Ronald, 300, 326, 330
Rebozo, Charles G. (Bebe), 239–40, 286, 293
Reciprocal trade program, 166
Reed, David A., 9
Reed, Stanley F., 49, 107, 122, 525–26
Rehnquist, William H., 281–82, 305, 533
Reid, Whitelaw, 375
Resor, Stanley, 200, 226, 288, 348, 465–66
Ribicoff, Abraham, 180, 181, 217, 458
Richardson, Elliot, 241, 245, 246–47, 251, 269–70, 274, 276, 289, 301, 346, 482, 499
Richardson, Sid, 156, 166, 178, 193, 243, 287–88, 298, 329
Richberg, Donald, 35
Richmond Junto, 359
Roberts, Clifford, 126
Roberts, Owen J., 10, 47, 66, 107, 272, 391, 525
Roberts, William A., 150
Robertson, Reuben, Jr., 131, 132, 159
Robertson, Walter, 158
Robinson, Charles W., 292, 301
Rockefeller, David, 125, 162, 189, 209, 224, 233, 234, 291, 310–11, 346, 356
Rockefeller interests, 7, 16, 22, 24, 39, 41, 51, 56, 64, 94–95, 114, 124–25, 145, 156, 157, 159, 161, 162, 163, 177, 186, 204, 216, 219, 225, 241, 291, 293, 311, 349, 387
Rockefeller, Nelson A., 113, 140, 161, 162, 174–75, 215, 235–37, 286, 300
Rogers, William P., 135–36, 240, 286, 293, 295, 441, 478
Rohaytn, Felix, 265–66, 346
Romney, George, 251–52, 291, 487–88
Roosa, Robert, 311, 347, 356
Roosevelt, Franklin D., 20–68, 87, 193, 213, 381, 394, 400
Roosevelt, Kermit, 147, 164
Roosevelt, Theodore, 7–8, 20, 380

Roper, Daniel, 29–30, 40, 41, 58–59, 394, 405
Rose, H. Chapman, 129, 130
Rosenman, Samuel, 60
Rostow, Eugene V., 198, 224–25
Rostow, Walt W., 198, 200
Roth, William M., 224
Rowe, James H., Jr., 195
Royall, Kenneth C., 421
Ruckelshaus, William D., 270
Ruml, Beardsley, 110
Rumsey, Mary H., 31, 36, 55, 60
Rumsfeld, Donald, 493, 495
Rush, Kenneth, 242, 245, 277, 291, 491, 503
Rusk, Dean, 83, 176, 197, 208, 451
Rutledge, Wiley, 107, 372, 528

St. Clair, James D., 299
Sale, Kirkpatrick, 233, 235, 272, 283, 300
Salles, Walther Moreira, 147
Sampson, Anthony, 151, 296
Samuels, Nathaniel, 287
Saunders, Stuart T., 188, 215, 228, 229
Sawhill, John C., 279, 355, 357
Sawyer, Charles, 89, 116, 202, 428
Saxbe, William, 247, 482, 496
Schiff family, 34, 397
Schlesinger, Arthur, Jr., 42, 184, 220
Schlesinger, James R., 245, 257, 274, 325–26, 336, 338, 350, 495, 513
Schmidhauser, John, 50
Schroder Banking Corp., J. Henry, 97, 146, 148, 164, 218, 311, 317, 321, 357
Schultze, Charles, 204, 327–28, 347, 351, 352
Schwellenbach, Lewis, 88, 431
Scranton, William W., 223–24, 260, 286
Scribner, Fred, 130, 159
Seaborg, Glenn T., 220
Seaton, Fred, 136, 393, 442
Seidman, L. William, 300
Seignious, George, 347
Seward, William H., 389
Shanley, Bernard, 162
Shapiro, Irving, 316, 331, 340, 347
Sharp, Dudley C., 133, 167, 393, 440
Shepardson, Whitney, 111, 148, 164
Shoup, Laurence, 315
Shriver, R. Sargent, 226, 253, 346, 474
Shultz, George P., 243, 250, 256, 257, 259, 263, 390, 479–80, 486
Simon, William E., 244, 274, 278–79, 288, 295, 301, 303, 344, 480, 495
Sirica John J., 269–70, 271
Sisco, Joseph H., 301
Skakel family, 181, 219
Sloan, Alfred P., Jr., 18, 19, 42, 159, 165
Sloan, George A., 37, 38
Smith, Alfred E., 12

Smith, C. Arnholt, 238–39, 285
Smith, Cyrus R., 201, 470
Smith, Gerald C., 158, 317–18
Smith, Walter Bedell, 90, 97, 158, 432
Smoot, Reed, 64
Smyth, Henry D., 105–06
Snyder, John W., 83, 114, 419
Social Security Act (1935), 42
Solomon, Anthony M., 320, 347
Sorensen, Theodore, 184, 222, 328, 351
Spofford, Charles M., 91, 433
Sprague, Robert C., 150
Stahr, Elvis J., Jr., 178–79, 453
Standley, William H., 79, 416
Stans, Maurice H., 145, 242, 248–49, 266, 267–68, 287, 290, 295, 298, 484–85
Stanton, Frank, 151, 214
Stein, Herbert, 258
Steinhardt, Laurence, 79, 113, 415
Stetson, John C., 322
Stettinius, Edward R., 78, 112–13, 410
Stevens, John Paul, 282, 305, 534
Stevens, Robert, 133, 149, 437–38
Stevenson Adlai, 127, 174, 176, 216, 217
Stewart, Potter, 154, 210, 280, 531
Stimson, Henry L., 9, 67, 70, 92–93, 111–112, 117, 373, 381, 411
Stock market regulation, 40. *Also see* U.S. Securities & Exchange Commission
Stoessel, Walter J., Jr., 277, 318, 491, 515
Stone, Harlan Fiske, 47, 67, 106, 391, 524, 527
Stone, W. Clement, 285, 298
Straus family, 26, 33
Straus, Jesse, 32–33, 51, 381, 408
Strauss, Lewis, 105–06, 122, 138, 139, 163, 444
Strauss, Robert, 328–29, 351–52
Strausz-Hupe, Robert, 303, 505
Stuart family (Quaker Oats), 37, 73, 74
Sullivan, John L., 115, 423
Summerfield, Arthur, 161
Sutherland, George, 46–47, 66, 523
Swanson, Claude, 28, 58, 404
Swope, Gerald, 19, 35, 36, 37, 38, 42, 62
Swope Herbert B., 30, 32, 38, 56, 59, 62
Symington, W. Stuart, 86, 424

Taft-Hartley Act, 121
Taft, Robert A., 121, 127, 158, 160, 163
Taft, William Howard, 8, 391, 397
Talbott, Harold E., 133, 439–40
Taney, Roger B., 362, 373, 379
Taylor, Maxwell D., 200, 202, 210, 476
Teagle, Walter C., 19, 36, 37, 38, 42
TFX (airplane) controversy, 189–91, 220–221
Thayer, Walter, 175, 223, 237, 292
Thomas, Charles S., 133, 134, 159, 438
Thomas, Franklin A., 349

Thompson, Llewellyn, 142, 167, 183, 226, 449, 461, 475
Thorp, Willard, 98, 114, 120
Thurmond, J. Strom, 249, 298
Tidelands oil issue, 165–66
Tilden, Samuel J., 386
Tobin, Maurice J., 88, 431
Toon, Malcolm, 318, 516
Traylor, Melvin, 55, 57
Trilateral Commission, 234–35, 276, 301 311, 314, 316–19, 320, 321, 328, 342, 344, 346, 347, 356, 387–88
Trowbridge, Alexander B., 201, 226, 470
Truman, Harry S., 80–122, 127, 155, 213, 381, 417
Tugwell, Rexford G., 34, 58
Turner, Donald, 228–29
Turner, Stansfield, 328

Udall, Stewart L., 179, 181, 200, 456, 469
Union Pacific Railroad, 22–23 and passim
United Corp., 16, 44, 65
United Fruit Co., 147–48, 165, 218
U.S. Atomic Energy Commission, 104–06, 121–22, 163, 171, 220, 225, 292
U.S. Central Intelligence Agency (CIA), 70, 95, 97, 145–46, 164, 185, 203–04, 219, 227–28, 257, 290, 328
U.S. Chamber of Commerce, 19, 43, 53, 64, 72, 104, 111, 114, 119, 161, 234, 307, 308, 315, 334, 335, 353, 354
U.S. Council of Economic Advisers, 104, 163, 187, 220, 228, 257–58, 327–28
U.S. National Aeronautics & Space Administration (NASA), 163, 171, 186–187, 225, 292
U.S. Office of Defense Mobilization (Korean War), 103
U.S. Office of Management & Budget (formerly Bureau of the Budget), 121, 145, 187, 204, 256–57, 327
U.S. Securities & Exchange Commission, 32, 40, 63
U.S. Steel Corp. (JFK clash), 220
U.S. War Production Board (WWII), 79–80
Usery, Willie J., Jr., 275, 500

Van Buren, Martin, 385
Vance, Cyrus, 179, 199, 210, 225, 316, 344, 346, 347, 453, 465, 506
Vandenberg, Arthur H., 100
Van Devanter, Willis, 46, 522
Vesco, Robert, 298
Vietnamese war, 191–92, 208–10, 229–30, 259
Villard family, 43
Vinson, Fred M., 83, 106, 152, 418, 529
Volcker, Paul A., 287, 356
Volpe, John A., 252, 488

Wagner Act (1953), 42–43, 52
Wagner, Robert F., 38, 43, 65
Walker, Charls E., 287, 354, 356–57
Wallace George, 312–13, 344
Wallace, Henry A., 29, 58, 81, 88–89, 113, 405, 427
Walsh, Thomas J., 27
Walters family (Md.), 21, 32
Warburg, James P., 22, 23, 34;
   Warburg family, 53, 56, 61, 112, 346
Warner, John W., 288
Warnke, Paul C., 319, 347
War Production Board (WWII). *See* U.S. War Production Board
Warren, Earl, 152–53, 166–67, 210, 230, 280, 382, 530
Watergate scandal, 267–73, 297–300
Watson, Arthur K., 253, 291, 489–90
Watson, Jack H., 326
Watson, Thomas J., 126
Watson, Thomas J., Jr., 179, 214, 355–56, 516
Waymack, Walter W., 105
Weaver, Robert, 226, 472
Webb, James E., 82, 187, 220, 225
Webster, Daniel, 6, 392
Weeks, Sinclair, 66, 137, 138–39, 161, 443
Weinberger, Casper, 251, 256, 487
Weinburg, Sidney J., 18, 37, 54, 55, 79, 103, 127, 130, 135, 175, 196, 215, 222, 224, 225, 284
Weisl, Edwin, 179, 194, 199, 223
Welch, Leo D., 191
Welfare reform (Nixon plan), 293
Welles, Sumner, 26, 41, 56–57
White, Byron R., 210, 217, 280, 531
White, John C., 348–49
Whiteside, Arthur D., 36, 80
Whitney, C. V., 55, 116
Whitney, George, 53
Whitney, John Hay, 126, 141–42, 175, 224, 237, 397, 447
Whitney, Richard, 40, 63
Whitney, William C., 142, 397

Whittaker, Charles, 154, 167, 372, 531
Wickard, Claude, 77–78, 413
Wiggin, Albert H., 24, 39
Wiggins, A.L.M., 114
Williams, G. Mennan, 217
Williams, Harold, 351
Williams, S. Clay, 62–63
Williams, Walter, 161
Willkie, Wendell L., 41, 43, 66, 397
Wilson, Charles E. (GE), 79, 103
Wilson, Charles E. (GM), 131, 159, 436
Wilson, Hugh R., 60, 409
Wilson, William B., 377
Wilson, Woodrow, 6–7, 8, 380, 390, 394, 397
Winant, John G., 42, 64, 78–79, 89, 113, 414
Winn, Peter, 267
Wirtz, W. Willard, 180, 181–82, 200, 458, 471
Wisner, Frank, 119, 164
Wolf, Robert E., 149
Wolman, Leo, 38
Wood, Robert E., 149
Woodcock, Leonard, 222, 313, 318, 323, 344, 517
Woodin, William H., 26, 41, 401
Woodring, Harry, 28, 58, 393, 394, 403
Woodruff, Robert, 55, 345
Woods, George D., 119, 186
World Bank, 70, 93–95, 118–19, 302
Wright, Edwin K., 95
Wriston, Henry M.,, 125
Wriston, Walter B., 125, 310, 316

Young, Andrew, 344, 347, 349, 356
Young, Owen D., 38, 55, 56, 99

Zarb, Frank, 279
Zellerbach, James D., 101
Zinsser, John S., 75, 89, 162
Zuckert, Eugene, 122, 178, 190, 200, 208, 455, 467